A Statistical and Agricultural Survey of the County of Galway
with
Observations On The Means of Improvement;
Drawn up for the Consideration, and by the Direction of the
Royal Dublin Society.

By Hely Dutton

A Statistical and Agricultural Survey of the County of Galway
With Observations On The Means of Improvement; Drawn up for the Consideration, and by the Direction of the Royal Dublin Society.
By Hely Dutton.

Clachan Publishing
3 Drumavoley Park, Ballycastle, Glens of Antrim,
Northern Ireland.
BT54 6PE

Email: info@clachanpublishing.com
Website: http://clachanpublishing-com.
ISBN - 978-1-909906-05-1

This edition published 2013

Original edition:
University Press, Dublin
Royal Dublin Society
1824

Copyright © of annotated and indexed edition, Clachan 2013

This book is sold under the condition that it is not sold, by way of trade or otherwise, be lent, resold, hired out or in otherwise circulated without the publisher's prior consent in any form of binding or cover other than that in which it is published and without similar condition, including this condition, being imposed on the subsequent purchaser.

Clachan
Publishing

A

STATISTICAL AND AGRICULTURAL

SURVEY

OF THE

County of Galway,

WITH

OBSERVATIONS ON THE MEANS OF IMPROVEMENT;

DRAWN UP FOR THE CONSIDERATION, AND
BY THE DIRECTION OF

THE ROYAL DUBLIN SOCIETY.

BY HELY DUTTON.

LANDSCAPE GARDENER AND LAND IMPROVER; MEMBER OF
THE FARMING SOCIETY OF IRELAND; AUTHOR OF AN
ADDITIONAL SURVEY OF THE COUNTY OF DUBLIN, CON-
TAINED IN OBSERVATIONS ON A FORMER SURVEY, BY
CAPTAIN ARCHER; AND AUTHOR OF THE STATISTICAL
SURVEY OF THE COUNTY OF CLARE.

DUBLIN:
PRINTED AT THE UNIVERSITY PRESS,
BY R. GRAISBERRY,
PRINTER TO THE ROYAL DUBLIN SOCIETY.

1824.

Editorial

This work was commissioned by the Royal Dublin Society and earnestly undertaken by Hely Hutton in order to establish the state of agriculture in County Galway and to see what improvements could be made. It remains an invaluable source of information about the history, social conditions, agricultural practices and major personalities in the Church, town and county of Galway in the early nineteenth century. It remains a wonderful historic source and is cited regularly by historians of Ireland, both national and local, as well as genealogists and family historians.

The Royal Dublin Society was founded in 1731 with the aim of improving Ireland's economic condition by promoting the development of agriculture, the arts, industry and science. To these ends, Hely Dutton sent requests for information to numerous landlords, agent and clergymen in the county. His approach in using a mass survey reflects the growing influence of more scientific methodologies both in collecting information and in agriculture, typical of the development of empirical and scientific methods at the time. However, the more traditional members of landed classes did not appreciate this approach and a large number did not even respond. Dutton seized upon this - probably justifiably - as indicative of the hidebound attitudes that typified many of the landed classes who themselves were the source of the problems.

His critique emphasises the need for efficiency, rationality and moral reform, and perhaps lacks a thoroughgoing analysis of the political and social conditions that resulted in the failings he so clearly saw and understood. However, this work is also important as Dutton goes beyond an analysis of the social problems and agricultural practices of the day and gives us a history of the churches, monasteries and convents of Galway as well as a chronology and outline of some of the major personalities of Galway town and its government.

As this is a reprint of an historic document, we are particularly keen that the material is edited in a manner that makes it more accessible to the modern reader. We have therefore added explanatory footnotes to the text to throw light on obsolete and obscure references and turn of phrase. Also, some paragraphing, spelling and punctuation have been modernised; in particular Dutton's extensive use of italicizing for emphasis has not been followed, as his words speak for themselves. Neither have we followed his practice of using inverted commas on every line of a quotation. Furthermore, we have added an index to the original in order to help the reader navigate the text easily,

As this is a copy of an earlier publication, we cannot take responsibility for errors that may have occurred in the original. We do, however, take responsibility for any that may have resulted from the editing, formatting and printing processes.

We make no claim to ownership of the original text, but feel we have added substantial elements to make it more accessible to the modern reader and request that anyone who uses materials from this publication acknowledge both the original publication and this reproduction.

Dr Seán O'Halloran, editor,

24 September 2013.

Table of Contents

Editorial	ii
Table of Contents	iii
To the Reader	viii
To Earl Talbot	ix
Preface	x
Advertisement	xv
CHAPTER I	1
SECTION I	*1*
SITUATION AND EXTENT	1
SECTION II	*3*
DIVISIONS	3
SECTION III	*5*
CLIMATE	5
SECTION IV	*7*
SOIL AND SURFACE	7
SECTION V	*16*
MINERALS	16
MOUNTAINS	21
SECTION VI	*27*
WATER	27
CHAPTER II	33
AGRICULTURE	*33*
SECTION I	*33*
MODE OF CULTURE	33
EXTENT OF CULTURE AND OF EACH SPECIES OF GRAIN SOWED	38
SECTION II	*41*
COURSE OF CROPS	41
SECTION III	*46*
USE OF OXEN — HOW HARNESSED	46
SECTION IV	*48*
NATURE AND USE OF IMPLEMENTS OF HUSBANDRY	48
SECTION V	*52*
MARKET FOR GRAIN	52
SECTION VI	*54*
USE OF GREEN FOOD IN WINTER	54
CHAPTER III	58
SECTION I	*58*
PASTURE	58
SECTION II	*61*
BREED OF CATTLE — HOW FAR IMPROVED, AND HOW FAR CAPABLE OF FURTHER IMPROVEMENT	61

MARKETS, OR FAIRS FOR THEM, AND LIST OF FAIRS	66
LIST OF FAIRS IN THE COUNTY OF GALWAY	67
SECTION III	*69*
GENERAL PRICES	69
SECTION IV	*70*
MODES OF FEEDING, AND HOW FAR HOUSED IN WINTER	70
SECTION V	*72*
NATURAL GRASSES	72
SECTION VI	*75*
ARTIFICIAL GRASSES	75
SECTION VII	*76*
MODE OF HAY-MAKING	76
SECTION VIII	*78*
DAIRIES — THEIR PRODUCE AND MANAGEMENT	78
SECTION IX	*81*
PRICES OF HIDES, TALLOW, WOOL, AND QUANTITY SOLD	81
CHAPTER IV	**82**
FARMS	*82*
SECTION I	*82*
THEIR SIZE	82
SECTION II	*83*
FARM HOUSES AND OFFICES	83
SECTION III	*85*
NATURE OF TENURES— GENERAL STATE OF LEASES AND PARTICULAR CLAUSES THEREIN	85
SECTION IV	*88*
TAXES OR CESSES PAID BY TENANTS	88
SECTION V	*89*
PROPORTION OF WORKING HORSES AND OXEN TO THE SIZE OF FARMS	89
SECTION VI	*90*
GENERAL SIZE OF FIELDS AND ENCLOSURES	90
SECTION VII	*91*
NATURE OF FENCES	91
SECTION VIII	*94*
MODES OF DRAINING	94
SECTION IX	*97*
NATURE OF MANURE	97
CHAPTER V	**107**
GENERAL SUBJECTS	*107*
SECTION I	*107*
POPULATION	107
SECTION II	*109*
NUMBER AND SIZE OF TOWNS AND VILLAGES	109
SECTION III	*189*

HABITATIONS, FUEL, FOOD, AND CLOTHING OF THE LOWER RANKS, AND THEIR GENERAL COST	189
HABITATIONS	189
FUEL	193
FOOD	194
CLOTHING	197
SECTION IV	*199*
PRICES OF LABOUR, WAGES, AND PROVISIONS	199
PROVISIONS	201
SECTION V	*201*
STATE OF TITHE — ITS GENERAL AMOUNT	201
SECTION VI	*203*
USE OF BEER OR SPIRITS, WHETHER EITHER OR WHICH IS INCREASING	203
SECTION VII	*205*
STATE OF ROADS, BRIDGES, &c. &c.	205
SECTION VIII	*212*
NAVIGATIONS AND NAVIGABLE RIVERS	212
SECTION IX.	*213*
STATE OF THE FISHERIES.	213
SECTION X	*226*
STATE OF EDUCATION, SCHOOLS, AND CHARITABLE INSTITUTIONS	226
SECTION XI	*229*
STATE OF RESIDENT AND NON-RESIDENT LANDLORDS	229
Resident Proprietors.	230
SECTION XII	*233*
STATE OF CIRCULATION OF MONEY OR PAPER	233
SECTION XIII	*234*
STATE OF FARMING AND AGRICULTURAL SOCIETIES	234
SECTION XIV	*236*
STATE OF MANUFACTURES — WHETHER INCREASING	236
SECTION XV	*241*
STATE OF MILLS OF EVERY KIND	241
SECTION XVI	*243*
STATE OF PLANTATIONS AND PLANTING	243
SECTION XVII	*248*
STATE OF THE EFFECTS OF THE ENCOURAGEMENT HERETOFORE GIVEN BY THE ROYAL DUBLIN SOCIETY, PARTICULARIZED IN THE ANNEXED LIST, AND ANY IMPROVEMENT WHICH MAY OCCUR FOR FUTURE ENCOURAGEMENT, PARTICULARLY FOR THE PRESERVATION OF TREES WHEN PLANTED	248
SECTION XVIII	*251*
STATE OF NURSERIES IN THE COUNTY, AND EXTENT OF SALES	251

SECTION XIX	*252*
PRICE OP TIMBER, AND STATE OF IT IN THE COUNTRY	252
SECTION XX	*254*
QUANTITY OF BOG AND WASTE GROUND — THE POSSIBILITY AND MEANS OF IMPROVING THEM, AND OBSTACLES TO THEIR IMPROVEMENT	254
SECTION XXI	*258*
HABITS Of INDUSTRY, OR WANT OF IT AMONGST THE PEOPLE	258
SECTION XXII	*259*
USE OF THE ENGLISH LANGUAGE, WHETHER GENERAL OR HOW FAR INCREASING	259
SECTION XXIII	*260*
ACCOUNT OF TOWERS, CASTLES, &c. OR PLACES REMARKABLE FOR ANY HISTORICAL EVENT	260
ROUND TOWERS.	261
PLACES REMARKABLE FOR ANY HISTORICAL EVENT	264
SECTION XXIV	*266*
LIST OF PARISHES.	266
SECTION XXV	*269*
ABBEYS — ECCLESIASTICAL DIVISIONS — RESIDENT CLERGY	269
ARCHBISHOPS OF TUAM.	269
CLONFERT	271
KILMACDUAGH.	273
KNOCKMOY ABBEY	275
ABBEYS AND MONASTERIES IN RUINS	276
ABBEYS AND PRIORIES OF REGULAR CANONS OF ST. AUGUSTINE.	276
MONASTERIES AND NUNNERIES OF CANONESSES OF THE ORDER OF ST. AUGUSTINE	277
ABBEYS AND PRIORIES OF THE ORDER OF THE CANONS REGULAR PRAEMONSTRATENSES.	277
PRIORIES AND PRECEPTORIES OF KNIGHTS HOSPITALLERS OF THE ORDER OF ST, JOHN OF JERUSALEM.	277
BENEDICTINE NUNNERIES.	277
CISTERCIAN OR BENEDICTINE ABBEYS, EXTANT AT THE TIME OF THE DISSOLUTION OF THE MONASTERIES IN IRELAND	277
CONVENTS OF THE FRIARS PREACHERS, OR DOMINICANS, COMMONLY CALLED BLACK FRIARS	278
CONVENTS OF THE FRANCISCANS, COMMONLY CALLED FRIARS MINORS.	278
CONVENTS OF THE EREMITES OF ST. AUGUSTINE, COMMONLY CALLED AUSTIN FRIARS	279
CONVENTS OF CARMELITES OR WHITE FRIARS	279
SECTION XXVI	*286*
WHETHER THE COUNTY HAS BEEN ACTUALLY SURVEYED	286

SECTION XXVII — *287*
    WEIGHTS AND MEASURES, LIQUID OR DRY — IN WHAT INSTANCES ARE WEIGHTS ASSIGNED FOR MEASURES, OR VICE VERSA — 287
SECTION XXVIII — *290*
    MORALS, MANNERS, AND CUSTOMS OF THE PEOPLE — 290
        MANNERS. — 291
SECTION XXIX — *295*
    CONCLUDING OBSERVATIONS — 295
APPENDIX — **297**
    TRIBES AND NON-TRIBES — 297
    POPE'S BULL — 310
    Innocent, Bishop — 310
        Servant of the Servants of God, &c. — 310
    CHARTER GRANTED BY QUEEN ELIZABETH TO THE TOWN OF GALWAY. — 314
        Copy of Mr. Cole's certificate of the translation. — 331
    CHARTER GRANTED BY CHARLES THE SECOND TO THE TOWN OF GALWAY — 331
APPENDIX — *349*
    THE BATTLE OF THE CHAUNTERS. — 349
        BY DR DOMINICK O'KELLY OF BALLYGLASS, — 349
        A CELEBRATED PHYSICIAN. — 349
    MR. KNIGHT'S DIRECTIONS FOR MAKING CIDER — 360
Index — *362*

To the Reader

This Report is at present printed and circulated for the purpose merely of procuring further information respecting the state of husbandry in this district, and of enabling every one interested in the welfare of this country to examine it fully, and contribute to its improvement. The Society do not deem themselves pledged to any opinion given by the author; and they desire that nothing contained in this Survey be considered as their sentiments. They have published it only for the comments and observations of all persons, which they intreat may be given freely and without reserve.

It is therefore requested, that the observations on reading this work may be returned to the Royal Dublin Society, as soon as may be convenient, and they will meet with the fullest attention in a future edition.

To Earl Talbot

My Lord,

Allow me to follow you into your retirement with that small but sincere tribute of respect, which you were so good as to permit me to dedicate to you when his Majesty's worthy Representative for Ireland.

To no one can a work professing to detail the agricultural practices of a county in Ireland be more appropriately offered, than to a noble man who has on every occasion manifested so warm a regard for her agricultural interests and general prosperity.

Your lordship has evinced this, by not only giving liberal premiums for improving the breed of Irish stock, but by affording that countenance which your acknowledged skill in rural affairs has rendered invaluable.

I trust your lordship will join with me in regretting, that so good an example has not influenced the landed proprietors. That it has not, I am sorry to be obliged to point to the deplorable falling off from the cheering appearance at the former shows of the Farming Society of Ireland, and to contrast it with the late thin attendance, which seems to have sordidly fluctuated with the funds of that patriotic society.

That your lordship may long continue to enjoy that *otium cum dignitate*[1] which can only be obtained by the influence of a good heart on an enlarged understanding, is the very sincere wish of your lordship's

Most obedient,

And very devoted Servant,

HELY DUTTON.

---

[1] 'leisure with dignity' Latin, [Clachan ed.].

Preface

I MUST begin by returning the most heartfelt thanks to my numerous friends in the county of Galway, for their unceasing acts of kindness in every respect, except in furnishing me with written information; of that, I have not to acknowledge the smallest, but from the late Rev. Mr. Russell, Mr. D'Arcy of Clifden castle, Mr. D'Arcy of Galway, Mr. Blake of Merlin Park, Mr. Reddington of Ryehill, and the late Mr. Edmund Costello of Galway, to whom I feel particularly obliged: had every one to whom I applied taken the trouble to make even a small portion of Mr. Costello's research, this Survey would have been much more worthy of public approbation than I am but too conscious it is: of one thing I feel I can congratulate myself; that in no instance have I knowingly deviated from the truth. If I have been deceived into the insertion of what is unfounded, at their door who stooped to this meanness it must lie; and if this humble attempt should ever be thought worthy of a second edition, I shall be delighted to expose the fraud, and the author of it. At an early period I published in the Galway newspapers, and I also distributed many hundreds of letters with printed queries of those matters of which I wished to receive information, but I have unfortunately the same complaint to make that I had of the gentlemen and clergy of the county of Clare. In my Preface to the Survey of that county I expressed my hopes as follows:

"I trust and hope I shall not have the same complaint to make of the gentlemen of the county of Galway, amongst whom I expect a continuance of that politeness and intelligence which I have formerly experienced; I have no fears on this head from the inhabitants of that county."

Alas! I reckoned without my host. Their "politeness and intelligence" no one ever doubted, but except in the very few instances above mentioned, I could not get a line. I need scarcely bring to the recollection of this county the many gentlemen who from their local knowledge, and the resources of good libraries, could easily have furnished me with even heads only of the necessary information on each subject; but I regret to state that I found a languor, not to say a reluctance when I have pressed them, and only as table talk have I been able to extract any information. I need not remark that the hours of conviviality are not in general those of inquisitive research, except as to the comparative excellence of different vintages, or the merit of different racers or hunters. I feel great pleasure in acknowledging that Mr. Bellew's extensive and choice library was ever accessible to me.[1]

---

[1] Had not some of the gentlemen and clergy of the county of Clare absolutely *refused* me the information I so often requested, I had avoided probably many inaccuracies, and perhaps some misstatements; they must be sensible that I could write only from the information of others; if I was deceived I cannot be accountable for what I published. I can solemnly assure them I was not influenced by any party motives; a stranger unconnected in the county, could have no party views whatsoever to answer: on the contrary, as a professional man, *it has probably been of no service to me.* There are some

The account of the minerals of Connemara¹ from Mr. Nimmo's very scientific report to the Commissioners for improving the bogs of Ireland, will be found, I presume, highly interesting. It must be evident that in a work of this nature I could not dwell as long as I wished on the improvement of our extensive bogs, nor on planting, green crops, irrigation, draining, &c.; they would each require a volume. It must be also equally evident what an arduous task I have undertaken, and from the little assistance I have received, how imperfect a work embracing such various subjects, must necessarily be. With this conviction I have waited thus long, and trespassed so much on the forbearance of the Royal Dublin Society, in hopes that a proper and enlightened view of the importance of the inquiry would have influenced the gentlemen of the county to have given me such information as would have enabled me to lay before the public a much more satisfactory view of the county, its manners and resources, than their indolence has permitted me to do. I am indebted almost entirely to my own research, which has been much retarded by a necessary attention to the duties of extensive professional engagements. When I reflect on the able reports drawn up by the clergy of Scotland, I turn with regret to the almost total neglect of my queries by those of this county whom I many years since applied to. They cannot say they had not leisure; they cannot say they had no information to give, for they could have furnished me with a much more perfect kind than a stranger can possibly be supposed to acquire. I am at a loss to account for this apathy. But I am not singular in this complaint, for in almost every *Irish Survey* the same is made. In Scotland, where those admirable surveys have been published, the protestant clergy have arduous duties to perform; here, from the majority of the county being catholics, the protestant clergy have not the excuse that might have been made there. I am by no means inclined to impute it to a want of intellect or less virtuous propensities than their neighbours, for I am happy to bear testimony to the full possession of both by the clergy of every persuasion. We must then consider it to proceed from the same cause that has influenced the other gentlemen of the county, *indolence*.² Had they a proper feeling on this subject, the survey should never have been committed into my hands, and I had been saved a very irksome task, and one by which I shall probably be a loser to an amount that I should be ashamed to mention; but I was induced, at an early period, by the solicitations of a partial friend, to undertake it, and a regard to the fulfilment of my promise alone has impelled me to give it birth. I most heartily congratulate the county that I have not much to say on the subject of *road jobbing*; and I trust the rising generation of Grand Jurors will scout this disgrace to the names of Christian and gentleman out of their jury-room.

---

characters, I understand, who instead of feeling any compunction for their ungentlemanlike behaviour, still pursue the same rude and vociferous mode of recrimination, I leave them to the laugh of their acquaintance, [original footnote].
¹ Modernised spelling. Spelt 'Cunnemara' throughout in original, [Clachan ed]..
² I was weak enough to think that every person to whom I enclosed the list of queries would travel with it in their pockets, and note down every thing they observed tending to throw any light on such query! , [original footnote].

What a delightful thing it must be to the proud feelings of Connaught men to be told by a Judge "Gentlemen of the Grand Jury, I most heartily congratulate you on the total abolition of road-jobbing; and that you seem now to feel that consideration for the distresses of your poorer fellow-subjects, which should actuate every gentleman. I trust I shall always have to praise you for making those roads, which are merely for your own convenience and pleasure, out of your own pockets. I most sincerely hope I shall never hear of presentments for *visiting roads*, (as they are properly called by the country people) constructed from the u public purse."

As in the Survey of Clare, I have avoided here a description of gentlemen's seats. The reason must be obvious to those who know that in very many of them I have been concerned in the embellishment or improvement. Were I to point out the defects of any place, it would, independent of its rudeness, probably be said my motive was the hope of being called in to amend them. On the other hand, I could not stoop to flatter the proprietor of a place into an idea that it possessed picturesque merit, when perhaps it was composed of *tame screens and circular clumps*.

If a man is satisfied with his hobby, it would be very ungracious, not to say cruel, to put him out of conceit with him; in fact, it would be a difficult task. The only remark I shall make is, that I have not seen any place, in any part of Ireland, that could not be much improved, especially by *thinning*. I wish that anything I could urge would induce the landed proprietors to emulate those noble plantings in Scotland. I imagine nothing of this kind has as yet been attempted in this county, though many parts of it are equally adapted for it as those of Scotland. I trust I have thrown some useful light on the fisheries, a matter highly deserving of the marked attention of not only those proprietors who have estates on the sea-coast, but of every landed proprietor, and more especially the merchants of Galway, who have now the high road to wealth opened to them by the legislature. I hope they will meet the offer by energy, and not only in this branch, but in the export of butter, and that trade in beef and pork, which by some former mismanagement they lost.[1] I have given copies of the charters of Queen Elizabeth (rectifying and confirming those of Richard the Second, Richard the Third, Edward the Fourth, Edward the Sixth, and Henry the Eighth,) and that of King Charles the Second.

I have been favoured by a kind friend with copies of several other charters, for, exclusive of those I have given, there are those of Richard the Second, Richard the Third, Henry the Sixth, Edward the Fourth, Edward the Sixth, James the Second, and probably some others, but I did not think myself warranted in laying my friends under contribution for what probably most of them would consider merely literary curiosities, except by a few in Galway. I trust it will be perceived that I have avoided

---

[1] I am delighted that one enlightened merchant, Mr. Maclachlan, has this year (1823) slaughtered a considerable number of cattle for exportation.. It is to be hoped this renewal of a former trade will not be damped by sending any but the very beat description of beef, [original footnote].

the insertion of much corporation matter with which I have been favoured, that would be considered agreeable by those only engaged in party, and any observations of mine must not be in prejudgment of a question with the merits of which I must be very imperfectly acquainted, and I do not write to serve any party. On the never-dying subject of *tribes* and *non-tribe*s of Galway, I have given the arguments on both sides; professing a perfect neutrality; I have, I trust, many friends of each party.

I have given a specimen of Galway poetry, that I flatter myself will be enjoyed by every lover of genuine humour. Since that period, we have had plenty of coarse satire, some daubing, some rhyming, but no poetry. It must be evident to every person of the least reading, that though I have not stopped to acknowledge it, I have drawn largely on several authors, particularly on Dr. Ledwich[1], Butler's *Lives of the Saints*, Grose[2], and any others that were likely to enlighten my subject. I trust therefore, that any living authors whom I have quoted may not be offended, nor think I could be mean enough to stoop to such acts of piracy, or vain enough to think I could escape detection. The fact is, that many of my notes were taken at moments of such great hurry, that the names of many of the authors have escaped my recollection. I may say with great truth, *Non mi ricordo*.[3]

To Mr. Hardiman's[4] admirable *History of Galway* I am deeply indebted for many articles that his indefatigable research has brought to light, and which the difficulty of acquiring put out of my reach. I must confess, had I seen his excellent book at an earlier period, probably the town of Galway would have been left entirely to him; but my Survey had been so far advanced, and so much of the town affairs intermingled with those of the county at large, that I had neither time nor indeed inclination to make a new arrangement. I flatter myself that from the union of Mr. Hardiman's book and mine, there will be found a more perfect county report than has hitherto appeared in Ireland. To Mr. Hardiman the town of Galway, and indeed the literary world, are highly indebted. To appreciate the intense labour and expense of his research through the different offices of record, a man must have been an author and in a similar situation.

Most sincerely do I wish him that remuneration which a discerning and grateful public should bestow; and I cannot think that any person of this province, where such multitudes are descended from the Galway families, can be so destitute of taste,

---

[1] Edward Lewich (1737?–1823), born in Dublin, was an Irish historian, antiquarian and topographer. His *Antiquities of Ireland*, now holds little authority. However, it is now valued for its numerous engravings by J. Ford depicting castles, abbeys, and round towers, [Clachan ed.].
[2] Francis Grose, (1731–1791) was a popular antiquarian and draftsman, publishing many antiquities of the British Isles. He published two *Antiquities of Ireland* in 1797, [Clachan ed.].
[3] I do not remember, (Italian), [Clachan ed.].
[4] James Hardiman (1790-1855)(Séamas Ó hArgadáin) b. Westport, Mayo, and native Irish-speaker published *History of the Town and County of Galway, from the Earliest Period to the Present Time: Embellished with Several Engravings* (Dublin: W Folds 1820), [Clachan ed.].

or even curiosity, as to be without the book; and even to those who are unconnected with the county I can promise a high treat, if indefatigable research, exquisite arrangement, manly style, and unimpeached veracity can deserve it.

To Mrs. Blake of Merlin Park I feel highly indebted for procuring me an inspection of the old map of Galway at Castle-Mount-Garret, (a *fac simile* of which Mr. Hardiman has published); also for communicating the old corporation book in her possession, from which much useful and entertaining matter has been extracted.

I shall feel highly honored by receiving the corrections of any person better acquainted with the county than I can pretend to be; they shall be gratefully acknowledged if this work should ever be thought worthy of a second edition.

HELY DUTTON.

Mount Bellow, Castle Blakeney.

Advertisement

From an extensive and very varied practice, and an attentive study of the higher branches of *Landscape Gardening*, the Author hopes he may claim the notice of his countrymen.

His designs for Water, and its picturesque accompaniments, he trusts, are more from Nature than those usually executed in Ireland, and perhaps even in England, if we may judge from the tame frontispiece to Mr. Pontey's new work "The Rural Improver," which, it may be reasonably concluded, is a chosen specimen of his practice, and of English taste.

In *thinning plantations*, so little known or attended to in Ireland, he endeavours to unite future profit with picturesque effect, and gives instructions for pruning plantations, which any intelligent hedge carpenter can execute, and thus spread this grossly and obstinately neglected, but highly necessary practice, for those who have a due regard for the interests of posterity.

A very considerable experience in drawing and irrigation enables him in many cases to lessen the expense, by making each contribute to the benefit of the other.

The plan he has for some time adopted, of giving occasional visits by the year, has been found so very satisfactory, he is induced to extend it, by which a very considerable saving in expense will be obtained by those who have extensive designs in contemplation.

A STATISTICAL AND AGRICULTURAL SURVEY,

&c. &c.

CHAPTER I

SECTION I

SITUATION AND EXTENT

THE County of Galway is situated on the western coast of Ireland: its greatest length is about seventy-five miles, and breadth about forty. On the west it is bounded by the great Atlantic ocean; on the north by part of the counties of Mayo and Roscommon; on the east by a part of the counties of Roscommon, West Meath, and King's county; and on the south by a part of the counties of Clare and Tipperary, and the bay of Galway. It is generally estimated to contain 775,525 plantation acres; but probably, like that of other counties, it is an erroneous calculation, for by Mr. Nimmo's estimate, the three baronies of Moycullen, Ballynahinch, and Ross, alone contain 350,000. A map upon a large scale has been lately published by the late Mr. Larkin, at the desire of the Grand Jury. Amongst many other useful purposes the true contents will be ascertained, and many false returns of lands paying cess will be rectified: great abuses of this nature have been detected by Mr. Davis of Hampstead, who has accepted the troublesome office of high constable for this very purpose. When the maps of each barony are published, the best lines of roads will be easily pointed out, and many jobs prevented; at the same time, I must confess this county is far behind some of their neighbours in this species of mean fraud, so disgraceful to the character of a gentleman.

The South Islands of Arran, at the entrance of the bay of Galway, contain about 7000 acres, and are the property of Mr. Digby; they let, or did let for about £2000 per annum, and the rents well paid. The largest island alone contains 4607 acres, Innismore 1338, and Innis Leer 909. Their chief trade consists in fresh and cured fish, feathers, a superior kind of yearling calves, much sought after by the Connaught graziers: formerly might be added great quantities of whiskey and smuggled goods of many kinds. Arran was anciently called *the blessed*. No less than ten monasteries were built by the pious *Endeus*, besides thirteen churches; and so great were the number of Saints and Hermits interred here, that the writer of the life of St Kieran thus expresses himself: *"In qua insula multitudo virorum sanctorum manet, et innumerabiles sancti, omnibus incogniti, nisi solo Deo omnipotent!, ibi jacent!*[1]*"* The family of Gore purchased these islands from Erasmus Smyth, and derive their earldom from this island, which was formerly in that of Butler; they are called South Isles, to distinguish them from one on the coast of Donegal, called the North Isle of Arran. A lighthouse has lately been erected on the large island. These islands are called by Ptolemy *Ganganii*, — a corruption of the Irish words *Cean-gan*: Cean signifies a head or promontory, and *gan*, external, — the people off the external promontory Burrin, in the county of Clare, opposite to these islands, had the same appellation from Ptolemy. The cattle on these islands are sometimes greatly distressed for fresh water, in so much that, in 1810 and 1821 every beast was brought to Connemara until the rains had supplied the wells. There are vast numbers of black birds and thrushes, but no frogs (as I am informed) in any of she islands. At a very remote period those in lands were inhabited by the Druids; many of their altars and other remains are visible and there are strong proofs that they were at this period covered with woods.

The late Mr. Richard Kirwan seemed to think that the bay of Galway was originally a granite mountain, shattered and swallowed up by some dreadful convulsion that left a vast mass of granite, called the Gregory, standing on limestone rocks, one hundred feet at least above the level of the sea. This curious circumstance occurs very frequently in the calcareous region in the neighbourhood of Galway, probably occasioned by the same convulsion that also gave entrance to the sea between the islands of Arras, according to O'Flaherty[2].

In the great island of Arran may be seen the remains of a fort, celled *Dun Ængus*, so called from *Ængus* of the *Huomerian family*, who flourished a little before the birth of Christ under Mauda, queen of Connaught. This island was formerly the residence of St Ende, and afterwards of a multitude of Anchorites and holy men; ever since it has been called, by tradition of the inhabitants, the Down of Conquovar the son of *Huomar* who flourished at the same period with *Ængus*. It is mentioned in the Ogygia that the bay of Galway was anciently called *Lough Lurgan*; the sea broke through between the islands of Arran, and formed it into the present bay of Galway: this rests on the testimony of Mr. O'Flaherty. He says also, that the Belgians gave names to the following places: Lough *Kime*, at present Lough Hacket, above the *Moy-sneang*, in the rectory of *Muntir-Moroghow*, in the barony of Clare Galway;

---

[1] 'In what remains of the holy island of the multitude of men and innumerable holy women, unknown to all, but only by the God Almighty, there they lie', [Clachan ed.].
[2] Ruaidhrí Ó Flaithbheartaigh, last *recognised* Lord of Iar Connacht and chief of the O'Flaherty clan. He became an historian and collector of Irish manuscripts. His published works included *Ogygia* and *Iar Connacht*. (see following footnote), [Clachan ed.].

Rhintumuin, in Madrigia, a peninsula on the south of Galway; also Loughcoutra, near Gort; Lough Buadha, Lough Baa, Loughrein, Loughfinney, Loughgrene, Loughriach, in the barony of Moenmoy, now Clanrickard.

A very curious natural production occurs at Barna, that would seem to countenance this assertion of the *Ogygia*[1]; many feet, probably ten, *below* high water mark, may be seen on the strand a turf bog of several feet in depth, in which are the stumps and roots of large trees, and many branches of oak and birch intermixed. On this bog there are rocks of many tons weight. The same phenomenon occurs at the west side of the island of Omey, which is very far advanced into the boisterous Atlantic Ocean. Probably few things in natural history are more worthy of scientific investigation, whichever of the following cases may be considered: — 1st, The tides cannot formerly have risen so high on this coast as at present; 2nd, The land must have extended an immense distance into the Atlantic Ocean farther than at present, to enable trees of such magnitude as those at the island of Omey and at Barna even to exist, or the winds from the west must have been of a very different nature from those that prevail at present.

It must also be recollected that woods must have existed to produce the bog. At a still earlier period we might cut the Gordian knot, by saying these bogs were formed before the deluge; but I wish some of my scientific friends to help me to untie it.

SECTION II

DIVISIONS

The County is comprised in the following sixteen baronies:

Athenry,	Dunkellen,	Leitrim,	Ballynahinch,
Killconnel,	Longford,	Half Ballimoe,	Kiltartan,
Moycullen,	Clare,	Killyhan,	Ross,
Clonmacow,	Loughrea,	Tiaquin,	Downamore.

At a remote period this county was thus divided amongst tribes of families:

Clankonow	amongst the	Burkes.
Clan Fargail	"	O'Hallorans.
Hy-maine	"	O'Dalys & O'Kellys.[2]

---

[1] *Ogygia: seu Rerum Hibernicarum Chronologia & etc.*, (1793) translated into English by Rev. James Hely, as
Ogygia, or a Chronological account of Irish Events (collected from Very Ancient Documents faithfully compared with each other & supported by the Genealogical & Chronological Aid of the Sacred and Profane Writings of the Globe. Ogygia is the island of Calypso, used by O'Flaherty as an allegory for Ireland. Drawing from numerous ancient documents, Ogygia traces Irish history back to the ages of mythology and legend, before the time of Christ), [Clachan ed.].

[2] At a still more remote period, the O'Layns were lords of this territory, which was then called Moy-Sachnoly, [original footnote].

Maghullen (Moycullen)	"	O'Flahertys[1].
Lilanchia (now the barony of Longford)	"	O'Maddens.
Hy-Fiacria Aidne	"	Clanrickard.

Conmacnemara, or the chief tribe on the great sea, comprehending the western parts of the county of Galway on the sea coast; it was also called Conmacne-Ira, or the chief tribe in the west; and Iar-Connaught, or West Connaught; likewise Hy-Tartagh, or the western country, the chiefs of which were denominated Hy Flaherty, or O'Flaherty, that is, the chief of the nobles of the western country, it contained the baronies of *Morogh*,[2] Moycullen, and Ballynahinch.

The meaning of the word *Galway* has been differently construed. Some say it is derived from Gal, a stranger, and Ibv, a territory; the country of strangers. It is also called Galliv, rocky or stony; also, Galmbaith, (Galway,) pronounced Galiv, a rocky barren country. In Syriac, *Galmitha*; in Chaldean, *Galmodh—durus silex, figurate, pro sterilitate solitudinis*. At some former period, in one of the Pope's bulls, it is called "the village of Galway." Many think it took its name from *Gaillimh*, or Galiv, the daughter of *Breasail*, who was drowned here; and in the old map of Galway, published in 1651, (of which a copy is given in Mr. Hardiman's admirable history of Galway,) the rock near which she was drowned is delineated: the map, however, is of little authority, as the publisher had the account only from tradition. The general opinion seems to be, that the name is derived from the words *Gail*, merchant, and *ibh*, pronounced *iv*, a territory; and Tacitus and Ptolemy countenanced this idea. Mr. Hardiman also says, that in all the ancient documents down to the year 1400, it is invariably written *Galvy*. "In process of time the word Gal-iva was altered into Gal-via, the literal translation of which, Gal-way, first occurs about the year 1400, and From that time it has remained uniform and unchanged, by any variation to the

---

[1] Moycullen is the birthplace of Roderick O'Flaherty who wrote the Ogygia, where he says, — "This is my native soil and patrimony, enjoyed by my ancestors time immemorial. There was a manor exempted by a patent from all taxes; it likewise enjoyed the privilege of holding a market and fairs, and was honored with a Seneschal's court to determine litigations; but having lost my father at the age of two years, I sheltered myself under the wings of royalty, and paid the usual sum for my wardship. But before I attained the proper age of possessing my fortune, I was deprived of the patronage of my guardian, by the detestable execution of my king. Having completed my nineteenth year, and the prince half a year younger, then I was compelled to take refuge in a foreign clime. The Lord wonderfully restored the prince to his crown, with the approbation of all good men, without having recourse to hostile measures; but he has found me unworthy to be reinstated in the possession of my own estate.— Against thee only, O Lord, have 1 transgressed; blessed be the name of the Lord for ever!" The estate mentioned here,. I am informed, is now possessed by Mr. Lynch of the Castle in Galway.— Note, Mr. Hardiman says he was bora at Park, near Galway, and died in 1718, aged eighty-nine. , [original footnote].

[2] There is no such barony at present. Mr. Nimmo mentions in his Report, "the hill of Mulrea in *Morisk*," and there is a parish called *Meirus* in Connemara. In the county of Mayo there is a barony of *Merisk*, [original footnote].

present day." Campion[1], in 1571, says that "Connaught hath as yet but the county of Clare, the towns of Athenry and Galway, a proper neat city at the sea side." At a very remote period the county of Cavan was reckoned part of Connaught.

SECTION III

CLIMATE

The climate of this county is in general peculiarly healthful; the strong and almost constant gales from the Atlantic, though frequently productive of rain, and unfriendly to the growth of trees exposed to their influence, seem to agree with most constitutions. A great improvement in the climate might be produced by planting extensively, and by the drainage of the extensive bogs and moors which form so large a portion of this county. The opinion entertained by many, whose education *should* enlarge their ideas, that trees will not succeed in situations exposed to the western gales, is a very erroneous one, and frequently dictated by a want of spirit: how is it possible such *patches* and their *screens*, as we see in almost every place, can stand exposure; even where they are thrown into a more extended form, they are on so pitiful a scale that they can only exist under the head of "Plantations and Planting". I shall enlarge on a subject peculiarly interesting to a county like this, so subject to storms. If there had been any meteorological observations made and continued for a number years, the change of climate could be ascertained; but it seems to be the general opinion of the oldest inhabitants, that for some years past storms and rain have been more frequent from the west than formerly[2]. As some corroboration of this idea, the encroachment of the sea near the Recorder's quay on the west side of Galway, may be adduced, where the marks of the potato ridges may be seen, and which only a very few years ago were in cultivation, though they, are now covered at every tide.

This ground could easily be recovered from the sea, and made more productive than formerly. There can be little doubt the sea is encroaching on the land where it meets resistance from rocks or high banks of earth: where a gradual sandy shore occurs, the highest tides do no injury. Those who make embankments against the sea or rivers should imitate this. In Ireland they are wretchedly constructed; at Borna instances may be seen of both the above effects of the sea. Lately the ground near the Recorder's quay, has been reclaimed by Mr. Bulteel, and promises to remunerate his very spirited exertion.

---

[1] Saint Edmund Campion, S.J., (1540 –1581) was an English Jesuit priest. He was arrested by priest hunters, convicted of high treason, and was hanged, drawn and quartered. He briefly acted as a tutor in Ireland where he wrote his *A Historie of Ireland* (1571), [Clachan Ed.].
[2] It is a curious circumstance that rice was sowed here in 1585, and was raised in England in the last century, [original footnote].

The medical gentlemen of Galway inform me that the town is generally very healthful, and where disorders do occur, they cannot be imputed to the climate or want of pure water, but to a want of cleanliness in the inhabitants, and a total neglect of every ordinance to enforce it by the magistrates. The fish market, and the adjacent quays, are particularly filthy at some seasons, when fish are very plenty. The fishers are permitted to cut off the heads and gut the fish in the market and on the quays, and leave them there unheeded, until they rot and emit a most offensive and dangerous stench. I cannot conceive what sort of organs the magistrates must possess; it is astonishing what nuisances indolence and habit will permit some people to doze over or overlook.[1] Disorders are sometimes caused by an immoderate use of fish, especially by strangers not used to good fish, but more especially from a too plentiful addition of melted butter, and that frequently very indifferent. The poorer inhabitants, who at certain seasons consume great quantities of fresh fish, have seldom cause to complain; butter is generally above their reach, and the more wholesome potato is substituted. The water of the town is also generally supposed to cause a disorder to strangers usually called *the Galway*, and they are put on their guard against its use; but if it is taken up above the town, or at Nun's Island, I imagine there can not be better water any where; but whilst the inhabitants through indolence permit their servants to take up water near the fish market, they cannot be surprised at its unwholesomeness, after passing through all the sewers, slaughter houses, tan pits, and barracks in the town. I assure the fair ladies of Galway I have frequently seen their tea-kettles filling between the old county gaol and the fish market; and within a few feet of their servant I have observed one filthy drab beetling dirty clothes, and another gutting fish. There are several excellent springs around Galway, but few make use of them, except those in their immediate neighbourhood, chiefly from the difficulty of getting their servants to go to them.

It is very easy to obviate much of the complaint against impure water by procuring a tin filtering machine of the annexed shape filled with fine and clean sand, which must be taken out and washed occasionally; the top or trumpet part should contain about four quarts of water, and if it is covered with canvass, it will prevent the necessity of washing the sand so frequently; the expense eight or nine shillings.

There have been many machines for this purpose on a larger scale invented lately, which no large house should be without, but this simple one will answer for a small family. Connemara is particularly healthful, so much so, that I was informed by a respectable Catholic clergyman, that in a parish containing upwards of 3000 inhabitants, only 40 died in 37 years; and of that number only 3 under 90 years of age. Frost or snow seldom remain on the sea coast of Connemara.

---

[1] Since I composed these strictures, several years ago, a most material change for the better has been made in every respect by the present Mayor, James Hardiman Burke, Esq. and many others are in a state of progress, [original footnote].

I was there in December 1816, when the inland roads were impassible from the depth of the snow; here, it was not more than three inches deep, and remained only 3 or 4 days. Cattle of all kinds remain out all the winter, and very rarely ever taste hay, for it is a scarce article in Connemara. I do not know any part of Ireland where watered meadows would so amply remunerate the proprietor, or where they could be so easily and cheaply constructed. This shall be noticed more fully under its proper head.

SECTION IV

SOIL AND SURFACE

The greater port of this county, if we except the immense tract west of Oughterard, is limestone; the divisions between this and the granite are generally well defined; even the superior verdure discovers immediately the limestone. Almost the entire of the county, beginning at either Bannagher or Ballinasloe and continued to Galway, is calcareous. From Galway to Oughterard, in a western direction, the highroad nearly marks the division between the two regions; all the country to the north of that road and extending over Loughcorrib into the counties at Mayo and Roscommon, except the neighbourhood of Dunmore, is limestone; that to the southward of this road, comprehending the baronies of Ballinahinch, Ross and Moycullen, extending upwards of forty miles long and sixteen broad, with the exception of some detached masses of primitive limestone, and which occur frequently near the road from Oughterard to Clifden, is all either granite or other minerals of great variety of appearance.

All the mountains of Sliebhbaughta that divides this county from Clane, beginning at Mountshannon, and running by Dalyston and Roxborough, and ending near Gort, are, I believe, silex. A remarkable tongue of fine limestone runs boldly into the mountains at Ballynagieve, the estate of Earl Clancarty, but no use is made of it by his tenants, as far as I was informed. There is also a considerable bed of limestone with large shells, in the river near Mr. Martin's at Oughterard, part of which forms a charming natural cascade. Limestone of various kinds has been discovered by the late indefatigable Mr. Donald Stewart in the Sliebh-baughta mountains, as shall be mentioned in the list of minerals.

The soil of this county generally produces every crop in abundance. The wheat, particularly that which is produced to the southward of Galway, is amongst the best in Ireland, producing that fine bread to be found in Galway, Tuam and other towns, and in almost every gentleman's house.

The barley and oats, from the introduction of better kinds than were formerly sowed, from the benefit of an extensive export, and from the establishment of extensive breweries at Newcastle and Galway, have been greatly improved in their quality, and the quantity astonishingly multiplied: this shows plainly, if it could be doubted, the incalculable benefit of a free export of corn.

From the general mode of fencing in many parts of this county, by dry stone walls, a stranger riding through the country is at a loss to know where so much corn as he sees in November around every village and cottage is produced; for where this fence is used, except immediately under the eye on each side of the road, he can perceive nothing but stone walls as far as the sight can reach, but the building of those walls enables the farmer to clear his land, and produce fine crops of potatoes and corn on land that before this improvement was not worth five shillings an acre.— It must be confessed that the country between Gort or Monivue and Galway is not calculated to impress a stranger with a favorable opinion of its tillage, yet there is scarcely any part of the county so susceptible of improvement as that extensive, and at present dreary tract. It has been all formerly under tillage of the most destructive kind, the usual running out one of Ireland, and has in most instances reverted to its original heath, If, on the contrary, limestone gravel, which I am informed is in almost every field, was liberally used, fences made with good hedges and ditches (in which this county is very deficient), and a proper rotation of crops pursued, followed by clover, ray grass, and other green crops, it would change the face of this desert, and instead of being, as at present, used for winterage for a few cattle or sheep, would in a short time become uncommonly productive of corn, and at the same time maintain more cattle and sheep than at present. I shall have occasion to mention this subject again.

Compared to many other parts of Ireland, this county, with the exception of Connemara and Slieu-brechten mountains, is generally flat and uninteresting, and requires considerable skill and patience to produce picturesque effect; it must almost generally be effected by planting alone, without much assistance from water or rocks; for though the first frequently occurs, yet it is generally accompanied by flat, uninteresting ground, and requires more time, patience and taste to produce picturesque effect by trees, than most improvers posses; and the latter, though in many places scattered over the ground in great profusion, are seldom of that character, or so happily placed that a man of taste would wish to introduce them into his scenery.

A great quantity of ground has been cleared of stones, which seems to be the favourite improvement of this county, and it is astonishing the expense some gentlemen go to, that would not lay out a guinea in draining or improving their bogs, or planting; but it is the Galway hobby horse, and it must be confessed, has been rode frequently with great address and profit I only wish that my hobby should be occasionally rode; if *with skill*, he will be found as pleasant and profitable as the other; if not, he is apt to leave his rider in the dirt. There are very extensive tracts of ground too full of rocks to be cleared with any profit, and which at present rear only a few sheep, that could be planted with infinitely more profit than can be made by dwindled sheep or half starved cattle. They occur to a large amount near Castle Taylor, that great range of country beginning at Persse lodge, and running for several miles into Burrin in the county of Clare; also in the neighbourhood of Galway, Rahasane, Cregg-clare, Menlough, Rahoon, Craghowell, &c. &c.

About thirty years ago one third of this county was estimated to be bog, mountain or lake; but since this calculation was made, great improvements have taken place in the mountains, and some in the bogs, and since the beneficial, but much abused practice of burning the surface in such situations has been adopted, a still greater portion of our waste land must be added to tillage; but I regret I cannot say any land has been added by the drainage of lakes. An immense addition could be made by lowering Lough Corrib, which could be easily effected, I imagine, near Well-park. An attempt was formerly made in a good direction to accomplish this, why it did not proceed I am to learn.

I should think the mill-sites on this outlet would more than pay the expense of the work, as the fall it so considerable, and the supply so abundant that they might be near each other, and the materials for building and supply of corn and fuel, &c. could be brought by water from the counties of Mayo and Clare; and, as a further inducement, there is fine limestone on the spot. Amongst the many lakes or Turloughs that could be drained, or at least lowered, Turlough-more, near Tuam, that near Rahasane, and that extensive chain from Castle Hacket to Shruel, are the most conspicuous: they are only occasionally flooded in winter, and want chiefly an enlargement and deepening of the outlet, or a confinement of the stream to a bed sufficiently capacious to accomplish this. The proprietors of these Turloughs have been wishing these fifty years this had been done, but speak to individuals on the subject, and they are unanimous in nothing but a desire to throw the expense on any one but themselves. — These Turloughs maintain about seven or eight sheep to the acre for about four months, but in wet seasons they are of little value.

The country about Ballynahinch, the seat of Thomas Barnwall Martin, Esq. is extremely bold and highly picturesque, totally different from anything to be met with many other part of this county. I am grieved to say, that nature has all the merit; she has had little assistance, though an almost constant residence for upwards of fifty years would lead one to expect that a small part at least of a large income would have been annually expended in improvements. Mr. Thomas Martin, who is a young man, and has only lately got possession of Ballynahinch, is, as I am informed, making preparations to plant extensively, and may hope to see his plantations of considerable size and value; but the scale of planting here must be totally different from that usually adopted; here it must be reckoned by the hundred acres, by whole mountains; not like the tame thin screens or belts of the followers of Browne, disgracing many places in this county; the outline must agree in character and extent with the bold and picturesque one of the stupendous Twelve Pins, rising majestically from the charming lake of Ballynahinch, and connecting it with the other beautiful lakes and rivers in its neighbourhood. What a paradise would Ballynahinch be now, had the same spirit and taste that actuate the men of fortune in Scotland, or many of the gentlemen of this county, been exerted here; but from Mr. Thomas Martin's love for planting, and every improvement, we may hope Ballynahinch may become *what it should have been.*

The neighbourhood of Loughrea, before very beautiful, has been greatly improved by a new line of road to Dalyston, the noble seat of the late Right Honorable Denis Bowes Daly. The grounds around this lake are most happily adapted for planting, and I am not a little surprised they have not been long since thickly inhabited.

A very fine vein of land begins at Gort, runs through Roxborough and Castleboy, spreading for some distance chiefly in a northern direction; from thence it proceeds towards Loughrea, and continues in a southern tract to Dalyston. This line includes *Coorine*, the estate of Earl Clancarty; Park, the estate of the late Right Hon. D. B. Daly; and *Grola*, the estate of Sir John Burke of Marble-hill: it continues in this line, and comprehends the fine lands of Pallas, Potumna, Eyrecourt, &c. and from thence with some variation to Aghrim. It has been said that this is a continuation of the celebrated golden vein of the county of Limerick; which, after running through the county of Clare, is continued in this line. From Loughrea this fine vein takes another direction, beginning at Ballydugan it continues with little interruption to Ballydonndan, Killrinckle, Eastwell, Oatfield, Aghrim, and Ballinasloe; for several miles beyond that, on the road to Athlone, it is a miserable country. The lands just mentioned are some of the best in the county, though there are many others equally good, but they are more detached or demesne lands; they will fatten cattle of any weight, and bring a price in proportion. The principal part of the lands of this county are, however, better adapted to sheep feeding, chiefly to rearing for the Leinster graziers, who usually buy them at the fair of Ballinasloe in October and May, and complaints are seldom made of unsoundness, the lands converted to this purpose being generally light and rocky soil, or heathy mountain. Between Clare, Galway and Tuam, the qualify of the ground is good, about Tuam still better, and improves as you advance to Dunmore, about which town the country is exceedingly picturesque, alternate hill and dale, and almost all either rich pasture or tillage. The grounds between Oranmore and Monivae are very indifferent; a sterile surface, covered with short heath and fern, but in general has, at two or three feet beneath the surface, limestone gravel, yet I could not learn that any use is made of it; if there was, the scourging system would infallibly take place. This kind of land extends for several miles on either side, and is highly improvable.

In the neighbourhood of Shruel the land is very fine, and lets for high rents. It is the property of Mr. Kirwan of Dalgin. — Note. It is such land, such a climate, and a country containing upwards of seven millions of inhabitants, that Malthus has the *candour* and geographical acumen to call a *remote and inconsiderable country*.

The bogs of this county, occupying to considerable a portion of the surface, have hitherto been too generally reckoned of little use, except for fuel; some improvements, however, have been made; the most material are those of Woodlawn, made by Lord Ashtown and his late father, of venerated memory, and by the late Mr. French of Monivae, — both detailed in Mr. Young's admirable *Tour in Ireland* upwards of thirty yean ago. Lord Clonbrock has improved many acres of bog, and is every day adding to his improvements. The late and present Mr. Burke of St. Clerans has converted a large tract of bog into excellent meadow. Mr. Burke, of Ballydugan, has also highly improved some bog; Sir Ross Mahon of Castlegar, and his brother the Rev. Dean Mahon, have also reclaimed much bog. Mr. Bellew, of Mount Bellew, has made an admirable improvement of 20 acres of cut-away bog, which, from not being worth five shillings per acre, is now (1817) under a crop of oats, after a fine crop of rape: he is continuing his bog improvements with great spirit. There are many other gentlemen who have reclaimed bog, but, as far as I could learn, nothing has been done on an extensive scale, or an unbroken progressive system. A few years since the celebrated Mr. Elkington was induced, by very liberal terms (if I am rightly informed 100 guineas a month, and travelling expenses), to come over from England. I have frequently seen his works; they were excellent, but differing little from the practice of every experienced drainer[1], except in the use of the auger for tapping the springs; a very beneficial practice in many situations. When be was in Ireland a bog-mania was very prevalent, but the paroxysm was too violent to continue. There is not any species of improvement requires more patience and skill; the evil has been accumulating for centuries, the greater part, I apprehend, since the 9th century, when, from the neglect of agriculture, and the rains of many centuries subsiding in the lower grounds, many of our bogs have been formed, and cannot be at once overcome. It requires higher powers of discrimination than falls to the lot of an illiterate itinerant drainer, one who mistakes neatness of execution for correctness of design. Many persons put themselves to great expense (I have known it as high as £12 per acre) in drawing what they call limestone gravel, with little good effect; it should have been known by those to whom I allude, that it was worth little. The bog was imperfectly drained; cattle, for the sake of a scanty pasturage, was permitted to poke it full of holes, which were filled with rushes, and the gravel, bad as it was, applied too soon. I have heard one of the gentlemen whom I mean, frequently assert in large companies, "that improving bogs would never repay the expense;" certainly not by his erroneous method. I must here remark that I have seen in this county little, if any, of that black, slaty, rich limestone gravel that occurs in some parts of the counties of Meath and Dublin; there is, however, an abundance in almost every field of that which is highly beneficial. From what I have seen it is necessary to caution those that use this valuable manure, that almost invariably the surface, and in some places to a considerable depth, the gravel in pits is worth little; but from ignorance, indolence, or from being generally executed by task, it is used, and must always disappoint the hopes of the improver. I have seen a good deal of this kind of bad gravel used, which with shallow, open, surface drains, in bad direction, produced little beneficial effect. The process of proving bog in skilful hands is so simple, the success with good management so certain, and the profit so considerable, that I am at

---

[1] It has been frequently asserted that Mr. Elkington was the inventor of the method of draining by cutting off the springs: it might have been so in England, where draining seems to be very little understood, especially clay soils, but in Ireland it has been practised time immemorial, [original footnote].

a loss to account for the neglect of the proprietors hitherto. The introduction of Fiorin grass[1] by the praiseworthy exertions of the late Dr. Richardson, (who deserves a statue to his memory in the Dublin Society's rooms,) and the knowledge of burning unproductive clay to ashes, have added greatly to the facility of improving bogs, especially those that produce a small quantity of light white ashes, of little use as a manure.

In all the mountains of this county fertile vales frequently occur, and those are the parts that are chiefly inhabited; but if a steady and liberal encouragement was given, and on honest observance of promises, many parts of those mountains, that at present return little or no rent, would be made as productive as land which seemingly has a better appearance. Lord Riverston, by pursuing a liberal and judicious plan of letting his lands, is rapidly reclaiming a large tract of the mountains of Slieuboghta. Mr. D'Arcy is pursuing the same plan in Connemara. The benefit of these improvements has become so evident, that I trust they will steadily adhere to them, and even extend them until they make Connemara and Slieuboghta a home for those mistaken people who cross the Atlantic; and I will venture to assert, that the money spent even in their passage, if they have a family and furniture, &c. &c. would stock and cultivate a large farm; and if they have a turn for fishing, they may add considerably to their comforts and emolument. The ground immediately about Monivae is good sheep walk, but between that and Galway, especially beyond Cussane, it is a dreary country of many miles square, and though at present covered chiefly with short heath, it is highly improvable by calcareous gravel, which abounds in almost every field. That its value was formerly well known is evident from the pits that have been opened at a remote period in every field, but the scourging system has been pursued, and as the surface of the pits was chiefly used, it could not be expected that the usual beneficial effects of destroying the heath could have remained to this day. I have seen few places in Ireland where capital and skill would be more amply remunerated, and instead of poor heathy pasture, rearing (not fattening) only two sheep to the acre, would, under the improved system in which green crops make a material part, produce abundant crops of corn, and fatten much more stock than they at present barely subsist. If only eight miles square were improved, (but I know it occupies much more,) and only six barrels of corn to the acre, the produce would be upwards of 80,000 barrels; but under such a system as I mean, beginning with restricted burning, much more than that average would be obtained. I am informed by a person who knows Norfolk well, that this tract of land is much superior in quality to the greater part of that country. It is evident that almost the entire of the lands under consideration have been in tillage at a remote period, but all in the running-out system, which left it much poorer than it was originally. There must have been a much greater population there than at present, and more corn consumed, which probably was the case before the introduction of potatoes. It is also probable,

---

[1] A variety of English bent grass, [Clachan ed.].

that when the scanty turf bogs in the neighbourhood were exhausted, the inhabitants emigrated, as for several miles, indeed to Galway, there is very little fuel to be had. As Galway, at the period when these lands were under tillage, did not export any corn, and the inland bounty had not been established, we are at a lost to know how the corn of ten miles square was disposed of. The land lets, or did let, on an average, for about 10s. per acre; but under an improved system, with ample capital and a long lease, it would be well worth more than twice that sum.[1] The following extract from Mr. Nimmo's admirable Report to the Commissioners for improving the bogs of Ireland, will, I trust, be considered a most valuable addition.

"The whole tract between Lough Corrib and the Atlantic ocean, is frequently termed Connemara, and for want of one general name, I shall sometimes call it so. It is, however, subdivided into three separate districts, which are nearly, if not exactly, conterminous with the baronial divisions; of these, Connemara proper, or the barony of Ballynahinch is the most western, having on the east a line drawn from the head of Kilkerran bay, by Lough Ourid, to Shanonafola mountain, and from thence along the ridge by Mamturk to the Killeny bay; the remaining boundary is the Atlantic. The name signifies "Bays of the Ocean" and, in a loose sense, is supposed to extend to Costello bay. The remainder is again divided by a line from Shanonafola Mountain to the upper part of Lough Corrib. The southern part is the barony of Moycullen, commonly galled Iar Connaught or western Connaught. The northern area is usually called Joyce's country, (from the prevailing family name,) or the half barony of Ross; the Isles of Arran containing the other half barony. The eastern part of Iar Connaught, ancient called Irras Dannan[?] to the distance of four miles from the town of Galway, is included in the county of the town. This district appears, not undeservedly, to be considered as one of the most uncultivated parts of Ireland: on a general view, indeed, it seems one continued tract of bog and mountain, the quantity of arable land not amounting to one-tenth, perhaps not one-twentieth of the whole.

"Where cultivation has made the greatest progress, on, the south shore of Lough Corrib, the arable or dry land is interspersed with extensive tracts of naked lime stone rocks of a most desolate aspect; and it appears to be only after incredible labour that a few patches of soil have been won from the general waste. Nevertheless, such is the general fertility of these spots, and the value of the pasture amongst the limestone, that this land, even including rock, produces a rent of 15s. per acre, and where tolerably cleared, lets as high as in any part of the kingdom. The other parts of the district are for the most part bare moors, consisting of bog of various depth, upon a bottom of primitive rock of difficult decomposition, and affording little soil; but several strings or beds of limestone run through the country, and are distinguishable by the verdure and cultivation which have taken place in their vicinity.

"Some conception of the present value of this district may be formed from the following particulars: the population amounts to about 30,000 of which one-half is in Connemara proper, two-thirds of the remainder in Iar Connaught: of the Connemara population, more than nine-tenths are settled along the sea shore; the inhabitants of the

---

[1] Since this was written, the fall in agricultural produce has made a very material change for the worse in every description of land, [original footnote].

interior do not amount to three hundred families, and these chiefly along some of the bridle roads that have been made through the country. In Iar Connaught, the population is either on the sea shore or on the northern slopes of the hills next the limestone country. In Joyce country the upland parts are uninhabited. The rental of the whole district I find to be about £50,000 per annum, of which the kelp may produce about £6000, so that the land averages at 2s. 7d per acre: from this also should be deducted the value of some salmon fisheries, and the export of turf. The profit rents may amount to about £25,000. So that each individual pays about £2. 10s.; but of this £2. only can be in money, the remaining 10d. arising from the sale by the landlord of manufactured kelp.

The soils of the three baronies may be thus arranged:—

Arable land,	about	25000
Bog,	—	120000
Mountain and Upland pasture,	—	200000
Rock, much of it limestone,	—	5000
	Total	350000 Irish acres.

"Though the general improvement and cultivation of Connemara would seem an undertaking of the most arduous description, it is not without facilities, which might, upon a candid consideration, make it appear a subject more worthy of attention than many other of the waste lands of the kingdom. The climate is mild, snow being little known during the winter; the cattle are never housed; the mountains on the north, and general variety of surface, afford considerable shelter. The summers, however, are wet, and it is exposed to heavy easterly winds. Although Connemara be mountainous, it is by no means an upland country like Wicklow; at least, three-fourths of Connemara proper is lower than one hundred feet over the sea. Great part of Iar Connaught rises from the shore of Galway bay, in a gently sloping plain, to about three hundred feet, at the upper ridge of which there are some hills of about seven hundred feet, and beyond them a limestone country extends to the edge of Lough Corrib, and but little elevated above its level, which is only fourteen feet higher than the sea; but Joyce's country on the other hand, is an elevated tract with flat topped hills of 1900 to 2000 feet, interspersed with deep narrow valleys. This district is nearly surrounded by the sea, on the south and west; and the great lakes, Mask and Corrib, on the east, the latter navigable into the town of Galway, and could easily be made so into the sea. Various great inlets penetrate the district, so that no part of it is distant four miles from existing navigation. There are upwards of twenty safe and capacious harbours, fit for vessels of any burden; about twenty-five navigable lakes in the interior, of a mile or more in length, besides hundreds smaller; the sea coast and all those lakes abound with fish. The district, with its islands, possess no less than four hundred miles of sea shore. On Lough Corrib it has about fifty miles of shore, so that with Lough Mask, &c. there are as many miles of the shore or navigable lakes as there are square miles of surface. This extent of shore is particularly important from its produce in sea weed, either for manure or the manufacture of kelp: the value of the last article, a few years ago, amounted to about £50,000; at present, from the low prices, it does not exceed £16,000. There are extensive banks of calcareous sand around the coast in almost every bay; and in the interior there are numerous beds of limestone, nearly all the navigable lakes having some on their banks.

"The supply of fuel is evidently inexhaustible. Connemara is very destitute of wood, a few scrubby patches only being thinly scattered through it. The country, however, possesses an extensive stool of timber, for in almost every dry knoll or cliff, the oak, birch, and hazel, appear shooting in abundance, and require only a little care to rise into valuable forests. Several bloomeries[1], which were erected about a century ago, consumed much of the timber, and copsing was afterwards neglected. The sheltered vales, navigations, and abundant water power, would form great advantages in the cultivation of timber. On the whole, it appears to me, that the improvement of this district, so far from being difficult or hopeless, is a thing highly feasible, and, if vigorously and steadily pursued, is likely to meet with fewer obstructions, and greater ultimate success, than perhaps in any other part of Ireland.

"The soils of this district may be ranged under four grand divisions or zones, in each of which the style of culture is tolerably uniform. In the first place we cut off a triangle along the shore of Lough Corrib by a straight line from the town of Galway to Oughterard. The culture crosses the lake to near Cong, where it turns westward by the north side of Ben Leva, and then runs through Lough Mask. This is the western edge of the great limestone field of Ireland, and in this division many hundred acres of that rock are laid bare. Along the edge is a narrow stripe of fertile country, with hillocks, of gravel, partly calcareous, but much encumbered with tumblers of Granite, &c. and not always cultivated. The hollows are usually filled with bog. The next draw one line from Oughterard, westward to the bay of Ardbear, leaving on the south, nearly one half of the whole district. Another line from Oughterard through the hill of Glan, and by the north side of Lough Corrib to the north side of Ballynakill bay. Between those limits are found many rocks of primitive limestone. The southern part is a continued granite moor, covered with bog of various depth. It contains no limestone; considerable quantities, however, are brought from Arran and the county of Clare, as ballast, by turf boats, and thrown out on the shore. This supplies what is necessary for building; it has not been yet applied to agriculture, but could be procured for that purpose, and burned on the shore for somewhat less than one shitting per barrel. There are banks of shell and coral sand on all the coast, but especially in the bays of Kilkerran, Birterbuy, Bunown, Mannin; &c. this sand is raised by dredging, and by beaching the boat on it at low water: that of Kilkerran, Birterbuy, and Mannin, is pure coraline[2]. There are also dry banks of calcareous sand on the especially at the western extremity, which are accessible by land; nevertheless calcareous sand is not much applied to agriculture as yet, though its value is generally acknowledged.

"A good deal of turf (peat) is cut on the shore, and carried to Galway, or sold on the spot to boats from Arran and Clare. Turf in Galway is worth about a guinea per four ton boatload; price in the bogs 1s. 1d. per ton (of the boat). A man cuts in the day a six ton boat load, or slane; two spread it, one foots, or dries it, one stacks, and twelve take it to the shore, producing 1s 1d. to 1s 2d per day for wages."

---

[1] Early Iron Forges, [Clachan ed.].
[2] Coralline is limestone which contains fossilised coral, [Clachan ed.].

SECTION V

MINERALS

By the annexed list of minerals, taken from the Museum of the Dublin Society, it will appear that this county is by no means deficient in mineral productions. The numbers correspond with those on the specimens of the Galway minerals in the Museum, if the arrangement is the same as it was in Hawkins's-street.

No.

2740 Black limestone with shells in it, in great abundance in the bed of the river at Cheviot Chase, the estate of Robert Persse, Esq. near his lodge. Before this discovery Mr Persse's brother brought limestone a great distance to improve his land.
2741 Grey limestone from the same place.
2742 Black limestone coated with calcareous earth from the same place.
2743 Brownish limestone from the large flat mountain adjoining to Cheviot Chase, on the estate of Lord Gort, near the wood of Gortnacarnane.
2744 Reddish concretion of limestone from the same place.
2745 Limestone with large pebbles of calcareous stone in it, from same place.
2746 Red heavy limestone with fine clear pebbles in it, from the mountain near where the remarkable long stones are standing in regular order, on Lord Gort's estate.
2747 Red, more compact limestone, from the same place.
2748 Purple coloured concretion of limestone from near the wood, on the same estate.
2749 A remarkable concretion of yellow and red limestone from said estate.
2750 Black limestone coated on one side with black calcareous earth, like coalsmute or coalslate, from the rubbish where a small trial was made for coal in the face of the mountain at Roxborough, on black slaty soil; but this stone was detached, and appeared to be round like the balls the colliers call coal measures, on the estate of Robert Persse, Esq.
2751 Remarkable heavy reddish limestone, in the land of Gortnacarnane aforesaid; in the wood are many strong Spas.
2752 Grey limestone coated with a concretion of stones, in the bed of the river in the lands of Killeen; in this river are beds of brown free stone on which the add fermented.
2753 Pale yellowish earth, on which the acid fermented strongly; it is a good manure, from the same place.
2754 Crystal calcareous spar, from a large course of it near the old Castle in the lands of Chireryorry; it runs in a right line across the road; in a like course of it, near Drumoland, in the county of Clare, pure lead ore was got.
2755 Black limestone with shells in it, from the bed and banks of the large river that is the mearing between the counties of Galway and Clare, in the lands of Sliebh-an-oir, or the gold mountain.
2756 Manganese, from a large bed of it in the bank of the river in the lands of Gortnacarnane.
2757 Manganese, from the Eelweir; also, good potters clay in the flat land adjoining Lord Gort's estate.
2758 Manganese, from the wood of Gortnacarnane; same estate.

2759 Black heavy ocherish stone, coated with the appearance of Manganese, found in the rock in the wood, from whence Mr. Peresse told me he has often seen smoke rise, near the lodge on Cheviot Chase.
2760 Manganese from said place.
2761 Strong blue day, with a round hard earth in it; from same place.
2762 Red heavy fire earth, from a large bank of it in the large moor in the lands of upper Killeen; it was proved to be as good painting stuff as that which I discovered in the island of Rathline in the year 1774; it was approved of by the painters of Dublin. Two cargoes were sent to the grand canal as tarras, but I believe it is better for painting.
2763 Iron stone from the same place, the estate of Lord Gort.
2764 Lead ore from upwards of three tons of it, got near the surface in the low flat lands on the side of Lough Corrib, within a few miles of Oughterard barrack, the estate of Mr. French, where a small pit and open cast were made.
2765 Lead and copper in a greenish stone and spar m the bed of the river near Oughterard, that divides the estates of Mr. O'Flaherty and Mr. Martin. A vein of it is in a rock near Oughterard.
2766 Lead ore from a mine Mr. Chamber and Co. were working on the shore of the bay of Galway.
2767 Yellow and rose-coloured copper and lead, from the river of Oughterard.
2768 Lead ore from a second mine Mr. Chamber and Co. were working.
2769 Lead ore, from near the summit of the mountain in Connemara, the estate of Robert Martin, Esq.
2770 Lead ore and sulphur, in a large course of white spar, from the same mountains.
2771 Lead ore, iron and sulphur in spar, from the same mountain.
2772 Lead ore in hard stone, with a small piece of the spar of Terra ponderosa, from one of the many trials made in those mountains by the late Robert Martin, Esq.
2773 Lead ore, from the same mountain.
2774 Very uncommon lead ore, found in detached pieces in the bed of a river in said mountain.
2775 Green and yellow copper and lead intermixed, from said mountains.
2776 Lead ore, sulphur and iron, from the same mountains.
2777 Lead ore and sulphur, coated with a group of pyritous crystals, from said mountain.
2778 Lead ore, from the same mountains
2779 Blue, black, lamellar slaty stone, from a vein of it in Gortnacarnane wood, the estate of Lord Gort.
2780 Heavy red earth, with small shining particles, from the large river from the lands of Gortnacarnane.
2781 Fine potters clay, from the demesne of Monivae.
2782 Manganese of a softer kind, from Sliebh-an-oir.
2783 Manganese, from various parts of Sliebh-an-oir, on the estates of Lord Gort and Mr. Persse.
2784 Blackish, heavy, porous iron stone, found near the long stones in the level dry mountain near Gortnacarnane.
2785 Heavy micaceous red and yellow earth, in the lands of upper Killeen.
2786 Dark purple coloured stone, coated red on one side, from same place.
2787 Purple fine grained stone, from same place.
2788 Yellow ochre, from same place.
2789 Yellow ochre, made by strong spa waters.

2790   White marl in the demesne of Monivae, in the canal near the house — good.
2791   Soft fine grained stone from a rock of it at Lady Grove, near Gort; it lies nearly horizontally: there is a stratum nine inches thick in this rock like coal-bind,
ccc   Spar from Cong.

The limestone in almost every part of this county, except the primitive one of Connemara, contains shells and other petrifactions of various kinds, and in different quantities, from that at Oughterard, disfigured by sections of large shells, to the beautiful marbles of Angliham and Merlin Park, near Galway, which are a fine black, nearly without shells, highly prized in England and in Dublin, to which they are exported in blocks, and a large quantity worked up into chimney pieces in Galway: they are much superior to Kilkenny marble, but until the quarries are worked, and the chimney pieces executed by machinery, they can never meet those of Kilkenny at market, as there, almost every operation is performed by machinery worked by water. I am informed a cubic foot of the Galway marble generally weighs 168 lb.; the workmen say the marble of Merlin Park is tougher than that of Angliham or any other in the county. At Ballyleigh near Gort, a fine black marble has been long used, and some of a fine quality has been lately discovered near Athenry.

A very beautiful grey marble has been discovered at Woodbrook, the estate of the Misses Netterville, much superior to any in this county, perhaps in Ireland. I discovered a very beautiful red and blue coloured marble at Merlin Park, greatly admired by the manufacturers, but all the trials that have been made are very defective; the quarries have been worked only near the surface, the deeper they go the better the marble has been found, and probably will increase in goodness with the depth. A very beautiful green marble has been discovered on the estate of Mr. Martin near Ballynahinch, which promises to excel any as yet discovered in Ireland.

Iron ore was formerly raised in the neighbourhood of Woodford, and after being mixed with that brought up the Shannon from Killaloe by a Mr. Croasdale, was smelted near that village, part of the estate of Sir John Burke. The works were carried on so extensively, that they devoured all the great oak woods with which that country abounded, and were then abandoned. Mr. Berry, I understand, at present raises ore on part of Lord Clanrickard's estate; and indications of iron are everywhere visible in the mountains between Woodford and Mountshannon. The refuse of those bloomeries has been used for making excellent roads by the late Sir Thomas Burke.

A very fine kind of grit stone is raised in considerable quantities near Dunmore, of every thickness, from that of slates to the largest mill-stones, which are frequently sold for ten guineas a pair, and when well chosen, are esteemed for some purposes superior to French burr stones at £30 or £40. a pair; but they must be selected by a judge of their quality, or those of a very inferior kind may be given.

On the mountains near Roxborough, a very fine kind of whetstones, and for polishing marble, have been found, nearly equal to the best hones, and are frequently hawked about the country for Loughneagh hones.

Marl abounds in many places, particularly in, and on the banks of the Shannon, in a small lake near Marblehill, which it is probable was formed at a remote period by sinking for marl, as traces of extensive improvements may be seen in the neighbouring mountains; it is also found in most of the low grounds between Portumna, Marblehill, and Eyrecourt. Formerly a great quantity of ground in the neighbourhood of Mountshannon was improved by marl raised by dredging in the Shannon: it is used in small quantities near Loughrea, from some pits on the banks of the lake near Cowreen. The late Sir Thomas Burke has used it more extensively than I believe any other person in this county, on a large tract of heathy mountain of little value before; it has since produced fine crops, is perfectly reclaimed, and a very valuable farm. Beds of marl several feet thick, and occupying many acres, may be seen on the road between Hampstead and Ballymackward, and has been formerly used in large quantities, as may be seen by the extensive excavations; but I could not perceive any traces of a recent use of it: a very large tract may also be perceived on the side of the road between Ahaseragh and Lowville, on the estate of Sir Ross Mahon; I believe little use has been made of it: as Sir Ross is a very spirited and intelligent improver of land, I suspect it is of inferior quality; it is also in great abundance between Mylough and Mount Bellew. This manure has been often tried alone on deep bog with little effect, but whether from not previously draining the bog, or using too small a quantity, I could not ascertain. I understand from those who have tried it on bog, that alone it produces but a trifling improvement, but that mixed with a very small portion of animal manure, the effects were astonishing; either manure or marl uncombined, very inferior in their effects. I have frequently seen a patch of deep bog that had formerly been marled, and after cropping according to the custom of this county, was let out without sowing grass seeds of any kind; though the herbage was neither good in quality or quantity, there was not the least appearance of heath, though the surrounding bog was covered with it: certain I am, that if this patch had been covered with either lime or limestone gravel, it would have been covered with white clover and other valuable plants.[1]

In the midst of a large bog and heathy mountain near Marblehill, the property I believe of Lord Riverston, an extensive bed of fine limestone presents itself; for many miles to the south and west no such thing is to be found: what a treasure lies here quite neglected, probably unknown to the proprietor, where a profusion of fuel is on the spot, and the carriage next to nothing; but no advantage is taken of this circumstance, whilst in the county of Wexford, where fuel is very scarce, there is a competition for limestone at 3s. 6d. per ton, and is in that state drawn 10 or 12 miles, frequently much further; but instead of improving what they have, the monied men of this county are more anxious to add to their unimproved rent-roll at an interest of

---

[1] In the Statistical Survey of the county of Cavan, we find that marl exposed to the influence of salt water becomes quickly petrified [original footnote].

3 or 4 per cent frequently much less, when the improvement of the grounds they have, would produce from 10 to 20 per cent at least, if judiciously expended; and what too many overlook, would give employment to their tenantry, and furnish them with a beneficial example. It is probable that many of those who purchased at war prices have not, from the sudden depreciation in the value of land, one per cent, for their money.

Near Ardfroy, and also in Mr. D'Arcy's demesne in Connemara, large beds of oyster shells may be seen, many feet above high water mark; lime has been some times made of those in Connemara before the discovery of limestone in so many places on Mr. D'Arcy's estate. In many parts of Connemara beautiful crystals of quartz and felspar[1] may be found, and I was informed that on the banks of Lough Inagh, crystals of various colours may be procured.

A crystalline sand of very superior kind for making scythe-boards, occurs at Loughcoutra, the estate of Lord Gort; mowers come for it upwards of 80 miles, and prefer the rifles made of it to those imported from England; the same kind of sand may be seen at Lough Greene, in the county of Clare, and is held in the same estimation for this purpose. That several trials have been made for the discovery of minerals is evident from the number of shafts which have been sunk in many places; they may be seen in many parts of Knockmoy, and the remains of some of the works for melting the copper ore may be still seen. I have been informed by an intelligent friend that the ground at the foot of this hill (Knockmoy) to the southward of Brooklodge, the estate of Mr. Blake, and close to the high road, has every appearance of minerals, probably copper. A shaft was sunk near Lawrencetown, the estate of Walter Lawrence, Esq. many years ago: tradition says they did not discover any ore, but that they threw up a considerable quantity of coal. A very remarkable range of limestone runs along the river at Oughterard; it projects over the river like half of a broken arch, covered in a very picturesque manner with ivy, juniper, &c. It continues to present this appearance for a considerable length along the river. It seems probable that at some former period the river was subterraneous, as remains of a corresponding part may be seen at the opposite side near the inn, and in the yard of this inn may be perceived another subterranean cavern of limestone, and a very fine spring well. Near this, a very charming view of a waterfall may be seen through the arch of a bridge in the demesne of Mr. Martin.

The following is from Mr. Nimmo's very scientific Report

"The geological structure of Connemara, &c. from the extent of rock which is exposed, and the connection which it exhibits between the primary and secondary formations of the island, possesses no small degree of interest. The various soils also, and the means of their improvement, will be best understood by being previously acquainted with the various rocks which form their base, and with their particular position.

---

[1] Probably 'feldspar', a common silicate mineral, [Clachan ed.].

"The country from Galway to Sline Head, is a sheet of granite, or rather sienite, with few mountains of any remarkable elevation. To the north of this tract, a hollow valley runs through the whole extent of Connemara, distinctly marked by a chain of narrow lakes, from Lough Corrib to Mannin Bay; its greatest elevation is only 164 feet above the sea; a cross valley runs from near the middle of this over to Killery bay; and various plains and vallies stretch southward from it towards the ocean, across the granite country, and forming at their mouths the several inlets that distinguish the mouth of the bay of Galway. The country, strictly mountainous, is from Lough Corrib to Aghris point, where the summits are from 1200 to 2000 feet; they are composed of quartz; round their bases, and in the valley aforesaid, they are gneiss and mica slate, with bands of hornblende and primitive limestone. Along the north side of Lough Corrib, and to Ballinakill, the mica slate and hornblende rise into mountains, but the limestone disappears. From Lough Mask to the Killery, a transition country of greenstone and grauwacke slate, covered by the old red sandstone or glomerate, which also forms the hill of Mulrea in Morisk. The upper beds of this and of the green stone, are frequently porphyritic; to the north of this in Mayo, greenstone and clay slate, and to the mountain of Croagh Patrick, the summit and west side of which are quartz; the east side, slate and serpentine; but still without any limestone, none of which is found until we come again upon the secondary limestone field.

MOUNTAINS

"Of the mountains of Connemara, the first place belongs undoubtedly to the group of Binabola, commonly called the Twelve Pins; they are situated about midway between the head of Lough Corrib and Aghris point, and between Birterbuy bay and the Killery, occupying a space of about five miles square; but with the lesser connecting hills to the north and west, they may be said to extend over seven or eight miles square, This mountain consists of two distinct ranges or groups of summits, connected together by the elevated pass or neck of Maam Ina, from which the steep and abrupt vale of Glan Ina, sending its waters to Lake Ina, descends to the east; and on the west, the stream of Clifton, which after a course of eight miles, falls into the bay of Ardbear. On the sooth of this pass, or Maam, the deep hollow of Glen Hoghan sends its waters to join the lake of Ballynahinch, and separates the hills of Lettery and Derryclare, which, with a lower ridge that descends gradually to the westward, compose the front range of the mountain. To the north, four summits surround the central map of Knockonhiggeen, the highest of the group. The deep vale and lake of Kylemore bound the mountain on the north, as the lakes of Lough Ina, Derryclare, and Ballynahinch do on the east and south; low ridges, or tails, pass off to the westward, run in parts out into the Atlantic, and reappear in the small isles off the coast The component rock of this mountain (especially on the south) is quartz, in general distinctly stratified, or at least schistose. The position of its beds its various; they seem to lap on the swell of the mountain. At Clifton[1], towards the western shore, and at Cleggan head, the beds are vertical, and splitting easily by intervening mica slates, afford a good, and not unsightly building stone. In the mountain the quartz is usually grey or brown, especially where the stratification is distinct, and in some places reddens into sinople; but it is frequently massive, and traversed by veins of milk quartz, or rock

---

[1] Thus in original text. Probably 'Clifden', [Clachan ed.]

crystal. The quartz hills are all steep-sided, and exhibit much naked rock. The cliff on the south side of Glen Ina is particularly grand, being a naked perpendicular precipice of about 1200 feet; a considerable stream of water falls over it. The height of the brow of Littery is 1930 feet above Ballynahinch Lake, or 1955 over the sea. Bengower, the summit of Littery, is about 9100 feet Knockannahiggeen may be about 9400 feet. Derryclare is 2000, and the other summits about 1800. Limestone occurs in some places along the foot of these mountains, particularly at Derryclare. On the north of Glen Ina it appears in patches, or shield-shaped formations, as they have been termed, at very considerable elevation. There is a still more considerable mass at Kylemore; and this formation, which can be traced into and across the opposite mountain of Mamturk, towards Lough Corrib, seems also to pervade the north side of the Benabola, since we find it at Miveel, Letterfragh, Ballynakill, and Cleggan. It is probable, therefore, that some other patches exist amongst the western arms of the mountain. The northern side, along the lake of Poulacopple, exhibits lofty cliffs of hornblende rock, large blocks of which have detached themselves and tumbled into the vale. The opposite mountain of Bencoona or Poulacopple is also of hornblende, and the limestone now ceases. This rock continues to the Lough Fea, and is succeeded by a tract of brown slate (grauwacke) at the little Killery, which I have not sufficiently explored. The insulated hill of Renville is quartz; at the northern side on the shore, the mica slate passes into a very peculiar kind of porphyry. On the south side we have a little limestone. The remaining hills from this to Ardbear are mica slate, and seldom exceed 500 feet elevation. Omey Island and Aghris point are low fields of granite; some veins of granite are found traversing the mica slate; but the particular situation of that rock, and of its foreign beds, will be described hereafter. On the east side of the Twelve Pins we have the vale of Lough Ina, at the mouth of which stands the insulated hill of Coolnacarton, affording from its summit, though only about 900 feet high, one of the best views of these vales, the lakes, and mountains, that is to be found. This hill is also composed radically of quartz, but on the west side cliffs of mica slate, in nearly horizontal beds, occupy the greatest space.

"Here is also a remarkable elevated patch of limestone, under which is some green serpentine, and a regular broad vein of granite directed towards the Binabola Mountain. The southern parts exhibit hornblende rock, and hornblende porphyry, which are also found in the hill of Cashel, (about 1000 feet,) which is the highest part of some rough but comparatively low ground on the south of Ballynahinch. On the east of the vale above mentioned a chain of hills runs along the boundary of the barony of Ross or Joyce's country, and terminates about one mile and an half down the south side of the lake. This chain has no particular name; the passes over it are known by the name of Ma'am, a term also used in the highlands of Scotland.

"The summit of Shanonafola is perhaps the highest, and may be about 2000 feet. Those hills are round-topped, with steep sides, exhibiting frequently naked sheets of quartz, the component rock of the range: but on the north side, beds of granular limestone run from near the head of Loughcorrib, and penetrate the chain in various places: of these the most remarkable are, 1st, at Eilen, opposite to Coolnacarton, where several patches appear in the side of the hill, with various other primary rocks; 2nd, on the side of the road of Maanean, descending into Joyce's country. It seems to continue down through Cower, towards the river, and at the point of the ridge Maamgawney it appears in large cliffs, accompanied by hornblende slate. On the opposite side of the quartz hills we have another great bank of limestone, beginning in Derryvreeda, and running through the farm of Finniesglen, along the eastern side of Lough Ina. This limestone is very tender and large grained: some more appears in Glenglass, and crossing the range in two or three places descends into Letterbrickaun. At Mamturk it appears a regular slate, being separated into very thin sheets by intervening mica. None is found to the north of that: the mica slate and horneblende now predominate, and the chain quickly ceases at the hollow of Glencraw; beyond which is a country of different formation. At the eastern extremity of this chain we have a low opening for about a mile along the shore of Lough Corrib, then the hill of Glan, which rises to the height of 1060 feet, steep to the west, and descending gently on the other side to the village of Oughterard.

"The northern base of this mountain, which is properly called Glan, is tolerably cultivated almost everywhere, else it is covered with bog. The structure of this hill is particularly interesting, as it exhibits in a small compass all the formations which occur in the district. It is also very metalliferous; a particular description of it, however, would be out of place here; I shall merely observe, that the western end, like the hills in Joyce's Country, is composed of quartz; the north side is mica slate, the middle is penetrated in a winding manner by beds of mica slate, containing hornblende and granular limestone, covered by thick beds of pyritous green stone. On the south and east are granite and syenite, which runs under the sandstone conglomerate, towards Oughterard, and this again passes under the fletz limestone, which subsequently passing Lough Corrib, occupies the greater part of the provinces of Connaught and Leinster. The boundary of this rock, it has been already observed, runs from Galway along the foot of the hills, nearly in a straight line to Oughterard; boggy hollows, with ridges of gravel constantly intervene between it and the mountains. From Oughterard it turns to the north, and crossing the lake appears on the opposite side, a little to the west of Cong, and occupies the southern margin of Lough Mask, as far west as the house of Petersburgh. The boundary now is lost in Lough Mask, but re-appearing at the upper or northern extremity, turns off towards Westport. It does not however reach that town, but about three miles short of it turns north east to Castlebar. The limestone of Westport, though of the same kind as the great lime stone field, is unconnected with it. It is particularly worthy of remark, that along the borders of the fletz limestone there are series of vast caverns, usually with subterraneous rivers traversing them. Though this be a common occurrence in the limestone countries, there are few instances, I believe, so remarkable as in this tract. A succession of lakes, having no visible outlet, occurs in the same situation: of these Lough Mask is by far the most considerable. The drainage of a country of 250 square miles sinks here in a bason[1] of forty square miles, and after a subterranean course of two miles, rises in several magnificent fountains to join Lough Corrib. On the south of Lough Corrib also, the Ross Lake has no visible outlet, though it receives the waters of a large tract of mountain; a bog of 2000 acres is thereby deprived of the advantage of applying these streams over it. The waters of Lough Mask are visible on the passage in several large caverns near Cong; but those of Ross probably rise in Lough Corrib, by on inverted syphon: I never could trace them in any intermediate situation. There are two or three other smaller lakes to the east of Ross, and of a similar description.

"The succession of the stratified rocks is very distinctly seen at the waterfall of Oughterard. The fletz lime stone near that place having lost some of its upper beds, from being perfectly horizontal, gradually becomes more elevated, and at length above the first fall at an angle of about fifty degrees; it is immediately succeeded by strata of sandstone,

---

[1] A basin, [Clachan ed.].

the tipper parts of which are somewhat calcareous, and effervesce slightly: this stratum is a part of the great formation of red sand stone or conglomerate, (semi Protolite of Kirwan,) which constitutes the immediate support of the lime stone strata throughout Ireland, and the component rock of the greater part of its interior mountains. This rock rises in Slieve Meesh, in Kerry; the Gaulties, Knocktopher, &c. in Kilkenny; the Keepers, Devil's bit, and Slieve Bloom; Slieve Bogtha, between Galway and Clare, and Fermnamore between Galway and Mayo. It seems to appear uniformly skirting the exterior edges of the great limestone field; forms also the most common land stones on that base, and in all probability a chief component part of the soil. At the falls of Oughterard, however, its thickness is but small, and it is only by a careful examination that its connection with the general mass can be perceived. A little way to the north it becomes more distinct, and is then readily traced in low ridges and knoles down to Lough Corrib, and in some of the islands; beyond the lake it is not so readily perceived in the isthmus between Lough Corrib and Lough Mask, although the numerous blocks attest its existence, until at length, near the northern boundary of the county, it rises into an elevated upland, occupying the country between Lough Mask and the Killery bay, and again the mountain Mulvea, on the north of that harbour in Mayo. Some beds of this conglomerate of sandstone in the mountains, assume a pophyritic appearance; it is then capable of receiving a polish: blocks of it are found at great distances on the low lands. The lower beds of the sand stone are a complete congeries of rounded or flatted pebbles, usually of white or brown quartz, frequently interspersed with specks of shorl. Many beds of this rock, and even of the granite, are intimately impregnated with iron pyrites, which decomposing on exposure to the air, are evidently the cause of its redness. Beneath the red sandstone are argillaceous strata, which a little to the north of the falls have the aspect of the plate or slate clay of the coal fields; but I do not find the least trace of coal. I therefore suspect them to belong to the transition slate, which occupies so great a portion of the south of Ireland, and of which a second band seems to pass from this neighbourhood, and sinking under the limestone, &c. until it reaches the Shannon, though there are not wanting traces of its existence; it rises near Newtown Forbes in Longford, and passing along the north edge of the province of Leinster, through Down, crosses the straight, and traverses the south of Scotland. An argillaceous rock is found generally skirting the limestone field, and immediately succeeding the red sandstone throughout Ireland, but it is much more varied in its aspect; I should be inclined to say that the sandstone conglomerate reposes in unconformable stratification over a brown slate, (argillite of Kirwan, grauwacke slate,) which is interbedded with greenstone of various grain; for though, usually fine, it is frequently large, and passes into a very beautiful green porphyry, very fine masses of which are found on the west of Lough Mask. The schistus or grauwacke slate of this district is most distinct on the north shore of the southwest arm of Lough Mask, and we also find it on the south side of the Killeny bay, near to its mouth. The slate on the north of the Killery is regular clay slate, though much intermingled with greenstone. The mountain Benleva, between the arm of Lough Mask aforesaid and Lough Corrib, is also composed of trap-rocks; at the south side a kind of coarse serpentine or green porphyry is found, which also appears in other places, and seems an accompaniment to the grauwacke slate in Cavan, Monaghan, &c. Towards the west this passes into mica slate and hornblende, which forms the component rock of the mountains along the north side of Lough Corrib, (the peninsula of Doon excepted, where there is granular limestone) and along the river of Bealnabrack, Minterowen, &c. to Kylemore. This rock seems to afford a fertile soil by its decomposition; some of the best lands in

Joyce's country are composed of it, as well as a fine black mould at Glencraw. The mica slate country is hardly, if at all visible at the falls of Oughterard; it occupies the north base of the hill of Glan, the whole of the low grounds between the mountains from Lough Corrib, westward, to Slyne head, and Aghris point: it is particularly beautiful near Clifden or Ardbear bay: in many other places the quantity of mica is but minute, and it assumes the appearance of a brown rubble stone or granite, as in most part of Urrismore. This rock passes through the low land in narrow ridges, and the troughs which are thus formed become lakes, many of which are now filled up by the accumulation of fibrous bog, though many hundreds still exist, The plain of Urrismore, for example, in the west of Connemara, is a complete labyrinth of bog and water. The stratification of the mica slate is usually east and west; several foreign beds run through it, and in particular the hornblende and granular limestone, which I have so often already mentioned.

"The importance of this last, in an agricultural point of view, is so great, independent of the metallic formation with which it is accompanied, as to require a more particular description. I have marked on the map[1] the extreme limits beyond which this limestone has not yet been found, and have already described the various beds found in the mountain tract; a continuous vein passes through the central vale of Connemara on the south of those mountains. The most eastern is in the form of Bunagippaun, about a mile south of Oughterard, and in the north front of the granite field, with a hill of syenite to the north, towards the fletz lime stone; from this westward it is found in the farm of Rusheena, where a ridge of it crosses the valley into the farm of Glengowla, and, after some interruption, appears at Derryadglinne; it also arises through the fatal of Learwan, on the south of the river, in broken ridges, to a considerable elevation, beyond Derryglinne; it occurs again in Letterfione, and crossing the hill in three or four beds, appearing on the very summit, it descends into the farm of Derrowra, where it forms the mining field, and where I have shafted down upon it at four fathoms, where it was not before suspected: beyond this farm it is unknown, and does not reach the lake; but on the north side it appears in Doon, &c. singularly mingled with the hornblende; and to the westward we have it in the vale of Bealnabrack, &c. In the central vale we have an island in Lough Bofin, and some ridges of limestone passing down the hollow towards Lough Corrib; again along the lake of Arderrow and Shindela; also in Lough Elan at Bunscanive on the summit; on Lough Oured at Boheshul, Cappahoosh, Garomin, to Ballynahinch; again at Imlagh, Munga, and Ballinaboy, on Ardbear harbour, and at the village of Clifden a little limestone also, though much intermixed with silica; it occurs between Ballynahinch and Cashel hill in Cloonile: the name is obviously derived from that circumstance, as is that part of Elian near Mameen. None of this limestone is accessible by water from the southern bays; and from the particular position of the strata it is impossible at any reasonable expense to form artificial navigations to extend the benefit of it to the southward; nevertheless the existing navigable lakes will greatly facilitate the transport of limestone whenever an extended agriculture shall call for it The position of this limestone is usually vertical, with conformable beds of hornblende slate, very irregular in its thickness, from the fraction of an inch to 126 feet, and frequently contorted and interrupted: it is in general white or grey, sometimes striped green; grains of lead, copper, and iron pyrites sometimes occur in it: it is granular and micaceous, and sometimes there are thin plates of silica running through it; the quantity of carbonate is

---

[1] Nimmo's map not included, [Clachan ed.].

various, according to the portion of foreign matter, but is some times as high as 96 per cent and it is in general easily calcined. Where there is a choice, it is preferred by the country people to the secondary limestone, for the purposes of agriculture. The only other remarkable rock, is that occupying the great granite field on the south of the district, and appears under all the others at the falls of Oughterard. This rock has little variety of structure, and contains few foreign beds; excepting hornblende, though frequently micaceous, yet the hornblende must refer it to the syenite of the German mineralogists. The north part from Oughterard runs in steep cliffs by Magheramore, Doon, Drumcong, Woodstock, and Dangan, to Galway, where it enters the sea in the east of the harbour. Low hillocks of silicious and limestone gravel mark its separation from the great limestone field on the north east; and in some places the successive beds of intervening rock are also visible. The rock is composed of quartz, feldspar, (which is usually cream coloured in the western, and flesh-coloured in the eastern districts, rarely greenish,) and shorl or hornblende, black usually, but frequently green (action lite). In some places the rock is of a porphyritic structure, with large and very beautiful crystals of felspar (as to the south of Drumcong, &c.) rivalling in beauty the finest Egyptian specimens I have seen.

"The western parts are more micaceous, and having less hornblende have the aspect of regular granite. At Urid the schistose structure gives the appearance of true gneiss. Along the northern front occur beds and veins of black hornblende, which rock also, with the beds of limestone, distinctly rest on it at Bunagippaun. The hornblende is hardly to be found further south: There are various metallic veins in this formation, which need not be here specified, but not an atom of limestone of any description, some fluor only excepted, in some of those veins. A few tumblers, and some gravel of the fletz limestone, occur towards the east end, as at Tonebricky, Corbally, Barna, &c. in the county of the town.

"I have already observed, that the great granite field contains no mountains of great elevation. The hill of Killegraly rises to about 700 feet on the northern edge, but the greatest part is a kind of platform, ascending gently from the level of the sea to nearly 800 feet.

"In this great moor are numerous lakes, being shallow basins in the granite, but in general the wells are such as afford a free descent to the numerous streams, and if the tract was well provided with roads, there seems little to hinder the extension of its cultivation. The map of Mr. Larkin does not give a faithful representation of this moor, as it seems there interposed with mountains. The only mountains of note in the granite field to the west of Leam are, the ridge of Leam, and Glentrasna, about 900 feet, which runs along the eastern tide of Glentrasna, from Lough Bofin to the castle bog, gently descending as it passes southward. From hence to Kilkerran, the hill of Commas, and two hummocks in Letterfore island, about 500 feet, are those only worthy of note. Urid, and a range behind it, run to near Screeb, and are about 600 feet high; a wide plain then intervenes to Knockmaiden, a range which occupies the west of Kilkerran bay of nearly 1000 feet; then the wide boggy plain of Orrisannagh has only the hills of Glynsk and Culleen, 300 feet each, the whole still a bed of granite. Beyond the bay, Urrisbeg rises to nearly 100 feet, and though numerous granite blocks encumber its side, the mountain seems rather a mica slate, passing into granite. The remaining tract, to Slynehead, is a plain of similar composition".

SECTION VI

WATER

In winter many parts of the county have the appearance of large lakes; they are formed by two narrow or shallow outlets; they are called Turloghs; of this description is that large body of water near Rahasane, and a much larger called Turloghmore, which covers a great tract of land between Tuam and Clare Galway: it is a curious circumstance that horse and boat races are held on the same ground, but at different seasons; and it has happened that at Christmas the Turlough has been completely dry, and on the 24th of June a flood as great as that usually seen in winter.

There are many other Turloghs, which, though individually they cannot be computed to those two, yet the aggregate covers a very extensive surface of the county. An attempt to drain Turloghmore was made about 50 years ago, by a Mr. Bodkin of Lackagh, who had an idea of making a navigable cut between Tuam and Galway: it is reported that the difficulty be encountered from the bed of rocks near the bridge of Lackagh, on the road to Galway frustrated this spirited attempt. It is probable be undertook this without professional assistance, and probably, like most country gentlemen, totally ignorant of the probable difficulty or expense of the undertaking. The Turloghs of Rohasane and Turloghmore alone cover many hundred acres of fine land from September or October, sometimes sooner, until May, often longer: when the water subsides, the greater part is used as a common by the adjoining tenants, who are greatly distressed for food for their cattle and sheep if a continuance of wet weather keeps the water on longer than usual, which was the case in 1811, and many other years. The expense of draining these Turloghs by acreable assessment would be a mere trifle to each individual, but it is almost a certainty that this never can be accomplished without an act of parliament, as one stubborn ignorant booby would render every effort of the other proprietors nugatory. I must consider it a strange neglect in the Legislature that they will not bring in one comprehensive act, to prevent the necessity and expense of getting an act which costs £900 for every trifling improvement.

Lakes abound in this county, some very insignificant, but there are others very beautiful. In Conamara there are many picturesque lakes. Along the road from Oughterard to Ballynahinch, a distance of nearly 20 miles, there is a chain of lakes; some are planted, and are very pretty, but they are generally destitute of trees. The margins of those lakes are mostly free from weeds, which adds much to their beauty.

Lough Corrib is the largest in this county; occupying upwards of 30,000 acres. It originates in several streams from Joyce's country, and assumes the form and magnitude of a lake near Castlekirk island, and spreads to a considerable breadth near Cong, where it has a subterranean communication with Lough Mask, in the county of Mayo, from which it is about two miles, with a fall of above 30 feet. It gets narrow at the ferry of Knock, and again suddenly increases in size until, about two miles from Galway it assumes the appearance of a river, which it preserves, to the sea. In the Annals of Donegal it is called *Galvia* or *Galiva*. Ptolemy called this river *Ausoba*, probably from Lough Orbsen. It receives many large rivers, and at its outlet, under the bridge of Galway seems to be fully equal to the Shannon at Athlone, but much more rapid. It possesses a multitude of islands, mostly inhabited, such as Inishgile, Inishgan, Castlekirk, and several others.

Note, *Inish* is the Irish for Island. To be able to navigate it with safety requires a considerable degree of skill, for it is in some parts very shallow, particularly near Galway. The Buachaly shoal, about four miles from Galway, and some near Newcastle, are very dangerous to those unacquainted with them; also some sunken rocks and islets that should have buoys placed on them. From want of a sufficient outlet it rises in winter considerably above what is requisite for the different mills in the town of Galway. An outlet has been proposed near Newcastle and Strawlodge, and formerly, as I have mentioned before, an attempt was made to give it egress at Wellpark, into Lough Athalia, and from ignorance of its utility was, and is to this day, called *Lynches Folly*. A considerable progress was made in the excavation, and seems to have been sketched with judgment; a moderate sum would complete it, and I imagine the mill sites would more than pay all the expenses. I trust the idea will be revived; the expense can be easily ascertained by an experienced engineer. In the *Ogygia*[1] it is asserted that this lake was anciently called Lough Orbsen, from a merchant of that name, who traded extensively between Britain and Ireland; he was commonly called Mananan Mac Lir, that is Mananan, from his intercourse with the Isle of Man, and Mac Lir, i.e. sprung from the sea, because he was an expert diver. He fell in the battle of Moycullen, on the banks of Lough Orbsen, having been run through by Ulinn the grandson of Nuad, the monarch of Ireland, by his son Thady: the place of engagement was denominated after Ulinn, therefore Magh Ulinn, the field of Ulinn, where the battle was fought is now, by a small change, called Moycullen. Keating[2] says, Oirbhsion Lough was so called, "because when his grave was digging, the lake broke out!" Keating was always fond of the marvellous, and it is not a little curious that all the lower class of schoolmasters in this county believe implicitly in his and other fabulous accounts of Irish affairs.

"A little learning is a dangerous thing."

---

[1] *The Ogygia,* refers to a work by Ruaidhrí Ó Flaithbheartaigh (1629-1718), also known as Roderic O'Flaherty, an Irish historian and the last recognised chief of the O'Flaherty clan. The full title is *Ogygia seu rerum Hibernicarum chronologia,* (1685). Ogygia, the island of Calypso in Homer's Odyssey, as an allegory for Ireland, [Clachan ed.].
[2] Geoffrey Keating, the English name for Seathrún Céitinn, as was a 17th-century Irish Roman Catholic priest, poet and historian. He was born in County Tipperary c. 1569, and died c. 1644. His major work, *History of Ireland*, more properly known as *Foras Feasa ar Éirinn* (literally "Foundation of Knowledge on Ireland") was written in Early Modern Irish and completed ca. 1634.

This lake, so highly interesting to the town of Galway, has been hitherto most shamefully neglected; it extends above 30 miles from Galway, communicating with the most populous parts of Mayo, and presents an extensive field for speculation; it is about 14 feet above high water mark of the sea, and rises about three feet in floods; this rise is chiefly caused by the want of proper mill weirs; at present they are only loose stones piled up, and let so much water through, they are obliged to raise them higher than they ought, to make up the deficiency caused by their indolent neglect; if, on the contrary, the weirs were substantially built with hammered stone to the summer level, an immense quantity of land on the banks of a lake like this, occupying above 30,000 acres, would be reclaimed. Probably there would be some opposition from the millers; but if they do, as has been suggested, I cannot perceive any ground for opposing an improvement so highly beneficial to every party, as the additional rise in winter is worse than useless. The occupiers of the mill sites are wealthy; they cannot therefore plead poverty as an excuse. Mr. Ninno, an eminent engineer, has advised the adoption of two large locks to admit a communication with the sea, which, with the assistance of ample overfalls adjoining, and building permanent overfalls to the mills, would not only give them water carriage to their mills, but would prevent the expensive necessity of unloading the great quantity of sea weed (brought up the lake) on the sea shore, drawing it on cars through the town, and reloading it into boats at the wood quay, which chiefly causes an expense of at least six pounds as acre for this manure, whose beneficial effect seldom lasts longer than one crop, two at the most.

Mr. Nimmo states the expense of the locks, and the purchase of property for this purpose, to be only £6000.; that they would give to Galway all the advantages of wet docks, and that by executing two weirs at the upper level, the mills will be better supplied, and they will enjoy the advantage of water carriage up the lake and down to the sea. There is an extensive tract of bottom, covered with water in floods, to the east of the causeway leading to Terrylan, the ancient seat of Lord Clanrickard; this could be drained, and would make valuable watered meadows.

Loughrea, containing about 470 acres, viewed from the town or from the road to Dalyston, has a charming effect, accompanied by the wood of Coureen,[1] and environed on the opposite tide by the picturesque and ever verdant hills of Park &c. &c. which are continued almost round the lake until they touch the town of Loughrea on the south. The view of Grouse lodge, backed by the Slieubh Bogtha mountains, adds not a little to the charming effect, and the mountains close the scene in the happiest manner. It is not a little surprising that these charming hills are not studded with villas, surely a much more desirable residence than the town of Loughrea for those whose business does not confine them to the town, where the houses and accommodations for private gentlemen are by no means inviting and where those who have been all their lives used to good gardens and every comfort of the country,

---

[1] This picturesque wood has been lately cut down, [original footnote].

must suffer many privations of those things which from habit are absolutely necessary to their health, especially fruit and vegetables. It has been said that short leases are the chief obstruction to building on those charming hills; if so, the proprietors must be blind indeed to their own interest, for no grazier or farmer can pay so large a rent as a man of property will for a few acres to build on, and it is impossible that at any future period they can come into competition[1]. Great loss is sustained by the proprietors of ground adjoining the lake, by the water being kept above the necessary level in winter, by a board thrown across the arches at the bridge near the Artillery barrack, which was evidently intended as an outlet for flood water; surely this board should be removed in winter, and only used in very dry weather, as only at that period it is wanted for Mr. Dolphin's mills. It is imagined by many that the water of this lake is impregnated with copper, and that the greenish hue it assumes is caused by it; but that this opinion is erroneous, is probable from its producing on its banks a profusion of the best kind of grasses, on the subsidence of the water in summer. It is caused by the extreme clearness of the water on a marshy or rocky bottom, that reflects the perpetual verdure of the hills.

It is very badly supplied with fish; pike, that lives in every situation, being almost the only kind caught in it; probably the chief cause of this is the extreme hardness of the water. This lake empties itself by two small outlets, one working a flour mill, and both taking a westerly direction, after passing through the town of Loughrea, adds considerably to the beauties of St. Clerans, the charming and improving seat of James Hadiman Burke, Esq. and joins the tide water at Kilcogan. Lough Coutra, the estate of Lord Gort, is very beautiful; and when his magnificent house and picturesque plantations are finished, will be amongst the finest places in Ireland. This place, naturally picturesque, has been greatly improved by the taste and skill of Mr. Sutherland, a very celebrated landscape gardener. The new approach is particularly well conducted. — Note, the house has been finished, and is an additional proof, to many others, of the taste of Mr. Payne, the architect. The river Suck[2] is the principal river of this county. It rises in the county of Roscommon, and after watering Castlerea, it begins to divide the counties of Galway and Roscommon near Ballymoe, runs by Athleague, Mount Talbot, Ballyforan, Ballinasloe, and adds very considerably to the waters of the Shannon. Its course, in general is very sluggish and consequently overflows its banks in many places, and almost every year damages great quantities of meadow, though at the same time it contributes much to their fertility. This evil might be somewhat abated by judicious embankments, and cutting off the water from the higher grounds, especially the bogs, but chiefly by levelling all the petty eel weirs on the river, which, instead of walls, should be made

---

[1] Since writing this I understand the minority of Lord Clanrickard has prevented it, as that terminates in 1823. I hope to see my suggestions carried into effect, [original footnote].
[2] It was from this river Mr. O'Kelly, a well-known poet of this county, in one of his poems elegantly calls the man of this county "*ye sons of Suck*." O'Flaherty says, about the year 2944, "the three rivers Suc sprung up between the lands of Galway and Roscommon." [original footnote].

entirely of wattles, that would permit the water to pass through them. A canal on this river from the Shannon, and carried to Galway, has been in agitation. The canal is now (1823) excavating. It will be a means of improving the agriculture of the surrounding country to a great extent. I trust it will not stop until it communicates with Tuam.

I imagined canal companies had long since seen the impropriety of meddling with rivers. Keating says this river was formed in the reign of Heremon. The Shannon touches only a small part of this county, beginning near Clonfert, and ending at Mountshannon. The river of Shruel, which divides this county from Mayo, injures many acres of ground; its only discharge at present is through apertures in the rocks under a hill, and emerges again near Moycastle. If these apertures, called swallows, were enlarged, and boys prevented from throwing sods and stones into them to facilitate the catching of eels, much injury might be prevented, but the obstructions are every day increasing, and the river is completely stopped, then possibly the proprietor will be sensible of this neglect, when he sees the country for many miles inundated, and property to a great amount destroyed, and perhaps many lives lost.

Formerly the mills of Shruel threw back water for several miles and injured a great quantity of land, the estate of Mr. Kirwan; but lately that gentlemen has, with great judgment, run a back-water drain parallel to the river, which gives him a power of draining a great tract of valuable land; but though executed for several years, no assistance has been given by cutting off the springs from the high ground, of much more consequence than even the back-water, drain. It has been proposed lately, by an eminent engineer, to prevent the water from sinking through the swallows, by bringing the river on the surface; but I understand one of those petty objections so frequently made by ignorance, has been raised to prevent it. The injury by the obstructions in this river, and which are very much increased by the mill at Shruel, extends through a great tract of country as far back as Castle Hacket and Thomastown. This county is almost every where blessed with springs of the purest water; there is one at Eyrecourt, whose water, I am informed, is six ounces in a quart lighter than any other in the county; it is certainly excellent, but I very much doubt the extent of its superiority. Another at Oranmore, near the bridge, remarkably fine, and from which a copious stream always flows; by analysis it has been found two ounces in the pound lighter than any other within twenty miles of it (that at Eyrecourt is not twenty miles off); a very fine spring near Killconnel Abbey; very fine springs near the east suburbs of Galway, called St Augustine's wells, where people do penance by parading in their bare feet round those wells a stated number of times. — See Rutty on mineral waters. A spring well near the summit of the rocky hill of Knocknay; it is never dry, and very fine water. Chalybeate wells[1] abound, — the most remarkable I shall mention. One at a short distance from Woodford has been used with great success, and has been analyzed by Dr. Donnelan of Portumna;

---

[1] natural mineral springs containing iron salts, [Clachan ed.].

one of great repute near the white gate on the estate of Mr. Burke of Tintrim. In the same neighbourhood, at the village of Quose, on Lord Clanrickard's estate, a well that instantly kills poultry that drink of it. A chalybeate of great efficacy in the demesne of Kiltulla, the seat of John D'Arcy, Esq. and on this gentleman's estate at Kingston, in Connemara, there is one that Mr. Kirwan, who often explored this country, considered as one of the best in Europe. Another at Cahertinne, near Dunsandle, often used. A fine spa between Clonfert and Lawrencetown; it has been taken with great effect in liver complaints; it is thought to be at least equal to that at Castleconnel; one near Athenry much frequented; another at Rathglass, near Kilconnell, much used; another near Woodbrook has been used; another at Killimor much used; one on the road side, near Abbert, has been greatly used; another of great repute near Hampstead; a far famed chalybeate spa at Oughterard, which induces many invalids to take lodgings there. This well is badly built, and no care taken, by a drain round it, to prevent the mixture of rain water: indeed the same neglect attaches to every spa well; they are uniformly neglected and dirty. Probably there are many others that escaped my notice.

CHAPTER II

AGRICULTURE

SECTION I

MODE OF CULTURE

WHEAT[1] is the crop at which almost every farmer aims, and to which almost every other is subservient: it must be confessed this predilection has one good effect attending it — the inducement to cultivate potatoes on a much larger scale than otherwise would be done: too many fallow for this crop, but not near so many as formerly, thanks to the potatoes for it. Wheat produced on fallow is usually sown in October. Where potatoes have been the previous crop, seldom until December, and sometimes, if the season is wet, defer the sowing until spring; twenty stones are usually allowed to sow an acre, but some few, where the ground is in high tilth, sow only ten stones, but always less seed in spring than in autumn. It is sowed both under the plough and by shovelling; the latter mode generally by cottiers. Oats are usually sowed after potatoes, produced by burning the surface, especially in moory soil not fit for wheat; but in ground adapted to it, wheat is the favourite crop; two barrels, or twenty-eight stone of oats, are generally sowed on the acre; some few sow less, but usually the quantity allowed is more than is necessary. The general mode of those who have not a sufficient quantity of manure for their potatoes, (and which are by much the greater number) is to hire land and pare and burn the surface; they pay various prices, from three to ten guineas an acre, according to the quality of the ground, but more frequently the price is regulated by the demand. Where there is little ground to be let for this purpose, it is astonishing the prices they will pay, or frequently promise to pay, and when the price of the seed and their own labour are added to the rent, one is at a loss to account for it, except that they must have the land at any price. Those who have land to let often take advantage of this necessity,

---

[1] In Henry the Second's time, our wheat was so small and shrivelled as scarcely to be cleaned by the fan; there was much straw but little corn, probably from the richness of the soil and a defective tillage. It is thought we had this grain from a Scandinavian tribe of Picts, called *Cruthnii*. *Cruithneacht* is the Irish for wheat, and it is likely we received an imperfect knowledge of the cultivation of it from them. Baron Finglass informs us that in the reign of Henry VIII. "No man having a plough of his own buy any corn, upon pain of forfeiting 12d. for every peck he shall buy, until his own corn be all spent. Also, that no man shall export corn out of Ireland, if the peck of wheat be above the value of 12d. and malt above the value of 8d. upon pain of forfeiting the same, and that no license be given to any man for the exportation." By a statute of Edward IV. "All persons were prohibited from exporting grain from Ireland if the peck of grain exceeded 10s. upon pain of forfeiting the grain, or the value thereof and the ship, half to the king and half to the seiser. Likewise, that no merchant shall buy corn in the sheaf, upon pain of forfeiting the same." [original].

and frequently suffer by it, for it is nothing uncommon to let whole fields in this manner at a high rent, and after a part is pared, some other person in the neighbourhood advertising ground at a lower price, they abandon what they have pared, and the ground is left on hands at a season too late to prepare for any other crop. The usual mode of settling for this ground is, after the potatoes have been planted, to get the ground surveyed, and notes are taken payable at various dates, but usually the 17th March following: frequently a considerable time elapses before the notes are paid, and is the cause of much litigation at every quarter sessions; for if from any cause whatever the crop is unproductive, whether from bad seed, too late sowing, or bad management, they are ever ready to take advantage of it, and by leaving the crop on your hands think they are exonerated from the promised payment; and even if they are willing they are often unable, the goodness of the crop being often the only security for the rent. Amongst the very few exceptions to demanding exorbitant rents for ground let in this way, it would be an act of injustice not to mention Mr. Daly of Dunsandle, who, though he could easily get eight guineas or more, desired his steward not se take more than six, and to give a preference to his own tenants. Preparatory to burning, the surface of the ground is skinned by spades, (provincially called screwed,) which for this purpose are always sharp and broad at the end, with a considerable bend in the blade, to prevent the necessity of stooping too much. From sixteen to twenty men will skin an acre in a day when they work for themselves; sometimes eight men have accomplished it; indeed any work appertaining to the potato seems to be more cheerfully executed than any other, as they say, "their heart warms to it," and every person must be sensible of the warmth of an Irishman's heart for any person or thing he likes. Some of the better kind of farmers use the plough for this purpose, but the general mode is by the spade or loy. When labourers work by the day it may probably take from thirty to forty men per acre.

Potatoes are usually planted in ridges of about six feet broad, the furrow about three feet; some few gentlemen, but scarcely any farmers or cottiers, plant in drills; the superiority of the practice only wants to be known to make it general. It saves manure, seed, and labour, and the produce is nearly equal; and as to quality of size, greatly superior. It leaves the ground in a much cleaner state and fitter for a crop. When ground is to be laid down with grass seeds, it is the only method; for it is almost impossible to level ground after ridges, the unequal sinking at the ground alone must prevent it: another material objection to ridges is that almost all the manure that should be retained near the surface and equally spread over it, is commonly buried in the furrows.[1] This mismanagement is always visible in the following year, in the superiority of the crop where the furrows have been, and is

---

[1] I have observed an excellent practice in the bogs near Athlone, when the potatoes are dug, they scrape all the surface into a sharp ridge in the middle of the potato ridge; it lies dry all the winter, and is ready to spread in a highly pulverised state in the ensuing spring, [original footnote].

still further visible for many years by the poverty of the herbage where[1] the ridges were. There are various methods of putting the potatoes into the ground[2]; they are

---

[1] "were" in original, [Clachan ed.].

[2] The following, from the Horticultural Transactions by the late Right Honorable Sir Joseph Banks, Bart. I imagine will be new to many of my readers. "The potato was brought to England by the colonists sent out by Sir Walter Raleigh, under the authority of his patient granted by Queen Elizabeth, "for discovering and planting new countries, not possessed by Christians," which passed the great seal in 1584. Some of Sir Waiter's ships sailed in the same year; others, on board one of which was Thomas Harriott, afterwards known as a mathematician in 1585; the whole however returned and probably brought with them the potato on the 27th July, 1586. This Mr. Thomas Harriott, who was probably sent to examine the country, and report to his employers the nature and produce of the toil, wrote an account of it, which is printed in De Bry's *Collection of Voyages*, Vol. 1. In this account, under the article of roots, p. 17, he describes a plant called *openawk*. "These roots," says he, "are round, some as large as a wallnut, others much larger; they grow in damp soil, many hanging together as if fixed on ropes; they are good food, either boiled or roasted."

Gerard, in his *Herbal*, published in 1597, gives a figure of the potato, under the name of potato of Virginia, otherwise called Norembega. The manuscript minutes of the Royal Society, December 5, 1693, tells us, that Sir Robert Southwell, then president, informed the fellows, at a meeting, that his grandfather brought potatoes into Ireland, who first had them from Sir Walter Raleigh, This evidence proves not unsatisfactorily, that the potato was first brought into England, either in the year 1586, or very soon after; and sent from thence to Ireland, without delay, by Sir Robert Southwell's ancestor, where it was cherished, and cultivated for food before the good people of England knew its value; for Gerard, who had the plant in his garden in 1597, recommends the roots to be eaten as a delicate dish, not as common food. It appears, however, that it first came into Europe at an earlier period, and by a different channel; for Cluaius, who at that time resided at Vienna, first received the potato in 1597, from the Governor of Mons in Hainault, who had procured it the year before from one of the attendants of the Pope's legate, under the name of Taratoufle, and learned from him, that in Italy, where it was then in use, no one knew certainly whether it originally came from Spain, or from America. Peter Cieca, in his Chronicle, printed in 1553, tells us, Chap, x p. 49, that the inhabitants of Quito, and its vicinity, have, besides Mays, a tuberous root, which they eat, and call Papas; this Clusius guesses to be the plant he received from Flanders and this conjecture has been confirmed by the accounts of travellers, who have since that period visited the country.

From these details we may fairly infer, that potatoes were first brought into Europe from the mountainous parts of South America in the neighbourhood of Quito; and, as the Spaniards were the sole possessors of that country, there is little doubt of their being first carried into Spain; but as it would take sometime to introduce them into use in that country, and afterwards to make the Italians so well acquainted with them as to give them a name (Taratoufli also signifies Truffle) there is every reason to believe they had been several years in Europe, before they were sent to Clausius. The name of the root in South America, is Papas, and in Virginia it was called Openawk; the name of potato was therefore evidently applied to it on account of its similarity to the battata, or sweet potato: and our potato appears to have been distinguished from that root by the appellation of potato of Virginia, till the year 1640, if not longer. Some authors have asserted, that potatoes were first discovered by Sir Francis Drake, in the south seas, and others, that they were introduced into England by Sir John Hawkins; but in both instances the plant alluded to is clearly the sweet potato which was used in England as a delicacy long before the introduction of our potatoes; it was imported in considerable quantities from Spain and the Canaries, and was supposed to possess the power of restoring decayed vigour. The kissing comforts of Falstaff, and other confections of similar imaginary qualities, with which our Ancestors were duped, were principally made of these, and of Erin's roots. The potatoes themselves were sold by itinerant dealers, chiefly in the neighbourhood of the Royal Exchange, and purchased, when scarce, at no inconsiderable cost, by those who had faith in their alleged properties. The allusions to this opinion are

usually spread by women on the manure before the planters, at about 6 to 9 inches asunder, and covered with spades; sometimes they are planted under the manure, and where sea weed (Algae of various kinds) is used, they are planted on the sea weed after it has had time to dry, for they find by exposure that if it is used fresh from the sea, it would injure the potato-sets. If the season for procuring this kind of manure has been protracted beyond the usual one for planting, they put the sets on the land, and give them a very slight covering of earth, and as fast as they can procure the sea weed, they spread it over this covering of the earth, and finish the covering by adding more earth from the furrows. An experiment has been tried, by throwing the sea weed in heaps to putrefy, but it was found that the fresh weed was much better, and much time and labour saved. The method of dibbling is used sometimes, but not often: the practice of using small potatoes for seed, prevails too much, nor can any thing convince them it is erroneous. A dry spring always ensures a plentiful crop of potatoes, and a wet one, which prevents the burning, on the contrary is the usual forerunner of a scarcity; for a very great proportion of the potatoes in this county, indeed I may say of the province, are raised from burned ground; the abolition of this practice (bad only from its abuse) is under the present wretched state of agricultural knowledge, and capital, impossible: until better practices are established, especially feeding in the house winter and summer, and a total change in the mode of letting land in villages, it can never take place. After potatoes in burned ground, oats are frequently sowed, and for which people are often charged six guineas an acre, sometimes less; this, under their mismanagement of late sowing, bad tillage, and generally very indifferent seed, is frequently a losing speculation, unless the produce brings a war price; but the competition is generally so great, that they are induced to offer more than the value of the land, and are sorely pinched to make up the rent, which is often done, in part money, part labour, and perhaps part produce at a low price. The proprietor of the ground, instead of laying it down with grass seeds with this crop, often sows repeated crops of oats, until the exhausted soil will produce nothing but weeds of the humblest growth, especially Fiorin grass of so diminutive a size, that by those who had seen it in bogs, it would scarcely be thought the same plant. In some places the ground is fallowed after the oats, and a crop of wheat taken, followed by one of oats without grass seeds, and left to nature to produce them, which in our favored isle is generally the case; but where the ground is of an inferior quality, this does not take place for many years, and in the interim the farmer suffers a loss proportioned to his rent: frequently, as soon as the surface is covered sufficiently with the roots of grass to retain the earth, this process is repeated preparatory to a renewal of this scourging system. I beg again to repeat that in most cases I am a warm advocate for restricted burning of land. Did landlords pay more

---

very frequent in the plays of that age. "Let it rain potatoes, and hail kissing comfits. MERRY WIVES OF WINDSOR Act V, Scene 5." — Note, it is curious enough that the potato has presented the same character to the present day in Ireland; but we add milk to make the charm complete, [original footnote].

attention to their estates, or did agents reside, and could be brought to consider that they have more duties to perform than the mere receipt of rents, much of this injury to land would be prevented. It has been a practice with some landlords to receive a large sum of money in hand for permission to wealthy middlemen to let large farms for burning, to poor people, at exorbitant rents; I do not know a fairer ground for breaking a lease, by the heir at law, and making this destructive tenant disgorge some of his ill-got wealth; however, this practice is not so prevalent as formerly; the mother of invention is often the mother of improvement.

On the sea coast, sea weeds (Algae) and coralines of various kinds, are their never-failing resources; on this manure they plant potatoes, which are followed by a crop of wheat, oats, and in sandy soils barley,[1] and then potatoes with a fresh manuring again. Potatoes produced from sea weed are, if planted early, as good as those produced by any other kind of manure; but if planted late, are generally wet, which is the case often with other manures. In many places on the sea coast, very fine early potatoes called *Windeleers* (the same I believe as the county of Wicklow Bangers) are produced in several feet depth of pure sea sand, manured by sea weed, and after that fine barley, which is all consumed by the innumerable private stills of Connemara.

A considerable portion of the tillage of cottiers is effected by the spade, and they scarcely ever fallow: their rents are too high, and their patch of land too small, to admit that wasteful practice; it is also the practice with some gentlemen to dig in oats in spring, and where the ground is too wet to plough with safety, or for those who permit such ploughing as I have often seen, it is a safe practice, however expensive. But why should any man of fortune have wet land, or permit bad tillage?

On Mr. Lawrence's estate, and elsewhere, the tenants plant potatoes in furrows made by the plough; they first spread a small quantity of manure on the surface, and plough it in, then throw it into furrows, in which they plant the potatoes; in a few days they second spit, and finish with a shovel; by this means they avoid the necessity of bringing up a quantity of bad earth; but in wet land the furrows between the ridge should be well dug, without throwing any part on the surface; this practice permits the wet to percolate, and if steadily persisted in, would prevent the necessity of throwing lac liagh (a clay) soils into high ridges, by which means, on many estates, one-third of the soil is unoccupied, and is a very material cause of the difficulty of paying rents.

---

[1] The Irish had not originally barley or rye, [original footnote].

EXTENT OF CULTURE AND OF EACH SPECIES OF GRAIN SOWED

There is a vast deal more corn produced in this county than a cursory view of it would lead one to think. In the rocky districts, where walls are almost exclusively the fence, and the enclosures small, the corn is seldom seen from the road, yet in these patches is produced most excellent wheat; the flour millers prefer it to that produced in deeper and stronger soils, as having a thinner skin, and though not so large a grain, producing more and better flour. The oats and barley produced in these calcareous soils partake of the valuable qualities ascribed to the wheat; but from a general neglect of landlords in providing good seeds for their tenants, are greatly inferior to what they would be both in quality and quantity of produce. If the same benign spirit actuated them that has so materially improved the live stock of the county, by giving gratis the best sires of each kind, an increase and improvement beyond conception would be the result, more especially as this county has lately become a considerable exporting one. It would be much for the advantage of the corn merchants in Galway if they pursued the enlightened practice of Messrs. Persse, late proprietors of the Newcastle brewery, of importing the very best of each kind of grain, and selling them first cost, there can be little doubt it would be fully repaid to them in a more ample and better produce to their stores, and do away that disgraceful stigma we perceive laid on Irish corn in every market note from Liverpool, where it is rated even lower than that produced in Scotland; and it must be highly gratifying to their feelings when they perceive the beneficial effects of their exertions.

In the neighbourhood of Oranmore, parish of Kilcolgan, Tartarian oats are very generally cultivated; they are esteemed better for light impoverished soils, and are said to give nearly half meal. In almost every part of this county a variety of very bad black oats makes a large proportion of the crop, and as the poor people have not better for seed, the evil is increasing: they say that the best potato oats become black in their ground; this I very much doubt, — but that it proceeds from a careless mixture of the corn. Crops of every kind in the lands of cottiers are generally carefully weeded, as I have often seen with pleasure in my rides through the country; and if indolence forms any part of the character of the inhabitants of this county, it is certainly not in the lower ranks it will be found, when working for themselves. There have been few improvements made in agriculture until very lately, indeed until Farming Societies were established, and they are still too much confined to the demesnes of men of fortune; to become general, the smaller landed proprietors must be induced to shake off their old prejudices, and turn their eyes to those gentlemen's seats, where they will see two horses in a plough without a driver, ploughing much deeper and better in every respect than they do with four horses, two leaders, and frequently a lazy fellow keeping or pretending to keep the plough in the ground by pressing on the beam with a pitchfork. I must confess were I a landed proprietor I should blush at seeing such practices, and much more if some of our travelling agriculturists from Great Britain were witnesses of such disgraceful practices. Why should not every landed proprietor have a little farming society on his estate? —

Could he lay out a very few pounds with more advantage? I regret to state I have more than once heard, "I do not care a damn what they do, or how dirty their houses are, so I receive my rents." Can there be a stronger proof of the little interest they take, than that little or no advantage has been taken of the liberal offer of the Farming Society of Ireland, of ploughs of the best construction, iron and wood, at very reduced prices, for the use of their tenants. Did a proper feeling actuate them, a great addition of carpenters would be necessary at the implement manufactory.

Like most parts of Ireland, tillage is despised in those districts where grazing prevails; yet a doubt does not remain on my mind, that the richest land would be more profitably employed in a union of tillage with grazing; but where tillage is practised, it is almost uniformly the scourging system that is pursued, without the intervention of an ameliorating green crop; yet this is the tillage which I have frequently heard put into the scale against grazing, or in other words, the most execrable tillage with the best grazing. How blind to their own interest must those farmers be who pursue this wretched system of deterioration, yet what better can be expected when men of large fortune and liberal education, seeing only through the eyes of an ignorant prejudiced steward of the old school, permit their lands to be scourged in this barbarous manner. How can it be expected their tenantry will make any change, when I assure my readers that more than once or twice I have heard the hackneyed cant of the common labourers used by those men of large fortune, and otherwise liberal education, "I wonder how our fathers and grandfathers did when these fine improvements were not thought of." And sometimes from those men who, by the industry of their ancestors, an extraordinary coincidence of fortunate circumstances, or from an unfeeling disposition, taking every advantage of the distresses of the poor, have jumped into a large fortune, and perhaps possess many rich grazing farms for a few shillings per acre, men of a plodding penurious disposition, and so rich that their frequent losses can never be known by the usual signs, those are the men that are compared with your New light farmers, as they are sneeringly called; men, who if they had the same capital, and farms at the same rent of the drones, would not only enrich themselves, but greatly improve their country. Graziers are seldom improvers of land; they are ready enough to build wall enclosures, but as to draining, many of them laugh at it. The prosperity of many ignorant illiterate farmers has often been adduced to prove their superiority over what they style book farmers; it must, however, be allowed, too many of the latter description have deserved this title, though a rational theory should be the foundation, yet too many find, when too late, that experience gained by an extensive practice is also absolutely necessary. Dr. Hales says: "Though I am sensible, that from experience chiefly we are to expect the most certain rules of practice; yet the likeliest method for making the most judicious observations, and for improving any art, is to get the best insight we can into the nature and properties of what we are desirous to cultivate and improve." Is this the case with Connaught farmers? Certainly not; for how few take even the *Farmers Journal*, though the annual expense is only thirty shillings. It requires little argument to show that many of those rich farmers owe their success to several causes — to their living little better than their labourers, whatever their increase of income may have been, an increase that has arisen from having rich lands at very low rents, and a very great and sudden rise in the price of every article of agricultural produce, and not infrequently they are money lenders to their poorer neighbours, from whom they extort illegal interest, which is often paid in labour at a low rate, &c. &c. Little argument is required to prove that repeated corn crops exhaust the soil; we see but too many proofs of it in every part of Ireland. It requires as little to prove, that alternate green crops, manured, give an increased fertility to the ground.

It is too generally imagined that green crops pay a very small proportion of what could be obtained for corn crops. I shall endeavour to prove, under the head "Course of Crops," that this opinion is the result of ignorance of the subject. It is not an easy matter to give the quantity of each grain produced on the acre; but I imagine, from an increase of the potato culture, the average is higher than when Mr. Arthur Young, so very beneficially to this country, travelled through it in 1779. I think it may be stated per acre, wheat, six to ten barrels, of twenty stones each; oat, twelve to twenty barrels of fourteen stones each; barley, fourteen to twenty barrels, of sixteen stones each; potatoes, thirty-two to eighty barrels, of thirty-two stones each, sixteen pounds to the stone[1].

A considerable quantity of fine wheat is produced in the baronies of Dunkellen and Athenry, also in the neighbourhood of Ardrahan, Gort, Caeggclare and Kirvara, which is mostly sent by water to Galway for home consumption and for exportation; many other parts of the county also furnish a supply for exportation, as there are few gentlemen that have not some tillage; but there is no such thing in this county, (at least I have not been fortunate enough to meet him,) as an extensive tillage farmer; many have occasionally a large haggard[2], produced by lands thrown on their hands,

---

[1] By the following statement from Mr. Young, it is seen what may be done by a high state of cultivation; it has been accommodated to the Irish acre,

			Barrels.	
Eastern Tour	Vol. I. p. 46	Oats per Acre,	$29 \frac{2}{5}$	of 14 st. each.
Annals of Agriculture	Vol. XI. P. 159	Do.	$29 \frac{7}{8}$	Do.
Do.	Vol. V. p. 240	Do	$30 \frac{9}{14}$	Do
Eastern tour	Vol. I. p. 48	Barley per acre	$25 \frac{11}{15}$	of 16 st. etch.
Do.	Vol. III. p. 19	Do	$28 \frac{5}{15}$	Do.
Annals	Vol. II. P. 79	Do	29	Do
Do.	Vol. II. p. 245	Wheat per acre	$18 \frac{4}{5}$	of 20 st. etch.
Do.	Vol. XII. p. 45	Do	$19 \frac{14}{20}$	Do.
Do.	Vol. II. p. 93	Do	$21 \frac{1}{20}$	Do.

In my surrey of the County of Clare, it is stated from good authority, that Mr. Singleton and hs father have had on rich Corcass lands 40 barrels of Bere, of 16 stones each, and 39 barrels of Beans, of 20 stones each, per Irish acre, [original footnote].

[2] An enclosure on a farm for stacking grain, hay, etc., (dialect, Manx, Ireland), [Clachan ed.].

lands unset, or from some other accidental circumstance, but they are not what would be called farmers in the counties of Meath, Kildare, Kilkenny, or Fingal. Some of the greatest haggards I have seen in this county were produced by a very wretched system, that of fallowing a worn out soil, taking a crop of wheat, preparatory to throwing it on the landlords' hands in that very impoverished state.

SECTION II

COURSE OF CROPS

This, although the most material branch of agriculture, is in general the least understood; without a change in our mode of cropping, little improvement can be made; we may continue to import English and Scotch ploughs, and ploughmen, but unless we import at the same time their good practices, and resolve steadily to pursue them, it only tends to bring them into disrepute with those who are but too ready to catch at every opportunity to decry practices they do not understand, or are too indolent to adopt. It is nothing uncommon to hear some gentlemen, after having been a few months in England, enlarge with rapture on the superiority of the agricultural practices of Great Britain; this may, in some measure, be accounted for, from their associating only with those English gentlemen who have made improved husbandry their pursuit. But had they made excursions into some of the remote counties, they would perceive practices to the full as reprehensible as our very worst. I need only desire them to read the *Annals of Agriculture*, and the Agricultural Reports of Counties, &c. &c. to convince them that we want English capital even more than their skill; this shows how necessary it is for our travelled countrymen to discriminate. That the improved practices of Great Britain are superior to any in the world, will, I imagine, be readily granted; but *caeteris paribus*[1], they are not universally so very far before us as their improvement in other branches of science would lead us to think, or as those who only take a prejudiced peep at agricultural practices would have us believe. In this county there is not much variation in the course of cropping; that of the small farmer and cottier adjoining Banagher, is, 1st, Pare and burn, or manure for potatoes; — 2nd, Rye; — 3rd, Oats, and manure for potatoes again. In the vicinity of the bay and coast of Galway the usual course is, 1st, One, or perhaps two crops of potatoes manured with sea weed of various kinds;— 2nd, Wheat;— 3rd, Oats. Often, whether from poverty of soil, scantiness, or bad quality of the seaweed, only one crop of potatoes and one of oats are taken, perhaps two of oats. The wheat produced by this manure, added to the usual effects of a calcareous soil, of which the southern coast consists, is generally of a very superior quality, and in great estimation at the flour mills; and the potatoes, if planted early, are usually of the best quality, and produced in great abundance; if planted late they are generally wet and soft, but are reckoned best for seed. In every other part of the

---

[1] Literally translated as "with other things the same," or "all other things being equal or held constant", (Latin), [Clachan ed.].

county the too general mode is, to hire land if they can get it, and pare and burn for potatoes, of which it is customary to take two crops in succession; if the ground is good, and every thing as they could wish, the second is better than the first; then wheat or oats as they can agree for the ground; it is then given up to the landlord, who is generally a middleman, and he frequently takes as many crops of oats as it will probably produce, and in this impoverished state it is permitted to lie for several years, until it in some measure recovers its former fertility, which, if it has been originally of a good quality, it will do in a period that would astonish an Englishman. As to laying it down with grass seeds or clover, (which must be done in most parts of England or they would have nothing,) sowed with the last crop, it is scarcely ever practiced, especially as this ruinous system generally takes place during the last five or six years of the lease[1].

If this wretched course (if course it can be called) was pursued only by small farmers or cottiers, they might well plead ignorance of better practices in extenuation; but when we see them constantly in use by those who from their education and fortune have no such excuse, they are, in their consequences, highly pernicious and reprehensible: what improvement can be expected from tenants, when landlords are guilty of those wretched modes of cultivation? I have frequently expostulated with farmers on the ultimate ruin they would bring on their families by such a system of deterioration, and endeavoured to impress them with the superior immediate and future profit of alternate green and Corn crops, but the answer has been almost universally here as well as in the county of Clare "what will you have us do, when our landlord or rich neighbours pursue the same system, though they pay their stewards thirty or forty pounds a year?" Until landed proprietors see with their own eyes, or procure those from whom the mist of prejudice has been cleared, to conduct their affairs, this must ever be the case. The ignorance and consequent obstinacy of old-light stewards, who maintain that nothing but corn or cattle can pay any rent, I am perfectly convinced has tended more to retard improvement in Ireland, than all other causes put together.

For the information of those farmers who may not have had an opportunity of seeing, better practices, or of reading those books where they are detailed, I shall endeavour to suggest such a course, as will not only give a superior immediate profit, but after any length of time leave their land in still better heart then when they began. The usual bad course I have before mentioned, is either to pare and burn the surface, or manure with black mud [2] and a little manure mixed, for 1st, potato— 2nd, wheat, —

---

[1] There are some great land sharks in this county who are all their lives in a constant scene of bustle and litigation with their landlord, from pursuing a knavish system of breaking up ground they have no right to do; they lay their plans so dexterously, and they have their creatures so very well trained, and so dependent on them, that they too generally succeed especially where the land belongs to an absentee, or a non-resident agent acts for him. [original footnote].

[2] For the information of such as may not know what is meant by black mud, it ii necessary to inform them, it is part of the bog, usually the surface, brought home in summer, and spread about their doors,

3rd, and 4th, oats, and frequently this grain continued until the productive quality of the ground is completely exhausted. After this it remains for several years producing scarcely any thing but half starved weeds of the worst kinds. Instead of this exhausting course, I would advise the following course should be adopted in light soils (but not sandy) of which the greater part of this county consists. — 1st, potatoes in ridges as usual, after burning, or with manure; 2nd, wheat, barley or oats; 3rd, clover and rye grass, or clover alone sowed with the preceding corn crop[1]; this to remain for two years if good; if not, it should remain only one year. The ground should then be broke up in autumn, and laid dry all the winter; at the usual season it should be manured for potatoes in drills, and the same course pursued as before; the clover should be mowed every day, and should lie in the swath until the following day, and given to stock of every kind in small quantities at a time; for this purpose a good ass and small well formed cart will, where the number of cattle is not very great, be found to answer best, as there is not that temptation to storing large quantities at a time, than which nothing is more to be dreaded, as it would heat very soon, and be refused by the cattle; then, indeed, the old-light steward, and the man who attended the cattle, would be in their element. "There now my lord, didn't I tell you the cattle never would thrive in the house in summer; it is against nature, &c." If the cattle have been well littered with the straw produced along with the clover, a vast heap of manure will be produced, and will bring their ground to an uncommon state of fertility; they will find that if this course is pursued for any number of years, the ground will be in better heart than it was originally. The introduction of rape, vetches, turnips, mangel worzel[2], &c. &c. must be gradually introduced, when a taste for improvement dawns on the mind, and the value of the soiling system is better known; until that period arrives (and the acceleration of it depends much on landlords), it would only perplex, perhaps deter those for whose benefit this course is suggested.

Whilst the small farmer or cottier is pursuing this course, it is to be hoped that those of information and larger income will lead the way in the introduction and cultivation, on improved and steady principles, of the best kinds of green crops, cultivated in a superior style, and consumed in the house by stock; then, and not before, will be the time to expect such good practices will be generally adopted. Irish farmers are not that race of obstinate fools they are sometimes called, they are not more wedded to the customs of their ancestors than the inhabitants of any other country of the same rank and neglected education; I have ever found them willing to

---

this is mixed with any manure they can scrape together, and remains an offensive black puddle until spring. If they are near a road, the sides are cut away to mix with it, (original footnote).

[1] In general the quantity of clover seed is not sufficient; not lest than twenty-one pounds to the acre should ever be sowed, though the ground may appear to be covered, yet when this crop has too much room, and not cut at an early stage of its growth, it becomes woody and unpalatable to cattle (original footnote).

[2] a variety of the beet *Beta vulgaris*, cultivated as food for livestock, [Clachan ed.]..

be instructed, if gentle methods are used, and they have reason to think they shall not lose by their experiment; but the language of petulance too often used to them, is not calculated to make proselytes; for instance, within two or three years, the practice of ploughing with two horses by those who formerly used four, has been in many places adopted, especially in the neighbourhood of those gentlemen who practice ploughing with a pair, without a leader; it is true, the boy to lead has been too generally retained; but lately I have in a few instances seen even him discarded; probably he is oftener retained for the sake of society than use. A gentleman in this county asked his ploughman could he plough with reins; "to be sure I can, Sir, but *the horses cannot speak to me*." — Example here, as in most cases, is worth volumes of directions, and when it is furnished by one of their own rank, it may be expected that other good practices will be extended amongst the small farmers and cottiers who stand most in need of it; to enable them to discharge the high rents they usually pay, made still higher by their own defective management.

Fallowing is still practiced very much, but not to the extent it was formerly; the increased cultivation of potatoes has, in a great measure, rendered it unnecessary; the great rise in rents too have contributed to this desirable abolition; farmers will at length become sensible of the loss they sustain by this triennial tax on their profits, besides fallowing; according to the careless method generally practiced, has not the extended effect of cleaning the land, but quite the contrary, for it helps to divide and transplant the roots of perennial weeds; and we frequently see fallows covered with thistles, ragweed, and other pernicious weeds in full seed, blowing about the country; in fact they are generally green fallows. Two crops of wheat are sometimes, but not often, taken in succession; the want of capital, even more than ignorance of the bad consequence is the chief cause of the defective tillage before mentioned. It is by no means uncommon for a man scarcely possessed of a guinea, to take fifty or an hundred acres of land; if the land has been under grass for some years, he is certain of setting almost every acre of it for eight to ten pounds an acre, for burning for potatoes for each of the two succeeding years; the third year he gets perhaps five or six pounds per acre, for sowing oats, and as long as he can get any one to take the ground, and then perhaps leaves it on the landlord's hands, in the wretched state I have before mentioned. As the fondness for money generally increases with possession, our landjobber becoming possessed of a sum he never had reason to expect, extends his views to new and larger undertakings; to accomplish this, regardless of future loss, he grasps at present gains, grows expensive in his living, becomes a tippler at dram shops, and not infrequently in a few years gets an abatement in the rent (as a reward for his good management) from his unthinking absentee landlord, or his Dublin agent, totally ignorant of country affairs,[1] and then

---

[1] Mr. McEvoy, in his excellent *Survey of the County of Tyrone* coincides most fully in this idea, page 128.— "Agents not acquainted with country business may be considered a great bar to improvement." The improvement of land depends very much on the activity and knowledge of agents, [original footnote].

lets the farm in small lots to poor cottiers (who must have land) at an exorbitant rent, and becomes one of those pests of society, an unimproving middleman[1], and a lender of money in small sums, for which he exacts usurious interest in various articles of produce and labour: if he wants the re-possession of a piece of land, he lets the tenant run in arrear, and then pounces on him with an ejectment, sells even the bed from under him, and turns him out to beg: every one acquainted with the county of Galway can easily find the original of this picture.

The exertions made by small farmers and cottiers to procure manure is extraordinary, often to the great injury of the roads; this ascertains to a certainty that a little attention on the part of their landlord, or his agent, would accomplish this *sine qui non* of good tillage; most of them keep cows in the house in winter, and frequently feed them with small potatoes, of the value of which they are perfectly sensible; then how easy would it be to induce them to cultivate a small portion of their land with rape, vetches, clover, or any other of those green crops, so very beneficially introduced into modern husbandry. It remains however to be proved by experiment, whether the potato should not take place of every other species of winter or spring food for stock of every kind. If we advert to the variety of soils in which it succeeds, to the intimate knowledge of its cultivation, which every person from the peer to the peasant possesses, its ameliorating effects on the soil, its fattening quality, and not like many other vegetables, communicating a bad flavor to the meat, the superiority it possesses over every other vegetable production, of keeping perfectly good for upwards of ten months; when all those advantages are added to their freedom from being pilfered, their leaving the ground free for another crop in October, whilst most other plants remain until far in spring, and many others which must occur to every agriculturist, they will perhaps obtain a very high rank amongst vegetable productions for stock. Long as we have had the root in Ireland, and much as the public attention has been turned towards its cultivation, I imagine from some trials I have made of propagating it from seed (a highly amusing pursuit) that we have yet but a very slender knowledge of it, and are very far removed from perfection.

The introduction of Fiorin grass in our bogs, or rather the extension, for it has been always there, has caused a revolution in our agricultural system, that promises to overturn many of our vegetable productions. In such soils its produce is, without almost any trouble, superior to most others; is always ready for use, and on ground frequently not worth two shillings per acre. I shall resume this subject in the section of green crops. — Nothing would elevate the poor man's tillage more than sowing red clover with his crop of flax; they both require ground in good heart and fine tilth; are sowed at the same time; the small leaves of the flax permit the clover to flourish, and it is pulled so early that it permits the clover to make such a growth, that if the

---

[1] I beg it may be understood that I consider the man of substance and skill who takes a tract of unimproved land for the purpose of improving, and then re-letting, is a blessing to his country, [original footnote.

ground is rich, and the proper quantity of seed sowed, there may be a cutting for green food obtained before winter, but this is not a good general practice.

SECTION III

USE OF OXEN — HOW HARNESSED

Oxen are not generally used in this county in husbandry. The following gentlemen, amongst perhaps a few others, use them in most kinds of work:

Sir John Burke — Marblehill.
Lord Ashtown.
Lord Riverston.
Mr. Browne — Moyne.
Mr. Thomas Martin — Ballynahinch.
Mr. Bellew — Mount Bellew.

Though those gentlemen harness them properly, they may be seen some times drawing very heavy loads with yokes and bows, a most cruel method,[1] the poor animals heads almost touching the ground, endeavouring to avoid the galling pressure of the yoke on their bare necks; how much easier must be the collar, or even the *sugan* of straw. I have seen with much pleasure several pairs of oxen working for Mr. Martin at Ballynahinch and Oughterard, much better appointed than I have witnessed elsewhere.

Spayed heifers are sometimes used, and are generally allowed to be superior to oxen; they are much quicker steppers, insomuch that the heifers belonging to the Rev. Mr. Symes of Ballyarthur in the county of Wicklow, which obtained the cup at the ploughing match of the Farming Society of Ireland in 1804, though very small, performed their work in much less time than excellent horses that started with them. I am surprised the spaying of heifers that are intended merely for fattening, has not been more practised; the advantages they possess over those not spayed are many. Every person who buys cattle at any of the fairs in this county, must know how very frequently they buy heifers in calf that they intended to fatten, which obliges them to sell before they are fully fattened. If on the contrary spayed heifers were bought, there can be no disappointment, and the grazier can take his own time to sell; they are also much quieter both in harness and in the pasture; as to the quality of their flesh, they possess a great superiority, and produce more inside fat at an early age, than those that are not spayed. The question so long agitated, whether horses or oxen are most economical for farming purposes, remains still unsettled. The advocates for horses contend, that though they cost more to purchase, require more expensive keeping, and eat more than oxen, and are of infinitely less value when past their

---

[1] In 1610, Mr. Ledwich says, ten shillings were levied for every plough drawn by the tail in Ulster; there were 1740 forfeitures, amounting to £270. !! — Yokes without collars, are little less cruel.

labour or are injured, yet the superior quickness of their movements, especially in the hurry of spring work, they think more than compensates for the small price, cheaper keeping, and superior value of the ox when past his labour.

Perhaps the comparison has not in general been fairly made; it has been almost always between large, heavy, sluggish oxen, ill fed, and middle sized, and quick stepped horses; one purchased for from £5. to £7. and the other from £20. to £40. Whoever thought, when he went to a fair to buy plough oxen, of seeing them moved before him; he only looks (or at least his wise man) to those who are likely to grow to a large size when fattened, without ever considering whether they step quick or slow; on the contrary, the horse is made to go through all his paces, and rejected if his movements are not good. Put a pair of those heavy limbed, lubberly black horses, that were so injudiciously endeavoured to be established in Ireland a few years ago, into a field with Mr. Symes's heifers, and a more forcible light will be thrown on the subject than from my pen. An additional, and a still more forcible light has been shed by the result of the ploughing match of the Farming Society of Ireland in March 1821. — 25 pair of horses, 2 pair of mules, 3 pair of oxen, and a pair of bulls, started for the prizes: we may rest satisfied that the horses were selected for the purpose. To the astonishment of the prejudiced, a pair of oxen belonging to Richard Cotter, Esq. won the cup; the second premium of £10. was carried off by another pair of oxen, the property of Joseph Atkinson, Esq. and the third prize of £5. was awarded to the bulls, the property of John Brown, Esq. In the present depressed state of agricultural pursuits, it becomes a matter of the utmost consequence to compare the expenses of horses and oxen, which every farmer can easily do, and make up his mind to sacrifice the pleasure of the eye to dictates of his judgment The proper feeding of oxen whilst working is generally most grossly neglected; if they get indifferent hay they are generally esteemed well fed; no wonder they are slow in their step; horses on the same bad hay without oats would not be found very quick stepped.

I have observed at a very celebrated place near Dublin, oxen fattening for the Farming Society's show, pampered with every vegetable delicacy the farm afforded; within a few yards stood a pared of miserable working oxen, nothing but skin and bone; they frequently lay down in the plough; not a potato, cabbage, turnip, or head of rape was given to those unfortunate animals, nothing but the worst kind of hay, the leavings of the fattening cattle. The steward, an Englishman from a part of England where oxen are seldom used, forsooth *"understood all the best practices of England; aye, that he did, knowed oxen never could stand work"*. The consequence was, that instead of turning them out to fatten in good store order, as they would have been if well fed, besides performing twice the labour, they were obliged to be kept two years before they were fat; the first year barely recovered them. The expense of feeding horses and oxen may be brought more on a par, if horses get Swedish turnip, steamed potatoes, or bruised furze (Ulex Europeus). I must not be understood, however, to mean that they will perform hard spring work without a portion of corn, but I am perfectly convinced that some of those vegetables should make a considerable part of their food; for riding horses, Swedish turnips or potatoes as a part of their food, will be found very wholesome, and even for hunters, given in small quantities (perhaps seven pounds) on the days they do not hunt; they will cool the body and keep it moderately open.

Mr. Young, in his *Farmer's Calendar*, page 263, says, "Swedish turnip is, next to carrots, the very best food that can be given to horses." Oxen are not so liable to be injured by accidents, nor to be rode by lazy or vicious servants; where only one beast is kept, a horse will be generally preferred, and probably where many are necessary, some of each will be found most useful, but the greater number should consist of oxen. Those graziers who buy large lots of store cattle have opportunities of picking out those oxen that are most likely to step quick; if they do not answer it is no loss, as they may at any time be turned out to fatten. It is highly probable that long legged lathy oxen are most likely to turn out light movers. The slow step of oxen is frequently caused by the laziness of the ploughman or drivers; I have often observed them at work, and was surprised they did not lie down and sleep, both ploughman and cattle.

SECTION IV

NATURE AND USE OF IMPLEMENTS OF HUSBANDRY

The common ploughs of this county are very ill calculated to perform good work; one of the greatest defects is the sole not lying flat on the ground, it has a tendency to run out of the furrow, and small ribs of hard clay are left unploughed; these ribs prevent the surface water from running into the furrows, which in winter is very prejudicial, and greatly retards the sowing in spring. It may be set down as an agricultural axiom, that when the ploughman does not preserve an erect posture at his work, he is either a bad ploughman, or his plough is defective or improperly set, of course his tillage must be imperfect. What is generally called the Scotch plough on improved principles, seems to be one of the best we have yet adopted; if well set and kept sufficiently sharp, it turns a sod nine or ten inches broad and five or six inches deep in stiff soils, with the assistance of only a pair of horses or oxen without a leader, in a much superior manner and with more ease than the same work is usually effected by four beasts and a driver; frequently two drivers and a man pressing on the beam to keep the plough in the ground, and the ploughman's elbow almost touching the ground. It very rarely happens that the furrows are straight; the person who leads the horses cannot possibly guide them in a right line, and the furrow is, from the faulty construction of the plough, generally so badly defined the horses deviate from it, and form curves not unlike some of those tame outlines for plantations that have continued a reproach to the taste of Ireland. If on the contrary, the ploughman holds the reins, his eye is constantly kept on some object on the headland, which he sees between the horses heads, and as from the cleanness of the furrow the horses can scarcely deviate, the work is performed with the greatest exactness. At ploughing matches, poles are set up on the headlands, to which the ploughman runs his furrow nearly as exact as if it had been cut by a line; a leader to the plough would find it almost impossible, as has been often (with no small share of ridicule on those ploughmen who so obstinately used him) proved at several ploughing matches.

The increase of ploughs with two horses without a driver has been very rapid; even the farmers of Fingal, who were as steadfast in the use of four beasts as those of any other part of Ireland, now begin, thanks to the Farming Society of Ireland, to see the superiority of the new method, and have multitudes of two horse ploughs at work. The old ploughman, backed by the steward of the old school,[1] have always endeavoured to throw obstacles in the way, but by training up a few young lads under an expert ploughman, this has been in many places counteracted, and emulation between the young ploughmen has done wonders, which must be the result in every branch of farming if judiciously and steadily directed. The rewards given by farming societies for good ploughing have had the most beneficial effects. The Scotch plough requires to be set for working by a person acquainted with its use; a man attempting to plough with it if set in the usual way of the common ploughs of this county would be defeated.

It has frequently occurred, that many have imported Scotch ploughs without providing proper persons to use them, and they have been laid by with a total loss of character, at the instigation of ignorance and obstinacy. But such attention has been lately paid to this interesting subject, that the importation of either Scotch ploughs or ploughmen is no longer necessary. Leicestershire wheel ploughs are in use with a few gentlemen, and are highly praised by those who have used them; but from the comparative trials that have been made, I could not perceive any superiority over the Scotch plough, and as they are more complex, are not likely to be used by small farmers. The general harrow of this county is of very rude workmanship, and defective in its operation, for the teeth are so fixed that several follow each other in the same track, consequently it leaves much of the ground untouched, which in seed

---

[1] The steward of the old school may be easily known by the following description: he generally wears a large bushy wig, or his long uncombed ringlets hanging down his shoulders; his stockings about his heels from never buttoning the knees of his breeches, or a pair of old boots without stockings; his frieze great coat, worn in the warmest weather, hanging off the shoulders, for he scorns to put his arms into the sleeves; he smokes out of the same pipe, and drinks whiskey with the labourers, who always accost him with "Paddy" or "Phelim," &c. &c. He buys and sells cattle, of the value of which he knows no more than to ask much and offer little, and laughs into scorn every attempt at improvement, "your honor's father did very well without all this new fashioned nonsense." The practice prevails here, as in the County of Clare, of permitting stewards to become small farmers; it is impossible they can attend to their masters' business; — the wages should be raised and this foolish practice abolished. I have known a footman go home to plant his potatoes for a week, and spend another in digging them!!! — Comparing the amount of what the enlightened steward gets, with the wages, land, grass for cattle, house, turf &c. &c. besides the loss by the idleness of every one under him, it will be found that the balance will be largely in favour of the first. The generality of "old light" stewards are mere lookers on of labourers.,[original footnote].

sowing is highly injurious, as it leaves much of the corn uncovered. The double harrow, in which the rings of the swingle-tree play on two iron bars, seems to be the best that has been invented, from its hustling motion, and from every tooth forming a separate small furrow, it stirs the ground in every part, and lies better to each side of a ridge; a very material advantage arises from each horse drawing his own share, a mode that should be adopted as much as possible in all farming work, and indeed in all kinds of draught. The couch rake, or harrow, is also used by a few, and is an admirable instrument for gathering the roots of perennial weeds and small stones; but particular care must be taken that the ground is previously well ploughed and harrowed; I have seen sad work where it was expected that it would answer for both plough and harrow. As few have had a sufficient quantity of tillage to keep a threshing machine constantly at work, very few are to be met with in the hands of farmers. The late Mr. Lambart, of Creggclare, was, I believe, the first who erected one; but many have lately availed themselves of the benefits attached to their use. As it has been well ascertained, that a farm under the improved alternate system of corn and green crops, will produce more cattle than it did whilst under grazing alone, we may expect to see those admirable machines brought into general use, more especially as I understand there has been one lately contrived by an Irish artist, of which the expense will not exceed twenty pounds. Where there is a sufficient supply of water it should be applied to work the machine; but if the levels are such that the water can not be used without injuring the watered meadows, (if any,) horses should be substituted; the periodical labour of two horses is of infinitely less value than the water for irrigation. I mention this from the experience I have had of the bad consequence of their interference at Marly, the seat of the late Colonel Latouche; I finished about ten acres of watered meadow, and made preparation to water many acres more; the stream that supplies them also turns the wheel of a threshing machine, and the levels not answering to supply both at the same time, the meadows were defrauded of their proper supply, and I understand have at the instance of the then steward been sacrificed to the threshing machine; two horses work the machine equally well; now supposing they were constantly at work, they may be rated high at sixty pounds per annum; and supposing that only fifty acres should be watered, (but much more could be done, for the supply could be increased from another river,) it is a very moderate calculation to rate the produce, including feeding in spring for ewes and lambs, and meadow and feeding in autumn, at eight pounds per acre, — we can easily perceive what a loss was sustained by such management. The steward understood tillage admirably, but was ignorant of the value of irrigation. At the time the machine was erected, the watered meadows were made, but the millwright never considered any one's advantage but his own. Drill machines are used by very few; drill barrows are more used. Carts are little used, except by gentlemen; they are too expensive for small farmers, and inside cars (those with the wheels under the body) are generally used, though very unfit for farming purposes, as both from their weak construction, and being shut up behind, a load of manure or any other substance must be taken out by shovels, instead of throwing back the car to disengage the load as practised in Leinster. Another objection to them arises from the wheels not turning on the axis, by which means in turning, one wheel makes a hole in the ground whilst the other describes a circle; besides from the clumsiness of the wooden axis, an additional share of friction is caused. What are usually called Leinster cars (the wheels without side the body) are a good deal used, but generally so weakly and badly made they can bear but small loads, and are seldom thrown back to disengage the load, but must receive some assistance from the shovel or pitchfork, which consumes much time and labour; the wheel should turn on the axis, and the line of draught should be nearly in a line with the side of the cart or car; the observance of this, and the proper proportion necessary to be thrown on the horse's back, are the principal cause of the superiority of the drays, which are now almost universally preferred by carriers of goods, to the almost total exclusion of the car; this formerly carried only at the utmost about 12 cwt. but the dray now, with the same horse, carries with more ease from 20 to 25 cwt. To prevent the injury the roads must receive from this additional pressure on a wheel of only two or three inches, I imagine a law should be enacted to oblige the proprietors to use wheels eight inches broad. Probably from not understanding the subject there might be an outcry raised at first against the change, but it is well known that the additional weight would be much more than counterbalanced by the facility it would give them of avoiding many ruts and shocks from the wheels getting between stones that the broad wheels would roll smoothly over, — and a considerable share of friction on the edges of the wheels would be prevented; at present, carriages so heavily laden, and with such small wheels, do considerable injury to roads, especially after hard frosts.

In Connemara and other hilly countries, slide-cars shod with iron are used; they are the only kind that could be used for carrying loads down a steep hill; in this situation wheels would precipitate the horse down the hill and destroy him. Wheelbarrows are uniformly of bad construction, the weight is almost entirely thrown on the hands instead of the wheel. That simple and useful machine a potato washer, is scarcely known; where much potatoes are used it saves much time and trouble. Winnowing machines are much used, but from not keeping them oiled you may hear them grating and spoiling the wheels a mile off. The machine for dressing flax, invented by Mr. Lee, introduced here by the Farming Society of Ireland, had better never have been introduced at their show, for from the bungling exhibition at Ballinasloe it only helped to confirm the prejudices against it; the person showed the process had never worked it before, so was excusable. From the result of a small trial I made, I am almost convinced the process might be much shortened and simplified; I fear prejudice has operated strongly against it. When I have leisure I purpose making some further experiments on this, and a method to avoid the troublesome and nauseous process of steeping the flax, or provincially "bogging." There is scarcely an implement in the county with a good and light handle, or well and permanently fixed; they are constantly running to a stone to fix them, for they seldom ever think of repairing their tools at home at night; a few examples of sending them home from work, where it evidently appeared from indolence, would soon cure the evil. Scythes are uniformly badly set, especially when they mow for others, of course the grass is left uncut and in waves; when they mow for themselves they shave the grass to the earth. The beaters of the flails are generally too long and too light, and instead of being straight, as they should be, are usually crooked. Scutching boards for flax are always too long and too narrow, by which means at every stroke the flax laps round the board, much of it is torn off; they should be heart shaped and a foot broad. The plough I have mentioned before. The teeth of the harrow are usually too short as well as those of hay rakes, and leave much of the hay behind.

Pitchforks are uniformly too short in the prongs, and cannot lift half the load they should do. Spades very un handy, and so slightly fixed to the handle cannot bear the least effort of strength, and the head always loose or coming off the handle; when worn they are most unfit for moving loose earth, to the loss of many thousands of pounds in this county. Shovels in many places are made of wood, edged round and pointed with thin iron, and so easily broken, they are useless for breaking hard lumps of earth, or properly beating the face of a ditch, a thing, by the bye, I have never seen done in this county. I once tried the experiment of watering and hard beating, often repeated, on the face of the ditch; the result was, that it became like a hard flag and remained uninjured by frost, and quite free from weeds.

SECTION V

MARKET FOR GRAIN

The market towns of Galway, Loughrea, Tuam, Ballinasloe, Gort, Eyrecourt, and lately a market established at Mount Bellew, which promises to be of great utility, are well supplied with grain, chiefly wheat and oats, and when the distilleries are at work with a considerable quantity of barley, but much less now than when malt only was used at the distilleries and breweries.

The numerous flour mills which have been established within a few years, have helped greatly to increase and improve the cultivation of wheat, affording to the former a certain and ready sale for his corn; and as there is always a smart competition between the millers, especially of Galway, he is certain of receiving the full market price of the day. Tuam, Loughrea, Gort, and Eyrecourt, have market houses, whilst Galway, where there is so much grain sold, is without one; that at Loughrea, from its small size, is almost useless. The erection of one in Galway has been talked of these fifty years past, but nothing has been done. Until 1810, the market house was a cellar in Market-street; at present a coach-house near Meyrick-square is thought sufficient by the corporation, who, if ever they awake from their doze, I advise to view the market house of Drogheda, as particularly worthy of notice; it combines utility with ornament. The exportation of grain from the port of Galway was scarcely known before the union, and was first carried on to any extent by the late Mr. Thomas Appleyard, about the year 1804, who continued this most useful traffic during his life. It has been also greatly extended by the Mr. Joyces, Messrs. Clarke, and several other merchants during the war. Since that period it has declined much.

The mode of payment at the mills is generally cash; sometimes notes at short dates, according to the credit of the miller or the wants of the farmer, and until lately, country bankers notes were preferred to those of the Bank of Ireland. It was a common thing to hear a countryman ask a friend to change a bank of Ireland note for one of Lord French's. Corn is usually sold by sample, and some caution is necessary when receiving it at the mill. The millers generally send their flour to Dublin by land carriage; they prefer this mode to sending it by the canal, as the uncertainty of the time of its arrival has been found inconvenient to many. It has not been found, though often prognosticated, that the want of the inland bounty formerly paid, has in the least diminished the quantity of corn cultivated.

Whatever objections may have been made against the act for granting a bounty on the inland carriage of corn to Dublin, it cannot be denied that it caused the erection of a multitude of very fine flour mills, of course promoted the cultivation of corn in districts, that from want of this encouragement scarcely produced as much as supplied the home consumption: at the same time the good effects of either bounties or restrictions (with some exceptions) on any kind of produce, are at least doubtful, the steadiness of the demand being a much better stimulus than an act of parliament. How many exposed themselves to ridicule a few years ago, when they proposed acts of parliament to oblige farmers to bring their corn to market, and to establish a maximum of price.

How indignant these wise heads would be, if a maximum of rent was proposed, or a maximum on any commercial production; but it seems they considered that agriculture was of less consequence than any other branch of traffic; the plough, a less useful implement thin the loom or shuttle, or less intellect necessary than for conducting manufacturing or mercantile pursuits. — How totally ignorant of agriculture?

SECTION VI

USE OF GREEN FOOD IN WINTER

THE inestimable value of green winter feeding is now, or at least ought to be, so well established in Ireland, that it were almost needless to use any argument in its favor, and nothing but the greatest perversity could induce many who should know better to treat it with neglect. It is a most fortunate circumstance that bog or moor is peculiarly fitted for the production of several kinds of green crops; under a proper system they not only produce the best rape, potatoes, turnips, cabbages, mangle wurzle, &c. but carrots and parsnips, as may or might have been seen at Woodlawn, the seat of Lord Ashtown, at Lord Norbury's near Nenagh, and several other places; but the vegetable above all others that claims our notice is certainly Fiorin grass (*Gramen Richardsonium*) whether we advert to the ease with which it is produced in soils of otherwise little value, the certainty of a crop, the quick return which takes place in producing a crop of six to seven tons of dry hay to the acre in the course of a few months after planting, which cannot be said of any other vegetable fit for hay; the undoubted fattening quality it possesses, from the extreme greediness with which all animals devour it, and its capability of being made into good hay in weather that would make any other kind only fit for the dunghill; it also possesses the valuable quality of preserving the banks of lakes or rivers from being disturbed by violent surfs, which has been exemplified at Mount Bellew, especially where it had grown previous to the admission of water into the new lake; it floats to a considerable length on the water, and on the return of every wave is doubled against the bank and preserves it: the propagation of this grass is so simple, that the most ignorant labourer can do it. Where an extensive plantation is in contemplation, the method is to set apart a large piece of good ground, suppose an old potato garden, for a nursery; an acre this way will give a supply the following season for a great extent of surface; the ground should be well ploughed and harrowed, and the grass scattered thinly over it, and as much earth laid on as will just place the stolones[1] in contact with the earth, into which they emit roots like a strawberry at every joint: it has one quality which I do not recollect any other vegetable production to possess, that of growing freely after it has been made into hay and stacked. The stolones can be easily procured from the banks and margins of rivers and bog ditches, at a very trifling expense. I saw in 1816, at Mr. Burke's, at Killimore, the ground where a crop of above seven tons to the acre of dry hay in the hay yard had grown; it was part cut-away bog, of little, value, and part was the high bank of very wet red bog, worth little. Mr. Burke left part of the crop uncut, to show to any person doubting the goodness of it; it was remarkably heavy, and in fine order for either hay or soiling. The process, after levelling the bog holes, was to spread a small quantity of manure for potatoes; shortly after they were dug, the stolones were spread and very lightly

---

[1] That part of a plant which anchors it, [Clachan ed.].

covered. This year he has made a considerable addition to his plantations, and intends to extend it over considerable tracts of bog; it was in February 1816, I saw this additional plantation just finished; it was made from hay that had been in stack in the yard, and had a flourishing appearance. There were many parts of the bog where a man would sink, if not prevented by the Fiorin grass; and on the high bank of red bog, that bad been left as a proof piece, a heavy beast might walk, though in its original state a sheep dare not attempt it; there seemed to be uniformly the best crop where the ground was wettest. If bog has been well drained, the drains should be stopped in May, and the water thrown back into the drains, to keep the bog moist in dry weather. This will be found a useful practice in most cases, in all kinds of land. It may be objected that in many situations manure cannot be procured in any considerable quantity, so many other branches of agriculture and horticulture requiring a share: the objection would have some weight if success depended on farm-yard manure alone, but where irrigation can be practised, the objection falls to the ground, because the water, if judiciously applied, obviates every difficulty: where irrigation is impracticable, recourse can be had to clay ashes, which can be procured in almost every situation, and the method of burning is known to almost every Irish labourer.[1] Where Fiorin meadows, from want of water or manure begin to fail, they can be easily renovated, by burning the surface and replanting; for this purpose the moss should be mowed, and brought to some adjacent land, not left too thick, and occasionally turned whilst the process of burning is going forward; no apprehension need be entertained of the loss of its vegetative quality for a much longer period than will be necessary for burning the surface: this process can be repeated as often as necessary in boggy soils that will produce yellow ashes only; white ashes are of little or no value. How must those ignorant sneerers in the sister country feel at Dr. Richardson's success? the value of Fiorin is now too well established in every part of the world to be injured by sulky ignorance, or agricultural vanity; if it has failed with some, it must have been from mismanagement, or possibly the true Fiorin has not been obtained, for I am well convinced there are many seminal varieties. In the same soil and situation I could perceive some that produced very scanty herbage, and the strings not larger than a knitting needle, and quite different in colour; I have also observed a variety that threw out very few stolones, but grew almost in one close tuft.

It is highly probable if the seed was sown in drills, and the plants singled out, many varieties might be perceived, and perhaps better than that so generally cultivated; for after all that has been said and done, our knowledge of Fiorin is far from perfection. Several gentlemen who have seen Mr. Burke's Fiorin grass are now planting it, so much more useful is example than precept I have not a doubt the practice will spread

---

[1] It is amusing enough to see the fuss that it made in England about the method of burning clay into ashes, a process completely known by the most ignorant Irish labourer. I trust the English agriculturists will not adopt the abuse of so good a practice — over-cropping, [original footnote].

rapidly; seven tons of hay, worth at least £14. from ground scarcely worth any thing, speaks a language that every man understands; it speaks through his head to his pocket.

Except in some few extreme cases, I imagine Fiorin should be preserved for soiling in the house, for which perhaps no vegetable that we are acquainted with can bear any comparison, still keeping in mind that it is the produce of ground of little value, though no ground can be too rich for it. The value of Fiorin has been long known in the county of Mayo. Mr. Bellew's, gamekeeper, a native of that county, has been frequently employed by poor cottiers, who value it highly, to instruct them in its propagation. In the county of Galway it is frequently called *hare* grass, from the decided preference given to it by that animal. I understand a very good ardent spirit has been distilled from it:[1] I wish the experiment had been rather made on beer. I perceive there is no getting away from Fiorin. — I fear my readers will think it has multiplied under my hands rather too much.

The following gentlemen, amongst a few others, cultivate green crops:

Lord Clonbrock,	Mr. Hen. Blake — Renville,
Lord Ashtown	Mr. French, — Monivae,
Lord Clancarty,	Mr. St. George — Headfort,
Archbishop of Tuam,	Mr. Burke — Ballydugan,
Bishop of Clonfert,	Mr. Burke — Kylemore,
Rev. Dean Mahon,	Mr. Kirwan— Castlehacket,
Mr. Bodkin— Armagh,	Mr. Blakeney — Abbert,
Mr. D' Arcy— Killtullagh,	Rev. Mr. Kelly— Castle Kelly,
Mr. Daly— Dunsandle,	Rev. Archdeacon Butson,
Lord Gort— Loughcoutra.	Sir Ross Mahon.

I regret I cannot publish a longer list: through the ignorance in which I have been left from want of information, I may have omitted the names of others who know the value of green food, but I trust the good sense of the gentlemen of the county will, before long, prompt them to pursue this very profitable branch of rural economy. I wish I could add that the proper rotation of crops steadily followed this good beginning, but I have seen few instances in this or any other part of Ireland, where the alternate course has been undeviatingly pursued. Perhaps a rotation of three years has been once or twice attempted, but either from the supineness of the proprietor, or too often the ignorance or perverseness of the old-school steward, has seldom had a fair trial: it is something like the improvement of bog; a few years back a great splutter was made; — Mr. Elkington was brought over from England, paid one hundred pounds a month and his travelling expenses, and we heard of nothing but

---

[1] I have been informed lately that the effects of the spirit produced from Fiorin has not been such as to encourage repetition; but on the other hand I have been told that the experiment was tried on green Florin. What would the effect be if green barley had been used? [original footnote].

the improvement of bogs, yet little was done; and now we hear complaints made of the expense of reclaiming bog.

Improvers of bog are generally too impatient; they begin to be a little sore when they have laid out some money, and see nothing immediately coming in, and frequently leave off just when they should go on with spirit. Most of the gentlemen I have mentioned cultivate Norfolk, Swedish, and other kinds of turnips, generally in drills; they also usually plant rape, vetches, and many have begun to propagate mangle wurzle, but little or no carrots or parsnips for cattle: in bog I should prefer Fiorin grass to any of them. At Mount Bellew, the grass of the plantations, and after grass of the lawn, are used for soiling through the winter, with very beneficial effects, for dairy cows and other stock.

If any person should hesitate to admit that cattle to a great extent can be not only fed but fattened, by soiling in the house in summer, I must refer them to the account of Mr. Muir in England, who fed to a state of great fatness 240 oxen by soiling in summer, and by the work of one scythe: considerable injury may arise from the indolence of the feeder, who, if not closely watched, will, to save himself trouble, lay in a large quantity of green food at once; in a short period this ferments, and is refused by the cattle. The proper method is to employ one man with a small wickered cart, that will contain only as much as will give some to each beast, — fresh and fresh, is the fattening principle of feeding, and also prevents the danger of hoving; but attention must be paid that even this is not carried too far to save trouble. There is no farming servant so difficult to procure as an attentive and intelligent herd.

I must also refer my readers to the soiling system, that is now actually carrying on to a great extent, by Mr. Curwen of Workington; he has successfully tried it with all kinds and ages of stock; but every agricultural pursuit of that gentleman is on a great scale, and carried on with a spirit and indefatigable activity that I fear, will have but few imitators in Ireland.

CHAPTER III

SECTION I

PASTURE

PASTURE occupies by much the greater part of the lands of this county, and varies infinitely from the rich feeding grounds of Ballydonnelan and its vicinity, to the light, heathy sheep walks which occupy so large a tract of dreary country, ten miles square at least, between Monivae and Galway, and extending for many miles into the county of Clare. Between Tuam and Castlebar the land is light and sound, and lets, or did let in 1814, on an average for about 34s. per acre. At present, (1823,) probably from 15s. to 20s. would be as high a rent as the present depressed state of agricultural affairs would permit for those lands. Between Cahir, Morris, and Shruel, mostly light sheep walk, with a little very bad tillage. A considerable quantity of pasture is obtained from the different Turloughs, especially that of Turloughmore, which extends from Clare Galway to near Tuam; they feed seven or eight sheep to the acre for about four months, the remainder of the year they are generally under water. There is also an extensive country of many miles between Athenry and Ardrahan, and stretching down to the sea at Kinvara, chiefly occupied by sheep, and a little tillage, mostly wheat. Between Croghwell and Galway, for several miles square pasturage is the general occupation of the ground; here too there are some spots of tillage producing excellent wheat, but often a fallow.

Almost the entire of the baronies of Ballynahinch, Ross and Moycullen is pasture; in the valleys there are many patches of tillage, and about the town of Moycullen a large quantity of excellent wheat is produced for Galway market. There is also along the sea coast, from Galway to Connemara, a good deal of tillage produced by manuring with seaweed chiefly, and sometimes by a very productive coraline sand; there is also produced here, for Galway market, a large quantity of very early potatoes, called *windileers*, resembling, if not the same as the Wicklow bangors. The surface of the three mountain baronies, before mentioned, is chiefly covered with heath, intermixed with large proportions of a plant called *black keeb*, and another species called *white keeb*, both I believe are carex[1]; the first continues green through the winter, the other does not; the mountains where the first prevails are let much higher than where the last predominates; the mountain that produces black keeb, I understand, uniformly produces white ashes when burned, the contrary takes place where the white keeb prevails; here the ashes are red or yellow, and produce excellent crops after burning, but unfortunately the running-out system is always pursued. The pastures of this county are greatly neglected; if they are dry grounds they are frequently covered with heath, small thistles, dwarf briars, (which you will

---

[1] Carex is a vast genus of sedges, [Clachan ed.].

often see covered with sheep's wool,) and all sorts of weeds usual in such soils. In moist pastures they are delivered down from generation to generation, full of swamps covered with rushes, and other pernicious aquatics; and this shameful neglect is frequently to be seen on the lands of very wealthy graziers. I must confess, did I possess property in this county, I would reject all proposals for a renewal from such characters; it would be a prudent method for landlords when they have proposals for their ground to look at the farms of such proposer, and reject all negotiation with him where his ground was not well drained, his fences in perfect order, and his gates and farm buildings in good repair. It is very much the custom in this county for graziers to add farm to farm to a great extent, and much beyond their capital, and even without looking at them; they send their wise man to view them, and on his report they propose a rent; if possible they will get permission to burn the land from weak, needy proprietors, or their ignorant agents, (who should be called receivers of rents,) and after taking crop after crop until they completely exhaust the ground, they send a notice of surrender, or expect an abatement of the rent: though they have not liberty to burn they frequently take it, and as perhaps the rent is regularly paid in Dublin to an agent who never sees the ground, no discovery is made until the mischief has been done, then probably a lawsuit commences, and it is so difficult to prove the burning, that the defendant, surrounded by his own creatures, often succeeds; besides, even if he has been obliged to pay the penalty, he is still in pocket from the high prices he will receive during perhaps five or six years.

		£.	s.	d.
The first year,	Per acre	11	7	6
Second year,	Do.	10	0	0
Third year, for Oats	Do.	7	0	0
Fourth year, Do.	Do.	6	0	0
Fifth year, Do.	Do.	4	1	0
		38	1	6
Deduct rent, penalty, and costs,		25	0	0
	Nett profit,	13	1	6

So that he may very well pay the penalty, and then, after taking all those crops, throw up the ground, as few graziers take land without a clause of surrender. That there are many who are above such mean shifts, I have great pleasure in acknowledging, but on the other hand, every one in the county knows who has often sat for the picture — he cannot be mistaken. That many kinds of soils would not bear all this cropping will be readily granted; but graziers of the above description seldom take poor land.

To many farms large tracts of moory bottoms are attached, for which in the survey there is an abatement of the rent. I have seen many of those that were considered by the proprietor as worth little, that would be worth twice the value of their best land; in their present state they feed cattle in very dry weather or hard frosts; but if they were drained, burned and gravelled, or limed, would produce more pasture at all seasons than their best upland; but most graziers seem to have an aversion to draining land, and if they do attempt it, they do it so injudiciously, that, after incurring a great and unnecessary expense, the land in a short period reverts to its original state. I had an opportunity, lately of seeing an instance of money thrown away by bad draining. A wealthy grazier accidentally met a Tipperary gentleman, who advised him to make sod drains at two perches asunder, and instead of being drawn across the declivity, they were in its direction, down the hill. They were accordingly made to the amount of above thirty, though only about half of what was intended; how they were made, by men who had never seen a sod drain made, and without any person to instruct them, we may easily conclude. The wetness of the ground (above 50 acres) proceeded from springs from very high ground, and their natural outlet was so accurately defined, that one intercepting drain, probably not more than three feet deep, would have drained the whole; but it was a travelling opinion my friend got, which is generally worth little. It is intended to plant the whole with florin grass, and as it can be all irrigated, it will then be many times the value of the adjoining upland, though at present it is esteemed of little value, and indeed I believe rent free.

The pasture of cottiers is uniformly bad; it is generally ground converted to this purpose after a scourging rotation of crops, without the benefit of any kind of hay seeds, frequently wet and poached through the winter by their starving cattle; they persist in this wretched mode, though the ground is perfectly bare of any kind of herbage. The ground they intend for meadow is generally used in this manner until far in the month of June, by which means, as well as from a wish to scrape all they can, they seldom mow until September or October, consequently their land produces little or no after-grass; Some few pastures possess a peculiar fattening quality; it seems to be the received opinion, that old pastures only will give inside fat to animals in any quantity, and that grounds newly laid down will not do so, though it will make them fat on the outside of the carcass; butchers are well aware of this when they buy.[1] I have examined many of those famous fattening pastures in this county, and that of Clare, and have uniformly found a large portion of the herbage to consist of:

      Crested dogstail grass, (Cynosurus cristatus,)
      White clover, (Trifolium repens,)
      Perennial red clover, (Trifolium pratense,)
      Yarrow, (Achillea Millefolium,)
      Small plaintain, (Plantago lanceolata,)
      Ray grass, (Lolium perenne,)
      Ladies bedstraw, (Galium verum,)
      Birds-foot trefoil, (Lotus corniculatus,)
      Fiorin grass, (Agrostis stolonifera,) a very large proportion.

---

[1] As there is no difference made in the sales, the profit lies with the butcher, [original footnote].

I have made many inquiries into the probable cause of this peculiarity of old ground, and the only answer I ever could receive was, "that it was so indeed." The graziers knew no more the names of plants than the cattle that fed on them. It seems to be highly probable, that as new soils are laid down with clean hay seeds, in which the seeds of many of the plants I have mentioned are not permitted to mix, this fattening quality in the soil does not take place until nature stocks the ground with them. There are two of those plants (birds-foot trefoil and yarrow) that never lose their verdure in the driest weather, and seem to be highly valuable, especially as they flourish in the sand banks of the sea coast, where I have traced their roots to ten or twelve feet deep, how much further I could not ascertain.

SECTION II

BREED OF CATTLE — HOW FAR IMPROVED, AND HOW FAR CAPABLE OF FURTHER IMPROVEMENT

The breed of cattle are almost entirely long horned; the produce of bulls many years since, and still continued to be imported from England. I am informed by many who have seen the common stock of long horned cattle of England, that ours are much superior, and if the practice pursued by sheep breeders, of reserving the best always for breed, was generally followed, the cattle of this country would be superior to any long horns in the United Kingdom; but the contrary practice usually prevails, and, except by a few amateurs, the best heifers are all sent to the great May fair of Ballinasloe, and other places. If a reserve of the best was made, with the use of none but the best bulls, they would rival the best of the sister country. With almost every extensive grazier, a few favourites have been preserved in the family for breed, which shows what might be expected if the scale was extended.

In the baronies of Ross, Moycullen, and Ballynahinch, the original breed are middle horned, usually a black or rusty brown colour; they are larger than the produce of the mountains of Kerry, and I think not so fine in their shape. The bulls generally have their horns set wide like bullocks, and do not in general possess that peculiarity of appearance, especially about the head, that the bulls of other breeds do. The cattle at the fair of those baronies, particularly that of Clifden, are generally very reasonable, and I am at a loss to know why the graziers do not speculate in them. There are a good many Devonshire cattle in the hands of different gentlemen, but they are confined to them; the graziers imagine a cross with their long horned breed would not be beneficial; but the same objection cannot be made by those who have estates in the baronies of Ross, Moycullen, or Ballynahinch; I imagine for them the Devon cross would be very valuable. The opinion of the inhabitants of those baronies of the long horned cross, is, that there is little improvement, except in the length of the horns; that their lands are too poor to maintain them. It is highly probable that the Devon cross would produce good plough cattle, as the native Irish are very quick steppers.

The Hereford, or middle horned breed of cattle, is also only in the hands of a few gentlemen; the Teeswater, or short horned, in still fewer hands. Of their comparative merits I shall not presume to judge, especially after the opinion so decidedly expressed by Mr. Coke at one of his shows, of cattle at Holkham; who, after regretting that the late Mr. Bakewell had not chosen a better breed than the long horned Leicesters to display his great talents upon, asserted, "that he really considered them rather the worst breed in England." He called upon Mr. Child, and other men eminent in their breed of cattle, who strongly corroborated the justness of Mr. Coke's assertion. I leave it therefore to the long horned breeders to fight their own battles; but it will take many more and better arguments to effect a change in Ireland. It must also be considered, that probably the meeting at Holkham were mostly breeders of Devonshire and short horned cattle.

A strange idea prevails in Ireland, that Devonshire cattle are small; the fact is, that some of the largest fat oxen in England have been of that breed. A few Kerry cattle occasionally find their way to this county; they are frequently good milkers, and their milk is productive of much butter. Many gentlemen have attempted to fatten them for killing in the summer months, when a larger beast would be too much for most families in hot weather, but have been generally disappointed; they did not fatten, but continued to increase in size; the reason is, that they purchased those that were too young; they should be four years old, at least, when they have done growing, and will then fatten well.

Mr. Browne of Moyne, and many other graziers, either go or send into the island of Arran to purchase calves, for which they generally pay high prices; the calves are frequently bought in the market of Galway, shortly after being calved, and are fed in Arran until the jobbers[1] buy them. In this island the enclosures for feeding the calves are divided into very small parts, well sheltered by stone walls; the grass, naturally very early and sweet, is always kept very good, and they are fed with boiled potatoes in winter. Cattle in Arran are sometimes so much distressed for water, that every beast has been sent to the opposite shore, until rains supplied the wells; many say that Arran calves do not fatten well, that they are tender, &c. &c. others, that they fatten well and quickly, when of the proper age, but that they do not produce tallow in proportion; the very active competition of the buyers puts an end to all doubt of the goodness. Cattle in the mountains are subject to a disorder called "the cripple;" they are cured by bringing them to the sea shore, or sandy beach of rivers, or by feeding on bran; in other words, bringing them from wet to dry ground, and good feeding.

Formerly, in Connemara, the horse, cow, rabbit, and rat, were all black. Cattle, in 1803, were much leaner than in former years, from a general want of water. I have often attempted to point out in many situations, where water could be easily

---

[1] *Jobbers* usually refers to wholesalers. [Clachan ed.]

obtained; I have been more than once answered, "I imagine Mr. Dutton if this could be effected, my steward would have long since perceived it!" There is a good deal of quackery about the care of many disorders in cattle and sheep; every herd has his infallible nostrum, which is generally handed down from father to son as a profound secret.

One of those very celebrated cow doctors, when applied to by a gentleman near Eyrecourt, who had a sick cow, said, "the cow had eaten a snail!" Probably, on a close inspection, the snail might have been seen in the same place that it appeared in the poor duck, in the old popular ballad of *Gossip Joan*[1]. It must be evident to every person, that in dewy nights - every cow must devour myriads of all kinds of insects, especially slugs and snails, and probably they contribute to their fattening, as the richest soils are most productive of those kinds of insects. Connemara has been long famed for its breed of small hardy horses; but from an injudicious cross with large stallions, they have lost much of their celebrity, and it is now difficult to procure one of the true breed.

A few years ago I saw some stallions in the stables of Mr. Martin at Oughterard, that were sufficient to destroy the breed of any country, especially of Connemara; before he introduced such horses, he should have showed his tenants how to provide food for their progeny. Mr. D'Arcy, of Clifden, has acted more judiciously; he procured a very beautiful small sire, who, I am informed, has left a very improved breed in Connemara. It is thought that the general breed of horses in this comity is far from improving. That old breed of strong hunters, for which this county was famous, has almost disappeared, and given place to a breed of mongrel racers, who are not able to carry weights, and who cannot bear to stand a moment without exercise, they are so bandaged up with sheets and rollers, and carefully shut out from all air in their stables. Probably it is not considered that within a few years the speed of the hounds has been so much increased by selection, that none but horses with a considerable share of blood can keep in with them, so much so, that the hounds of Mr. French, of French Park, will not permit so much as alighting to open a gate. No person, I believe, will deny the necessity of blood; but they will also I hope agree, that blood without strength will not carry them to the end of a long fox chase in a heavy country, with sixteen stone on their back. The breed of horses in the hands of farmers and cottiers is a wretched one; I do not know a greater want in this county than good middle sized compact sires; those in use at present are generally too large, and are usually heavy, ill shaped animals, whose high condition blinds the judgment of the poor countryman. I do not recollect to have seen a Suffolk punch horse in this

---

[1] The lyrics of this ballad are "Good morrow, Gossip Joan, Where have you been a-walking? I have for you, for you for you, for you for you... a budget full of wonders." The wonders are listed: A cow with a calf that cannot eat hay, a duck which died from eating a snail, [Clachan ed.].

county, but I imagine they would be well adapted to it[1]. Surely it is incumbent on every man of fortune to furnish his tenants with the use of good sires of every description; they may rest assured it will help to enable them to pay their rents.

The improvement in the breed of sheep has been most rapid. When I first came to Ballinasloe, having always heard so much of Connaught sheep, I was not a little surprised at seeing such multitudes with thick legs, booted with course wool down to their heels - and such a bushy wig of coarse wool on their -heads, that you could scarcely perceive their eyes; at present they have nearly all disappeared, and given place to a fine breed, not to be equalled by the general stock of long wooled sheep in England; this must be imputed to the introduction of Leicester rams, who, though they might and did deteriorate the wool, from an injudicious, indeed a ridiculous idea, that "so as the shape was perfect, no matter if the wool was as coarse as goats-hair, &c." I recollect to have seen a ram at Ballinasloe, that was purchased in England for three hundred guineas, and he completely answered this description; he was of the most perfect form, but what little wool he had on was as coarse as goat's hair.

The wished-for shape has been obtained but the Farming Society of Ireland, perceiving the injury this wool had received, are now anxious to cover that fine form with fine wool; for this purpose they give premiums for the best rams' fleece, and so rapid a change for -the better has taken place, that I have little doubt in a few years we shall export rams to England. The breed of Merino sheep is confined to a few gentlemen in this county. The Rev. Dean Trench produced two hundred and forty-six fleeces of Merino on Ryland, of first quality, which sold for 1s. 11d. per pound; also, twenty-one of third quality, at 1s. 8d.; Mr. Athy, thirty-three fleeces pure Merino, which sold, for 2s. 2d. per pound; Rev. Mr. Vincent, twenty fleece of pure Merino, for 1s. 9d. per pound. I do net perceive that any of those gentlemen have crossed with native sheep; I imagine Lord Gort might cross with the native sheep of his neighbourhood with good effect. We may perceive the good effect produced by crossing the native short wooled sheep at the last sales of short wool in October 1881, at the Farming Society home in Dublin; the Rev. Thomas Quinn received 2s. 7d. per pound for the wool of the third and fourth crop of Merino on Wicklow ewes; Mr. Wynne 2s. 5d. for South Down or Leicester; Rev. Dr. Truel Is. 10d. for South Down or Wicklow, four pound each fleece.

There are a few deer parks in this county; some of them ill calculated to produce high flavoured venison; for they are deficient in that variety of browsing which it seems is necessary to communicate that fine favour it should possess; most gentlemen think if they can enclose any piece of good land with a high wall, every

---

[1] Since writing this, I have seen the breed with Mr. George of Headford, and he has obtained premiums for the best stallion at Ballinasloe show in 1819 and 1820; and Mr. Blake of Renville, in Connemara, I understand is very partial to them, [original footnote].

thing is accomplished — there is nothing so difficult to procure as a sufficient tract of land for this purpose. Few parks are confined to the feeding of deer alone, they are usually stocked in part with all kinds of cattle, sheep, and horses; though cattle might be beneficial, it can scarcely be deemed judicious to permit sheep or horses, (except a few brood mares,) who bite too close to leave any thing for deer; on the contrary, a moderate stock of cattle helps to keep down the rank grass, and permit the short sweet herbage, which deer love to feed on, to spring up. Deer are frequently neglected in winter; consequently the venison season is either lost or protracted. Some few of the old stock of red deer are still to be seen in the mountains of Connemara; when they apear, however, the hue and cry is raised, and they are frequently killed. Mr. D'Arcy's deer park at Kiltolla, is said to produce the best and earliest venison in the country, but is greatly injured by the admission of horses. Some few gentlemen procure males for the use of their tenants, especially bulls, but the practice should be general for their own sake; for every improvement the tenant makes in either cattle or land, ultimately ends in the landlord's pocket, in either a rise of rent, or a certainty of its payment: the interest of a good landlord, and good tenant, are inseparable; above all things, they should procure good boars, for pigs are the poor man's chief stock, and constitute a very material part of their means of paying their rent: every person must be sensible there is much room for improvement in this stock.

It has been often asserted that swine, left at their liberty to roam about, thrive better than those confined in a sty: I grant that where they are kept in the usual filthy state, and neglected in the quantity or quality of their food, they certainly do, and probably whilst they are young it may be useful to give them liberty. When landlords are absentees, the procurement of good males should be given in charge to their agents, whom I suppose to be resident. The non-residence of an agent appears to me the most extraordinary mismanagement of an estate: I should nearly as soon suppose the conductor of an extensive manufactory or brewery, to live in Dublin, or at any considerable distance from the concern, as an agent; they should be called receivers of rent, and not agents.

The South Down sheep are not much liked in Connemara, they say, the wool is too short, and their own wool longer and finer. If a selection was made of the native breed, they might probably arrive to a high degree of perfection; at present not the smallest is ever made. In contradiction to this, many say that South Down wool would be preferred, if a price adequate to the fineness could be procured for their stockings, but the women complain that they are at the mercy of the peddlers, who are their only customers, and who often enter into combinations to lower the price. Note —I am informed a Mr. Mullarky in Connemara, is, remarkable for fine wooled sheep of the native breed.

In the 4th vol. of the 2nd series of the Repertory, p. 461, it is asserted, that inoculation with the cow-pock has succeeded completely in preventing the scab in sheep. If this has any foundation in truth (which I confess I very much doubt), it would be a valuable discovery. Has any breeder tried it yet?

MARKETS, OR FAIRS FOR THEM, AND LIST OF FAIRS

Ballinasloe is the chief fair for fat cattle, to which the buyers from Cork, Limerick, all parts of Leinster, and frequently from England and Scotland, repair in October: the fair usually continues for four days. The Leinster graziers here also lay in their stock of sheep for the winter and spring. This fair, though established at a very early period for the accommodation, it is imagined, of the Galway merchants, who had a considerable export of beef, long before the cities of Cork or Limerick had monopolized it, yet no patent appears for it until 1757, when Richard Trench, Esq. of Gurbally, got one for holding a fair at Dunlo on the 17th of May, and 13th of July. The great fair for fat cattle in October, it is probable, was established long before this period. I regret I have not been able to procure a list of the number of cattle and sheep sold at this fair. I wished to have ascertained the sales as far back as any record could be procured. For this purpose I wrote to Mr. Sinclair, Lord Clancarty's steward, who, from being Baron of the fair, was competent to give me the information. I was so unfortunate as not to have been thought worthy of the slightest notice. There is also at Ballinasloe a very considerable fair in May, at which many graziers from Leinster lay in their stock of lean cattle: here may be seen numbers of fine heifers, selected by graziers and jobbers, for their size and fine shape, a practice which has greatly retarded the perfection to which cattle would be brought, if the best were selected for breed; there are also a considerable number of sheep at this fair, but bearing no comparison to those in October.

The fair in October produces a good number of horses, but greatly inferior in number and quality to. those produced 20 years ago. A very considerable number of store cattle and sheep are sold at Loughrea on the 26th of May. In every considerable town there is a market for a small number of fat cattle and sheep, once a week. In Galway, there have been sold on one market day in September 1806, 20 head of fat cattle and 200 fat sheep. In several places there are fairs chiefly for the sale of turkeys, to which the neighbouring gentlemen usually send to lay in their stock for winter and spring; they find this much cheaper than rearing them at home, as the cottier's wife and children take better care of them, than it could be expected their own servants would; they are usually sold full grown, and frequently fit to kill, for from 1s. 8d. to 2s. 6d. each; in 1821, they could be purchased in many places for 10d. and a shilling: at the fair of Aughrim alone, on the 14th of October, there are frequently 20,000 turkeys sold; they are greatly inferior, especially in the breast and wings, to those produced in Meath, and many other parts of Ireland, and also much smaller, which probably proceeds, from not getting corn at an early period of the growth.

LIST OF FAIRS IN THE COUNTY OF GALWAY

Castle Blakeney,	**Jan.**	2	Moylogh,	do.	10
Ballyraoe,	**Feb.**	1	Gort,	do.	11
Clogheea Beg,	do.	1	Clonfert,	do.	12
Barna,	do.	6	Creggs,	do.	12
Kilcreest,	do.	6	Newtown Eyre,	do.	12
Longhrea,	do.	11	Claddagh,	do.	14
Portumna,	do.	15	Portumna,	do.	15
Clarun Bridge,	do.	16	Claren Bridge,	do.	17
Bellymoe,	**Mar.**	13	Abbey Knockmay,	do.	21
Ahascragh,	do.	27	Ballynamore,	do.	21
Ballynasloe,	do.	27	Ballymoe,	do.	21
Eyrecourt,	**April**	3	Loughrea,	do.	21
Drumgriffio,	**May**	1	Lawrence-town,	do.	22
Kilcreest,	do.	1	Kilnalag,	do.	24
Tynagh,	do.	4	Ahascragh,	do.	25
Athenry,	do.	5	Isserkelly,	do.	25
Barna,	do.	6	Mount Shannon,	do.	28
Newtown Eyre,	do.	6	Tynagh, 2 days,	do.	31
Portumna,	do.	6	Clifden,	**Sept.**	1
Claddagh (Galway)	do.	8	Fairhill,	do.	4
Dunlo (Ballinasloe)	do.	8	Kiltarton,	do.	4
Lawrence-town,	do.	8	Eyrecourt,	do.	8
Mount Bellew Bridge,	do.	8	Ardrahan,	do.	12
Aghrim,	do.	9	Derrymactoghny,	do.	18
Kilconnel,	do.	9	Kilcorban,	do.	18
Gort,	do.	10	Tubberindony,	do.	20
Tuam,	do.	10	Caltragh,	do.	21
Ballymoe,	do.	11	Galway,	do.	21
Headford,	do.	11	Claremore,	do.	26
Kiltarton,	do.	11	Mt Bellew Bridge,	do.	29
Clonfert,	do.	12	Castle Blakeney,	**Oct.**	2
Creggs,	do.	12	Castle Hacket,	do.	2
Monivae,	do.	12	Meelick,	do.	2
Woodford, 2 days,	do.	12	Woodford, 2 days,	do.	2
Cappataggel,	do.	15	Ballinasloe, 4 days,	do.	5
Caltragh,	do.	15	Dunmore,	do.	10
Tubberbrackin,	do.	15	Tubberpadder,	do.	10
Castle Blakeney,	do.	16	Tuam,	do.	10
Claregalway,	do.	16	Newtown Bellew,	do.	11
Claran Bridge,	do.	15	Monivae,	do.	12
Kinoura,	do.	18	Aghrim,	do.	14
Ardrahan,	do.	22	Headford,	do.	14
Ballymote,	do.	22	Clifden,	do.	14

Oranmore,	do.	23	Claregalway,	do.	17
Ahascragh,	do.	24	Kinvara,	do.	17
Tullinadaly,	do.	24	Portumna,	do.	17
Kileorban,	do.	25	Ballinakill,	do.	20
Claremore,	do.	26	Oranmore,	do.	20
Loughrea,	do.	26	Galway,	do.	21
Kilnelag,	do.	27	Tubberbracken,	do.	23
Dunmore	do.	29	Ballymoe,	do.	25
Mount Shannon,	do.	29	Athenry,	do.	26
Newtown Bellew,	**May**	29	Kilcreest,	do.	30
Galway,	do.	31	Newtown Eyre,	do.	30
Ballinakill,	**June**	1	Barna,	**Nov.**	6
Mt Bellew Bridge,	do.	9	Gort,	do.	7
Creggs,	do.	12	Moylogh,	do.	8
Kilnelag,	do.	20	Kilconnel,	do.	11
Aghrim,	do.	21	Newtown Bellew,	do.	11
Isserkelly,	do.	21	Ardrahan,	do.	13
Moylough,	do.	21	Claddagh,	do.	13
Ballymoe,	do.	24	Portumna,	do.	15
Kilcreest,	do.	24	Claran Bridge,	do.	16
Clifden, (Connemara)	do.	26	Kiltarton,	do.	21
Portumna,	**July**	1	Tullfoadaly,	do.	21
Atheary,	do.	3	Clonfert,	do.	22
Ballinasloe,	do.	4	Killimore,	do.	22
Tuam,	do.	4	Ahaseragh,	do.	24
Dunmore,	do.	10	Mount Shannon,	do.	28
Eyrecourt,	do.	10	Aghrim,	**Dec.**	1
Tubberpadder,	do.	10	Loughrea,	do.	5
Tubberindoney,	do.	12	Dunmore,	do.	11
Dunlo,	do.	13	Newtown Eyre,	do.	11
Caltragh,	do.	17	Tynagh,	do.	11
Mt Bellew Bridge,	do.	25	Galtragh,	do.	14
Castle Blakeney,	do.	26	Lawrence-town,	do.	15
Derrymacloghny,	**Aug.**	1	Clifden,	do.	18
Kilconnel,	do.	4	Creggs,	do.	19
Barna,	do.	5	Claremore,	do.	20
Clareraore,	do.	9	Eyrecourt,	do.	20

SECTION III

GENERAL PRICES

It is almost impossible to ascertain the prices of cattle at different periods; fluctuating with the quality; demand, the prospect of peace or war, plenty or scarcity of grass, and many other circumstances. The war which has recently, closed, contributed chiefly to keep up the prices for several years; peace has lowered them considerably, (1816,) and probably they may be lower, but not in the degree apprehended; for the prices offered for calves were so very low, that many fattened and killed those, which at a former period they would have sold to graziers for stock: that this conjecture has some foundation, may be proved by the great plenty and cheapness of fat veal in all the different markets. In 1807 cattle were uncommonly cheap and an universal slaughter of calves and young cattle took place; the consequence was, that in three years the prices rose and I have little doubt the same effect will take place, though not I hope to a war price. The graziers however, have no right to complain; they have generally become purchasers of land, and it is now-high time they should share a little of their incomes with their neighbours; those who speculated in land as if the war was to be eternal, have been justly rewarded for their unfeeling folly. There has not been any fall in the price of sheep, but rather a rise, and wool sells now (1815) for 26s. per stone. In 1819 it rose to 32s. per stone, but in 1820 it fell to 20s. Horses have had a rapid fall in price, and probably may be lower for a short period. The high prices given for cavalry horses helped greatly to improve the breed; from, the general neglect of most farmers to breed, it is highly probable in a few years there will be a considerable demand for horses. Swine still keep up their price (1819); chiefly caused by a brisk demand from jobbers from Waterford and other places, and also for exportation to many parts of England, chiefly the neighbourhood of Manchester. In 1820 they have experienced a very sudden and great fall in price. The great fall in the price of cattle and sheep at Ballinasloe, in October 1820, spread a general gloom over the province of Connaught; the prices for cattle were from three to five pounds each less than last year, and sheep from ten to fifteen shillings under the last year's price; to those who had bred their own stock this was not quite so disastrous as to the jobbers who purchased in spring; many of those gentlemen sold their stock at Ballinasloe for less than they paid for them, consequently such as could not draw on their banker were nearly ruined. Towards the end of 1820, and the beginning of 1821, the prices for stock improved greatly. The demand for pigs in February and March was extraordinary, consequently the prices kept pace with it. The multitudes that have left this province are astonishing, insomuch, that I am inclined to the opinion of some author, (whose name I do not recollect,) "that there are more pigs than sheep in Ireland." In October 1821 the prices fell again, even still lower than before, but were something better in November. It is generally agreed, however, that though the prices were low, the demand was still brisk. Not withstanding the former losses, many were induced, from an idea that things could not be worse, to give prices for stock in 1822 far above their value; the consequence has been, that many who were much injured in their property before, are now entirely ruined; even an abatement in the rent has been a very partial relief, as the capital has vanished.

In 1823 the prices for sheep at Ballinasloe improved much from the former year, but such as were kept over from that fair have been since sold at a loss. Cattle at that fair were rather better than it was expected they would be, but paying very little for their feeding.

Many have been induced to send their fat cattle to Leicester and other parts of England, which I understand has succeeded well. Probably if there was sufficient feeding, they would go to a better market in spring, but few, if any, are prepared to feed in winter, consequently they must sell. I imagine a few acres of early sown rape or turnips would prevent this necessity, but I am aware the great graziers in this province will join their 'wise man' in a laugh at this proposal; and yet in Scotland such things are common. There has been a considerable demand from England for horses fit for hunting and carriages, and high prices given, which is likely to improve the breed much.

SECTION IV

MODES OF FEEDING, AND HOW FAR HOUSED IN WINTER

The mode of feeding is chiefly confined to what the bounty of Providence furnishes; few cultivate green food for winter, and as to soiling in the house in summer, the most beneficial practice that ever was followed, the person who proposed it would be laughed at by the graziers: the answer of ignorance and prejudice is always ready; "have not Mr. A. and Mr. B. &c. made fine fortunes by the present practice?" the fact is well known to be, that Mr. A, and Mr. B, and multitudes of others, on the death of their fathers, jumped into a large tract of rich grazing land, at a few shillings an acre, and a large stock of cattle laid in at low prices; a sudden rise in every article produced by land elevated many, from being middle men (without an acre of estate) paying £800 or £1000. a year rent, to 4, 5, or £6000. a year; but the question here is, what they might have made by better practices: let any of those gentlemen begin at the present prices of land and stock, and see what would become of them, especially after the October fairs of Ballinasloe in 1820, 1821, and 1822. We have seen lately great tracts of land given up, at a rent which would formerly have created a fortune. In general hay is the only winter feeding, except where winterage is kept; a beneficial practice much followed: there are some rich lands on which the herbage will not stand the severity of winter, but there are extensive tracts of dry ground, possessed by almost every extensive grazier, that preserves the grass until the rich feeding lands are ready in May: where they do not possess any of this description of ground, they are obliged to use hay, as few, if any, of those who may be called graziers, ever think of green winter food. Cattle and sheep are seldom housed even in the severest weather, and range about the land, poking it full of holes; for not a grazier in a thousand drains his land; even if he did, it would be by shallow, open, surface drains. Cottiers always house their cattle at night in winter, and frequently give them potatoes, hay, or straw, in small quantities. On the 1st of June 1810, upwards of 6000 sheep were destroyed in this county alone, by a severe storm of hail, snow, and rain. The mornings of the end of May were frosty; many lost upwards of 60, mostly ewes, that had been shorn two days before: how highly beneficial would a sheep house have been at this time?[1] I imagine ewes with lambs should not be sheared until the lambs are weaned. Near Galway, and any town possessing a brewery, grains are very much used; they usually sell for 1s. 8d. per barrel, and they carry them on their backs into the mountains, west of Galway, upwards of two miles; a barrel gives about eight feeds to a cow.

Under the article "use of green food in winter," the names of the few who cultivate green winter food may be found; but it will be perceived that this very beneficial practice is confined to gentlemen, not a single grazier being in the list: if I should through ignorance have omitted any, I shall feel a singular gratification in publicly acknowledging it. It must be here understood, that I do not give the cultivator of a random crop of rape to reclaim a bog, and whose chief inducement is the value of the seed, the enviable title of cultivator of green winter foods, it can be only a strictly systematic cultivator that can deserve it. In the numberless advantages of toiling in the house in summer, may justly be added the following opinion of enlightened and scientific Sir: Humphrey Davy:

"The plants are less injured when cut, than when torn or jagged by the teeth of the cattle, and no food is wasted by being trodden down; they are likewise obliged to feed without making a selection, consequently the whole food is consumed; the attachment or dislike to a particular kind of food, exhibited by animals, offers no proof of its nutritive powers. Cattle, at first, refuse linseed cake, one of .the most nutritive substances on which they can be fed."

Almost every gentleman has a few stall-fed cattle for his own use in winter; but, except in the distilleries, few are fed for a market. Galway takes a good many. There are very few, if any other markets, that would encourage the feeding of any quantity, and Dublin would be too great a journey for fat cattle. A few years ago fat cattle and sheep were brought to Dublin by the grand canal, in cattle boats, and seemed for some time to be much approved of; for what reason they have been given up, I am ignorant.

---

[1] A sheep house is a useful appendage to any farm for many purposes; as dressing, shearing, branding, or examining, &. &; it might be made highly ornamental, by being placed in the centre of a group of trees, with the shepherd's house attached, and communicating with four fields, &c. &c., [original footnote].

SECTION V

NATURAL GRASSES

The natural grasses are the same in general produced in every part of Ireland, in similar, soils and situations. A bountiful Providence provides the seeds, and the constant feeding keeps it good, otherwise it might be anything else; the grazier takes no pains; he neither drains, sows hay seeds, nor destroys weeds; and his fences, if any, are bad. The plants that predominate in most lands remarkable for fattening, are chiefly the following:

White Clover,	(Trifolium repens,)
Trefoil,	(Medicago lupulina,)
Ladies bedstraw,	(Galium verum,)
Small Quaking grass,	(Briza minima,)
Crested dogs tad grass,	(Cynosurus cristatus, or *thraneen* in Irish)
Yarrow, very abundant,	(Achillea Millefolium,)
Small Plaintain,	(Plantago lanceolata,)
Red Clover,	(Trifolium pratense,)
Ray grass,	(Lolium perenne,)
Sweet scented vernal grass,	(Anthoxantum odoratum,)
Creeping bent grass,	(Fiorin-Agrostis stolonifera)
Birds foot trefoil,	(Lotus corniculatus.)

Meadow foxtail, (Alopecurus pratensis) is by no means a common grass in this county; I perceived it only at the Bishop of Clonfert's, Mr. Charles Seymour's, Summerset, Mr. Bellew's, Mount Bellew, in very small quantity, and in a field between Galway and Rahoon, on the top of a granite rock, with scarcely any earth on it; in each of those places it was produced in small quantity, and looked as if it was not indigenous, but probably had been brought in hay seeds from Dublin, in the neighbourhood of which it abounds in many fields.

In addition to the list I have given, there might have been some other kinds, probably perennial red clover (Cow grass), &c. but those I have mentioned were most abundant, indeed, almost to the exclusion of all others: I do not recollect to have met with any ground remarkable for its fattening quality, that did not abound with yarrow, and Birds foot trefoil: — except by the late Dr. Anderson (whose works are not so much read as they should be) they are not probably mentioned by any agricultural writer as food for cattle, yet there are no two plants that could be propagated with more ease by seed, of which they are very productive. The few fields that are sowed with hay seeds are too generally stocked with what is sold in the seed shops as white English hay seed, (*Holcus lanatus*) a small portion of Ray grass, and a very small quantity of red clover. Probably it will be found that there are few more worthless grasses than the *holcus lanatus*,[1] as it possesses, amongst many others, the bad property of retaining, nearly through the entire day, the rains and dews: it is the kind usually sowed in reclaimed bog, and generally gives a great return of seed, but declines rapidly afterwards; it is for this situation greatly inferior to Fiorin grass, which has now established itself, aided by the indefatigable exertions of Dr. Richardson, who, (instead of the sneers of ignorance) for his unwearied dispersion of it all over the world, deserves a statue to his memory; and I must be permitted to suggest, that the Farming Society of Ireland are not as much alive to his merit as he deserves: though he is above all pecuniary remuneration, they should rank their deep sense of his merit, by a handsome piece of plate, made still more acceptable, by a consciousness of deserving it.[2] There is not perhaps in all the range of agricultural improvement, any vegetable more highly deserving of encouragement, especially, when it is considered, that it thrives best on bog. It would be amusing, if it was not disgusting, to hear the doubts expressed of the truth of the statements of its produce by different gentlemen: will those sagacious men tell the following gentlemen they lie? — The Bishop of Derry 7½ tons of dry hay per acre: in December 1812, the Rev. Thomas Radcliffe, secretary to the Farmers' Society, and well known for his scientific knowledge of agriculture, sent in a report to the Farming Society of Ireland of Dr. Richardson's Fiorin meadows; it is inserted in the *Irish Farmer's Journal* of January the 9th, 1813, to which I must refer, as being too long for this publication; and as I cannot possibly suppose any agriculturist can be so stupid as not to possess this valuable publication; — I also publish the following statement from the same Journal of the 27th May, 1815, — The late, much lamented Mr. Travers Adamson, near Moate, county of Westmeath, received a premium of £50. from the Farming Society of Ireland, for two acres of Fiorin hay: it was stated by sworn viewers, to be perfectly well saved, for either rick or loft, (a doubtful point with some wiseacres); it was planted only in November 1813, on a dry pasturable bog, with ten or twelve spit of turf under it; — the bog was pared and burned; the crop was mowed between the 12th September, and 1st of October; it was weighed and ricked in November and weighed 16 tons, 2cwT. Sqrs. and 16lb«: it was weighed again in May, before Mr. Anthony Robinson of Moate, and weighed 12 tons, 6cwt and 3 qrs. and was, as he affirms, of prime quality; this was equal to

---

[1] Humphry Davy says, "it appears to be disliked by all sorts of cattle; the produce it not so great as a view of it in the fields would indicate; but being left almost entirety untouched by cattle, it appeals as the most productive part of the herbage. The hay which is made from it, from the number of downy hairs which cover the surface of the leaves is soft and spongy, and disliked by cattle in general."—After this opinion from so competent a judge, I feel strengthened greatly in my dislike to this unjustly fashionable grass, [original footnote].

[2] Since I composed this eulogium, the subject of it has gone to that place where virtue meets its reward. It is curious to see the opinion expressed of Fiorin grass, in his *Elementary Treatise on the Indigenous Grasses of Ireland*. "There is also a grass which grows in our low grounds, that I have heard some farmers talk of with much delight; they call it Florin or Floreen grass; I have taken pains to procure some plants of it, but have not succeeded", [original footnote].

upwards of 31 Smithfield loads, of 4 cwt. weight each, per acre. The expense of procuring this very valuable crop (exclusive of burning, probably forty shillings), was only £4. 10s. 2d. Every person can appreciate the value of this immense crop, on ground of very little value; it must be also recollected, that it was produced in one year from the time of planting, which could not be accomplished from any other plant usually made into hay. — Mr. Morley Saunders, of Saunder's Grove in the county of Wicklow, at the same time received the second premium of £30. for the second best two acres; the produce, by the affidavit of Mr. James Critchly, appears to be 9 tons, 15cwt,: "the hay was remarkably dry, (if any thing too dry) and on the 13th of May, 1815, it had been weighed when it was fit to rick, and weighed 11 tons per acre; it is necessary to remark, that this crop was of spontaneous growth:[1] at the same time Mr. David Watty received a premium of £90. for the third beet crop; the produce of well saved hay on two acres was 9 tons, 14 cwt. and 2 qrs.; the ground, a bog of little value. The following extract, from the Caledonian Mercury comes so strongly in aid of the above statements, that I cannot refrain from re-publishing it: —

"In the *Caledonian Mercury* of Thursday last, there is an advertisement offering to let the farm of Pennyland, part of the estate of Dalswinton, in Dumfriesshire, Scotland, belonging to Patrick Miller, Esq. of Dalswinton. The farm contains 1000 Scots acres; 289 acres have been laid down with clover, rye-grass, &c: and there are also 76 acres laid down with Fiorin grass; and it is the intention of the proprietor to lay down, in the course of the present year, 194 acres more with that grass. The following extract from the advertisement shows the great utility of cultivating Fiorin grass, and is in the highest degree honourable to our countryman, the Rev. Dr. Richardson.

"As Mr. Miller has cultivated Fiorin grass for five years, upon all kinds of soil, and to a much greater extent than any other person in Britain or Ireland, he is now perfectly satisfied that the Rev. Dr. Richardson has been the means of calling the attention of agriculturists, by his persevering and patriotic zeal and diligence, to the knowledge and value of a grass which will prove of the greatest importance to the United kingdoms of Great Britain and Ireland. Although it may not yet be known to what extent this grass may become valuable; or to what purposes it may be most probably employed, nor the number of sheep or cattle that may be fed and supported upon one acre's produce of this grass; Mr. Miller is nevertheless happy, that he can, without hesitation, declare, from his own experience, that Fiorin grass is a most valuable acquisition in the way of agriculture. Upon grounds which were let for twenty-one years, at one shilling per acre, and for which he could not, after advertising the same ground to be again let, obtain a higher rent, this ground had been laid down by him with Fiorin at an expense of about £10. per acre, which has produced 300 stones of excellent Fiorin hay, per acre, 24lbs. to the stone, and he believes that there are many thousands uncultivated acres in Scotland, of the same

---

[1] I much doubt the propriety of giving a premium for spontaneous growth, [original footnote].

quality with his, which, if properly laid down with Fiorin, after being enclosed and drained, would produce crops equally good with his. Mr. Miller is also happy, that he has it in his power to affirm, that the second and third year's crops of Fiorin are superior to the first, and require only a top-dressing the second year. For how many years the Fiorin may continue to be equally productive, he cannot from his own experience say; but what he considers of the greatest importance is, that sheep and cattle may pasture with great profit and advantage, if not after the first, yet always after the second year's crop, upon ground which, before being laid down with this grass, would not have supported their weight. All the sheep he has slaughtered, during some weeks past, for the use of a numerous family, have produced mutton, at twenty months old, after seven weeks feeding upon the aftermath of Fiorin, equal, if not superior to mutton of any age, however fed, and he has no doubt of having mutton of the same quality for some months to come, from sheep of the same age fed upon Fiorin hay. During the three months of last Autumn, Mr. Miller fed twenty-eight work horses, at work every working day during that period, upon Fiorin fresh cut, without any other kind of food, and no work horses could go on with their work, and be in better condition at the end of that time."

SECTION VI

ARTIFICIAL GRASSES

The use of those is confined to a few gentlemen; very few farmers ever think of saving artificial grasses; if they sometimes do, red clover is the only one, but as to soiling with it in the house, the only beneficial way of using it, it is almost unknown; it is always pastured on, a most wasteful practice, as, if the clover is good, a great proportion of it is destroyed by the feet of cattle, besides the danger of losing cattle by eating too much at one time. Soiling, unless carelessly managed, is free from this objection, and cattle are obliged to eat without selection, for according to Sir Humphry Davy, "the attachment or dislike to a particular kind of food, exhibited by animals, offers no proof of its nutritive powers." I have seen colts brought from the fair of Hospital in the county of Limerick, toss about good oats with their noses, and leave it behind them in the manger. I have also frequently seen sheep refuse turnips at first, but contrary to the opinion of Dr. Lawrence in his *Farmer's Kalendar*, I scarcely ever knew any animal refuse potatoes, though he says, page 424, "I have given them in large quantities, with bran and wash, to large store pigs, in styes, without any good effect; also to young pigs, running the yard, with ill effect. I tried my stables round, with the same success that a certain German cultivator experienced," (see Annals of Agriculture,). I could only persuade one old mare to bite a raw potatoe, and she spat it out again; so horses it seems, as well as doctors, disagree." That horses will not be able to perform hard work, if fed on raw potatoes without corn, who ever doubted? but that they injured young pigs running in the yard, I shall not stop to remark on, but to state that the best pork I ever have tasted, was fed entirely on raw potatoes and grass; the general fact is, that pigs, as well as most other animals in Ireland, (I do not know how it might have been with Dr. Lawrence's epicures,) except those put up for fattening, seldom get enough, they are only kept alive; the same may be said of fowl.

I think it is incumbent on every proprietor of land to try experiments, on a small scale, of every vegetable for the use of cattle. Several of our young gentlemen would find it a very pleasing antidote to ennui; they would be more healthfully employed than lounging on sofas, when they are not occupied in the sports of the field: Lord Kaims says, "violently active in the field, supinely indolent at home:" and I should imagine, that conversations on the comparative value and mode of cultivating land and its produce, would be far more useful than the general topic, and kept up for whole nights, on the powers of different horses to leap walls, and the short time it took them to ride a certain distance; the entire merit in both cases remaining with the horse. I am, however, happy to state, that this worthless character is wearing out fast, and in nothing has the benefit of the frequent intercourse with England been more visible than the change of manners. Vetches or tares are little known in this county; if they were tried by farmers, they would be found to preclude the expensive necessity of fallowing; they have been proved to prepare ground for wheat much better than a naked fallow; the one pays rent, the other adds a year's to the expense of the wheat crop; but to make them produce their best effects, they must be sowed thick enough (four bushels to the acre) to be a smothering crop, and consumed in the house by stock; the value of the manure produced by this practice must be added to the comparative account against the naked fallow.

There are two varieties of vetches, winter and spring; the winter vetch, sowed in spring, frequently mildews and is spoiled; the spring vetch, sowed in autumn, at the same time with the winter vetch, has been entirely destroyed by frost, whilst the other has escaped. It is not very easy to distinguish the difference in the seed or plant, and frequently one kind is sold for the other. It is an excellent practice to sow with the vetches a thin crop of rye, beans, or even oats; they help to support them. Where this crop is used for soiling, it is seldom cut in time, by which means a great proportion of the crop becomes too old, and the stalks too hard for cattle; though many think they are most beneficial in this forward state. Swine, and all kinds of fowl, especially geese, will fatten on them at this period of their growth.

SECTION VII

MODE OF HAY-MAKING

The general mode of making hay is very injudicious; the meadow is usually cut at a very late period, when much of its value is lost; with an idea of getting as much as possible from the land it is frequently deferred until October, especially by those who buy the meadows standing; the evil of this practice is not confined to the injury the hay receives, but extends to the future crop, which is prevented from shooting as early or vigorously in spring, as it would do if the after-grass covered the ground in winter; for it will probably be found, that, as a general practice, eating the after-grass is not a good one, though in many rich lands, or those that can be assisted by yard manure or clay ashes, it may be done, especially where the mowing has been performed at an early season; few, if any, ever think of using manure for this purpose; it is too much wanted for potatoes, which generally consume all the produce of the farm yard. When the grass is cut, it is generally thrown out of swathe, be the weather wet or dry; though certainly it would be much safer in the swathe in wet weather. It is also usually turned so often, especially in hot sun, that it loses much of its value; even after it is fit to put into field cocks, it is frequently spread about the field, and often caught by showers, and all the process of drying had recourse to again, to the great injury of the hay. There are very few who employ hands enough for this purpose, which requires more than any other farming operation, as every thing depends on catching the favourable moment. The very common oversight of not obliging hay makers to bring spades and other tools, according to the work they may have to perform, very frequently occurs here. Early in the morning, whilst dew is on the grass, or after a shower, whilst the hay is drying, much useful work aught be performed; cleaning and sinking ditches, making drams, picking stones, and various other works, of which there can be no want in any farm in this county. It is a disgusting thing to see a number of labourers, at such a season of hurry, sitting smoking under a hedge, waiting for the hay to dry, &c. The usual lazy method of mowing is injurious to both crops; it leaves much of the grass uncut, and the stumps that are left, are worse than useless. When they cut meadow for themselves, that they buy standing, they not only shave it into the earth, but defer it to so late a season the grass has not time to recover before the winter sets in. In letting meadow on the foot, there should be always a restriction as to the time of cutting; in that case, if cut at an early period, the closer it is cut the better; but not so low as to injure the crown of the plant There is a large portion of the hay of this county produced on callows, (meadows near the banks of rivers,) and though they are frequently lost by sudden floods, after being made into hay, yet so indolent are the proprietors, that they usually procrastinate their removal until, though they are not caught by flood, the bottom of each cock is much injured. Nothing is more common than to see haycocks standing like small islands in the midst of water, especially along the river Suck.

Hay should always be shaken out of swathe after the mowers, by hand, and not in the customary lazy way with forks, which leave it in wisps, impervious to wind and sun; no grass cut after one or two o'clock should be spread out until the following morning when the dew evaporates, nor should any hay be left spread during the night, except it has received wet. "Oh never fear, Sir!" has spoiled much hay in this county, and in every other, for every thing is left to chance. Both tramp cocks and grass cocks are always left on too broad a base, they should be well pulled at the bottom, and every handful frequently crossed over each other on the top of the cock; the observance of this very simple process will, in a great measure, prevent the admission of rain water. The northern method of making the hay in lap cocks or muffs, is, I imagine, scarcely known in this county. The fermentation of the hay is carefully prevented; if the cock gets the least warm they are frightened, and it is instantly taken down, I certainly am no advocate for that excessive high fermentation that makes the hay of a foxy colour, and though preferred in many parts of England, I agree with my horse in preferring green hay that has undergone a gentle fermentation. Although I am convinced our hay generally receives too much making, yet the generally succulent state of our herbage, and a more humid atmosphere, compared to that of England, make more time necessary than would be required in that country.

When the hay is fit to make into tramp cocks, (field cocks of about a ton each,) if time will permit, it will be found a beneficial practice to draw it home to the rick yard, to be made into the same size as field cocks, and so ranged as to be easily built into a rick or large cocks, when sufficiently seasoned. It is nearly impossible to give directions suited to every case for the best method of making hay. Any one can make hay in good weather; the only danger then is too much making: wet weather is what tries the skill of the farmer; at this period an abundant supply of labourers, of all ages and sexes, enables the farmer to take instant ad vantage of every favourable moment.

It is a very common practice to spread out more hay than can be well made up the same evening; trusting too much to chance, nine times in ten they are caught by rain, or at least heavy dew, and have not sufficient help to prevent the effects of a coming shower, which in summer can be generally prognosticated by most country people sufficiently early, if help is at hand. It will be found a good general rule to spread hay as little as possible after it has been made into grass cocks, but frequently to re-make them from small into large, increasing the size with the state of dryness; always carefully shaking with the hand each time of re-making, and pulling well the bottoms of the cocks, and spreading it on the tops, and the hay smoothed neatly down the sides of the cocks, so as to have the appearance of being thatched.

It is needless to detail the process of making clover into hay; he must be a wretched farmer that does not consume it by soiling in the house; also, Lucern, St. Foin, or any other green crop. The farmer should watch his field cocks to prevent too great a state of fermentation, which may easily be perceived at the leeward side of the cock, not only by the hand, but by an appearance of moisture, as if the cock was wetted on the surface in one spot near the top. Sometimes a hole made into the cock will check it, if not, it must be well shaken and re-made.

SECTION VIII

DAIRIES — THEIR PRODUCE AND MANAGEMENT

Dairies, on the extensive scale they are in the counties of Cork, Limerick, Waterford, or Carlow, are, I imagine, unknown in this county. Near Galway, especially on the west side, a large quantity of excellent butter is produced, and near every town as much as supplies the home consumption; any not used in this way is salted, and generally sold in Galway. The merchants of Galway have lately very laudably offered premiums for the best butter, and I trust they will shortly become exporters. Mr. Dodd, who was formerly an eminent provision merchant in Dublin, and who is now weigh master and butter-qualifier of Galway, has taken every pains to improve and extend the butter trade; though it commenced with such favorable prospects, that the butter brought the highest prices in the London and Spanish markets, yet I understand it has lately rather declined. The merchants are making every exertion for its advancement The butter made at Barna, near Galway, is of very superior quality, and its character so well established, that there is always a competition for it by the inhabitants of Galway. Dare I say, that to my taste, (especially that made by one woman near Barna,) it is superior to any I have ever tasted elsewhere; it is made of the natural colour of butter, and not spoiled by the addition of too much hot water, which almost every dairy maid, from habit, uses to hasten the process. Many seem to overlook the bad taste caused by dirty vessels and hot hands, — which should never (nor indeed any hand) touch the butter so as the butter looks nice, and floats in clear water in a cut glass cooler[1]. In excessive hot weather, cold spring water may be necessary to bring the butter to the breakfast table, but surely not in cold weather.

I trust the use of turnips will not be established in the dairies here, as they are beginning to be in the county of Carlow, where, if the practice becomes general, the merchants will have to regret it, in the loss of that high character their butter has obtained at foreign markets.

Almost every cottier near Barna has a cow, some perhaps two: the temptation of so good and near a market as Galway, frequently leaves little milk for the children. In other parts of this county there are too many cottiers without a cow, who endure great misery where there are children, even of those who have a cow, many are without milk great part of the year, waiting most anxiously for the calving of the cow, which generally does not take place until May or June, which leaves them without milk in winter when it is most necessary. It is an almost universal practice with those even in good circumstances, to pursue this losing method; frequently where four cows are kept, only one gives milk in winter: where little land is occupied, the cow should be sold out immediately when she grows slack in her milk, and replaced with one in full milk.

I do not think any cheese is made in this county, except cream cheese, and that not as general at the table of a man of fortune as it should be; it only appears on state days. Butter may be preserved sweet for several years, by the following receipt; it never becomes hard or too brittle, but continues to look and taste like butter fresh churned. It requires to be a month made before it is used.

---

[1] I have frequently heard "some bad weed that the cows eat" accused for the ill taste occasioned by dirty vessels. I beg to point my readers' attention to the Survey of Kilkenny, by Mr. Tighe, for the filthy method of making Waterford butter , [original footnote].

> 10 ounces of common salt,
> 2 ounces of saltpetre,   } made very fine;
> 2 ounces best brown sugar,

they should be all intimately mixed; to each pound of butter, put one ounce of the mixture, with which it should be well incorporated, and packed close in tubs or crocks in the usual way, and the sides of the vessel well closed.

It is not a little extraordinary that the filthy custom of permitting the calf to empty two teats, whilst the dairy-maid is milking the other two, prevails in this county: the economy is certainly praiseworthy, as nothing is lost; the calf contributing to the milk pail any thing that dribbles from his mouth. Will it be believed in other parts of Ireland, that the reason given for this vile, lazy practice is, "that the calves would not thrive if fed in any other way." By this method there can be only a guess at the quantity each calf gets, the strong calf drinking more than the weak one. As the calf is always permitted to finish the milking, the cow habituated to this method often retains the strippings or last milk, for the calf. It is well known that the proportion of butter produced from milk drawn at this period, and the first milk has been ascertained to be in some cows from 16 to 1, and 8 to 1 in favor of the strippings. It is highly probable that calves suffer much from getting milk only twice a day, and even then, the quantity is given at the discretion of the dairy maid. The method practised in some parts of England of feeding them three times a day, seems to be much better, and probably an extension of the plan would be still more beneficial: I only allude to those calves fed by hand, and not those by the cow, as those can be fed only when the cows are milked; it is also a good practice to milk cows three times a day, when they are in the height of their milking. From the general bad feeding that cows receive, they yield but a small proportion of the quantity of milk they should do; and it diminishes rapidly as winter approaches.

The cows that poor people are able to buy are of the very worst description, they are wretched animals, half fed from their infancy. Near large towns where there are breweries, cows often get grains, which increase the quantity of poor thin milk. In winter there is frequently a division made between the cow and pig of small potatoes, but far from what either could consume. In general the cows of this county are very far behind other parts of Ireland as milkers, whether this proceeds from the breed, or want of early feeding, I am ignorant, probably both causes may operate.

SECTION IX

PRICES OF HIDES, TALLOW, WOOL, AND QUANTITY SOLD

The prices of hides and tallow vary so much, that it would require better information than I could procure, to make any satisfactory statement. The hides are all tanned in Galway and other towns; the quantity tanned, bears but a small proportion to the consumption of the county, for which purpose large quantities of leather are brought from Dublin, Athlone, and some from England, and esteemed much better than that tanned at home, especially heavy hides: the tallow is all consumed in the country by the chandlers[1]. The price of wool varies with the quality, and often with the period at which it is sold. A demand from England raises the price, as this year (1818), owing to a demand for woollen goods in the manufacturing towns in England, wool has risen to 52s, per stone of 16lb. The great wool fair of Ballinasloe, that used formerly to bring together all the graziers of three or four counties, and buyers from Leinster and Munster, has dwindled to almost nothing, and now almost all the wool is sent to Dublin to different commission houses, where the most honorable dealings are observed. Formerly above six weeks were ridiculously lost, and great expense incurred by the competition between buyers and sellers, which should name a price first; to such extent was this carried, that the buyers have made excursions to view the country, and the sellers in the mean time have either gone home, or too often have been tempted into habits of drinking or gambling: the present mode is much better for both parties. The wool is generally sent to Dublin in packs containing about 7cwt: each pack takes 21 bundles of coarse home-made canvass, at about 10d. per bundle: the expense of carriage, commission, &c. may be about 10d. per stone.

Except in Connemara, and a few places in the hands of gentlemen, there is little short wool grown in the county. In Connemara a very considerable quantity, indeed I believe the whole, is worked up in stockings, of which there is a very considerable sale. There may be some flannel and frizes made, but I imagine not much; The genius of the women seems to lean to knitting stockings, which only wants encouragement to make them superior to any in the world for the same price: the usual retail price of the peddlers is twenty pence per pair. What can be expected from so inadequate a price, when their profit is deducted?

---

[1] candle maker, [Clachan Ed.].

CHAPTER IV

FARMS

SECTION I

THEIR SIZE

THE size of farms varies infinitely from one acre (if such can be called a farm) to those in mountain districts of many hundred acres, set by the bulk, I rather think that any piece of land that does not give constant employment to a plough, cannot be with propriety called a farm. Those that do not, may be called cottier holdings, a most wretched mode of occupation if too large, for by aiming at crops which can be only cultivated to advantage by the plough, they are generally the most distressed kind of tenants; a mongrel race between farmer and labourer. It is not easy to say what the size of a cottier holding, cultivated entirely with the spade, should be; it depending much on the quality of the land and the assistance that may be derived from grown-up children. Probably six acres of good land would be sufficient. That question, which has been so often agitated about the proper size of farm, and whether large or small farms are most advantageous to the public, may be easily answered by considering that every size will meet with corresponding capital, us in truth it should do; and as to the comparative value of large or small farms, much depends on management; however, there is little use in arguing on what always must subsist — farms of every gradation; and if every farmer takes no more than he has capital to till properly, I presume it is of little consequence to the public what the size may be. It is well established that four farms of fifty acres each, will bring a higher rent than if all let in one farm. We have been not a little surprised to read in the public papers about the tenants of Mr. Coke of Holkham, some having an interest worth £2000. per annum, and upwards. We have nothing to do with the motives of Mr. Coke, but I can scarcely be persuaded that a much more useful tenantry, and higher rent, might not be obtained by dividing those great farms into holdings of one to two hundred a year rent. If the tenants had obtained those great interests by reclaiming the land, they would richly deserve any income they might have. I imagine our Irish landlords will not be very ready to imitate Mr. Coke, indeed, in any respect; in fact, very few have the income. It is a very common error with Irish farmers to take more land than they have capital for; the contrary is the more prudent practice, and at the same time the most profitable; for if he has spare capital, he can employ it profitably in various ways, until be feels his way, and he is always ready for a bargain; for ready money enables a man to purchase many things on low terms.

Farms in Connemara, and the mountain baronies west of Galway are generally very large, and set by a bulk rent from perhaps fifty to three hundred pounds a year, and are chiefly occupied in grazing young cattle. On the sea coast, and in the valleys of this extensive region, the farms are small, and generally held by occupying tenants from various parts of Ireland. Probably a labourer should have only as much land as will give his family abundance of potatoes and milk, but he should be certain of employment from his landlord when not occupied by his own affairs, and his wages should be increased; for I am convinced the rate of wages has not kept pace with the rise in land and the late fall in produce. Some humane landlords, I am happy to say, have raised the wages of their labourers; but it is not as general as it should be. I am aware, it will be said, that labourers are paid sufficient for the small quantity of labour they perform; — I often regret their habitual idleness; but what are stewards for? Probably on a comparison of Irish labourers with those of other countries, taking into the comparison the difference of wages, it will not be found so very much against- them as some of our travelled agriculturists seem to think: one gets 5d. the other 2s. per day!

The practice of taking many farms, and some very distant from the residence of the tenant, is much followed in this county. These cannot be so profitably managed as by an occupying tenant, pursuing a good system of alternate tillage and grazing. Every person possessing distant farms must be well aware that he loses much grass by trespass, either permitted or unheeded. I recollect once being told by an extensive land jobber, that he was convinced he lost upwards of £1000. a year in his different farms by trespass: what a system this must be! It is really astonishing that landed proprietors do not perceive the losses they sustain by letting to any but occupants. Formerly the great reputed wealth those land jobbers possessed blinded the judgment of proprietors; but we have seen some of the highest and most imperious heads brought very low lately, by a fall in stock and other produce. It is the practice very much of shopkeepers in county towns to take large farms. I much doubt if they had not the till to draw on, whether those farms could be kept. I know several instances where money has been accumulated by those shopkeepers, but it was at a period when war prices were received for every thing. I imagine if they had not other resources the October fairs, 1820 and 1822, would try their bottom. I presume to think an extension of the business they are used to would be much more profitable.

SECTION II

FARM HOUSES AND OFFICES

As farmers generally build their own houses and offices, they have commonly every defect, both as to site and execution. The offices placed without any previous plan; a stable here, a cow-house there, and every thing so badly arranged and finished, that they do not answer fully any purpose for which they should be erected. The very general practice in Ireland of placing almost every building below the level of the adjacent ground, may be seen in great perfection in this county; even the dwelling house has usually a step down into it, by which means it is always damp; and as pigs and fowl are usually permitted to range through the sitting room, it adds to the general filthy state of the dwelling. Though the pig is not in general permitted to take up his lodging in the house at night, the fowl almost universally do, with an idea that the warmth and smoke of the house are beneficial to them. In contradiction to this idea I know several instances where the fowl sleep throughout the year in trees, and are as productive, in every respect, as those kept more tenderly. Farm houses have often a sufficient number of small windows, but the greater part are stopped up, and frequently the only light comes in at the door; as to a window opening to let in air to a room, it is a rarity, and even disliked by the country people: even houses of the first rank, will it be believed that servants' apartments have seldom this convenience. I regret to state that the sleeping accommodation of servants is most grossly neglected in many houses that have no excuse but great indolence. This has been carried to such a length, even in one of the first houses in the county, that a physician was obliged to order the window of a housemaid's room, ill of fever, to be broken open: the house-keeper declared it had not been opened for twenty years! High rank is no excuse for this cruel neglect, but rather an aggravation. Make servants comfortable, and make them do their duty. In many parts of this county the cabins are built of clay, generally very badly tempered, on a foundation of a foot or two of stone; but as the thatch seldom projects far enough over the wall, the rains and frost melt it away, and in a few years the house falls, or is propped with sticks or a buttress of loose stones. If they were originally built with a projecting roof of at least two feet, this evil in a great measure would be prevented; but until landlords or their agents either build houses or superintend their building, this must be the case. I have been often at a loss to account for the callousness of many landlords in this county, that could patiently see around them such miserable dwellings for their tenants, whilst their horses and bounds have every attention paid to their comfort The gentlemen of this county have been accused by their neighbours of possessing a great deal of pride, if so, it certainly does not consist in an attention to the superior accommodation of their tenantry. Any person who has travelled from Athy to Cork, or in many other counties, must be painfully struck with the great difference, not only in their houses, but in their general appearance. I am most happy to say, however, that there are many exceptions to this stigma. I only forbear to mention them from a conviction that a speedy change in others for the better will take place. There can be less excuse for it in this county than perhaps any other in Ireland, as there are very few absentees, and the properties are generally ample; but it does not so much require property as exertion and a proper feeling of its consequences; for it will be found that those tenants who are remarkable for any superior degree of cleanliness in their habitations or family are the most regular in their payments.

There is one office which should be indispensable in every yard; yet it must be at the house of a man of some rank only where it will be found! Very few stables have racks with mangers so construed as to save the hay seeds, and in many of those very places they are often brought from Dublin at a great expense, and not so good as those saved at home. I imagine it is incumbent on every landlord or his agent to superintend the plan, site, and building of every house on his estate. As they generally contribute nothing else, they may well contribute their advice[1]. I am convinced there is scarcely a tenant that would not conform to the wish of his landlord: the chief objects to attend to are, the site; levels of the floor of the house and yard; arrangement of the offices; a prevention of dunghills in front of the house; and the roof so contrived as to project at least two feet beyond the wall of both house and offices.

SECTION III

NATURE OF TENURES— GENERAL STATE OF LEASES AND PARTICULAR CLAUSES THEREIN

Leases are generally for thirty-one years, or three lives; but lately leases for twenty-one years, or a life, have become more general. Very few landlords are now so blind to the interest of their children, however imprudent their ancestors might have been, as to grant leases renewable forever. Formerly leases for thirty-one years and three lives were sometimes granted, but I imagine not lately. A good deal of land is held by bishops' leases; an uncertain kind of tenure, that gives rise to many bickerings between landlord and tenant, and prevents all manner of improvement. A power to plant is reserved by many landlords, but it is a power, I fear, that is too seldom used. Too much of the land of this county is let in partnership; this wretched mode of letting land must have originated at a remote period, when the state of agriculture was very low, and the means of stocking a farm still lower. Whilst the war continued, a high price for every kind of agricultural produce enabled village tenants to pay their rents punctually; and many landlords, not adverting to the sudden fall there must be on the conclusion of the war, nor on the taxes it must create, insisted it was the best mode of letting land. Happily we are now at peace, and they are convinced that this cause (the peace) and an unthought of increase of population far beyond their means of support, have rendered it the very worst mode of letting land, and instead of being the most punctual tenants they are the reverse. At the rate at which population has increased, if the land of many villages was even given rent free, the tenants in a few years could not exist. Surely landlords must, or at least ought to have seen that the permission either openly or tacitly given to villagers to subdivide their shares amongst their children, or with strangers who tempted them with a trifling profit rent, must ultimately have the present effect. It is a very general custom with village tenants, and indeed with those who hold separate tenures, to give a part of their division of land as a marriage portion with a son or daughter, and this so often repeated, that ground sufficient to maintain them has not been had by any of the parties. On an estate that I had the superintendence of in this county, I knew many villages that originally consisted of six families, now have above twenty: and

---

[1] Lord Clancarthy makes an addition to his tenants of two-thirds or more of any sum they choose to expend in building, and in many instances expends the whole amount, [original footnote].

on another estate, one village has increased to six. There is another evil attendant on this erroneous system, the great decrease of bog for fuel on many estates. In the original lease above mentioned, turf banks sufficient for six houses were allotted. Now there are twenty necessary, and very frequently others from adjoining estates are permitted to cut turf. This has been unobservedly decreasing the value of many estates. How many circumstances tend to prove the great necessity of a resident agent? Those who do not understand the future of turf bogs (Dublin agents) imagine they are inexhaustible. According to the improvident mode of cutting and managing bogs the carriage every day becomes more difficult and expensive. Landlords too often, instead of laying out the line for cutting with some system of improvement in view, permit their tenants to act at random; not adverting to the certainty that bogs will hereafter, and probably at no distant period, be some of the most valuable part of their estates. Very few leases are taken, especially by graziers, without a clause of surrender, to prevent a loss if the price of land or produce should fall. At the same time, I do not see why a clause of re-assumption should not be inserted in favor of the landlord; always making full remuneration for any permanent improvements; and if to a certain amount, probably the clause should be void[1]. I shall probably be thought visionary by at least one party, but I do not write for any party. I apprehend too many took advantage of the late sudden depression of the value of agricultural produce, and worked on the fears of timid landlords to obtain a permanent abatement of their rents; -and some, I am informed, took advantage of the pecuniary obligations their landlords were under to them, to force them to give leases at a rent far below the value of the land. That any land taken within the last ten years at least, was entitled to a temporary abatement was but fair; but why the proprietor of the land should not have a reciprocal chance of a rise, is not consonant to my idea of the compact that should exist between landlord and tenant. Many, I am well aware, are biting their nails that their surrenders were accepted. Fee simple estates frequently sell for upwards of twenty years purchase; the rate depending on various circumstances. Freehold property much the same as in Clare, sixteen or seventeen years purchase. A very high portion of the county is let, especially to cottier tenants, without any lease; they universally assign this uncertain tenure as the principal cause for the non-improvement of their farms and houses, and doubtless this, added to the reasons I have before given, will account for the ruinous state of the village system. As to the length of the tenure which should be given, I apprehend twenty-one years, or a life, a very fair term for any land that is delivered to the tenant in reasonable good order, with a comfortable house and offices on it, always holding in

---

[1] A farmer in this county waited on his absentee landlord, in Westmeath, to get a renewal of his lease, and, as an inducement, he stated, that in addition to the other improvements he had made, he had planted a great number of trees; his intelligent landlord, curling up his nose, "Sir, I give you no thanks for planting trees, my agent tells me they only encourage sparrows to destroy the corn!" [original footnote].

remembrance to give a decided refusal to the former tenant leaving his farm, house, and offices in an untenantable state. Nothing could ever tempt me to give a renewal to the tenant that run the ground out of heart the last years of his lease. Where improvements are to be made, and an house and offices built, a term of thirty-one years, or three lives, seems to be mutually advantageous; this very much depends on the sum expended; in many cases a longer term would be necessary. The clause against burning is very necessary in the present state of agricultural practices; but if the clause was only against over cropping, the burning in most cases would be highly beneficial. The clause also against breaking up more than a certain proportion of the land until that formerly broken up was laid down, has been to my knowledge most shamefully evaded; in those cases there was unfortunately no restriction as to the number of crops, nor the state of the ground when laid down. I have seen the clause also evaded by sowing hay seeds after the plough, without harrowing, and with that most worthless of all grasses called in the seeds shops white English hay seeds (*Holcus lanatus*). An attention to those matters forms a very material part of the duty of an agent. Dr. Lawrence says, "It is to be lamented, both on public and private grounds, that estates are ever superintended and leased out by other than able judges of cultivation." I know many agents that do not know the difference between St. Foin and Lucern.

Many landlords exact the payment of their rents a few months after it is due, some in a few days; but the usual mode is to leave half a year's, often a whole year's rent in the tenants' hands, called the *hanging gale*, and many are often obliged to take their rent in small sums, as the tenant receives it at fairs or markets.

Non-resident agents cannot do this, and very often the money is dissipated. Probably no money laid out by a proprietor of land would make a more ample return than that laid out in the improvement of the farm previous to letting it. In most cases, at least in this county, a tenant getting a farm in an impoverished state, is neither able nor capable of improving it; and I have no doubt many would be better able to pay an ample interest annually, as an additional rent, than expend the money the first year or two of his lease; besides, the superior productiveness of the farm would give him such a lift, as would enable him to keep up his farm in the good state in which he got it. It must be understood I mean here that the landlord should fence, drain, repair the house and offices, and leave a crop of clover and grass seeds in the stubbles; a power to sow which the year before the termination should be reserved in every lease. Cottier tenants should never be permitted to alienate without permission from their landlord. From a want of this clause, or indolence in enforcing it, many bad and turbulent characters have been introduced into a peaceable country. I should be very cautious in advising restrictions on the mode of cropping, but really the ruinous practice of taking successive corn crops without any kind of manure or green crop, has arrived to such a pitch, that a restriction becomes necessary for the interest of both landlord and tenant; also that they should be obliged to sow clover and grass seeds with every spring corn crop. No one practice would elevate the agriculture of

Ireland from its degraded state more than this, considered either as to its immediate effects on the land, or as furnishing the means of future improvement by the feeding of immense numbers of stock, without which, improvement is nearly impossible. This system could be greatly assisted by the use of ashes of clay, the material for which every farm furnishes; but what can be expected from poor tenants, when rich proprietors do not set the example? A most extraordinary and oppressive power is claimed by some landlords near Ballinasloe, of turning in cattle and sheep on the 29th of September, into ground he has let, at perhaps a very high rent, for corn acres[1]. I have seen cattle and sheep intended for the fair of Ballinasloe on the 5th of October, turned into potatoes, which were unfit to dig at that season, and were very much injured by the treading of the cattle in wet weather.

SECTION IV

TAXES OR CESSES PAID BY TENANTS

The taxes are a cess, generally called public money, for repairing roads and various other purposes, fluctuating almost every year from five to ten pence, and sometimes eighteen pence per acre for the spring half year; but in summer it is much higher, as provision must be made for the expense of roads, &c. accounted for at the Summer Assizes; but the tax differs in almost every barony. Formerly this tax has been as high as six shillings per acre, when illicit still fines were levied on the barony. — Quit rent is another tax of two pence halfpenny per acre. Vestry money for church repairs, about three halfpence per acre. There are several other heavy taxes which few grumble at because they are voluntary; for instance, the tax caused by the depredations of vermin of all sorts, is beyond all calculation, but seems to be little noticed. I am convinced, however, it is much more than those necessary ones imposed by the legislature. Another heavy tax is the drunkenness which every fair, market, or funeral induces. Many of those who take every opportunity to evade the tax of a few pence for custom at a fair, would think little of spending five shillings in whiskey. I do not know of any other taxes but the usual ones of hearth, window, dog, horse and carriage; to evade which many mean precautions are taken of locking up, or sending away dogs, horses and carriages, and giving false returns of every thing taxable; yet those men would send a message to any one who should dare to express a doubt of their honor! what a degrading idea for a man of fortune!

> "There are a variety of little meannesses of which persons, otherwise of reputation and credit, are guilty, to save trifles in expenditure; but surely none at once so senseless and reprehensible, as the endeavour to defraud government of the taxes legally imposed upon us. It is the same thing as defrauding a private individual, and indeed comes to that at last. It is bidding defiance to the law; hurting fair dealers; and robbing our rulers of

---

[1] It must be understood here that Corn acre, vulgarly called Con acre, means land let for one or two crops; — it is not confined to that let for corn, but includes potatoes or any other crop, [original footnote].

their due, to the diminution of those duties which must be made good by new levies on the public.[1]"

SECTION V

PROPORTION OF WORKING HORSES AND OXEN TO THE SIZE OF FARMS

It is difficult to ascertain the proportion of working horses or oxen to the size of farms; but I imagine in general it is far below what a well cultivated farm would require, where manure is to be brought from any distance; this indeed, except near large towns on the sea coast, is very seldom thought of. It is true that many use a good deal of limestone gravel, but the carriage of this is usually done by hired horses or asses with baskets, and seldom farther than the adjoining field or bog. A farm of one to three hundred acres, may perhaps possess six horses, but frequently the farmer hires others when there is a press of work in spring: small farms one or two horses, but they also hire or borrow additional horses. Where villages possess horses, they generally assist each other. Oxen are not as much used as they should be. Poor people sometimes yoke a horse and a cow together in a plough or harrow. I have often seen a very small heifer drawing three large sacks of oats to Ballinasloe market; it were much to be wished this practice was more general; of their superior fitness for the work of a poor man, there can be little doubt; for independent of many other advantages, an ox or heifer will thrive and work on the food that would not be sufficient for a working horse, and when past their labour, they will probably bring more than their original cost, whilst the horse is worth little or nothing: I believe the cause of the preference is merely custom; a powerful opposer to every kind of improvement. A few farmers use oxen, but always four in a plough for the slightest work; they are never fed as they ought to be, either in summer or winter. In summer, after a hard day's work, instead of being turned into good grass, where they would fill their bellies quickly, they are almost always consigned to some bare pasture, where they can merely exist: instead of this unfeeling mode, they should be soiled in the house in summer with some kind of nourishing green food; in winter with turnips, cabbage, potatoes, mangel worzel, Fiorin grass, &c. &c. and plenty of the best hay or good oaten straw fresh threshed: if they are fed in this manner, they will be able to bear any work that a horse would, and be always ready to turn to fatten in forward condition; where this management is observed, scarcely too many can be kept, as, if they do not work, they are in such high condition, as always to command a ready market, whilst on the contrary idle horses would ruin a farmer.

---

[1] Quotation from '*The monthly mirror: Reflection Men and Manners*, J. Wright – 1804, [Clachan ed.].

SECTION VI

GENERAL SIZE OF FIELDS AND ENCLOSURES

There is an endless variety in the size of fields: those of graziers and the better kind of farmers vary from five or six to twenty acres or more, but frequently in the farms of graziers, especially those stocked with sheep, several fields are thrown into one by gaps or prostrate walls, though some are very careful in the building, and maintaining the permanency of their walls.

The ancient cantred[1] of land consisted of thirty townlands, each as much as would pasture three hundred head of cattle; every townland had eight carricates or ploughlands of 120 acres each, so that a townland contained 960 acres, and a cantred would pasture 9000 head of cattle. The name of cantred or carrucate is now little used, but that of townland still subsists, but not confined to any limited number of acres. The size of fields appropriated to tillage, is also very various, running from one to perhaps thirty acres, but fields of that extent do not frequently occur. The fields that produce the fine wheat which supplies the numerous mills of Galway, are generally small; those also that feed the much prized calves in the island of Arran are very small, and the ground rocky. On an average, tillage bears but a small proportion to grazing, but varies much in the different baronies; in the mountainous baronies of Moycullen, Ballynahinch, and Ross, beyond all calculation in favor of grazing.

There are many advantages attending enclosures of a moderate size, not one of the least, is the shelter they afford from westerly winds, which prevail most destructively for the greater part of the year, especially to the crops of potatoes; they were ruinously so in the Autumns of 1816 and 1817, by breaking or bruising the stacks so much, that the produce was far below the usual quantity in favorable seasons. Contiguous to a house, a few small enclosures are highly convenient, more especially where the soiling system is pursued; one of these used as a kitchen garden, cultivated by a small iron plough drawn by one horse, or still better by an ox or heifer, would be found one of the most beneficial appendages to a farm. I am well aware of the many objections that will be made against this practice: "we are not in the habit of doing so in our county," or, "our cattle are not strong enough to be used singly in a plough, where we find two insufficient." As to the first, why do not the landed proprietors lead the way; they cannot presume to say that the intellectual powers of Connaught men are below the English or Scotch standard. As to the other objection, no person can be so stupid as to imagine that ground taken from pastures or a stubborn, wet, unworked soil, could be at once tilled by one beast; but why not bring it gradually into tilth equal to that of Mr. Ducket of Esher, of which every kind of soil is capable; certainly to accomplish this on a large scale would be beyond the pocket or manure of most farmers in this county; but the space of ground necessary

---

[1] A term originating and usually only associated with Wales meaning a district comprising a hundred villages, [Clachan ed.].

for this purpose need not in general exceed four acres, keeping in mind the gradual extension of this plan, until the whole farm is a garden. The short cut to this is by the liberal use of the ashes produced by burning the substratum of clay instead of the surface, or by burning into mountains of ashes the margins of bogs, which generally produce great quantities of the best ashes —— I shall mention this very interesting subject under another head. No person can suppose that the common run of weak ill fed horses would be equal to the necessary exertion. If improvements are intended, improved implements, and proportional strength must be adopted; those mistaken economists who sell all their good oats and keep the bad for their working horses, had better follow their old system than furnish additional arguments to those who are rejoiced at the failure of experiments.

SECTION VII

NATURE OF FENCES

In the greater part of this county, stone walls prevail as fences: in many situations none other could be so easily or beneficially procured, for the clearing of the ground contributes the material for building the wall. Formerly the usual wall was composed of stones piled up without order, which may be called filigree work, easily built up, but as easily thrown down, and a very unstable fence for corn fields: within the last twenty years, however, a very material change for the better has taken place; the war prices for all kinds of agricultural produce, and the facility which country banks afforded of raising money, gave a powerful impulse to every kind of improvement, very visible in the substitution of good double stone walls in lieu of the former, and in many cases accompanied by gravelling the surface, but in few by draining or laying it down evenly, or with grass seeds. In those districts where stone walls are much used, the labourers are very expert, and will execute them well if the stones are reasonably good and they are well watched. Prices vary; sometimes double stone walls three feet wide at the bottom and battering to 18 or 20 inches at the top, and five feet nine inches high, finished with two sods, are built for two shillings and sixpence per perch, the stones brought to the place by the proprietor, and no foundation to be dug, which in general, especially where there is a sod, is an erroneous practice. The prices vary much in different districts, much depending on the goodness of the stone. When the wall is carefully built and dashed with good mortar, and in a proper season, it makes an excellent and permanent fence; but an eye must be occasionally kept on the workmen, or they will not run stones long enough through the wall to tie it. By much exertion a man can earn about one shilling and four pence per day, if the stones are good and not too small: in many places the prices are much higher, as high as four shillings and four pence per perch for double stone walls two feet wide at bottom and six feet high. In other places, where long thin stones can be procured, the longest are placed upright on the largest end, and those of the next size wedged in an upright position between the first, and the wall brought to about four feet high by a repetition of this operation with the smaller stones, which key them like an arch, and render them very difficult to be thrown down by a beast; for this reason they keep out hunters, who though very allowable in their proper place and season, are very unwelcome visitors to a well improved place, or to a breeding sheep farm. Those kind of keyed walls may be seen admirably executed in the demesne of Creran, the seat of Mr. O'Kelly, and a few other places, where the stones are sufficiently long for the purpose. In some places all the small stones are preserved to finish the top of the wall, whilst in others the better practice prevails of placing the heaviest stones on the top, which are with more difficulty moved by cattle. A great deal of the expense of building walls may be saved by making them, only three feet high; and where they should act as a fence on both sides, two drains, three feet wide and three feet deep each, should be sunk about a foot from the bottom of the wall: if it is necessary to fence only one side, as for plantations, one drain only will be necessary; this will probably be found a much better fence than the generality of six feet walls, as no beast can get near to disturb the stones, or take a leap on the wall. The earth at the foot of the wall should be sloped off to prevent sheep leaping on it to graze; where it surrounds plantations, it is not such an abominable object as a high wall, as it may be completely covered by mending the earth at the outside to a sufficient height for this purpose, and if it obtains a gradual inclination, and sowed with grass seeds, will not be perceptible at any distance.

I regret I cannot commend either the number or workmanship of the ditches of this county, indeed I may say province. Except in the demesnes of a very few gentlemen, they cannot be called either fences or drains; few are deeper than two or three feet, and, as in most cases, hedges are scarcely ever thought of, cattle can so easily run them up or tear them down with their feet, that they are usually bearded with either thorns or furze, which never last longer than one year, and must be renewed annually, to the destruction of many a charming thorn; and this is not confined to their own trees, they frequently encroach on their neighbours.

Where materials for bearding are not easily procured, recourse is had to sods, which, if the fence joins the high roads are cut from the sides of it. This has been a loss of many thousand pounds to the county, by the necessity it occasions of obtaining presentments to widen roads to the statute breadth, by filling up the chasms occasioned by the very culpable inattention of the magistrates and resident proprietors. A ditch less than seven feet broad and six feet deep can scarcely be called a fence; and they may be taken for axioms, that where a ditch requires bearding, or that a beast can get into the gripe to graze on the sides, it cannot be called a fence. It may be some consolation to the Galway ditch-makers to hear, that in many parts of England practices equally bad prevail, and with a most comfortable obstinacy. Every ditch should be planted with thorn quicks or other trees, and the back made so high and sharp on the top, that a beast will be deterred from walking on it There is a necessary operation well known in Meath and elsewhere, that I can scarcely get gentlemen to comprehend, or their workmen to practice, that is, beating the ditch very hard with the back of the spade; in fact, the spades called *loys* are of such flimsy construction, that a sufficient blow from a strong man would demolish one of them: this practice is so very necessary, that if (which does not often occur) the earth is too dry, water should be frequently poured on it during the operation of beating. The ditch should be always faced with the lowest stratum, generally consisting of limestone gravel, which should be preserved for this purpose. If this simple process is observed, the face of the ditch will be impervious to rain, consequently little liable to be injured by frost; to prevent any danger from this grand enemy to new made ditches, they should be planted with thorns or other trees in February, and not finished until all danger of frost is over.

In many situations I should recommend, instead of thorn quicks, to plant two years old bedded seedling forest trees, disposed in masses of one kind, of considerable breadth; indeed there are very few cases where I would not exclude thorns entirely; indolence I know will say they will be cropped by cattle and sheep; so they will if the usual fences are obstinately made. I know that they will succeed in this situation better than in many others, especially if kept scrupulously clear from weeds.

Where double ditches are made, they are generally too wide on the top, and as the ends are generally left open, cattle graze on them and thrust out the banks over the quicks which they destroy by browsing on them; independent of this cause the great breadth receives a large quantity of rain water, which runs in gullies down the banks, and helps to destroy the quicks. Instead of this method they should be brought nearly to a point by hard beating, and particular care taken that no beast can jump up upon them. In most parts of this county, especially the barony of Killyan, where I have made upwards of sixteen miles of ditches and drains on one estate, it is necessary to leave a considerable set off to the bank of the ditch, for the land is so overcharged with water that when it gets wet it washes away the stratum in which the chief supply originates, and ruins the ditch. Where I have any apprehension of this, I generally the first year cut the drain much less than it is intended finally to be, and the following year cut off all that has fallen in, which, with the widening, makes a sufficient back to the ditch. As to paring a ditch so as to look neat and workmanlike, as every one should be, and as may be seen in Meath and other counties, it is frequently impossible, as in most instances the ditch is composed chiefly of *lack liagh*, a kind of earth that slacks like lime with frost, and washes away with the first shower. It is a very rare thing to see a well laid or plashed hedge; it is not understood by any person of this county that I have met with: those who may be desirous of having this very necessary operation performed, should apply to some friend in Meath or Fingal, where the practice is known. There is a most shameful want of field gates to almost every farm in this county, even in the demesnes of many men of fortune, though there may be a superb entrance gate, the demesne is nearly destitute of this great comfort to any man who has stock. Where some provident ancestor had built gate piers, they are usually filled up with loose stones, which must be taken down if stock are to be viewed or moved; to prevent this becoming too troublesome, the herd (proverbially lazy) generally cuts down a fine thorn or two to stop the gate way; when this becomes a little dry, it is stolen for firing, probably by his own children, and new trees are substituted, to the destruction of many a beautiful thorn, for the most destructive animals that ever ruined hedges are the herd and his family: speak to him, or indeed to any peasant, against cutting thorns, and they are astonished at your partiality to them; indeed where thorns or other trees are attached to holy wells or any other remarkable place, they are fortunately protected by the superstitious veneration of the people.

Many object to furze (*Ulex Europeus*) on the backs of ditches, but I confess the injury they may do to the land by ejecting their seeds into it, is in my mind more than counterbalanced by the shelter and security they afford; even if they do appear in the land, such as escape the teeth of sheep are easily pulled up after a thaw or heavy rains in winter, when it may contribute to the employment of some poor aged man, able to do little else. In many parts of Ireland and Wales much use is made of them, when bruised, for cattle in winter, and are an excellent food. It is also highly probable that they are an antidote to the rot and many other disorders of sheep.

SECTION VIII

MODES OF DRAINING

Hitherto draining has not been much practised in this county: the general mode was by open surface drains, which, except in bog, are the most useless and disgraceful kind to an improver of land. A few gentlemen of fortune have lately made considerable drainages in their demesnes, but the practice is far from being as general as its importance deserves, it would be a happy day for Ireland if they extended this improvement to their numerous bogs and mountains.

Hitherto, from not understanding the subject, and from Irish impatience, and often want of capital, little has been done on an extensive and unbroken scale; a spirited effort is sometimes made, but seldom continued with that perseverance which the subject requires, and from which only a beneficial result may be expected. A few years since Mr. Elkington, nephew to the celebrated drainer in England, came over to this country under an engagement to a few spirited gentlemen, at (if I am rightly informed) one hundred guineas a month and his expenses paid; this gave such an impulse to draining that hopes were very generally entertained that great and permanent advantages would accrue to Ireland; certainly his works were excellent, and more neatly executed than the general practice had been, but the direction of his drains, depth of sinking, and mode of covering, were little or nothing different from those in practice by every other scientific drainer. His auxiliary mode of tapping the springs in the bottom of his drains was almost unknown in Ireland before his arrival.

But the general idea at that time, that nearly the virtue of the rod of Moses was attached to his auger, was found to be much exaggerated, and in a multitude of trials it was discovered that success was frequently very partial and accidental; however, I deem it a very valuable discovery, and in many instances it may be highly useful. Since that period many itinerant quacks have started up in this branch, as well as in irrigation, whose low terms have blinded the judgment of some landed proprietors, that in this, as in landscape gardening, have mistaken neatness of execution for correctness of design, and then parsimony has been justly punished by failure. Mr. Hill, a native of North Britain, followed Mr. Elkington; he was imported by the Farming Society of Ireland, and as far as I can judge from what I have seen of his works, is an excellent drainer, and a general good judge of the value of work; as such I highly recommend him.

Since that period I have not heard of any person of eminence; probably there may be many; if I knew their names I would with great pleasure give them publicity. A Mr. Howley, a native of the county of Mayo, but many years a pupil of the celebrated Mr. Webb in England, has executed a big improvement at Mount Bellew, with great credit to his professional acquirements. I shall never imitate the illiberal remarks Mr. Hill has thought proper frequently to make on my works; I feel myself, from the partiality of my friends, high enough to look down on them[1]. Some draining by covered stone shores has been made, but the amount has been trifling: when they are made in the proper direction, sunk to the proper depth, and carefully finished, they are very effectual; but I have seen much money thrown away on those drains by ignorance and carelessness. Sod drains, if properly executed, are very useful as auxiliaries, but not for principal drains where much water is to be conducted; they are scarcely known in this county, and consequently there is little likelihood of their being well made; for this reason they have been decried by those who have executed them badly. I have discovered a method of draining in these soils with an impervious substratum, that I presume to think will supersede every other kind in such soils; the materials are to be had in almost every field, the expense trifling, and it cannot be injured by the plough or the tread of cattle. When the immense quantity of land of this description in England and Ireland is considered, and that it is the most difficult of any to drain, I presume to hope for parliamentary reward, which I shall not claim unless I can prove my statement in the fullest manner.[2] An immense quantity of land could be reclaimed in this county by draining, but there seems to be an almost total neglect of it, except by a few, and even many of those get tired after making a few efforts* I venture to think I have made more ditches and drains in one estate in this county in two years (1816 and 1817) than perhaps have been made in the whole county of Galway, and they are only the outlets to other intended drains. In two

---

[1] One of those itinerant gentlemen, I understand, has done me the honour to assume my name in many places where I am not known, and has arrogated to himself the designing of the lake at Mount Bellew, &c. A letter to Mr. Bellew, Mount Bellew, Castle Blakeney, will immediately detect the impostor. I never pay a professional visit without a previous invitation. , [original footnote].

[2] Some years since I mentioned this officially to late secretary of the Farming Society of Ireland, but was not fortunate enough to create the slightest interst in any favour — Alas! it was an Irish invention and probably may die with mc, [original footnote].

summers upwards of 5000 perches were made, and they are still going on with the same spirit; this is not the drainage of a demesne, but part of a design to drain an extensive estate, the property of three young ladies. Blush, ye landed proprietors, who spend your property in countries where your vanity is so frequently mortified, or who, more from fashion than liking, fritter away your time and estate, and injure your health in gaming houses!! — There is nothing so easily drained as bog, nor is there any kind in which more money has been thrown away, under an idea that very deep draining was necessary. It has, to be sure, a very imposing appearance to stand on the edge of a bog drain neatly cut to the depth, perhaps, of sixteen feet and eighteen feet wide, and probably of considerable length; but it is frequently, alas! a great drawback to this pleasure, to observe the bog within a few feet of it still like a wet sponge; a drain, however capacious, will have little effect, especially if drawn in the direction of the fall, unless many surface drains assist it, and the bog frequently stirred or turned to assist the rain in washing out those acids that prevent its decomposition; for this reason, the nearer to the approach of winter the better, as alternate rains and frosts are powerful assistants in the process. It is this frequent turning that fits the turf mould usually brought to the door or yard of every cottier near a bog for manure, (called black mud or *mooreen*,) it cannot be supposed it is the very trifling addition of earth or dung alone they are able to add that produces this effect; it is to the washing or steeping in a damp or wet situation that its effect is to be attributed, for in too many instances they have nothing to add to the heap. There cannot be a more mistaken idea than making bog too dry; it may make it into turf, but will never decompose it, on which depends in a great measure the improvement of bog. In nothing is this more clearly ascertained than the propagation of Fiorin grass; in very dry bog it is little worth, but in that kept nearly in a state of pap it will flourish, provided some manure has been previously used; indeed even without this help we frequently see it flourish in very moist situations. Surface drains in bog should have but little fall, merely as much as will give the water a gentle currency. I venture to assert that our bogs, which are now a bye word of reproach to our country, will, at no very distant period, have their value properly appreciated. It may not be generally known that Mr. Roscoe, the well-known and ingenious improver of Chatmoss in Lancashire, sold 1000 acres of improved bog for £10,000. which he had held for a lease of 99 years: this will scarcely be credited by those gentlemen who cover their own want of industry, by throwing doubts and difficulties in the way of this high road to wealth.

Sir Humphrey Davy, who has thrown a brilliant and lasting light on every subject connected with chemistry, says, "bog is a soil covered not only with fuel, but likewise with manure. It is the excess of manure only which is detrimental, and it is much more easy to destroy, than to create it". — Speak of draining at any public meeting, and you would think every demesne in the county of Galway was perfectly drained; but view them, and you will probably find that this improvement has been confined to the ground immediately in view of the house. Much money might be saved by using the plough instead of the spade in making ditches and drains, in soils not rendered unfit by too many stones.

SECTION IX

NATURE OF MANURE

The principal manure of this county is what is generally called black mud or *mooreen*, which is the raw face of some adjoining bog, brought home generally in baskets or kishes, and spread about the yard, and up to the very door of the dwelling house; on this is laid any dung, clay, or gravel, they can scrape together; if they are near the high road, they are sure to dig away part of it, or the ditches on either side, for this purpose, even where magistrates pass almost daily. This is mixed with the black mud, and lies until used for potatoes in spring. In some places they trench in hot dung stratum super stratum, which is very near the practice recommended by Lord Dundonald. I have seen this practised on the Miss Netterville's estate by one of their tenants, who I am convinced had never heard of the practice. The collection of this mud is highly injurious to many estates, as it is taken away down to the barren earth, called *Lack liagh,* that can, when thus stripped, be with great difficulty ever reclaimed. This practice, where there are extensive villages, is a serious injury, and is one proof amongst many others, to show how little attentive agents generally are to everything but receiving the rents. A remarkable instance of this abuse occurs near the new schoolhouse, between Clonbrock and Ahaseragh. If tenants were obliged to leave a foot at least of the bog over the earth, it would be sufficient, when mixed with the gravel, which generally lies under the *lack liagh*; a mixture of this last with bog, or any other soil, I am inclined to think produces rushes. The next manure is ashes, produced by burning the surface sod, and forms a very large part of that used for potatoes. On many estates, as well as by an act of the Legislature, this is prohibited under a large penalty, but this should be on the over cropping.

Those who do not discriminate, show a very limited and prejudiced knowledge of the subject. A respectable and intelligent correspondent, though a little angry, answers my query on burning, thus: -

> "Burning is generally prohibited; but to my certain knowledge, not injurious, if the land be not over-cropped. Clover, &c. &c. has flourished with me better after it, than after dung or folding. Most of our landlords are chymists [*sic*], or think themselves so; theory and practice are thrown away on them; they are above listening to such trash; experiments laughed at, and thrown into the keenest and wittiest ridicule, for we have such geniuses here, as you have mentioned in the County of Clare Survey, &c."

Much attention has been lately paid in England to the burning of clay, that is, the substratum, and as a general practice, is much preferable to burning the surface; but in bogs or moory ground, or that in which many perennial weeds predominate, I should give a preference to burning the surface. Burning clay has been long practised in the north of Ireland; it is a highly valuable manure, if not followed by too many corn crops. Mr. Curwen of Workington Hall in Cumberland, has introduced it on his extensive farms, and as he has very justly obtained great celebrity as an agriculturist, the practice may be expected to advance rapidly in England, or rather in Scotland, as they are less bigoted to old customs than the middling ranks of farmers in England. Great and unnecessary expense and trouble were at first incurred from not pursuing the simple mode of Ireland, and help to show, that notwithstanding the advanced state of agricultural knowledge, how little one country knows the practices of another; I might say, how little one county knows of the practices of the adjoining one.

This ignorance, in a great measure, helps to confirm bad practices. In the year 1815, it began to be practised to a great extent in Scotland, as the following short extracts from the Dumfries and Galloway Courier will plainly prove, and at the same time the enterprise of Scotland, and our want of knowing the practices of our own country. Mr. Alexander Craige, in a letter to Mr. Boyd of Morton Hall, says, "last season, by way of experiment, I manured part of my turnip field with well rotted stable dung, which was ploughed in the same day it was led out; the remainder with ashes; that sown on the ashes sprung much earlier than that on the dung, continued more vigorous during the season, and when I pulled them lately, the turnips produced from the ashes were more than double the size of those from the dung." Again, "Mr. Wallace has a considerable quantity of ashes on land for his Swedish turnip this season, and he means to have at least sixty acres of turnips from ashes; so fully convinced is he of the superior efficacy of clay ashes, that he has repeatedly declared to me, he would not now be at the trouble of carting dung from Kirkudbright to his farm, though only one mile and half distance, even if he were to get the dung as a present: to burn the clay ashes has cost me one shilling the cart load."[1] Again, "no rule can be laid down for regulating the size of the lumps of clay thrown on the kiln, as that must depend on the state of the fire, but I have found every lump completely burned in opening the kiln, and some of them were thrown on larger than my head. After a kiln is fairly set agoing, no coal, or wood, or any sort of combustible is necessary, the wet clay burning of itself, and it can only be extinguished by inattention, or carelessness of the operator." I imagine limestone broken small and burned with the heaps of clay, would be a material improvement. To this mode of burning, landlords can have no reasonable objection: if they have, it must proceed from the grossest ignorance or obstinacy; on the contrary, they should encourage it, especially in this county, where the stratum of clay, which almost invariably intervenes between the surface and a stratum of calcareous gravel, is pernicious to vegetation. The only difficulty in burning clay is at the commencement of the process: it requires a good quantity of dry turf, (peat) or some other convenient combustible, to set it completely on fire, after that, if a little gradual attention is paid,

---

[1] There is a provoking inaccuracy in many English reports, where the quantity it not mentioned. The cartload aforementioned may be a double or single horse cart. If the number of *bushels* had been mentioned, we would then have a datum to direct us, [original footnote].

clay fresh from the pit, if not absolutely soaked in water, will burn without any further preparation, and the moister the earth is that is burned, the better the ashes, as they will not be so likely to approach to the state of brick, for it is well known that ashes should not be burned, if possible, further than a grey colour.[1] I have seen a steward of great eminence, who, totally regardless of the simple process pursuing in an adjoining field by poor people, whose heaps were probably not ten feet from each other, made immense piles of sods, about four to the acre; independent of the expense of carrying the sods to those heaps and wheeling out the ashes again in barrows on the field, the ground did not receive near so much benefit, for it is well known that the most luxuriant produce is where such heap has been burned, though the ashes are always carefully scraped off those places, and frequently the heaps are removed to allow the ground to enjoy the benefit of this torrefaction[2]. I well recollect at the time making those remarks to the proprietor. "Pooh, pooh! don't you think a man that I give fifty guineas a year to, knows more than those poor people, and to tell you the truth Mr. D. I do not think you seem to have read the late publications on the subject!" On the estate of Mr. Joseph Kirwan of Hillbrook, near Tuam, a very singular practice takes place: for at least thirty years past his tenants have burned their ground every second year; they dig up the stubble in winter into small sods, which they leave to dry until March or April, when they burn them and have fine crops. The last Mr. Kirwan informs me as good as thirty years ago. A few years since I strongly advised the burning of a heathy, moory mountain, worth about two shillings per acre to a gentleman in a neighbouring county; he objected at once to the practice, and said he could produce one of his tenants who had tried it with every bad effect. To convince me of my error the farmer, a keen fellow, was sent for; he informed me, very gravely, "that burning the surface was very prejudicial to land; that he had tried it, and the ground "was much impoverished:" his course of cropping was, after burning, 1st potatoes, very bad, all stalks and no potatoes;— 2nd. potatoes, very fine, 3, 4, 5, 6, 7, oats, "all excellent:" after this course, without sowing any hay seeds, had good meadow, yet still he insisted the ground was impoverished, "and he never would advise any one to burn ground." I admired nothing more than the patience of the landlord that could listen to such a farrago of nonsense, except, that even after this display of ignorance or roguery, he continued steadfast in his opinion of the "impropriety of burning land." The fact is, he possessed great tracts of rich, fattening lands, and did not discriminate between those worth four pounds an acre and the mountain above mentioned, worth only two shillings.

---

[1] In some English publication lately, (I forget which) an author gravely asserts that "he believes burning day for ashes is an Irish practice." He will be astonished when he is informed that more than half the potatoes of Ireland, especially the western part, are produced by this manure. But the practices of this "remote and inconsiderable island", as Mr. Malthus calls it, seem to be little known in the sister country, [original footnote].
[2] Process of heating to remove water, [Clachan ed.].

A species of manure called "oyster bank sand" (a coraline) has been used on the coast of Galway, especially in Connemara, with astonishing effect[1]. In one place, at Ballynakill, Mr. Lynch's estate, it had been spread on a piece of wet moory land, worth little; it immediately became rich meadow, mostly Fiorin grass, and has continued for upwards of forty years to produce meadow, though to this day, to the disgrace of the proprietor, it remains undrained. Mr. D'Arcy, of Clifton, has used it lately with very great effect, 20 to 30 tons to the acre, the expense from three to five pounds per acre. A considerable quantity of lime is used between Oughterard and Olan; it is brought by water from Portacarron: on enquiring I was answered, "Sir, we could have nothing without it:" but every pains is taken to run the ground out of heart, by repeated crops. A ton of limestone, if very good, produces about 11 cwt of lime, weighed whilst hot before it imbibes fixed air; when exposed to the air it increases daily about 1 cwt. per ton, for the first five or six days. Two cubic yards of good turf will burn one of broken limestone; four pence per ton for burning lime, the fuel and stone laid down at the kiln.[2] Limestone gravel has been formerly used in this county to such extent, that there is scarcely a field that has not an old gravel pit, and in some there are several. A very large proportion of the county was formerly covered with heath, which has nearly all disappeared where the land has been gravelled; but it is not a little extraordinary that, though every person acknowledges the beneficial effects of this process, yet at this day very little use is made of it: where it is used, it is frequently in the most slovenly manner, without previously levelling the ground, and sometimes on bog, before it has been drained, without which, it must be the grossest ignorance of the subject to attempt it, for in a short time it sinks into the bog, both by its own weight, and the treading of cattle, and becomes of little use, and probably the proprietor comes to the Farming Society, and complains that "he gravelled bog at a great expense with little permanent effect." This invaluable manure abounds in almost every part of the county to the south of Galway; beyond that, and into Connemara, it is very rare, though I perceived very fine manuring gravel in the neighbourhood of Rahoon and Dangan, where the use of it would be highly beneficial.

When the carriage is short, land can be amply manured for two to three pounds per acre. The greater part of the demesne of Belview, the seat of Mr. Lawrence, which formerly did let for £3. per acre, was so completely covered with heath, that "when a cow lay down, the horns could not be seen above it". The late Mr. Lawrence gravelled it, and took two fine crops of potatoes without manure, and laid it down

---

[1] There are inexhaustible banks of this manure, and calcareous sand round the coast, and in almost every bay; and in the interior there are numerous beds of limestone, which have been more particularly mentioned under the head of minerals, [original footnote].

[2] In page 331, Vol. 4. of *Communications to the Board of Agriculture*, a Mr. Dodgson of Cumberland county, found out that lime could be burned with peat,— wonderful! [original footnote].

with a crop of oats.[1] It is well known that a great deal of land will rear the largest ox, but will not fatten him, but if gravelled will fatten him perfectly.

Irrigation is another manure that is little used in this county. Formerly some ill conducted efforts were made at Marble Hill, St. Cleran's, &c.; but have been most unaccountably abandoned by the present proprietors. There is scarcely any demesne that could not be, in part, watered, A few years since upwards of twenty acres were prepared for this purpose at Ballynahinch, which, after an expenditure, if I am rightly informed, of £700. have been also neglected. If this was expected to operate as an example to Mr. Martin's tenants in Connemara, nothing could be devised more likely to prevent it, as, independent of the enormous expense, the kind of irrigation pratised there, *(Trunk work)* though it might be proper for that situation, was little adapted to a hilly country, where an infinite quantity of catch work could be cheaply effected; but I have frequently perceived in many parts of Ireland, that many professional men who come over here, bring with them a decided aversion to any practices different from those they have been used to. A strong instance of this occurs on the banks of the grand canal, near Salins, the property of Mr. Griffith. I was informed by the ingenious Mr. Hamilton, formerly secretary to the Farming Society, and whose death will be long deplored by agriculturists, that those meadows were formerly very productive as catch water meadows, but that Mr. Griffith was induced, from the suggestions of a man who had but a very partial knowledge of the subject, to throw them into Trunk work, which caused such a quantity of bad clay to be thrown on the surface, that they have never since recovered the injury, and they remain as a strong auxiliary to the prejudices of those who, obstinately ignorant of the subject, seize on every opportunity to point out the failure of those meadows, as decisive against the advantages of irrigation. I have scarcely ever passed them in the canal boat without having a battle to fight for them, and the rushes with which they are covered generally decided against me. I am convinced I lose many pounds in the year by them; but I think worse of the manner in which I am dismounted from, I confess, a very favourite hobby horse, whom I wish to carry double. Lord Conbrock and Mr. French, of Monivae, have lately had some ground laid out for watered meadows by Mr. Chisterman, a very celebrated irrigator from England, the same who conducted those at Ballynahinch. Very extensive irrigation could be practised at Roxborough, Castleboy, Gort, Woodlawn, many places near Tuam, and others that I do not immediately recollect. It may be safely assumed, that wherever there is running water, or extensive bogs, or mountain, there can be irrigation. But the most favourable place for the purpose of extensive and highly valuable irrigation occurs between the 24 and 26 mile stones on the road between Oughterard and Ballynahinch; several large streams pour down from the extensive mountains in the

---

[1] I doubt much the accuracy of my information, "that two crops of potato were produced without any additional manure." I think it probable the ground was burned. [original footnote].

course of those two miles, and many more could easily be added to them. I do not recollect ever to have seen any place so well calculated for this purpose, nor any place that capital could be so profitably expended on, and, unlike many other speculations, there would be here a return, in one year, of probably at least four times more than the expenditure. Situations for this improvement abound in Connemara, where meadow is particularly valuable. I cannot account for that apathy, nay, aversion to irrigation, that some of the gentlemen of this county seem to feel. Few places I have seen to offer more facilities for this improvement than Turo, near Loughrea; Dunsandle also is very fortunately circumstanced for it.

The next manure I shall notice is sea weed (Algae, of several varieties); it is much used on the sea coast, and produces excellent potatoes, if planted early enough, and vegetables of all kinds, particularly cabbage, of a fine flavour. This manure must remain spread for a few days to dry, otherwise it will injure the potatoes; the quantity used for this purpose varies according to circumstances. It seldom produces more than two good crops; one of potatoes, and one of corn, mostly barley, for the private stills. The weed mostly used for this purpose is that torn from the rocks by Atlantic storms, and washed ashore by a violent surf, when it is gradually gathered into heaps, and carried on the land at leisure times. The weed that is cut from the rocks at low water is esteemed too valuable for this use; it is generally reserved for making kelp. I am strongly of opinion, however, with Mr. Nimmo, a most intelligent civil engineer, that the most profitable use that could be made of sea weed would be for manuring the mountains of Connemara. In his luminous report to the directors for improving the bogs of Ireland, he says, -

> "The great supply of manure on the coast is the red sea weed, which is cast ashore in considerable abundance, and frequently it is cut in the deep water by people in boats: two or three boat loads, of about six tons each, are usually applied as manure over an acre of land; the usual course being 1st, sea weed for potatoes; 2nd, oats or barley; 3rd, natural meadows (without sowing any hay seeds) for four or fire years, and then sea weed, &c. as before; the grass mostly Fiorin. On the second breaking up, the surface is frequently pared and burned: this, in a district where most of the soil is only a thin red bog upon bare granite, cannot but be very destructive.[1] It has produced much naked rock amongst the cultivated parts. Another manure is found in considerable abundance among the rocky creeks, the use of which might help to diminish this pernicious practice, that is, *sea ooze*, or sludge. It seems to be partly decayed marine vegetables, partly mud or bog stuff, which has been transported to the sea, and a considerable portion of decayed animal substances mixed with broken shells."

This has never yet been used in Connemara, though the shell sand is known to be considerably improved by being near a river mouth, where it is, perhaps, impregnated with this substance. Perhaps it might be even worthwhile to float off bog into some of those creeks, where the sea would convert it into manure. The

---

[1] This will probably be adduced in favour of the anti-burners, but they must not think I advocate the abuse of the practice, [original footnote].

value of the sea manure is abundantly shown by the numerous patches of cultivated ground which occupy the shore from Galway westward, and where the soil must have been originally of the most uninviting description, being nothing but bog and rock: a vast extent of it is now reclaimed, and seems fitted for crops of any description, even wheat having been tried with success. It is commonly supposed that grain is apt to run to straw, without filling the ear, on reclaimed bog; this must arise from the wont of manure or improper drainage, as I have seen in various parts of these shores as good barley as on any dry land in the kingdom; and it must be observed that it is not the defect, but the excess of drainage which is thus injurious; for as bog parts with its moisture by evaporation more speedily than almost any other soil, unless a proper supply be preserved in the sub-soil towards the latter end of summer, the crop runs the risk of perishing from drought. In this quarter the perpetual moisture from the Atlantic renders such an accident less probable.

The original population of this district seems to have been entirely confined to the seacoast. This is in a great measure still the case. The old churches and chapels are all on the shore, and the only occupation was fishing: even now there are few persons who can be considered as farmers alone. Farming and fishing, it is well known, do not assort well together; and however active the natives appear in the latter occupation, they are little inclined to exertion in the former. The pursuit of the sun fish or basking shark, in the months of April and May, employs a good many hands at a season particularly inconvenient. The usual size of boats is about 9 tons, costs £40. exclusive of tackle, and the number being considerable, (for scarce a farm but has one or two of them, besides smaller,) shows that a considerable capital is applied to navigation, though very little in agriculture, for the only implement of husbandry is the spade. The manufacture of kelp from the black sea-weed is now very general, and though tolerably productive, abstracts a great quantity of manure from the purposes of agriculture, insomuch, that it is very questionable, the great advantage of reclaiming the wastes being considered, whether it would not be better for the proprietors to apply the whole of the kelp used to the land. The quantity manufactured in the whole of Connemara is about 4000 acres, which may require about 50,000 tons of the sea weed, and it is probable might suffice for manuring 4000 acres of land; and this, after one course of cropping, would be let in permanent pasture, worth five to ten shillings an acre at least; whilst, during the cropping, the produce can not be reckoned at less than £12. to £20. and the rent to the landlord at two to three pounds per annum. The present price of kelp is under £4. per ton, for, from the inferiority of the manufacture, it does not bring so much as the Scotch kelp: the expense of cutting, burning, &c. is reckoned at 30s to £2. per ton, but in truth cannot be ascertained, being combined with the rent of the lands, for kelp burning is not a particular profession, but is always done by the cottagers and tenants on the spot. They begin cutting in May, after finishing the tillage, and employ on it all the time can be spared from turf and potatoes until Michaelmas. An able kelper may make three tons; the average is two, and three men in one house may make from seven to eight in a season; the number employed would therefore appear to be 2000.

About twenty days work are required to cut and land the weed for one ton; the quantity of weed which makes one ton and an half is amply sufficient to manure an acre, which would be done at the rate of forty-five shillings, seeing that the expense of carrying out the weed to the field is as great as that of drying and burning the kelp. In Galway, seaweed for manure is usually sold at half a guinea per ton.

Though the red weed is equally fit for kelp making yet as it comes mostly in bad weather, when it cannot be dried, it is seldom made use of for that purpose. The kelp in 1808 sold in Galway at £13. per ton; freight thither from the bays 5s. per ton; at present the price is so low as £3. 10s. to £4., so that many of the farmers found it more for their interest to employ the weed in agriculture. This disposition is likely to become general in the present state of the markets, and seems deserving of encouragement. The benefit that would come to Connemara from the transfer of the manure and labour to the improvement of the land, is perhaps not rated too high, when we say it would be annually as much as the present rental, £50,000. Near the town of Galway seaweed is so valuable that a small space occupying only about a rood, sells for £10. 16s. In some places about thirty yards in length of seashore sell for four guineas, but this is given for that only washed in by the tide; they are restricted from cutting any, but if they are not closely watched, they sometimes tear the weed from the rocks that it may be washed ashore, which greatly injures the future crop, it is computed that in the town and neighbourhood of Galway alone, upwards of £500. is expended in the purchase of sea weed; great part is brought through the town on cars, put into boats at the wood quay, and carried some miles up Lough Corrib; the expense, besides the buyer's labour and time, is at least seven shillings each car load, which only covers about twenty perches in length of a potato ridge six feet broad; this amounts to at least six pounds per acre, and seldom produces more than one or two good crops. In the usual season the shore is covered with boats landing seaweed, which is divided into heaps and sold by bulk, according to the means or consumption of the buyer, and almost always for ready money. Since writing this section, I have found amongst my papers the following: it was written by me as an answer to a paragraph in one of the Galway papers; it may serve as an antidote to the dangerous, and I trust ill founded doctrine endeavoured to be established by that writer, who, I regret to say, has sheltered himself under an anonymous signature.

> "Having seen a paragraph in your paper from a respectable and intelligent correspondent, which from the host of respectable writers he adduces, may tend to injure a practice that in the present low state of agriculture, and increasing population in this county is absolutely necessary, permit me to make some remarks on it. When your very industrious correspondent took such pains to collect so many proofs of the injurious tendency of the practice, he was not probably aware that he was writing the severest satire against the majority of his friends in the county; for it is against the abuse of this practice that all writers, except your correspondent, have declaimed: I should imagine he has suffered by this abuse. Whilst gentlemen will let their lands for this purpose without restrictions, or whilst they employ agents totally ignorant of rural economy, who think

they have no duty to perform but to receive the rents, accept bills, and drive the tenants, they cannot with justice complain of the injury their land receives. I am perfectly aware of the beneficial effect of a union of chemistry with agriculture, which your correspondent recommends, and have every degree of respect for, and admiration of the abilities of Professor Davy, who has thrown new and brilliant light upon this subject, as he has upon every other, yet, when I read in the Treatise on Manures of our celebrated and lamented countryman Mr. Kirwan, p. 15. 'White turf ashes have been found useful, red turf ashes useless, and generally hurtful." I may be allowed to doubt, as the most ignorant countryman knows the reverse of both positions is the fact. The recommendation of Mr. Marshall to "men of landed property (quoted by your correspondent) to regard the practice with a watchful eye," is precisely the advice, if worth anything, that I would give them; but I would not wish to see them obstinately close their eyes on the proper use of the practice. Sir Humphry Davy chiefly objects to burning "sandy, dry, silicious soils, containing little animal or vegetable matter." Few, I imagine, will deny the absurdity of burning sand. Dr. Anderson (also quoted) in his Treatise on Peat Moss (our bog), has denied the abuse of the practice as followed in Ireland.

'Your indefatigable correspondent has been at no small pains to collect evidence; but like other evidence, he has made all his selections lean to the side he has adopted. Now permit me on the other side to adduce a few arguments from practical farmers, writers, and chemists, which I trust will turn the scale in favour of the practice, under a judicious system of management. Every agriculturist knows this is an old subject of dispute in husbandry; but what I have seen, and the evidence I have read of the practice, inclines me to be its decided advocate, without however, entirely condemning the conduct of those landlords who interdict it to their tenants, because being a great provocative to fertility, farmers of a certain description make use of it to run the land entirely out of heart. Paring and burning are, by the enemies of the practice, supposed to diminish the staple of the soil; an idea purely chimerical. Mr. Young's arguments on this head, with the facts he has adduced, appear to be entirely conclusive. It is admitted that some land in this country (England), as well as in Ireland, has been entirely exhausted and ruined by the practice, whilst large tracts of a staple equally thin, have been immemorially burned, not only without perceptible diminution of their staple, but to their obvious great improvement. The exhaustion and rain of the land after burning, have in all probability resulted from the unfair treatment of plying them with successive corn crops without rest or manure; a method, in truth, fully adequate to the destruction of the richest lands, without the aid of paring and burning: but in order to prove fairly the evil consequence of the practice, it behoves the enemies of it to produce examples of lands injured thereby, which at the same time have been cultivated in a fair and husband-like manner, namely, by having a single corn crop taken at first, to be followed by hoeing crops and grass seeds, a due proportion of manure being allowed to the succeeding corn crops. After detailing the mode at cropping, &c. Dr. Lawrence resumes in p. 68. "Thus is finished the most beneficial operation, which, at a stroke, as it were, effects more than could be achieved in many laborious and expensive seasons. The soil is purified, and its natural fertility revived, by that grand destroyer and restorer of all things, fire. After all which has been said about the lost of staple by burning, it is highly probable, or rather certain from experience, that the loss of substance is not perceived, before it is recovered from the air, from the accumulating process of vegetation, and from the addition of manure. If the hoeing system be early and well pursued, burned land will remain clean and free from all weeds for many years, or indeed forever, and the benefit of the original operation will be felt during half a long lease; but if in a few years a renewal of paring and burning should appear necessary, it evinces either very defective or shameful husbandry, or that the former operation was superficially and improperly conducted. Old hidebound meadow, or cold infertile clay, is recovered and improved by no other method, so effectually and speedily as by burning." Thus far Dr. Lawrence in his *New Farmer's Kalendar*. — Mr. Kirwan in his *Treatise on Manures*, p. 20 says, "paring and burning reduces the roots of vegetables to coal and ashes, and thus prepares both a stimulant and nutriment for plants." Page 80, "many," have imagined that it diminishes and consumes the soil, but repeated experience has shown the contrary. I need only mention that of Colonel St. Leger in Yorkshire, related by Mr. Young in the first volume of his Eastern Tour, p. 182. "It is well known that clays and loams are rather hardened than consumed by heat; however, unless fresh seeds be committed, the soil will be unproductive for a number of years; the coaly principle may also be exhausted by too many crops." I imagine I need not pursue the subject farther.'

CHAPTER V

GENERAL SUBJECTS

SECTION I

POPULATION

THIS part of every Statistical Survey must remain very imperfect, until the fears of the people are removed, that some object of taxation is concealed under the anxiety to obtain the amount of it. In a county so decidedly catholic, any return given by the protestant clergy must be very erroneous. To accomplish this very desirable object the catholic clergy must be induced to take an interest in its attainment; but even this would fail, were their flock not well convinced that nothing connected with taxation was intended. I shall, however, give what information I have received, which every person will have an opportunity of correcting or forming an opinion on. In 1762 the population was estimated at 14,000. By the census taken in 1782 the population of the town of Galway was 14,000; by statistical tables in 1788 only 9000. In 1803 it was computed to be 20,000. In 1817 upwards of 40,000 in the town alone; in the wardenship, which extends about four miles round Galway, 100,000. In the Cloddagh alone, almost entirely occupied by fishermen and their families, it is computed there are between four and five thousand inhabitants: What an increase since 1695, when the fishermen were only 88! By the return of Mr. Conolly of the male population between the age of 18 and 46, the parish of St Nicholas contained 2301; that of Rahoon 1006. So that if we take the general estimate of the twelfth part of the population as able to bear arms, it will amount in those two parishes only to 39,684, and it may be fairly assumed that a census taken for this averred purpose must be considerably under the truth. In the town and liberties of Galway, 1971 houses pay the hearth and window tax; this, at only six to each house, makes but 8226; if this is correct, what a vast proportion pay neither of those taxes.

By the census taken in 1815, it appeared that the population of the entire of the town and county of the town, extending four miles every way round Galway, was only 24,684. I cannot conceive for what purpose the town was put to the expense of making this census, so evidently incorrect. When the census taken by Mr. Conolly of those able to bear arms between 18 and 45 years of age, amounted to nearly 40,000, exclusive of the parish of Oranmore, even this must have been below the amount, though only for the two parishes of St Nicholas and Rahoon. This Census gives not quite five and an half to a house at Bohermore; every person must be sensible how much below the real amount this mast be. Of what use were the tables also of Mr. Bushe? they tended only to mislead; in 1788 he returned the population of Galway as only 9470, allowing ten to each house; in 1792 only about 12,000.

The islands of Arran contain a population of upwards of 2400 souls. Mr. Hardiman in his return of the population of Galway, as given by Mr. William Shaw Mason, though he says the persons who pretended to take the census "were deterred by menaces from venturing among the villages", yet he says he gives it "as a curious document, intimately connected with the modern description of the town." I am at a loss for what useful purpose this census could have been given in his publication, except to show the arrangement by Mr. Mason, which is excellent; the most curious thing is, that the public should be put to such great expense for a thing confessedly erroneous. The persons employed to take this census were the laughing stock of every one acquainted with the country. As to the population of the county of Galway, I have not any data to guide me, and I can venture to say, that any computation Mr. Mason may give must be erroneous, if not corrected by the catholic clergy. Whatever may be the amount of the population, it is certain there has been unfortunately a vast increase, and from the mode generally practised of dividing farms, already too small, into very smallholdings, totally inadequate to the maintenance of a family, this evil must rapidly increase. Many treatises have been written on this momentous subject; the majority of them tell us what we but too well know; some are fanciful, some impracticable, and almost every plan that has been devised helps the emigration of those that are best able to stay at home. Some authors advise the improvement of our bogs and mountains as a means of employing our redundant population; but they forget to point out from whence the fund is to come. Did county gentlemen do their duty, there would be little occasion for the interference of government. Their apathy is most unaccountable, and they must, in a great measure, be answerable for the riotous proceedings of the populace that so lately disgraced this county: an employed population is always peaceable. An intelligent correspondent informs me that he has known Galway intimately for upwards of forty years, and it is now twice as large and populous as at that period, but not by any means twice as rich. The import trade has greatly increased, and the export, except in corn, has decreased.

Of the population of the other towns I have been left in ignorance by those to whom I applied. Formerly great apprehensions were entertained that population was decreasing, but most unfortunately Mr. Young's prediction, forty years ago, has been fulfilled: — "Let population alone, and it will take care of itself" But those who were so anxious for an increase of population, did not discriminate between an employed and half employed one. It unfortunately happens that neither the parents or children are actuated by those prudent feelings that govern the generality of the lower classes of the English; there they consider how children are to be provided for, and will avoid any contract until they have some prospect of doing so: in Ireland the same class think of little else but the means of getting the children. I recollect many years ago being astonished at the assertion of an old and very intelligent clergyman, "The introduction of potatoes into Ireland was the greatest curse she could have received." Every day's experience helps to convince me of the truth of the assertion. I know it is very generally said, "what would become of our dense population without them?" but I would much rather be told what is to become of them with them? Until the practice of reletting and portioning children with small divisions of land is cut up, root and branch, it is vain to expect a change for the better. It will be asked how is this to be effected? By landlords considering an attention to the welfare of their tenantry an imperative obligation, or by agents recollecting that the receipt of rents is not the only duty they have to perform. Many landlords have clauses in the leases of cottier tenants, to prevent reletting, but none against dividing their scanty farms with their sons or daughters on their marriage. This is the prolific cause of much of the wretchedness of Ireland. Unimproving middlemen should be repulsed in every offer they make for land, as they add considerably to the poverty of Ireland, by reletting to the poorest class of tenants. It is imagined that the population of Connemara and Iar Connaught double every ten years, very much assisted by emigrants. If houses were built by the landlords, Conamara would be soon found to hold out advantages that would prevent emigration to distant countries.

SECTION II

NUMBER AND SIZE OF TOWNS AND VILLAGES

The town of Galway contains, within the walls, 21 acres, 1 rood, and 21 perches; but the town outside the walls is of considerable extent, probably as much as the old part, including Dominick-street, the Claddagh, Meyrick's-square, Nun's Island, Bohermore, &c. &c. It was a town of considerable trade so far back as 1280; vessels of 400 tons can come up to the quay. They traded with France, Spain, the West Indies, and North America, very extensively; especially for wine and brandy. Of the former article they imported so much as 1200 tons a year, which they enjoyed for several centuries, and supplied the entire of Connaught, Leinster, and great part of Munster. The tradition is so well preserved, that on my remarking to a gentleman the resemblance of several doors in Athboy, in the county of Meath, to those in back street in Galway, he informed me, "they were anciently used as wine vaults by the merchants of Galway, and from whence they supplied Dublin, Drogheda, and several other towns." Mr. Anthony Lynch still keeps up the credit of the Galway wines. His port is much superior to the generality of that to be had in Dublin, and much lower in price. It is so well known in the counties of Galway and Mayo that several gentlemen buy from no other merchant. They exported to the wine countries, beef, pork, fish, butter, wool, &c. They also formerly supplied the British navy with beef and pork of their own curing, but by some means were tricked out of it by the Cork and Limerick merchants. It is generally thought that the fair of Ballinasloe was at a remote period established there for the accommodation of the Galway exporters. It may be cited as an instance of their former opulence, that a house which now would let for £50. per annum, was then mortgaged for £14,000.

Before the year 1790 this town was in a state of great decay; at the period of the union it began to flourish. At this time Dominick-street was built; also houses about Meyrick's square, some near the infirmary, and in other places, began to appear, and gave an air of improvement to the town. The old useless town wall was nearly demolished, to make room for extensive stores and other buildings, and helped to clear the town of contagious disorders, to which it had been very subject before. Galway is a county of a town in itself, the liberties extend upwards of four miles round it. It is governed by a mayor, who is, by his office, a magistrate of the county at large. A recorder, four magistrates, aldermen[1], and two sheriffs. No criminal or civil process from any other place can be executed here without permission of the magistrates or sheriffs, enjoying the same immunities as Cork, Waterford, and Limerick.

They levy their own taxes for bridges, roads, jail, and other public works, by presentment. The Claddagh, (in English, *a dirty place,*) a suburb to the west of Galway, at present possessed, almost exclusively, by fishermen, was, it is generally imagined, inhabited by the first settlers, who emigrated from Athenree, under king John. It is a small town in itself, with well-paved clean streets. Previous to 1808 it was proverbial for filth, as the name expresses, but the exertions of Captain Hurds of the Royal Navy, then commanding the sea fencibles[2], overcame this difficulty; by his influence he persuaded them to appropriate a small part of their pay weekly, and under his inspection it assumed the comfortable appearance it presents at present to the traveller. In return for this they have cleared their settlement of contagion, which, before that period, swept away multitudes.

Their population is thought to exceed 3000. They seldom permit a stranger to live amongst them, calling them "transplanters" and despise them greatly. They are exempt from the payment of all taxes whatsoever, by what law, except that their houses in general are not taxable, I am ignorant. They seldom marry out of their own village, and generally at a very early period of life: it is highly probable that they will shortly feel the ill effects of a superabundant population. The parents generally contrive between them to give a boat, or at least a share of one, which secures a maintenance for a more than ordinary share of children. In the months of May (ever propitious to lovers) and September the young couples frequently elope, which always concludes with a wedding, and a faithless Strephon[3] has never been known. St Patrick's night is usually set apart for weddings. They are lamentably ignorant, and seem to have a very decided aversion to instruction, scarcely ever sending their children to school, and few speak any language but a harsh sounding Irish, scarcely intelligible to the inhabitants of Galway. When not out fishing they are usually repairing their boats and nets, and they are generally so well prepared for sea, that we seldom hear of lives lost. When not employed in this way, they are generally

---

[1] At present we do not hear of aldermen; but that they were formerly it is obvious, for on a tomb stone in the Franciscan Abbey there is, "Pray for the soul of Alderman Domnick Browne and his posterity:" he died in the year 1596. I find also that in 1727 money was ordered to be paid for the funeral of aldermen and other officers, &c. and at Alderman Fisher's funeral, Sibby Lee received 6d. for rosemary, [original footnote].
[2] Home guard, [Clachan ed.].
[3] Strephon lover, from name of the Arcadian shepherd lover in Sidney's *Arcadia,* [Clachan ed.].

drinking, at which they spend a great part of their earnings, and often remain in this state until necessity obliges them to go to sea again; preparatory to which, the strand is covered in every direction with their wives and children procuring bait of many sorts, but mostly what are called lugs, the same name used in Fingal. Their sea store consists of oatmeal cakes, potatoes, water, and firing, but never any kind of spirits. When they are longer at sea than usual, their return is hailed with great joy by their families, ushered into the whiskey shop by their wives, and in a state of intoxication put to bed. The boat is then unladen, and the fish carried to market by the women, who exclusively take possession of it, the husband never interfering, and it is sold to hawkers and women who keep standings in the market. The women pay for every thing, having the complete control of the purse. An instance occurred of a man wishing to keep his own money, but the indignant companions of his wife threatened to burn his house and actually proceeded to such violence that poor Jerry Sneak was forced to succumb.

The fishermen elect a mayor and sheriff from amongst themselves on every St. John's, day. They march in noisy procession through the town of Galway, preceded by men carrying bundles of reeds fastened on poles, which at night they set fire to at their bonfires; it is always a scene of drunkenness and riot, but seldom proceeds further. On St John's eve it is the custom to light immense fires of turf, bones, &c. in different parts of the town of Galway; they are surrounded by young people, mostly females, who ask some trifle from each passenger; they are usually armed with bundles of the seed, stocks of docks, tied up like small brooms with which they touch lightly the passengers or lookers on, saying, "honor the bonfire," which every person is expected to do by touching their hat, or if a woman, by a slight courtesy. I have seen some of your mighty sensible people refuse to do this, and I confess enjoyed the touching they received with the dirty brooms. They are tried for offences amongst each other, and always submit to the decision of their mayor or sheriffs; and is was not until, very lately they would submit to the control of any other jurisdiction, but they are now gradually losing that idea of exemption they formerly, insisted upon, and which has been exceedingly troublesome. It is a remarkable circumstance, that during the rebellions of 1798 and 1820, and indeed at every other disturbed period, not a single man has been found disloyal, and I must say with great pleasure, it is a characteristic of the inhabitants of Galway. They have a patron saint, to whom they pray on all occasions of distress, such as storms, unproductive seasons, &c. &c. and on their safe return make an offering of three fish for the poor. It is remarkable that they never suffer their parents to beg, but all their wants, and even whims are indulged. Very few have either a cow or potato garden. The Claddagh is the estate of Mr. Whaley, whose ancestor; a colonel of Cromwell's, also formerly possessed Rahoon, near Galway.

There are three barracks for infantry, which can contain about 900 men, and temporary barracks for about 600 more. There are few towns in which the military can be better or more cheaply accommodated, of which the general abundance of fish constitutes a very material part; there is also, a very abundant supply of potatoes and other vegetables, especially cabbages, excellent butter, &c. &c. Until lately there was only one bridge, which is upwards of 400 years built; at the suggestion of General Meyrick a considerable increase in the breadth of this bridge has taken place, but still inadequate to the great pressure at some periods; to obviate this, and at the same time to open a communication between the new court house, and the two jails, a very beautiful new bridge has been lately erected by presentment, which does infinite credit to the taste of Mr. Behan the architect. A handsome meat market was built in 1802, by Mr. Francis Blake, which is well supplied with, excellent meat of every kind except fat fowl which must be purchased lean from the country people on every Saturday, and fattened by the consumer; sometimes a fat fowl may be picked up, but this is mere chance. Four or five women, forestallers[1], frequently buy up the fowl to retail again in the same market, and often abuse the servants of those who send to market. I am at a loss to conjecture why they are not brought fat to market; there can be little doubt they would pay well in a town where good living is so much practised. Small, but fat and high flavoured mutton from the neighbouring coasts and islands is generally to be had in the market, weighing from ten to fourteen pounds per quarter; larger mutton may be frequently purchased, but much inferior in the flavour. The beef, in general, is excellent in the season, lamb and kid of the best quality abound, and generally at reasonable rates. Before this market was erected, the meat was to be seen hanging in the most disgusting manner against the walls of houses in different parts of the town, and so blind were the butchers to their own comfort and convenience, that it was at last necessary to use military force! I regret to state that this market is generally very dirty, and sheep and other animals are permitted to be slaughtered in it. The vegetable market kept near the main guard is generally well supplied, and at reasonable rates; all kinds come to market washed, by which means any imperfection is easily detected. The cabbage raised near the seaside on seaweed, is particularly delicious; those who have been used to those cultivated on ground highly manured, cannot form any idea of the difference. There are also in the season, peaches, strawberries, gooseberries, apples, pears, &c. In 1801 General Meyrick had a handsome square of two acres laid out and enclosed with walls for a parade for soldiers; it is at present also the principal walk for the *beau monde*, if they are content to wade through puddles to get to it. Unluckily it is also the fair green, which I hope may be changed to some less objectionable situation. Under the same auspices also, a commodious fish market was erected, well supplied, in general, with fish on moderate terms.

To express their opinion of his meritorious exertions, the inhabitants have inscribed over the entrance, "This fish market built by subscription, under the patronage of General Meyrick, who during his residence here acquired the praise of a grateful people, for his administration of justice and benevolence, 1800" Several regulations

---

[1] People who buy up goods in order to force high prices, [Clachan ed.].

were at that time made and strictly observed; but latterly the fish-women have returned to their old filthy practices of heading and gutting their fish in the streets; they frequently throw them over the quay wall into the river, and at every ebb tide they emit a most offensive smell in warm weather, which may be perceived as far as the lower four corners. The general also proposed to light, pave, and clean the streets of Galway, but (as on a late occasion) such opposition was given that he was obliged to abandon the idea. From those two circumstances, and from the treatment experienced by the Honorable William Le Poer Trench, who, from the most praiseworthy motives, interested himself warmly to accomplish the same business, it may be fairly concluded that the majority of the inhabitants of Galway are fond of dirt and darkness; if not, why did they not step forward and put down the sordid opposition of a few dirt-loving individuals?

The county gaol. —

"This truly superb structure has been erected on Nun's Island, in the west end of the town; it is built in a plain manly style of architecture; one is pleased with the arrangements and cleanliness of this extensive prison, which for salubrity of situation and convenience rivals any prison in the empire, and as such may be truly termed a national institution. The form is a crescent of two stories high, within an area exceeding two acres, surrounded by a wall twenty feet high, strengthened by pilasters at equal distances on the outside. The minor yards, which separate the wards, unite and terminate in a point precisely in front of the Governor's house; the entire within view of his windows, of course he may at a glance, survey the state of the whole. Each ward has its water closet, which is washed every morning by means of a canal and conductors running under the entire building: these wards enjoy at all times an abundant supply of wholesome water. In the centre of the crescent is a handsome chapel for the prisoners where both Protestant and Catholic chaplains regularly attend in rotation. No intercourse is ever allowed between the sexes, each being confined in separate wards: the debtors have also comfortable apartments separate from both. It is but justice to observe that every attention has been always paid to their individual comfort that the state of the prison can admit of. This gaol is under wise and wholesome regulations, and the whole are more comfortably lodged, as far as their respective situations will admit, than any other prison in the empire. No prisoner is ever ironed here, nor is it necessary. The Governor's house, with suitable accommodations, stands exactly opposite the centre of the crescent; it is a handsome building of two stones, with well finished apartments, where prisoners of the higher order are lodged; also a guard house on each side of the entrance gate, with accommodations for turnkeys, &c. and on the outside the fatal drop. The prison is at present under the government of Mr. Fitzsimons, who unites great humanity to a steady observance of the useful regulations of the prison. On the arrival of a prisoner, after being well washed and cleaned, he is equipped in the prison dress, which is numbered. They are allowed sufficient firing, and particular care taken by the inspector that their bread is of a good and wholesome quality. Their beds are comfortable; they are of merit, and hung on swivels, about two feet from the ground; there are at present about 75 beds: the entire building is vaulted; the doors are of metal, and there is not any timber used in the building. A handsome gravel walk surrounds the prison, where the debtors are allowed occasionally to recreate themselves. In the intervening part of the yard, the governor has generally a large supply of potatoes, vegetables, fuel, &c. much of which he humanely distributes gratis to the poorer prisoners; had an hospital been erected here for the benefit of sick prisoners, it would have completed the whole. The plan is said to have been taken from York gaol, but greatly improved by Mr. Morrison, whose great taste is well known in this county; it was entirely finished under his inspection, and cost about £27,000."

It is a curious circumstance that there was no county gaol in Galway until 1686. It was established in Loughrea in 1685, when the county of Connaught was divided into five counties.

Before the removal to their new county gaol, the prisoners were confined in an old castle near the fish market, the property of Mr. Morgan of Monksfield: Mr. Howard says, "in two long rooms, with dirty floors, and no fire place." What a happy change has taken place?

A new court-house has been lately erected; the design by Mr. Morrison; its appearance is very pleasing, and it possesses convenient apartments for the judges, jury, and all the officers attached to the court; there has been also a tavern established, which is well conducted by Mrs. Eddington, widow of the late governor of the county gaol, and is a singular convenience to those who are detained late in court at the assizes. Very extensive stores have been lately built by Messrs Joyce, Messrs. Clarke, Mr. Moore, Mr. Fitzgerald, and other merchants, which have contributed greatly to the good appearance of the town, and tend to show that business is increasing. When such intelligent, wealthy, and enterprising men as the Messrs. Clarke establish themselves in a town, they throw life and vigour into a decaying trade, such as until very lately was possessed by Galway. The stores of those gentlemen are well worth seeing, not only for extent and superior arrangement, but for the variety and magnitude of their contents. Mr. Wakefield, a late traveller, has been so uncandid (from report) as to impute the decay of the town of Galway to a want of punctuality in the merchants. Before he made this unfounded attack he should have been better informed on the subject. There seems to be more want of capital than of faith in the mercantile part of the community.

Many of the old houses of this town are single, as they generally surround a small square, to which there is a common entrance under the houses next the street; on either side of this passage is the entrance to those houses, for formerly, when this town was the great mercantile depot of several surrounding counties, and even of Dublin, for Spanish wines and other commodities, the under parts were stores, as may be seen by the low pointed arch, which is so different from, and inferior to the usual elegant style of those intended for entrances, as not to be mistaken.[1] There are three circulating libraries, and two booksellers. The Amicable Society have a good library, and a large room for newspapers and conversation; they consist of about 80

---

[1] I am informed that the houses in Badajos, and other towns in Spain, are built very much like the old houses in Galway, and here, like them, a common entrance, and the kitchen at the top of the house, [original footnote].

members. If I am rightly informed (I hope not), several men of large fortune are upwards of ten years in arrear, though the subscription is only one guinea a year; if so, I should venture to think that the society must have been under a bad regimen, or, that men of fortune and gentlemen are not synonymous. This society was established in 1791: their chief object is the discussion of the principles, improvement, and encouragement of agriculture, trade, commerce and science. The arrangements are under the direction of a president, vice-president, treasurer and secretary, a committee of four members, and a librarian, all chosen half-yearly; every person proposed for admission, and seconded, must remain a week on the books previous to a ballot, at which there must be at least twelve members; two black beans are fatal: this difficulty of admission they say makes them select, but I apprehend it might be used in so numerous a society to answer a party, if such a thing could be found in an amicable society. Their funds are ample: besides periodical works, they take in several English and Irish papers, but shame to say, (if I am rightly informed) they take neither the English or Irish Farmer's Journals, or Munster Magazine, &c. Before 1791, so far from a reading room, there was not even a coffee room in Galway. There is one very praiseworthy regulation that is strictly adhered to in this society; not to introduce either religious or political subjects for discussion. In 1641, a society called the Tribune Society, was established, and continued for some years; their proceedings were kept secret; they were armed horsemen, and their avowed purpose was to keep down Papists: such was the temper of that period in Galway! what a happy contrast the present liberal feelings of Protestants and Catholics present?

There is a ring of six bells in St. Nicholas' church; they have tongues in the usual way within side, and at the same time have hammers, which are worked by a wheel and strike on the bells; they chime some unintelligible tunes. The belfry was built by Nicholas More Lynch in 1561, and this munificent man also gave two organs and a great bell to the church, but he always kept the key in his own custody. Galway also possesses an exchange, nearly in ruins, over which, at the risk of their lives, the corporation affairs are transacted; also elections for the town, and the assizes for the town are held here. The situation is particularly inconvenient, it is in a very narrow part of the street: it formerly was ornamented with a lofty cupola, but it was imagined the roof from which it sprung was too weak to support it, and it has been removed: a new one is much wanted, and probably opposite to Meyrick square would be an appropriate situation for it, and also for a corn-exchange, which is equally necessary, as in an old coach house the extensive corn trade of Galway is transacted; — also four nunneries, three monasteries, and an infirmary, an institution that reflects great credit on the country, and on Dr. Veitch, whose excellent management and humane treatment of his patients have obtained universal approbation; it was opened in June 1802.

As it may serve an useful purpose, I insert the following rules and regulations, to be strictly, adhered to in the county Galway hospital.

I. No person can be admitted as (an intern) patient of the hospital who does not produce a letter of recommendation from a governor or governess of the infirmary.

II. The hours of general attendance at the hospital are from 11 to 12 o'clock every day. All out-patients to attend at those hours. No out-patient to proceed farther than the hall of the hospital, without orders from the surgeon.

III. The days of admission (only) on Mondays and Thursdays, except in cases of accident.

IV. The patient, upon his or her appearance in the hall of the hospital, at the hours and days above-mentioned, and producing the recommendation, will be immediately inserted upon the books of the hospital.

V. Each patient, after being inserted on the books, to be taken to the bath room to be well washed and cleaned by the person appointed for that purpose, and the barber directed to attend; afterwards to be taken to the vesting room, and dressed in the hospital clothing, and directed to the ward and bed appointed by the surgeon; and on his or her dismissal their own clothing to be given to them, and the hospital clothing delivered up to the proper person appointed, to be well washed and fumigated, and put upon the proper number in the vesting room.

VI. The nurses to count over the bed clothes and clothing, &c. to the patient; and are to be responsible that he or she leaves every thing in the same state, allowing for necessary tear and wear; and no patient (except allowed by the surgeon) to visit the other wards; if found in any but their own, to be immediately dismissed the hospital.

VII. No patient to be allowed to spit or dirty the walls or floor of the house, as spitting boxes and bed pots are provided for the purpose; and no smoking of pipes allowed on any account in the wards.

VIII. Immediately on the bell ringing, every patient that is able (or who is ordered by the surgeon) are to attend in the dressing room.

IX. Any patient who acts impertinent to the house keeper or nurses, to be immediately dismissed, and to be reported to the governor or governess who recommended him or her.

X. All medicine to be given by the surgeon or nurses; and they are immediately to report, should they refuse either medicine or diet as directed.

XI. The wards of the hospital to be washed and fumigated twice a week, and oftener if necessary.

XII. The housekeeper to visit the wards twice a day, and to report any deviation from the above rules, as she is responsible for the cleanliness of the whole hospital; and no filth or excrements of any kind to remain one minute in the patient's ward.

XIII. The nurses or housekeeper are to see the patients take their meals, according to the dietary annexed; and the patients to report any neglect or deficiency in their diet: — first to the nurses, then to the housekeeper, and if immediate redress is not granted, to the surgeon.

XIV. The rules and regulations to be read to each patient on admission to the house; and their name, age, and disease, posted up on the head of their bed.

DIETARY OF THE PATIENTS

FULL DIET

Breakfast — One quart of good stirabout, with one pint of new milk, or one quart of sour ditto;— the same at night.

Dinner — One pound of good household loaf bread, and one quart of new milk, four days in the week;— and half a pound of boiled meat, one quarter stone of potatoes, with as much broth and vegetables as they can eat, the other three days.

CONVALESCENT DIET.

Breakfast — One quart of flummery or stirabout, and one pint of new milk.

Dinner— One pint of broth, with half a pound of boiled meat; or one pint of milk, and a pound of loaf bread.

LOW DIET.

Breakfast — One quart of flummery, or gruel, with half a pint of new milk.
Dinner — One pint of milk, or two of gruel, half a pound of loaf bread, with as much drink as ordered.
Drink — (When ordered by the surgeon) to consist of milk-whey, barley-water, water-gruel, cream of tar-tar-whey, (in proportion) as directed.

J. VEITCH, M. D.

Surgeon county Galway hospital

There was formerly a Charter house, but it has been discontinued for some years. Galway gives a title to the family of Monckton. The armorial bearings of Galway are an antique galley, or probably a herring buss, and not the ark, as some fanciful people would wish us to suppose. I imagine the tribes do not go quite so far back as the deluge. The herring buss seems to be much more appropriate, as the herring fishery was the foundation of their former prosperity, and also the foundation of many large estates in this and the neighbouring counties, and if pursued with the same spirit and intelligence, would still create many more, for gambling and extravagance are daily making opens [*sic*] for those who make a more prudent use of their wealth. The old town gaol was formerly the town court-house, and the market cross stood opposite to it.

It speaks highly for the morals of Galway, that before the removal of this gaol to the main guard, the prisoners were confined in a small room under the old tholsel[1]. It was determined to remove the old gaol and guard house, and build a new town gaol; and in 1810, they were removed to the new prison. It is under the same good regulations of the county gaol; and every comfort consistent with safety, is afforded

---

[1] Tholsel (Irish *Tólsail*) refers to former public buildings in Ireland's towns. The meaning of the word is uncertain, [Clachan ed.].

to the unhappy inmates. A man died not long since who remembered when there was neither tea-kettle or sash-window in Galway; they were first used by Sir John Kirwan, (of the Castlehacket family) in Middle-street, where Mr. Fahy, an eminent architect, now lives; all others were leaden lights. There was formerly a Foundling hospital; it was converted to an artillery barrack in 1798, but is now occupied by the nuns of the Presentation order.

It is a curious circumstance that the separate apartments of many houses are the estates of different proprietors; this arose in a great measure from the former opulence of Galway when a floor of apartments, or even a single room, was given as a portion to a child.

Galway swarms with beggars, and frequently of high pretensions, as they often ask for "half a crown." There are no lamps lighted in Galway, except a few in Back-street. Formerly the streets were better lighted, but it was obliged to be given up; "the smugglers broke them" The town wall was originally built by the corporation about the year 1280, by a duty on different articles of consumption. At a later period another wall was built outside the former, and several bastions added, on which cannon were mounted. The ramparts, bastions, and other fortified works at the east side, were built by Cromwell. Some old people remember the embrasures; many recollect when the town wall was a favorite walk, and when the gates were shut every night, and a chain hung across the street: the place where it was fastened is still visible at the house of a chandler at the upper four corners; the date of the building of the house is 1558. It has been said that this chain was originally intended to prevent the clan of the O'Maddens from galloping into the town, and plundering the inhabitants, which they were in the habit of doing, even in day light. What a situation those industrious people must have been in! the O'Flahertys at one side, and the O'Maddens on the other, always ready to pounce on them. The most perfect part of the wall is near William's gate, and is now a garden belonging, I believe, to Mr. Puxley; it is very high, and was surrounded by a deep ditch, which has been nearly all filled up, and at present occupied by gardens or buildings. On several parts of the wall may be seen the name of the mayor and sheriffs in office when they were erected. For repairing the wall, the corporation in 1780 ordered one shilling and nine pence halfpenny. It is evident therefore, that a minute attention was paid to its repair. On the west gate, at the end of the present bridge, there was for merely a stone, which is still preserved; on it was in scribed "Oh! God deliver us from the ferocious O'Flahertys;" and it was decreed that any person of that name found in the town should be put to death: at present some young ladies are the only dangerous persons of that name, and I hope before long they may be confined.

It has been asserted that Galway formerly belonged to the O'Hallorans, from whom it was purchased by a company of merchants — adventurers, living at Athenry, which was a walled town long before Galway, and, as before mentioned, this was not walled until 1280, above a century after their arrival, under King John. It has also been said that the tribes settled first as fishermen, at the Cloddagh, and moved from that to Galway at the opposite side of the river. It would seem from such different statements, that little better than conjecture can be given. However one thing we are certain of, that they were a wealthy and respectable colony of merchants at a remote period. The Athys were of some note at an early period, for "William D'Athy was appointed treasurer of Connaught 8th December, 1388, with the fee of £10. yearly." The Blakes, formerly called Caddell, were also a very ancient family, for one of them was sheriff of Connaught in 1306. The Bodkins are also very ancient, and highly descended. At an after period the Costellos and some other names were admitted, and were called half tribes. In the reign of Edward IV. money was coined in Galway, for that king made a grant to Gormyn Lynch of the office of warden and master of the mint in Ireland, empowering him to coin money for Galway. — Note, I had one of his groats, which I gave to the late General Valiancy to add to the collection of the Royal Dublin Society. It is also asserted that letters were directed to Galway, near Athenry. St Stephen's island, near the Wood-quay, was anciently in the county, and the county court house built there, on the same site occupied by Mr. Joyes the distiller. The descendants of the original settlers of Galway are called the thirteen tribes, from the numbers of each name that almost exclusively possessed the trade of that town; and it is asserted that the appellation was given by Cromwell's officers from this circumstance. In one list, with which I have been furnished, the name of Morris is omitted, and in another that of Font; if both stand there must be 14 tribes. There were many other names of those living in Galway long before the tribes, such as Valley or Wallin, Kerwick, Call, Lawless, Dillon, Calfe, Verdon, Frehine, Tierney, Coppinger, Moore, Brunt, Brannegan, Moylan, Bardon, Blundell, Conkeragh, Ffarty, Butler, Penrise, Hoth, Fallon, Weider, Bermingham, Muneghan, Quirke, Sage, Killery, Quinn, Develin, Biggs, Lemper, Le Fickhill, Lang, White. How the 13 tribes came to have the exclusive preeminence I am to learn, and probably the public will feel little interest in it. I have been furnished with a voluminous statement, which may be found in the supplement; but I must leave this weighty affair between the tribes and non tribes. The thirteen tribes (or according to my list the fourteen tribes) have some whimsical attributes attached to their names, probably given at the time they received their name of tribes from Cromwell's officers, such as

Athy — suspicious.	Faunt — barren.
Blake — positive.	Joyce — merry.
Bodkin— dangerous.	Kirwan— stingy.
Brown — brave.	Lynch— proud.
Dean —devout	Morris— plausible.
D'Arcy — stout	Martin — litigious.
French — prating.	Skerret— obstinate.

The following verse seems to countenance the above list: Athy, Blake, Bodkin, Browne, Deane, D'Arcy, Lynch, Joyce, Kirwan, Martin, Morris, Skerret, French.

It must be evident to any person who knows the county, how much misapplied they would be at the present day, one only being remarkable, *Font-barren*, the family being nearly, if not entirely extinct. I have been informed that only four or five of the Galway tribes can claim a right of burial in the cathedral or collegiate church, viz. Lynch, D'Arcy, Browne, French, and Kirwan, though the privilege of the last has been always disputed, and never allowed. If this circumstance is correct, how truly ridiculous to carry those antiquated claims even to the grave. — The blood of the vulgar to mix with the Mirabels! However, I wish a general prohibition to burying in churches extended to every part of Ireland; it is a shocking and dangerous practice. Formerly church-yards were on the outside of every town, but Cuthbert, Archbishop of Canterbury in 750, obtained a dispensation from the pope for making church-yards within towns and cities. — It is remarkable that there is not one of the Society of Friends in Galway: about thirty years ago there were a few in Galway, but from some ill usage they deserted the town, to the great disgrace and serious loss of that town.

The first authentic account we have of Galway begins in the year 1280. It will probably be the best method to throw the history of Galway into the form of annals, I shall therefore adopt that form.

1280 The youngest son of a Mr. Lynch of Castleknock, near Dublin, came to Connaught, and married the daughter and heiress of the Lord Marshal of Galway, whence all the family of Lynch are descended. They were originally from the town of Lintz in Austria, where one of the family was governor, and defended the town against a powerful enemy *whilst there was a blade of grass to be had within his reach*, and for that reason he got the trefoil as his coat of arms; the lynx, the best sighted creature, for his crest; and the motto, "Guarded by its own virtue." From Lintz one of that family settled in Normandy, where he was allied to some lords of that country.

From Normandy one of the same family came to England as a general to William the Conqueror, and from this family spring the Lynches of Galway. Mr. Hardiman states, from the old volume of pedigrees in the herald's office, that "William Le Petit came to Ireland in 1185 with Sir Hugh de Lacy, who granted him by his charter, Macherithimar, &c. (now the barony of Magheridernan in the county of Westmeath,) except the Logh and town of Dysart; that they were palatine barons of Molingare, and that William Le Petit had a son, Nicholas, who was ancestor to the family of Lynch of Galway." "William, (or according to other accounts,) John de Lynch was the first settler of the name in Galway; he was married to the daughter and sole heiress of William de Mareschall, and it is stated that the eldest branch of the family were called Mareschall until the male line became extinct." "Their mansion house occupied the extensive square on which the present lower citadel, or shamble barrack stands." — Note, there are two families amongst the lower classes, Linchee and Lynsky, that are probably derived from the same stock.

1300 The town of Galway was built by a colony of Englishmen of the names I have before mentioned, denominated tribes. — Note, there seems to be some confusion in the chronology here, as in the preceding article one of the Lynches was said to have married the daughter of the marshal of Galway in 1880. It will be perceived by the following article that the marshal's name was also Lynch, though under the date 1280 it is said that the first of that name came from Castleknock, near Dublin.

1312 The great gate and the old works adjoining the same were built by Nicholas Lynch, the black marshal, or marshal dubh[1].

1316 The 4th of August William de Burgo and Richard de Bremingham encountered Phelimy O'Connor, king of Connaught, and a numerous army of Irish, near Athenry, with prodigious success, for they slew the king and 8000 of his men. The valour of Hussey, a butcher of Athenry, was very remarkable on that occasion, for he fought with O'Kelly and his squire together, and slew them both; for which he was knighted, and is the ancestor of the reputed Barons of Galtrim. It was said that Athenry was walled with the plunder of this battle, and that the brave Bremingham was made Baron of Athenry for this noble service, and his heir is now the premier Baron of Ireland.

1433 Two of the Burkes seized upon most part of the estates of De Burgo, which by marriage had reverted to the crown, and divided it between them; and knowing they could not hold it by the law of England, they confederated with the Irish, and changed their language, apparel, customs, and manners, nay, their very names were altered into those of Mac William Eighter and Mac William Oughter, (that is, upper and lower,) and by these means they have made shift to keep some part of that mighty estate for many score years.

1442 The west bridge of Galway was built by Edmond Lynch Fitz Thomas (commonly called Emuin a Thuane) at his own expense. He possessed Newcastle, and was descended, from the eldest branch of the family, called in Irish *Canmore*, the great tree or head of the Lynches. The great influence they possessed is proved very plainly by having in 169 years upwards of eighty mayors of Galway.

1460 William Lynch Dubh, sovereign, enacted that no houses or lands belonging to the town should be set to Irishmen, without the consent of the council and officers for the time being. This act was confirmed in 1485, by the then mayor, Pierce Lynch, and the commons.

1462 In the reign of Edward IV. money was coined in Galway, by Gorman Lynch, who had a patent to coin money in Dublin Castle, Trim, and Galway — of such consequence was Galway at this early period; four-pence, two-pence, half-pence, and farthings. — Note, I was fortunate enough to purchase one of those groats, which I presented to the late General Valiancy for the Dublin Society's museum.

---

[1] In 1376 there were four cities in Ireland; Dublin, Waterford, Cork; and Limerick; and five towns, Drogheda, Kilkenny, Roes, Wexford, and Youghal. If so, where was Galway at this, period, as no mention is made of it as a town? In the Pope's bull in 1484 it is called "the village of Galway." [original footnote].

1467 Amongst other grants to Lord Dunboyne, he had the prizage[1] of Limerick, Cork, Ross, Youghal, Kinsale, Dingle, and Galway, during his life.

1468 Edward IV. enacted a law against forestalling and regrating[2] in Galway. In this reign also it was enacted that every Irishman shall take an English surname of a town, as England, Ireland, Scot, Kilkenny, Chester, &c; or a colour, as white, black, brown, grey, &c; or an art or science, as carpenter, smith, brewer, baker, &c; or from his office, as cook, butler, servant, steward, gardener, &c; which name their issue shall use on pain of forfeiting his goods yearly until it be done; to be levied twice a year, to maintain the king's wars, according to the discretion of the king's lieutenant or his deputy. How little reason some of our high heads have to be proud of their ancestry!

1473 Galway was almost entirely destroyed by fire.

Mr. Hardiman gives the following list of provosts, portreeves[3], and sovereigns:

1274	Thomas De Lince, provost
1290	Richard Blake, alias Caddell, bailiff or portreeve.
1353	Stephen Penrise, provost; he was afterwards collector of the new customs. He died in 1383.
1378	Richard Scared, alias Scaret, provost; now called Skerrett.
1414	Walter Skeret, ditto.
1417	The same, ditto.
1434	Emund Lynche, sovereign.
1444	The same.
1448	William Allen, alias Den, provost
1460	William Dubh Lynche Fitz-James, sovereign.
1461	James Develin, ditto.
1462	William Oge Allen, alias Den, ditto.
1476	Thomas Lynche, ditto.
-------	John Skeret, provost.

1485 The same, last sovereign, John Lynch Fitz-Edmund, last Provost.

------- Dominick Lynch, commonly called Black Dominick, got a grant from king Henry VII. of letters patent, authorizing a yearly election of a mayor out of the corporation of the town of Galway, and the first mayor was his brother.— Much of the property of the Lynches is derived from an intermarriage at a remote period, with an heiress of the ancient Irish family of O'Halloran.

------- Pierce Lynch, first mayor of Galway.

Andrew Lynch Fitzstephen, and James Lynch Fitzmartin, bailiffs.

------- The Bull of the college, which the corporation bought, was published and read in the court house on the 3d and 6th days of November.

---

[1] A form of customs duty, [Clachann ed.].
[2] Forestalling and regrating are both ways of manipulating prices through creating scarcity and bulk buying, [Clachan ed.].
[3] A portreeve or port warden is an historical official possessing authority over a port town, [original footnote].

1486   Dominick Lynch Fitzjohn, mayor.
       Richard Morris, and Jeffiry Blake, bailiffs.
       This year it was enacted by public assent, that none of the corporation should be served with any writ or process, until the matter had been first tried by the mayor and council of the town, under a penalty of £20. This mayor bequeathed a great deal of money for charitable purposes. He made several additions to the cathedral, and left to every convent in Ireland, 15s. 4d.
1487   William Lynch Fitz Sandy, mayor.
       No bailiffs.
1488   Jeffry Lynch, mayor.
       No bailiffs.
1489   John Lynch Fitz John, mayor.
       No bailiffs.
       No bailiffs.
1491   John Skerrett, mayor.
       No bailiffs.
       The Skerretts were originally called Huscared or Scared. One of that name was provost of Galway in 1378. The estate of Ardfry, now the property of the Blakes, belonged to him, and also the lands on which the abbey of Clare Galway was erected, now, I believe, the property of Lord Clanmorris. They also possessed the estate of Headford, now the property of Mr. St. George.
1492   Thomas Lynch Fitz Edmond, mayor.
       No bailiffs.
1493   James Lynch Fitzstephen, mayor.
       No bailiffs.
       This mayor built the choir of St. Nicholas' church at the west end, and put painted glass in the windows. "He hanged his own son out of his window for killing and defrauding strangers, without either martial or common law, to show a good example to posterity, so tender were they of their credit". His fellow citizens seemed to be sensible of his merit, by electing him to the chair three times. The history of this more than Roman act of justice seems to be that he sent his only son to Spain on some commercial affairs, who returning with the son of his father's Spanish friend, and a valuable cargo, conspired with the crew to murder him and throw him overboard, and convert the property to their own use. One of the party, as providentially happens in most such cases, discovered the horrid transaction to the mayor. He tried and condemned his son to death, and appointed a day for his execution. It was imagined by his relatives that through their intercession, and the consideration of his being an only son, he would not proceed to put the sentence into execution.
       He told them to come to him on a certain day, and they should have his determination. Early on the day appointed, they found the son hanging out of one of the windows of his father's house: it was commemorated by the cross

bones in Lombard-street[1]. It is not a little extraordinary that the commemoration should not have been put up until the year 1624, the date on the stone, and that 131 years should have elapsed. In another account of this affair it is laid in the year 1526, when Stephen Lynch Fitz-James was mayor. It is, I imagine probable, that the present front of the house where those emblems are placed, was formerly the back, for the windows of the back are ornamented, whilst those of the present front are plain; and at and after the time it happened, a street ran from Lombard-street into the present church-lane, then called *Boher-cran-more*, which from the circumstance was called *dead man's lane*, at present taken into the church yard, which may be seen by consulting the map of 1651. — Another instance of this stern virtue occurs in the person of Strongbow in 1172, who executed his only son, by cutting him across the middle, after having reproached him for running away from the Irish at one of his battles in the county of Wexford. — **Note**, Mr. Hardiman has worked up this melancholy transaction into a very interesting little tale, and to give the better effect, has introduced a fair lady as the cause of this tragedy. But I am inclined to think the cross bones allude to a horrid murder mentioned in Archbishop King's collection, said to have happened in 1625.

1494 John Lynch Fitz-Edmond, mayor.
No bailiffs.
He contributed greatly towards finishing the college house opposite to the church.

1495 Thomas Blake, mayor.
No bailiffs.
No person to sue an inhabitant until the cause be first heard in the tholsel by the mayor and council — penalty £20.

1496 Walter Lynch Fitz-Robert, mayor.
Valentine Blake, and Thomas Bodkin, Bailiffs ----- Note, why there were no bailiffs for the last nine years I am to learn.
The inhabitants were ordered to keep arms, each according to his calling — penalty 12d.
It was enacted this year that no person shall take part with any lord or gentleman, or uphold any variances in word or deed, as in using the words *Cromaboo*, *Butleraboo*, or such other words, but to call only on Saint George or the name of the King. The offenders to be committed to prison without bail, until they have made fine at the discretion of the lord deputy and council. At this time the country was kept in a state of warfare by the factions of Fitzgerald and Butler,

---

[1] This if a flag with skeleton head and cross bones; as it is inscribed:
1624.
Remember death.
All is vanity of vanities.

whose parties used those words as the warhoop of each party[1]. It was the custom of those turbulent times for every great clan to have watch words, which may be more fully seen in Harris[2]. The word of the Clanrickards was *Gal-riagh-aboo*, or the cause of the red Englishman.

1497   Domnick Lynch-Fitz-John, mayor 2d time.
Walter Lynch and Oliver Lynch, bailiffs.

1498   Andrew Lynch-Fitz-Stephen, mayor.
Peter Martin, and Martin Fount, bailiffs.
This mayor began the work from Lough-a-Thalia to Poulavourline, at the cost of the corporation. He was employed as agent from the corporation to oppose the *presumes* against Pierce Butler, Earl of Ossory, and died in prison. This year a considerable part of the work from Shoemakers tower, was built out of the king's customs. There is a continuance of said work to the quay out of said customs. This year Edmond Deane, son to William Deane, came out of Bristol; of course he could not have been one of the tribes to whom the pope's bull in 1484 was directed. Also this year the bell called Clogherafine, was begun to be rung in this town, which was the curfeu first ordained by William the conqueror in England.

1499   James Lynch-Fitz-Martin, mayor.
Peter French and Stephen Lynch, bailiffs.

1500   Jeffrey Lynch, mayor.
James Lynch and Nicholas French, bailiffs.
This year Galway was accidentally burned.
Richard Begge made free, on condition of keeping an inn for stranger; and Donell Oge O'Volloghan (O'Nolan) goldsmith, made free, on condition of maintaining Andrew Fallon, who is old and impotent.

1501   Roebuck Lynch, mayor.
David Kirwan and John Morris, bailiffs.

1502   John Lynch-Fitz-John, mayor.
Patrick Lynch and Walter Lynch, bailiff.

1503   Edmond Deane, mayor.
Cornel Fallon, and William Kirwan, bailing Note, the first non-tribe elected into office.

1504   Walter Lynch-Fitz-Thomas, mayor.
John Bodkin and William Murtin, bailiff,.
After a most complete victory obtained by the Earl of Kildare over Clanrickard and his confederates at Knocklow, the towns of Galway and Athenry were surrendered to the Lord Deputy and his associates, and the whole country destroyed, and the conquerors overloaded with booty.

1505   Stephen Lynch-Fitz-Domnick, mayor.
Edward Athy and Robert Lynch-Fitz-Martin, bailiffs.

---

[1] Common Irish war cries involved the use of the clan name followed by *abú*, e.g. *Clann Fearghaile Abú*, [Clachan ed.].
[2] Harris's 'Hibernia,' 1778, [original footnote].

This mayor built the poor house in High-street, and his wife Margaret Athy, in his absence, built the Augustinian Monastery on Fort-hill, which he finished and endowed with rents of lands. He paved part of the town: he also founded an hospital. If any outlandish man or enemy of the inhabitants shall take any of them for any discord or words between any brother or neighbour of Galway, so that one neighbour shall procure for evil-will to his neighbour, so be taken as aforesaid; that then he that procureth such taking, shall ransom and restore again that person, rendering to him all his loss and damages, and the remainder of the goods to the prince and officers for the time being.

That no householder be an hostler, nor no maintainer of the common horse *[sic]*, or harlots, on pain of 6s. 8d.

1506 Thomas Bodkin, mayor.
Richard Deane, and Leonard Lynch, bailiffs.
This family (Bodkin) were descended from Maurice Fitz-Gerald, lord of Windsor, who came to Ireland with Strongbow. He was the ancestor of the ancient Earls of Desmond and Kildare. This seems to be confirmed by their motto (Cromaboo) being the same. In the reign of Richard II. they possessed large property in and about the town of Galway; and Richard Bodkin was a burgess of Galway and provost of Athenry in 1454. In the late history of Galway it is stated, that the original name of this family was Poiticin, and were descended from Maurice Fitz-Gerald, the lineal descendent of Otho, a noble prince of Italy. His descendants intermarried with the families of Lynch, Burke, D'Arcy, O'Flaherty, French, Blake, Athy, O'Shaughnessy, Martin, &c.

1507 Arthur Lynch, mayor.
William Joyce and Anthony Lynch, bailiffs.
In November, 250 people, with the mayor, fell over the bridge.
It was ordered in council that the warden and bailiffs be first served at market — Note, what a watchful shepherd the warden must have been! Ordered, that no butcher take no *cnaye-goulle* nor *skeingh-glac* out of no cow that he selleth: — the first is probably the tripes, and last the sticking piece.

1508 Stephen Lynch-Fitz-Domnick, mayor.
Richard Lynch and William Morris, bailiffs.
It was enacted this year, that every dweller should make clean before his door once a week, and that no dung heaps should be made in the streets, under the penalty of 12 pence; also that whatsoever man, woman or child be found prowling the streets or walls, shall lose 2d.

1509 Stephen Lynch, Fitz-James, mayor.
Edmond French and Adam Faunt, bailiffs.
Whatsoever man or woman have any kyne[1] in town, shall keep them in their houses both summer and winter; and if they be found on the streets, to pay 4d; and no swine or goat to be kept in town above fourteen days, on pain of killing.

---

[1] *Kyne* or *kine* is an old plural word for cattle, [Clachan ed.].

1510 James Lynch-Fitz-Stephen, mayor.
William Kirwan and Valentine French, bailiffs. This mayor built at his own expense the chapel of St James in the new fort in Galway. In this reign (Henry VIII.) it was enacted, that none of the king's Irish subjects shall be shaven above the ears, or wear the hair on their heads like long locks called Glibbs, (I wish this act was still in force,) or use hair on their upper lips called a *Crommeale*, or wear any shirt, smock, kercher, *bendell*, neck-kercher, *mochet* or linen cap coloured with saffron, or wear above seven yards of cloth in their shirts or smocks; and no woman to wear any *kirtel* or coat tucked up, or embroidered with silk or laid with *aske*, after the Irish fashion, &c. penalty for a lord spiritual or temporal £6. 13s. 4d.
Knight or esquire £2.
Gentleman and merchant £1.
Freeman or yeoman 10s.
That every cooper shall give two tun hoops for a penny, three pipe hoops for a penny, three hogshead and barrel hoops for a penny. That the shoremen, or cottoners shall give five *baunlac*, (bundles) six, seven *baunlac* of frize for two pence; eight *baunlac*, nine *baunlac*, ten *baunlac* for three pence, and a shore mantle for 10d. subpoena 12d.

1511 James Lynch-Fitz-Gregory, mayor.
Stephen French and Nicholas French Fitz-Arthur, bailiffs.
That all idle men and women not able to pay watch tax retalladge, be expelled the town: that the fishers of the lough shall bring into the market three days in the week, and to give an hundred eels for 2d. That no butter be sold above one penny a pound, and no dearer, on pain to lose 12d.; and his body to be put in prison that doth the contrary. — Note, can we be surprised at the hostility of the native Irish, after this detail of oppressive restrictions, and those that follow? D.

1512 James Lynch-Fitz-Martin, mayor.
William Athy and Laurence Bodkin, bailiffs.

1513 Walter Lynch-Fitz-Thomas, mayor.
Jonack Kirwan and James Skerret, bailiffs.
The house for poor and religious women near St. Nicholas' church, which now belongs to the nuns of the third order of St Francis, was given by this mayor; he had his daughter, a virtuous and religious woman in it, where he died.
It was ordered that no honey be brought to town except it be good and merchantable; and that no dweller shall become surety for any gent of the country, nor ransom none of them.

1514 Stephen Lynch-Fitz-Walter, mayor.
Robert Lynch Fitz-John and Edmond Athy, bailiffs.
That none of the town buy cattle out of the country, but only of *true men*. That the mayor, warden and bailiffs, shall be first served with all provisions at market, and then who first comes is first served.

1515 James Lynch-Fitz-Stephen, mayor, third time.
John Lynch-Fitz-Domnick and John Morris, bailiffs.

1516 Stephen Lynch-Fitz-James, mayor.
John William Lynch-Fitz-Andrew and Thomas Kirwan, bailiffs,
Ordered, that no man of the town shall lend or sell galley, boat or barque, to an Irishman.

1517 Stephen Lynch-Fitz-Domnick, mayor.
Martyn Lynch-Fitz-John and Gabriel Lynch, bailiffs.
It was ordered that no person shall give nor sell to no Irish, any munitions, as hand porins, caliones, powder, lead, nor salt petre, nor yet long bows, cross bows, cross bow strings, nor yarn to make the same, nor no kind of weapon, on pain to forfeit the same and an hundred shillings.
That every ship that cometh a fishing within the haven of Galway, shall pay half tithes to the college of all such fish as they shall take, if they take fire, water, and service within the said town or haven. Also, that every top man pay 40s. and every small man 20s. and four pounds of gunpowder to the town and corporation.

1518 John Bodkin, mayor.
Domnick Deane and Martin Lynch-Fitz-James, bailiffs.
It was ordered by the corporation that no free man should quit the town without leave from the mayor, penalty 1s. 8d. Also, if any man shall bring any Irishman to brag or boast upon the town to forfeit 12d. Also, that no man of this town shall *oste*[1] or receive into their houses at Christmas, Easter, nor no feast else, any of the Burkes, McWilliams, (Burkes,) the Kellys, nor no sept else, without licence of the mayor and council, on pain to forfeit £5. "That neither O' nor Mac shall strutte ne swagger through the streets of Galway."

1519 William Martin, mayor.
Bartholomew Faunt and Richard Martin, bailiffs
It was ordered that if any man, free or unfree, be found by night in any man's house to give copulation, or to do with the good man's servant maid, or daughter, by way of advowtery, to lose 20s. and also to the man in whose house the same person is found, to lose to that man 20s. That no Irish judge nor lawyer shall plead in no man's cause within this town or court; for it agreeth not with the king's laws, nor yet the emperor's in many places. — Note, until the reign of James the First the Brehon laws only were in force, except in the counties of Dublin, Meath, Kildare, Louth, and the cities of Dublin, Cork, Limerick, Waterford, Drogheda, and a few other places.
Also, that he that gets, a freeman or merchant's daughter with child, shall either marry her or give her a sufficient portion with another man. — Note, this was put in force in 1521.

1519 This year the town wall was brought so far to the west, as forty yards beyond Michael's tower; also part of the quay was built at the charge of the king and the

---

[1] To host or receive as an inn-keeper, [Clachan ed.].

corporation. The young men of the town began to go under bond, and to have a company by themselves, which was approved of by the corporation.

1520 Martin Faunt, mayor.
Richard Blake and Oliver French, bailiffi.
Ordered, that no priest, monk, canon, nor friar, shall keep no w-----e nor lemon in any man's house within this town, and that man which keepeth or hosteth the said w----e or lemon to forfeit £20. *Query lemon?*

1521 Anthony Lynch, mayor.
Arthur Lynch and Ulick Lynch, bailiffs.

1522 Stephen Lynch-Fitz-Domnick, mayor.
John French and John Fallon, bailiffs.
That no man of this town be free of the corporation unless he speaks English and shaves his upper lip *weekly*. And that no man of this town shall sell nor lend to any outlandish-man (poor paddy!) no kind of armour or shirt of mail, nor sell no harness, on pain of 20s.

1523 Stephen Lynch-Fitz-James, mayor.
John Kirwan and Peter Lynch, bailiffs.

1524 Adam Faunt, mayor.
Richard Faunt and Ambrose Lynch-Fitz-James, bailiff.
The family of Faunt or de Fuente settled in Galway in the fifteenth century, and came from Athenry, where they had probably come with the other English settlers of king John's reign. One of this name died in Galway in 1814, aged 105, probably the last of the name. — I recollect seeing a man of this name (Jemmy Faunt) many years since working in a nursery in Drumcondra, near Dublin. The Faunts were connected by marriage with many very respectable families in the counties of Meath, Mayo, &c.

1525 William Martin, mayor.
Walter Lynch-Fitz-John and Henry Joyce, bailiffs.
The Martins are a very ancient family in Galway. The first of the name was Oliver Martin, who was one of Strongbow's invaders: some antiquaries think they are derived from the Firbolgs *Martini*. They were eminent merchants of Galway, and branched out into different parts of this county, and those of Mayo, Limerick, Clare, &c.

1526 Stephen Lynch-Fitz James, mayor.
Marcus French and Thomas Blake, bailiffs.
Ordered, that no carpenter or mason shall have for his wages but two-pence each day, with meat and drink.

1527 William Morris, mayor.
Richard Bodkin and Thomas Lynch-Fitz-Stephen, bailiffs.
This year Thomas Moore was made a freeman.
The family of Morris were originally called Mares, and sometimes and still by the Irish Moresh: they were very old settlers, for we find Richard Morris was one of the bailiffs in 1486.

It was ordered that whoever plays at quoits or stones, but only to shoot in long bow, short cross bow, and hurling of darts or spears, to lose at every time 8d.

1528 John Lynch-Fitz-Andrew, mayor.
Richard Kirwan and Jonack Lynch, bailiffs.
That in what house, shop, or cellar, there be found players at cards, dice, tables, or other unlawful games for money, by young men, especially by apprentices or Irishmen, on pain to lose the money they play for, and also where they play to pay 20s.

1529 Richard Gare Lynch, mayor.
Edmond Lynch and Francis Blake, bailiffs.
When this mayor first went to sea, he set off from the Black-rock in the middle of the bay of Galway, and fired a gun there: he made a fortunate voyage; in testimony of which this custom was observed by his posterity, and to this day every vessel that has one of that name on board observes the same custom.
That whatsoever countryman shall spoil, rob or wound any of the inhabitants of this town, either by land or water, shall have no privilege in any man's house within the town, unless for debt.

1530 Jonack Kirwan, mayor.
Marcus Lynch and Stephen Lynch-Fitz-Arthur, bailiffs.
It was ordered by the corporation that any priest or vicar of the college found with any fault or crime, to lose one hundred shillings and their benefice; and also if he or they keep any w— e being with child, or bearing him children, to pay the above penalty.— The clergy of the present day, of each religion, are shining examples of every virtue. — The Kirwans are a very ancient and respectable Irish family. It is generally thought they are the same with the family of Kerwick or Keroyk, mentioned amongst the original inhabitants; the name has been spelled Kyrvan, Kerovan, Kirevane, O'Quirivan; the pronunciation at present by the old inhabitants is Kirovane, and from them the true pronunciation is generally to be had of all names originally Irish. One of this family, John Kirwan Fitz-Stephen, who was mayor in 1686, was the first possessor of Castle Hackett, which originally belonged to the Hacketts.

1531 James Skerrett, mayor.
Walter Skerrett and John Lynch-Fitz John, bailiffs.

1532 Anthony Lynch, mayor.
Marcus Lynch and Jonack Lynch-Fitz-Stephen, bailiffs.

1533 Richard Blake, mayor.
Anthony Blake and Thomas Martin, bailiffs.
Any inhabitant who should begin any strife, debate, or quarrel, or draw out swords, dagger, or knife, to pay 100s.; the weapon to be nailed and put up in the pillory. — Note: the offender should have been put there instead of the instrument.

1534 Thomas Kirwan, mayor.
Christopher Lynch-Fitz-Stephen and William Lynch, bailiffs.

1535 Richard Martin, mayor.

Dominick Lynch and George Skerrett, bailiffs.

Upon a return from his voyage the mayor fired a gun at the little castle on Multon island, which is still observed by all the Martins to this day.

1536 Richard Martin, mayor.

Dominick Lynch and George Skerrett, bailiffs.

Whatsoever woman, of what degree she be, bearing child, shall not make *common bancks*,[1] and great expense as in time past, but shall keep her accustomed beads during her pleasure, without any resort of common house haunters, save only her friends, such as she list, on pain to forfeit 20s.; and also whatsoever man or woman goeth into any such house, asking or seeking for meat or drink, unprayed or bidden, to pay 6s. 8d.

Henry VIII. ordained that the town of Galway should use the English language, order, and habit, and not to forestal the market of Limerick, nor correspond with the Irish. Also, that his deputy shall receive the fee farm and customs of the city of Waterford, and half the fee farm of Cork, Youghal, Limerick, and Galway, and the other half to the reparation of their walls, and to their defence.

That no man of Athenry, although he bought his freedom in this town, be free, unless it be a young man having no house here or there.

1537 Martin Lynch-Fitz-James, mayor.

Nicholas Lynch and Patrick Lynch, bailiffs.

That no person under a penalty of 20s. shall send any meat or drink to any that keepeth sanctuary in the abbeys, east or west, fearing to come into the town to pay their debts.

1538 John French, mayor.

Nicholas Blake and William Skerrett, bailiffs.

That any person or merchant of this town that shall make any bargain or contract in Spain, France, or any other lands, for wine, salt, *yeone*, [?] or any other kind of wares, shall, before he put the said shop or wares in book or custom, find to the mayor and officers of this town sufficient and substantial sureties, that he or they shall well and truly content and pay the stranger of his payment, for the discharge and credit of the town and inhabitants thereof.

This mayor was generally called *Shane ne Sallin*, from the great quantity of salt he brought from Spain into Galway. He built the north side of St Nicholas' church from the north pinnacle to the chapel of the Blessed Sacrament, and the great chapel which lieth on the south side of St Francis' abbey, together with the stone house that stands over the river, annexed to the west pinnacle of the said abbey, called John French's chamber to this day. — The family of French came to England with William the conqueror, and to Ireland with Strongbow. They settled first in the county of Wexford, from whence one of the family came to Galway in the reign of Henry VI. and another in the reign of queen Elizabeth, from whom the Frenches of this county and Roscommon are descended. I have

---

[1] Open house. [Clachan ed.].

beard it asserted that the first of the Frenches was a judge of that name, sent over from England to try the Blakes for the murder of the Athys. The lord deputy Grey came into Clanrickard from Thomond, and took the castle of Ballyclare, and delivered it to Ulick Burke, and on the eleventh day he came to Galway, where the corporation treated the lord deputy and all the English soldiers, gratis, for seven days, and Ulick Burke did the same with the Irish. The mayor and aldermen followed the example of Limerick, and took the oath of the king's supremacy, and renounced the pope's usurped authority. Here likewise O'Flaherty, O'Madden, and Mac Yoris made their submission. The deputy was a violent reformer, and seized to his own use the rich ornaments of the church of St. Nicholas.

1539 Arthur Lynch, mayor.
Andrew Lynch-Fitz-Stephen and James Oge Lynch, sheriffs.
This mayor died shortly after his election, and Arthur French-Fitz-Geoffry was elected in his place. — It was enacted that widows should have a third part of all such goods as were in the lawful possession of their husbands, and not disposed of before their death, but not otherwise. This year Andrew Browne of Athenry was made a freeman of the town.

1540 Domnick Lynch-Fitz-James, mayor.
Ambrose Lynch and George Lynch-Fitz-Walter, bailiffs.
Nicholas Browne, Robert Browne, and Domnick Browne-Fitz-William, were made freemen of the town. The lord deputy Grey on his return to England was accused by his enemies, amongst other things, with carrying the artillery in a small vessel to Galway, and making the town pay thirty-four pounds for that carriage. Like wise that he destroyed the castle of Lackagh and Derry vic-Clogny in favour of Ulick Burke, though the rightful possessor offered submission and rent to the king.

1541 Thomas Lynch-Fitz-Stephen, mayor.
Peter French-Fitz-Waden and James Kervick, bailiffs.
Richard Browne was made free of the town. It was enacted that no sanctuary should be allowed for debtors longer than twenty-four hours. The Spittal, or St. Bridgid's house in the east suburbs, was founded as a maintenance to some of the poor members of this town falling to decay, and upon each Sunday every burgess of the town was bound to send a maid to collect alms for the said house, which was usually observed afterwards for many years. In this reign a law was made that no merchants wife should use any tavern or ale-house, upon pain of forfeiting twenty shillings, *toties quoties*, as often as any of them do the contrary, "but to let them be occupied in making of cloth and linen."

1542 Henry Joyce, mayor.
Edward French and Patrick French, bailiffs.
Ordered, that no person of this town shall buy or sell with merchants of Limerick, Cork, Waterford, Dublin, or other towns or cities for any goods, or cause the same to be transported by land or sea, unless they come to this town as other strangers and merchants in ships, on pain of forfeiting the goods and £20.

About this time the bishops of Tuam and Clonfert, and Captains Wakely and Ovington, were appointed commissioners to decide controversies instead of the former Brehons. — The family of Joyce, or Joyes, or Jorz, Jorse, is very ancient, and allied to some of the British and Welsh princes. The first of that name, Thomas Joyce, came to Ireland in the reign of Edward I. He acquired extensive property in Iar connaught, (since called Joyce country,) and from him are descended the Joyces of that country; of whose size and strength I have seen and heard many instances. I saw an elderly man of that name of uncommon stature and strength, whom, I was informed, when in his youth and elevated with the native, never was satisfied until he had driven every man out of the fair green: those who knew his humour, and also his strength, generally retired beyond a certain small bridge: when his whim was satisfied by submission, he permitted them to return quietly, and no further notice was taken on either side. Resistance would have been not only useless, but almost certain destruction, for nineteen in twenty were of that name, and all related. When I saw him he was the remains of a noble figure, remarkably gentle and kind to every one, and heard with great regret the pranks of his youth mentioned.

1543 Jonakin Lynch, mayor.
Edmond Kirwan and Edmond Bodkin, bailiffs.
Nicholas Coin or Quin, and his son, Thomas Coine, were admitted freemen.

1544 Edmond Lynch, mayor.
William Lynch and Thomas Lynch, bailiffs.
It was enacted that the warden and vicars should not set any of the lands, tithes, or other revenues of the collegiate church of St. Nicholas for more than one year. Before this, longer tenures had been given to friends and relations, to the great injury of the institution.
The sweating sickness carried off numbers of people.
On his submission to Henry VIII. Ulick Burke was created Earl of Clanrickard, and his estate was regranted to him, and the abbeys and patronage of all benefices within his precincts.
The cocquets[1] of Galway were excepted in the patent; but in lieu of them the earl had a pension of £30. per annum, the third part of the first fruits, and the Abbey of Via nova, or Clonfert. He also gave to the earl a house and parcel of land, near Dublin, to encourage him to make his appearance frequently at court

1545 Thomas Kiwan, mayor.
Ambrose Lynch and Stephen Faunt, bailiffs.

1546 Stephen Lynch-Fitz-Arthur, mayor
James Faunt and Walter Skerrett, bailiffs.

1547 Thomas Kirwan, mayor.
Ambrose Lynch and Stephen Faunt, bailiffs.

1548 Dominick Lynch-Fitz-John, mayor.

---

[1] Documents or payments related to custom duties, [Clachan ed.].

John Joyce and Domnick French, bailiffs.

Richard de Burgo, called Richard Sassanagh, (English Richard,) for £1000. obtained from Henry VIII. a grant of all Connaught, after the death of the then king of Connaught; and on the 10th June a writ was issued to the Lord Justice to seize on Connaught, forfeited by O'Connor, and to deliver it to Richard de Burgo at the rent of 300 marks for the first five years, and afterwards for £500. per annum, except five choice cantreds near Athlone, which probably were designed for the support of that garrison. Shortly after this period the earl intended to put all Iar connaught under contribution, or chief rent; he took the whole prey of the country, and they coming to *Trabane*, within two miles of Galway westward, were set upon by a small party and the prey taken from them, and they were forced to turn their backs, and the most part of them were either drowned in the sea or river of Galway. Some got over the river, but such was their apprehension of death, that they knew not how.

Timor pedibus adidit alas[1].

1549 Thomas Martin, mayor.

Givane Faunt and James French, bailiffs.

For sundry and divers injuries and wrongs that the septs of Clan Donze, Clan McConchour, Clan Caleboy, the O'Hallorans Slought-Etaggard, and O'Flahertys, their chief captains, doth daily to the inhabitants of this town, that when any of the said septs with their captains be found in town, to be taken and arrested until restitution be made for all hurts and damages as he or any of his sept doth to the inhabitants; and that the mayor or officers shall not licence nor pardon any of the said septs to come within this town, without licence of those on whom they commit the trespasses, or owing debt.

This mayor built the west gate and tower at the end of the bridge. In consideration of which the corporation gave him the plot of ground whereon the mill was built, and was lately called Thomas's mill; over the gate was inscribed — "This gate was erected to protect us from the Ferocious O'Flahertys."

1550 Richard Kirwan, mayor.

Denis Kirwan and David Bodkin, bailiffs.

Ordered, that the mayor, for the time being, shall have of the fishers of the lough or river every fish day, betwixt Michaelmas and Hollontide[2], but two hundred small eels, and every of the bailiffs one hundred; and from Hollontide forth it is ordered, that the mayor, for the furnishing his table with fresh fish, shall have the election of two fishers whom he list, and every of the bailiffs to have in like manner a fisher to keep their house with fish.

1551 John Oge Lynch, mayor.

John Lynch and Persse Lynch, bailiffs.

1552 Jonack Lynch-Fitz-Stephen, mayor.

---

[1] Latin, *Fear gave him wings*, [Clachan ed.].
[2] Welsh calendar festival for 1 November, a counterpart of Irish Samain. Again we see the preference for Welch terms in statements from the city rulers. [Clachan ed.].

Andrew Browne and Robuck Lynch, bailiffs.

1553 Patrick Lynch, mayor.
Anthony French and Domnick Browne, bailiffs.
Ordered, that the mayor and bailiffs do sustain four masons annually to work on the murage and pavage[1] of the town.
King Edward VI. granted a charter of incorporation to the reformed warden and vicars, and annulled the pope's bull.

1554 Nicholas Lynch-Fitz-Stephen, mayor.
Henry Lynch and David Kirwan, bailiffs.
The mayor was also called Nicholas-more-Linchee.
At his own expence he built the work adjoining his grandfather's work in St Nicholas's church, and is to this day called *Lynch aisle*.

1555 Nicholas Blake, mayor.
Peter French-Fitz-John and Pierce Lynch-Fitz-John, bailiffs.

1556 William Skerrett, mayor.
John Blake-Fitz-Robert and Martin French, bailiffs.

1557 James Oge Lynch, mayor.
Richard Lynch and Walter Lynch, bailiffs.
This mayor built the south end of St Nicholas's church. The east end of the tholsel was built. The Burkes of the county of Mayo, under the conduct of Mac William Eighter, were defeated at Shruel, by the Burkes of the county of Galway, under the conduct of Richard Burke, Earl of Clanrickard. In July the lord deputy made an expedition against the O'Maddens, whose country, called *Silanchia*, (now the barony of Longford,) was last year, on the murder of John O'Madden, divided between Malachy Modher and the murderer, Brasil Duff. The deputy sent a summons to the castle of Meelick, but the warder, though he boasted how stoutly he would defend it, and threatened to hang the herald if he brought any more messages, sneaked off in the night.

1558 Ambrose Lynch-Fitz-Martin, mayor.
Domnick Lynch and Richard Lynch-Fitz-Patrick, bailiffs.
A petition from the town of Galway was presented to queen Elizabeth, stating that they were greatly oppressed by the O'Flahertys, who had forcibly dispossessed the O'Briens of the island of Arran, who had agreed for a stipulated tribute to protect the town from pirates, and had so well fulfilled the agreement for many years, that this petition was preferred to restore them to their ancient possessions. In June the lord deputy, the Earl of Essex, marched into Galway, and was well received by the archbishop of Tuam and the bishops of Clonfert and Clanmacnois, who with the clergy met him in procession. In this reign Sir George Carew and Henry Sidney had orders to destroy all the manuscripts they could find, and which they too effectually accomplished. In this reign also the king of Denmark was anxious to have the Irish manuscripts in his possession,

---

[1] The town walls and pavements or streets, [Clachan ed.].

which had been brought from Ireland by his countrymen, translated. He applied to queen Elizabeth to send him a person well qualified for this task; for this purpose one Donald O'Daly, fit in every respect to engage in this business, was chosen. But a council was called, and a certain member opposed the scheme, lest it might be prejudicial to the English interest.[1]

1559 George Lynch-Fitz-William, mayor.
Peter Lynch and Robock French, bailiffs.

1560 Stephen Lynch Fitz-Arthur, mayor,
James Lynch and Nicholas French-Fitz-Oliver, bailiffs.

1561 Nicholas Lynch-Fitz-Stephen, mayor.
Nicholas Lynch and Martin Lynch, bailiffs.

1562 Thomas Blake, mayor.
Patrick Blake and Walter Blake, bailiffs.

1563 Thomas Oge Martin, mayor.
James Lynch-Fitz-Arthur and Patrick Martin, bailiffs.

1564 Nicholas Blake, mayor.
John Lynch-Fitz-Thomas and John Fits-Henry Blake, bailiffs.
This mayor was fined £40. for issuing the queen's writ against the warden and Richard Joyce, "young man," his farmer, "without first suing them before the mayor and council, according to a law enacted by the corporation in 1486".

1565 Peter Lynch-Fitz-Vaden, mayor.
Nicholas Lynch and Andrew Morris, bailiffs.

1566 James Kyrvicke, mayor.
William Martin and Richard Browne, bailiffs.

1567 Edmond Kirwan, mayor.
James Lynch and Martin Kirwan, bailiffs.

1568 Domnick French, mayor.
William Lynch and George French, bailiffs.

1569 George Faunt, mayor.
Gregory Bodkin and Valentine French, bailiffs.

1570 Denis Kirwan, mayor.
John Martin and Ambrose Bodkin, bailiffs.

1571 Robert Lynch, mayor.
Roland Skerrett and Nicholas French-Fitz-Vadien, bailiffs.

1572 John Lynch, mayor.
John Lynch Fitz-William and Marcus Lynch, bailiffs.

1573 Pierce Lynch Fitz-Oliver, mayor.
Charles Lynch Ulick and Oliver Oge-French, bailiffs.

1574 Andrew Browne, mayor.
Anthony Lynch Fitz-Marcus and Nicholas Kirwan Fitz-Denis, bailiffs.

---

[1] I trust some of our Irish antiquaries will take advantage of this notice. Probably many valuable documents would be obtained in Denmark, [original footnote].

This mayor died in office, and James Kirwan was elected. It is imagined the Brownes came over with Strongbow. It is evident they were not of much consideration at an early period in Galway, for this is the first mayor of that name.

The Brownes of the county of Mayo settled there in the reign of Queen Elizabeth, and were different families from those settled in Galway at an early period. — Quere - do the Mayo Brownes vote as tribes?

1575 Domnick Browne, mayor.
James Lynch Fitz-Stephen-Arthur and Michael Lynch Fitz-Stephen-Arthur, bailiffs.

Seven of the family of the Clandonnels, and Mac William Eighter, junior, who could speak Latin though he could not speak English, submitted by oath and indenture, and agreed to pay 250 marks *per ann.* for his country, besides contributions of men on risings out, and consented that the clan of the Clandonnels should hold their lands of the Queen; whereupon he was knighted, and had some small present from the deputy, and an English sheriff sent into his country as he desired. The town of Galway at this time was poor and disorderly, and the country destroyed by the Earl of Clanrickard's sons, against whom infinite complaints were made.

Nevertheless they had the confidence to come unexpectedly into the church of Galway in the time of divine service, and upon their knees to make their submission; and at the same time they humbly begged pardon for their extravagancies, which by the advice of the privy council was granted to them. Although for the present they were confined, and afterwards carried to Dublin; and so the lord deputy having stayed three weeks at Galway, set out towards Dublin, and kept sessions in every county he marched into, and settled garrisons in all places convenient. He finished his progress on the 13th day of April, 1576. — In a letter of the lord deputy he says, amongst other things, that Athenry was the most miserable spectacle in the world; the whole town was burned by the Macan Earlas, and the church itself not excepted from the general ruin, although the mother of one of those vipers was buried therein; but this was so far from mitigating their fury, that the son being told his mother was buried in the church, replied, that if she was alive, he would sooner burn her and the church together, than that any English church should fortify there; that these Macan Earlas hated each other, and yet like Herod and Pilate joined together against any third person whom they thought to be a common enemy. That the deputy had laid a tax of two thousand pounds on the county, towards rectifying of Athenry, and took from the Earl of Clanrickard the castles of Ballyclare and Ballinasloe. — That O'Connor duh, and O'Flyn, submitted to him at Roscommon, (their country being destroyed), and desired the English laws and government.

That the whole province of Connaught was much annoyed by the Scots whom the Macan Earlas brought to their assistance. Shortly after this the deputy received letters from the bishop of Meath, and the mayor of Galway, which informed him that the sons of Clanrickard, who had lately submitted (with the connivance of their father) passed the Shannon, changed their English for Irish apparel, sent for their friends and the Scots, and being met went to Athenry, sacked the town again, and set the new gates on fire, defaced the Queen's arms, drove away some, and slew others of the masons that were building. The industrious deputy made such haste, that in three days he was with them; at the report whereof the rebels were amazed, and fled to the mountains; but Clanrickard's castles were taken, and himself sent close prisoner to Dublin, though he made many excuses, to no purpose; which done, the deputy restored Castlebar to Mac William Eighter, and went to Galway to comfort and save the townsmen. Not long after this the Macan Earlas, Clanrickard's sons, were up again in Connaught, and had gotten 2000 Scots to their assistance; they besieged Ballyriagh (Lough rea), one of the Earl of Clanrickard's castles but Thomas L'Estrange and Captain Collier, who lay in garrison there with fifty horse and one hundred foot, defended the place so gallantly, that they forced the rebels to raise the siege, with the slaughter of six captains and 150 soldiers; whereat the rebels were so nettled, that they immediately fell upon Mac William Oughter and wasted his country; but upon the approach of the lord deputy the rebels dispersed, and thereupon the deputy divided his forces, and by the help and intelligence of Mac William Oughter, he met with and defeated several small parties of the Irish, and killed many, and executed some; and so having restored Mac William to most of his castles, and being informed that the Scots were retreated to the rocks and the glens, he knighted Sir Nicholas Mulloy, and according to the Queen's orders, left him governor of Connaught, and then returned to Dublin. He also, during his time, again repaired the town of Athenry, and built the bridge of Athlone.

1576 Peter French Fitz-John, mayor.
      Thomas Kirwan and George French Fitz-Ed ward, bailiffs.
1577 Pierce Lynch, mayor.
      John Blake and Francis Martin, bailiffs.
      This year John Burke, alias Shane-ne-shammer, or Far-more, was put to death by his own cousins at Ballyfenton, assisted by the country people. He intended to be Earl Clanrickard, or at least the head of his family.
1578 John Blake Fitz-Richard, mayor.
      Christopher Lynch and James D'Arcey, bailiffs.
      St. Nicholas church was repaired and much beautified.
1579 Martin French, mayor.
      Marcus Lynch Fitz-Stephen and Richard Butler, bailiffs.
      An order was made that no grown timber should be exported.
1580 Domnick Lynch Fitz-John, mayor.
      Thomas Lynch and John Skerrett, bailiffs.
      This mayor erected a school at the quay, which was afterwards converted into a place of defence called *cean-a-walla*, or head of the wall. He had a chief rent in all provisions to be sold within the town or exported: he also built the west side of the town house. Sir William Pelham, lord justice, marched to Galway, and

confirmed the privileges of the town: he thence marched through Athenry, Ballinasloe, and Athlone, to Dublin.

This year William Burke, younger son to the Earl of Clanrickard, and the Earl of Thomond's son, were apprehended near Galway, and were both hanged near the king's walls, by William Martin, marshal of the team, they being in rebellion against the crown; which act he did to prevent the coming of the pardon, which was procured by the said mayor. — This year died Connor-mac-a-Righ (the son of a king), an inhabitant of the island of Arran, who was 220 years old. He remembered when there were but three stone houses in Galway, the Abbey, the red Earl's house, now inhabited by Staunton, a publican in Court-house lane, (formerly called the Red Earl's lane) next door to the old court house and Athy's castle; and that there was only a small chapel where St Nicholas church now stands, and another at our Lady's chapel.

He remembered the building of Rosiella Abbey,[1] and that he killed 180 beeves[2] in his own house, reckoning one for every Christmas.

Whereas many and sundry greedy, detestable and inordinate gains of living of interests or *Cambies*, after the rate of wheat, or a good hide for the marke, by the year, has been taken up by such as lent money; ordered that none be here after taken but by such as are authorised by her Majesty's laws.

1581 Peter Lynch Fitz-Marcus, mayor.
Domnick Martin and Marcus Lynch Fitz-Peter, bailiffs.
A contention arose about this time between the Mac-an-Earlas, Ulick arid John Burke, on the death of their father; but it was referred to commissioners, who ordered that Ulick Burke should have Loughrea and the Earldom of Clanrickard, and that John should have Leitrim, and they both agreed that if either proved a traitor to the Queen the other should have all.

1582 Robuck French Fitz-John, mayor.
Walter Joyce and Edmond French Fitz-Robuck, bailiffs.

1583 Nicholas French, mayor.
Anthony Lynch Fits-Thomas and Oliver Browne, bailiffs.
An addition was made to St Nicholas church.
Any inhabitant comforting, lodging, or maintaining in his house or otherwise, any bawdry or harlots, shall forfeit every time 20s.

1584 Nicholas Lynch, mayor.
Richard Martin and Jeffrey Martin, bailiffs.
At this period the Earl of Ormond revived his claim to the prisage[3] of the wines of Galway, from which they imagined they had been exempt, and established his claim with costs.

1585 James Lynch Fitz-Arthur, mayor.
Stephen Kirwan and Thomas Browne, bailiffs.

---

[1] I imagine this it Ross Abbey, called sometimes Ross-Traleg and Ross-Reilly, [original footnote].
[2] An adult ox, bull, cow, etc., reared for its meat, [Clachan ed.].
[3] the right, usually of the king to take a certain quantity of every cargo of wine imported, [Clachan ed.].

Ordered, that no inhabitant henceforth pay any cess, tax or tallage, but according to his ability of goods and lands. — The province of Connaught was divided by Sir John Perrott into the counties of Galway, Roscommon, Sligo, Mayo and Leitrim. Before this period there were only the counties of Connaught and Roscommon. The following curious articles, touching reformations in the common-wealth, were presented the 25th February, 1585, by the advice of Sir John Perrott, who was remarkable for the kindness with which he treated the Irish people.

That the young English tailors and their boys be vagrants, the most in the town, using all unlawful plays and lascivious expences both by day and night, yea, and withal playing the whore whose names partly will hereafter ensue. That none be suffered to use any kind of unlawful games or plays to deceive and make the people idle, and shun to earn their living by good and lawful means.

That no young man, apprentice or otherwise, shall wear no gorgeous apparel, nor silks either within or without their garments, not yet fine knit stockings either of silk or costly wise; wear no costly long riffs thick and started, but be contented with single riffs, and that also they shall wear no pantwofles[1], but rather be contented with shoes. That generally all artificers in town do exact and take up for their works far more than is allowed unto them by the assize of the town, and beside that their exaction of money, they exact and take aqua vitae, wine, meat and drink, bread, broth, flesh, candles, and flax, with many other things. — That all sellers of victuals do take of the people very unreasonable gains, far beyond that reasonable allowances allowed them by the assize of the town, according to the rates laid by the market. That many in town, and especially nurses, are engrossers and encroachers of the markets, and also they who are better and most provided, besides the market, and have most store of corn, be the first that engroseth and encroacheth the market there. — Great laches[2] and slackness in our watch and ward armour and weapon, and worst of all, a great want in this town, viz. of powder, match, and munition, which we protest to be prevented as well by the governor of the realm, as also by the corporation, so far forth as the power corporations ability will reach, and that the same be provided in time, fearing of any imminent danger.— That no fry of fish, viz. of eels, be taken by no way whatsoever, beginning the 15th day of April to the spring following the same; and also that no red salmon be taken, nor crew of salmon as in the statute in that behalf is provided, *Act-na-howly* always excepted, for that we found it so by antiquity; and fearing the destruction of the fish, to prevent the same, that no limed hides or flax be suffered to be put into the river. — That all artificers, craftsmen, and common labourers, do take more than they should for their hire, both by the year, quarter, month, and day, far over the assize set down by the corporation.— That the shoemakers, glovers, and skinners of this town do not well tan their leather, nor yet utter the same according to the market; and to prevent the

---

[1] Pantoufles - soft sheepskin slippers, [Clachan ed.].
[2] Negligence, [Clachan ed.].

same, it is good to establish and order that they make good stuff, and utter the same according to the market — That the new statute made by the goldsmiths, concerning their own facultie or art, is commendable, so as they shall observe the same, and mend their former faults.— That many merchants and handy craftsmen have relinquished their mansions in town, and keep themselves in the country, without answering tax and tallage[1], scot and lot[2], within this town, from time to time, as appeareth by the names in Nicholas Lynch, the town clerk, his book; and, to prevent the same, it is good to establish, that every of them do come to dwell in town, or otherwise to order a fine lesse their liberty as appertain. — That a more stricter order be taken to bar the making of aqua vite of corn than hitherto hath been used, for that the same is a consumption of all the provision of corn in the commonwealth. — That no freeman within age shall have no utterance in the trade of merchandize, until he come apprentice to an householder that shall pay tax and tallage, except only a man's heir. — No craftsman, or, as it were, grey merchant, go abroad to buy or sell (under pretence of being servants to free men) any kind of merchandize, cattle, or other things, that shall not be of their own faculty; and that no weaver shall weave either linen cloth or single frize under the breadth of three quarters of a yard, on pain of forfeiture. — That neither porters, harpers, messengers, millers, bakers, butchers, or any nurses, or any kind of craftsmen, do at no festival times, or at any other time, come to any man's house to crave either for *ben bridge*, offering, meat, or any drink, by any way whatsoever, in vayne, on pain of imprisonment and loss of a crown, as well of the giver, as also of the offender. — That if any honest man's wife be convided (invited,) that she bring no more in her company but one, on pain of a crown. — That none do presume to enter into any house of banquet, without he be invited; and if he be invited, to have his billet under the inviter's hand, on pain of a crown. — That no cow or bullock under the age of three years be killed to be sold, upon pain of forfeiture. — That no kind of salt, in respect of wages or gift, be given to any boatman, either for sail of wages, nor yet to any horseman, for his carriage or sack, nor yet for the sack itself, but money. — That none shall either cut truffs or dig the meadows and pastures of this town, either by east or west, especially Conssuckin to the crag of Castlegar, by Pollmorydine, and all about the salt water lough, and in like manner in the meadows and pastures of the waste, within our franchise, in no place and in any wise; that the highways be neither hedged or manured to encroach the common way, on pain of forfeiture for every these defaults, not only all the labour and manurance, but also 20s. *toties quoties*[3]. — That no seaman or seamen, or, as I would say, fisherman or fishermen, do take in hand either the plough, spade, or *teithe*, that would bar them from fishing, both to serve themselves and the commonwealth with fish; in consideration whereof that the said fishers and their

---

[1] Royal tax, [Clachan ed.].
[2] A payment; lot, a portion or share applied to householders who were assessed for a tax paid to the borough for local or national purposes, [Clachan ed.].
[3] "As often as the thing shall happen", [Clachan ed.].

wives and family, be reasonably served before others with all necessary sustenance and food of provision as cometh to the market, whereby they might be the better able to earn their said livings that way, and have the better hope. — That, according to the ancient statutes, the course of the running water, that is to say, the little gate ditch water, all along that entereth through Nicholas Lynch's mill, and the water that entereth into the gut, all along to the issuing out of the same in Martin's mill, be always kept clean, as well within the walls as without — That the *aqua vita* that is sold in town ought rather to be called *aqua mortis*, to poison the people, than comfort them in any good sort, and in like manner all their beer; and all wherein the officers, in reforming the same, have need, to be more vigilant and inquisitive than they be. — There is no good bread made to be sold, neither well made, nor well baked, nor yet good, cheap as the market goes, but rather by half and half to deceive the people: for the reformation whereof we find, that men and women of good skill in making and baking of bread be thereto appointed accordingly, and as the rates of the market will be set down by the officers, so as it be a penny, half-penny, farthing, always to be found. — That no victualling house, cellar, or shop, where any victual, wine, or aqua vita is, be not in any honest sort kept clean, wherein there is neither sitting place, cloth, dish, or any other service, which have great need of reformation, — That all the meat that is thought to be either sodden or roasted by the bowcherous [?] cooks of this town is not worth the eating, and therefore is not sufferable, which also hath need of reformation, so as all to be clean, and retailed by penny, halfpenny, farthing, and wear their clean aprons; and that there be no horns suffered to be where the meat is dressing. — That, according to the ancient statutes, hogs be not suffered to be fed within the town, and especially upon the market place. That no man shall draw, or cause to be drawn, the wool of his sheep at no time, but rather shear them in due time, and not otherwise.

That no mutton or sheep be burned with the skin or wool, to the end that both might very well serve their own turns otherwise.

That candle-makers have very great need of reformation, for that they sell neither light nor sight, neither good tallow nor good thread, nor yet any good stuff at all for candles.

That no artificer, or man of occupation whatsoever, not suffered to be idle, wandering and wagginge[1] abroad the streets, taverns, or other places, upon working days, without a special good cause; during which time they must go either without cloak or mantle, having in their hands some token of their own crafts tools.

That no woman shall make no open noise of an unreasonable cry, after the *Iriskrie*, either be fore, nor yet after, the death of any corpse, much less in the house, street, and before all in the church, the house, nor yet in the fields; we mean their singing songs, long to praise of men, both dead and also alive, and not to God ever-living. —

---

[1] Gossiping, [Clachan ed.].

That no woman shall wear no gorgeous apparel, but as becometh them to do, according to their calling; and in especial they shall altogether forego the wearing of any hats or caps otherwise, coloured than black, and upon them they shall wear no costly hatbands, or cap bands, of gold thread; the mayoress only excepted.

1586 William Martin, mayor,
 Valentine Blake and Marcus Lynch, bailiffs,
1587 John Blake, mayor.
 Walter Martin and Anthony Kirwan, bailiffs.
1588 Andrew Morris, mayor.
 Patrick Kirwan and George Morris, bailiffs.
 This year a piece of the wall near the point of *Cean-a-walla* was built at the expense of the corporation. — One of the Spanish Armada was wrecked in the bay of Galway, and upwards of seventy of the crew perished; and several other vessels were lost on the coast, and the greater part of the crews that escaped were massacred by order of Sir William Fitz-Williams, lord deputy of Ireland, who had several beheaded near St Augustine's monastery
1589 Richard Browne, mayor.
 Oliver Kirwan and P. French Fitz-Valentine, bailiffs.
1590 James Lynch Fitz-Ambrose, mayor.
 John Martin Fitz-Patrick and William French Fitz-Nicholas, bailiffs.
 A belfry was erected this year, and several bells added; one of them remains in use; on it engraved "renewed be Master James Linche, mayor, and Hugh Butwall, founder of this bell, 1590 T.W.
1591 Ulick Lynch Fitz-Edmond, mayor.
 James Lynch Fitz-Martin and Peter Blake, bailiffs.
 The castle of Menlo demolished, for hindering turf boats to come to Galway by Lough Corrib.
1592 Valentine French, mayor.
 John Lynch and Geffry French, bailiffs.
1593 John Martin, mayor.
 Roebuck Martin and Arthur Lynch Fitz-James, bailiffs.
1594 Ronald Skerrett, mayor.
 Pierce Lynch Fitz-Jonack and Patrick Lynch Fitz-Ulick, bailiffs.
1595 Marcus Lynch Fitz-Nicholas, mayor.
 Thomas Lynch Fitz-Domnick and Gregory French, bailiffs.
1596 Oliver Oge French, mayor,
 P. Oge French Fitz-Peter and William Lynch Fitz-Peter, bailiffs.
 This mayor married Margaret Joyce, daughter of John Joyce; she had been formerly married to Domingo De Rona, a rich Spaniard, who had taken a liking to her, on seeing her going to the water bare-legged to wash clothes. He died and left her very rich, and without issue. Whilst the mayor her husband was at sea, she built the greater part of the bridges of Connaught at her own expense. One day reviewing the workmen, an eagle flying over her head, let fall a stone ring: the most skilful lapidary was ignorant of the kind: it has been preserved in the family

since!! ¹— Richard Martin was the first recorder, and continued so for thirty years.

1597 Anthony Lynch Fitz-Morris, mayor.
Patrick Kirwan and Andrew Blake Fitz-Patrick, bailiffs.

1598 Nicholas Kirwan Fitz-Denis, mayor.
Marcus Blake and Patrick Blake, bailiffs.

1599 Michael Lynch, mayor.
Christopher Lynch Fitz-Richard and Patrick French Fitz-Oliver, bailiffs.
John Quirke, and James Codegan or Conegan were made freemen.

1600 Francis Martin, mayor.
Marcus Lynch Fitz-Martin and Edmond Lynch Fitz-Pierce, bailiffs.
The fort of Galway was built at the King's charge.

1601 Christopher Lynch Fitz-George, mayor.
Robert Blake and Nicholas Lynch, bailiffs.

1602 James D'Arcy (*Riveagh*, or swarthy), mayor.
Robert Blake and Nicholas D'Arcy, bailiffs.
This mayor, who was also vice president of Connaught, died in June following, and was succeeded for the remainder of the year by Christopher Lynch Fitz-George, who had been mayor on the preceding year.²
Robert Blake purchased a patent from the king, of the chief rent the Red Earl had in Galway.
The lord deputy kept his Christmas at Galway, and there received into favor the O'Flahertys, Mac Dermotts, O'Connor-roe, and others. He ordered that the fort of Galway should be finished. At this time the county of Clare was taken from Connaught and added to Munster.

1603 Marcus Lynch Fitz-Stephen, mayor.
Martin Gauldy Lynch and Oliver Martin, bailiffs.

1604 Marcus French Fits-John, mayor.
Martin Font and Christopher Blake, bailiffs.
This year, Andrew French, a native of Galway, with his two sons, Edmond and Geoffry, went to Spain, where, through their good breeding and education, his eldest son Edmond, was made receiver of the King of Spain's estate, and Geoffry made governor of a considerable place in the West Indies; he was very much honored and respected there, and was knighted of the order of St Jago, and made

---

¹ Eagles, it seems, were very watchful of the affairs of this family (Joyce), for one of the family who had been taken prisoner, and for many year a captive by the Saracens, after many surprising vicissitudes of fortune, escaped after many years confinement, into Spain; where this guardian eagle or angel led him to a place where immense treasures were hidden. On his return to Galway he expressed his gratitude to Heaven by building churches, the town wall, and other useful works!!! [original footnote].
² This is the first mayor of that name, as the family did not settle in Galway until the reign of Queen Elisabeth. They deduce their pedigree from Charlemagne. Sir John D'Arcey came over to Ireland at chief justice to Edward II. in 1323. He married a daughter of De Burgo, Earl of Ulster, from whom probably all the D'Arceys of Ireland are descended, if this is correct, what claim can they have to the name of Tribe? , [original footnote].

general of the Spanish fleet coming from the West Indies with the king's plate and treasure, and his son Anthony, made a page to his majesty, and a captain of horse in the wars with France, and by them taken prisoner, and ransomed by the king of Spain for £3000. He had been formerly married in Spain, and died without issue, but left a sister honorably married in Spain. — This year the Roman Catholics repaired several abbeys and monasteries; amongst others Kilconnel, Loughrea, Knockmoy, and Clare Galway.— At this time the circuit for judges of assize commenced in the county of Galway, and for many years was held alternately in Galway and Loughrea.

1605 John Skerrett Fitz-William, mayor.
Geoffry Lynch Fitz-Domnick and John Lynch Fitz-Marcus, bailiffs.
That every freeman, being a merchant, dwelling in town, keeping crock and pan, and paying tax and tallage[1], shall have a voice in electing officers yearly, and also in all general matters which shall happen.

1606 Edmond French-Fitz-Robuck, mayor.
Peter Lynch-Fitz-Marcus and Pierce Lynch-Fitz-Jonack, bailiffs

1607 Richard Martin, mayor.
Martin D'Arcey and Robert Martin, bailiffs.
The law to prevent the alienation of the church property by the warden and vicars was renewed, under the penalty of expulsion out of the college house and church, as an unprofitable member, and also forfeiting £20.

1606 Stephen Kirwan, mayor.
Martin D'Arcey and James Oge D'Arcey, bailiffs.
"This year there came to Galway a gentlewoman called the lady Jacob, to look for her pedigree, she being repulsed in England. She had a good equipage, well attended, and much made of her. She was the daughter of one Ulick Lynch of Hampton in England, whither she returned with her genealogy". Galway, because it had submitted to the king's pleasure, as to the customs and poundage! his majesty did by letter of the 3rd March, 1606, order the lord deputy to renew their respective charters, with the addition of reasonable charters.
At this period there was a famous school, containing 1200 scholars, kept in Galway by Alexander Lynch.

1609 Oliver Browne, mayor.
Nicholas French and Domnick Browne, bailiffs.
This mayor, refusing to take the oath of supremacy, was deposed, and Thomas Browne elected in his place; he also refused to take the oath, was also deposed, and fined £100. and Ulick Lynch was elected for the remained of the year.

1610 Richard Bodkin, mayor.
Patrick Martin and Christopher Bodkin, sheriffs.
This year Geoffry French-Fitz-Domnick and Patrick French-Fitz-Robert were sent by the corporation to England, to renew their charter and get further

---

[1] Royal tax, or tax levied by a lord, [Clachan ed.].

privileges from his majesty, James I. which were granted to them, with an extension of their liberties for four miles east and west of the town; the corporation was made a county; and the high sheriff of the county had nothing to do with the town and liberties, and the king's sword was brought hither. The corporation at this time consisted of a mayor, two sheriffs, twelve aldermen, a recorder, and common council. Previous to this year the customs of Galway amounted only to £672. 17s. 6d.; for Dublin, £1890. 2s. 1d.; Limerick, £141 9s. 6d.; Carrickfergus, £399. 6s. 1d. But it seems this was only the custom of prohibited goods, and the three pence per pound for the other goods due by common law.

Aldermen first mentioned; before this period they were called *masters*, and sheriffs were called *bailiffs*.

1611 Val. Blake Fitz-Walter-Fitz-Thomas, mayor.
Andrew Lynch-Fitz-John and Thomas Blake, sheriffs.
This mayor was deposed for refusing to take the oath of supremacy, by Sir Oliver St John, in the presence of William O'Donnell, Archbishop of Tuam, (who had shortly before translated the New Testament and book of Common Prayer into Irish,) and his place was supplied by Richard Martin. He built a chapel in St Francis Abbey, on the south side of the choir, where he and his posterity were buried. This chapel was afterwards converted to a sacristy.
October 2nd, the Earl of Thomond, Sir Oliver St John, vice president of Connaught, Sir Thomas Rotheram, knt. governor of St Augustine's fort, and Roger O'Shaughnessy, esq. were elected freemen.
The company of young men got a charter from the mayor and corporation, constituting them a body politic of themselves, and empowering them to make bye laws for the well governing of the company, and their captain should sit next the sheriffs of the town at all public meetings, and should be an *esquire*[1] for that year, and the whole company exempted from the payment of any taxes; in consideration whereof they were bound to watch and ward[2].

1612 Sir Thomas Rotheram, mayor.
Marcus Lynch-Fitz-Christopher and Adam Faunt, sheriffs.
This year no person eligible to the office of mayor could be found in town, who would take the oath of supremacy; in consequence of which, Sir Thomas Rotheram, governor of St Augustine's fort, and privy counsellor of Connaught, was appointed. Many excellent ordinances were made in this and the former mayoralties.

1613 Walter Martin, mayor.
James Oge D'Arcey and George Martin, sheriffs.

1614 Nicholas D'Arcey, mayor.
James Oge D'Arcey and Francis Martin, sheriffs.

---

[1] Originally an Esquire was a rank above just "gentleman" and below "knight", [Clachan ed.].
[2] Service as a watchman or sentinel, [Clachan ed.].

Sir Valentine Blake, of Menlough, was returned to sit in parliament for the town of Galway, and for many years afterwards. — Note, in the list of baronets in the almanack, the date of the creation is 1622.

1615 Pierce Lynch-Fitz-Jonack, mayor.
Pierce Martin-Fitz-William and Jonack Lynch, Fitz-Pierce, sheriffs.
Peter French-Fitz-Valentine was elected mayor; but having refused the office was fined £100, and Pierce Lynch elected in his place, as no other would take the oath.—-This year upwards of 1200 tuns of Spanish wine was landed here for account of the merchants of Galway.

1616 Pierce Lynch-Fitz-Jonack, mayor.
John French and Emond Lynch, sheriffs.

1617 Francis Lynch-Fitz-Peter, mayor.
Thomas Lynch-Fitz-Pierce and James Semper, sheriffs.

1618 Nicholas Lynch-Fitz-George, mayor.
James Semper and Marcus Lynch-Fitz-George, sheriffs.
Sir Charles Coote, knight, Sir John Burke of Derrymaclaughney Castle, knight, John Bourke, of Downsandle, esquire, and John Jacob, of Galway, admitted freemen.
The work called the *new work* was began by consent of the merchants of Galway, intending to make a more commodious place there for trading; which walls they were bound to finish within a limited time. Forty families of Hollanders offered to execute the work for thirty-five thousand pounds, and undertook to finish the whole in fifteen years; yet nothing was done.

1619 James D'Arcy-Fitz-James, mayor.
Marcus French-fitz-Marcus and Peter Martin Fitz-Walter, sheriffs.
The town was burned on May day; it took fire on the east side of the town, occasioned by a shot from a musket, being a usual day for the sports of the youth of the town.

1620 Andrew Lynch-Fitz-John, mayor.
Marcus French and James Semper, sheriffs.

1621 Robert Martin, mayor.
Luke Rawson and Manus Cunnine, sheriffs.
This mayor died in office, and was succeeded by his father, Richard Martin, who had been mayor in 1607, and was also elected in 1611 to fill the place of Valentine Blake, who had been deposed for refusing to take the oath of supremacy.

1622 Patrick Martin-Fitz-Walter, mayor.
James Lynch, and Pierce Martin, sheriffs.

1623 Marcus Oge French-Fitz-Marcus, mayor.
James Lynch-Fitz-Arthur and Geoffrey French Fitz-Arthur, sheriffs.
Donell McRoebuck Bermingham, Edmond Burke of Kilcornan, and Walter Bourke of Turlogh, in the county of Mayo, and their heirs, were made freemen,

they paying *scot and lot*[1]. Lord Falkland took his circuit and came to Galway, where he knighted Sir Richard Blake-Fitz-Robert, and Sit Henry Lynch, baronets. He left as a legacy three hundred pounds towards building a college, and five hundred pounds towards the preferment of fatherless children of the natives of the town.

1624 Robert Blake-Fitz-Walter-Fitz-Thomas, mayor.
Geoffry French and John Blake, sheriffs.
Before this period the choice of the mayor was only in the aldermen and sheriffs of the town; the aldermen were those that had been mayors or in election to be such; and none were ad mitted to that dignity but Protestants, so that for thirty years before this, time all the mayors were obliged to swear that the king was head of the church. To avoid this, the corporation thought fit to give every freeman of the town a vote, and by this means Robert Blake was the first Catholic mayor that had been elected for upwards of thirty years.

1625 Thomas Lynch-Fitz-Nicholas-Fitz-Stephen-Fitz Arthur, mayor.
William Blake-Fitz-Christopher and Walter Browne-Fitz-Thomas, sheriffs.
This year the fort of Ballymanagh, at the foot of the bridge, was built also new leads to the gate, at the expence of the corporation. — Ordered in council, that any person who shall scandalize and unmannerly behave himself in speeches to the mayor, shall forfeit £20. Also, that no howling or shoutings be made in or out of the streets of this town at the burial of any deceased person; but that all such barbarous courses be given over, on pain of five shillings for each abuse; whereby all and every corpse here be carried to his grave in a civil orderly fashion, according to the form in all good places observed. — Note, it would be highly desirable if the present mayor would prevent the repetition of this national disgrace. D.

1626 James Lynch-Fitz-Martin-Fitz-William, mayor.
Jasper Martin-Fitz-Nicholas and Marcus Skerrett, sheriffs.
Murrough O'Flaherty, called O'Flaherty More, died this year at Bunowen Castle, in Connemara, and was interred in St. Francis' Abbey in Galway.

1627 Sir Richard Blake-Fitz-Robert-Fitz-Walter-Fitz-Andrew, knt., mayor.
Edmond Kirwan and Nicholas Blake, sheriffs.
This year king Charles I. granted to the mayor, for the time being, to be of his majesty's council for the government of the county of the town and the county at large; and likewise to join him with the governors of the said county in commission for the execution of martial law.

1628 John Lynch-Fitz-Richard, mayor.
Richard Lynch-Fitz-John and Stephen Martin, sheriffs.
May 17. For as much as the grace of God is the best revenue of this town, and his blessing our greatest rents; and that charitable distributions are, according to his divine promise, an hundred fold rewarded, both in this and the other world; it

---

[1] A municipal tax formerly levied in proportion to the ability to pay (from Old French *escot*, a payment, [Clachan ed.].

is ordained, that the collectors of the rents and revenues of this town shall, once every year, distribute £10. between the poor widows of the birth and blood of the town, in imitation of that good widow, commanded by our Saviour, who cast her two mites into the treasury; and in hope that the supplying the needful exigents of the poor may increase our comings in, and thereby enable us to do works tending to God's glory, and the good of the commonwealth. It was also enacted, that sturdy beggars and poor scholars be banished; and that such poor and needy men, born in the town, as shall be allowed to beg, shall have leaden tokens fastened to their caps, to distinguish them from others. And for as much as divers strangers, and some of the town, do keep blind ale-houses, which are the relievers of idlers and malefactors, who, by cheating, cozening, and villainy, do disturb the quiet and peace of the town, it is ordered that the several constables of the several quarters and franchises do, every quarter session, present the names of such, and of all other persons selling beer, ale, &c. that a certain number of select men may be named and licensed to do the same.

1629 Nicholas Lynch-Fitz-Jonakine, mayor.
Martin French and Alexander Bodkin, sheriffs.
Aldermen Marcus Blake had been chosen mayor, but died on the morning of the 29th September, before he entered into office; "it pleased God Almighty to call him out of this transitory life to the everlasting, and out of the chief chair of this town (whereof he was to take possession) unto a better and more glorious one in heaven".

1630 Sir Valentine Blake-Fitz-Walter-Fitz-Thomas, knight and baronet, mayor.
Francis Blake and Richard Kirwan, sheriffs.
It was stipulated that the mayor's salary should not exceed £12. sterling, "the same being the stipend all the old mayors had." And that the recorder should have but £10. per year, "which was all that our first recorder, Mr. Domnick Martin, and Sir Harry Lynch elected recorder after him, received." Since the mayoralty of Sir Thomas Rotheram in 1612, the mayor's salary amounted to £100. yearly. On the 1st of August, Oliver Martin was chosen mayor, and Andrew Brown Fitz-Oliver, and Edward French-Fitz-Patrick, sheriffs; but Sir Thomas Rotheram having on the 12th September following come into the tholsel and produced a letter from the privy council, ordering that the magistrates should take the oath of supremacy; the mayor and sheriffs elect, requested until the 27th for consideration, upon which they declined to take the oath, and the officers above mentioned were accordingly chosen. It was then ordered that the mayor should have the former stipend of £100. a year for his salary.

1631 Geoffry Martin, mayor.
Robert Kirwan and John French-Fitz-Stephen, sheriffs.
This Robert Kirwan left £10. per annum, to relieve the poor prisoners of Galway.

1632 George Martin-Fitz-Walter, mayor.
Pierce Martin-Fitz-Walter and Jonick Lynch-Fitz-Pierce, sheriffs.

1633 Patrick French-Fitz-George, mayor.

George French-Fitz-Patrick and Walter Blake-Fitz-Andrew, sheriffs.

1634 Sir Domnick Browne, knt. mayor.

Michael Lynch-Fitz-Stephen and Domnick Lynch-Fitz-John, sheriffs.

This year the street from the great gate to the cross was paved.

Thomas Wentworth, lord lieutenant of Ireland, came in great state to Galway, where he was honorably entertained in Sir Richard Blake's house, whom he much commended for his hospitality. He then knighted Sir Domnick Browne. In this reign, when Lord Wentworth was governor of Ireland, the sheriff and jurors of Galway shewed so independent a spirit in opposing his wishes to establish the king's right to some estates, that they were fined £4000. each, their estates seized, and themselves imprisoned until it was paid, which was the sentence passed in the Castle chamber, at the same time saying, "it was fit their pertinacious carriage should be followed with all just severity;" they were also to acknowledge their offence on their knees in open court

1635 Nicholas More-Lynch-Fitz-Marcus, mayor.

William Lynch-Fitz-Andrew and Christopher Bodkin-Fitz-Thomas, sheriffs.

Carte, in his life of Ormond[1], (upon what authority appears not,) says, that by the interposition of the Earl of Clanrickard in England, the fines of the sheriff and jury of Galway were afterwards reduced, the plantation laid aside, and the inhabitants confirmed in their estates, upon the like terms as the rest of the kingdom, without suffering the hardships, change of possessions, and other disagreeable circumstances which attended a plantation. This must be a misstatement, for the sheriff and jury were imprisoned, and on Lord Wentworth's making a report of his proceedings to the king in council in 1686, his majesty told him "that it was no severity, and that if he had served him otherwise, he should not serve him as he expected;" and it appears that they still continued in prison in 1637. It was in Lord Clanrickard's house that Wentworth held his court of inquisition; and the death of that lord, which happened soon after, inflamed the popular odium against the deputy.

It was imputed to the vexations conceived by this nobleman at the attempt against his property by an insolent governor, who possessed himself of the earl's house at Portumna, and in his hall held that court which impeached his title to his lands. It may not be amiss here to give the character of Lord Clanrickard from Carte, vol. I. p. 212, — "He was a man of great piety and strict virtue, regular in his devotion, exemplary in his life, and considerate in all his actions. His natural parts were very good, and much improved by study, observation, and reflection; but whatever were the accomplishments of his head, the perfections of his heart were still more eminent. In a word, he was truly wise, truly good, and truly honorable, and ought to be conveyed down to posterity as one of the most perfect and rarest patterns of integrity, loyalty, constancy, virtue and honor, that the age he lived in, or any other, has produced." — Note, how gratifying must

---

[1] The life of James, Duke of Ormond: containing an account of the most remarkable affairs of his time, and particularly of Ireland under his government (1753) by Thomas Carte, [Clachan ed.].

this eulogium be to his present noble and youthful descendant? I sincerely hope and trust it may have due influence on his future progress throughout that life which he is about to enter on, and of which his present actions give such a happy presage. D.

1636 Anthony Lynch-Fitz-James, mayor.
Geoffry Faunt and Domnick French, sheriffs.

1637 Sir Thomas Blake, bart. mayor.
Marcus Lynch-Fitz-William and James Lynch-Fitz-Stephen, sheriff 25th November Stephen Lynch-Fitz-Nicholas Fitz-Jonaken, recorder, died; he had continued in office since 1624.
The lords justices, Viscount Ely and Sir Christopher Wandesford, received orders to call upon corporations for a return of their pretended privileges; to issue money to finish the fort of Galway; to suspend the Lord Courcey's pension, and to quicken the admeasurement of lands in Connaught. This year the east town gate and the *horolege*, or hour clock, were built at the expence of the corporation.

1638 Sir Robuck Lynch, bart. mayor.
Thomas Lynch-Fitz-Ambrose and Peter Lynch-Fitz-Peter, sheriffs.

1639 John Bodkin-Fitz-Domnick, mayor.
John Kirwan and Francis Athy, sheriffs.
This year the market-house near the church yard was begun at the charge of the corporation.

1640 Francis Blake, mayor.
Geoffiy Blake and Martin Lynch, sheriffs;

1641 Walter Lynch-Fitz-James-Fitz-Ambrose, mayor.
John Martin-Fitz-Geoffry and Matthew Martin-Fitz-Nicholas, sheriffs.

1642 Richard Martin-Fitz-Stephen, mayor.
Domnick Skerrett-Fitz-Edmond and John Bermingham, sheriffs.

This mayor was such a favourite in Galway that he was chosen alderman and mayor in his absence; he refused the office, but was afterwards prevailed on to accept it. He bequeathed £800. to build a chapel in St Francis's abbey, and another in the church of St Nicholas. He left legacies to all the convents and abbeys in Connaught An order was made, declaring the right of precedency in station, and public meetings within the town of Galway; wherein nevertheless, it is meant and intended, that baronets and knights shall hold and enjoy the places and precedencies to them of right due; and that none shall challenge and enjoy any place but such as go in gowns, except the captain of the young men: 1. the mayor. 2. the recorder. 3. mayor of the staple. 4. aldermen who bore office by their seniority. 5. sheriffs for the time being. 6. captain of the young men. 7. lawyers that were recorders, with their gowns. 8. aldermen peers according to their seniority, in their gowns. 9. the coroner, in his gown. 10. the chamberlain and escheator[1], in their gowns. 11. lawyers and barristers, in their gowns, who did practise, according to their seniority. 12. constables of the

---

[1] Officer in charge of reversion of property to state. [Clachan ed.].

staple, or late sheriffs. 13. all other sheriffs that bore office, according to their anquity.[1] 14. the four captains of the four quarters. 15. burgesses, according to their seniority of house keeping. — The aldermen were usually chosen on the evening of the last day of July, at a meeting of the mayor, recorder, and such aldermen as had borne the office of mayor, commonly called "short council;" and one or two were chosen yearly, to supply the place of the new mayor, and such aldermen as might happen to die.

In June, some regiments were dispatched for Connaught by the lord lieutenant, who in that expedition took Knock-Lynch, lord Clanrickard's estate, a strong castle of Mr. Lynches. The besieged, except women, not accepting quarter, were put to the sword. Sergeant Redmond Burke of Lord Clanmorris's foot company, and two more, were hanged by the governor of the fort of Galway, the said lord being then of his majesty's army; for which action, no reparation being made to his lordship, he alleged it to be the occasion of his revolt from the lord marquis of Clanrickard. A party of the garrison of the fort murdered six people in Renville, amongst whom one Geoffry Fitz-Thebot, aged about 170 years, and in a burning fever, with his wife, who was also very old, were murdered in their beds, which action provoked many of the neighbours to stand on their guard against the fort. At this time two protestants were murdered in the county of Galway, whereof one was a minister; and it is certain that the marquis of Clanrickard caused the three men who murdered one of them to be hanged in gibbets in three several places; and by his lordship's order. Sir Roger O'Shaughnessy hanged the two cow herds who murdered the other. Lord Clanmorris having declared against the said fort for hanging his sergeant as before expressed, took sergeant Rowbright and two or three more of the soldiers of said fort, pillaging a village near Galway, and hanged Rowbright and the soldiers. — The 13th of February the inhuman massacre at Shruel was committed on the English soldiers, by the Burkes of Mayo. Until this period the Irish had always a school for poetry *alone*, and it seems it was in one of those that Dr. Keatinge learned most of his real and fabulous Irish history: it seems before his death, from a conviction of their falsity, he wished to have recalled the few copies that had escaped into the world, and requested they might never be translated into any other language[2]. Though there are many authorities in Keatinge, yet the multitude of fables with which they are intermixed has brought the whole, in the minds of those who are disposed to doubt the great antiquity of our country, into disrepute. It is astonishing with what a ridiculous pertinacity schoolmasters uphold those fables.

---

[1] An obsolete term for an old person, [Clachan ed.].
[2] Seathrún Céitinn, known in English as Geoffrey Keating, was a 17th-century Irish Roman Catholic priest, poet and historian. His major work, *Foras Feasa ar Éirinn* (literally "Foundation of Knowledge on Ireland", more usually translated "History of Ireland") was written in Early Modern Irish and completed ca. 1634.

In April, Galway submitted to the earl of Clanrickard, who was governor of the county, and was by him taken into protection until the pleasure of his majesty (then expected over) should be known; but the lords justices did not approve of that protection, unless the town would admit an English garrison. However, Clanrickard made use of that opportunity to relieve the fort of Galway, where the archbishop of Tuam and thirty-six ministers, and many more English, were in very great distress. The August following lord Forbes came into the bay of Galway, landed some guns, and seized on the abbey, and being joined by the lord president the earl of Clanrickard, they pretended to besiege the town; but they wanted necessaries, and therefore the lord Forbes compounded with the town for a sum of money, which was never paid, and drew off from the siege, and proceeded up the Shannon.

1643 Sir Valentine Blake, junior, knight and baronet, mayor.
Oliver French and John Kirwan, sheriffs.
This year the Catholics celebrated Mass in the church of St Nicholas, and continued in possession of it until 1652, when it was possessed by the Parliamentarians.
In August, the fort of Galway was surrendered to the Irish; whereupon the rebels marched to the siege of Castlecoote, to which the town of Galway subscribed £300.

1644 James D'Arcey Fitz-Nicholas, mayor.
Domnick D'Arcey and Robert Martin-Fitz Jasper, sheriffs.

1645 Edmond Kirwan Fitz-Patrick, mayor.
Domnick Browne-Fitz-Nicholas and Martin Kirwan-Fitz-Andrew, sheriffs.
This mayor was accounted a rich man, and left £800. to the Jesuits to build a college. A little before he died he was completely exhausted by the excessive contributions, and drawn in a cart to Loughrea for the same, being unable to hold out. This year the strong bulwark about Shoemakers' tower was built, but not altogether finished in his time. The 27th of April a warrant was issued to make Henry lord viscount and Thomas lord viscount Dillon and the survivor of them, lord president of the province of Connaught, except the county and town of Galway, the government whereof, with 10s. per day, were granted to the lord Clanrickard.

1646 John Blake-Fitz-Nicholas, mayor.
Domnick Blake-Fitz-Robert and Nicholas Bodkin-Fitz-David, sheriffs.
The tholsel began to be built, but was re-built in Queen Anne's reign. Upon the taking of Athlone, the Pope's Nuncio went to Galway, which town had agreed to a cessation, and therefore all divine offices were interdicted, and the churches were shut, and the very ensigns of authority were forced from the mayor's house; but that insolence caused such a tumult, that if those badges of office had not been immediately returned to the mayor by the same hand that took them, it certainly had come to blows and blood in the very streets; as it was, two or three men were slain in the scuffle, when the archbishop of Tuam caused the church doors to be opened by force. The Nuncio also summoned a national synod to sit

in Galway on the 15th of August; whereupon the supreme council sent him a letter, shewing the inconvenience of that congress; but it had no effect on him, for, as he was used to do, he persisted obstinately in his own sentiments.

1647 Walter Brown, mayor.
Domnick Martin-Fitz-Thomas and Peter Browne-Fitz-James, sheriffs.
At a general assembly of confederate Catholics held at Kilkenny the 10th January 1647, we find the following names for the county of Galway:

John Bermingham,	Galway,
Francis Blake,	ditto.
Domnick Bodkin,	ditto.
Edward Browne,	ditto.
Jeffry Browne,	ditto.
John Burke,	Castle Carre.
Theobald Burke,	Buolly Burke.
Ulick Burke,	Glynsk.
Patrick D'Arcey,	Galway.
Christopher French,	ditto,
James French,	ditto.
Martin Lynch,	ditto.
Nicholas Lynch,	ditto.
Roebuck Lynch,	ditto.
Anthony Martin,	ditto.
Dermod O'Shaughnessy,	Gort

In the month of August, the Marquis of Clanrickard, assisted by the forces of the province, and some English and Irish sent to him out of Munster by the Lord Inchequin, blocked up the town for the space of twelve or fifteen days; but being paid £2000. raised his camp.

1648 Sir Walter Blake, knight, mayor.
Martin Blake-Fitz-Andrew and James Blake-Fitz-Nicholas, sheriffs.
Sir Walter Blake was knighted by the Marquis of Ormond, Lord Lieutenant of Ireland, for his Majesty King Charles I. who notwithstanding the great power of the parliament party, and the several ordinances made by them, and published against his Majesty's succession and right to the crown, was joyfully proclaimed as usual with his predecessors within this town, King of England, France, Ireland, &c. This year the flanker about *the work* was built, and the new flanker adjoining to Lyons' tower, together with the wall and ramparts. "it may be well supposed that these three ensuing things brought no good success to the town; but rather ambition, discord, and discredit, viz. knights, lawyers and *bomery masters*. The knights brought pride; the lawyers intricacy and licentiousness, where all matters formerly were tried and determined by two honest burgesses or friends. The bomery masters [?] brought discredit in the highest degree. In old times they would rather hang themselves than break and discontent strangers, which is now made a common trade, to the great dishonour of the good and famous report evermore held of the said town. Now, the town is infested with

pride, none being accounted worthy of good marriage or portion, however so well bred or educated except he had a stone house or good estate. Likewise in the said town the sin of lechery abounded". — Note, I have given this curious article verbatim. D.

Ordered, that lieutenant colonel O'Shaughnessy (in consideration of his alliance in blood to *the whole town*, and for the good nature and affection that he and his whole family do bear to it) shall be hereafter freemen of this corporation. — Note, this very ancient family possessed the greater part of the present property of Lord Gort, who has derived it from Sir Thomas Prendergast, the son of the patentee.

1649 Thomas Lynch Fitz-Marcus-Fitz-Martin, mayor.
Stephen Lynch-Fitz-Nicholas and Anthony Lynch-Fitz-John, sheriffs.
This mayor left £280. to the Dominicans, to keep two of his own kindred of the same order in Paris to study. He was appointed a judge in Connaught in the mayoralty of Sir Oliver French— This year a grant was passed by the corporation to the nuns of St Clara, of island Altanagh, to build a convent.

1650 Sir Oliver French, knight, mayor.
James French-Fitz-Edmond and Peter Lynch-Fitz-Anthony, sheriffs.
Charles I. wrote a letter, dated 4th of February, expressing his approbation of the loyalty of the town of Galway.
The plague raged in Galway from the first of July until the following spring; many thousands lost their lives, and for a long time the town was almost deserted by the inhabitants. The citizens met in the country and voted 200 marks to pay physicians and other persons, to purify and clear the town. They exerted themselves so well, that it was completely eradicated.

1651 Richard Kirwan Fitz-Thomas, mayor.
Thomas Lynch-Fitz-Patrick and Arthur Lynch-Fitz-Stephen, sheriffs.

This year, in the month of May, Sir Charles Coote was made commander in the province of Connaught, after the rest of Ireland was reduced; he also possessed himself of Athlone, Sligo, Loughrea, and other strongholds in this province. The parliament forces having forced a passage over the river Shannon, he besieged the town of Galway on the east, and having taken Terrylan, Oranmore, and Clare castles, he pitched his camp between Loughathalia and Suckine, about the 12th of August, and there continued still, notwithstanding many sallies and interruptions from the town, until the 12th of April following, and then the town, despairing of any relief by sea or land, and much impoverished and exhausted in paying four hundred pounds per week to soldiers, and making various works, surrendered itself up on very good and honorable terms; so, without committing any act of disloyalty, they became subjects to the parliament of England in April 1652. Upon the surrender, there was a dearth in the country, by means whereof many thousands died; and by a second plague that came upon the town and country, God's severity punished their ill doings with death, plague and the sword, and many that lived had no means to support themselves. Colonel Peter Stubbers, governor of Galway, upon the information that multitudes of vagabonds and idle men were in the county, obliged and ordered them to be shipped to Barbadoes; whereupon there was such a general press and taking up of the people, that many a house-keeper going into the fields to see their cattle, or from one field to another, were pressed and sent on board, and all others that were not entered in the contribution book were also sent; so that there were 800 persons sent to the island of Carabia, (I suppose Barbadoes) and there sold as slaves, or as Turks would use them, which brought such a general scarcity of servants, that scarcely any could be had for love or money, and were come to that height that they rather became masters than servants, which was a great addition to their former miseries; for instance, a plough man's wages, besides meat and drink, being £4. 13s. he being but an ordinary servant; 30s. to an ordinary maid servant; so, as the commons of England bearing and holding the government, so likewise the servants and commons of Ireland did rule and bear sway over their superiors, lords and masters. The second plague or pestilence abovementioned began in June, and continued for two years, wherof a great many of the natives and freemen died. The old natives in general being much impoverished by the in supportable contributions laid upon them, and were so tired of their lives, that they did not shun the infection, but submitted to its vehemency, and withal not knowing where to go from it, the country being totally ruined and wasted. This year the east and west citadels were built at the cost of the state, or rather of the country. In September Captain Bond, being governor of Arran, was set upon by the Irish under the command of Murtogh O'Brien, who took the island.

New troubles were also raised in Iarconnaught, which occasioned great ruin. The marquis of Clanrickard issued an order that Sir Robert Lynch and 200 musqueteers, with three pieces of ordnance and ammunition, should be sent to the island of Arran. The duke of Lorrain offered to lend £10,000. for king Charles the second's use, on a mortgage of any town or fort that was considerable; whereupon the lords Taaffe and Athenry, and Jeffry Browne, were appointed to treat with him, and proposed to mortgage Galway for that sum; but at length it was found a juggle on Colonel Sinnot's part, who was agent for the duke of Lorrain.

Commissioners of trust appointed by the marquis of Ormond were desired to treat with the committee of congregation of Galway, and made several proposals to them, which they rejected.

The marquis complained, amongst other things, that the corporation of Galway did, last summer, unwarrantably assume to itself the power of judicature in maritime affairs; and that the mayor for that time being (with what assistance we know not) adjudged and accordingly disposed of a ship and her lading as a prize, notwithstanding our inhibition to him at that time, as the like power had never been assumed before, but all prizes were adjudged by commission from the supreme council of the confederate catholics. They also refused to admit their governor, the marquis of Clanrickard, and a garrison. They likewise published an excommunication and declaration against any one that should obey or adhere to his majesty's government; and that the mayor and aldermen, with a multitude of others of the said corporation, were present, countenancing and abetting the said traitorous excommunication. Also, that the captain of the guard of the town, commonly called Captain of the young men, made search for the marquis, thereby endeavouring to bring contempt on him and his majesty's authority. — Note, queen Elizabeth's charter constituted the mayor of Galway admiral of the bay and liberties of Galway.

D.

1652   Michael Lynch-Fitz-Stephen -Fitz-Nicholas, mayor.
Alexander Lynch-Fitz-Andrew and William Martin-Fitz-Stephen, sheriffs.

On the 12th of May Galway surrendered to Sir Charles Coote, and it was at that time considered so very strong, that the loss of it carried with it the fate of Ireland, and was the determination of the rebellion. On the 15th May Lord Viscount Mayo was shot to death in Galway for the murders at Shruel in 1641. The account of this deliberate act of treachery is as follows: upon the surrender of Castlebar, it was agreed that the English should march away with their arms, and be safely conveyed to Galway; and though they were deprived of their arms contrary to the articles, yet the Lord Mayo and his son, Tibbot Burke, with their followers, conveyed them safely to Ballynacarrow, and the next day to Ballinrobe, and the third day to the Neale, where they left Sir Henry Bingham on pretence of his being sick, but as was suspected to preserve him from the subsequent massacre. The fourth day they came to Kinlough, and the next day to Shrule, (which it seems was two miles out of the road to Galway,) where they lodged that night; and on the next morning, the 13th February, 1641, an ambush was laid on the other side of the bridge, which, as soon as the English get over the bridge, fell upon them, and by the help of the convoy murdered about eighty of them[1]; the protestant Bishop of Killaloe, and a few others, only escaping. It was proved by four witnesses that the prisoner, Sir Tibbot Burke, was present at the massacre, and did not oppose it; that the convoy were the murderers; that the Lord Mayo's fosterers, servants, and followers, were of that number. It was also proved that the Lord Mayo engaged by a capitulation to convey the English safe to Galway; that they were disarmed by his command, and some of them were stripped and plundered on the way by the convoy; that the convoy *pricked forward* the English over the bridge, towards the murderers. The old Mayo went to a little hill hard by to look on; and that the prisoner, Sir Tibbot Burke, was seen to come over the bridge from the murderer, after several Englishmen had been killed, and had been actually amongst them with his sword drawn. In his defence he said he had no command of the party, but with two servants only came to attend his father; that on the contrary he went over the bridge, and drew his sword, with design to preserve the English; that being shot at by one of the murderers, he got an horse, having lent his own to the bishop of Killaloe to make his escape, and rode away

---

[1] The scene of this horrid act of treachery is at present the estate of Mr. Kirwan of Dalgin, to whom Shruel belongs, [original footnote].

before the murder was committed, and if he had not fled, he had been killed himself; &c. &c. But this defence, whether false, or from the temper of the times, had no effect, and he was executed on the 15th June, 1662. This year the island of Bofin surrendered, and Arran was restrained.

O'Connor, Sligo, and many others of quality were hanged at Boyle and Galway for several murders in the beginning of the wars. There were 2,500 soldiers sent to Spain and France, and the great dearth continued, together with the contribution; so that a full third of the people of the province died of the plague, and their goods, even their household stuff and body clothes, were canted, and sold for very considerable sums, being taken for the contribution.

Richard Burke, a colonel in his majesty's service, had quarters given him by some of Colonel Coote's men; he being taken in a skirmish between Colonel Grace and some of Cromwell's party, and being a prisoner for some time, Colonel Henry Ingoldsby ordered his head to be cut off. It was a usual practice at this time with Colonel Stubber, then governor of Galway, and others commanding in said county, to take people out of their beds at night, and sell them for slaves to the West Indies; and by computation he sold out of this county above 1000 souls.

1653   Arthur Lynch-Fitz-Anthony, mayor.
       Nicholas French and Arthur Lynch, sheriffs.
       "Shortly before this period, Colonel Richard Grace, of Moyelly Castle, in the King's county, (one of the bravest officers of his time, and also one of the most steadfast adherents of the ungrateful Steuart family,) while defending an important pass in the neighbourhood of Galway, at the head of 3000 men, was defeated in a sanguinary engagement by Colonel Ingoldsby. This defeat was followed by the speedy reduction of the entire province."
1654   Thomas Lynch-Fitz-Ambrose, mayor.
       Richard Lynch and Anthony French-Fitz-Peter, sheriffs.

On a petition of the English protestant inhabitants of the town, on the 29th September, it ordered by the lord deputy and council, on the 25th October, that the mayor and chief officers, as set forth in the charter, should be English, and protestants; whereupon Colonel Peter Stubbers was elected mayor, and Paul Dodd and Marcus Lynch-Fitz-Thomas[1] were elected sheriffs. The old corporation were disfranchised, and the English soldiers made free, and also coblers, butchers, bakers, tinkers, and all sorts of mechanics. The pressing of people for Barbadoes continued. The unruly crew of soldiers garrisoned in the town under the command of Colonel Stubbers, broke down the monuments and coffins of the interred, and taking from them their winding sheets, expecting treasure in the coffins. They also took down the

---

[1] "This individual, according to tradition, was the only native of Galway who changed his principles and religion, and joined the common enemy of both; in consequence of which, all communication was denied him by his friends during his life, and he is said to have died of a broken heart, occasioned by remorse and shame for his apostacy."--Hardiman's History of Galway, [original footnote].

crucifixes and such spiritual and costly work, engraved in fine marble, both in the church and in the abbey. Amongst the rest Sir Peter Frenche's tomb, or monument, gilded with gold! and carved in fine marble, which stood in the Abbey, and cost in the building thereof £5000 (in 1653!) by Lady Mary Brown, a virtuous woman, wife to the said Sir Peter French, and which monument was converted by the governor of the town into a chimney piece, and the rest of the stones sent beyond seas, and there sold for money by the governor, and the said tomb left open for dogs to drag and eat the dead corpse there interred. They likewise razed down the king's arms, and converted the churches and abbeys to stables, and divine books were broken up, and put under goods, wares, tobacco, &c. &c. they being for the most part illiterate and covetous to hoard money, to the great ruin of the poor inhabitants, without regard to conscience or observance of public faith; the sword being then in lieu of the law. In June, Charles Fleetwood, lord deputy of Ireland, took his circuit and came to Galway, where he gave a definite sentence for removal of the old inhabitants of Galway; which order was immediately sent from Dublin and executed, contrary to their conditions and articles. One Hurd, deputy governor of Galway, and Colonel Stubbers, issued an order to prohibit the wearing of the mantle, which he enforced (as was usual with Cromwell's officers) with such severity, that it came to be every where laid aside, and they cut a laughable figure, who having nothing but the mantle to cover their upper parts, ran half naked about the town, shrouded in table cloths, pieces of tapestry and rags of all colours and forms, so that they looked as if they had escaped from bedlam. On the 24th December, a general assembly of the kingdom met at Loughrea; they declared their obedience to his majesty's authority, and to that of the marquis of Clanrickard, or any other chief governor of the kingdom, duly appointed by his majesty, but not to any governor whilst under the influence of the presbyterian party, and whose prisoner he then was.

At this time the town of Galway was divided between twenty-four of Cromwell's officers, but much of it was afterwards purchased back by the former proprietors. Some of the descendants of those officers still have very considerable property in the town; amongst others, that of Whaley, who possesses, or did lately possess the Claddagh, inhabited by fishermen. Also, the families of Eyre, Boyce, Stubber, Atkinson, Cottingham, Lawrence, &c. &c. One of the family of Whaley was recorder in 1664 and afterwards. Of those of Eyre, many were mayors and recorders in the reign of Charles the second, William and Mary, and George the second; and the family at this time have large possessions in the town and county, exclusive of large estates in other parts of Ireland. The earl of Uxbridge has an estate in a house in lower Abbeygate street, nearly opposite to the new chapel; he obtained it in right of Sir Nicholas Bayley, his mother's ancestor, and which he got as a debenture from Cromwell. Thomas Deane, a shop-keeper of Galway, (and one of the tribes too!) was the only person who had power to sell tobacco and snuff in Galway, which he obtained from Colonel Stubber, Cromwell's governor of Galway, who was also a partner in the monopoly. He was enabled to purchase the estate of Ballyrubbuck, near Creggan. He was the great grandfather of the late John Skerrett, of Ballinduff, near Headford. He paid Colonel Stubber a large bribe for this monopoly. — Note, it is probable that about this period the name of tribes was given to the families whom I have mentioned before.

1655 Colonel Humphry Hurd, mayor.
John Campbell and John Mathews, sheriffs.
The mayor was a joiner, and Mathews a weaver.
This year the archbishop of Tuam, the bishop of Killaloe, and many more of the clergy, were banished, and sent over seas. A court of claims was erected in Athlone to try the qualifications of the Irish. On the 18th October Colonel Richard Lawrence and Thomas Richardson, esq. were deputed to value the castles and houses.
Their appointment was renewed on the 30th, and they were directed to survey and appraise the houses in Galway; and all the proprietors that desired it, under their hands, were to have liberty until the 10th November, 1656, to make sale of their interests to any protestant that had not been in arms or otherwise disaffected: the third part of the purchase money to go to the commonwealth. Such houses as should not be sold by the proprietors before the 14th of December, 1655, to be disposed of for a year's time by the governor, to any protestant not having been in arms against the commonwealth; provided that the governor "do engage such as shall take the same, that no waste or spoil should be committed on the houses that stand empty and undisposed of, or suffer the same to be despoiled or wasted by the soldiers."

1656 Paul Dodd, mayor.
John Peters and Mathew Forth, sheriffs.
This year the transplantation went forward, and lands accordingly assigned to the Irish in Connaught and the county of Clare, the commissioners sitting at Loughrea, which was carried on with such partiality, that such as had but coarse land, or no land at all, were best served, and others that had great estates were postponed, and for the most part had no lands at all. Those that had most money and the best friends in court carried the gain, and the poor Irish being utterly beggared, attending them to no purpose, sold their decrees to the English at a crown an acre, who had lands assigned to them of that value, by which means and other courses, and by debts bought of the soldiers, the English vested themselves of most part of the country.
"The town of Galway for the most part fell to decay, so that at this time you might see whole streets not having six families in them. The soldiers and butchers, that would before content themselves with cellars and cottages, had now houses to live in, until they burned all the costly lofts and wainscots and partitions, and then would remove to other houses, until they almost destroyed all the fine houses, and left them so full of excrements and filth, that it was poisoning to enter one of them, though formerly fit to lodge kings and princess being the best fitted town in the kingdom, and the inhabitants thereof the most gallant merchants in Ireland, for their hospitality, liberality, and charity at home and abroad, and accompanied with good education.

In the midst of frost and snow, after being turned out, they were forced to shelter themselves by hedges, and poor miserable smokey huts, and brakes in the country, being all removed but six families, who were forced to quarter the most part of the garrison soldiers, and pay excessive bribes, and at last were all turned out, with the best of the catholic clergy, about fifty in number, and committed to Arran and Bofin islands, where they were almost starved to death, being allowed but two pence a day, and that at last not paid, and a strict proclamation against the lives and goods of such as would entertain any clergy man. Images of our blessed lady and other saints burned, and the chalices made common drinking cups, and priests vestments turned into secular clothes."

1657 Gabriel King, mayor.

Jervis Hinde and Thomas Hervest, sheriffs.

The north Abbey of Galway, belonging to the order of St. Francis, was demolished. It was built by Sir William Burke, as before mentioned. This year the prince of Burrin died.

1658 Sir Charles Coote, mayor.

John May and Richard Ormsby, sheriffs.

Sir Charles was Lord President of Connaught. He persecuted the catholic inhabitants of Galway, and so heavily taxed them, that most of them were obliged to quit the town.

This year the usurper, Oliver Cromwell, died.

Also Ulick Burke, Earl of Clanrickard. It may not be amiss to give, from Borlase[1], this noble man's character; who had been in such busy scenes: "He was not a man of shining abilities; but of great humanity, courtesy, and generosity; strongly attached to his friends, a true lover of his country; above all sordid views or motives of private interest; he adhered to the crown from principal, and had a particular affection for the king's person; the English resorted to him with as much security, and by him indeed were relieved with great hospitality, to an incredible charge to his own purse; hanging many, though of his own kindred, whom he found imbrued in blood[2], greatly resenting the barbarity and in humanity of the Irish, inasmuch as Hubert Boy Burke and Sir Ulick Burke, his near relations, preying on the English, he often frustrated by discovering their designs, and furnishing Sir Charles Coote from time to time with supplies of arms to oppose them.[3]

The Earl of Clanrickard mortgaged Galway and Limerick to the Duke of Lorrain. The recorder and principal inhabitants made over to him the protectorship of Galway as long as his disbursements remained unpaid, but this was so warmly opposed by the Lord Clanrickard, that an end was put to the negotiation, and the Duke of Lorrain lost £26,000. that he had advanced.

1659 John Mathews, mayor.

---

[1] Possibly Borlase's 'History of the Irish Rebellion' (1643), [Clachan ed.].
[2] It seems by this that he possessed the power of life and death. H. D., [original footnote].
[3] Not clear in original where quotation ends, [Clachan ed.].

Richard Bernard and William Speed, sheriffs.

This year Sir Charles Coote and the Protestants seized all the garrisons in Ireland, and amongst the rest Galway, and took and committed all the Anabaptists, who were then and before in the height of their power, and were chief commanders in Ireland.

1660 John Morgan, mayor.

George Scanderbeg Bushell and John Pope, sheriffs.

A palace was erected by the citizens of Galway for the reception of Charles II. Who purposed paying them a visit. It was, when entire, the largest structure in Ireland under one roof: it extended from the corner of Shop-street opposite to Lyche's castle, generally called the upper four corners, to the house where the amicable society meet. It must be evident that it was constructed of some materials easily put together, and as easily removed, as it was merely to answer a particular purpose. A visit from the king would have been only a just return for the many miseries they endured from Cromwell's officers and soldiers.

1661 John Eyre, mayor.

John Murry and Robert Brock, sheriffs.

1662 Henry Greenway, mayor.

Benjamin Veil and Walter Bird, sheriffs.

1663 Edward Eyre, mayor.

Richard Walcott and John Barrett, sheriffs.

1664 John Morgan, mayor.

William Fleming and Thomas Semper, sheriffs.

1665 Colonel John Spencer, mayor.

Robert Warner and George Younghusband, sheriffs.

1666 John Spencer, mayor.

George Davidson and William Jackson, sheriffs.

1667 John Spencer, mayor.

Christopher Sirr and James Berry, sheriffs.

1668 John Spencer, mayor.

Richard Barnard and John Pill, sheriffs.

John Spencer had been chosen mayor on his journey to England, but John Peters was sworn into office.

1669 John Peters, mayor.

William Hardiman and Robert Mathews, sheriffs.

1670 John May, mayor.

Robert Warner and Abraham Cowell, sheriffs

1671 Richard Ormsby, mayor.

John Geary and John Vaughan, sheriffs.

27th March, proclamation was made that the old inhabitants be restored to their freedom.

1672 Gregory Constable, mayor.

Thomas Andrews and William Hill, sheriffs.

They were appointed by the lord lieutenant and council.

1673 Gregory Constable, mayor.
Thomas Revett and Thomas Cartwright, sheriffs.
Twelve aldermen were added, making in all twenty-four; also as many burgesses added as made them twenty-four, of which the common council were to consist. This was done to bring in money, of which they were in great want.
At this time the whole body of the gentry of the county of Galway offered to surrender their estates to the army, and for that purpose sent a letter of attorney to the earl of Clanrickard, then in London, signed by 125 persons of the best quality in the county: at the same time the sheriff and other persons who were still in prison for acting uprightly, instead of seeking redress, petitioned, but in vain for pardon, offering to acknowledge the deputy's justice and their own errors of judgment, upon conditions only that they and the rest might be put upon the same footing with the other planted counties; for in these cases the general rule was, that a fourth part of their land should be taken from the natives, with an increase of rent upon the remainder; but the county of Galway, on account of its former refractoriness, was planted at a double rate, so that they lost half.

1674 Colonel Theodore Russell, mayor.
Thomas Buck and Marcus Harrington, sheriffs.

1675 Colonel Theodore Russell, mayor.
John Flower and Richard Poole, sheriffs.

1676 Colonel Theodore Russell, mayor.
John Clarke and Richard Browne, sheriffs.

1677 Colonel Theodore Russell, mayor.
John Clarke and Richard Browne, sheriffs.
The corporation received a new charter from Colonel Russell, who made a bargain with Madam Hamilton for the grant she had from his Majesty Charles II. For the part of the revenues and town lands mortgaged by the natives in the year 1647, to several forfeiting persons, by which it was vested in the king, and so granted as aforesaid.

1678 Colonel Theodore Russell, mayor.
Thomas Staunton and John Amory, sheriffs.
A proclamation was issued, forbidding the papists from coming into the castle of Dublin, or any other fort or citadel, and ordering the markets of Drogheda, Wexford, Cork, Limerick, Waterford and Galway, to be kept without the walls; and not long afterwards the lord lieutenant and council, by their letter, ordered the popish inhabitants to be removed from Galway, Limerick, &c. except some few trading merchants, artificers, and others necessary for the said towns and garrisons, and by virtue thereof many were expelled, but by the stupidity of the Protestants, at their request and upon their security, the papists were readmitted into those towns. — When lord Wentworth, in the reign of king Charles I. attempted to destroy the titles to estates in Connaught, and throw them into the hands of the king, he fined the jury of Galway £4000. each, because they would

not submit to his arbitrary measures. At this time he ransacked and destroyed old records of state and memorials of ancient monasteries.

1679 Colonel Theodore Russell, mayor.
Thomas Staunton and John Amory, sheriffs.

1680 Colonel Theodore Russell, mayor.
Thomas Simcocks and Samuel Cambie, sheriffs.
The corporation petitioned the lord lieutenant and council that the assizes should be held in the town of Galway; also that notice be forthwith given to all persons that are not free of the corporation, that they do not presume to trade by retail within the town, either in shops or houses, or their goods shall be seised and sold.
Alderman Mathews, for abuse given to colonel Russell, the mayor, was suspended from council; and it was ordered, that such persons as have borne offices in the corporation (masters of companies excepted) shall, every Sunday in the forenoon, attend the king's sword to church in their gowns; every person neglecting, to pay half a cob[1] each time; and upon refusal be expelled the council; and that no person presume to sit in the mayor's first seat without his gown.

1681 Colonel Theodore Russell, mayor.
Thomas Simcocks and Samuel Cambie, sheriffs,

1682 Colonel Theodore Russell, mayor.
Marcus Lynch and William Hoskins, sheriffs.

1683 Colonel Theodore Russell, mayor.
William Hoskins and Thomas Yeaden, sheriffs.
That any of the council who shall depart without taking leave from Mr. Mayor, shall forfeit a cobb.

1684 Colonel Theodore Russell, mayor.
Thomas Yeaden and Thomas Wilson, sheriffs.
The steeple was raised, and two bells hung.

1685 Colonel Theodore Russell, mayor.
Thomas Wilson and Richard Wall, sheriffs.
Ordered, that no cattle be hereafter slaughtered within this town, nor suffered to come into it; that no milch cows be permitted in it; and that 2s. 6d. fine be imposed on any one throwing garbage into the river. Every inhabitant was ordered to pave before his door, in such manner as the mayor and sheriffs shall direct.

1686 John Kirwan Fitz-Stephen, mayor.
George Staunton and Jonathan Parry, sheriffs.
He was the first Catholic mayor, after a lapse of thirty-two years, and was the first proprietor of Castle Hackett, which originally belonged to the Hacketts, who were driven to the county of Mayo in 1641.

---

[1] A coin which as not been struck, often associated with Spanish currency from the New World, [Clachan ed.].

In this reign Sir Thomas Southwell and lord Kingston were taken by the opposite party, and sent prisoners to Galway, where they were brought to trial by judge Martin, who persuaded them to plead guilty, assuring them of the king's mercy, who had just landed. The judge after having prevailed on them to confess themselves guilty, passed sentence of death upon them: after which they were closely imprisoned, and removed from gaol to gaol until the victory obtained by king William many months after. In that time they were once summoned by lord Clanrickard to prepare for execution (although he had no orders for it), and the sheriff appeared with all the necessary preparation for the same on the day appointed; this the earl did by way of jest, giving them no other reason for putting them into this terrible fright, but that they were hereticks.

1687 John Kirwan Fitz-Stephen, mayor.
James Browne Fitz-Gregory and Marcus Kirwan Fitz-Domnick, sheriffs.

1688 Domnick Browne of Carra Browne, mayor.
Francis Blake Fitz-Andrew and Domnick Bodkin Fitz-Patrick, sheriffs.
Galway received a new charter from king James II. The quay and new pier were erected and repaired at the charge of the corporation.
The church of St Nicholas was again possessed by the Catholics, and Father Henry Browne chosen warden.
In the summer of this year vast numbers of beetles destroyed the country between Galway and Headford.

1689 Domnick Browne, mayor.
Francis Blake Fitz-Andrew and Domnick Bodkin Fitz-Patrick, sheriffs.

1690 Colonel Alexander Mac Donal, mayor, until the 9th of December, when Arthur French was appointed mayor.
William Clear and Oliver French, sheriffs.

A few days after the battle of Aghrim, general Ginkle led his troops to Galway, which it was necessary to reduce, before Limerick should be attempted. The garrison of Galway consisted of seven weak regiments, but they expected to be considerably reinforced. D'Ussona, a French officer of distinction, then in the town, assured them of succours from his master the king of France. An Irish partisan, known by the name of Balderoy O'Donnel, promised to march to their relief at the head of 6 or 7000 northern rovers, and some assistance was expected from the garrison of Limerick. With such hopes lord Dillon returned a defiance to the summons of Gingle, and declared that he, D'Ussona, and all his officers, were unanimous in their resolution to defend the town. But after a resistance of a few days, it was found that the attempt made to throw some troops into the town from Limerick, was frustrated by the vigilance and bravery of the besiegers. That O'Donnel's followers, alarmed at the defeat at Aghrim, had deserted him with the usual instability of the old Irish; and that he, with the remains of his wild troops, amounting to 600, were preparing to make terms with the English government.

The townsmen and magistracy declared warmly for surrendering, and though they were at first imprisoned for their presumption, yet the garrison quickly adopted the same sentiments.

The Irish had been busily employed in finishing a fort at the south end of the town, which commanded a great part of the wall on that side.

A detachment crossed the river, and conducted by a deserter, surprised and seized on the fort[1]. The governor parlied, a cessation was granted, and a treaty of capitulation commenced. Talmash, and other officers, elevated by success, were utterly averse to granting any terms; but Ginkle wisely considered that the season for acting was gradually wasting; that the Irish war was a grievous embarrassment to the continental interests of the king, and a dangerous encouragement to the disaffected in England. To prevent another year of bloodshed in a country already wasted by distress, to extricate the king at once from difficulties at once grievous and dangerous, he resolved to grant, at once, such conditions to Galway, as might convince the whole Irish party of the infatuation of their perseverance in a desperate cause, and dispose them to an immediate submission. The garrison was allowed to marsh out with all the honors of war, and to be conveyed to Limerick, with liberty to those who desired it, to continue in the town, or repair to their respective habitations. A free pardon was granted to the governor, magistracy, freemen, and inhabitants, with full possession of their estates and liberties under the acts of settlement and explanation.

The Romish clergy and laity were allowed the private exercise of their religion, their lawyers to practise, and their estated gentlemen to bear arms: nor was those favorable terms without their effect; several considerable parties daily revolted from the Irish, and were either entertained in the army, or taking the oath of fidelity to the king and queen, or dismissed peaceably to their habitations at their option. Leland says, that in the battle of Aghrim, and in a bloody pursuit of three hours, stopped only by the night, 7000 of the Irish were slain. The unrelenting fury of the victors appeared in the number of their prisoners, which amounted only to 450. — "Ginkle gained reputation by the defeat of the Irish, but his army lost all claim to humanity, by giving no quarter!" — At the battle of Aghrim above 2000 who threw down their arms and asked for quarter, and several who had quarter given them, were afterwards killed in cold blood; in which number were lord Galway, and colonel Charles Moore.

1691 Sir Henry Bellasise, mayor.
     John Gibbs and Richard Wall, sheriffs.
     The church was restored to the Protestants, and has continued so ever since.
     26th July, the town surrendered to general de Ginkle.
1692 Thomas Rivett, mayor.
     Richard Wall and John Gibbs, sheriffs.

---

[1] This fort may be easily traced, and the embrasure, still in part remain, [original footnote].

1693 Thomas Revett, mayor.
John Gibbs and Richard Wall, sheriffs.
After the surrender of the town to king William's forces, the catholic inhabitants were so ill-used by the soldiery and others, that such multitudes left the town on this account, as to cause a meeting of the corporation to devise measures to prevent it. It was agreed that no pass should he allowed to any person to leave the town, and that measures should be taken to prevent the licentiousness of the soldiers, which was by no means countenanced by the government, who allowed the full use of their rights as agreed at the capitulation, and were acknowledged by parliament

1694 Thomas Simcocks, mayor.
Thomas Coneys and Francis Knapp, sheriffs.

1695 Thomas Simcocks, mayor.
Francis Knapp and James Revett Vigee, sheriffs.

1696 Thomas Cartwright, mayor.
James Revett Vigee and Marcus Lynch, sheriffs.
It was ordered that no person but a freeman keep open shop in Galway, or the liberties thereof, (four miles in every direction,) or sell or expose to sale any wares therein, except on market days, and paying quarterage. "This oppressive law was entirely directed against the roman catholic inhabitants, none of whom were then free. They petitioned the lords justices and council against it, but without effect; it continued, therefore, rigidly in force for many years after, and was one of the principal causes of the decay of the town."

1697 John Gerry, mayor.
Marcus Lynch and Jervis Hinde, sheriffs.
On the 2nd August their excellencies the Marquis of Winchester and the Earl of Galway, Lords Justices of Ireland, on their progress came to Galway, and were on the following day entertained at the mayor's house, at the charge of the corporation.
Peace proclaimed with France 7th November.
A bill was prepared to remove the archiepiscopal see of Tuam to Galway, and that £500. should be granted to repair the cathedral, and £1500. should be granted to provide a residence for the archbishop: a petition against it was presented, and the measure was lost

1698 John Gerry, mayor.
Jervis Hinde and Thomas Poole, sheriffs.
The mayor was allowed one hundred pounds of his salary to pay debts.

1699 Thomas Andrews, mayor.
Thomas Poole and Samuel Simcocks, sheriffs.
This mayor gave a case to hold the king's sword in the church of St. Nicholas.

1700 Richard Browne, mayor.
Samuel Simcocks and Robert Blakeney, sheriffs.

1701 Thomas Staunton, mayor.
Robert Blakeney and John Broughton, sheriffs.

It was computed that 1000 barrels of herrings were taken by seventy boats, on the night of the 15th of September, and sold for four shillings and sixpence per 1000. The following year such multitudes were taken that they sold for eight pence and ten pence per 1000. The winter and spring before, so great a quantity of cod fish were taken that they sold generally for one penny each. So great a scarcity of money prevailed, that good mutton sold on market days for four pence to six pence per quarter, and ordinary sorts for three pence.

It was ordered that the two last mayors do pay £50. each (out of the arrears due to them) towards building the exchange or the tholsel; and that the present mayor shall have £200 salary, allowing £50. for the same purpose.

At this time Mutton Island was fortified; the town gates were repaired, and three companies of foot, consisting of 250 men, were raised in the town.

Some progress was also made in building the exchange.

1702 Thomas Staunton, mayor.

John Broughton and John Fouquiere, sheriffs.

The mayor gave one hundred pounds towards building the exchange. Herrings sold this year for a halfpenny per hundred.

1703 James Ribett Vigie, mayor.

John Fouquiere and George Gerry, sheriffs.

In the summer of this year so great a quantity of cod fish were taken that they sold for one half penny each, and were very seldom taken at that season before.

1704 John Eyre, mayor.

George Gerry and William Hinde, sheriffs.

It was ordered that no mayor should have more than £150. Until the tholsel should be built, and that the number of aldermen should not exceed twenty-six. Also, that all popish shop-keepers do appear before council, and show cause why they should not pay quarterage.

1705 John Eyre, mayor.

Mark Wall and William Hinde, sheriffs.

This mayor allowed two hundred pounds out of his salary towards building the exchange. Ordered, that all popish shop-keepers do appear before council, and show cause why they should pot pay quarterage.

1706 John Eyre, mayor.

Mark Wall and William Fisher, sheriffs.

1707 Richard Wall, mayor.

William Fisher and Henry Lardner, sheriffs.

This mayor died the 3rd July, and alderman Gibbs was elected for the remainder of the year. Alderman Edward Eyre objected to Lardner being sheriff for having a popish wife.

It was ordered that the mayor's salary should be reduced to £100.

1708 John Gibbs, mayor.

Henry Lardner and Edward Barrett, sheriffs.

On the rumour of the landing of the Pretender in Scotland, several gentlemen and merchants were imprisoned, and all the other catholic inhabitants turned out of the town, and several priests also imprisoned; so great was the apprehension that the markets were held outside the town walls, and no mass permitted. But shortly after permission was given to them to return to their dwellings, and the markets restored to the town.

1709 Jervis Hinde, mayor.
George Staunton and Charles Gerry, sheriffs.

1710 Edward Eyre, mayor.
Robert Mason and David Tenant, sheriffs.

1711 Edward Eyre, mayor.
Edward Roads and Robert Coates, sheriffs.

1712 Edward Eyre, mayor.
Charles Morgan and William Moore, sheriffs.
May 12. The necessity and advantage to the town and corporation, of having a spacious entrance open and unbuilt before William's gate, leading to the east suburbs, and to Bohermore, having been this day presented in council, alderman Edward Eyre, (whose father in 1670 obtained a lease of part of said ground, with several other parcels,) declared that, he would agree to grant a piece, of ground containing about thirty perches, for that purpose; in consideration of which the corporation, (himself being mayor) on the 19th of May following, extended the term of his lease to lives renewable forever.

1713 Edward Eyre, mayor,
Bruno Browne and John Bird, sheriffs.

1714 Robert Blakeney, mayor.
James Lynch and Thomas Smyth, sheriffs.

1715 Robert Blakeney, mayor.
Samuel Blood and Doctor Hendron, sheriffs.

1716 Robert Coates, mayor.
John Gibbs and Doctor Hendron, sheriffs.

1717 Robert Coates, mayor.
Jeffry Cooke and Richard Hutchinson, sheriffs.

1718 Marcus Wall, mayor.
John Marmion and John Grindleton, sheriffs.
That the several persons who in November and December last were elected members of the common council, having been so elected manifestly with a design to evade the statute which on the 25th of said month of December was to be in force, and in order to perpetuate the government of this corporation in several gentlemen and others in the county of Galway and else where, who have no interest or concern in the town, or pay any scot, lot, or other contribution therein, by means whereof the protectant inhabitants are greatly discouraged, and that part of the statute whereby protestants are encouraged to come and dwell in the town, will be frustrated, if not prevented; ordered, June 30th, that these persons be no longer members of the common council.

1719 Samuel Simcocks, mayor.
Robert Andrews and John Hautenville, sheriffs.

1720   Samuel Simcocks, mayor.
Francis Wheeler and Thomas Holland, sheriffs.
In Bowie's Geographical description of Ireland, he says at this period, "Galway an ancient corporation, of good trade; both rich and populous ".

1721   William Hinde, mayor.
Edward Roades and Howell Price, sheriffs.

1722   William Hinde, mayor.
John Mannion and James Ribott Vigie, sheriffs.

1723   William Hinde, mayor.
John Mannion and John Cox, senior, sheriffs.

1724   George Gerry, mayor.
Francis Wheeler and Richard Huchinson, sheriffs.

1725   George Staunton, mayor.
Charles Rivett and Erasmus Irwin, sheriffs.
At this period the tolls for the market and gateage were £418.; water bailiff, £20.

1726   Charles Gerry, mayor.
Robert French and Robert Mc. Mullin, sheriffs.
Two bells were hung in the church of St. Nicholas.
George Dollard gave a certificate that the organ was in tune; by this the organ must be at least ninety-four years in the church, and as organs were first introduced into Irish churches in 1641, probably the present organ is in the church since that period— 179 years. At this period £10. was allowed for the judges' lodgings each.

1727   Charles Rivett, mayor.
John O'Hara and Robert Cooke, sheriffs.
20th January. For celebrating the prince's birth day the following articles were ordered by the mayor:

	£	s.	d.
5 quarts of Rum,		5	0
24 Lemons,	4	0	
Sugar,	1	0	
6 bottles of Wine,		8	0
Bread, Butter, and Cheese,	1	8	
Pipes,		0	1
5 mugs of Ale,	0	10	

As they grew a little mellow there was a second order:

	£	s.	d.
5 pints of Rum,	4	2	
20 Lemons,	2	4	
2 bottles of Wine,		2	8
Sugar,	0	10	
Tobacco,		0	1
	£1	10	9

This is somewhat different from the present lord mayor's feast in Dublin.

At this period, and afterwards, money was advanced to pay for the funeral of several aldermen, and other officers. At the funeral of alderman Fisher Sibby Lee received sixpence for rosemary.— Note, I am to learn why we never hear of aldermen at present

1728 Richard Rivett, mayor Henry Morgan and Francis Simcocks, sheriffs.
The corporation made a present of the organ in St Nicholas' Church to the town.
Henry Morgan died in office, and was succeeded by John Johnson, clockmaker.

1729 John Gibbs, mayor.
Patrick Blake and Andrew Holmes, sheriffs
Oatmeal sold in Galway for twelve shillings the bushel.
It was ordered on the 14th September, that Richard Rivett, late mayor, have a donation of £100. added to his former salary of £200, in reward of his upright conduct.

   Market and gateage, £474.
   Water bailiff,   £12.

1730 John Staunton, mayor.
Richard Fitzpatrick and Neptune Morgan, sheriffs.
At this time the mayor's salary was £200. per annum.

   Sergeant at Mace, £3.
   Exchange Porter, £2. 10s.

A box for the bishop of Clonferf's freedom, £1. 6s. 3½d.
10th February, the chamberlain, Samuel Simcocks, was ordered to pay, for the encouragement of the new fair at Bohermore, for a shift to be run for, as follows:

	s.	d.
2½ yards fine linen,	5	10
3 nails of muslin for ruffles	0	9
Thread,	0	1
Making the Shift,	0	3
1 yard of red ribbon for a knot for the head	0	10
Tape,	0	1
¾ yards red ribbon for the sleeves,	0	3
Also,		
A fine felt hat to be cudgeled for,	4	4
A yard of red ribbon for a cockade,	0	10

17th June, paid for the expences of getting a patent for fairs and market lately granted, £27. 1s. 5d.
Andrew Lynch and his sons were discharged from gateage, customs, and taxes, for seven years, for keeping the streets clean.

1731 Walter Taylor, mayor.
George Staunton and Henry Ellis, sheriffs.
Mayor's salary, per annum, £300.; town clerk, £6. 10s. paid by the corporation in lieu of all other emoluments.

14th June, £3. 3s. 9½d was ordered for three boxes for Lord Muskerry, Lord Mountcashel, and the Hon. Mr. Mac Carthy's freedom. Also, a silver box for Lord Jocelyn's freedom, 17s. 10½d.; for the fashion, 8s. 1i½d,; six yards of blue, red, and white ribbon for a tassel for the judges' freedom.

1732 Charles Morgan, mayor.
Nicholas Staunton and Patrick Blake, junior, sheriffs.
At a common council held in Galway, the chamberlain was ordered to advance money to the mayor for prosecuting Simon Lynch and others of popish inhabitants of the town of Galway, not being registered, and that alderman Simcocks, alderman George Gerry, and alderman Charles Gerry do inspect the laying out of the money.

1733 Jeffry Cooke, mayor.
William Fairservice and Richard Barrett, sheriffs.

1734 John Bird, mayor.
John Simcocks and Hugh Wilkinson, sheriffs.
Simcocks died in office, and Edmond Staunton was elected sheriff.
Ordered, that the recorder for the time being, quatenus[1] recorder, but no longer, shall sit and vote in the common council, though not admitted a member thereof (repealed 27th July, 1772.) Also ordered, that £30, be paid to alderman Charles Rivett, apothecary, to furnish his shop with drugs, proper for supplying the Protestants and others.

1735 Domnick Burke, mayor.
Robert Cooke and Anthony Taylor, sheriffs.
Taylor died, and Henry Ellis was elected.

1736 John Staunton, mayor.
Henry Ellis and Patrick Blake, jun. sheriffs.

1737 Domnick Burke, mayor.
Robert Macmullen and Thomas Northeast, sheriffs.

1738 Richard Fitzpatrick, mayor.
Richard Barrett and William Fairservice, sheriffs.

1739 Henry Ellis, mayor.
Henry Vaughan and Simon Truelock, sheriffs.
A great frost rotted almost all the potatoes in Ireland in half an hour. The ice on the river from the west bridge to Ferryland was so thick, that hundreds of people played football on. It from the wood quay to Newcastle.

1740 Thomas Holland, mayor.
Aston Swannick and Henry Lewin, sheriffs.

1741 Robert Cooke, mayor.
Croasdale Shaw and John Johnson, sheriffs.
A fever raged this year that occasioned the judges to hold the assizes in Tuam. Numbers of the merchants of Galway died this year, and multitudes of poor

---

[1] In the capacity of, [Clachan ed.].

people, caused partly by fever and by the scarcity, as wheat was twenty-eight shillings per hundred weight — Note, in 1812, wheat was thirty-two shillings per hundred weight

1742 John Disney, collector, mayor.
George Simcocks and John Hamlin, sheriffs.

1743 Thomas Shaw, mayor.
Michael Fairservice and Josias Sherwood, sheriffs.

1744 George Purdon, mayor.
Charles Hamlin and Thomas Sherwood, sheriffs.

1745 John Mills, mayor.
John Johnson and John Shaw, sheriffs.
A great fall of snow this year that smothered vast numbers of cattle and sheep, which caused a great many farmers to surrender their lands.
The best land in Connaught, after this period, let for five shillings per acre, and numbers who had courage to take lands enriched their families. Wheat rose now from six shillings to eighteen shillings per cwt. — Fourteen sail of East Indiamen anchored in the road of Galway; and in spring following, six sail of men of war came to convoy them: they all sailed away together, a glorious and unusual sight.

1746 Croasdale Shaw, mayor.
George Thomas and Francis Hardiman or Wad man, sheriffs.

1747 James O'Hara, mayor.
George Shaw and Edward Shields, sheriffs.
George Shaw died, and Thomas Sherwood was elected.
Ordered, that £900. be granted to alderman Richard Fitzpatrick, his heirs and assigns, by mortgage of all the corporation lands and revenues, to reimburse him his expence for several years, in assiduously supporting the rights, privileges and immunities of the corporation. Also, that no succeeding mayor be allowed any salary whatever, but by the appointment of the majority of the common council.

1748 James Disney, mayor.
Francis Hopkins and Henry Covey, sheriffs.
O'Hara, the former mayor, held over the office until dispossessed by captain M'Kenzee and a party of soldiers.

1749 John Eyre, mayor.
Elias Tankerville and John Mandeville, sheriffs.

1750 The honorable Francis Annesley, mayor.
John Morgan and John Softlawe, sheriff.
The mayor died, and was succeeded by John Eyre.

1751 James Staunton, mayor.
Richard Mathews and George Drury, sheriffs.

1752 John Hanlin, mayor.
Aston Swanwick and Joseph Seymour, sheriffs.

1753 Ambrose Poole, mayor.
John Mandeville and James Jones, sheriffs.

1754 George Simcocks, mayor.

John Johnston and Samuel Shone, sheriff.
Wheat sold this year for six shillings per cwt.

1755 John Shaw, mayor.
George Dunn and Hugh Wilkinson, sheriffs.
Wheat eleven shillings per cwt.

1756 Patrick Blake, mayor.
Charles Lopdel and Elias Tankerville, sheriffs.
Wheat fifteen shillings per cwt.

1757 Robert Cooke, mayor.
Edward Murphy and James Galbraith, sheriffs.
Wheat six shillings per hundred.

1758 Edward Shields, mayor.
Francis Tomkins and George Lewis, sheriffs.
An act passed this year to prevent the distillation of spirits from grain for one year.

1759 Crosdell Shaw, mayor.
Richard Blake and Hugh Montgomery, sheriffs.

1760 Thomas French of Moycullen, mayor.
Henry Covey and James Foster, sheriffs.

1761 Charles Rivett, mayor.
John Mandeville and James Galbraith, sheriffs.
10th November, a petition was presented to parliament to prevent Catholic shopkeepers from manufacturing or selling their goods, or employing journeymen for this purpose; it was signed by the mayor, sheriffs, warden, and Protestant inhabitants of Galway. — Such was the temper of the times. How different from their feelings at present.

1762 Charles Daly of Callow, mayor.
Richard Blake and Hugh Montgomery, sheriffs.

1763 Henry Ellis, mayor.
Edward Murphy and James Galbraith, sheriffs.
Andrew Carroll, spearing salmon at the west bridge, was drowned, by the cord getting entangled about his legs.

1764 John Eyre, mayor.
Elias Tankerville and Charles Lopdel, sheriffs.
There was a double return for mayor.— The candictates were Richard Fitzpatrick and Richard Martin of Dangan. Neither being approved of by the privy council, another election was directed, when John Eyre was approved of, and sworn.

1765 James Daly, mayor.
Hugh Wilkinson and Luke Dodgeworth, sheriffs.

1766 Henry White, mayor.
Hugh Montgomery and George Lewis, sheriffs.

1767 John Gibson, mayor.
Charles Davy and Edward Shields, sheriffs.
The infirmary outside Williams' gate began to be built this year.

1768 Thomas Taylor, mayor.
Samuel Grace and Robert McMullen, sheriffs.
Francis Lynch of Rahoon, was the first Roman Catholic sworn on a grand jury since the revolution.

1769 Denis Daly of Dunsandle, mayor.
Richard Blake and Edmond Fitzpatrick, sheriffs.

1770 Anthony Daly of Callas, mayor.
Elias Tankerville and George Drury, sheriffs.

1771 Patrick Blake of Drum, mayor.
Thomas Clutterbuck, who died in office, and Luke Thomas, sheriffs.
From a remote period the judges had been entertained free of expense, but this year the corporation was possessed with a fit of economy, and ordered that the payment for the judges. lodgings should be discontinued.— This was shortly after rescinded, and £10. per annum has been since paid for that purpose. At this period, and for some years after the town, and indeed the county, was kept in a most unpleasant situation between the partisans of Mr. Daly and Mr. Blake. Some blood was shed, and the ferment did not completely subside for many years: this was attributed to the choice of Mr. Blake as mayor. To prevent any repetition of such disgraceful proceedings, none but one of the Daly family has been chosen since 1776.

1772 Denis Daly, mayor.
Thomas Bodkin of Carrabeg and John Thomas, sheriffs.

1773 Charles French of Clogher, mayor.
John Morgan and Robert Squib, sheriffs.

1774 Key Edmond French, mayor and warden.
George Thomas and Samuel Grace, sheriffs.
This year the immense granite rock called the Gregory, on the island of Arran, was shattered by lightning.

1775 Elias Tankerville, mayor.
Robert O'Hara and James Shee, sheriffs.

1776 James Shee, mayor.
Samuel Grace and James Burke, sheriffs.

1777 Denis Daly, mayor.
William Burnet and Robert Squib, sheriffs.

1778 Peter Daly, mayor.
John Morgan and Michael Kelly, sheriffs.

1779 Hyacinth Daly, mayor.
James Burke and Samuel Grace, sheriffs.
Ordered, that the freedom of this corporation be presented, in a gold box, to the right honourable Walter Burgh. — 31st of May, the Galway volunteers were embodied, and the following officers elected:
    Richard Martin, Dangan, colonel.
    James Shee, deputy mayor, lieutenant colonel.
    John Blake, Coolcun, major.

>J. O'Hara, recorder, captain of grenadier company.
>Mark Lynch, captain of battalion company.
>Michael Blake, Frenchfort, captain of light infantry,
>Jasper Lynch, adjutant

1780 Denis Daly, mayor.
Samuel Grace and John Bradley, sheriffs.

1781 Hyacinth Daly, mayor.
Samuel Grace and Michael Kelly, sheriffs.

1782 Anthony Daly, mayor.
Michael Kelly and John Bradley, sheriffs.

1783 Denis Daly, mayor.
John Lynch and William Frazer, sheriffs.
A contested election for the county of Galway took place between Denis Daly of Dunsandle, William Power Trench, Edmond Kirwan of Dalgin, and Richard Martin of Dangan, esqrs. It continued fifty-two days, when Mr. Daly and Mr. Trench were elected. It cost the parties immense sums, and very much injured their properties for many years after.
About this period Mr. Andrew French imported the first cargo of flaxseed into Galway; it amounted to 300 hogsheads, of which he sold only 100. In 1789 the importation from 1500 to 9300 hogsheads. In 1815, 3000 hogsheads; most sold into the counties of Mayo and Roscommon, but very little in the county of Galway: the greater part saved at home.

1784 Denis Bowes Daly, mayor.
John Morgan and John Bradley, sheriffs.

1785 Denis Daly, mayor.
Luke Thomas and John Bradley, sheriffs.

1786 Ralph Daly mayor and warden.
John Morgan and Luke Thomas, sheriffs.

1787 Denis Bowes Daly, mayor.
Michael Kelly and Charles Donnellan, sheriffs.

1788 Denis Daly, mayor.
William Frazer and Robert Squib, sheriffs.

1789 Peter Daly, mayor.
Michael Kelly and Edmond Fitzpatrick, sheriffs.
The quantity of herrings taken this year was so great, that they sold for 4d. to 6d. per 100.

1790 Denis Bowes Daly, mayor.
John Bradley and Robert Squib, sheriffs.

1791 Denis Daly, mayor.
John Bradley and Robert Squib, sheriffs.
The mayor died in office, universally lamented in the county of Galway. St. G. Daly was elected for the remainder of the year.

1792 St George Daly, mayor.
John Bradley and Robert Squib, sheriffs.

1798 Richard Daly, mayor.
   John Bradley and Robert Squib, sheriffs.
1794 Denis Bowes Daly, mayor.
   Thomas Browne and Charles Morgan, sheriffs.
1795 Hyacinth Daly, mayor.
   Peter Daly and Edmond Fitzpatrick, sheriffs.
   18 sail of East Indiamen, and five men of war, anchored in the bay of Galway.
1796 St George Daly, mayor.
   Hyacinth Daly and Michael Burke, sheriffs.
1797 Hyacinth Daly, mayor.
   Denis Bowes Daly and Edmond Fitzpatrick, sheriffs.
1798 Denis Bowes Daly, mayor.
   Hyacinth Daly and St George Daly, sheriffs.
   St George Daly resigned, and John Burke of St Clerans served the office for the remainder of the term.
   The merchants in an hour collected fifteen hundred guineas, which they presented to General Hutchinson, who commanded in the town: without this supply he could not have joined General Lake to meet the French at Killala. The yeomanry of the town joined in this unfortunate expedition. This year the old charter school was occupied as an artillery barrack, and at present by the Presentation convent
1799 Colonel Peter Daly, mayor.
   Denis Bowes Daly and John Thomas, sheriffs.
1800 Hyacinth Daly, mayor.
   Thomas Browne and John Thomas, sheriffs.
   The Dominican chapel, near Galway, was built. A few years ago the late alderman Patrick Bride, a native of this town, enclosed the cemetry of this abbey with a wall; before this it was subject to great abuses by pigs, &c.
1801 Colonel Peter Daly, mayor.
   Thomas Brown and John Thomas, sheriffs.
1802 Hyacinth Daly, mayor.
   John Strogen and Michael Dillon, sheriffs.
1803 Denis Bowes Daly, mayor.
   John Strogen and Michael Dillon, sheriffs,
1804 James Daly, mayor.
   John Strogen and Michael Dillon, sheriffs.
1805 Hyacinth Daly, mayor.
   Michael Dillon and Charles O'Hara, sheriffs.
1806 Hyacinth Daly, mayor.
   Charles O'Hara and William Mason, sheriffs.
   Denis Bowes Daly was elected mayor, but not attending, Hyacinth Daly held over another year.
1807 Denis Bowes Daly, mayor.
   Charles O'Hara and William Mason, sheriffs.

This year the foundation of the new town gaol was laid, on Nuns' Island.
1808   Hyacinth Daly, mayor.
Charles O'Hara and William Mason, sheriffs.
1809   Denis Bowes Daly, mayor.
Charles O'Hara and William Mason, sheriffs.
1810   James Daly, mayor.
Charles O'Hara and William Mason, sheriffs.
1811   Hyacinth Daly, mayor.
Charles O'Hara and William Mason, sheriffs.
Charles O'Hara died, when John Strogen was sworn into office.
This year the extensive burial ground on Fort Hill was enclosed by Mr. Robert Hedges Eyre, "As a mark of his respect and esteem for the inhabitants of the town of Galway, in August 1811". In this place lies interred Mr. Thomas Leggett, a very celebrated landscape gardener, who, after beautifying almost every demesne in the county, is most ungratefully suffered to lie here neglected, without even a "Hic jacet!" — I proposed some years since to receive subscriptions to enable me to raise an humble monument to his memory, but, alas! I felt a freezing indifference, except from one gentleman, who would give twenty guineas, provided it was erected in his own demesne.
I was much pleased with the following tribute in this church yard, so creditable to the living as well as to the dead:— "Sacred to the memory of Peter Rogier, native of France: this stone is placed as a tribute to his memory, by his friend and master, Charles Bingham. Galway, October 25, 1807.
1812   Denis Bowes Daly, mayor.
Francis Eager and Thomas Browne, sheriffs.
Thomas Browne died, when Jethro Bricknell was sworn into office.
This year the foundation of the new sessions house was laid at Newtown Smyth. Richard Morrison, architect.
1813   Hyacinth Daly, mayor.
Francis Eager and Jethro Bricknell, sheriffs.
This year the governors and trustees of the will of Erasmus Smith laid the foundation of a school house in the east suburbs of Galway.
1814   James Daly, mayor.
Francis Eager and Jethro Bricknell, sheriffs.
1815   Hyacinth Daly, mayor.
Francis Eager and Jethro Bricknell, sheriffs.
The tolls and market set for £665 N. B. The kelp, butter, and potato cranes are not included in the above sum.
A light-house, forty-five feet high, was erected on Mutton Island, near Galway, which has been of infinite use to all vessels entering the bay; especially fishing boats, which were frequently in a most dangerous situation when adverse winds prevented their entrance before night. The new county court house was opened this year. It stands on the site of the old Franciscan Abbey, and is not included in the county of the town.

1816 Hyacinth Daly, mayor.
Jethro Bricknell and Francis Eager, sheriffs.
1817 Parnell Gale, mayor.
Michael Dillon and Matthew T. Smith, sheriffs.
1818 James Daly, mayor.
Michael Dillon and Matthew T. Smith, sheriffs.
The foundation of the new catholic chapel of St. Nicholas was laid on the 1st July, by the late Hyacinth Daly, esq. mayor. It has been lately finished, and is of the ornamented Gothic style.
1819 James Daly, mayor.
Michael Dillon and Matthew T. Smyth, sheriffs.
1820 James Hardiman Burke, mayor.
Michael Dillon and Matthew T. Smyth, sheriffs.
1821 James H. Burke, mayor.
Michael Dillon and Matthew T. Smyth, sheriffs,
1822 James H. Burke, mayor.
Matthew T. Smyth and Michael Dillon, sheriff.

LIST OF RECORDERS

1595 Domnick Martin.
1610 Damian Peck bart.
1610 Domnick Martin.
1625 Sir Henry Lynch, Bart.
1633 Stephen Lynch.
1635 Stephen Lynch.
1636 Thomas Lynch Fitz-Marcus.
1642 John Blake.
1652 Marcus Martin.
1654 Robert Clarke.
1655 Henry Greneway.
1657 James Cuffe.
1659 Edward Eyre.
1663 Henry Whaley.
1666 John Shadwell.
1670 William Sprigg.
1686 Sir Heny Lynch,
1687 Thomas Lynch-Fitz-Isidore.
1691 Nehemiah Donnal-Ian.
1694 William Handcock.
1695 Robert Ormsby.

1706 John Staunton.
1717 Arthur Ormsby.
1718 Robert Shaw.
1725 John Staunton.
1730 Thomas Staunton.
1738 Edward Eyre.
1739 Domnick Burke.
1747 Eyre French.
1749 John Staunton.
1750 John Morgan.
1759 James Staunton.
1761 John Staunton.
1774 James O'Hara.
1775 John Morgan.
1779 James O'Hara.
1787 Robert Shaw.
1819 James O'Hara, jun.
1820 James O'Hara, jun.
1821 James O'Hara, jun.
1822 James O'Hara, jun.
1823 James O'Hara, jun.

TOWN CLERKS.

1674 Richard Revett.	1757 James O'Hara.
1679 Robert Shaw.	1774 Robert O'Hara.
1728 Robert Mc Mullen.	1775 James O'Hara.
1729 Richard Revett.	1777 Robert O'Hara.
1736 Alexander Lynch.	1778 James O'Hara.
1741 Robert Mc. Mullen.	1789 Robert O'Hara.
1742 Robert Cooke.	1812 John O'Hara.
1742 Robert Cooke.	

The town clerk was formerly called Notary, but by the charter of Charles II. the tide of town clerk was given to this officer, and Jerome Russel appointed, though it appears that in 1585 Nicholas Lynch was town clerk.

A LIST *of the* REPRESENTATIVES IN PARLIAMENT *for the town of Galway since tie reign of Queen Elizabeth, before which period there is no correct list.*

1539   Jonoke Lynch, of Galway.
       Peter Lynch, of the same.
       (For the parliament of 1568 no list extant)
1585   Peter Lynch.
       Jonoke -Lynch.
       Robuck French Fitz-John,
1613   Valentine Blake, of Muckenis, alderman.
       Geoffry Lynch-Fitz-Domnick, of Galway.
1634   Sir Thomas Blake, of Menlogh, bart.
       Nicholas Lynch, of Galway, alderman.
1639   Sir Robert Lynch, of Galway, bart.
       Sir Valentine Blake, Menlogh, bart.
       (Expelled 22nd June, 1642, for the rebellion.)
1661   Edward Eyre.
       John Eyre, of Eyrecourt
1689   Oliver Martin.
       John Kirwan.
       (Parliament of James II.)
1692   Sir Henry Bellassyse, knt Nehemiah Donnellan.
1695   Richard St George.
       Robert Ormsby.
1703   John Staunton, of Galway.
       Edward Eyre.
1713   John Staunton.
       Samuel Eyre, of Eyrecourt.

1714	John Staunton.
	Robert Shaw.
	Edward Eyre.
	(John Staunton miselected.)
1727	John Staunton.
	Thomas Staunton, alderman.
1732	Thomas Staunton.
	(Alderman Thomas Staunton, deceased.)
1735	Domnick Burke.
1747	Richard Fitz-Patrick.
1761	John Eyre.
	Richard Fitz-Patrick.
1767	Denis Daly, of Dunsandle.
1768	James Daly, of Dunsandle.
1773	Robert French.
	Anthony Daly, of Callow,
1776	Denis Bowes Daly.
	Anthony Daly.
1783	The same.
1790	Rt Hon. Denis Daly Sir Skeffington Smyth, bart.
1792	Rt. Hon. Sir Skeffington Smyth, bart.
	Peter Daly.
	(Sworn 19th June, 1792, in the room of his brother, the Rt Hon. Denis Daly, deceased.)
1799	St George Daly.
	George Ponsonby.
1804	Denis Bowes Daly.
1805	James Daly, of Dunsandle.
1812	Hon. Frederick Ponsonby.
1814	Valentine Blake, of Menlo.
	(The Hon. F. Ponsonby miselected.)
1818	Valentine Blake, of Menlo
1820	Mathew George Prendergast

TUAM. — The residence of the Archbishop, is a handsome town, of considerable inland trade; it possesses several fairs, and a weekly market well supplied with excellent meat of every kind, especially veal in the proper season; also with fish from Galway, which is frequently to be had in this market when the inhabitants of Galway are without it, because the dealers in fish called jolters or cadgers, are generally supplied before the housekeepers, as being much better customers. There is an extensive brewery kept by Mr. Blake, who supplies the country for many miles round.

The bread is particularly good: this town possesses a market house, and a billiard table and reading room over it, which is a great relief to many shopkeepers, as it takes away from them that great nuisance in country towns, idle loungers, who fill their shops, and frighten away many timid country people, especially women, who cannot encounter the broad stare and second hand wit of those idlers. The archbishop's palace, without possessing much architectural beauty, is exceedingly commodious and very spacious. It is highly ornamented by a handsome and extensive demesne, and excellent gardens. There is a dispensary, which, under the skill, conciliating manners, and excellent management of Dr. Little, has been of infinite use to the poorer classes of society. There are also two newspapers well edited, and uninfluenced by either religious or political party. The Roman Catholic archbishop has lately erected a handsome house, which, with the Catholic college of St. Jarlath (late French's bank) adds much to the appearance of the town. An abundant and clear stream of water runs through the town, supplying the brewery, several tanneries, &c. &c., and after spoiling a great deal of choice land by the grossest neglect of the proprietors, turns an insignificant flour mill, that should never have been permitted to be erected there, as throwing back water on land of ten times the value of the mill, and falls into Turloghmore, from whence it runs to Lough Corrib, and through the town of Galway to the sea. There are two good inns, at which the mail and canal coaches stop, which, as Tuam is the entrance to the county of Mayo, is highly useful to the inhabitants of that opulent county. This town is built on a low situation, yet I understand is very healthy. There is a constant intercourse with Galway, from whence the shopkeepers are supplied with many articles for an extensive home trade. Much to the credit of this town, religious distinctions are almost unknown to have any influence on their actions; from the archbishop to the lowest inhabitant they live in the greatest harmony: once for all, I must say this is the characteristic of every part of this extensive county, and their firm adherence to a monarchial government has from the earliest period been conspicuous in every change, and for which they have often suffered severely. A wretched attempt has been made in the establishment of a meat and vegetable market; nothing can be more disgraceful than the appearance and site; after every heavy shower of rain it is flooded up to the stalls, and a pool of water of some depth in the centre.

LOUGHREA— Is a considerable market town, chiefly the estate of the earl of Clanrickard; the agent to whose extensive estates lives in the town. There are several very extensive fairs, and two weekly markets, on Thursday chiefly for corn, and on Saturday for all kinds of provisions, with which it is so well supplied that many respectable families have settled here: the number of gentlemen's seats in the surrounding neighbourhood is another strong inducement, as they are mostly resident proprietors. This town is charmingly situated on the lake from whence it derives its name; it is more remarkable for its extreme clearness than for its goodness, being extremely hard and unfit for drinking. It is, I suppose, from this cause, nearly destitute of fish, except pike, and of those I am informed there are comparatively very few. It has been suggested that its general green hue proceeds from a mineral cause; this must be erroneous, for it possesses neither this colour nor any mineral taste after being taken from the lake. The colour probably may be caused not only by the ever verdant hills which round it on the east and south, but by the reflection of a clear sky from a bottom of white marl; the marl also may account for the hardness of the water.

Loughrea has a large linen and yarn hall, in a wretched state of neglect and decay, but in which there is a considerable quantity of coarse linens and yarn sold once a week. The linens are mostly of a coarse and narrow kind, of very inferior quality; a small quantity also of coarse diaper is frequently exposed for sale. A few years ago very fine diaper for table linen was made by a weaver from the north, but I imagine he has left the country, probably from want of encouragement: there are about 120 looms in this town. There is a large and commodious barrack for cavalry, and one for artillery, which has been occupied by infantry since the disturbances in 1820. There is a walk called the Mall, much frequented on Sundays, but in a state of gross neglect. It was laid out and planted by the late Mr. Robert Power, a very intelligent, and extensive nurseryman, and was formerly well kept, but seems to be at present totally neglected.

The greater part of the country round the town is very beautiful, both naturally and from the number of gentlemen's seats in its vicinity, — Dunsandle, Dalystown, St Clerans, Porsselodge, Holly Park, Kiltolla, Ruford, Benmore, Woodlawn, Roxborough, Castle Boy, Rahasane, Tyrone, Monksfield, Creggclare, Ballydonnellan, Ballydugan, Eastwell, &c. &c. and many in the cottage style. I wish I could praise it for its cleanliness, but it is generally, especially the suburbs, in a most filthy state.

I recollect riding some years since with the then agent to the estate, and wondering he did not make the inhabitants keep the town clean, and put their dunghills behind their houses. I was answered "indeed I cannot get any good of them:" what an answer from an agent and a magistrate! The principal street is covered with loose stones, brought there by those who keep standings; they are suffered to lie there, a most dangerous nuisance, and seem to be entirely unnoticed by the proper officer, the seneschal[1], and magistrates, several of whom doze in the town. A very beautiful new church, from the tasteful pencil of Mr. Paine, has been lately erected. It is unfortunate that a better site had not been chosen, and which I am informed the Countess of Clanrickard offered, rent free, and a large subscription. It would have been well in this, as in many other public works, if the choice had been left to professional taste and skill, and the interference of those who can have but a very superficial knowledge of such affairs disregarded.

Since the Messrs. Clarke of Galway have become such extensive exporters of corn, and frequently buyers to the amount of above 200 barrels of oats on each market

---

[1] Steward of great house, [Clachan ed.].

day, the increase has been astonishing; as they purchase none but oats of the best description, and always pay ready money (Loughrea usage), the farmers have every inducement for exertion, and the effect is very visible.

HEADFORD, — The estate of Richard Mausergh St George, Esq. is a town of good inland trade, as it is the thoroughfare between the counties of Mayo and Galway into Connemara. Much to the credit of Mr. St George the streets are kept very clean and free from swine, which, with the exception of Ballinasloe and Mount Bellew, is an uncommon circumstance in this province. There are several fairs, and a weekly market held here, and Mr. St. George gives premiums for the encouragement of the linen and flannel manufactures, which have been of infinite use. This town is improving much in its appearance, under the auspices of an intelligent and spirited resident landlord, who lives near the town, and possesses a fine demesne, extensively planted from his own designs, which have evinced a considerable degree of taste. This demesne is ornamented by a small lake capable of being much enlarged, and possessing a superiority over most others, of having an abundant stream of the most limpid water running into it on a high level, which gives a power of not only an enlargement of the lake, but an extensive scene of irrigation. The views of the mountains of Joyce country and of those of Mayo, which assume a sublime outline, with those of Lough Corrib, contribute highly to the beauty of the environs of Headford; the ruins of the abbey of Ross, near the town, is also a very fine object. Ower, the seat of Mr. Burke near Headford, possesses great capability, not only from highly picturesque views, but from the shape of the ground and water; it adds much to the cheerful appearance of this neighbourhood. If every landlord possessed half as much energy and taste as Mr. St. George, the county would assume a very different appearance, and how much more rational, healthful, and eventually more pleasing, would their time be occupied than at a gaming table!

BALLINASLOE.[1] — The estate of the Earl of Clancarty stands preeminent for cleanliness, and the regulations for maintaining a rare and effective system of police. This herculean task has been accomplished chiefly by the Hon. and Rev. Charles Le Power Trench, brother to Lord Clancarty, in a very few years. When I first saw Ballinasloe it was not outdone by even Galway in either filth or a vicious police; the doors of the houses were almost inaccessible through dunghills, as high as the eves of the cottages, and an uncontrolled ingress given to all kinds of vagabonds, male and female. In the daytime, in even the best part of the town, it was difficult to pass from one house to another, the foot path was so blocked up with cars, pigs, and other

---

[1] In the inquest held before Sir Anthony St. Lager, then Master of the Rolls, and Peter Palmer, second Justice of the Common Pleas, in which the limits of the county Galway were accurately ascertained, it is stated that 'it goeth under the middle arch of the middle bridge of Ballinasloe," and from thence with the course of the stream it falleth into the Shannon, &c. I make this extract from Mr Hardiman because I believe it is generally thought the mearing of the county is under the middle arch of the North bridge, near Cuff's Inn, [original footnote].

nuisances. In the night you were obliged, from a regard to your neck or your shins, to wade ankle deep through puddles, in the middle of the street; even here, you were lucky if you escaped a tumble over a pig or a large stone, or escaped a Scotch salute, without the Edinburgh caution of " 'ware heads." Now, what a contrast! The foot path well paved, and swept every day; not even a bowl of water permitted to be emptied into the streets (what a hardship!) not a car or carriage, even those of gentlemen, permitted to stand in the street without horses; not a dunghill or loose stone. Every alehouse shut up at an early hour; not a shop open during divine service; vagabonds and idle women sent to bridewell; the footpaths well gravelled for a considerable distance on every road round the town, and posts fixed to keep off the wheels of carriages, &c. &c. All this, and much more, has been accomplished by a steady, yet discriminating adherence to regulations calculated for the general good. They were at first violently opposed, as lately in Galway, by those, who blinded by prejudice and old habits were insensible to the blessings of cleanliness; yet they now seem to be sensible that the health and comforts they enjoy, have more than compensated for the loss of any of their former imaginary and filthy conveniences. The change has been effected by a well digested and impartial system of rewards and punishments, and I think the motto to Lord Clancarty's printed regulations might very justly be "The wreath or the rod." Portarlington has long been held up for a model of cleanliness, and very justly; but the merit here is much greater; there the inhabitants are composed chiefly of those in good circumstances, who have retired on their fortunes; here the number of that class is very trifling, whilst a great part of the town and extensive suburbs are chiefly inhabited by those of humble rank. I must confess that I, who have seen Ballinasloe before its regeneration, never go there without feelings of delight, which probably may be heightened by my mind always reverting to Bohermore, the leading suburb to Galway, faugh!— Ballinasloe possesses an excellent market for every species of grain, usually of superior quality; also a well supplied meat market, and generally fish from Galway.

A new and commodious market house has been lately built by Lord Clancarty, which is a very desirable improvement for both buyer and seller, who before were obliged to transact their business in the open street, which was very injurious to all kinds of agricultural productions. There are two extensive barracks for infantry, and one for cavalry; they have been for some time unoccupied, until in 1820 they were filled by troops called in to quell the ribbonmen. There are fairs held on the 27th of March, 8th of May, 4th July, and 4th October. That held on the 8th of May has been long celebrated for a superior breed of store cattle from the several adjoining counties; they consist chiefly of heifers, and are usually purchased by the Leinster graziers for fattening, a system, which though it shews the superiority of the breed of Ireland over the general breed of England, is contrary to that which should actuate the breeders. That system is to select the best at the different fairs for this purpose. If, on the contrary, those were kept for breed only, to what a height of perfection they would arrive in a few years, I need only mention the beneficial tendency of the contrary practice in sheep, of whom the best only are kept for breeding.

The farming society are at length, (though it has been often brought to their recollection) sensible of the national and individual loss sustained by this antiquated and stubborn folly, and have offered premiums for this very desirable purpose. As it has not been long in operation, an opinion cannot well be formed on the result, yet it is highly probable it only wants a little perseverance to establish its superiority, not only prospectively, but immediately. I shall have occasion to speak of this in another section more appropriate to the subject.

GORT— The estate of Lord Gort, as it stands near the county of Clare, to which it is one of the passes from Connaught to Munster, has a considerable share of inland trade; it possesses an excellent weekly market, and several fairs; there are extensive barracks. The appearance of this town, naturally very cheerful, has been lately much improved by the erection of a beautiful church by Mr. Paine, which is a proof, amongst many others, of this gentleman's architectural taste.

Lord Gort's residence in this town, accompanied by a very picturesque reach of the river, gives a very favourable impression, on entering it from Loughrea, and with the spaciousness of the streets, and the new houses that have been lately erected, has changed its former gloomy and neglected appearance into cheerfulness, and a promise of increasing trade. The environs are very beautiful, containing many natural curiosities. Ryndifin is exceedingly picturesque. The river, which is considerable, runs against a very high and bold rock, nearly perpendicular, and sinks so completely and quickly, that one is at loss to know where it goes. It communicates with the *punch bowl* and the *churn*, and breaks out again at a very considerable distance under a fine natural arch of considerable breadth, and again becomes a river.

The punch bowl is a large circular basin exceedingly deep and always supplied with water, and grassed down to the brink; it has every appearance of the crater of a volcano, but probably has been occasioned by the same convulsion of nature that produced the churn at a considerable distance, and which is like a very deep and large well. I do not know any part of this county that will so amply repay the picturesque traveller a day's stay at Gort, where there is a good inn, especially when a view of Lord Gort's highly picturesque demesne of Lough Coutra is included. A view of a magnificent castle, designed by Mr. Paine, placed on the brink of an extensive and charming lake (Coutra) surrounded with wood, and a noble background of mountains, will add to the pleasure. The recent improvements, including a front and back approach, do infinite credit to the long established taste and skill of Mr. Sutherland. An inspection of the ruins and round tower of Kilmacduagh will add considerably to the pleasure of an excursion from Loughrea, and an attentive view of the architectural beauty of the columns of an ancient arch, between the nave and altar of a chapel at some distance on the north west, will, I imagine, be amply repaid. The country between Loughrea and Gort is highly beautiful, comprehending Roxborough, Castleboy, Cool, Cappard, and other seats, and fine hills, accompanying the road the entire way.

ATHENRY,— In an old map is called Kingstown, and was anciently called *Athnery*; it was at a remote period, even before Galway, a town of some eminence, of which some remains may be seen in the ruins of the town wall and gate, and an old abbey, &c. An hundred years ago it was reckoned the second town in the county of Galway; at present it has every appearance of decay, not possessing any kind of manufacture of any note. Mr. Grose, in his Antiquities, gives the following account of this town:—

"Athenry[1] was formerly an handsome town, surrounded by walls by King John in 1211. Meyler de Bermingham, second baron of Athenry, granted land to build a Dominican monastery on, and an hundred and sixty marks. St Dominick, it is said, wrote to Bermingham for this purpose, and a noble fabrick was erected in 1241. Florence O'Flin, archbishop of Tuam, Thomas O'Kelly bishop of Clonfert, Walter earl of Ulster, William de Burgh, and others, were great benefactors to this church. In 1400, Pope Boniface the 9th granted a bull of indulgence to those who visited and contributed to the repairs and preservation of this monastery. An accidental fire having consumed the church in 1423, Pope Martin the fifth issued another bull for the reparation; and in 1427, William Ryedymar and Richard Golber and other Dominicans, having represented to the said Pope Martin that there was a want of religious men to instruct the natives in the Catholic faith, petitioned him for a licence to found two chapels or oratories, with a belfry, bell, cemetery, house, cloisters, and other offices. Where these chapels were built is not well known, but it is supposed they were at Tombeola, at the head of Roundstown bay, in the barony of Ballynahinch, and at Ballindown in the county of Sligo.

Pope Eugene the fourth, in 1445, renewed the bull of Pope Martin for the repairs of the church, at which time it had thirty monks; and in 1644, it was erected into an university *(studium generale)* with four others for the Dominicans, by order of a general chapter held at Rome. The little dependence to be placed on Monkish inscriptions, where the honor or interest of their order is concerned, will evidently appear from the following certificate: "We the underwritten do by these presents testify to our posterity and future ages, that we seen and read with our eyes this inscription placed over the door of the refectory of the Dominicans of Athenry. *Carolus Manus rubrae me fieri fecit*. As time will erase these letters, we have given this testimony the 24th day of October, 1725.

      Thomas Power Daly, Corrownakelly, esq.
      James Browne,
      Andrew Semper,   } Athenry.
      Andrew Browne,

---

[1] Not clear where this quotation ends, [Clachan ed.].

  Michael Berny, deputy
  R. P. Fr. Raymundus de Burgo.
  R. P. Fr. Augustinus de Burgo."

Without doubt these respectable persons saw what they testified, but the inscription is a palpable forgery, and allowed to be such by the historiographer of the Dominican order, for, says he, "how could Cathal-croove-derg, the person alluded to, who was titular king of Connaught, and died in 1224, cause this refectory to be made in 1241, the true time of its building?" The cemetery of this monastery was a great place of interment. In it were laid the De Burghos, Mac Davoes, O'Heynes, Kilkellies, Moghans, Brownes, Lynches, Colmans, and Dalies. In the 16th of Elizabeth this monastery, with its appurtenances, thirty acre of land in Athenry, and twelve in the town of Belindana (*quere* Ballindona) were granted forever *in capite* to the portrieve and burgesses of the town of Athenry, at the yearly rent of 26s. 4d. Irish money.

The remains of this monastery show it to have been a noble and extensive pile. Part of them are converted into barracks, and the barrack yard was the ground where the cloisters stood. The tower is unequal, the lower being larger than the upper part. The eastern window is in good style. — In 1295, Peter de Bermingham of Athenry sat in one of Edward I's parliaments.

This abbey is the burial place of many respectable families, amongst others William de Bermingham, archbishop of Tuam and son to the founder, was buried here in 1289. In 1312 a charter was granted by Edward II. for walling the town.

There are a multitude of villages not possessing any claim to a particular notice; with the exception of Mount Bellew, they are uniformly dirty and ill built, owing chiefly to that criminal indifference which too many landlords seem to feel for the comforts of their tenantry. In some few places an attempt has been made by a few pennyworth of white-wash to imitate the example set by Lord Clancarty, but a lamentable difference subsists; his tenants have the entire of their little cottages and concerns uniformly clean and comfortable; the others, though the front of their cottages may be dabbed with white wash, the back and interior exhibit every reality of filth and wretchedness. Lord Clancarty's tenants are assisted by a contribution of two-thirds or more of their expenditure, the other tenants must help themselves.

It would be unpardonable to omit mentioning Mr. D'Arcey's infant town of Clifden in Connemara, which promises at no very distant period to arrive at great celebrity; it only wants a mercantile man with a capital and enterprise to accomplish this; such men as Mr. Patterson of Kilrosh, Mr. Patten of Wesport, or the late Mr. Anderson of Fermoy. Clifden possesses almost every material for cheap building; stone, sand, lime, and cheap labour on the spot, and the sea open for the carriage of timber and

---

[1] Portreeve is a bailiff or mayor charged with keeping the peace and with other duties in a port or market borough, [Clachan ed.]

every other article. The roads to it were formerly very hilly and difficult; at present, by the unceasing and well directed exertions of Mr. D'Arcey, they run for many miles nearly on one level, and when the new line of road is finished, the communication between Clifton and Oughterard, a distance of upwards of thirty miles, will be nearly all the same level, by conducting it in the valleys instead of the present dangerous one over and on the edge of precipices. He has been ably assisted in those roads by Mr. Thomas Martin, through whose estate the greater part of the road will run. Mr. D'Arcey has erected a very commodious hotel for the accommodation of those who may be induced by the desire for sea bathing or pleasure. He has also built a very beautiful gothic church from the picturesque pencil of Mr. Coneys. A Catholic chapel and market house are in a state of progress; also stores for salt, and all other necessaries for either the fishery or for shipping in distress, are intended to be immediately built.

SECTION III

HABITATIONS, FUEL, FOOD, AND CLOTHING OF THE LOWER RANKS, AND THEIR GENERAL COST

HABITATIONS

The habitations of the lower ranks, with the exception of Ballinasloe, Headford, Mount Bellew Bridge, Woodlawn, Clonbrock, and, perhaps, a few others, are wretched in the extreme. That attention to the comforts of their tenantry, which should actuate every liberal minded man, seems to be almost unknown, and one is led to imagine that the idea I have heard expressed by more than one, is general: "What the devil do I care how they live, so as they come to work when I want them, and pay me my rent!" I regret to have to remark here, that extreme hauteur of manner that some landlords observe to their tenants; one would be tempted to think that they did not consider them of the same species; they can know nothing more of their dispositions than of so many cattle. Did they relax a little, and treat them with a dignified kindness of manner, they would find a warmth and sincerity of return, much dearer to a feeling mind than that heartless hat-offering that seems to tickle their pride so much. I would beg of them to look to the meetings at Holkam, Wynnestay, and many others. Do they imagine that those enlightened proprietors of estates, that would equal half the estates of this county, lower themselves in the estimation of sensible men, when they collect around them at those meetings, their noble and humble friends? In ancient Persia a festival was yearly celebrated, in which husbandmen were freely admitted to the king's table, "From your labours," said the king, "we receive our sustenance, and by us you are protected; being mutually necessary to each other, let us, like brethren, live together in amity." Many landlords are attentive to the wants of their cottiers, but too careless of their comforts; of which they should be instructed that cleanliness is the very first. There is scarcely a cottage that has not a step down into it, and the dunghill uniformly near the door.

The common cant of many is, "they could not help it," the fact seems to be, they would not take the trouble to help it. Are we to be told that a poor cottier, totally dependent on his landlord, will not build on any site or level laid out for him, and keep the dunghill at the back of the house, and sufficiently far from it as not to incommode the family; but perhaps all this neatness would be too far from the road to be seen by travellers, the chief inducement, I fear, for the expenditure of much white wash; if this was not the inducement, why not, like lord Clancarty, extend to it to the whole estate? If the landlord is a non-resident, his agent should take delight in doing it; but I have had occasion before to remark, that the generality of those gentlemen are mere receivers of rent. My idea of an agent is, that he should consider himself a working partner at a certain percentage, rising or falling with the state of the concern, for farming must, to all intents and purposes, be considered a manufacture, and a very complicated one too, and I regret to say, one of which many agents are deplorably ignorant[1].

To the bad effects of a damp situation may be added, the want of ventilation, (which occurs also frequently in some great houses,) which in general is confined to that between the doors; for if there is a hole in the wall with a pane of glass fixed in it, it is the most they generally possess; as to a window that opens, that is a luxury

---

[1] I dare say it will be said here by some of my sagacious friends, "Aye, aye, Dutton wants an agency himself." I certainly would have no objection to one where I could have an opportunity of practising what I have suggested; but they will, perhaps, accuse me of arrogance, when I assure them that no emolument that would be offered, could tempt me to undertake the management of the affairs of a distressed or extravagant proprietor, nor indeed many others, though of great extent; I do not wish to fish in troubled waters like those gentlemen whom we so often see in the public papers, proposing to advance a sum of money to entitle them to the agency of the estate. I know an estate in this county that has frequently changed the agents, who are obliged to advance a sum of money; the tenants have been ruined, the rents have been screwed up so high above their value. God help the unfortunate tenants, and indeed the landlords that comes under the claws of one of those harpies, whose practice is to *flay* the tenants; mine would be, according to queen Elisabeth's advice to one of her Irish lieutenants, only to *shear* him. At the same time I am of opinion there cannot be a more ruinous or cruel practice than permitting tenants to run in arrears. Here the resident agent has the superior advantage of being able to distinguish between the tough rogue and the industrious unfortunate; for he is not fit for this situation that cannot form a near estimate of the circumstances of every tenant. An agent should be almost always on horseback amongst the tenants, laying out for them where drains should be made, where and how they should irrigate where plant, &c. &c. This could be accomplished by a steady and impartial system of rewards and punishments in fact, every large estate should have a little farming society for itself. Emolument with me is a secondary consideration; I have no pecuniary inducement; I have no reason to provide for but myself. It will be seen by the following advertisement which I inserted in the Farmer's Journal in September 1806, what my wishes were at that period. "He wishes for a resident agency, and presumes to think that any person having extensive designs to execute, or wants lands to reclaim, will meet with knowledge of rural economy, vary different from the generality of non-resident receivers of rent. Those who may wish for a more detailed statement of his acquirements, he trusts, will find that he can meet a liberal engagement with a very superior degree of exertion, and general knowledge of what should constitute the duties of a resident agent to landed property. Anonymous applications, or from any but principals, will not be noticed."

possessed by very few except show cottages. In too many instances, the cow and pig keep their places in the house; certainly not so frequently as formerly.

The general mode of thatching in this province, with a neatly twisted ridge of straw, is much superior to that usually practised in the county of Dublin, where mortar or road dirt are substituted, and occasions the thatch to decay very soon. The mode of building cottages here is nearly the same throughout the province; they are usually of stone without mortar. In some places a foundation of stone, and the remainder of the wall either of sods or tempered clay, at which work the labourers of this county are very far behind those of other parts of Ireland. As a proof that they are conscious of their instability, they put uprights of wood in building the wall, on which the rafters rest, instead of a wall plate; they are generally about six feet asunder; across those there are *ribberies* stretched, consisting of branches of trees, and on those, smaller sticks, (wattling,) which support the *scraws* (sods cut thin) into which the straw is thrust with an iron instrument, and neatly smoothed with a rake; sometimes the straw is fastened on with scallops, or with ropes stitched to the ribberies. Frequently the roof is covered with heath or potato stalks, which very soon decay, and as there is very seldom an eve stone, and the thatch does not project far enough over the wall, the rains are admitted, and in a very short period the wall either tumbles, or is propped until it becomes so bad that a new patch must be built, and not infrequently the wretched inmates are obliged to place their beds close to it in this wet state. What the consequences of this are, may be perceived in the numerous cases of colds, consumptions, and fevers, &c. that daily occur at every dispensary, which, much to the credit of many gentlemen, are becoming very general, and are of infinite use. I must still think, however, that much of the necessity for medical aid might be prevented by an attention to the habitations of the cottier tenants, and that if they even received the attention that the pigs receive in many places, much might be done. If the agent lives too far from the estate, which is too frequently the case, or that it would interfere too much with the amusements or indolence of the proprietor, a person might be appointed for this sole purpose, a rural conservator, or agricultural agent. I must confess when I reflect on this culpable neglect, I probably feel too irritable to think or write calmly; when I see the expence incurred in erecting stables, dog-kennels, and piggeries, I cannot help immediately thinking on the unfortunate man and his family, lying in a wisp of damp straw by the side of a new built mud wall. I am not so cynical as to deny every comfort and cleanliness to those noble and beautiful animals — horses; or those other animals that contribute to our health or amusement; I think much should be conceded to induce an occasional residence of landed proprietors, for I do not think they should be always *cotting* at home; they should see the world, especially the younger part. I also agree that architectural beauty should accompany the arrangement of those offices, according to a man's rank and fortune, but surely a reflecting mind would conceive that a frequent visit and close inspection of the condition of their tenantry would not be incompatible with their other arrangements. How delightful would it be to extend the usual visit after breakfast from the dog-kennel and stables, to examine the stalls of those other animals that would not be less grateful, and on whose prosperity depends the means for the maintenance of every other. I presume to think that lord and lady Clancarty, and their family, have a delicious gratification when walking through their tenantry, that can never be felt by those who think of nothing but an increase of their rental. Were I a landed proprietor I should be ashamed to ask one of my tenants "what his name is and where does he live?" when at the same time there is not a hound of forty couple whose name I would not know, and from what dam and sire, &c. In a late advertisement in one of the public papers, a pack of hounds was advertised, "whose blood can be accounted for during fifty years careful breeding". I do not give this extract from any cynical motive, for I think if hounds are kept they should have every attention paid to their goodness and keeping; I pity the man whose spirits are not raised by the cry of the hounds. On this subject I am proud to have the countenance of Mr. Kent in his hints to landed proprietors, page 206:—

> "Estates being of no value without hands to cultivate them, the labourer is one of the most valuable members of society; without him the richest soil is not worth owning; his situation then should be considered, and made at least comfortable, if it were merely out of good policy. There is certainly no object so highly deserving the country gentleman's attention; his interest and his duty equally prompt him to do all he can to place him on a better footing than he is at present The first point to be taken under consideration is the state of the cottages which those useful people inhabit; and next, how far their condition can be improved by better regulations. The shattered hovels which half the poor of this kingdom are obliged to put up with is truly affecting to a heart fraught with humanity[1]. Those who descend to visit these miserable tenements testify that neither health or decency can be preserved in them. The weather frequently penetrates all parts of them; which must occasion illness of various kinds, particularly agues, which more frequently visit the children of cottagers than any others, and early shake their constitutions. It is shocking that a man, his wife, and half a dozen children should be all obliged to lie in one room together, and more so, that the wife should have no more private place to be brought to bed in. This description is not exaggerated, offensive as it may appear. We are all careful of our horses, nay of our dogs, which are less valuable animals; we bestow considerable attention upon our stables and our kennels; but we are apt to look upon cottages as encumbrances and clogs to our property, when in fact those who occupy them are the very nerves and sinews of agriculture. Nay, I will be bold to aver, that more real advantages flow from cottages than from any other source; for, besides their great utility to landed property, they are the greatest support to the state, as being the most prolific cradles of population. Cottagers are indisputably the most beneficial race of people we have; they are bred up in greater simplicity; live more primitive lives; more free from vice and debauchery than any other set of men of the lower class; and are best formed and enabled to bear the hardships of war and other laborious services. Great towns are destructive both to morals and health, and are the greatest drains we have." In page 216, "Almost every parish is, in a great measure, subject to some particular gentleman, who

---

[1] It is a gloomy satisfaction to think that this is a description of English peasantry. Some of our travellers would wish us to think the poor are (or at least were) in the most enviable state of cleanliness and comfort, [original footnote].

has sufficient power and influence over it to correct the present grievance, and to set a better example. Such gentlemen should consider themselves guardians of the poor, and attend to their accommodation and happiness; it is their particular business, because they and their families have a lasting interest in the prosperity of the parish; the farmers only a temporary one. If a gentleman's estate be so large that he cannot attend to objects of this sort, he should at least recommend the cottagers to the attention of his agent, and give him strict instructions to act as their friend and protector; for unless some check be put upon great farmers, (in the county of Galway middlemen) they are very apt to contribute to the demolition instead of the protection of cottages". Page 254, "The landlord, tenant, and labourer, are intimately connected together, and have their reciprocal interests, though in different proportions; and when the just equilibrium between them is interrupted, the one or the others must receive injury. At present the balance is considerably against the labourer; and yet though it may seem a paradox, if the other parties ultimately derive no advantage from it. Sir William Molyneaux, who lived in the reign of Henry VIII., on his death bed gave this advice to his son, "let the underwood grow; the tenants are the support of a family, and the commonality are the strength of a kingdom. Improve this fairly, but force not violently either your bounds or rents above your forefathers."

The rent paid for a hovel, such as I have described, with a very small garden, is in many places from thirty to fifty shillings; and grass of a cow, badly kept, from a guinea and an half to three pounds; this frequently on ground that would be well let at fifteen shillings per acre. A few years since I was delighted with the appearance of the tenantry of Mr. Lawrence, near Headford. In the month of May there was scarcely one without a stack or more of corn and hay, a small meadow in good heart, neat gardens, and every appearance of comfort: now, alas! (1822) we may look in vain for them; they have disappeared. Mr. D'Arcey builds excellent stone cottages with a porch for his tenants in Connemara, and they have every appearance and reality of comfort.

FUEL

This, with few exceptions, is turf or peat[1]. — In the town of Galway a large proportion is sea coal. Also in a district of country bordering on the southern coast of the bay of Galway, and running for several miles inland, coal is much used, as the

---

[1] It is amusing to read a letter in the 4th volume of the *Communications to the Board of Agriculture*, from John W. Willaume, Esq. on this subject. He says very gravely, "It has been rejected from the parlour, the kitchen, the brew-house, &c. as being injurious to grates, and to all sorts of vessels put on it; it cannot be employed in the roasting of meat, as it will impart a disagreeable taste, and it is destructive of all sorts of furniture by the effluvia which it emits, or by the dust or ashes that may chance to be blown from it. If these disagreeable consequences could be obviated, it might be made an article of general consumption, as a substitute for coal, much to the advantage of the seller and consumer." Every thing we read shews how little Irish affairs are known in England, and to what a ridiculous pitch prejudice must have arrived in that enlightened country. Can it be necessary to inform Mr. Willaume, that at least four-fifths of the noblemen and gentry of Ireland are obliged to cook with peat, and probably Mr. Curwen can tell whether the roast meat has a disagreeable taste. I do not know what kind of peat Mr. Willaume used. It may possibly be highly sulphureous; but in Ireland I imagine no such complaint can be made, [original footnote].

country is possessed of very little turf, and the greater part of what they so burn is brought chiefly from the coast of Connemara. In general, fuel is plenty and cheap, except in the district before mentioned, and in that line of country beginning at Galway and running to Athenry and Monivae, a distance of several miles, with scarcely a turf bog. In some places the poor are obliged to gather dried cow dung, and frequently may be seen piles of it near their houses as large as turf ricks: this must injure the land much, but necessity has no law. A good workman will in two days, if the bog is good and deep, cut as much turf as will supply his consumption for the year: his family usually finish the process of drying, &c. In many bogs, from want of draining, much of the best of the turf is left uncut; in numerous instances, this will hereafter become a treasure when the bogs are cut out, which, notwithstanding the general plenty, has really happened in many places. This great plenty has hitherto caused great waste in the mode of cutting.

By the total neglect of many agents, bogs are frequently cut into pits or holes, which retain the wet, and add much to the expense of reclaiming them. In fact there are many agents that have never set a foot on the bogs of the estate. The verge of almost every bog is inhabited by cottagers for the sake of easy carriage of turf and black mud, which is an object of great consequence to a poor man, who frequently possesses no means of carriage better than two baskets on an ass's back; sometimes the human back is obliged to bear the burden, and often the female part of the family.

In the island of Arran, and all the other islands on the coast, they are obliged to procure their fuel from the opposite coast of Connemara, and the boats generally bring back limestone as ballast, which answers for domestic purposes, but not in sufficient quantity as to be of use as a manure to a soil highly adapted for it.

FOOD

In this county, as in many other parts of Ireland, the potato constitutes the greater part of the food of the peasantry; indeed this partiality is entertained by every intermediate rank to the palace, no table being without them. It would be in vain to attempt to produce evidence of the ruinous tendency of this propensity of the lower ranks; the current runs too strong against me; yet I imagine, on a candid enquiry, it will probably appear that much of the misery of the lower ranks of society in Ireland may be attributed to the ease with which a family may be subsisted on this vegetable. Possibly it is not generally known that an English acre of potatoes will produce food for one meal for 16,875 men; whilst the same quantity of ground will not grow wheat for more than 2745; the expenses of raising both crops nearly equal. I am aware that it will be asked, what would become of our dense population without potatoes, could they afford to buy bread, &c. &c.? but the question is, why the indolence of landed proprietors have permitted this increase of a starving population, by permitting the minute subdivision of land? for to this chiefly is owing this rapid increase. How many wretched hovels do we see in every part, of Ireland, thrown up hastily either in a dry ditch, or against a bank of earth, and with scarcely an article of even the meanest kind of furniture. It is true on some estates a clause against reletting is inserted in the leases, but in very few is it strictly enforced. The proprietor, except it is near the high road, never sees it, and the agent, perhaps of a rank little higher than the tenant, overlooks it, as he has the tenant as security for any under tenants who may creep into the village. On an estate in this county, of which I had the improvement, much of this kind of reletting had occurred; some of the villagers, from an increase of their family (to each of whom, when grown up, some ground was allotted) had not sufficient to support them comfortably, yet in many cases, from the promise of a profit rent, they permitted renegades from different parts of Ireland to occupy a part of their little cottage, or perhaps converted a cow-house into a wretched habitation for perhaps a murderer or a robber, and of this description many of the disturbers of the peace of the country were composed.

A cottier has seldom less than from three roods to an acre of potatoes; of this he plants as much as he has manure for, the remainder he raises on land hired for burning from some adjacent landholder, and generally at exorbitant rates; sometimes as high as ten guineas an acre[1]. For the setter of the land this is frequently a most uncomfortable mode, as multitudes will take it at this high price, that, if a bad season or other untoward accident happens, will leave it on his hands; and even if they do take them, it is frequently on credit, and payable at a distant period. If it is a ready money bargain, the potatoes are put into pits in different parts of the field, and frequently remain there in the way of the plough; in few cases can they be induced to dig their crop until the appearance of frost compels them, and the proper season for wheat sowing is lost. The letting is usually committed to some wise man, a species of shark that many country gentlemen have about them; he exacts money for earnest, and as he is not generally answerable for the solvency of the takers, he lets either to his favourites, or perhaps to those who give most whiskey. If those kind of people were always made answerable for the rent, they would be more careful, and justice requires they should be liberally rewarded for an attentive and honest discharge of a very troublesome duty.

The quantity of potatoes used by a family consisting of six people, is commonly about twenty-two stone per week, and this may be about the average quantity raised on about an acre of such ground as the poor generally occupy, allowing some for

---

[1] I have great pleasure in stating, that a few years ago when Mr. Daly of Dunsandle broke up his lawn by this process, he gave directions to his steward to charge only six pounds an acre, and not to let to strangers until his own tenants were supplied; for this ground he could easily have got ten pounds an acre. Nor can I omit mentioning that the steward of the late Mr. Andrew Brown of Mounthazel, having set a large quantity of land near Ballinasloe for eight guineas per acre, Mr. Browne thought it too high, and desired him to return a guinae per acre. With equal pleasure I have to state that in the year 1812, a very trying year for the poor, lord Clonbrock sold all his pigs, and turned out his horses to grass to save their food for the poor: in every respect his lordship is an excellent landlord, of course much beloved by his tenants, and very universally esteemed, [original footnote].

beggars, who are seldom refused, and also for the pig, dog, cat and fowl: frequently in winter the cow and horse get a small share of potatoes, also reserving about 170 stones for planting an acre in spring.

In many parts of this county the cottiers have a very scanty share of milk with their potatoes; for as they seldom have more than one cow, and too many not any, they are for a part of the year without any milk. In many instances they get nothing but the buttermilk, as the butter is frequently sold to pay the rent, or clothe the family, &c. In some places much use is made of sheep's milk, which is a great relief to many poor families, but often at the lambs' expense: those useful animals sometimes give four quarts of milk a day; on this stirabout is made with oatmeal, very white and nourishing. On the sea coast much use is made of fish[1], and in general the inhabitants are much more comfortable than those more inland; those on the coast of Connemara are particularly so, as few have less than two or three cows, and many have from eight to twelve, and both men and women are in their persons and dress much superior to those of any other part of this county; they look like another race of people: in Connemara they call brandy and milk *Cow — Cow*, and to which they are very partial in the morning. No cottage is without a cabbage garden, but they seldom have any succession, as they use almost exclusively the large flat Dutch cabbage, which before winter they generally bury in the earth, a practice that universally prevails in this province, producing a rank substitute for what a little attention would give them abundance of.

Not one in an hundred ever think of having greens all the winter, by sowing a pinch at a time of cabbage or borecole[2] seed, every month from March to September: even the sprouts from the cabbages are usually destroyed by the cattle or goats, these most destructive animals, that no landed proprietor should permit, where there are trees or hedges. The kind of potatoes cultivated in this county are:

Grenadiers.	Cork reds.	Turks.
Red apple.	Barbers wonders.	Ox noble.
White apple.	Bangors.	Yams or bucks
Black.	Red nose kidney.	Coppers.
Early Prussians.	Leather coats,	Purple kidney.
Cups.	White eyes.	American dandies.
Lumpers.	Windeleers.	
English reds.	Pink eyes.	

Lumpers are much used, at they are more productive from a little manure than any other kind, but they are a wretched kind for any human creature; even pigs, I am informed, will not eat them if they can get any other kind. Cups are in great estimation, *as they stay long in the stomach*, of course require strong powers of

---

[1] I am informed that children that use this food, are never troubled with worms, [original footnote].
[2] Kale - a vegetable with green or purple leaves, [Clachan ed.].

digestion, especially as they are usually dressed by the country people "with a bone in them" That potatoes are a wholesome food, I believe there can be little doubt; and I can have little feeling for the distress of an English manufacturer that can procure good potatoes and new milk for his family for at least a part of each week;[1] I say good potatoes, because in general they are in England much inferior in quality to those used in Ireland. I should strongly recommend the opinion of Mr. Arthur Young, who has always advocated the cause of truth, virtue, and loyalty. In his Irish tour, when speaking of the food of the Irish, he says, "when I see the people of a country, in spite of political oppression, with well formed vigorous bodies, and their cottages swarming with children; when I see their men athletic, and their women beautiful, 1 know not how to believe them subsisting on an unwholesome food."

One would imagine the libeler before mentioned had been reading Mortimer, who wrote in the year 1721; he says, "the potato is very near the nature of the Jerusalem artichoke, but not so good or wholesome! they are planted either of roots or seeds, and may probably be propagated in great quantities, and prove good for swine." How wonderfully opinions are changed since the French revolution! then, they were "food for republicans," now, "they are only fit for swine;" but any thing to serve a purpose.

We have seen lately in some of the public papers, that potatoes are, in some districts in India, taking the place of rice. It is a curious circumstance, that about one hundred years ago, potatoes did not last longer than about August; and only sixty years ago a boiling was generally reserved to make colcannon on all hallowed eve; since that we have obtained kinds that continue good until the following season. In the neighbourhood of Galway they use manure brought from that dirty town, which for that reason is particularly fertilising. They pay about eight pounds for as much as manures an acre of land; they spend usually four months collecting it on their ground. Most of the crops, except oats, are sold in Galway.

CLOTHING

The majority of the population of this county are clothed in frieze, especially the elderly; much of it is made at home by the females of the family; the remainder purchased at the different fairs and markets in country towns. Frieze or coarse flannel jackets, and petticoats of a muddy red, are much worn by the females, when occupied about their domestic concerns; but in general, on Sundays they are dressed

---

[1] But an English manufacturer has been so long used to his porter and cheese, and gin every night at some ale house, and his wife to tea, that they reckon potatoes and milk, starvation; and writers of a certain kidney know well how to take advantage of this feeling. One of this nefarious class says "potatoes are only fit for swine;" a potato is the worst of all things for man; there needs nothing more to inflict the scrofula in a whole nation, (and the potato feeders in Ireland, where the lower classes exist on that vegetable, are a proof of this)! It distends the stomach (wonderful!) it swells the heels (unless the eater labours hard) and it enfeebles the mind. If the potato has this last effect, it were devoutly to be wished that writer had used them freely, since he has turned his strong mind to the worst of purposes, [original footnote].

in coarse cotton fabrics, but mostly accompanied by red petticoats. On the coast of Connemara the men are very generally dressed in blue jackets and trousers, as they are mostly amphibious, which gives them an appearance of cleanliness and neatness much superior to those of any other part of the country. Any other articles of dress the women may want are frequently received in barter for the produce of their farms, or of their industry: eggs are very much used in bartering for tobacco and small articles, and coarse linens and yarn for those of more value: sometimes they will come several miles with a pennyworth of eggs, half a pound of butter, a few greens or cabbage, chickens, &c. The men scarcely ever go without shoes and stockings in winter; but with the women the practice is almost universal; they walk several miles to a fair barefooted, and in some retired spot where they can have water they wash their feet, put on their shoes and stockings, let down their gown, comb their hair, settle their cap, and adjust every article for the fair or market[1]. Two pair of shoes, worth from seven shillings to half a guinea, are generally sufficient for the year, with the addition of two pair of soles, at two shillings each. The stockings worn by both men and women are generally of home manufacture, and, except in Connemara, very few are made for sale: sometimes we may see a belle dressed in white cotton stockings on a Sunday or at a fair. Hats are usually of felt, made of wool, and low priced, from three to five shillings each. Breeches worn by elderly people are commonly of frieze, the same as the coat and waistcoat; but the young men are ambitious of getting thicksets or cords of different fading colours; the beaux are fond of black or pearl colour, made so very tight about the knees that they get very little wear from them: you will frequently see one at the top of the fashion with his stockings gartered below the knee, and the knees of his black breeches open, and a profusion of long black tape strings hanging loose about his legs. It seems to be a universal practice with most country tailors to make every article of dress too tight; probably it may be by the directions of the rustic dandies. Whilst about their daily avocations they are frequently in tatters, but on Sundays generally cut a very respectable figure. The women of the Cloddagh, near Galway, never wear any ribbons, but are very expensive in lace for their caps. Most country women are chemists, and prepare different vegetable substances for dyeing. With a species of bog earth, strongly impregnated with iron, alder leaves or branches, and copperas[2],

---

[1] From the outcry railed against me in the county of Clare for meddling with the ladies legs, and with whom the ladies of this county seem to have joined, it is necessary to remark, that an attentive perusal of that part of the surrey of Clare, page 180, would have convinced them that I touched their legs very gently. Some ladies seem to insinuate that I said all the ladies of that county go bare legged. I only said, "I have seen even some young ladies not averse themselves to appearing *in shoes without stockings.*" I cannot think of making a serious reply to this, but I can assure them that since they seem to wish it, I shall for the future set such ticklish subjects aside. The ladies I alluded to in the county of Clare, though not of that rank that, by the rules of heraldry, entitled them to that distinction, yet they were of a rank in life that should have placed them above such a filthy custom. In no part of Ireland need the ladies less fear to show their legs; the more we see the more we would wish to see, [original footnote].
[2] ferrous sulfate, [Clachan ed.].

they make an excellent and permanent black. With briar roots, or elm or oak bark, and copperas, red wood (I suppose logwood) and galls, a good brown, and several intermediate shades.

Almost all kinds of clothes are washed by beetling,[1] which is usually performed by a woman standing up to her knees or higher in water, beating on a large smooth stone the article to be cleaned; this they frequently do for hours, and often in winter, with seldom any worse effect than spoiling the shape and colour of their legs; for after this operation they run to the fire, which causes their legs to swell and become discoloured. It was from those, that *Zwiss*, several years since, formed his idea of Irish legs, and probably knew no farther.

SECTION IV

PRICES OF LABOUR, WAGES, AND PROVISIONS

The rate of wages varies in different parts of the county; in some places, only five pence in winter, and seven pence in summer; others sixpence and eight pence; others eight pence and ten pence; a few give a shilling in the harvest, but it must be understood that those rates are for tenants who have land. On one estate the wages are sixpence half-penny per day, and the rent for indifferent land from thirty shillings to three pounds per acre. Where they are what are called *spalpeens* or strangers they receive more, and frequently get their diet, especially in harvest, turf cutting, or potato planting; though in some few instances, and they are very few, the rate of wages, and the rent of land occupied by labourers may be on a par, yet the general rate of wages is far below a remuneration for active services, and by no means keeps pace with the value of the inferior kind of land usually occupied by labourers. Those who do not know the customs of Ireland must be on their guard when they hear Irish gentlemen boast at the duke of Bedford's or Mr. Coke's shows, that they charge only so much for a house and garden, and an acre of land, or grass for a cow, &c. &c. They must be told that the general run of cottages (at least in the province of Connaught) are damp houses, built by the poor cottager himself. Perhaps some benevolent landlord may give him some of the thinnings of his plantations for roofing it, and may, as a compliment, permit him to quarry a few stones for a foundation, but he is left to choose the site and levels himself, which, to save trouble, is generally built where some advantage may be taken of either some damp hollow, or the bank of a ditch, &c. The garden is generally very small, merely sufficient for a few cabbages; the remainder of the acre is occupied with alternate crops of potatoes and oats, manured by a scanty portion of dung, made by an ill fed cow and a pig, mixed with black mud; the grass for a cow almost universally on the very worst part of the land, and often overstocked.

---

[1] the pounding of linen or cotton fabric to give a flat, lustrous effect, [Clachan ed.].

For these favours it is expected the most active exertions shall be made. Can we be surprised that under those circumstances labourers are indolent? Warner, who wrote on Irish affairs many years since, gave good advice on this subject: — "Were the common people once made warm and thriving by their industry, they might better spare their gentry than they can do now." Probably it will be found advantageous, first, to raise the wages, or lower the rents, and then to exact better attention to early hours and an increased exertion. It will be found that reward will be better than coercion; it will take away from stewards that excuse, which with some reason they make, for not obliging labourers to perform more work than they usually do.

According to the present system, turning them home by way of punishment produces little beneficial effect; for the trifling sum they receive, when put into competition with their own domestic occupations is often below their notice. In fact, except in the middle of winter, it is frequently very difficult to bring them from home, and recourse must be had to driving[1]. The practice of task work is increasing much in this county, and only wants to be better known to be generally adopted. It requires some experience to ascertain the value; but the simple method of devoting one day to superintend the execution of a given number of perches, or part of any kind of work, will enable any person to estimate the value; but a resolution must be formed to insist that the pattern, when properly arranged, shall be implicitly followed, making ample allowance always for unforeseen obstructions. In most cases it will be necessary to enforce the accomplishment of the work in a given time, otherwise it may be executed at a season that will not only increase the difficulty of the execution, but ditches or drains executed, or at least finished in winter, suffer severely from frost or heavy rains. In very few cases should a ditch be made at once; in land that will run at the bottom, (and which is the general case in this county,) if the ditch is intended to be seven feet by six deep, it should be sunk only about three feet deep and three feet broad the first year; the following year it may be finished, and in many situations it will have run so much on the sides from the issue of water long pent up, and the action of frost, that there will be little more than paring the sides to make the ditch of the intended breadth. A great extent of draining by task has been executed at Mount Bellew; and on the Netterville estate I had executed in two years upwards fifteen miles of ditches and master drains, but in both cases a statement of the value, owing to difference of dimensions, and unforeseen obstructions, might only tend to mislead. At some future period I may probably give a table of the rate of wages, and hope I may be favoured with assistance from those

---

[1] As the meaning of the word 'driving', may not be generally known out of Ireland, it is necessary to state, that from the general poverty of cottier tenants, and I may say of most Irish tenants, half a year's rent, called the hanging gale, generally remains unpaid; this, on failure of coming to work, and frequently for some misdemeanor, is exacted, by driving some beast to pound, which is usually released on coming to work, or some other accommodation; if not, the animal is advertised and sold in a few days. I fear in many cases this is a great source of oppression, but in many others highly necessary, [original footnote].

who have pursued this method of executing work. The wages of a house carpenter is from two to four shillings per day; those of a plough or car maker, usually called a hedge carpenter, from eighteen pence to two shillings and six pence, and his diet; a thatcher the same; other trades men usually by measurement, at the usual rates, or according as advantage can be taken of his necessities.

Shepherds have usually a house, small garden, some tillage ground, and grass for a cow and heifer, and generally keeping for a brood mare. As they are servants of some responsibility, they have commonly many indulgences, and no person would take a herd without his possessing some stock, as they are frequently the only security from neglect or misdemeanor.

PROVISIONS

The prices of provisions are so very fluctuating, that I cannot see to what purpose I should give a list of them; they not only vary almost every week, but in different towns at the same period. The bread of this county, in general, is excellent, which does no little credit to the millers, for except in some particular districts the wheat is very inferior to the growth of other parts of Ireland, and where their flour frequently does not keep pace with the goodness of their wheat. The superiority of the flour of this county may be accounted for by the millers being mostly practical men, and superintending their own concerns; those, and their mills, are the description that are useful to the tillage of a country, (and I wish there were more of them,) as they bring the market home to the farmer, who, where those mills do not exist, loses, besides his expenses, two or three days by bringing his crop to Galway; and as his horses and cars are both generally very weak, the quantity he can draw seldom exceeds two barrels (forty stone) of wheat, or three of oats (forty-two stone).

This is a heavy tax on his profits, exclusive of the loss of seasons for his different operations. The farmers have also adopted the useful practice of selling by sample, which saves them much trouble, and does not put them so completely in the power of the miller as those who bring their sacks to market. Formerly there was a considerable export of beef and pork from Galway, but for several years that trade has been lost. The merchants of Galway have lately exerted themselves to encourage an export of butter; I fear there has not been much success attending their praiseworthy regulations for its encouragement. I cannot understand why it should not succeed, as a considerable quantity of good butter is made to the west of Galway, and in many other parts of the county, and I am informed has always brought the highest price at foreign markets.

SECTION V

STATE OF TITHE — ITS GENERAL AMOUNT

There can be no second opinion about the right the clergy have to tithes; the right to estates cannot be stronger; even those who are most adverse to this mode of provision for the clergy do not deny this, but they exclaim against the mode of collection, and as far as I could collect their opinions, they seem to think that every incumbent should, by immediate agents, collect his tithe, and not let it to others, who again employ proctors or inferior persons to view and set the tithe, and those frequently of very questionable character. Another great objection seems to be valuing tithe by the acre, without making sufficient allowance for inferior or bad crops. The prices charged for tithe, per acre, are very various; in some parishes, wheat a guinea to one pound six shillings; oats 12s.; barley 12s. to 20s.; sheep 45s. to 50s. per 100; lambs 50s. per hundred: in others, 9s. 9d. to 11s. 4½ . for wheat; oats 5s. to 7s.; barley and bere 8s. to 9s.; sheep a guinea to twenty five shillings: near Loughrea, 12s. to 14s. for wheat; 9s. to 10s. for oats and barley; 50s. per 100 for sheep: in another place, 10s. for wheat; 7s. for oats and barley.

The late Rev. Mr. Russell, for the parishes of Ballindoone, Moyne, Omagh, and Ballynakill, charged no more than he did fifteen years ago, and all by composition. The greatest hardship in my mind is the exemption of cattle. In 1735 the Irish house of Commons (what a house of Commons!) passed a resolution against tithe for cattle, called the *tithe of agistment*, which frees the rich grazier, and lays the burden on the poor tiller of the soil. Before this period it had been received by the clergy of Ireland as well as England; which appears by the act of Henry VIII. 93. chap. 12, which enumerates and provides for the due payment of corns, hay, pasturage, and other sorts of tithes and oblations commonly due. It appears that between the years 1722 and 1795, forty-three suits for agistment[1] tithe were instituted in the Exchequer in Ireland, and in all of which that were decided, the judgment of the court was in favour of the claims of the clergy. Surely the enormity of this exemption must strike every thinking mind.

How praiseworthy would it be to take the tithe off the crop of those who can so badly bear it, and lay it on that which requires so little exertion; and on no other terms do I wish it. I trust the legislature of the present day will view this affair in a very different light from their conscientious brethren of 1735. On the other side, I am perfectly convinced that many who complain most loudly of the hardships they suffer, have less cause than many others: I recollect one extensive farmer complained to me that he only paid formerly about £15. for his tithe, and indeed, truly, the incumbent had the conscience to charge him £60. I had heard the circumstance before, and a little cross examination at length brought out, that he had broken up a large additional quantity of grass land for corn, and increased to a great amount his stock of sheep; yet he was so unreasonable and uncandid as to expect his tithe at the old valuation.

It is ridiculous to suppose that if the land was made tithe free the landlord would not increase the rent to the full value of the tithe. In an examination of Mr. Emmet by the

---

[1] 'Agistment' refers to the proceeds of pasturage in the king's forests, [Clachan ed.].

house of lords in 1798, he says, "I am sure if tithes were abolished, the people taking new leases would be obliged to pay more in proportion for lands, than the value they now pay for tithes. There have been many modes proposed for making the burden of tithe lighter on the shoulders of the poorer class of farmers, but they have been all found objectionable.

I shall not take upon me to propose any other change in the present system than the one I have before mentioned, as I feel the subject too difficult to deal with; but it must strike every person that something must be resorted to that will do away a very general charge, *that as the prices of corn fall, and the farmers' difficulties increase, the rates of tithes increase*[1].

SECTION VI

USE OF BEER OR SPIRITS, WHETHER EITHER OR WHICH IS INCREASING

The use of beer has increased considerably, and if beer or ale could be had of pure quality, brewed from malt and hops only, the use would still increase; but the brewers have been so long in the habit of using drugs of various kinds, that all idea of drinking such wholesome pale ale as we were used to in the days of yore has been long abandoned. The brewers, I am aware, allege, and probably many with truth, that although they may use other ingredients than malt and hops, they are quite inoxious. As I am not skilled in brewing I cannot take upon myself to ascertain the fact, nor am I individually concerned, as I rarely drink brewers beer; I see too much vitriol passing by every day with carriers, confessedly for their use. The fine ale that is to be met with at some few private houses shows what could be done. At all events the very idea of the hurtful ingredients used in breweries, has made multitudes of water

---

1 From the following extract from Curry's Review, it will be perceived that the mode of paying the clergy in the reign of king Charles I. was more complicated than at present. "The bishops received 6d. per annum from every couple, (holy water clerk); of every man that dies a muttue, by the name of anointing money, but from a poor man that had but one cow, they take that for mortuary money; from one that is better able, his best garment for mortuary. If a woman, her best garment for mortuary; and a gallon of drink for every brewing, by the name of Mary gallons; for every beef that is killed for the funeral of any man, the hide and tallow, and they challenged a Quarter besides. 4d. or 6d. per annum from every parishioner for soul money: a ridge of winter corn, and a ridge of oats for every plow, by the name of St. Patrick's ridges: for portion-canons the tenth part of the goods, after debts paid, &c. &c. In the time of the Anglo-Saxons, besides a tithe of every thing, even merchandise, a silver penny was paid for every hide of land at Easter, under the denomination of plough-alms. At the feast of St. Martin a certain quantity of wheat or other grain was offered on the altar; it was called kirk-shot, and was assessed on each house according to its value on the preceding Christmas. Those who refused to pay it were amerced forty shillings to the king, and twelve times the value to the church. Thrice in the year was paid the lest-shot, or a certain quantity of wax of the value of a silver penny for each hide of land. There was also another tax, called soul-shot, for prayers in behalf of the dead. — I have selected these few passages to show our present that the present rates of tithe are light, compared to those of ancient days. And I presume to think an abolition of their ruinous, dirty fallows, and wretched mode of running out the soil, would more than enable them to pay their tithes, [original footnote].

drinkers. I am at a loss to know why every private house does not brew as formerly, when even small farmers brewed; the reasons generally given by many are, that they do not wish to be liable to the visits of guagers at all hours, and that they cannot get good malt to buy. As to the first objection I have never heard of any improper intrusion, nor need there be any apprehension if an honest return is intended; but I have heard of some mean practices, where an example of a different tendency should have been set to the tenants; at the same time I am convinced that the principal was totally ignorant of what was going forward, and that many domestics would think the beer much the sweeter if they could *jink the guager*. As to the second objection, it would not cost much to erect a small malt house, which might answer for several adjoining families, and might be conducted by the brewer, who also might brew for those families: the kiln would be highly useful for drying corn, &c. In most cases I imagine indolence to be the chief cause. There are several breweries in Galway, and a very extensive one at Newcastle near Galway, where an imitation of pale English ale is brewed, that is much liked by many people.

There are two at Ballinasloe, one at Tuam, two at Loughrea, one in Gort, by a highly esteemed brewer, and one at Oranmore, which I imagine are all the breweries in this extensive county. One great inducement to private brewing I omitted to notice; the production of pure barm[1], so material an article in house keeping, and which in many situations it is difficult to procure, and frequently, from the ingredients used in brewing, of bad quality. I imagine the consumption of spirits has not increased; at least of spirits paying duty. The poverty of the whiskey drinkers has prevented much of that drunkenness we had formerly to complain of. There are a few licensed distilleries in the county, but not at work in 1820. In spite of every exertion of the excise officers, unlicensed stills abound, especially in all mountainous situations. A very general idea prevails that poteen whiskey is much wholesome than parliament whiskey: it wants something to counterbalance the detestable taste of smoke which it generally possesses, but the palates of many are so degraded by habit, that they think no whiskey pure unless it has this smokey taste; and I am informed some distillers, taking advantage of this depravity of taste, have imitated it in their liquor. The unlicensed distillers add considerable quantities of vitriol, soap, &c. and set all the bad taste down to the account of malt dried with turf! and their customers swallow this, as well as their vile liquor. I understand in Connemara, where whiskey is the staple, it is distilled from barley malt, or at least barley brought generally from the coast of the county of Clare, and that they never use vitriol: certainly the best I ever tasted was in that country; it was nearly without any taste of smoke, and comparatively mild, though just taken from the still: that kept for two years was excellent. Vast quantities of spirits from this part of the county, and all along the coast, are consumed in Galway. Drunkenness amongst the higher ranks of society is now very rare; little of that mistaken hospitality remains, which locked the door

---

[1] The yeasty foam on liquor used as a leaven in baking, [Clachan ed.].

whilst it deprived you of your reason; a perfect freedom of action prevails, and though the decanter is pushed about as freely as ever, it is your own fault if you proceed to intoxication. In some fashionable houses care is most kindly taken to prevent long sitting, by permitting the fire in the dining parlour to go out, and by announcing that *coffee is ready*. Indeed in general the ladies of this rank possess every inducement to hasten a return to their society in the drawing room. The effect that was intended by the destruction of the small distilleries, has not been produced, but rather a diminution of revenue; it also had the effect of spreading unlicensed distillers through the country in every direction. No advantage has been taken of the late act, permitting stills of a smaller description to be worked. It has been computed that in Ireland there is consumed, of licensed and unlicensed whiskey, 8,650,000 gallons in the year; of this quantity a considerable share is drank in Connemara, where it is much the custom for all the neighbours to attend when a still is run off, and never quit the house until all is consumed, and another batch announced: happy country! The distillation of spirits from malt, was first practised in Ireland about the year 1590. Previous to this, a spirit was imported from France and England called aqua vitae, and from thence our whiskey was called Uisge-beatha, the water of life.

The Irish had formerly a liquor called Pimento composed of wine, honey, cinnamon, ginger, and other aromatics, which was called by foreigners Irish nectar, and was highly prized by them.

SECTION VII

STATE OF ROADS, BRIDGES, &c. &c.

The roads of this county are generally good: indeed there can be little excuse for bad roads; for the best materials, either broken stone or good gravel, abound in almost every part of it. In many places, either from indolence (the vice of this county) or ignorance, the stone is not broken as small as it should be: on this subject there seems to be some diversity of opinion.

One very intelligent gentleman, I am informed, insists that for the mail coach roads stones should not be broken small. The celebrated road maker in England, Mr. M'Adam, seems to countenance the same idea in his publication on this subject. A little discrimination would very probably enable us to account for this. In those parts of England where Mr. M'Adam has operated, the stone is probably of a soft or brittle kind, but in Ireland, especially in this county, the stone is usually a very hard limestone, bearing the chisel, and the fracture almost as hard and sharp as a broken bottle; besides the mail coach seldom or ever deviates from one track in the centre of the road, as the drivers entertain an idea that every carriage must give way to his Majesty's mail; and as the carriers generally follow in the same track, the stones are soon ground down sufficiently to answer the purpose of the mail coach drivers, and they look no farther than their own convenience; but to others who travel, those roads are most unpleasant and dangerous. Probably I shall be able to prove that the idea is unfounded. It must be evident to every person that the nearer any road approaches to a uniformly smooth surface, the easier the draft on the horses; the iron rail ways prove this beyond any cavil; surely then, a road covered with broken stones deviates from this axiom in proportion to the size of the stones of which it is composed. Every person who travels in a carriage must be a very competent judge, and the hobbling of the unfortunate horses speaks volumes on the subject, exclusive of the loss of time. Though in a national establishment like that of the mail coaches, where this may be overlooked or disregarded, it may not be so apparent from their weight and the rate at which they drive, yet it must have an effect on the feet of the horses, and the wear of the carriage.

I have invariably found that in proportion, as the stones were broken small, the road was good.[1] Another practice recommended by Mr. M'Adam, and advocated by several in Ireland, is to leave the stone uncovered with any sort of clay or gravel. This has its origin from the same source: the stones generally used in England are so soft, or easily broken down, as not to require that covering which our hard, compact, limestone does. I grant that the argument used by many that in process of time the, stones will be worn down, has some shade of reason; but what must the carriages and horses suffer until this tedious process takes place? In roads much frequented by heavy carriages, and the stone broken very small, this should be dispensed with, but surely the advocates for this cruel omission, where large broken stones are used, do not consider that the road does not become firm until there is as much of the asperities of the broken stones worn off as will make a uniting medium for them.

This may happen at no very distant period in roads much used by heavy carriages, but in those not much frequented, and the stones of a hard kind, they remain for a long time in a most disagreeable state. I must confess, on sufficient proof being given, I think on action should lie against the maker of such road, for laming a horse or breaking the spring of a carriage.

Probably it may not be adverted to generally, that every obstacle the wheels of a carriage have to surmount, gives a shock to the horses' shoulders proportionate to the amount of the difficulty, and that there are plenty of those in every rough road, need not be enlarged on here. This may be very easily proved by a man wheeling a loaded wheel-barrow alternately on a newly made road of this barbarous construction, and on a firm smooth surface, and the effect on the feet of the horses by walking on them in very thin shoes.

---

[1] In my *Survey of the County of Dublin,* I gave an instance corroborative of this assertion. The best and most lasting road I ever saw was made with the powder and very small broken stone that remained, after the larger stones had been expended. It must be also known, that this occurred where two roads intersected each other, [original footnote].

Another very material objection to those uncovered roads is, that where the stones can shift under the wheels, the difficulty of the draught of wheel carriages must be greatly increased, for the stones swell up before the wheels, and on the most level road produce the effect of going always up hill; this effect is strongly proved by carriages going down steep hills, where roads are newly made with loose broken stone; there is no occasion to lock the wheel. On the Tuam road we have a strong proof that they do not wear well; there, according to the idea that bare broken stones are most lasting on mail coach roads, they are generally constructed in this manner. There it may be perceived, especially as the broken stones are laid on the old hard road, (a wretched practice) that the wheels of the coaches in a short time wear a passage for themselves, and purge out the stones on either side, leaving a firm hollow in which the wet settles, and helps to wear the road; but this answers their purpose.

That there is some jobbing in this county I fear we must admit, but infinitely below the amount in some other counties; and I am happy to state that the practice is declining fast, and I look to, and call on the rising generation of grand jurors to scout this disgrace to them out of the county entirely. In no part of Ireland are there better grand jurors, and if they sometimes lend themselves to a job, it proceeds from a deception of some favourite or wise man, the pest of this province. The new road act, which empowers magistrates to hold baronial sessions previous to the assizes, to examine into presentments, will tend much to lessen the frequency of jobs. I am convinced that many who practise this meanness, do it frequently from seeing their fathers and others doing it when they were young and thoughtless, but they should consider, that putting this into plain language, every man who knowingly practises, or even countenances a job, is a rogue and a liar. One of the greatest and most frequent abuses of the roads, is the practice winked at, if not countenanced by many landlords, of cutting away the sides of roads, and forming large and deep ditches where none originally existed. I shall mention a few amongst multitudes of others, that I have noticed. From Abbey Knockmay to Galway; from Tuam to Shruel, particularly abused; not only ditches have been formed, but walls thrust several feet into the road, and large and deep gravel pits made near Shruel close to the road: here it is particularly disgraceful, as the road formerly, (much to the credit of the maker,) was left very spacious with fine hedge rows, and a level grass verge. The hedges are all nearly cut down to stop gaps, and the sod either cut away, or gravel pits made in their place. There is the less excuse here, as the proprietor, a gentleman of the most elegant manners and good taste, is almost a constant resident, It shows what a dangerous thing bad example is to the best informed minds.[1]

---

[1] Since I composed the above, I am gratified that an attempt has been made to level these gravel pits. I fear we may thank English liberality for if, as I understand it was done for meal money, which performed many other miracles, [original footnote].

Between Tuam and ClareGalway the road is most shamefully cut away, especially near the latter village, where ditches ten or twelve feet wide, and six feet deep, may be seen, and still going on. In some parts of this line of road, where the road is fenced by stone walls, particularly near the seven mile stone, the tenants have made ditches on both sides, totally disregarded by either their landlord or the magistrates, who frequently pass by them. Between Cahermorris and Clare Galway, the same bad practices are pursued. The road between Tuam and Knockmoy greatly injured by ditches at least two feet wide, where none formerly existed, as the fence is a high stone wall. In short there are very few exceptions to this gross neglect of the country gentlemen. I am strongly persuaded, that where the roads have been thus cut away, the proprietors of the adjoining land should be obliged to fill them up again; they may apply to their indolent agent, or those to whom they have let their lands, and who generally are the aggressors. This most useful punishment could not by any construction be called an *ex post facto* one, as the road acts have been explicit on the subject. I imagine those who have walls on the sides of any road should be obliged to cope them with mortar, to prevent the stones from rolling into the road; it is astonishing how this nuisance is overlooked by magistrates; it has however one advantage, the frequent shocks their carriage gets keep them awake; and it affords fine practice to the juniors of the whip to drive the wheel of a gig to rub a stone without going over it. Amongst other evils those abuses will tend, at some future period, to bring into a multitude of broils with the country people, any person who will have the honesty to insist on an abolition of such disgraceful practices. Chiefly to indolence, and a neglect of a steady, yet temperate enactment of the existing laws, may be attributed that systematic opposition to them amongst the lower orders, that has continued for half a century to disgrace Ireland. After being obliged to use the rod, I shall with much more pleasure confer the wreath. On Mr. Bellew's extensive estate, through much of which the high road runs, not a ditch or any part of the road is injured. The road between Galway and Oughterard, wide and remarkably well made; but the loose stones that are permitted to roll about the road are a serious drawback on the pleasure of travelling through this charming country. It is a common practice with the tenants in many places to pick the stones off their field and lay them on the sides of the roads; this has been practised to such extent between Dangan and Rahoon near Galway, that scarcely, room for a carriage has been left. Mr. Browne of Moyne has made a great improvement by widening and enclosing the road along his demesne wall, and has continued this road in a new line, that instead of going over the high hill of Dangan, runs on a level and communicates with the Tuam road at Horse-leap. When Mr. D'Arcey went first to reside at Clifden in Connemara in 1816, he could scarcely ride into the country; but now, in 1820, he is enabled to drive a coach and four horses in hand from Galway to Clifden, a distance of nearly fifty miles.

He has opened, at his own expense, a road along the sea shore from Clifden to the intended quay, and from thence to his house, worthy of an old Roman. He is also now perfecting a new line of road from Clifden to Oughterard, which, instead of going over steep hills as at present, will run for nearly thirty miles with scarcely any difference in the level.[1] Many others are making good, roads, and improving and shortening the old lines, and are deserving of every encouragement from the grand jury. I have heard some gentlemen boast that they never ask for a presentment; they should rather boast that they made many good roads. The late Mr. Arthur French of Monivae, who at that time represented the county of Galway in parliament, was the person who introduced a bill for making roads by presentment Before that period the roads were made by statute labour, as practised I believe at this time in England; a wretched mode, that rendered them almost impassable. The present representative of his house, Mr. Robert French, has lost nothing of his energy, as he is an excellent road maker, and a well known enemy to jobbing. Like every other part of Ireland many of the roads of this county are conducted over steep hills, and the senseless and expensive practice resorted to of lowering them instead of changing the line to the base of the hill: amongst others, the most prominent appears to be that leading over the hills between Tuam and Dangan; if the line was changed, and brought to the east of Mr. Kirwan's of Hillbrook, and Killoreran church, and united to the present line at Moylough, it would not only run nearly on a level, but, what few alterations do, it would shorten the present line by some miles. I beg it may be recollected I speak only from very frequently viewing the line of country from the high road; but the levels and line could be easily ascertained. A very beneficial change could be made in the road running over the hill of Liscopel between Ballinasloe and Aghrim; another at the hill of Culliagh near Ballinasloe, and many others that I do not immediately recollect. The benefit that would result to the public from altering the line of road over these and many other hills is so obvious, that I need not enlarge on the subject farther, than to state that in almost every hill the materials are within reach of wheel-barrows. It is highly probable that when those and all other roads on hills were made, the bogs or low grounds adjoining were woody swamps, and in some cases like the Esker near Banagher. The facility with which gravel could be procured, might be a strong inducement, nothing more being wanting than removing the large stones, and the gravel of which they consist formed the road. Formerly there were conservators in this county, but it was soon found it was a needless expenditure of the public money, because they did not do their duty. A very natural question arises here, why did not the magistrates and country gentlemen oblige them to do their duty? If they did their duty conscientiously, I do not know a more useful public officer, and the salary they were to receive was totally inadequate to the duties they should perform. I hope to see either them or some other officer encouraged by a

---

[1] Many of the under-tenants who hold immense tracts of ground at little rent, say that Connemara has gone to the devil since good roads were made: the value of land is too well known. Villagers in general do not wish for good roads to their villages; they say it only encourages others to bid over them. What a strong argument in favor of good roads! increasing the value of lands: recollect this, landlords! [original footnote].

liberal stipend to undertake this arduous and dangerous task, for I much fear he would be left as a scape goat by some of the indolent gentlemen of the country.

Some time since it was proposed to appoint surveyors of roads, with adequate salaries; but the acquirements necessary, or thought so, to the situation, were so many, that very few were found to be competent, and I believe the idea has been abandoned, at least for the present. Probably many applicants were mere young civil engineers, little acquainted with the detail or materials for road making; others, perhaps, were well acquainted with those requisites, but totally ignorant of the use of a spirit level. If baronial surveyors are ever appointed, probably it would be a useful regulation to oblige every such surveyor to take an apprentice or pupil, which would keep up an eligible stock of young men to fill situations in this department, subject to a yearly examination by a board of engineers, whose certificate would be a necessary preliminary to an appointment Emulation here, as in most other affairs, would be a powerful stimulus to exertion, both in master and pupils. Perhaps a medal of small value would be an useful auxiliary. I presume to think that in the outset of a new project like this, perfection should not be expected in the surveyors, but in a short period there will be an opportunity of selecting. The injury roads receive from the shade of trees is very great. To cut those down that have been already planted could not be expected, but an act to limit the distance of all future plantations from the road would be highly useful, and taken in a picturesque view, it is a churlish method of preventing a view of the demesne, and nothing can be pleaded in its favor but custom. It is a part of those same designs invented by Browne, and was introduced into Ireland by his followers. Nothing would contribute more to the preservation of roads than an increase in the breadth of the wheels of carriages heavily laden. The damage done to the roads by narrow wheels after heavy rains, or hard frost, is very great. The wheels of carriers' drays, that usually carry upwards of a ton, and are seldom more than three inches wide on the sole, many much less, are particularly injurious to roads. Probably it would be found a beneficial regulation to oblige them, and mail and other public coaches, to use wheels at least six inches broad, and private carriages instead of two inches should be at least four inches wide.

I imagine, that so far from this unusual breadth adding to the difficulty of the draft, by an increase of weight and more friction, it would greatly ease it, by enabling the wheels to avoid the many shocks they encounter from slipping into ruts, and the extreme degree of friction and exertion to extricate them. This must be manifest to every person travelling in a gig. On the contrary, broad wheels, by rolling over those obstructions, will ease the draft on the horse, and add much to the comfort of the traveller, and safely to the springs, I am not prepared to say how far this idea might be carried, but I trust the Dublin Society will take up the subject, as they possess many members fully competent to the task. It is a fine field for the attention of the implement society, and I trust they will notice this. It is not a little surprising that magistrates and country gentlemen do not seem to be aware of the injury roads receive from the narrowness of wheels. Frequently may be seen upwards of twelve hundred weight on cars whose wheels are not more than an inch and half broad.

The dishing of wheels adds much to the injury, as in general the whole wheel does not roll on the road, and to add still more to the injury, the wheels are frequently shod with iron, from which the heads of large nails project considerably beyond the periphery. After an angry and stubborn opposition of many years, it is at length found that cylindrical or upright wheels are best; and they are now adopted by the mail coaches, and are advancing fast into use by carriers. I expect before long to see the plough, harrow, and roller, a necessary apparatus for every road. I cannot conceive why a heavy metal roller has not been long since introduced.

As to the difficulty of ploughing roads, it is merely ideal, for if a proper plough is used, at a proper season, the difficulty vanishes. I had a road ploughed at the late Sir Thomas Leighton's, near Dublin, much firmer than the generality of roads, and it was ploughed at an improper season, in summer, after very dry weather.

It has lately become a very general idea, that nothing but broken stone will do for roads much frequented. This idea has been carried to such excess on the Tuam road, near Horse-leap, that close to a very fine gravel pit, broken stone has been used. In one part of this road, near Briarfield, some years since, a part for several perches was made with this gravel from Horse-leap. It is to this day (1822) the very best part of the road, and at either end of this gravelled part the road has been twice repaired with broken stone, and at present wants another coat, whilst the gravelled part is nearly at good as at first, and so firm that a heavy wheel makes little impression on it. On remarking this circumstance to the person who keeps the road in repair, he acknowledged it, but said he was not allowed to use any thing but broken stone. I do not think I remember an instance of a more stubborn adherence to an erroneous system than this use of broken stone, close to an inexhaustible supply of the best gravel. It only wants screening to separate the sand and large stones from the proper sized gravel, neither of which should ever be used on roads. It is the practice of the workmen on this part of the road to place large gravel under each heap of broken stone, and they are all measured as broken stone. I find it difficult to quit this subject, but many of my readers, I dare say, wish me off the road.

Many bridges are in a state of great decay, very much owing to carelessness in building the parapet walls; they are seldom coped with stones sufficiently large, nor are they properly fastened, by which means, in a few years, the entire wall is gradually taken away by the country people, and seems to be unnoticed by the passing magistrates, until a new presentment is obtained for repairing it. For what a parapet wall should be, I refer my readers to that under the battery at Shannon bridge. Many bridges are too narrow, especially those of Athlone, Banagher, Ballinasloe, and indeed, in general, all the old bridges of the county. I understand presentments have been granted for widening several of them.

The new bridge of Galway, opposite to the gaol, is a beautiful structure, and does great credit to the architect, Mr. Behan. The first stone was laid on the 29th June, 1818, by the Hon. William Le Poer Trench, and was entirely finished in October, 1819. Formerly such a bridge, and in such a rapid torrent, would have occupied several years in the building.

In many parts of this county great inconvenience, and often considerable danger, is suffered by travellers, from flood water permitted to remain on the roads. At Horse-leap there is a very prominent instance of this; a few pounds would abate this nuisance, by lowering the outlet. If, instead of going through the water, the road had been brought round the foot of the hill to the west, the expense of building a causeway of considerable length would have been saved to the county, and then the nuisance would only injure those who are too indolent to use any exertion to abate it. If country gentlemen would condescend to take professional advice, many abuses of the public purse would be avoided. Amongst many others, one occurs between Moylough and Mount Bellew, that a few pounds also would lower. Much to the credit of the Rev. Mr. O'Roarke a wall has been built to prevent travellers from falling into the very deep quarry holes on the north side of this water, but it is still dangerous to strangers, for at night, and if hard frost sets in, it will be impassible.

SECTION VIII

NAVIGATIONS AND NAVIGABLE RIVERS

There is at present a navigation on the Shannon which runs along this county for about thirty miles. Lough Corrib is also navigable for about the same distance; there is not any other water navigable for any length. It has been proposed to make the river Suck navigable from the Shannon to Ballinasloe, and from thence to Galway, but I believe it has proceeded no farther than conversation[1]. Some other lines have been formerly proposed, but nothing further has been done.

Of their usefulness there can scarcely be any difference of opinion, but whether the articles likely to be carried on them would remunerate the undertakers, I am not prepared to answer. I imagine the principle of using rivers for water carriage is a very hazardous one; the difficulties to be encountered in floods, and in making track ways, are very considerable. However, the river Sack has an advantage over many other rivers used for this purpose; its course is very sluggish, and the supply equal to any trade likely to be on it: under the head '*water*' I have more fully enlarged on Lough Corrib. The advantages of water carriage over those of land are very great, so much so, that one horse and three men to attend a boat of sixty tons, will draw as much as one hundred and twenty horses, carrying ten hundred weight each day, even allowing one man to drive three horses. The expense of drawing the boat will be about £110. per annum, and going twelve miles each day, the usual rate at which

---

[1] Since I wrote this the canal has been laid out and men at work on it. [original footnote].

carriers travel, whilst the expense of one hundred and twenty horses and forty men for the same distance will amount to £3,320.

"This is worth the serious attention of the landed proprietors, for it is highly probable, that at no very remote period, grazing and tillage will be more united than at present; for nothing but the grossest ignorance and prejudice will maintain that they cannot be conducted more profitably on the same land, when judiciously blended, than according to the present indolent grazing system alone. Did the graziers read a little more, and see and know what is going forward in the agricultural world, they would learn that by the improved practices of England and Scotland, more cattle are fattened on the same quantity of land, when united to tillage, than the same land formerly fattened when under cattle alone; they would then perceive the great benefit of having green food for their stock in winter and spring, and the superiority of the alternate green and white crops over the present wretched mode of running the ground out with repeated corn crops. Many may call this *book-farming*. The introduction of turnips and clover were once called book-farming; and I daresay Mr. Muir's feeding, to a state of great fatness, five hundred head of cattle in the house in summer, by the cutting of one scythe, will be called book-grazing".

SECTION IX.

STATE OF THE FISHERIES.

There are few subjects of more importance to this county than the fisheries, whether we consider the home consumption, the supply for which is in general greatly below the demand, or the exportation of a redundancy, which could be infinitely increased. To begin with the sun fishery. This usually commences in April, and continues for about six weeks. Custom has established this period, but they are found at various seasons.

Those fish are a harmless species of shark, called the basking shark, and produce various quantities of oil, from four to twelve barrels of about thirty gallons each, which sells for from four to six pounds per barrel, but the prices frequently vary from those rates, like every article of consumption, according to the demand or supply. As this fishery is carried on at present, it is mere peddling, but might be greatly improved and extended by employing larger vessels, that could meet or pursue the fish at greater distances from shore than those usually employed, from their small size, dare attempt; for it is well known that sun fish could be caught long before April at greater distances from land, for the best fish remain in deep water; and as the small vessels must wait for good weather, the most favorable season elapses, and they dare not venture out of sight of land nor lie out at night. To fish with the best effect, vessels of 120 tons, at least, should be employed, with at least 80 or 100 tons of cask; also, to attend them there ought to be three boats with eight men each, that is, six to row, one to steer, and one with a gun harpoon, with plenty of ropes, twine, &c. &c. Small boats could be beneficially employed in bringing the liver[1] ashore whilst fresh, upon which depends the goodness of the oil for burning, as producing a brighter flame, and more free from any offensive smell. Very frequently, from some mismanagement or carelessness, the fishers lose their spears; or something has been forgotten or goes wrong, and the season is lost before they can replace them. Mr. Young says, that in the year 1799 there were 40 or 50 boats employed in this fishery in Galway; at present there are not probably more than five or six. In the year 1761 a Mr. Nesbit killed, in one week, on the coast of Donegal, forty-two sun fish, each of which yielded from half to one ton of oil, whilst in the west of Galway it has often happened that all the fish that were struck, either from bad, rusty harpoons, or some carelessness, have escaped. Will it be believed that many proceed on the fishery with their harpoons so rusty and out of order since the former season, that they frequently break or are inoperative; even under this defective system upwards of £5000. worth of oil has been sold in a season at Westport and Galway, from fish caught on this coast. The following valuable document has been communicated to me by Mr. D'Arcey, who has a considerable estate in Connemara, as it throws considerable light on this interesting subject, its publication, I trust, will be deemed serviceable: —

> "From the experience of a number of years it appears, to an undoubted certainty, that the sun fish, white fish, and herring fishery, could be carried on with the greatest success on the north west coast of Ireland; the causes which have prevented its success to the extent that it might have been, will be detailed underneath, in which also is pointed out the advantages to be derived from the establishment of a company, the expense that would attend it, and the most convenient place for its establishment. To illustrate this, the following queries have been proposed, and the following answers given from the closest inquiry, and the fullest information that could be collected in the whole extent of the north west coast of Ireland:—

First query. — Why have not the fisheries on this coast been hitherto carried on to any extent?[2]

Answer. — The fishery on the north west coast of Ireland has been hitherto neglected, both from want of means and of experience.

Second query. — What would be the most probable means for now carrying it on with the best effect?

---

[1] Many people think the oil is produced from the blubber, like whale fishing, but it is the liver only which is used for that purpose. However, it remains for future research to ascertain if some use might not be made of the remainder of the fish, probably for manure, [original footnote].

[2] Dr. Stokes in his admirable "Observations oft the Population and Resources of Ireland." — "These shores afford an inexhaustible mine of wealth— a fresh harvest at every season, without tillage, seed, or manure, free of rent, tithe, or taxes; many acres of that sea are more productive of nutritious food, than the same quantity of moderate land, and require only boat, nets, and hardy hands to reap the never failing crop which Providence has supplied.", [original footnote].

Answer. — Twenty wherries[1], properly appointed, with proper crews, would be an establishment befitting a company with sufficient apparatus for the different qualities in the different seasons. The herring fishery begins about the first of February, and continues at various intervals to the 16th March, as they never come into any one harbour exclusively, but sometimes into one, and sometimes into another; and as the extent from one end of the north west coast to the other is spacious and extensive, the vessels best calculated to take advantage of the different situations are wherries, because they can work round from harbour to harbour in weather that vessels of another description could not stir, and that the common boats of the country are afraid to go out. The wherries to carry each of them two boats on their deck, with their nets, such as would suffice to load the wherry in case the take continued.

Third query. — What would be the average expense of carrying on an establishment sufficient to ensure success?

Answer. — The probable expense attending twenty wherries, building, stores, residences for the families of the crews of the twenty wherries, and such other artificers as such an establishment would require, and such necessaries for the building and repairing of Wherries, &c. &c. would amount, as per the following statement.

Fourth query.— What would be the probable profits arising from such an establishment? Answer.— The probable profits arising from such an enterprise would amount as per the following statement.

The cod and ling fishery commences at various intervals, from the first of February, every year, near the shore, where it is considered they come from the bank that lies seven or eight leagues from the land, and where they are considered always to be found, it stretches along the north-west coast of Ireland. The quantity that might be killed on the bank, and convenient to the shore, are beyond calculation. The number of ling exceeds that of cod in the proportion of five to one. When any of the Connemara boats (which is but seldom) have ventured out on the bank, in a few hours, with their hand lines alone, they have filled their boats. In the year 1815, in the month of March, a boat from Connemara, with only two spillards, in one day brought in thirty-six dozen, killed near the land; very few ling amongst them. Their hooks were so very small, and so unfit for heavy fish, that they lost near a fourth part of them, of course it may be computed they lost an equal number of cod as ling. Another boat, with one spillard, in one day, brought in 160 ling and two cod. Last summer a boat with one line and one hook brought in nineteen dozen, and would have killed more had they not, alas, I lost their only hook. Also in the same year, (1815) some Galway boats, of seven or eight tons burden, that were better appointed, returned, some on the fourth, others the fifth day loaded with split cod and ling, not

---

[1] Usually a light rowboat for one person; here it seems to refer to a larger vessel used locally, [Clachan ed.].

being able to carry the quantity they had unopened, and having no salt for curing them.

Last summer, and the summer before, a man came from Malbay in the county of Clare, in his horse-skin boat; he killed more fish than any six Connemara boats; as fast as he filled his boat, he came ashore and sold them, as they were killed near the land. Hence it may be computed that a good wherry, and crew well appointed, would kill ten times as much as any of the common boats, and fish ten days for one that the Connemara boats do, and that each of the wherries would kill and cure forty tons for exportation, and to which they would not be confined, having always the Galway and Westport markets open, and particularly in the spring of the year when fresh fish sells well. The sun fishery begins about the middle of April, and is considered by the Connemara people to be over about the first of June, at which time they discontinue looking for them, and apply themselves to their country occupations, though great sculls of them have often been seen by vessels sailing along the western coast in the months of July and August. Wherries lying out fishing on the bank, when the fish returns from the land, would always have a chance of meeting there the sun fish, (for that is the place to meet them) and lose no time in quest of them until they appear, as they would always have their boats, lines and spears ready at every opportunity that would offer. The sun fish liver produces from five to seven barrels of oil each, some as high as eleven or twelve. The Connemara boats generally come into harbour every night, by which they lose the beginning of every day. When they chance to kill one or two, they lose a week at least, loitering and providing casks for the liver, before they go out again, which a wherry need not do, as they would have a sufficiency of cask to hold the liver. The sun fish generally come from the southward, and sweep along the north-west coast of Ireland northward, in the line of the Rosses, seldom close to the land, and from thence along to the west of Scotland, as reported by the masters of vessels from that country. On the 4th and 5th of May 1815, there were such quantities of sun fish about the direction of the bank before-mentioned, that the Galway and Connemara boats killed between one and two hundred of them, with which they all returned to their respective homes quite content with what they had got: whence it may be computed that a wherry that would have continued out, would have killed three times the quantity of any Connemara boat, having it in her power to protect her men and boats in the worst of weather.

Fifth query. — Where on the north-west of Ireland would be the most convenient situation for such an establishment?

Answer. — In order to carry this scheme into full effect, under the direction of a company, the first object to be considered is the best harbour to secure in safety, near the fishing ground, the wherries, and the place best calculated for giving shelter and comfort to the crews, their families, and the different tradesmen such an enterprize would employ. M'Kensey's[1] drafts will show that the bay of Ardbear in Connemara is the safest, easiest of access, the best outlet, and nearest to the fishing ground of any on the north-west coast of Ireland. But M'Kensey did not point out all the advantages of that fine bay of Ardbear, which is capable of securing the largest ships. He entirely omitted the basin at the head of the bay, which dries at low water, and where two hundred wherries may lie aground at low water, on a fine even strand for repairing, or loading or unloading, and remain there for safety in the inclement season of the year. It is so well sheltered, that a three inch rope would hold the largest wherry in Dublin bay in the worst of weather. This basin comes up close to the new town of Clifden, where there might be salt pans, and such stores and houses as would be requisite for the building or repairing of wherries, and such houses as would be required for the accommodation of all the people concerned in the undertaking. It has also the advantage of lying midway between Galway and Westport, and lies most conveniently to the fishing ground. It also possesses the superior advantage over an island, of being at all seasons easily accessible. From the aforesaid observations it may be computed —

That each wherry may kill five sun fish, and that each would yield five barrels of oil, each to sell for £6. that is —	£3,000 0 0
That each wherry would kill and cure forty tons of well cured cod and ling, which if sold at 3d. per lb. would come to —	£22,000 0 0
That each wherry would kill and cure of black pollock, mackerel, and other fish, as much as would bring, in the course of the year —	£5,600 0 0
That each wherry would catch 180,000 of herrings, which if sold at £3. per per 1000, exclusive of bounties —	£10,800 0 0
	41,800 0 0
Cost of twenty wherries, with two boats, herring and mackerel nets, spillards, hand lines, sun fish spears, and lines, with casks to hold the liver, computed at £700. Each.	£14,000 0 0
Buildings necessary to accommodate the crews and	£3000 0 0

---

[1] Mr. Murdock M'Kenzie made a general survey of the whole harbours bays, and shores of Ireland, on the scale of one inch to an English mile, with general charts, in two volumes, [Clachan ed.].

their families of the twenty wherries (the ground will be given free by the proprietor for the use of the company.)

Stores and other necessary buildings for the use of the company.	£2000 0 0
Sundry articles that may be wanting in the course of the year for the twenty wherries.	£1000 0 0

Annual amount of wages and victuals for twenty wherries.

To twenty captains at £50. each,	£1000 0 0
To eighty fishermen at £20. each	£1600 0 0

The following bounties to the captains and crews, on the proviso that the quantity killed would amount to the within calculation, to be proportioned to the different quality of each quantity:

To the twenty captains £50. each	£1000 0 0
To eighty fishermen £30. each	£2400 0 0
To extra men during the herring and sun fish season	£500 0 0
To annual wear and tear of twenty wherries	£2000 0 0
To victualling twenty wherries at £91. 10s. each	£1825 0 0
To one of the captains to act as director at sea	£200 0 0
To one director on shore	£300 0 0
To two clerks	£200 0 0
To porters, splitters and salters	£50 0 0
	£11,275 0 0

N. B. It would be advisable to grant further bounties to all crews exceeding those quantities, which most likely are underrated. The spear or harpoon used for killing sun fish is a very curious instrument in its construction: it is composed of a steel spear barbed; for almost half its length it is grooved at one side; through the side of the groove there is a strong rivet, on which an iron handle turns; at the end of this handle there is a socket for the reception of a wooden pole, to which a strong rope line is made fast: the spear is launched with the handle closed up in the grove. When the fish finds himself wounded he flies off, which disengages the handle in the groove, and as it opens and turns across in the wound, it forms a barb of the whole length of the handle, from which no exertion of the fish can extricate it. The sun fish finding himself wounded, swims away rapidly, and tows the boat after him, until being quite tired, they kill him, take out his liver, and turn the carcass adrift, as food for various kinds of fowls and fishes.

The herring fishery is not carried on to that extent that it ought, and in general is greatly mismanaged; there is almost always something wrong or wanting. At one time there is a want of salt to meet an extraordinary take of this valuable fish; at other times the nets are out of order, or the boats are leaky, and a variety of other circumstances, proceeding often more from want of capital than good management or industry. It has frequently happened, that from want of salt immense quantities have been thrown on the sea shore and left to rot: sometimes a boat load has been sold for eighteen pence.

Herrings begin to be sold frequently at a guinea a thousand, and when the vessels are full, or salt scarce, for fifteen shillings: what a field is here for capital and skill? — To fish with the full effect for herrings, it is necessary to have two sets of nets, as the meshes of those used for the spring fishery would be too large for those used in summer, and the fish would almost all go through, whilst those not used for the summer fishery would be too small to mesh them in spring. In the winter and spring fishery the boats usually employed are so small, that the boatmen are afraid to venture where they are most likely to catch fish. The usual method of this coast, and I believe throughout Ireland, is to let down the nets, and the fish mesh themselves; whilst, if I am rightly informed, on the western coast of Scotland the nets are drawn against the scull of herrings, by which means a boat is immediately loaded. On enquiry in Galway why this beneficial practice was not adopted, I was answered it would disturb the fish, and they would leave the bay. It seems the Scotch herrings are not so easily offended as our proud Connaught ones[1]. When the herring fishery begins at Galway, almost the entire of the male population of the neighbouring villages run to the shore to assist, and have a certain share, amounting sometimes to a guinea or more for one night's work. The small rowboats, that are generally used along the shore, frequently take upwards of 20,000 herrings in a night, which sometimes sell for £1. 7s. per 1000, and they often make two trips if the fish are in abundance, and near the shore. Sometimes several men join in a boat and nets for this fishery, many of them tradesmen of different branches, and at this period abandon their profession; in this case they have an equal share of the produce, according to the share of money they have contributed. Sometimes the boat and nets belong to one person, and are hired out; the owner gets a clear half, and the remainder is divided amongst the crew. When not employed in fishing, they are

---

[1] "On the coast of Norway, the cod are taken in nets, spread vertically, and kept by weights and floats, at that particular depth at which the fishermen expect the shoal will move. The fish so taken are in better order than such at take the bait, and all of one size." DR STOKES, [original footnote]

usually employed in gathering sea weed for manuring ground for potatoes, or for burning for kelp. During the season for catching herrings, all other fishing is almost abandoned, consequently other kind of fish are scarce in Galway. Five thousand are reckoned a middling night's take of herrings for one boat: all they get are sold to supply the home demand, which is so far from being answered, that many cargoes are brought from the north west coast. The fish sells at from sixteen pence to two shillings per hundred, sometimes much higher, though often less. The fishermen say that the quantity of fish has decreased for the last fifteen years, but this may in some measure be imputed to their not being aware that the fish are often to be found in great abundance far below the usual depths at which they are generally fished for; this has been ascertained by an accidental breaking of the rope to which the corks were attached, which caused the nets to be brought down by the weight of the leads to a considerable depth: before this fortunate accident happened scarcely a fish was caught, but to their great astonishment, when brought up, the sunken net was found so loaded with fish, they could scarcely with safety bring it into the boat. Whether they have since taken advantage of this providential hint I am ignorant, but I rather fear they have not. For some reason not ascertained, the herring fishery commences at a later period than formerly; the fishing at present not beginning until February or March, though formerly it began in November, and generally concluded at Christmas.

The approach of the herrings to the bay of Galway is known by various signs, such as the appearance of vast numbers of those fowls that feed on herrings, and their making an unusual noise; by a great take of cod, hake, or black pollock, who follow the herrings; by the luminous appearance of the sea at night, and other signs known to the fishermen. When the appearance of the fish has been ascertained, the admiral of the fishermen dispatches boats to prevent all the boats in the bay from going out until his permission is obtained. Any persons presuming to act contrary to his orders are punished with the loss of boats and nets, and probably a sound drubbing. When it is his pleasure, an evening is appointed, and all the boats in the surrounding bay assemble at the Cloddagh, near Galway, or meet them on the way to the amount of 500 or upwards, and all sail out together, and preserve a profound silence until they arrive on the fishing ground; and a charming sight it is. Upon a signal given by the admiral's boat, they all at once drop their nets. As the great scull of herrings divide shortly after they enter the bay, and fill every creek and inlet of it, much time is lost by this nonsensical and tyrannical parade, for it is well known by the owners of small boats in those creeks many days before the admiral signifies his high and mighty pleasure, but they dare not fish. In my Survey of Clare, I have detailed the same silly regulations by the Shannon fishermen. Government, well aware of this abuse, have appointed an officer to prevent the ill effects of such arbitrary nonsense, and they can now, I believe, fish when it suits their purpose.

The bay of Galway, which extends from Black Head to Sline Head, abounds with fish of various kinds, such as turbot, sole, john dory, plaice, flounders, flukes, halibut, skate, cod, haddock, hake, ling, whiting, salmon, mullet, bass, white and black pollock (called black nuns), bream, mackerel, horse-mackerel, red and grey gurnard, nurse, scolobert, rock fish, sand eel, conger eel, silver eel, and lobsters, cray fish, crabs, oysters, cockles, razor fish, scallops, &c. &c. From the great abundance of hakes, this bay has been called the bay of hakes. There are at least 500 fishing boats belonging to this bay, besides those belonging to the Cloddagh fishermen, who have between 200 and 250, employing upwards of 2500 hands, who live almost entirely by fishing of various kinds. Before the year 1790 their boats were small, but since that period they have increased them to fourteen tons, with which they are now able to go to Limerick, Westport, Sligo, &c. Prior to this enlargement they seldom ventured beyond the islands of Arran, and on the appearance of a squall ran into the first sheltered creek they could make, and frequently lost their market. It is generally imagined that the fishing bank extends from Cleggan bay, on the coast of Connemara, to Newfoundland, and abounds with cod; but the boats are too small to encounter that part of the sea where the best fish abound. The late Rev. Mr. Russell, who paid great attention to this subject, informed me, that a fisherman that he knew set his lines for ling in the usual place near the island of Bafin; he had so little success that he removed his lines to a considerable distance further into the Atlantic ocean; the consequence was the loss of almost all his lines by the extraordinary weight of fish. He took advantage of the hint, and made a great deal of money, whilst his neighbours still continued peddling near shore. Vessels from England, Scotland, Cork, &c. wait for cargoes of fish, which they cure and make a great profit of. If the merchants of Galway possessed a proper spirit of enterprise this profit should centre in their pockets, and they would long since have formed an extensive fishing company, and not see themselves disgraced by frequent advertisements of "Scotch herrings just arrived." This is likely to be accomplished in Connemara on an extensive scale, on Mr. D'Arcey's estate; the report of which I have before given, — a fishing company is in a state of progress, under a system of regulations and bounties, that promise to reward the great exertions made for this purpose by the late collector, the Hon. William Le Poer Trench, whose unceasing endeavours to promote every plan beneficial to the town met with frequently an illiberal opposition.

Galway, in the year 1576, had a great import of wines and other commodities from Spain, all paid for in fish. The Spaniards and Dutch also fished on our coasts at a very early period, which caused an act to be made in 1465 to prevent them. Philip II. of Spain, agreed to pay £1000. per annum to the Irish treasury for liberty to fish on the Irish coast. In the time of Charles I. the Dutch agreed to pay £30,000. for a similar license, as a further proof of what value foreigners considered this permission. In 1650, as a great favour, Sweden was permitted to fish, provided she did not employ more than 1000 vessels. At some seasons turbot are in great plenty, and reasonable, and are, or were lately brought by the mail coaches to Dublin; but soles and other flat fish are not in that plenty they might be, if from a ridiculous prejudice of the fishermen, trawling was not prevented in the bay, which abounds with such fish; they say that it disturbs the spawn upon which they feed.

If this is correct, they should encourage the disturbance of it to induce turbot, soles, &c. to come after their food, for it is generally agreed that the spawn is mostly of black pollock, a worthless fish. It is well known that on the coast of England, where trawling has been practised for centuries, no diminution has taken place, and the company now so laudably established at Dublin, show the great advantages of the practice, for black soles, that were formerly very dear, are now to be had for a trifling sum. The Galway fishermen cannot suppose that the spawn of all the fish in the Atlantic ocean it deposited in the bay of Galway. Should they not rather consider it as one of the bountiful dispensations of Providence as a means of providing a delicate and nutritious article of food. It would be probably of much more consequence to enlarge the size of the meshes of their trawls, by which the destruction of the small fish would be avoided. To fishing in rivers and lakes with nets whose meshes are small, may be attributed the increasing scarcity of trout and salmon: it is a well established fact, either passed over or smiled at (as I shall probably be) by gentlemen, that every countryman, and even their own game keepers, will kill every fish in the net; trout not larger than sprats, and eels not larger than a straw.

They should pay particular attention to the nets of their sportsmen, and never suffer them to kill at any time more than is necessary for use, by way of amusement, and to show their superior skill in catching fish. In 1811 the fishermen of Galway, (a mulish race), aided by those whose education should have placed them on higher ground, petitioned the lord lieutenant against Captain Morris, commander of the Townsend revenue cruiser, who with several other gentlemen had established a trawl boat for fishing for turbot in Galway bay. It was referred to the commissioners of customs; who, after investigating the business minutely, gave it as their opinion, that "Captain Morris's conduct has been productive of much public good, and that the charges made by the fishermen are unsupported, and that he is a most zealous, active, and attentive officer."

In the *Galway Weekly Advertiser* we have the following strong proof of the indolence of the Galway fishermen: —

> "We may consider that our herring fishery is over for this season; our boatmen would not go out until the take was over every where else, and now that the weather is broke, and the nights getting long, it will be impossible for the miserable craft they go to sea in to stand the heavy seas on this coast. These unfortunate people cannot be persuaded that it would be wise to take herrings during the fine weather in the months of May, June, and July; and even last week, although the weather was favourable, they stayed at home; Monday, 4th September, being the fair day, they would not go out, and having got drunk they lost the whole week. In any other part of the world the boats would have gone out on Sunday night, and would have had three or four thousand pounds worth of fifth to sell at the fair, and by that means have kept a large portion of the money received here on that day in the town, as many persons from the country would have taken home a load of fish. We have long deplored the loss we sustained for want of a protecting force for the peaceable fishermen of this bay; but it seems in vain, although we have commissioners of

fisheries, with all their subordinate officers, aided by new acts of parliament, still the pirates command the bay, and prevent this town and neighbourhood from enjoying the blessings of a free fishing. When we had Captain Morris stationed here, he protected the fishery; and such persons as wished to go out every night were secured against assault; the consequence was, that fish in the greatest abundance were taken, and many square rigged vessels were loaded, and wealth flowed into the town, and no fish were imported here that season; every shop was full of business, and the demand for exciseable goods was very considerable, and the whole population of the town one busy scene of industry."

We do not know in what terms to speak of the ignorance and bigotry of those miserable creatures who follow the business of fishermen in Ireland. In all countries, no doubt, those engaged in seafaring pursuits are more superstitious than any other class, but in Ireland they seem to be immersed in the very depths of superstition. Exclusively of fifty-two days in the year held as the Sabbath of Christians, there are about sixty saints days observed by the half starved fishermen of Ireland. No nation could bear such a waste of time, and least of all can the people of this country afford so much idleness. Where are the Catholic clergy? What do they teach the ignorant? Do they think that the road to heaven is through a life of wretchedness, misery, and crime? It would really seem that a doctrine of this kind has become the creed of the lower classes of Irishmen. That crime accompanies the indolence of superstition is apparent from the above statement. The Galway fishermen will not catch the fish themselves, nor will they allow any others to do it; no, they destroy the nets and assault the crews of the boats which come from other quarters to fish in the bay, as if they had an exclusive privilege to the produce of the ocean. The fishermen of the villages on the sea coast of Dublin attacked the boats of the Dublin Fishing Company last year; but some notable examples were made of the ruffians, and the consequence is, that fish of all kinds are sold in the markets of Dublin at half the former price. It is thus that the whole country is interested in the success of the fisheries. We expected that the board of commissioners for fisheries, with all their subordinate officers, would have taken some trouble to fulfill their duties. We are confident no blame attaches to the respectable and intelligent secretary; but we shall say no more, than that it is a disgrace to hear of pirates commanding the bay of Galway, or in other words, that the industrious part of the community should not be protected by British laws against the outrages of the idle and worthless. The wealth that Scotland annually acquires by her fisheries, is one of the main sources of the prosperity of that country, and at this moment there are several boats from Ireland fishing on the coasts of Caithness. That every species of fish may be found in the Irish seas in equal abundance is certain, but saints days, superstition in its most hideous aspect, and mismanagement of every kind, seem to encircle Ireland with ignorance, poverty, and distress."— *Faulkner's Journal*, 25th September, 1820[1].

---

[1] Not clear from original where this quotation begins, [Clachan ed.].

Lobsters are generally in great abundance, and I am informed that on some part of the coast they are put into holes in the rocks that are covered at half ebb, and fed to a large size with fish and other food. Muscles are much used in Galway for soup on fasting days, and if well made is a delicious dish. Cockles are used frequently for sauce to fish, but, unlike those used in Dublin, are a very insipid addition, because they are brought to market ready dressed, and the liquor, the best of the sauce, is thrown away. Some idea may be formed of what extent the fishery of Galway might be, when it is known that in the first three days of lent upwards of five hundred guineas have been received for fish, mostly cod. Black pollock (black nuns) are sometimes sold for a penny or two pence, weighing upwards of ten pounds, and it has been proved by the experiment of an ingenious person in Galway, that the liver produced in value more of oil than the whole fish cost at market. There is a very extensive salmon and eel fishery at Galway. The salmon fishery has been thought of great consequence, so far back as the reign of Henry III. It was for a long time in the possession of the De Burghs family and several others. In 1520 the Franciscan friars had it. In 1521 Henry VIII. granted it to Anthony Lynch, in partnership with a widow Lynch. A further grant was made by the same king to them and their heirs for 13s. 4d. per annum. Several others received permission to establish fisheries upon the river. The families of Lynch and D'Arcy possessed the fishery until dispossessed by Cromwell's officers. In 1663 Sir George Preston became possessed of it, and had it secured by the act of settlement.

It descended to the Eyres of Eyrecourt, one of whom had married one of Preston's daughters. Their son, in 1710, disposed of his interest to Mr. Edward Eyre of Galway, whose family still possess it. For several years much altercation, at the point of the sword and pistol, and some litigation, has occurred about shutting or opening a part of the stream called the kings gap or main gap; the right to keep it constantly open has, very much for the interest of the lessee, been established.

Surely it must strike every person in the least acquainted with the subject, that if all the fish were caught, the fishery in a few years would be annihilated. This mistaken and avaricious practice, and above all, the destruction of them in every river at night, by millers' servants and country people, when they are worth little, have caused the increasing scarcity of salmon and trout. Salmon are frequently speared from the battlement of the bridge, a very curious but dangerous practice, which has been time immemorial in one family, of whom one, if not more, has lost his life by the entanglement of the rope, which is fastened to the spear, and is thrown with such force, and is so heavy, that it inevitably drags any person about which the cord is entangled into the river, which is here uncommonly rapid and deep, and dashed with great force against large sunken rocks, amongst which the salmon lie, and it requires an experienced eye and considerable practice to form the curve that will fix the spear in the fish. Salmon also abound in every river on the coast of Connemara, especially Ballinahinch, which are excellent, and almost always in season. Sometime since very fine fish from this weir were sent to Galway at an unusual season for this fish; yet although fish of every kind was at that time scarce, the epicures of Galway would not even be tempted to make a trial. In Lough Corrib there are a great variety of trout, especially the gillaroe, whose gizzard is so highly prized. The number of sail boats which are employed in the fishery of Galway may be about 200 to 250; they are from four to fourteen tons burden, and cost building about twenty to fifty pounds; nets and tackle, &c. fifteen to twenty pounds more. The nets are always of hemp, tanned with oak bark[1]. There are usually five or six hands to a boat; they fish for shares, divided into sixty. They have had this fishery time immemorial, and would not permit a stranger to settle amongst them. Since the year 1695 there has been a great increase, for at that time there were only 528; now the population of the Cloddagh amounts to upwards of 3000. Oysters of very superior quality abound on the coast of Connemara, and all round the bay of Galway, and are in season almost the whole year. Pearls of great beauty, but not very large, have been taken from the pearl muscle in several rivers, particularly near Oughterard, and some in Connemara.

I have lately seen in *Faulkner's Journal* some letters on the fisheries of the coast of Galway, from the scientific pen of Mr. Frazer. If this is the gentleman who took such pains to instruct the fishermen in the neighbourhood of Duncannon Fort and Ballyhack, in the county of Wexford, in the proper method of curing fish for exportation, it could not have fallen into better hands; for if I was rightly informed, when in that neighbourhood, shortly after it was said to happen, a cargo of dried fish was entrusted to the care of Mr. Frazer to sell for the fishermen's account. A statement, therefore, of the expenses and profit of the cargo would form a very useful document for the guidance of those intending to engage in the fisheries of Galway. Probably the introduction of some of those Wexford fishermen would help to enlighten their Galway brethren; and I am certain, from Mr. Frazer's ardour in the pursuit, he could have no objection to make an excursion to Ballyhack, from whence he might select some of those he had instructed in the process of curing fish.

TABLE OF TIDES.

	Galway Bay	Arran	
Neap tides rise,	6 or 7	8 or 9	feet
Ordinary spring tides,	12	15	feet
Extraordinary spring tides,	15	18	feet
High water on full and change days	H. M. 4 15	H. M. 4 15	o'clock. o'clock.

---

[1] I cannot find that the following receipt for preserving nets or lines is known in Galway. Five parts of tar and one of fish oil melted together; when quite hot, put in the nets or lines, and when they are completely soaked, draw off the composition quickly by a tap in the bottom of the vessel. Or if more are to be done, take out the first, and after well draining set them out to dry, taking care not to put them on any thing that would adhere to them, [original footnote].

SECTION X

STATE OF EDUCATION, SCHOOLS, AND CHARITABLE INSTITUTIONS

Until within a few years, the state of education was at a very low ebb, although 60 years ago there were many celebrated Latin schools, where the sons of respectable families were educated; but now many of the gentlemen of the county seem to be sensible of its importance, and several schools have been established by individuals highly to their credit: I trust before long we shall see one on every estate in the province. The school established by the will of Erasmus Smyth in the town of Galway stands pre-eminent; it is admirably conducted by the Rev. Mr. Whitley. The trustees have erected a handsome and very commodious school house and extensive range of offices with a spacious play ground. There is attached to the house about 15 acres of excellent ground, and a large garden. The house is built in an extremely healthful situation, near Fort Hill, commanding a fine view of the bay of Galway, Black Head, the Isles of Arran, &c.

"Erasmus Smyth was an Alderman of London, who came over to Ireland with the army as commissary in the year 1641 to suppress the rebellion. After it was put down, he purchased at very low rates many of the forfeited estates in various parts of Ireland, particularly in the county of the town of Galway, and neighbourhood of Sligo. Well knowing that his titles and tenures were very precarious, and liable at a future period to be litigated, he very cunningly made a grant of part of the lands for the founding and endowment of Protestant schools, and other charitable purposes, for which he obtained a charter, dated the 26th of March 1669, appointing the bench of bishops, the lord chancellor, the judges, the great law officers, all for the time being, governors and trustees, well knowing that if any flaw should ever appear in the patents, titles, or tenures, under which he got the estates, the law officers would always protect and make the title good to his heirs, and which has been really the case, as his heirs have possessed their immense property unmolested to this day…

The estate of Erasmus Smyth in the county of the town of Galway may amount to about 1400 acres, and may at a very moderate calculation, including mills, houses, plots, &c. in Newtown Smith and Bohermore be valued at five guineas per acre, or £7900 per annum; the tenants interest may be well worth three times that sum; of which the following statement, (contributed by an intelligent friend who is intimately acquainted with the affair) is strongly corroborative. Mr. Brabazon has about £400. per annum profit rent; Mr. Cummin £350. per annum profit rent: most of the old tenants have been turned out, and few of the occupying tenants have been left. Roscom, 232 acres, lately set, pays to the charity two guineas an acre, and was immediately let at four guineas to some of the former tenants, under the exploded and unfounded idea, and which is the bane of Ireland, that a middleman tenant is more secure than the former small tenants; had this been the case, it would not have been let to those very under tenants by the middlemen. The seaweed alone attached to Roscom is worth about £300. per annum, which brings down the rent to about a guinea an acre. The eastern and western parts of Roscom, 264 acres, pay to the charity about twenty five shillings per acre, and have been re-let to poor people at about four or five pounds per acre. The sea weed of these two divisions is worth about 200 guineas per annum, and reduces the rent to about fifteen shillings per acre. Ballybanemore (west) divided into five parts of twenty acres each, was let at the same time from £3. 5s. to £3. 15s. per acre, being of the same quality as the former, and without the advantage of the kelp shore. Ballybanemore (north) formerly occupied by resident villagers, who paid their rent immediately to the governor's agent, were turned out, to give compensation to the tenants who occupied the western part, who pay the charity twenty-five shillings per acre, and re-let to three of the former resident tenants at about two guineas per acre. Mr. Burke of Murrough, for 140 acres, pays about twenty-four shillings per acre, with a kelp shore, worth about £100. per annum: about 50 acres of this farm are re-let for three to four guineas per acre; the remainder is but indifferent land. Mr. Blake of Merlin Park offered to give three pounds per acre for 100 acres of east Roscom, and to go security for the resident small tenants, who offered £4. per acre for western Roscom, but was refused: the charity now receives but two guineas per acre; yet those small tenants who were refused are the very tenants thought eligible by the middleman tenant. Mr. Blake also offered to lay out £1000. in improvements, and in building comfortable houses for the former resident tenants. The five divisions of 20 acres each, would produce each £100. per annum profit rent if let to tenants. The tenants to three of the divisions were entitled to some preference, because they have laid out large sums in improving lands belonging to the charity in the town of Galway. If the lands had been let, according to advertisement, in small divisions, they would have been all taken by the inhabitants of Galway, who are anxious to get plots so near the town for building on, which would not only have improved the property, but would have added greatly to the beauty of the environs of that town, for the situation of the ground is very fine, commanding fine and extensive views of land and sea. A committee of two or three, assisted by a professional man perfectly acquainted with the nature of land, should have been sent to view the ground and its capabilities before the letting, and become acquainted with the tenantry and their circumstances, and take them from that scourge, a middleman, who takes advantage of that natural preference for their native soil, which tempts them to bid considerably above the real value of the land, and is one great cause of their general poverty and distress"

There are two charity schools established in Galway; the first was set on foot by the late Rev. Augustine Kirwan, Catholic warden, for the education of poor indigent boys, who are carefully instructed in the principles of their religion, and in reading, writing, and arithmetic: the school is chiefly supported by the occasional contributions of the charitable, which has created a fund that, with receipts of charity sermons, enable the trustees to take in and instruct 150 boys; one hundred of whom they are enabled to clothe yearly, and are also able annually to bind out 12 apprentices to useful trades, by which they are rescued from vice, and become useful members of society. Their funds and concerns are managed by a president, vice-president, treasurer, and secretary, annually chosen, and who are under the patronage of the Catholic warden, vicars, and parochial clergy of the town. In the year 1791 the late Mr. Kirwan, a merchant of London, bequeathed £400. to be vested in trustees, who were to divide the interest amongst old decayed Galway families, (being tribes only) every Christmas for ever; always giving a preference to his own poor relations. The principal has been laid out in the purchase of an estate in the county of the town of Galway, from colonel John Blake of Furbough, which at the expiration of a lease in a few years, will let for about £100. per annum; this will relieve many poor decent families, room-keepers, who are ashamed to beg. — The late Rev. Bartholomew Burke, who died in 1813, one of the Catholic vicars of Galway, by his last will and testament bequeathed £6000. (a great part of which was given to him for charitable purposes) for founding a nunnery of the Presentation order.

The nuns will be enjoined and obliged to instruct, lodge, and teach a certain number of poor female orphans for ever: they have lately taken the house in Galway formerly occupied as a charter school, and latterly as an artillery barrack, for this purpose, and have commenced their meritorious works with great ardour. There are several private schools in Galway, and very few villages are without a small school, but generally of very inferior description. The diocesan school of Tuam has been long celebrated, and what will be considered extraordinary by many, several of the sons of Roman Catholics have been educated there.

There is also in Tuam the college of St Iarloth for the education of Roman Catholics, under the superintendence of the R. C. archbishop of Tuam. Many young men are educated here for the priesthood, and are sent to the college of Maynooth previous to their taking orders. I am well informed it is admirably conducted, and every person who has been often in Tuam must bear testimony to the respectable appearance and remarkable propriety of behaviour of the students at such periods as are devoted to study.

In Connemara there are about a dozen schools, attended only in summer: in winter, which it much the custom elsewhere, the masters attend at the houses of their pupils. To the west of Galway the inhabitants do not wish that their children should learn English, as they say, from their almost daily intercourse with the town of Galway, the girls would be seduced frequently by the soldiers, and the sons tempted to enlist in the army. Formerly Mr. Eyre allotted the profit of the salmon weir of Galway, and a large brick house opposite to the exchange, for the maintenance of 20 poor men. I am at present ignorant if this bequest is fulfilled. The state of education in Ireland at a remote period must have been very high, and comparing it with that of any other part of the world at the same period, it would lose nothing; for we find from Dr. Ledwich[1] and other authors, that in the 6th century the British clergy fled to Ireland to avoid the tyranny of the Saxons, and opened schools here. The Irish clergy also at this period frequently resorted to the east, to receive episcopal ordination, by which their knowledge was much improved, and they were often accompanied on their return by the religious of those countries, prompted by curiosity and that high religious character we had so justly obtained at this time.

From this cause the Greek language was well under stood in Ireland. Pope Gregory the First discountenanced profane learning, the more to encourage sacred, and with that intent burned the Palatine library and the works of Livy (what barbarism!) hence

---

[1] Edward Lewich (1737?–1823) *author of Antiquities of Ireland*, originally published in 1790, [Clachan ed.].

the liberal and ingenious were necessarily driven to this isle to acquire the rudiments of knowledge, as papal injunctions had no force here. — Note, it was not until the 12th century that the discipline of the church of Rome in Ireland was established by the council of Cashel. In 1652, the New Testament was published in Irish by archbishop Daniel of Tuam, and the expense defrayed by the province of Connaught, and Sir William Usher, clerk of the council.

SECTION XI

STATE OF RESIDENT AND NON-RESIDENT LANDLORDS

There are very few absentees of large fortune in this extensive county; though some may be absent, yet still in most cases a small establishment is kept up, and improvements are carried on; but this is very inferior to the advantages to be derived from the cheering influence of the proprietor of an estate. There is scarcely a possibility of a man of fortune residing on his own estate without making some kind of improvements, and exclusive of the relief this affords to his cottier tenantry, the example is highly useful to the better class of farmers. I trust before long to see the example of Lord Clancarty followed by every landed proprietor, in the establishment of a farming society for the encouragement of his tenantry. I can venture to assure them, that every shilling they expend in this way will return them ample interest, exclusive of the delight they must experience from seeing around them a cleanly and happy tenantry. I wish much to impress this warmly on the minds of my younger friends in this county. To the old gentlemen I fear it would be too troublesome for adoption. The day has long since passed away when the pursuits of agriculture were thought to be derogatory to the rank of gentleman. Happily it is now cherished by men of the first rank in every part of the world. We may judge from what Cicero says in his Offices, how highly it was esteemed in the most polished period of Rome, when after discriminating between professions that are mean and those that are honourable, he says, "But amongst all the methods of enriching oneself, there is no better, no one more profitable, pleasant and agreeable; no one more worthy of a man and a gentleman than that of manuring and tilling the ground." One of the beneficial consequences of such a resident proprietary, is the number of excellent grand and petty jurors it produces. Of grand jurors I think there could be at least six sets selected, of ample fortune and sound judgment; and petty jurors are generally of a description and fortune rarely to be met with elsewhere. In a debate in the House of Commons in 1811, Mr. Fuller gave our absentees the following excellent advice: — "Let the great men of Ireland go home, instead of spending their money here; let them regulate their own tenantry and estates, and not hear of them through those secondary persons whom they employ. Lord Kaims says very justly, "It is a strange sort of ambition that moves gentlemen to spend their estates in the House of Commons, where most of them are mere mutes, instead of serving their country and themselves at home, which is genuine patriotism." How many fortunes in Ireland have been ruined by this mute propensity?

Resident Proprietors.

Lord Clanrickard (a minor), Portumna.
Lord Clonbrock, Clonbrock.
Lord Clancarty, Garbally.
Lord Riverston, Pallace.
Lord Gort, Loughcoutra.
Lord French, Castle French.
Archbishop of Tuam, Tuam.
Bishop of Clonfert, Clonfert
James Daly, M. P. Dunsandle.
Malachy Daly, Riaford.
John D'Arcy, Clifden Castle and Kiltolla.
Richard D'Arcy, Newforest.
Robert D'Arcy, Woodville.
Burton Persse, Sen. Tallyho- Lodge.
Burton Persse, Jun. Persse Lodge.
Robert Persse, Roxborough.
Robert Parsons Persse, Castleboy.
Henry Persse, Persse Park.
John Blake, Belmont Pierce Blake, Holly Park.
Charles Blake, Merlin Park.
Walter Blake, Oran Castle.
Martin Joseph Blake, Brookelodge.
Sir John Blake, Bart. Menlo.
Valentine Blake, Menlo.
Edward Blake, Castle Grove.
James Blake, Waterdale.
Henry Blake, Renville.
--------Blake, Corbally.
Robert Blake, Killeen Castle.
Colonel John Blake, Forbough.
Michael Blake, Frenchfort
Christopher Dillon Bellew, Mount Bellew.
Michael Bellew, Mount Bellew.
Hon. Arthur Nugent, Flower Hill.
Christopher Usher, Eastwell.
Michael O'Kelly, Creran.
Denis O'Kelly, Kelly's Grove.
Rev. Armstrong Kelly, Castle Kelly.
Denis H. Kelly, Castle Kelly.
William Kelly, Ashfield.
Francis Kelly, Liskelly.
James Kelly, Ballinamore.
George Kelly, Mucklow.
John Cuffe Kelly, Carrarea.
Festus O'Kelly, Licooly.
John Browne, Moyne.

Rev. Dean Browne, Ahascragh.
Michael Browne, Moyne.
Mark Browne, Rockville.
Bernard Brown, Ballymurphy.
Andrew Browne, Movilla.
John Blakeney, Abbert.
Sir John Ross Mahon, Castlegar.
Bernard Mahon, Beechhill.
Rev. Dean Mahon.
Walter Lawrence, Belview.
Christopher Reddington, Kilcornan.
Thomas Reddington, Ryehill.
Thomas Reddington, Glenlow.
Waller Lambert, Creggclare.
Walter Lambert, Lambert Lodge.
Walter Lambert, Castle Lambert
Walter Lambert, Castle Ellen.
Henry Lambert, Aggard,
Giles Eyre, Eyrecourt Castle.
Thomas Knutford Eyre, Eyreville.
Edward Burke Eyre, Cloone.
John Kirwan, Castle Hacket
-------Kirwan, Glan.
-------Kirwan, Blindwell
Joseph Kirwan, Hilbrook.
Edward Kirwan, Ballyturn.
Edward Kirwan, Gardenfield.
-------Kirwan, Cregg.
Marcus Blake Lynch, Barna
Mathew Lynch, Lavalley.
-----------Lynch, Drimcong
Mark Lynch, Galway.
-------Lynch, Rathglass.
-------Lynch, Moycullen.
-------Lynch, Cartron.
-------Lynch, Shannon Bridge,
-------Lynch, Clough.
Robert French, Monivae.
Robert Joseph French, Rahasane.
------------------French, Elm Hill.
------------------French, Portacarn.
John Bodkin, Anna.
John Bodkin, Bengarry.
Domnick George Bodkin, South Lodge.
James Bodkin, Rahoone.
Burke Bodkin, Mount Silk.
Arthur French St. George, Tyrone.
Christopher St George, Kilcolgan Castle.

Richard Mansergh St. George, Headfort.
Stepney St. George, Myer Hill.
Richard Martin, M. P. Clareville.
Robert Barnwell Martin, Ballynahinch.
Robert Martin, Ross.
Edward Martin, Tullyra.
----------Martin, Curraghmore.
----------Martin, Spiddall.
Edmond Henry O'Flaherty, Lemonfield.
Thos. Parker O' Flaherty, Derrymacloughy Castle.
John Burke, Tyaquin.
Sir John Burke, Marble Hill.
Hayacinth Burke, Killimor.
James Hardiman Burke, St. Clerans.
Robert Burke, St Clerans.
John Burke, Tintrim.
-------Burke, Orver.
Miss Cheevers Fallon, St Brendon's.
Miss Nettervilles, Neterville Lodge.
Walter Joyce, Merville.
Walter Butler, Richard Gregory, Coole.
John Blake Forster, Ashfield.
Edward Beatty, Cappagh.
Philip Lynch Athy, Renville.
----------------Basterot, Duras.
Edmund Concannon, Waterloo Lodge.
Robert O'Hara, Rahine.
Hayacinth Cheevers, Kellyheen.
Cornelius Duffy, Ballinamore.
Anthony Donnelan, Ballyeighter.
Stephen Donnelan, Killagh.
Donnelan, Hillswood.
Richard Galbraith, Cappard.
Thos. Edward Hearn, Hearnsbrook.
John Athboy M'Dermott, Rath more.
----------------M'Dermott, Springfield.
Michael J. Aylward, Ballynagar.
Bernard Connolly, Shannonview.
Francis Davis, Hampstead.
----------------Skerrett, Nutgrove.
----------------Skerrett, Drumgriffin.
----------------Skerrett, Ballinduff.
----------------Skerrett, Carnacrow.
Samuel Wade, Fairfield.
Thomas Wade, Fairfield.
Christopher Lopdel, Athenry.
John O'Neil Geoghegan, Bunown.
Charles Morgan, Monksfield.

James Cuff, Esker.
Non-Resident Proprietors
*Lord Ashton, Woodlawn.[1]
*Thomas Kenny.
*Colonel William Kenny.
*Sir John Burke, Glynsk.
Marquis of Sligo.
Earl of Charlemont, Joyce Country.
Earl of Leitrim,   do.
Lord Clanmorris, Clare Galway.
Martin Kirwan.
----------------Smyth, Spring Lawn.
----------------O'Connor, Benmore.
*-------------- Kelly, Newtown.
----------------Digby, Arran.
David Rutledge, Ballagh.
Matthew George Prendergast
----------------O'Connor, Colesmantown.
Malachy Donnelan, Ballydonnellan.

SECTION XII

STATE OF CIRCULATION OF MONEY OR PAPER

During the late extended war the circulating medium was almost exclusively country bankers' notes, chiefly those of Lord French and Co. and those of Messrs. Joyce and Co. and such confidence was reposed in the stability of both firms, that I have known a marked preference given to their notes by the country people, to those of the bank of Ireland. Much of this might arise from an idea that forgeries were more easily detected, as at almost every fair one of the partners, or a confidential clerk of each of the houses, attended to discount bills, and exchange their own paper for bank of Ireland notes; and such was their credit, and the grateful recollections of favours received, that they found little difficulty in this exchange. But, alas! this tide of success flowed only for a limited period, and both establishments stopped payment for a large amount, and spread ruin and misery through this county. The principals of both establishments died a few years since. Of Mr. Joyce's debts, I believe almost ten shillings in the pound have been paid, and it was the general opinion, that from his highly honorable character, activity, and skill in business, had he lived, the remainder would in a few years have been paid. Of the affairs of the Tuam bank little

---

[1] NOTE. — Those only who are marked thus * can be reckoned Absentees, for though the remainder may not reside in the county, they either live in some other part of Ireland, or some of the family keep up an establishment on the family estate. As I have inserted both lists from memory, I probably may have omitted many names, [original footnote].

is known. The estates of some of the partners have been sold, but how far they will go to liquidate the large amount of the failure I am ignorant.

That the facility with which discounts were made gave an extraordinary impulse to business in the province of Connaught, will not be denied, but like all violent efforts, the reaction debilitated the constitution. As the affairs of the bank of Tuam are before the public, it would be highly unbecoming in me to conjecture what the result will be.

Gold coin has nearly disappeared, and all the minor concerns are transacted by bank of Ireland tokens of different values. Those that are under the necessity of taking bills, find a considerable difficulty in discounting them. There are, I believe, only two discounting houses in the county, both in Galway, where bills on Dublin or bank of Ireland paper may be had for such bills as are of undoubted solvency. A want of attention to this very necessary qualification, I have heard, was amongst the causes of the failure of the two banks; but I think it more probable that the same cause that operated on all the southern banks lately, was the chief one, speculation beyond their capital. Mr. Walter Joyce also, at the period of the failure of his brother's bank, transacted a considerable share of separate business in Galway, but was not affected by those disasters. He has retired from the banking business with a large independent fortune, and highly honorable character. — At present scarcely any but bank of Ireland notes will be taken in any money transactions.

SECTION XIII

STATE OF FARMING AND AGRICULTURAL SOCIETIES

Some years ago there was a farming society established at Loughrea; but from some mismanagement (probably non-payment of subscriptions) it subsisted for a very short period. At present there is not any local society; probably thought unnecessary in consequence of the great annual meeting of the Farming Society of Ireland, which takes place in October at Ballinasloe.

This popular and numerous assemblage of the society has been generally attended with great satisfaction to the public. Here, exclusive of the encouragement offered for the improvement of Breeding stock, from which Ireland has received acknowledged benefit, the most important advantage has accrued from the harmonious and cheerful society which has uniformly prevailed at those meetings, uninterrupted by the distinctions of religion, politics, and party, which seem to have merged in a general wish to promote the objects of the institution, as essential to the agriculture and prosperity of the country. Many advantages have arisen from the establishment of this society, in which the chief of the nobility and landed proprietors are enrolled.

1st. — The increase and improvement of cultivation, acknowledged by the select committee on the corn trade in the house of commons in 1813.

2nd. — The increased export of corn resulting from this, and more than doubled since the date of the society's institution[1].

3rd. — The improved quality of corn, from the improved culture, and the wide dispersion of imported seed.

4th. — The introduction and method of using all the best implements.

5th. — This method of using taught by persons employed by the society.

6th. — The establishment of district ploughing matches throughout Ireland, by which the improved plough and its use have been particularly encouraged.

7th. — The distribution of premium ploughs amongst the working farmers.

8th. — The purchase and distribution of bulls, rams, and swine. To all these, and many other branches of agricultural improvement, has the society's attention been directed, and to those objects have its premiums been appropriated. Any person who recollects the October fair of Ballinasloe previous to the institution of the society, and who is now in the habit of attending it, can appreciate the great and manifest improvement which has resulted from its exertion. I have been favoured by an intelligent friend who possesses a considerable landed property, with the following remarks amongst many others: —

> "The Farming Society's shows are not quite as judiciously timed as they might be. Why not have premiums at the great May fair of Ballinasloe for fat cattle as well as in Dublin in March? But of all the injudicious arrangements, the show at October of horned cattle to obtain premiums for figure, size, and shape, is the most absurd: take the following reasons. In the first place, healthy cattle are too much in flesh to afford the best view of their shape, make, &c.; again, the breeding season for horned cattle is then past. The purchasers of prize heifers, cows, or bulls, must hold them over until the following month of August before turning them to breed. The possessors of prize bulls, or of those nearly of equal figure and value, may, and probably will have disposed of them before the breeding season following, and thus the farmer, already too indolent, and often taking his sires from the nearest quarter, however inferior, has another difficulty thrown in his way in the discovery of those of the superior kinds. Ballinasloe May fair should be the show period for breeding stock, whether bulls, cows, or heifers."

It has been proposed some time since to establish a Farming Society for this province, called "The Connaught Farming Society." If it was established under judicious regulations, and the funds not jobbed away amongst useless officers, totally ignorant of agricultural affairs, I am persuaded it would be of infinite benefit, as they might embrace several minor concerns not coming within the range of the Farming Society of Ireland.

As a *sine qua non* their secretary should be able and willing not only to give reports of the transactions of the different meetings, but also encourage a correspondence

---

[1] Total barrels of corn exported from Ireland from the year 1782 to 1799, - - 8,495,033
 Ditto, Ditto, from 1801 to 1818, each period being 17 years, - - - 19,223,671,
[original footnote].

with agriculturists of all ranks[1]. In England and Scotland several agricultural and horticultural societies have published their transactions, which have been of material benefit; in Ireland, as far as I am in formed, no such thing has ever appeared. One would be led to imagine the officers of our societies were merely actuated by the salary attached to their office. At the same time this exertion should not be expected without remuneration, which should be ample, but it should not be a sinecure. I recollect, some years since, when the late Mr. Hamilton, the then secretary of the Farming Society of Ireland, invited all descriptions of farmers to meet him once a week to communicate and receive information: I have often attended those meetings with great pleasure and advantage; but with him his salary was a secondary consideration, and I fear a carelessness in his pecuniary affairs, and the difficulties brought on by it, helped to hasten the effects of a weakly constitution.

As I have mentioned elsewhere, I think every landed proprietor should have a yearly show for his own tenantry, when premiums should be given for cleanliness, good husbandry, long service, &c.

SECTION XIV

STATE OF MANUFACTURES — WHETHER INCREASING

The manufacture of coarse linens forms the principal one of this county. They are generally what are called handle linen; in some places the handle is 30 inches, in others 32½ inches; again, 28½ inches, sheetings 37½ and 40½ inches wide. In fact, though there is a certain breadth prescribed by act of parliament, and a power given to inspectors, who do or should attend every fair and market, to seize those deficient in breadth, yet little or no notice is taken of it, and they are generally any breadth the owner or the weaver chooses to make them. There is a considerable quantity sold every Thursday at the linen-hall in Loughrea; and a great deal of sheetings are also disposed of at the inn at Tuam; but I understand they are not of such fabric as to do any credit to the makers, as they are of a very flimsy texture, and too often bleached with lime. There is little secret made of this by the country people, and though now and then a little stir is made by the inspector, and perhaps a few pieces seized, it is only laughed at. To make the regulations against this abuse effective rests with the landlords, but they most unaccountably neglect it, though under their nose. If they for a moment reflected that much of the means of paying rent is produced by the sale of linens, they might, perhaps, pay more attention to this affair. At every fair and market a considerable quantity of yarn is sold, but I am informed very inferior both in the spinning and mode of reeling. Many factors attend the fairs, and buy the yarn on commission; and as the weighing rests entirely with them by ouncels, which they

---

[1] I have been informed of a secretary of a Farming Society on being asked a simple agricultural question, answering in the most pettish manner, "Really, I know nothing about such things". If he had been asked a question on the rate of exchange, his answer would have been quite pat, [original footnote].

always carry with them, it is probable there are impositions practised on the sellers. The magistrates should look to this. It is the duty of the person who receives the tolls and customs, but in general I fear it is neglected; also, particular attention should be paid to weights and measures, in which it is highly probable much fraud is practised, by using weights made of stone, which, though frequently broken, still retain the original denomination.

I am not aware of any woollen manufacture existing in this county, except that of flannels and friezes for home use and sale, at from 1s. 8d. to 2s. 6d. per bandle[1] of 30 inches wide, of which almost every woman in the county understands the manufacture. It is not a little extraordinary that so extensive a county, possessing every facility for the manufacture of woollens, should be without it. It possesses the best clothing wool for both coarse and fine fabrics. In Connemara the wool of the country is of very great fineness, and if a little pains were taken by the proprietors of those extensive tracts of pasturable mountain, a wool might be produced equal to the finest manufacture. Probably the Merino cross would be most profitable, and the shape of the native sheep is more assimilated to that of Merino than any other that I am acquainted with. A few years ago South Down rams and ewes were introduced by some proprietors of estates, particularly by Mr. Blake of Renvyle; but of the result I am ignorant, except that I perceive, by an advertisement of that spirited gentleman, that he has near six hundred South Down fleeces for sale. The benefit to be obtained by the cross I have suggested, may be in some measure ascertained by a recurrence to the annual sale of fine wool at the Farming Society house in 1819, where it will be seen that the Rev. Thomas Quin received for 177 fleeces of the third, fourth, and fifth cross of Merino on Wicklow ewes three shilling per pound, whilst at the same time he only received the same price for one hundred and five fleeces of pure Merinos. As the N. B. at the end of the report, "When the wools are delivered, the weight of each parcel will be inserted in a future publication" has not, I believe, been fulfilled by the secretary of the society, no opinion can be formed of the nett profit. However, enough is proved to convince us that in the fifth, or even the third cross, they are equally valuable, and probably from a careful selection and crossing, an additional weight may be added to the fleece. I think I cannot give a better description of the Merinos than a few extracts from the excellent report (I wish we had mere reports from the same pen) of the Merino sheep at Messrs. Nowlan and Shaw's Merino factory, at Merino cottage, in the county of Kilkenny, by the Rev. Mr. Radcliff, secretary to the Farming Society of Ireland. In February 1820 they consisted of six hundred pure Merinos; he says,

"It is considered by the proprietors of this flock, who must be competent judges, being also principals of the Merino factory, that instead of any deterioration being

---

[1] An Irish measure of two feet in length, Irish. *Bannlam*, from *bann* - a measure + *lamh* hand, arm, [Clachan ed.].

perceptible, the quality and weight of the fleece has improved since the importation of the flock."

"The average weight of the clip of 1819, per fleece, was 6½ pound in the grease, rate of sale 3s. per pound. The proprietors of the factory wish to encourage the sale of Merino wool in the grease; it suits the operations of the factory; and three shillings in the grease is a better remuneration to the grower than 3s. 6d. river-washed on the sheep's back. From this, and a former statement of the number of sheep supported per acre, a very flattering estimate presents itself of the acreable value of the wool. It is ascertained that each fleece of the entire flock weighed six and a half pounds, and that it produced 3s. per pound, amount per fleece 19s. 6d. It is also ascertained that each acre supports eight sheep. Gross value of wool per acre, £7. 16s."

"This flock consists almost exclusively of pure Merinos. Nevertheless certain crosses have been tried, and wool of each description of Merino cross has been occasionally purchased for the use of the factory. The opinion which they have formed from those different trials is, that with respect to wool the Merino on Ryland is the most valuable. The Merino on Wicklow mountain remarkably good as a general wool, even in its first cross, and infinitely better in the deeper crosses. The Merino on Leicester, contrary to the common opinion, is considered by the proprietors of the Merino factory to be a very good wool in its second and third crosses, and very useful for general purposes. The first cross sells for 1s. 6d. per pound; the second for 2s.; the third for 2s. 6d. to 3s. This admixture of blood produces a greater weight of fleece than any other; and if in a third cross, it becomes so valuable the proprietors of Leicester sheep might surely try the experiment. The mutton would be improved, and the quantity of loose fat increased."

How wonderfully opinions are changed since this crop was first proposed some years since. "It would be of a description, neither long nor short wool, fit for no kind of manufacture," &c. A considerable quantity of white friezes and cadow[1] blankets are made and sold at Galway, Loughrea, the fair of Tubberbracken, and several other fairs. In the neighbourhood of Galway a considerable quantity of flannels are manufactured; some make upwards of 300 yards in a year, by which they frequently pay their rents; they pay for weaving about three halfpence per yard, and a good weaver can make twenty yards in the day. Two women are generally employed to prepare the yarn for the weaver; they receive at the rate of about two guineas per annum, and their diet. A linen manufacture was established by the late Mr. Lawrence at Lawrencetown; there were at one time upwards of 30 looms that wove linen and fine diaper. At present I am informed there are only four or five. There was also a flourishing linen manufacture established by the late Right Hon. Denis Daly, at Mount Shannon, but when he sold that estate the linen manufacture went to ruin. A great deal of linens are made at Woodford, which are esteemed better than those of Loughrea. In Connemara there is some fine linen made, but much more of a coarse quality; bandle linen for home consumption. There are about one hundred looms in Connemara, and are increasing very much.

---

[1] An article of dress or mantle, made mostly at Wexford, Ross, Waterford, and Trim, [Clachan ed.].

Cottiers generally sow from 1 to 5 pottles[1] of flax seed, and probably there may be about 1500 hogsheads of flax seed sowed each year in this county, the produce of this is generally made into coarse linen and coarse yarn for making canvas for sacks, &c.; and it is remarkable that coarse canvas for bags sells for 10d. or 11d. per handle of thirty inches, whilst a much finer sort will only sell for 8d. because, as the farmer is obliged to allow seven pounds for the sack in the sale of any article it may contain, he wishes for that which will weigh the heaviest. About five bandles make a sack. A large quantity of very coarse canvas is made from tow[2] near Tuam for packing wool, and a considerable deal sent to Cork, Waterford, Ross, and Limerick, for the purpose of packing bacon for exportation. Flax grows tall and well on reclaimed bog, but must be pulled green, or it is subject to have what is called *gluneduh*, or black joint, and though it may be softer than that grown in upland, there is more waste. It would be very material to ascertain the cause of this disorder. There is very little hemp seed in this county, though peculiarly well calculated for reclaimed bog. By some late trials also, it had been ascertained that a flax much superior to that usually cultivated, can be procured from nettles. It requires no watering or bogging, but simply to be well dried previous to breaking, scutching, and hackling in the usual way. It requires to be boiled for a short time in water with soap and a little ashes, and the water changed two or three times, when a flax is produced beautifully white, without further bleaching. It lasts much longer, when made into linen, than any other kind, and bears frequent changes from wet to dry better than that we usually wear. There can be little doubt it will flourish in reclaimed bog, and as it is a perennial, never injured by frost, it possesses a very great superiority over either flax or hemp, only requiring a little ashes once every year or two as manure.

Kelp is a manufacture of much consequence to those possessing property on the coast. The manufacture of this article was unknown here until about the year 1700, and the late Andrew French and his grandfather were the first, and for a long time the only exporters. At that period the price was 14s. to 20s. per ton. It continued to rise gradually to £16. a ton in 1810, since which is has fallen to £4. In 1810 great losses were sustained by those who speculated in this article; it fell from £16. to £4. per ton. A considerable saving might be made if the exportation of kelp was permitted direct from the coast where it is burned, without being brought to Galway; the saving, exclusive of loss of time, expenses in Galway, and waste, would be 30s. per ton. The craner in Galway gets 6d. per ton — 1s. for basket to weigh it in, and 1s. for each draught of the scales of 5¼ cwt. In some years the amount of sales has been upwards of £60,000. but lately has not exceeded £13,000. or £14,000. Except in a time of great scarcity Galway kelp, from its bad quality, is in little demand. It is generally thought to be inferior to Scotch kelp. The Galway merchants say there is much prejudice in this idea, and to prove it they shipped a cargo for Scotland, and re-

---

[1] A measure of liquid or seed of half a gallon, [Clachan ed.].
[2] Course, heavy linen, [Clachan ed.].

shipped it as Scotch kelp, and received under that delusion £4. per ton more than they would have had for it as Galway kelp. The makers of the kelp say, that there is so little difference made on the quay of Galway, between good and bad, it is not worth their while to take any pains; for they say, those whose business it is to appreciate it are grossly ignorant and careless.

There is a considerable quantity of knit woollen stockings sold in Connemara, to the amount of at least £10,000. per annum; though possessing the finest wool, they are of very inferior manufacture. The makers say they are so completely at the mercy of the pedlers, who are the only buyers, that they have no encouragement to make them better. If proper encouragement by some capitalist was given they would be superior to any in the world at the same price. They possess a softness and elasticity which no wove stocking, however fine, does; but from being made frequently with only a single thread, they give very little wear. Some times they are made in a superior manner, are then excellent, but they are by no means the general manufacture of Connemara. I have the authority of a very eminent stocking manufacturer in Dublin to state, that "if a hall was established in some central situation, and an honest intelligent inspector appointed, and some persons of capital were to embark in the business, the manufacture would be brought to such a pitch of perfection as not only to supply the whole consumption of Ireland, but to open a trade to all other parts of the world, and enable us to understand the English and Scotch manufacturers " in their own markets." One town alone in Scotland exports knit stockings to the amount of above £100,000. It is a curious circumstance, that in the mountains of Cunnnmara the sheep are generally sheared as the wool is wanted; frequently you will see one side only entirely shorn- another sheep with one shoulder or thigh shorn. When a woman wants a little wool to finish a stocking, she trips away to the mountains, claps the sheep's head between her knees, and shears just as much as she judges will complete her work. The same sheep is often shorn three times in the year; as this operation is not confined to the summer months, and the shelter is so great, and the climate near the sea so mild, that it is thought the animal suffers little from this singular practice. This frequent clipping has been assigned as the reason for the superior fine and soft texture of Cunnamara stockings.

There is a paper mill in Galway, which supplies Limerick, Ennis, and Westport, and some kinds are sent to Dublin for printers'· use. They find that making those sorts are more profitable than the finer, of those they manufacture a considerable quantity. It bas been well ascertained, that their paper has been sent to Dublin, and after having been cut has been turned to Galway in the form of letter paper, and purchased by those who would not use their own town's manufacture if they knew it. There is a considerable manufacture of black marble chimney-pieces in Galway from the marble quarries in Anglingham, Menlow, and Merlin Park. The two first quarries are worked by Mr. Ireland, who exports a considerable quantity of blocks to Liverpool, Bristol &c. where they are highly esteemed. This marble, if well-chosen is perfectly free from those white spots that so much injure the appearance of that of Kilkenny, and the generality of marble in this country. Mr. Hardiman, who knows the habits of the people of Galway so intimately, say in his history of the town of Galway, on this head: -

"The Merlin Park quarry was opened in 1814, and Mr. Blake, the proprietor, exported a few cargoes; but the industry, perseverance, and resolution to encounter, not only preliminary expenses, but even temporary losses, to bring a work of this kind to perfection, do not seem to have attended these undertakings. There is, however, little doubt but that, if these quarries were worked with spirit and judgment, they would in a short time, become a considerable source of emolument, and fully reward that attention which they so much deserve."

There is a manufactory of tobacco pipes in Galway, and another in Creggs; also several potteries of coarse ware, one near Dunsandle, lately established, where they make excellent garden pots at reasonable rates, there is a considerable number of feathers exported from the island of Arran, and the naked appearance of the poor geese throughout the country shows how much they contribute to our weary bones. They are plucked three times a year and produce 3d. or 4 d. for each plucking; but as the buyer generally plucks them, they are often greatly injured, especially in the wings, which are frequently broken. – There is a considerable manufacture of felt hats in Loughrea, and several other towns; they sell for 3s. to 6s. each. A good deal of straw hats and bonnets are made in several towns; the hats from 1s. 8d. to 2s. 6d., the bonnets from 2s. 6d. to 10s., perhaps more. Straw bonnets have been lately manufactured in Castle Blakeney, as high as three guineas each.

SECTION XV

STATE OF MILLS OF EVERY KIND

In the town of Galway there are about 23 flour mills, 6 oat mills, 2 malt mills, 4 tuck mills[1], 1 paper mill, and 1 bleach mill: there are also, in different parts of the county, upwards of 12 large flour mills, and several of a smaller though not less useful description, and several oat and tuck mills. As the Galway mills are almost always at work, it may be conjectured what a quantity of flour must be dressed annually, of which, after supplying the neighbouring counties and the adjacent country, the remainder is sent to Dublin. It is calculated that even at a very low average there are at least 12,000 tons annually manufactured by the millers of Galway alone. This, even at the low rate of £20. per ton, shows what an impulse must be given to the agriculture of the country, by the expenditure of upwards of £200,000, and, added to the great export of corn during the war, and the liberal discounts of the banks at that period, accounts for the high rents paid for land. If all the mills are now at full work, I trust the distresses of our farmers will be only temporary. The great increase of

---

[1] Mills used for the cleansing of cloth (particularly wool) to eliminate oils, dirt, and other impurities, [Clachan ed.].

flour mills has been chiefly since 1790; previous to that period there were but two; the late Mr. Patrick Ward and Mr. Rickard Burke's, near the fish market. There have been two capital mills erected a few years since on Nun's island, one by Mr. Fitzgerald, and the other by Mr. Regan, finished in 1814; they have every advantage of the late improvements in arrangement and machinery. Mr. Regan's, I understand, is composed entirely of metal, contrived and executed by Mr. Macky, a very ingenious millwright from Scotland.

This mill was begun in 1813; it is erected on five arches, is 80 feet long by 41 feet broad, has 12 floors, lighted by an hundred glass windows; it was finished and ready for work in one year, and considered to have cost £10,000. It has four pair of stones, which can be worked either together or separately, with only one undershot waterwheel. The power is so great, and the machinery so complete, it can grind with one pair of stones 20 cwt. in an hour. The machinery of this mill is highly worth the inspection of the curious, and reflects high credit not only on the ingenious man who executed it, but the spirited individual who has risked such property in the concern, and most sincerely do I wish him every success. Such men are a blessing to a country, as they assist the industrious farmer, upon whose prosperity every other class of society depends, an opinion, it were to be wished, prevailed more generally amongst our legislators[1]. About forty years ago a Mr. Waddlesworth erected the first flour mill in Galway: he was opposed by all the bakers, and at length they burned his mill, and from the injuries and insults he received, was obliged to quit Galway. Before his mill was erected, each baker had a large chest in the mill that ground for them, with a lock and key, in which he usually kept as much wheat as he judged would be sufficient until the next market day. As he wanted it, it was ground in the mill. When we compare this with the present number (23 flour mills) it must be with feelings of joy at the encouragement it gives to the farmer. Many of the millers of this county give a preference to the mill stones raised near Dunmore; which, if well chosen, they say, are for some species of the manufacture equal, if not superior to French burr, though not more than about one third of the price.

---

[1] It must be sincerely regretted that this gentleman's speculations have not been so fortunate as he deserves; but I trust his difficulties will soon terminate. I fear (a very usual thing in Ireland) his capital did not keep pace with hisardent mind, [original footnote].

SECTION XVI

STATE OF PLANTATIONS AND PLANTING

Planting has long been a favourite pursuit in this county, especially since the days of Shanley and Leggett, who certainly gave a considerable impulse to it; but there are scarcely any of such extent as to be called a wood, much less a forest. The formal style of surrounding the demesne with a screen, or called more appropriately, from its narrowness, a belt, (in many places it might be justly termed a thread) and the interior blotted with circular clumps (they could not from their general want of connection be called groups) prevented, in a few years, when they admitted light through them, all idea of extent. The designers of that period are not to be much blamed, for such works were the fashion of the day, and a tame copy of the Browne school. Probably in the days of London and Wise, of topiary memory, their works were esteemed of the highest order of taste, until, with the assistance of Addison and Pope, Kent and Nature prevailed over the Sheers. It is however disgraceful to the present age, that they obstinately pursue the same tame method as their forefathers. Many gentlemen have planted extensively, but still they have not planted forests. I have scarcely ever seen one that a quarter of an hour's ride would not bring you from one end to the other.

The late Mr. Lawrence of Bellevue, planted a great extent of screens and clumps[1], upwards of 370 acres; but from their narrowness, want of timely thinning, and a deficiency of underwood, they admit the light to be seen through them. This is the general fault of the Irish planting, and if we may judge from different publications, of English planting too. When, some years since, by an order from the court of Chancery, I thinned the plantations of Bellevue, I advised them to be carefully copsed, and an additional breadth, and more varied outline to be given to the screens and clumps.

These would in a few years have shut out the light, and relieved them from that wretched tameness that Mr. Lawrence, in conformity with the fashion of the day, adopted, and would have converted his clumps into groups. I regret to say that none of these ideas have been adopted; cattle have been admitted into most of the plantations, and something like an American improvement has been pursued.

It was the late Mr. Lawrence's intention to have added considerably to those screens, and I am informed he often wished his demesne extended seven miles, that he might have planted it all. The study of the demesne of Bellevue would, however, be well worth the attention of the lovers of this charming art; exclusive of those very general faults he would learn to avoid, he would perceive some of the best oak trees growing

---

[1] "But ah! how different is the formal lump,
Which the improver plants, and called a clump."
KNIGHT'S LANDSCAPE

in several feet of turf bog, badly drained; whilst in dry ground, apparently more appropriate to their growth, they have made little progress. Here also may be seen (or might have been seen) some of the most beautiful ash trees growing luxuriantly in upwards of three feet of turf bog, completely surrounded by stagnant water within a foot of the surface; and what is very remarkable, there are Scotch fir and alder amongst them, greatly inferior in growth and health. In the servants' hall there is a table made of pineaster, planted and cut down by the late Mr. Lawrence. The first length of the tree was nine feet, cut into boards nineteen inches broad; another length nine feet also, cut into boards sixteen inches brood, exclusive of a considerable top; the wood beautiful, and of excellent quality. There was a Weymouth pine of about forty-four years growth, (planted by Mr. Lawrence,) cut down for a pump stick; the circumference was four feet ten inches; the timber was very fine, very red at the heart, and full of turpentine: the top was decayed, which caused its conversion to this use; until then, I had been always led to think that Weymouth pine was a soft, white, worthless timber. Balm of Gilead fir uniformly decayed in every part of this demesne when about fourteen feet high. Indeed I do not recollect to have seen a flourishing tree of this species of considerable age, in any part of Ireland.

Pineaster invariably flourishing at the west side of every plantation, whilst on the south and east they have mostly decayed. I cut down many hundreds in that state. Larch, Scotch fir, and sweet chestnut, bent by the westerly winds; but oak, spruce and silver fir, and Weymouth pine, not bent; beech a little bent The following dimensions of trees, (if they have not been cut down) will show, in a forcible light, the spirit of planting Mr. Lawrence possessed; and, in addition to what I have just detailed, the profit of planting. That has been so often doubted by those who are eager to lay hold of every excuse to hide their indolence, that I give it with more pleasure than hope. They were all planted by the late Mr. Lawrence. They were measured in 1808, and were in circumference, at three feet from the ground, and about forty-four years growth, as follow:

	Ft.	In.		Ft.	In.
Acacia	5	4	Copper beech	5	4
Cedar of Libanus	6	8	Occidental plane	9	6
Scotch elm	10	0	Evergreen oak	5	0
Sweet chestnut	7	6	Horse chestnut	5	9
Oak	8	6	Scotch fir	4	4
Silver fir	7	3	Ash (sold for four		
Portugal laurel	4	7	guineas)	6	1
Weymouth pine	5	0	Pineaster	5	7
Tulip tree (60 feet			Hornbeam	6	2
high at least)	5	10	Beech	7	5
Common laurel	3	3	Larch	6	3
&c. &c. &c.					

The late colonel Hayes of Avondale, (dear to the memory of every lover of planting and polished manners,) measured the sweet chestnut in 1790; it was then, at six feet from the ground, four feet eight inches: as there is very little difference in the girth at six feet or three feet from the ground, there has been an average of two feet ten inches in eighteen years, nearly a foot diameter in so short a period. If this statement is correct, what an immense loss must be sustained by the premature and indiscriminate cutting at Bellevue since the death of Mr. Lawrence. The late colonel Hayes, in his admirable treatise on planting, sets this in a very clear light, "The timber of an oak tree of fifty years growth, is worth from twelve to twenty shillings: a tree of seventy-five years growth may be worth from four to seven pounds." — Note, I beg most earnestly to recommend an attentive perusal of this treatise to every person possessing woods. I cannot suppose any one who has either a taste or a love of planting can be without it The mistaken idea of planting trees of very inferior value for nurses, has been practised at Bellevue, as well as in every plantation in Ireland, England, and a recurrence to my Survey of the County of Clare, p. 279, will show it has been also adopted in Scotland. When thinnings of plantations are to be sold, the money received for those of larch, when compared with that of beech, alder, and many others, will throw a strong light on my position. The country people are all perfectly sensible of the superiority of larch over every other except ash, to which they are very partial, that any quantity of those can be sold, whilst beech, alder, or Scotch fir, may remain long on hands.

Mr. Lawrence showed great judgment in selecting hardy trees for the west side of his plantations; they are very much beech, hornbeam and sycamore. Many people, I have been informed, thought him a little deranged when he planted such a quantity of his demesne as 370 acres; but if his views had been seconded during the minority of his son, there would be an immense property coming to him and his children. He planted 100,000 oaks at the distance at which they were intended to stand for timber, and filled up the spaces with other trees for nurses. He calculated that each oak tree in forty years would be well worth at least 20s.; and had they been properly thinned in time, this calculation would have been greatly below the value. Some progress was made for this purpose when I commenced the thinning; and if it had been gradually carried on for a few years, his judicious intentions would have been more than realised. If I am rightly informed, since that period, oaks and nurses have nearly all disappeared. I made a valuation of what value the entire plantations of this demesne would be at a future period of thirty years, when they would be about seventy-four years old, and supposing the trees to stand twelve feet asunder, which is sufficient for trees not intended for ship timber, and even at twenty shillings each, they would be worth £181,300. but they would be more likely worth £3. each, when they would be worth £543,900. besides the value of the thinnings in the meantime. I am aware it will be said that there must be deductions for failures; I grant it; but I am convinced that it is more probable that many trees of this age (seventy-four years), will be worth from £5. to £10. each. It proves, amongst numberless instances in Ireland, that one or more sworn superintendents of the plantations of minors, under the control of the court of Chancery, (as my operations at Bellevue were) would be a most useful officer, and would prevent the gross frauds and dilapidations committed frequently by guardians and executors on the property of wards of chancery[1].

Immense losses have been sustained at Bellevue, by cutting, at a former period, the limbs of beech and other trees, eight or ten inches from the stem; holes were formed when the stumps decayed: if cut close at the time, the wound would have been healed over long since. I met another glaring proof of this erroneous practice at Rossborough, the seat of the earl of Milltown. Several years ago a person of the name of Smyth, who had been a long time planter to the late duke of Leinster and his father, commenced *a pruner of plantations*, and probably a designer. He was unfortunately engaged at Rossborough, where he pruned with a vengeance. To improve the body he cut off limbs a foot diameter of beech trees (some of the largest I ever saw). When I viewed them a few years ago, there was a well hole, filled with water, reaching from the mutilated timber to the ground in the centre of the tree. It may be well supposed what havoc such an improver must have committed at the duke of Leinster and other places, for I understand he was much employed, and I suppose he did this from *experience*, that *ignis fatuus*[2] of improvers of all descriptions. The picturesque appearance of many plantations has been completely prevented in numberless places by mistaking Mr. Pontey's excellent directions for pruning forest trees.

At Marble Hill, the seat of Sir John Burke, trees have made a rapid progress in a soil by no means favourable. They were planted in 1775, at four years old, and in 1803, when I took the dimensions, were as follows, at five feet from the ground:

	Feet.	Inches.	
Beech,	3	5	in circumference.
Ash,	3	5	do.
Oak,	2	11	do.

Which was a considerable growth for 28 years, and in such a soil. An excellent practice was adopted by the late Sir Thomas Burke, of planting two or three years old forest trees like quicks[3] in the sides of ridges, thrown up like potato ridges; this practice is well worth the notice of those possessing soils with a thin or wet surface over clay.[4] I have had many opportunities of witnessing the extreme hardiness of

---

[1] I took the liberty, some time since, to address a latter on this subject to the Lord Chancellor. At I have never been honored with an answer, I presume his lordship did not approve of the idea. I can only regret it, without having had any reason since to change my opinion, [original footnote].

[2] Something that misleads or deludes; an illusion, [Clachan ed.].

[3] Quickthorn. A fast growing hedging plant, [Clachan ed.].

[4] I regret exceedingly that I have not been honoured by Sir John Burke with an answer to a letter I took the liberty of addressing to him, requesting the girths of those trees at the present period. It might have been even an amusing document to Sir John or his son at some future period. I feel great gratification in acknowledging the urbanity with which the late Sir Thomas Burke acceded to my request for information. Not content with his own information during a very delightful week spent at Marble Hall

pineaster. At Cnuck-a-Donagh, the estate of Mr. Martin, near Bushy Park, two very flourishing pineasters may or might be seen on a very exposed hill; the west side of the tree as vigorous as the east, whilst Scotch firs in the same situation are in a miserable state of decay. At Rahasan also, pineasters are growing vigorously exposed to the westerly winds; and in the same plantation Scotch fir are only lingering out their lives. The largest oak probably in this province may be seen here; it is a noble tree, and spread with a charming canopy upwards of seventy feet The instances of the hardiness of pineaster almost convinces me that the immense fir trees found buried in bogs in exposed situations are pineaster, and not Scotch fir. An immense pineaster may be seen (1803) at Killeen, in the parish of Ballynakill, the estate of Sir John Burke. It was brought there by one Porter, one of Cromwell's soldiers; there is or was a large Scotch fir near it, greatly inferior in every respect, though tradition says they were planted at the same time. Great losses are sustained by permitting birch to occupy the place of better trees. In my survey of Clare, I have given an instance of it in the extensive woods of Cratilon. At Woodpark, near Woodford, consisting of about 40 acres, this mistake occurs. This wood, like most woods in this county, is grazed, and in a wretched condition, at least it was so when I saw it a few year ago. Miss Netterville's woods near Woodbrook are under the same mismanagement; birch and other inferior kinds encumbering the ground, the greater part a swamp from want of draining, and, as usual, they are grazed: to account for this ruinous practice, it is a part of the wood ranger's perquisites. Occidental plane stands the westerly winds at Merlin Park, the seat of Mrs. Blake, close to the bay of Galway, better than many trees that are esteemed more hardy; they shoot late in the spring, when all danger from frost or winds is nearly over. Canada and Carolina poplars also stand the western blast, and in a very dry, thin, limestone soil. A very strong proof of the losses that are suffered by the indiscriminating predilection for oak, in soils not adapted to them, may be seen near Craghwell; oak of about 26 years growth not more than about twelve feet high, whilst larch of the same age near them may be sawed into boards. It is a general idea that horse chestnut will not thrive in bog; I have seen many instances of a contrary tendency; amongst others, they are in a very thriving state in a bog at Woodlawn, where indeed most kinds of trees are flourishing in improved bog. At Clonfert also may be seen very fine old ash trees in bog of several feet in depth. I am fond of multiplying the proofs of the capability of drained bogs, to produce many trees and crops, that stubborn ignorance and the vanity of your mighty sensible people will not allow them to do. There are probably more fine ash trees than of any other kind in this county. An uncommon fine one at Mount Bellew, called Cromwell's tree, as tradition says it was planted when he was in Ireland. Also at St Clerans, some very fine ones may be seen. There are multitudes of other fine ash that I do not immediately recollect; I hope I shall be forgiven by those who possess them. It would be unpardonable not to mention the Doniry ash, on

---

he not only favoured me with letters of introduction to his friends, but sent intelligent men to show me everything worth seeing in his neighbouthood, [original footnote].

the road between Loughrea and Portumna. When I saw it in 1803, it was in a state of great decay. It was so large, that I was informed a weaver worked at his loom in it, and his family lived with him in it. It was surrounded with iron hoops, which I hope have preserved it. When Mr. Hardy saw it some years since, it measured at four feet from the ground, 42 feet in circumference; at six feet high, 33 feet round. About 25 years before Mr. Hardy measured it, a school had been kept in it. At Kiltolla there is an uncommonly fine and immense ash tree, called De Ginckle's tree. Tradition says that General and his officers sheltered under it after the battle of Aghrim, on their way to Galway. A decided preference is given to ash by buyers in general, and for this reason it is very difficult to protect them at all ages; this has hitherto prevented many from planting them, but latterly a great number have been planted. When they are plenty enough to be within the reach of the poor man's pocket, this complaint will scarcely ever be heard. Their value and scarcity must have been great even in the time of Henry VIII. when every Irishman within the English pale, having a plough, was obliged to plant 12 ash trees in the ditches and closes of his farm, on pain of forfeiting two shillings; a large sum at that period.

There are very few orchards in this county that produce cider for sale, and indeed, from the sample I have tasted in most private houses, the less they make the better, if the proprietors are determined to adhere to their present system of mismanagement I have scarcely ever drank any cider made in this county that did not require sugar to be added to make it palatable. In the appendix I have given the method of making the best kind of cider, from the scientific and practical directions of Mr. Knight; it seems to be the best that has yet been published.

SECTION XVII
STATE OF THE EFFECTS OF THE ENCOURAGEMENT HERETOFORE GIVEN BY THE ROYAL DUBLIN SOCIETY, PARTICULARIZED IN THE ANNEXED LIST, AND ANY IMPROVEMENT WHICH MAY OCCUR FOR FUTURE ENCOURAGEMENT, PARTICULARLY FOR THE PRESERVATION OF TREES WHEN PLANTED

The following list of bounties paid by the Royal Dublin Society, will prove the spirit of planting it gave birth to. The bounties have very properly been discontinued for some years; in this, as in most other affairs, the chief benefit to be derived is from pointing the attention to the subject. To make men think for themselves is the chief object to be obtained; in fact whatever wants a bounty to support it is seldom worth notice, and probably will be very short lived, if it has not some intrinsic merit of its own.— How much money has been jobbed away in Ireland formerly, by bounties to individuals for the establishment of ill-judged speculations?

Bounties given to nursery-men between the years 1768 and 1795.

		£.	s.	d.
To	James Mullowney	86	15	0
	Michael Madden	349	3	1

Fancis Madden	-	-	- 618	6	1
Robert Power	-	-	- 288	0	6
Richard and Thomas Clarke	-	-	- 979	4	5
Francis Kelly	-	-	- 119	4	1
			1680	13	2

Bounties for the following number of acres, received by gentlemen in the same period.

	Acres.		Acres
Mr. Lawrence	39	Mr. Joseph Kirwan	10
Right Hon. D. B. Daly	141	Lord Riverston	41
Mr. Charles Morgan	6	Mr. W. Taylor	20
Mr. Walter Lambert	20	Sir Thomas Burke	42
Mr. Edward Kirwan	10	Mr. Michael Burke	53
Mr. William Persse	3	Mr. Robert Dillon	10
Mr. Nicholas Martin	10	Mr. Richard D'Arcey	10
Mr. Chris. St George	10	Mr. Mark Browne	10
Mr. C. French	13	Earl of Clanrickard	125
Mr. Connolly	10	Earl of Clancarty	21
Mr. William Nugent	10	Mr. Charles Blake	25
Mr. Richard Martin	10	Mr. Marcus B. Lynch	20
Mr. Robert French	10	Mr. Martin Lynch	23
			702

The bounty to nursery-men was of infinite use, as several extensive nurseries were established in this county, that probably would not otherwise have been. Since that period the nursery business has been at a low ebb, as most gentlemen, as they should do, have their own nurseries[1]. The number of acres planted by gentlemen amount to 702, a considerable quantity in 27 years, when it is considered that those were only such as had obtained a bounty, for we cannot suppose that there was not infinitely more than that number, that did not obtain any, for nothing under 10 acres received the bounty. At the same time the names of many gentlemen occur here, that should individually have planted more than the whole amount; such were, among some others,

> The Right Hon. Denis Bowes Daly.
> Sir Thomas Burke.
> Earl of Clanrickard.
> Mr. Marcus Blake Lynch.
> Lord Riverston.
> Mr. Richard Martin.

---

[1] Latterly a considerable improvement has been made in the sales at the nurseries, as a spirit of planting has become very prevalent in this country, [original footnote].

All proprietors of extensive mountains, well calculated to produce timber trees. It would have been a desirable condition, and I believe was intended in giving those premiums, that they should be well fenced, and thinned at the proper age, both of which, the last especially, have been grossly neglected. But the planting that calls loudly for adoption is, that of the extensive mountains and bogs that occur so frequently in this county, with the exception of Dalyston, Roxborough, Portumna, and perhaps some few others, little has been done in this way. If the same spirit actuated the landed proprietors of this county, and I may say of Ireland, as those of Scotland, what a country would ours be! In that enlightened country (Scotland) probably more has been planted in that kind of ground by one noble proprietor, than in the whole of Ireland. There they reckon by the thousand acres, here by the acre. I suppose it was from a knowledge of this, that Mr. Loudon, a very celebrated landscape gardener in England, estimated the amount of Irish taste; for in his treatise on improving country residences, page 683, he says, with all the ardour of one solicitous for our improvement. "What might not be done in Ireland, in the civilization and improvement of the lower orders," (those wild animals with wings and tails I presume he meant) "by the introduction of taste amongst the higher and middling classes" We cannot sufficiently admire Mr. Loudon's knowledge of the taste of the higher classes, or his advice how to improve it. We are such a tasteless stupid people, especially the higher classes, that it would fail, unless administered by the picturesque superintendence of Mr. Loudon in *propria persona*[1]. Poor Ireland, how little either her capabilities or her people are known! I shall, not follow Mr. Loudon further, or it might be said it was *jalousie de metier*[2], or two of a trade could not agree; but probably we only differ in this one point, for judging from his writings on this subject, I most cordially join him in his reprobation of the followers of Browne, of whom we have had too many, gentle and simple, for the last fifty years in Ireland. I regret to state, that their tame style has taken such firm possession, that any picturesque deviation from it is generally designated *whim, caprice, flights of fancy, &c. &c.*

On the other hand, I have seen some gentlemanlike sketching, that forcibly brings to my recollection some appropriate lines in Knight's Landscape:

>*All art, by labour slowly is acquired;*
>*The madman only fancies 'tis inspired.*
>*The vain, rash upstart, thinks he can create,*
>*E're yet his hand has learn'd to imitate;*
>*While senseless dash and random flourish try*
>*The place of skill and freedom to supply.*
>*To improve, adorn, and polish, they profess;*

---

[1] In one's own person, especially without representation by an attorney, [Clachan ed.].
[2] Professional jealousy, [Clachan ed.].

But shave the goddess, whom they come to dress;
Level each broken bank, and shaggy mound,
And fashion all — to one unvaried round;
One even round, that ever gently flows,
Nor forms abrupt, nor broken colours knows;
But wrapt all o'er in everlasting green,
Makes one dull, vapid, smooth, unvaried scene.
Shaved to the brink, our brooks are taught to flow
Where no obtruding leaves or branches grow;
While clumps of shrubs bespot each winding vale,
Open alike to every gleam and gale;
Each secret haunt and deep recess displa'd,
And intricacy banished with its shade.

SECTION XVIII

STATE OF NURSERIES IN THE COUNTY, AND EXTENT OF SALES

There were formerly several eminent nurseries in this county, as may be perceived in section 17, but though they may not be diminished in number, they certainly are in the extent of sales, owing very much to almost every gentleman maintaining a nursery of his own, and without this it is in vain to think of planting extensively. Except very great designs are in contemplation, I would advise a purchase of seedlings from the nurseries, in preference to sowing seed, and in general never to permit forest trees, with some few exceptions, to remain longer in the nursery if (as it should be) it is rich ground, than one season; if in poor soil they may remain two summers, but seldom longer. At present there is an excellent small nursery at Kilchrist, lately the property of a very ingenious honest man, Martin Larkin. It is continued by his widow in the same neat style. Two or three small nurseries at Ballinasloe; — a small one at Mount Bellew bridge; — one or two near Bellevue; — one at Galway, and several small ones in the neighbourhood of Loughrea. There may be some more that I do not recollect. The demand for fruit trees or curious shrubs is very trifling; those who want either, usually procure them in the Dublin nurseries. The nurseries, with the exception of Mrs. Larkin's, are kept in a slovenly state; this, though it may appear to hurt only the eye, is very injurious to trees that are destined to bleak exposures; for if high weeds are permitted to grow up with them, they are rendered too tender to bear sudden exposure, and the roots of couch grass and other, perennial weeds are moved along with them, and are highly injurious to small trees. Another very blamable practice of many nursery-men, is planting trees too thick in the nursery; most kinds are planted out at two or three inches from each other, and the rows frequently not more than a foot asunder, often much nearer. When trees are permitted to remain two years or more in this crowded state, it is highly pernicious, and is the chief cause of the failure in many cases, where the fault is laid at the door of the poor planter.

It is very much the practice with nursery-men to put out one year old seedlings at once into the rows where they are intended to stand until four years old; by this practice, most kinds of trees, especially Larch and Scotch fir (naturally inclined to have a scanty supply of roots,) are very unfit to plant in shallow soils, as from want of room to spread, and the roots of seedlings never shortened when planting, as they should be, they run down perpendicularly, and when moved to shallow ground at an advanced age, the roots are obliged to be cut short; if, on the contrary, they were a second time transplanted, and had sufficient room, they would be well worth twice the price they usually sell for. The nursery-men say, with some truth, that few, if any, would give a remunerating price for this additional trouble. Most of my friends, when they are going to purchase trees, enquire only where they can get the cheapest trees at the age they wish to purchase: They in general look more to the head than to the roots; to the length than to the thickness of the stem.

SECTION XIX

PRICE OP TIMBER, AND STATE OF IT IN THE COUNTRY

There is very little of what can be called timber sold in this county. The sale is mostly confined to that of ash; even for this the market is soon over stocked, and water carriage is generally too distant to assist the sale[1]. It is not easy to state the rate at which timber sells, for it is usually by bulk. Where ash is sold by the foot, it is frequently so low as two shillings per cubic foot; a few of a large scantling, for particular purposes, may be had as high as four shillings. Firs of good size at about two shillings per foot. Elm 2s. 6d. to 8s. 6d. Oak 3s. to 4s. 6. but very few of any considerable size in the county; of course the quantity of bark is very trifling. It has been lately at a very low price; birch and blade sallow bark at about half the price of that of oak; the first reckoned much superior by the tanners. It is not a little extraordinary that the use of larch bark is totally unknown; yet in many parts of England it sells readily for about half the price of oak bark, and in Scotland the duke of Athol sold 100 tons of this bark for £10. per ton. Colonel Hays states that about 24 oak trees of 18 years growth, badly managed, will predate a barrel of bark of 12 stones. Alder, when it can be pictured of a good size, is much esteemed for bolsters for cars, and for bushing the eye of the lower mill-stone round the spindle, as it never takes fire by friction. In handles for tools it does not blister the hands. I have seen it made into tables, and a side-board, &c. very beautiful.

---

[1] The immense quantity of large timber of all sorts blown down by the dreadful hurricane of the 5th of December, 1822 has lowered the price of it considerably, [original footnote].

Many are often distressed for laths that have Scotch fir of their own fit for this purpose, but, from an idea that none but foreign timber will answer, have never tried them. I had the experiment tried at Bellevue, by which it was ascertained that a piece of a tree four feet long, and about ten inches in diameter, would make upwards of 600 laths, besides the top and branches. In general only one length can be procured from each tree fit for the purpose, on account of the knots; but, as many lengths as are free from this objection can be used equally well as the best. I had larch tried for this purpose, and contrary to the opinion of the workmen, it split into excellent laths, which are probably of much superior duration to those, from Scotch fir. Much use is made of kishes[1], which sell for about five shillings each; some made of small sallows, 3s. 4d., others of strong hazel rods, 6s. each; it takes about 200 sallow rods to make the kish. Rafters or couples for cottages from 2s. 6d. to 6s. Ribs, or stretchers over the couples, from 4s. to 6s. per dozen. Rods for making baskets 2s. to 3s. per 100. Scollops 6d. to 8d. Small kishes or baskets for horses from 1s. 8d. to 2s. 6d. or 3s. A hurdle, of which much use is made for floors, from 2s. to 6s. Bog timber, such as is usually dug up out of bogs, is in great request; it consists of oak or fir; the first is greatly esteemed for any work executed in damp situations; and the fir for all kinds of carpenters' work, for which it is excellent; also for laths, which are thought to be much more lasting than those from foreign fir. Sometimes this species of timber is twisted into ropes, much used for supporting the beds of the cottiers, as they bear damp better than hempen ropes. On the verge of most bogs oak is usually found, but further into the bogs fir is the kind mostly discovered. Bogs on mountains generally produce more timber than those in flat situations, which seldom furnish any timber, but on their borders. Yew of considerable size is frequently found buried in bogs. If it can be procured without what the workmen term shakers (cracks), it makes beautiful tables[2]. Timber buried in bogs is discovered by going on them early in a dewy morning, as the dew never lies on the bog over the tree; they ascertain with a long spear if the timber is sound and worth extricating from the bog.

Gross timber should be cut with a cross-cut saw whilst standing; the handles to be turned for this purpose at the forge. Where timber is sold by the foot, and very gross, a material saving will be made, at least a foot in length. In the progress of the work iron wedges of different sizes are used to give freedom to the operation of the saw, and a pit must be dug around the tree to give the workmen elbow room. In the

---

[1] A basket used in Ireland, mainly for carrying turf, from Irish *cis*, *ceis* ("basket, hamper"), [Clachan ed.].
[2] One of the most beautiful tables I have ever seen is of this wood, at the Rev. Dean French's near Elphin. It is about four feet diameter, and without the least flaw. I have lately been informed of an immense yew tree, growing in 1808, at Grassford, in Denbighshire, North Wales. At five feet from the ground the circumference was 27 feet 9 inches: it had originally eleven immense limbs; two are decayed; two are advancing fast to that state, but seven are in a thriving state. It has stood in the reigns of seventeen kings, three queens, and the commonwealth of Oliver Cromwell, from the reign of Henry IV. in 1392, [original footnote].

cutting of every species of timber in Ireland, a very careless method is pursued. The hatchet-men, to prevent the necessity of stooping, generally leave much of the best of the tree in the ground. In those that do not shoot again, as larch and all the firs, it obstructs the scythe, and in those from which it is wished to procure another growth, it is particularly injurious, as, instead of the shoots being produced from the roots, they are produced on the stump, in a brush; and to increase the evil, those, instead of all but one or two being rubbed off (not cut) are all permitted to remain. This is the chief cause of the wretched oak woods we generally see in this county, indeed I may say all through Ireland, and probably in England. Many gentlemen are now beginning to thin their oak woods, but when they have grown up for 10 or 12 years in a thicket, it is too late to expect much benefit from thinning. To produce the full benefit of the practice I have recommended, it must be commenced in the first, or at least the second year, when the shoots, as I have mentioned before, should be rubbed off, and not cut; for if not cut quite clean to the bark the evil will be increased by the multiplication of the shoots. Nothing can be more grossly neglected than the plantations of this county, I may say of Ireland. They are, with the exception of Mount Bellew, Clonbrock, and a few other places, scarcely ever thinned until they are like May poles, and the poverty of the original idea made manifest by the admission of light. I recollect some years since asking a wood-ranger at Dunsandle, why some small trees, that I had marked two years before, were not cut down, his answer, I imagined would be that of most gentlemen and wood-rangers, "Lord, Sir, do you think I am such a fool as to cut down my master's trees, when I could get nothing worth while for then." Probably they have remained uncut to this day, to the great injury of the standing timber.

SECTION XX

QUANTITY OF BOG AND WASTE GROUND — THE POSSIBILITY AND MEANS OF IMPROVING THEM, AND OBSTACLES TO THEIR IMPROVEMENT

In this county the quantity of bog and other ground is very great, especially in the baronies of Moycullen, Ballynahinch, and Ross, occupying that extensive country from Galway to Killeny bay, a distance of upwards of thirty miles, and nearly as much in breadth from the sea to Cong. Of this vast tract, containing upwards of 500,000 acres, very little is in cultivation, and that chiefly near the coast. There is very little of this country that could not be improved by burning the surface, and manuring with either sea weed or lime, as in many places there are quarries of limestone, and at Oughterard limestone is in great abundance. On the sea coast the means of improvement are easily had, as great quantities of limestone are brought from the coasts of Clare and Galway and the island of Arran, as ballast; this could be extended to any amount. A great extent of ground would be improved by irrigation on very moderate terms. Sea sand and a species of coralline also abound in almost every bay, and when they have; been tried, their fertilising effects have been astonishing. I have mentioned those means of improvement under another head.

There is also a large tract of mountain between Loughrea and the county of Clare, that could also be easily reclaimed by irrigation and planting. Of bogs there are immense quantities all reclaimable. In fact I have scarcely ever seen a bog that could not be reclaimed at a remunerating expense. Most of those who object to this on account of the expense, seem to think that it is all expenditure and, no return; but this, though a too common idea, is a very erroneous one. It is true there can be no improvement without a previous expenditure of money; but what species of agricultural, or any other pursuit can be carried on without this outlay? How much money must be expended before a crop of wheat can be put in the pocket, or what can be made of any kind of stock without it? — In many instances where bog or waste ground is of such a nature (as all the mountain generally are) as to produce red or yellow ashes, the return by rape, potatoes, and many other crops, is made the first year, and frequently a large sum beyond the expense. In red bog that produces only white ashes, the return will be longer delayed, but certain.

Mr. Young, in his tour in Ireland, "Whatever the means used, certain it is that no meadows are equal to those gained by improving a bogs they are of a value which scarcely any other lands rise to in Ireland; I should suppose it would not fall short of forty shillings an acre, and rise in many cases to three pounds." — If those were the sentiments of Mr. Young at the period be wrote, what would they be now since the introduction of Fiona grass on bogs? — Again, "Many potatoes, are planted in bogs that are drained; they are the first thing they plant, manuring, with, limestone gravel and dung; the first will not do alone, very little dung will do; the crop is superior in quantity to these of any other land; they will get fifty pecks more than from grass land." A remarkable instance of this species of improvement in the county of Mayo is detailed also in this valuable work. "A curragh of one hundred acres, that it, a wet quaking bog or *qua*, which will not do for turf with a long sedge grass on it, part of a farm at thirty pounds a year, lord Altamont (late marquise of Sligo) took it into his hands with the consent of the tenant; he drained it, at an expense of £30. by drains ten feet wide and five deep at 7d. per perch; this simple thing improved it so much, that without any other improvement he set it to the same tenant at seventy pounds per year, made so perfectly sound, that bullocks of 8 cwt could graze on it."

Lord Kaims gives a remarkable instance of the value of improved bog. "At the seat of Mr. Burnet of Kemnay, ten miles from Aberdeen, a kitchen garden, a flower garden, a wilderness of trees indigenous and exotic, are all in a peat moss, (bog) where water stagnates from one foot to two under the surface."

This subject has been so often and ably discussed, and the proofs both here and in Scotland are so clear, that I shall not dwell longer on it; which is no little self denial, as I confess it is a very favourite subject. Much ground has been cleared of stones, with great profit. An instance came under my own eye worthy of the attention of the doubters; a very numerous class in this county, indeed nearly as numerous as the sneerers. The late Mr. Hartley, parish priest of Kilconickny near St Clerans, cleared two acres of ground, at an expense of eighteen guineas: it was so very rocky that it was not previously worth five shillings per acre. The first year it was let for potatoes at six guineas an acre; the second year, for the same purpose, at seven guineas per acre. It was, when I saw it in 1803, under remarkably fine barley and clover, and perfectly clear of stones. It would readily let at that period for three guineas an acre on a lease.

	£	s.	d.
Four years rent and expenses of clearing	27	6	0
Received for rent of the two crops	29	11	6

Thus there was a profit of two guineas an acre on the clearing alone, exclusive of the permanent value, I fear there are few would have had so much spirit

An embankment at Bunoun, the estate of Mr. Geoghegan O'Neill, has reclaimed upwards of 80 acres from the sea. Mr. Bulteel has also made a spirited and valuable improvement, by reclaiming a large piece of ground from the sea near the town of Galway. It is highly probable that a large tract of land could be taken from the sea near Oranmore; it has a rich muddy bottom; also a large quantity of cut-out bog near Oranmore, the estate of the right honourable James Fitzgerald could be drained and reclaimed. There is a great deal of ground near Tyrone and Kilcolgan that could also be reclaimed. In many other parts of the county vast quantities of land on the banks of rivers or arms of the sea could be easily reclaimed. A great deal of money has been very unnecessarily expended in making very deep drains in bogs. One deep drain only is generally sufficient to intercept the water flowing into the bog from higher ground. The chief improvement in bog is putting the surface, by frequent turning in winter, into a state to be washed by the rains of that season, assisted by alternate, freezing and thawing. Nothing can be more erroneous than attempting to cultivate red bog in hot weather, which, instead of assisting in the decomposition, only converts it into turf fit for burning, in which state it will remain undissolved and unproductive for many years. The objection generally made to cultivating bog in winter, of not being able to get men to go on it at that season, may be easily obviated by procuring wooden shoes, or rather shoes with wooden soles of birch, alder, or any other light timber. These are a kind of shoes every landed proprietor should introduce on his estate; they are exceedingly cheap, last long every countryman can make them, and if properly shaped, are as easy to the feet as the generality of thick soled shoes worn by country people: the chief art is giving the sole a turn up at the toe like leather soles, instead of making them to lie flat on the ground: they must be lightly shod all round.

Much has been written on the subject of employing the poor in the cultivation of bog by parliamentary enactments. I have not seen any plan that is likely to succeed; they have all failed to point out from whence the funds for this purpose are to come, and many seem entirely to forget that bogs are private property. Did the landed proprietors consult their own interest, or that of their posterity, it is with them the improvement should originate.

In one of the public prints in 1880, it was with great confidence stated "that nothing could be made by improving bog." This ignorant and presumptuous assertion is so totally in the teeth of numberless proofs to the contrary, that it would be waste of time to attempt to refute it. I would advise the proprietor of that paper to procure some person who is not so totally ignorant of rural economy as the editor seems to be, to write for him on this subject.

Some years since I proposed the establishment of a waste land company and was authorised by some monied men to advertise for the purchase of waste land; I had many proposals offering great tracts of highly improvable ground on very advantageous terms, but it vanished into thin air. After incurring a considerable expense in advertising and for postage, I found that was all my reward. On stating, amongst other matters, the appointment of a person to conduct the improvements, I found that an affair of such magnitude I was expected to conduct for a salary of fifty pounds a year. I therefore retired in disgust, and the affair died with Mr. Hamilton, the late secretary of the Farming Society of Ireland. Notwithstanding the failure of this attempt, I still think that, by a company with an ample capital, is the only likely means to accomplish this very desirable object. It is unreasonable and unfeeling to expect that the means for this improvement should come from the public purse, that finds it so difficult to provide for those unavoidable demands on it, that a long protracted war has necessarily occasioned. — Note, it is a very curious thing to see algae of various kinds, sea pink, and many other plants that usually grow on rocks, flourishing in the banks of bogs, washed by the sea, at high water mark, near Ardbear.

In Bartram's travels in West Florida, a work highly esteemed for its veracity, we meet the following account of alluvial deposits, as difficult to be solved as the formation of many of our bogs.

> "On our return home we called by the way at the Cliffs, which is a perpendicular bank or bluff rising up out of the river nearly one hundred feet above the present surface of the water, whose active current sweeps along by it. From eight or nine feet below the loamy vegetable mould at top, to within 4 or 5 feet of the water, these cliffs present to view strata of clays, marie, and chalk of all colours, as brown, red, white, yellow, blue and purple; there are separate strata of these various colours, as well as mixed or party coloured; the lowest stratum next the water exactly of the same black rich soil as the adjacent low cypress swamps above and below the bluffs, and here in the cliffs we see vast stumps of cypress and other trees, which at this day grow on those low wet swamps, and which range on a level with them. These stumps are sound, stand upright, and seem to be rotted off about two feet above the spread of their roots; their trunks, limbs, &c. lie in all directions about them. But when these swampy forests were growing, and by what cause they were cut off and overwhelmed by the various strata of earth, which now rise above one hundred feet above the brink of the cliffs, and two or three times that height but a few hundred yards back, are enquiries perhaps not easily answered."

SECTION XXI

HABITS Of INDUSTRY, OR WANT OF IT AMONGST THE PEOPLE

I have had innumerable proofs, in my professional pursuits, that the lower classes of this county cannot with justice be accused of want of industry, when working for themselves. When working for others they do as little as they can, not only from a want of sufficient remuneration, but from the lazy habits they are permitted to grow up in from their boyhood, by the indolent stewards of the country. I have had occasion to mention this in another section. As there is no difference made in the wages of the industrious or indolent, one of the chief inducements to exertion is withheld. That they are extremely industrious may be seen in numberless cases, in cleaning ground from stones, of which they make immense piles and lose much land; if instead of this they could be induced to bury them deep in the potato furrows, they would find it a great improvement. If this practice is pursued, the stones fit for building should be reserved. In the improvement of bog they are also very industrious, where they have any capital (which they seldom have), and a sufficient length of tenure; but what can be expected from a cottier that can scarcely exist, or that, if he improves bog without having a lease, furnishes the certain means of dispossessing himself, by creating ground that will be measured on him by a new agent ignorant of country affairs, or of the poor man's exertions? Much bog has been reclaimed between Shannon-bridge and Ballinasloe by cottier tenants, and in many other parts of the county. [There is] scarcely a tenant near a bog that does not improve a little. In Connemara a great change for the better has been made in the habits of the people. When Mr. D'Arcey went first to live in that country, he found it very difficult to find any person on his estate inclined to labour for him. Indeed, prior to this happy era, there was scarcely any demand for labourers; but now they are at least as industrious as the inhabitants of any other part of the county, and anxious to procure employment. At a former period, smuggling alone occupied the minds of every class, and their whole occupation was either watching the approach of smuggling vessels or revenue cruisers, or helping to unload the vessels with singular dispatch when they appeared, and distributing their ill-got ventures through the country. Happily, at present, smuggling is little practised, and a consequent improvement in manners has taken place.

The number of holy days which, from the way they are usually observed, should rather be called idle days, are a great drawback on industry. I have had occasion to know frequently the sentiments of the Roman Catholic clergy, and the best informed Catholic gentlemen on this subject, and they were almost unanimous in a wish, that they were translated to the following Sunday; and it is not a little remarkable, that much country work is performed on Sunday, that the lower orders would scruple to do on some holy days, especially the lady days, of which I believe there are four or five, and two of them in harvest. From the number of holy days, the working days of Catholics cannot be reckoned more than about 260, so that if we add the Sundays, wet days, days at fairs, funerals, stations, holy wells, patrons, weddings, &c. we may perceive how few days are devoted to labour. Of the industry of the higher ranks, I fear I cannot say much; many are possessed of a "bastard industry, that prompts to activity without ever thinking of consequences." In the pursuit of anything amusing they are wonderfully active, but an industrious attention to the improvement of their lands is rather a rare quality. There are many praiseworthy exceptions to this character, even of those of the highest ranks, and I trust we shall shortly see many more; I ardently hope, that before long they will feel the delights resulting from a system of farming, combining pleasure with profit; and that they will pay no attention to the unfounded assertion of those who, wanting skill or perseverance, maintain that a gentleman can make nothing by tillage farming. The fact seems to be, that it requires more attention than they are inclined to bestow; whilst the grazing system requires little of either skill or trouble. I feel great pleasure in noticing the praiseworthy encouragement given to his tenants by Mr. Blake of Frenchfort, and also the spirt and intelligence with which this has been embraced by his tenant, John King {near Merlin Park), whose farm is or was in 1819 conducted in a very superior style of cropping and cleanliness. Everthing about him comfortable and clean, his corn and fuel drawn to the well-enclosed haggard long before others have their corn stacked, or their turf cut.

SECTION XXII

USE OF THE ENGLISH LANGUAGE, WHETHER GENERAL OR HOW FAR INCREASING

The use of the English language is increasing rapidly all through the county, but in no part more than in Connemara, and generally with a good accent. Many are emigrants from English and Scotch regiments, of which the Scotch Fencibles furnished many highly useful members. A considerable number are those who have evaded the pursuit of their landlords or other creditors, from many different parts of Ireland, particularly from the north, a few years since, when "to hell or Connaught," was the charitable denunciation of that unhappy period. It is somewhat curious that near Galway, and particularly in the town (at the Cloddagh), many do not speak English, but a harsh Irish, not very well understood in general. It has been generally allowed that the following scale may be given of the merit of the different dialects of the Irish language: "The natives of Ulster have the right phrase, but not the pronunciation. Munster the pronunciation but not the phrase. Leinster has neither. Connaught has both". Many understand English, who, from an apprehension they do not speak correctly, deny their knowledge of it. A witness at an assizes at Galway was proceeding to swear, in good English, that he could not speak a word of it, he meant that be did not speak English sufficiently well to give his testimony in that language.

English is always spoken in the country schools, as the parents are anxious their children should speak it. I may therefore safely assert that the English language is gaining ground fast. In the next generation there will not probably be a gentleman that will be able to speak Irish. It is remarkable that the most ignorant Irish man speaks in general the most correctly grammatical in his own language, and I believe, on a comparison with the natives of many shires in England, where they speak the most unintelligible jargon, he has no cause for much apprehension.

SECTION XXIII

ACCOUNT OF TOWERS, CASTLES, &c. OR PLACES REMARKABLE FOR ANY HISTORICAL EVENT

There are many old castles, or rather castellated houses, for of those that really can be called castle, I believe Portumna, built by the Burkes, is the only one. Before the arrival of Henry II. there were not more than four or five, except those built in cities. Probably the first building of this kind in Ireland of lime and stone was the castle of Tuam in 1161, by Roderick O'Connor, monarch of Ireland, and for that reason was called *Castrum mirificum*. In Henry eighth's reign there were upwards of five hundred of these small castellated houses; and since that period, chiefly in the reigns of Anne and Elizabeth, they multiplied exceedingly. "Queen Elizabeth's ministers obliged every grantee to construct a castle, fort, or bawn, for the protection of his family and tenants. The common small square castles were the residence of English undertakers, and all those built before the reign of James the First were executed by English masons, and on English plans." They are, with few exceptions, small, gloomy, and uncomfortable, and only calculated for defence by the English settlers against sudden incursions of the oppressed natives, or in the warfare carried on by different opposite chieftains who lived by plundering each other. When Cromwell arrived here he demolished the greater part of them, and a happy change in the manners of the people prompting landed proprietors to advance considerably in the comforts and appearance of their houses, they have continued to advance in refinement, not only in the mode of building, but in the arrangement and furnishing of them. In Connemara are the castles of Renvyle, Doon, Ard, Ballynahinch, and Bunown, the ancient seat of the O'Flahertys, one of whom, Murrough O'Flaherty, used to get on the hill of Bunown, which hangs over the sea, and "declare war against all the potentates in the world, but especially against that pitiful, pettifogging (it seems even at a remote period we have had pettifoggers) town of Galway;" and his dependents used to say "Murrough is angry and there will be bloody work." Aghnenure, within two miles of Oughterard, was a place of some consequence; it was anciently a seat of the O'Flahertys, and at a later period inhabited by the Earl of Clanrickard, who dates several of his letters from it; one on the 20th October, 1651: it was of considerable strength, according to the mode of attack of that early period. A river, communicating with Lough Corrib, runs under the castle; and tradition says that there was a bell attached to a trap in the kitchen for catching salmon, which gave notice to the cook when the fish was caught.

Lord Clanrickard also dates some of his letters from Ierrylan, a large ruined castle opposite to the town of Galway. On the 7th March, 1650, the Marquis of Clanrickard

gave audience to the Duke of Lorain's ambassador at this castle. It is a curious circumstance that this lord always, in his letters to the Irish commissioners at Galway, used the words *we* and *our*. In one of his letters from this castle, he says:—
"Whilst I was in treaty with lord Forbes, the commander of a parliament ship of war, and though lord Ranelagh, president of Connaught, was then in the fort of Galway, I saw the country on fire, my tenants' houses and goods burned, and four or five poor innocent creatures, men, women, and children, inhumanly murdered by Forbes's soldiers, who having taken possession of Lady's Church in Galway, the ancient burial place of the town, did, upon their departure, not only deface it, but digged up the graves, and burned the coffins and bones of those that were buried there." It is said that the castle of Cregg was the last erected in this county; it was built in 1648 by an ancestor of our celebrated countryman, Richard Kirwan, who in Cromwell's usurpation received the thanks of General Ireton, and a permission under his hand and seal to carry arms, in consequence of the protection he afforded to the protestants in 1641. The castle of Kinvara is in good preservation. There is the remains of a round castle between Gort and Kilmacduagh: I mention it as not being common. The castle of Athenry was built by Bermingham, and seems to have been of considerable magnitude. The castles of Loughrea, Castleconnel, and Portumna were built by the Burkes. There are a multitude of other castles that I either do not recollect, or are not worthy of further notice, except Lynch's castle at the upper four corners in Galway, inhabited by most respectable woollen drapers of that name;— the ancient Fitzgerald arms, and underneath, badly cut, the figure of an ape with a child in its paws. In Coat's History of Ireland, page 85, it is written, that Thomas Fitzmaurice Fitzgerald, Lord justice, was nicknamed, "*Nappagh*, Simiacus, or the ape, because when his father and grandfather were murdered at Calian, the savants, on the news of it, run out of the house as if distracted, and left this Thomas in the cradle; whereupon an ape that was kept in the house took up the child and carried it to the top of the castle of *Traly* and brought him down safe and laid him in the cradle, to the admiration of all the beholders". —On consulting Mr. Hardiman's drawing of this castle, the ape and child may be plainly perceived under the coat of arras.

ROUND TOWERS.

Those round towers, which have so much puzzled antiquarians, are to be found in the following places: — Ballygaddy, Kilbannon, Kilmacduagh, Meelick, Murrough, and Ardrahan; of that of Killannan about fifty feet remain, the door about twelve feet from the ground.

— Note, there is an uncommonly fine and copious spring well near this tower. — The tower of Kilmacduagh, which is of great height, leans, I am informed, upwards of seventeen feet from the perpendicular, and I fear, from the cracks in the wall in several places, we shall lose one of the finest specimens of this curious architecture in Ireland. I discovered one at Murrough, about two miles to the southward of Galway on the sea coast; I believe it escaped the research of Dr. Ledwich and Dr.

Beaufort. Also the remains of another very small one near the church of Ardrahan, which I believe also escaped their notice; it is the smallest I have ever seen. About forty feet of that at Murrough remains; it is only about ten feet in diameter in the clear; the walls four feet thick; the door about six feet from the ground: there are courses of stone to rest the timbers of the floor on. To attempt to say for what purpose those very curious structures were erected, at a period so remote as to baffle all enquiry, would be in me very great presumption. One eminent antiquarian thinks they were erected long before the churches were constructed of permanent masonry, or covered with anything but thatch. Another antiquarian, of great celebrity, maintains they were built by the worshipers of fire; this opinion seems to gain some countenance from Hanway's travels in Persia, where he mentions four temples at Sari, formerly belonging to the Gebers or fire worshipers, who formerly inhabited all this coast: these edifices are made of the most durable materials, and are rotund, and about thirty feet in diameter, raised to a point of near 120 feet in height.

Another very general idea seems to be, that they were belfries; if this was their use, it must have been at a period not so very remote as generally imagined, for Strabo says, that bells were first suspended in the ninth century; others say, that bells were invented by Bishop Paulinus, of Campania, in the year 400. It is probable, from their different size and finishing, those towers were erected at different periods, and at some after period, probably, were used as belfries. If they were originally intended for this use, why make the doors from 12 to 20 feet from the ground? There are many who maintain that they were built for places of penance, in imitation of St Daniel the stylite, who after the example of St Simeon, determined to take up his residence on the top of a pillar: for this purpose a friend built him two pillars, connected with iron bats, and on these another pillar, surmounted with a vessel surrounded with a balustrade. The lord of the ground, about 468, built him another pillar, higher and larger than the first, on which he lived until he was 80 years of age, and died on it. The prince built a third pillar, joined to the other two, and placed a roof over it. That this pillar was of some size, and accessible, is evident from his saying mass on it, and from his receiving visits from several. The Emperor Leo caused a small monastery to be built for his disciples adjoining to the pillar. It is probable that, from the fervour of their piety, they might have exceeded each other in the height of their pillars: at this day they are almost invariably contiguous to a church, and any that remain at their original height are roofed, and holes for joists are almost every where visible. I have thus thrown together the different opinions on this subject, without presuming to form any of my own, which could in truth be worth little.

Raths, or as they are commonly called, Danish forts, abound in this county; some are built of large stones, but in general they are composed of earth thrown up by digging a trench; in some few instances a second and even a third trench was formed: the bank was surmounted by a stake hedge. Though they have been attributed to the Danes, it is more probable they were formed by the natives to protect them from sudden incursions of the Danes, and from each other; and as Ireland at that period was overrun with wolves, many might have been used for protecting the numerous herds of cattle, which constituted the chief riches of Ireland, from those animals. The very meaning of the word *rath*, security, shows for what purpose they were constructed. Doubtless they were by the Danes to secure their plunder, and many might have been thrown up for this purpose by them. "Dun Ængus, in the great island of Arran in the bay of Galway, is seated on a high cliff over the sea, and in a circle of monstrous stones without cement, capable of containing 200 cows. The houses having been of wood, have long since disappeared." The violence of the surf is gradually undermining this highly interesting monument of antiquity. — Note, it resembles very much the Happahs or forts in the newly discovered island in Hawksworth's voyages[1].

There are several *Cromlechs*,[2] or Druids' altars, as they are frequently called; some of very rude workmanship, which shows their high antiquity, and others on which more pains have been bestowed. Some are of one rude flag supported by equally rude pillars; in others the flag is upheld by side flags; they are uniformly destitute of any inscription, which plainly proves their erection at a very remote period. There is a fine one in the demesne of Marble Hill, of one stone 30 feet long by eight broad; it was much injured by the hands of ignorance before the late Sir Thomas Burke became possessed of the estate, as many of the stones were taken for the purpose of building a common well. It is strange the little interest many gentlemen take in the records of antiquity, as to permit them to be mutilated, or perhaps entirely demolished. Some times these Cromlechs are called *Leabha Diarmuid is Grane*,[3] or from some whimsical allusion, Darby and Grane's bed. There can be little doubt they were used for some religious ceremony of the Druids, and in after times might have been imitated or used for places of sepulture; but they are so different in their form and workmanship as not to be mistaken. I do not recollect to have seen any of those pillar stones that are reckoned of such high antiquity, but that on the Countess's hill near Dunsandle; tradition says it is of a very remote period. A curious monument of antiquity may be seen near the town of Loughrea, on monument hill. There were formerly eight flat and rude stones, about four feet high and two feet broad, tapering to a rounded top; five are still standing, two are lying flat, and one wanting; they are at equal distances, about seven yards asunder, in a circular mound of earth raised about four feet above the adjoining ground. In the centre there is a tumulus of earth raised about two feet. There is a charming view from this hill of Loughrea, the Shannon, Dalyston, the Tipperary, Clare, Connemara, Mayo, and Burrin mountains,

---

[1] Hawksworth wrote the official record of the voyage of Captain James Cook's first Pacific voyage, published in London in 1773, [Clachan ed.].
[2] Grose says the derivation of Cromlech is from the Amoric word *Crom*, crooked, and *leh,* a stone. [original footnote].
[3] In Irish folklore cromlechs were reckoned to be where the mythical lovers Diarmuid and Gráinne slept, [Clachan ed.].

Croagh Patrick, &c. &c. the foreground uncommonly undulating and picturesque. There are some vestiges of a circular entrenchment round the foot of the hill. The interior of this Stonehenge should not, I imagine, have been planted; the very shape should have prevented it. About 300 yards to the S. W. of this hill may be seen a very rude Cromlech, consisting of two rude side stones, covered with a lozenge-shaped stone about three feet broad and four long. I give this from a note I made on the spot; but I have been since informed, that there have been doubts about the antiquity of this fort, and it is asserted that it is of modern date, and a mere imitation, a flight of fancy. If so it does infinite credit to the designer; finding it in company of the Cromlech helps the idea of its originality.

PLACES REMARKABLE FOR ANY HISTORICAL EVENT

"Lugad-Mac-Con, of the Ithian descent, being vanquished in the battle of *Kenfebrat* by his father-in law and his forces, having spent some time in exile, put into Galway with a great number of foreign auxiliaries; and seven days after his arrival, on a Thursday (as Tigernach has accurately remarked), he obtained a signal victory over king Arthur at Moy Mucroimhe, near Athenry, eight miles from Galway. Forga, king of Connaught, amongst others, fell on the side of Arthur; also on the same side seven nephews of king Arthur, Lugadlaga, the brother of Olill, but related to Lugad-Mac-Con by his mother, and Ligum of the Fotharts (whom Arthur banished) Lugad's companion in his exile, pursuing Arthur after the battle, stood at a brook in Aidhnia, and attacking him there, tumbled him to the earth, and as he lay almost breathless, cut off his head, and brought it to the conqueror. The brook has got the name of *Turloch Airt* in commemoration of this action, which it retains to this day, and is situate between Moyvaela and Killcornan."

"Gno-more and Gno-beg, the two sons of Lugad, fixed Delvin Feadha amongst the Cunmacnians,, to the west of Galway, (Connemara) between Lough Orbsin (Lough Corrib) on the north, and Lough Lurgan (the bay of Galway) on the south, nine miles from Thomond; their posterity have divided it into Gnonone and Gnobeg, which are at this day comprehended within the barony of Moycullen. The M'Conrys (sons of the king), who are descended from Gno-beg, within my recollection held lands in Gno-beg, under the O'Flahertys, who for a series of 800 years past have held the sovereignty of the Conmacnians and Delvinians there."

About the centre of Lough Corrib is an island called Innishgoile, about a mile in circumference, and thickly inhabited. In the middle of this isle there is a very ancient churchyard, and the ruins of an old dwelling house, which oral tradition and many corroborating circumstances represent as the retired abode of the heads of some monastic order in ages past. The island contains also an old chapel, dedicated to the memory of St. Patrick. The different arches and entrances into these buildings were of the common Saxon order, and the stones of which they are composed are carved into human features, and one of a red gritty substance, although there does not appear in the neighbourhood a single vestige of any quarries of that description[1]. Such parts of these decayed edifices as now remain are supported by woodbine and ivy, which entwine together, and forming a complete roof, present an uncommon picturesque appearance. The head stone of a grave in the south west part of the island, having lately attracted the attention of a military gentleman of much information and research quartered near the spot, he was induced to show it to an intelligent soldier of the Tipperary militia, well acquainted with the Irish language. The soldier, whose name is James O'Farrel, has ingeniously deciphered and translated the inscription upon it. It is written, he says, in the hard Irish, or virgin characters (the Ogham), and is in English "underneath this stone lye Goill, Ardan, and Sionan." These three are supposed to have been brothers, and the island it is believed was called after Goill, the eldest of them, who was the chief in the religions order on it, and esteemed for exemplary piety and devotion.

There is no mention made of Innishgoile in Sir James Ware's Antiquities of Ireland, nor do we remember to have seen any notice taken of it by Dr. Ledwich, or any other writer upon the subject, although many extraordinary traditions respecting this island are afloat, the truth of which is in many instances strengthened by strong corroborative testimonies: amongst others, the following is rather singular (if true). The noise of beasts and birds upon the island is said to have been so loud and so often repeated, as frequently to have interrupted the devotional exercises; in consequence of which an earnest appeal was made to heaven, and although the place still contains many of the quadruped and winged species, the former is not heard to bellow, nor the latter to warble. How unlucky that this exemption was not extended further; what a demand there would have been for wives from this island! — The above was extracted from a Galway paper.

---

1 I think I have seen the same kind of stone in the door of Tuam cathedral, in Dunbrody Abbey, in the county of Wexford, and many other similar places, H. D.

SECTION XXIV

LIST OF PARISHES.

Ardagh, Rectory,	Church.
Athenry, ditto.	Church.
Addergoole, Vicarage.	
Anhadown, ditto.	Impropriate[1].
Ardruhan, ditto.	Church and Glebe.
Abbeygormagan, ditto.	
Aghrim, ditto.	Church and Glebe.
Arranmore, Rectory.	
Ballymacward, Vicarage.	Church.
Ballynacourtney, ditto.	
Buiowna, Rectory.	
Ballynakill, ditto.	Impropriate.
Ballynakill, Vicarage.	
Ballynakill, Rector and Vicarage.	
Ballynakelly, Rector.	
Bellelare, Vicarage.	
Ballane, ditto.	
Beagh, Rectorage.	Glebe.
Ballindown, ditto.	
Clonkeen, Vicarage.	
Clonbraen, Rectorage.	
Carrigin, ditto.	
Clare, Vicarage.	Church.
Clonthuiscart, ditto. Glebe.	
Clonfert, ditto. Church.	
Clonish, ditto.	
Drumacroe, ditto.	
Dunmore, ditto.	Church.
Dunamon, ditto.	Impropriate.
Donaghpatrick, Rectorage.	
Duras, Vicarage.	
Donenaghta, ditto,	
Doneny, ditto.	Glebe.
Foghena, ditto.	Glebe.
Faghy, ditto.	
Galway, ditto.	Church.
Isserkelly, ditto.	Glebe.

---

1 'impropriate' is an ecclesiastical terms referring to the transfer of property, rights, etc. from the Church into lay hands, [Clachan ed.].

Inniscultra, ditto.	Church.
Innisbofir, Rectorage.	
Innismain, ditto.	
Innishere, ditto.	
Killimordaly, Vicarage.	
Kilconnel. Vicarage.	
Kilcluny, ditto.	
Kilgerril, ditto.	
Killikineen, ditto.	
Kilcolgan, ditto.	Church.
Killeroen, ditto.	Impropriate.
Kilbegnet, ditto.	Impropriate.
Kilconla, ditto.	
Kilbennon, ditto,	
Kilkerrin, Rectorage.	Church.
Kilyhan, ditto.	Impropriate.
Kileroran, Vicarage.	Impropriate.
Kilesolan, Rectorage and Vicarage.	Church.
Killoscobe, Vicarage.	Church.
Kileroran, Rectorage.	Church.
Knockmay, ditto.	
Kilmaglan, ditto.	
Kilbennan. Vicarage.	
Kilower, Rectorage.	
Kilkilvery, ditto.	
Kilfursa, ditto.	
Kileney, ditto.	
Kilcornagh, dittos	
Kilily, Vicarage.	
Kinvaru, ditto.	
Kilinvura, dittos	
Kileney, ditto.	Glebe
Killartan, ditto.	Church and Glebe
Kiltullagh, ditto.	
Kilconiran, ditto.	Glebe
Kilora, ditto.	Glebe
Kilconickny, ditto	Church
Kilogellan, ditto.	
Kilchrist, ditto.	Glebe
Kilnadeema, Glebe	
Kilrickle, Vicarage.	
Kilmeen, ditto.	
Kilane, ditto.	

Kilelaghton, ditto.
Kiloran, ditto.
Kiltormer, ditto.   Church and Glebe
Kilcooly, ditto.
Kilquane, ditto.
Kilinan, ditto.   Church and Glebe
Kilthomas, Rectorage.   Glebe
Kilteskin, Vicarage.   Glebe
Kilimore bulloge, ditto.
Kilmolinoge, Rectorage.
Kilmacduagh, ditto.
Kilcommon, Vicarage.
Killarmeen, ditto.
Liskeery, ditto.
Lackagh, ditto.
Lickrig, ditto.
Loughrea, Rectorage and Vicarage.   Church and Glebe.
Leitrim, Vicarage.
Lickmolasky, Rec and Vic.   Church and Glebe.
Monivae, (no parish).   Church
Moylough, Rectorage.   Church and Glebe
Meelick, Vicarage.
Moynes, Rectorage.
Moycullin, Vicarage.
Oranmore, ditto.
Rots, Rectorage.
Rahoon, Vic. (was formerly called St. James 9 parish.)
Stradbally, ditto.
Templetogher, Vicarage.
Tuam, ditto.   Church.
Teinagh, Rectorage   Church and Glebe.
Tienascragh, Vicarage.
Umond, Rectorage.

SECTION XXV

ABBEYS — ECCLESIASTICAL DIVISIONS — RESIDENT CLERGY

ARCHBISHOPS OF TUAM.

The See of Tuam, containing 1,135,650 acres, was united to Enachdoen or Annaghdown in 1324, and the see of Ardagh, formerly held in commendam[1] with Kilmore, held in commendam with it since 1742, at which time the see of Kilfenora, which was held in commendam with Tuam, was joined to Killaloe to be held in commendam with that see. This see is valued in the king's books, by an extent returned anno 28th Elisabeth, at £50. sterling. The chapter consists of Dean, Archdeacon, Provost, and eight Prebendaries; therefore five Stipendiaries. The church is dedicated to St. Jarlath, the son of Logu, who is looked upon as the first founder of the cathedral of Tuam, anciently, called Tuaim-da-Gualand; it was afterwards dedicated to his memory and called Teampul Iarlath, or Iarlath's church: the time of its foundation is placed about the beginning of the sixth century. In the year 1152 this cathedral was, by the aid and assistance of Tirdalvac O'Connor, king of Ireland, rebuilt by Edan O'Hoisin first archbishop of Tuam, at least the first who had the use of the pall; for some of his predecessors are sometimes called bishops of Connaught, and sometimes archbishops by Irish historians, although they were not invested with the pall. Some of the succeeding bishops built a new choir, and afterwards converted this church into the nave or body of the present church. The bishopric of Mayo was united and annexed to Tuam in 1559.

St. Iarlath sat in (he died in 540)		501
St. Briacas or Baecain (commemorated in Arran 1st May)		502
Ferdomnach,	died	781
Eugene Macclerig, Murchad O'Nioc,	do.	969
Aid O'Hoisin,[2]	do.	1033
Erchad O'Molomair,	do.	1080
Cannae O'Carail,	do.	1086
Catasach O'Cnail or O'Conml,	do.	1092
Murgesius O'Nisc,	do.	1118
Donald O'Dubhai,	do.	1122
Maurice or Muredach O'Dubhai,	do.	1150
Edan O'Hoisin, (succeeded in 1150)	do.	1150
Catholicus O'Dubhai,	Succeeded	1161
Felix O'Ruodan, a Cistercian monk,		1201
Marian O'Loghnan, dean,		1235
Florence Macflin, chancellor,		1250
Walter de Salem, dean of St Paul's, London, 1257		1257

---

[1] In canon law, commendam (or *in commendam*) was a form of transferring an ecclesiastical benefice *in trust* to the *custody* of a patron, [Clachan ed.].

[2] It is remarkable that several of this name (now called Hessian) live in and near Tuam, [original footnote].

Thomas O'Connor, translated from Elphin, 1259	1259
Stephen Fulburn, translated from Waterford, 1286	1286
William De Bermingham, 1289	1313
Malachy Macaeda, ISIS	1349
Thomas O'Carroll, Archdeacon of Cashel, translated to Cashel,	1365
John O'Grady, Archdeacon of Cashel,	1365
Gregory, ------, translated from Elphiu,	1372
Note — He was fined £100. for not appearing upon summons at a Parliament held at Castle Dermott in 1377. — He was deprived in	1386
Willam O'Cormacain, translated against his will to Clonfert,	1386
Maurice O'Kelly, translated from Clonfert, The See vacant from	1394
John Babynghe, Dominican friar,	1410
Cornelius, Franciscan friar,	1411
John Batterly, Dominican friar,	1427
Thomas O'Kelly, translated from Clonfert,	1438
John De Burgho,	1441
Donat O'Murry, Augustine Canon,	1458
William Shioy, or Ioy,	1485
Philip Pinston, Franciscan friar,	1503
Maurice De Porta, alias O'Fihely, Franciscan friar,	1506
Thomas O'Mullally, or Lally,	1531
Christopher Bodekine, translated from Kilmacduagh,	1536
William Lally, Dean of Tuam, at the same time he held Enaghdune,	1573
Nehemiah Donnelan, (resigned in 1609,)	1595
William Daniel,	1609
Rodolph Barlow, Dean of Christ Church,	1629
Richard Boyle, translated from Cork,	1659
John Maxwell, translated from Killala and Achonry,.	1645
He died in 1646; he was most barbarously treated by the rebels both at Killala and Tuam. The See remained vacant until the restoration of King Charles II.	
Samuel Pullen, Dean of Clonfert, He also held the bishopric of Kilfenora in commendam.	1660
John Parker, translated from Elphin, translated to Dublin,	1667
John Vesey, translated from Limerick,	1678
Edward Synge, translated from Raphoe,	1716
Josiah Hort, translated from Kilmore and Ardagh	1742
He held the See of Ardagh in commendam with this See, and it has gone along with it in like manner ever since.	
John Ryder, translated from Down and Connor,	1752
Jemmet Browne, translated from Elphin, 1775	
Honorable Joseph Deane Burke, translated from Leighlin and Ferns,	1782
Honorable William Beresford, (Baron Decies,)	1794
Honorable Power Trench,	1820

Note. —   In Mr. Hardiman's history of Galway, he says, "the late Archbishop Skerrett of Tuam," was descended from the tribe of Skerrett By the above list it does not appear that one of that name ever was an Archbishop of Tuam.

It has been said that in. the year 487 an abbey was founded here and dedicated to the Virgin Mary, which, in the beginning of the sixth century, was made a cathedral by St Iarlath, and a city was afterwards built here in honor of this exemplary bishop, whose remains were preserved in a chapel called Teampul-na-Serine, or the church of the shrine. After the death of this saint we find express mention made of three persons who were abbots of Tuam, viz. Cellagh, son of Eochad, who died in the year 808; Nuadat-Huo-Bolchain, abbot and anchorite, who died 3rd October, 877; and Gonach, son of Kiaran, abbot of Tuam and prior of Clonfert: he died in 879.

CLONFERT

The See of Clonfert,[1] containing 270,000 acres, to which the See of Kilmacduagh has been united since the year 1602, is valued in the king's books by an extent returned, anno 28th Elizabeth, at £80. The chapter of Clonfert consists of a Dean, Archdeacon, Sacrist or Treasurer, and nine Prebendaries.

St. Brendon, the son of Finlogue, contemporary with St. Brendon of Birr, and his fellow student, founded an abbey at Clonfert; near the Shannon, A.D. 558, over which he was abbot himself, and was buried in it after a life of 93 years; he died at Enachdune on Sunday the 16th May, 577, from whence his body was conveyed to Clonfert, and there interred.[2] His life is extant in jingling monkish metre in the Cotton Library at Westminster. In his time the cathedral of Clonfert, famous in ancient times for its seven altars, was founded. Colgan makes St. Brendon the founder and first bishop of Clonfert, and says that he abdicated and placed St Moaena in his rooms; others again say that Moaena was the first bishop.

We find in the Ulster annals under the year 571 or 572, the death of the first Bishop of this see, thus remarked: "Moaena, Bishop of Clonfert; Brenain went to rest." Brendon being yet alive, the day of Moaena's death is placed on the first of March. His true name was Nennius or Nennia, but it is common with the Irish to add the monosyllable *mio*, which signifieth *mine*, to the proper name of their saints, out of respect and tenderness.

---

[1] Clonfert signifies, in Irish, a wonderful den or retirement. It was also called Via nova. No female was permitted to enter into the abbey, [original footnote].
[2] He had been principal of the abbey of St. Mary of Portpure, in Galway, which was than a college much resorted to, [original footnote].

	Anno.
St. Moaena	Died 571
Fintan Corach flourished about the close of the sixth century.	
St. Senach Garbh,	620
St Colman, the son of Comgal,	620
Cummin Fodhu or long Cummin,	662
Rutmel, called Prince and Bishop of Clonfert,	825
Cathald Mac Cormac,	861
Cormac Mac-Ædain,	921
Gilla Mac Aiblin,	1116
Petero O'Mordai, Cistertian Monk, drowned	1171
Maetisa Mac Award, died	1173
Malcallen,	1181
Thomas,	1248
Cormac or Charles O'Lumlin,	1259
Thomas O'Kelly	1263
The See vacant almost three years.	
John, an Italian, the Pope's Nuncio, Translated to the Archbishopric of Benevento.	1266
Robert, a Monk of Christ Church, Canterbury	1296
Gregory O'Brogy, Dean,	1308
Robert Le Petit, Franciscan Friar, 1319, deprived,	1321
John Lean, Archdeacon of Tuam, The See vacant almost 60 years.	1322
Thomas O'Kelly, a secular Priest,	1347
Maurice O'Kelly, a secular Priest,	1378
David Come, Franciscan Friar,	1398
At this time the Pope translated William O'Cormacain, Archbishop of Tuam, to this See; but the Archbishop took this so much to heart, that he neglected to expedite his bull of translation in due time, and was therefore deprived	
Thomas O'Kelly, translated to Tuam,	1415
John Heyn, Franciscan Friar, provincial of that order in Ireland	1438
Thomas De Burgo,	1444
Cornelius O'Mullady, Franciscan Friar, translated from Emly,	1447
Cornelius O'Cunlio, translated from Emly,	1448
Mathew Mac Raik,	1507
David De Burgo, a secular Priest,	1508
Dennis, a Franciscan Friar,	1509
Richard Nangle, Provincial of Augustine hermits in Ireland,	1536[1]
Roland De Burgo, Dean of Clonfert	1541
Stephen Kirovan or Kirwan, Archdeacon of Enachdune,	1582

---

[1] The original date given is misprinted 536, [Clachan ed.].

Roland Lynch, Archdeacon of Clonfert,	1602
He held this in commendam; he also most fraudulently alienated much of the lands of both Sees.	
(The See vacant for near two years.)	
Robert Dawson, Dean of Down,	1627
William Bayley, (he did not get possession until the Restoration)	1644
Edward Wolley,	1664
(The See vacant from 1684 to 1691.)	
The Episcopal revenues were seized into the hands of King James, and paid to the Bishops of the Catholic Religion.	
William Fitzgerald, Dean of Cloyne,	1691
Theophilus Bolton, Chancellor of St Patrick's, and Vicar General of the Diocese of Dublin, translated to Elphin,	1722
Arthur Price, Dean of Ferns, translated to Leighlin and Ferns,	1724
Edward Synge, Chancellor of St, Patrick's, translated to Cloyne,	1730
Mordecai Carey, translated to Killala and Achonry,	1731
John Whitcomb, Rector of Louth, in the diocese of Armagh, translated to Down	1735
Arthur Smyth, Dean of Derry, translated to Down,	1752
Hon. Willian [sic] Carmichael, translated to Ferns,	1753
William Gore, translated to Elphin,	1758
John Oswald, translated to Dromore,	1762
Denis Cumberland, translated to Kilmore,	1763
Walter Cope, translated to Leighlin and Ferns,	1773
John Law, translated to Elphin,	1782
Christopher Button,	1804

In the reign of Cormac king of Ulster, who was killed in 257, Dunlong, king of Leinster, the son of Ennyniagh, and great grandson of Cathic, king of Ireland, attacking with more than savage cruelty a boarding school at Clonfert, most inhumanely butchered 80 young ladies of the first distinction, with their 300 maids; whereupon king Cormac put to death twelve Dynasts of Leinster, who were associates in the assassination, and exacted the Borian mulet of king Tuathal from the Laganians, with an additional increase.

KILMACDUAGH.

Kilmacduagh was united to Clonfert in the year 1602, and held in commendam with that see.

This see is valued in the king's books, by an extent returned anno 28th Elizabeth, at £13. 6s. 8d. Irish money, amounting to £10. sterling.

The chapter of Kilmacduagh consists at present, as I am informed, of a Dean, Archdeacon, Provost, Chanter, Treasurer, and two Prebendaries; they have no lands nor chapter seal that I could get any account of, and one of the prebends is worth but

£30. per annum; but in ancient books of visitation there are four more prebendaries mentioned. The church of Duagh is indebted for its original to St Colman, the son of Duagh. He was descended from a noble family of Connaught, the ancient chiefs of Fir Malgaid, and very nearly related to Guair, king of that country. To distinguish him from other Colmans, his contemporaries, he was usually called after his father Mac Duagh, or the son of Duagh. He was very fond of an ascetic life, and is said to have lived in a wilderness in the South part of Connaught seven years with only one companion. From this life of retirement he was in the end made a bishop, and fixed his see in a place which from his surname was called Kilmacduagh, or the church of the son of Duagh. This church was endowed with large possessions by Guair, king of Connaught, and his successors.

St. Colman flourished about the close of the sixth century or beginning of the seventh; his festival is kept on the third February[1]. The following is a very imperfect catalogue of the bishops of Kilmacduagh.

		Anno.
St Colman, promoted about		620
Indrect,	died	814
Rugnad O'Ruadan,		1178
Odo, Chanter,		1227
Gelasius Mac Scaelaga,	died	1249
Maurice Ileyan,		1283
David O'Ledaghan,		1290
Laurence O' Laughnan, Cistercian Monk,		1306
Luke,		1325
John , ------, Dean,		1347
Nicholas,		1371
Gregory Ileyhan	died	1395
Nicholas Ileyhan, Dominican Friar,		1399
John Icomaid		1401
John Abbott, of Curcumore, confessed by the Pope,		1418
Cornelius, resigned,		1502
Mathew, Archdeacon of Killaloe,		1505
Christopher Bodekine, translated to Tuam, and held this See in commendam		1533
Stephen Kirovan, translated to Clonfert,		1578
The See vacant for five years after his translation.		

---

[1] An ancient Crosier, said to have belonged to St Colman, is in the possession of an old woman at Kilconnel; she makes a livelihood by showing it, and frequently disputed points are settled by an oath on the Crosier, and it is said the veneration for it has hitherto prevented perjury, [original footnote].

Roland Lynch,   1583

In 1606 he was translated to Clonfert, and held this See in commendam, and they have ever since gone together.

KNOCKMOY ABBEY

This Abbey, about six miles from Tuam, was founded in 1189 by Cathal O'Connor, surnamed Croove-derg, or red hand. He was king of Connaught, and resenting the imperious behaviour of Hugh De Lacey, Lieutenant of Ireland, summoned the Irish chieftains to attack the English in every quarter. Almeric St. Lawrence, who had been informed of his danger by De Courcy, marched to Ulster, but was intercepted by O'Connor, and he and his men cut off, after having killed about 1000 of the Irish. In the height of the battle, O'Connor vowed to build an Abbey in his own country if he was successful, and he therefore erected this abbey, in Irish *Cnoc Mugha*, the hill of slaughter, and by monkish writers called *Monasteriun de colle victoriae*. It was bestowed on the Cistercians, the habit of which order the founder took on him, and dying in 1224, was interred in his own abbey. The most curious remains at Knockmoy are the fresco paintings which adorn the monument of O'Connor; one compartment represents Christ on the cross, another exhibits six kings, three deceased and three living; of the latter he in the middle is Roderick O'Connor, Monarch of Ireland. He holds in his hand the *seam roge* or shamrock, a plant greatly regarded by the Irish, from a legendary tradition, that St. Patrick emblematically set forth to them the mystery of the Trinity, by that three-leaved grass (white clover). This also expressed his being lord proprietor of the soil of the kingdom. The princes on each side are his vassals; he with the hawk on his fist is his grand falconer, the other with the sword his grand Marshal; these held their land by grand serjeantry[1]. Below them sits a Brehon with his roll of laws, having pronounced sentence of death on Mac Murrogh's son, for the crime of his father having joined the English, (see Giraldus Cambrensis, p. 770) [2]. The boy is tied to a tree, and two archers are executing the sentence, his body being transfixed by arrows. This supplied a good hint to such Irish chiefs as deserted their natural prince. "I do not believe these paintings are as old as the age of O'Connor; they seem rather to have been executed in the 17th century, when the confederate Catholics possessed themselves of the abbey, which they every where repaired, and in many instances adorned with elegant sculptures. The fresco paintings were executed in the 17th century, when the confederate Catholics repaired those abbeys and chapels, and when they had the aid of Italian and other foreign architects and artists to execute any history they should

---

[1] Tenure of lands of the crown by an honorary kind of service, due only to the king, [Clachan ed.].
[2] Gerald of Wales (c. 1146 – c. 1223), also known as *Gerallt Gymro* in Welsh or *Giraldus Cambrensis* in Latin, archdeacon of Brecon, was a medieval clergyman and chronicler of his times. As royal clerk and chaplain to King Henry II of England he travelled Ireland. He was proud of his Norman and Welch descent and reflected and shaped the view of the times tin presenting the Irish as barbaric savages, [Clachan ed.].

propose." Probably this conjecture is unfounded; for it is scarcely possible that any Italian would execute such daubing. It appears more likely they only renewed the original, and as a proof of their taste, left them unaltered from the rude pencil of antiquity. They bear some resemblance, I imagine, to the rude sketches of the Peruvians and Mexicans at the period they were cursed with the civilization of Cortes and his followers. The tomb of O'Connor has been greatly injured by people at funerals, the fresco paintings are growing very faint, and in a very few years will be entirely obliterated. In the reign of Henry VIII. Hugh O'Kelly, Abbot of Knockmay, surrendered that abbey, and made his submission to the king; he also covenanted to furnish the king with 60 horse, and a *battle* of galloglasses, and 60 kern, when the Lord Deputy comes to Connaught, and with 12 horse and 24 kern any where out of Connaught, and so that abbey was granted to him during pleasure. In 1620 Val. Blake held this abbey and its appurtenances. It is now the estate of John Blake Forster, Esq. of Ashfield. The masonry of this fine abbey is of superior workmanship, and quite different in the ornaments from any others I have seen; some beautiful remains of capitals, &c. may be seen scattered about the church yard. The stone of which the columns are made seems to be of a softer and finer kind of limestone than any in the neighbourhood, and the mouldings seem to be a composition of limestone. The wretched state in which this fine ruin is permitted to be by the proprietor of the estate, does but little credit to his taste. Until lately there was for many years a skeleton exhibited, (not much to the credit of family feelings) said to be that of Lady Evelina French, whose tomb is in the abbey. It has been very properly re-interred.

ABBEYS AND MONASTERIES IN RUINS

ABBEYS AND PRIORIES OF REGULAR CANONS OF ST. AUGUSTINE.

Tuam Abbey — founded by St. Jarlath, or Hierlatius (Iarlath, according to the Irish pronunciation) in the 5th century. He was of the noble family of the Dalfiatuses.

Tuam — Priory of St John the Baptist, founded by Terlogh O'Connor, king of Ireland, about 1140.

Cluan Fois— Abbey founded by St Iarlath before mentioned, in the 5th century.

Arran — In the great island of Arran in the bay of Galway — Abbey founded by St E Endeus, A.D. 449.

Tradition says that Ængus, king of Cashel, about 490, granted the great isle of Arran, called Arran Naomh, or Arran of the Saints, to Saint Enua or Endeus to build ten churches on. Another author says in 480.

Kill Conoil— Abbey founded by St Conail in the 5th century.

Clonfert — Priory of the Blessed Virgin Mary, founded by St Brendon, A.D. 558.

Killmacduagh — Abbey founded by St. Colman Mac Duagh, the first bishop of Killmacduagh in the 6th century.

Inis-Mac-hua-Cuin — (an island in Lough Corrib) Abbey founded by St Brendon of Clonfert, in the 6th century.

Rathmat, near Lough Corrib— Abbey founded by St Fursa, abbott in the same century. There is now there a parish church in ruins called Killfursa, From this Saint. 1

Kill-Cuanna— Abbey founded by St Cuanna in the sixth century.

Imaidh or Immagh, (now called Omey,) an island on the coast — Abbey founded by St. Fechin in the seventh century.2

Ardoilen, (probably high island,) another island on the coast, anciently called Iris Arthair — Abbey founded by the same saint in the seventh century, St Gormgul was a monk here, and lived in great veneration; he died in 1017.

Clountouiskart-O'Muny — Abbey founded by Saint Broaden, Abbott of it, who died in 809.

Aghrim — Abbey of St Catherine, founded by Theobald Walter, first Butler of Ireland in the thirteenth century.

Monaster O'Gormagan — Abbey of the Blessed Virgin Mary, mentioned in a record of 1308; this Abbey was founded by an Irish nobleman of the name of O'Gormagan.

MONASTERIES AND NUNNERIES OF CANONESSES OF THE ORDER OF ST. AUGUSTINE

Enachdune (Anneighdown) — Monastery of the Blessed Virgin Mary, founded by St Brendan in the sixth century.

ABBEYS AND PRIORIES OF THE ORDER OF THE CANONS REGULAR PRAEMONSTRATENSES.

Tuam — Abbey of the most Holy Trinity, founded by the Burkes in the thirteenth century.

PRIORIES AND PRECEPTORIES OF KNIGHTS HOSPITALLERS OF THE ORDER OF ST, JOHN OF JERUSALEM.

Kilnalekin — Preceptory of St. John the Baptist, founded by the O'Flahertys, formerly kings of Iarconnaught, in the thirteenth century.

BENEDICTINE NUNNERIES.

Kilcreunata, alias De Casta Sylva— Monastery founded by Cathaldus O'Connor, called Croovederg in Irish, king of Connaught, about the year 1200. Ardcane was a cell of this order.

CISTERCIAN OR BENEDICTINE ABBEYS, EXTANT AT THE TIME OF THE DISSOLUTION OF THE MONASTERIES IN IRELAND

Knockmoy — Abbey of St. Mary *de colle victoriae* founded by Charles O'Connor, called Croovederg, king of Connaught in1189 or 1190; others say in 1200. He there took the habit of a Bernardine or Cistercian, and was buried there. This house was a daughter of the Abbey of Boyle, of the line of Clairvaux. In 1262 Thomas O'Connor, Archbishop of Tuam, united the rectory of *Idermada* to this abbey, with the consent of the lord of Idormada.

---

1 There is a curious rude altar near a burial place on the east aide of this island; also a chapel in ruins, probably this abbey. It is now almost covered with sand, and probably will totally disappear in a few years, [original footnote].
2 In Dr. Beaufort's ecclesiastical Map of Ireland it is called Killursa, instead of Killfursa; it is situated near the confines of the Co. of Mayo, on the East side of Lough Corrib, [original footnote].

CONVENTS OF THE FRIARS PREACHERS, OR DOMINICANS, COMMONLY CALLED BLACK FRIARS

Athenry — Convent of St. Peter and St Paul, founded by Miler de Bermingham, the second Lord Baron of Athenry, A.D. 1241. He died in Munster, not far from Cashel, but was buried in this church.

Portumna — Convent of the Blessed Virgin Mary, and St. Peter and St Paul, founded by the O'Maddens, lords of the barony of Longford, before 1426.

Tombeola — Convent of St Patrick, founded by the O'Flahertys, kings of Iarconnaught, about 1427.

Galway — Convent of the Blessed Virgin Mary given to the Friars preachers of Athenry, by Pope Innocent VIII. in 1488. It formerly belonged to the Canons regular, Praemonstratenses of the abbey of Tuam, and was founded by the O'Hallorans.

CONVENTS OF THE FRANCISCANS, COMMONLY CALLED FRIARS MINORS.

Clare-Galway or Clare-yn-dowl — Convent founded by John De Cogan about 1290.

Galway — Convent in St. Stephen's island, by Sir William Leigh de Burgo, A.D. 1296. He was Lord Warden or Custos of Ireland in 1908, and dying in 1324 was buried in this convent. On a tomb-stone on the left hand of the porch of the Franciscan Monastery may be seen the following inscription, which corroborates the above account from *Butler's lives of the saints*.[1] "Memoriae G°. Illmo. Dno. Gull. De Burgo Suae nationis Principi et hujus monasterii fundatori. qui obiit A 1324 posuit F-V-B-G ✠ (Farther Valentine Browne, guardian of this monastery,) Frater venerabilis B. Guardias, 1645." — This was found in 1779 under the place where the high altar was formerly. It is a very large flag with the family arms, and a very long and broad sword, round the edge the above inscription is well carved. The remains of the old monastery were a few years since standing, but have been taken away completely for building the present chapel. The fees for burial here are part of the income of the Protestant warden.

Kilconnel — Convent founded by William O'Kelly, A.D. 1414. The O'Kellys were kings of Immany, where the chief families were seated at Aghrim, Gallagh, and Mullogh. It was reformed by the observants in 1467.

Roasrielly — Convent founded by lord Gannard, an English gentleman. A.D. 1498. I find in a Monasticum. Published in London in 1772, Ross-Traily Monastery in the Diocese of Tuam; "it was founded in 1431 and reformed in 1470," the founder not known; the author adds, "that this place is very lonesome, encompassed on all sides with water, and is only one way accessible, and was, not many years since, preserved entire by the interest of the earls of Clanrickard of the family of the Burkes." By the description of the site this must be the beautiful abbey of Ross, near Headford.

Meelick — Convent founded by one of the O'Maddens, lords of Longford, now a barony.

---

[1] In 1381 there being two popes at Rome, and the people of Ireland being doubtful to which they should pay obedience, pope Urban, to fix them entirely to his interests, empowered the guardians of the Franciscan Monastery to excommunicate every person in the province of Connaught who should adhere to Clement VII. who he assured them was antipope. In the year 1728 the judges held their court here. Queen Elisabeth granted to the corporation twelve gardens, containing three acres, two parts of a water mill, the ninth part of the tithes of two acres of land, called Portcalle, near Galway; a salmon every Wednesday out of the great weir, and three every Saturday out of the high weir, and one every Saturday out of the haul net, and as many eels as shall be taken one day in every week: out of the county eel weir on the river. [original footnote].

Kilnalechin— Convent founded before 1325.

Arran, in the bay of Galway — Convent, founded A. D, 1485.

Boilean-Clair — Monastery, founded in 1290; it was formerly very rich.

Athenry — Monastery of St. Michael, founded by Thomas earl of Kildare, and his wife, in 1464, and built one part of the cloister, but other benefactors finished it. Margaret Gibbon built the first chapel, and earl of Desmond the second, and one O'Tully the third. F. Raimund Burke, an observant, and bishop of Emly, was buried there, anno 1562, and at last this house was destroyed by queen Elizabeth.

CONVENTS OF THE EREMITES OF ST. AUGUSTINE, COMMONLY CALLED AUSTIN FRIARS

Galway — Convent founded, some say in the thirteenth century, by one of the Berminghams, lords barons of Athenry; others say in the year 1508, by Stephen Lynch and his wife Margaret.

Donmore — Convent founded by Walter Bermingham, the ninth lord baron of Athenry, A.D. 1425.

CONVENTS OF CARMELITES OR WHITE FRIARS

Loughrea— Convent of the Blessed Virgin Mary, founded by Richard de Burgo, earl of Ulster, and lord of Connaught, A.D. 1300, A Monasticon published in 1722, says, this monastery was founded by one Richard Harley, an English gentleman.

Crevebane— Convent founded in the fourteenth century, by the Burkes, ancestors to the earls of Clanrickard.

Ballynahinch — Convent founded in 1356, by the O'Flahertys, kings of Iarconnaught.

Galway — Convent founded by the Burkes.

Kaltrane-Palace — A Monastery built by the Berminghams, lords of Athenree.

Long Abbey was anciently of great celebrity: the abbott was mitred and sat in parliament, and the succession of abbotts has been preserved to the present day by the Roman Catholics. St. Fechin founded this abbey and Immey (Omey) and Ardoilon (High island).

In the 28th of Elizabeth's reign, amongst other bequests granted to Trinity College, Dublin, a part of the revenues belonging to the canons regular of Cong, founded under the invocation of the B. V. Mary, by Donald Mac AEd, king of Ireland in 624, who kept his court at Cong, where his successors resided; also the priory of Lisduffe, which was a cell to Cong Abbey.

Near the west gate of the town of Galway, without the walls, there was formerly the monastery of St. Mary of the Hill: on the Nuns forsaking it, the secular clergy entered into and kept possession of it for a long time; but on the petition of the inhabitants of the town to Pope Innocent VIII. it was granted to the Dominican friars by a rule dated 4th December 1488.— There are no remains of this foundation except the cemetery, the whole building being demolished by the townsmen in the year 1652, in order to prevent Cromwell from turning it into a fortification against themselves: there has been lately erected a new chapel here.

There was also an Augustinian friary on a hill near this town, founded by Stephen Lynch and his wife Margaret, in the year 1508, at the earnest request of Richard Nangle, a friar of the same order, who afterwards became archbishop of Tuam.

About the year 1300 Richard de Burgo, earl of Ulster, founded a monastery in Galway for Carmelites or white friars, dedicated to the Virgin Mary; this was granted to Richard earl of Clanrickard. — There was also a chapel or leper house.

The priory of St John the Baptist was founded at Tuam about the year 1140 by Tirdcloane O'Connor king of Ireland. It is not certain to what order this house belonged, but it was granted to Richard earl of Clanrickard. The abbey of the Holy Trinity was founded here, either in the reign of king John or of Henry III. for Praemonstre Canons. — Note, Tuam and all its churches were destroyed by fire in 1244.

The monks of the Cistercian Abbey of Dunbrody, in the county of Wexford, had for a long time a chapel at Portumna, dedicated to St Peter and Paul, but having at length forsaken it, O'Madden, Dynast of that county, gave it to the Dominican friars, who with the approbation of the monks of Dunbrody, erected a friary here, and a church which they dedicated to the blessed Virgin Mary and the original patron saints; at the same time they built a steeple and all other necessary offices.

Pope Martin granted a Bull to confirm their possessions, dated 8th October 1426; and the 23rd November following he granted indulgences to all who have contributed to the building. The walls are still nearly entire, and show that the monastery of Portumna was by no means an ignoble structure. The ancient choir is now the parish church.

There was formerly a small chapel of ease in Galway, dedicated to St Nicholas, where the cathedral now stands. — *Quere, chapel of ease to what church?*

The old free school in High-street, lately pulled down, and new houses erected on the site by Mr. Hynes, was formerly a nunnery or chapel; and some years since part of a subterraneous communication was discovered leading towards the cathedral. The date on this old house was 1522.

In the 9th century the Ostmen (Danes) introduced a new religious order, the Benedictines, into Ireland; they first erected stone roofed Crypts. — Note, one of these remains at Killaloe.

The Roman Catholic college or collegiate church of Galway is composed of a warden and eight vicars, and is, or has been possessed of a fund of about £3000. obtained chiefly by charitable bequests. The late Rev. Bartholomew Burke was treasurer. This fund has been accumulating since the Reformation, and is enjoyed by them in lieu of the tithe they lost at that period: the interest is annually divided amongst them. The warden receives about £36. and each of the vicars about £23. They also had formerly a much larger fund, which they transferred to France about the time of the Reformation, from whence they had a handsome yearly income, but this was seized at the period of the French revolution, together with all their church plate, worth upwards of £500. which they kept there to protect it from the rapacity of the reformers. They had also several burses; one at Louvain, very valuable, and in various parts of the continent, which they might either let or bestow to the students they might send there from Ireland. They have well-founded hopes that now the affairs of France are settled, they will be restored to them. The election of the Catholic warden and eight vicars is vested exclusively in the presentation or patronage of the thirteen tribes or Galway families, for all the parishes that compose the wardenship, with the exception of a few families that they liberally made free of the Catholic corporation a few years ago. This right of election they arrogated to themselves some centuries ago, alleging that they purchased, for the sum of £1500. the ten royalties of all the lands and parishes that at present form the wardenship, from Donatus O'Murray, the then archbishop of Tuam and Enaghdaen, which agreement Pope Innocent VIII. ratified, and issued his bull (which will be found in the Appendix), forming Galway into a wardenship in the year 1484,[1] This £1500. the tribes affirm was, from a conscientious motive, laid out by Donatus O'Murray, in the purchase of lands of equal value, and which now form the richest and fairest patrimony possessed at present by the see of Tuam. The lay corporation under which the Tribes act for the return of their warden and eight vicars, are composed of a mayor, recorder, sheriffs, and town clerk, all of whom must be Catholics, as well as the voters. On a vacancy for a warden or vicars, one or more candidates usually offer themselves each of whom is supported by his friends. On the day of election the most respectable of each party proposes his friend, which must be seconded. If no opposition appears, the sheriffs declare the candidate duly elected, and certify the same in an official form. The certificate is signed by the mayor, recorder, sheriffs and town clerk, and also by a few of the most respectable electors.

However if a contest should arise, which is usually the case, a poll immediately commences, with the same regularity and forms as a county member would contest his election, and sometimes with as much animosity. None are allowed to vote but tribes, (though living in any part of Ireland, or the universe, their votes are received, if Catholics) except three or four resident families who got their freedom by special favour, viz. the O'Flahertys, Costellos, and Keallys, After the election a scrutiny generally follows, cautiously rejecting the votes of any of the tribes that might be, or whose ancestors were bastards, or whose real names were not acknowledged real tribes, and various other equally weighty causes, by which it may be perceived that

---

[1] I am completely at a loss here; it is said above that the tribe, arrogated the right of presentation at far back as 1484, yet it is generally acknowledged that several of the tribes came in at a much later period. The Browns did not settle here until about the year 1540, and the Trenches many years after 1484, when a judge of that name arrived here from England to try the Blakes for the murder of the Athys. The family of Morris did not settle in Galway until 1485, a year after the date the Pope's Bull, [original footnote].

the election of a warden and vicars is vested solely in the laity, being a domestic nomination without the interference of any foreign power whatsoever. On the election of a warden by the people, as above-mentioned, he is presented to the dean — (Note. I do not recollect any mention elsewhere of a dean) — and vicars, who ratify and confirm the election. A warden of Galway is armed with the same spiritual powers as any bishop, except that he cannot ordain, confirm, or consecrate the holy oil on holy Thursday in lent. He also exercises the same jurisdiction over the convents and nunneries as any bishop in his diocese. By the bull of Pope Innocent, he may be removed every third year if the electors or tribes dislike him; he is therefore reelected every first day of August. No bishop can exercise jurisdiction within the limits of the wardenship, except the Metropolitan, the Archbishop of Tuam, who usually makes a triennial visitation, which he is obliged to finish in a limited period, so jealous are they of their privileges. The warden has a chair and a vote in synod, as a bishop would, and can always have two students at St. Patrick's College, Maynooth.

There are three convents and four nunneries. The Dominicans, Franciscans, Augustinians, and Presentation, lately established by the V. R. W. French, for the education of poor female children, of whom upwards of 30 are dieted, clothed, and lodged, and upwards of 300 day scholars are educated in useful works, and reading, writing, and arithmetic, &c. How praiseworthy would it be if every convent and friary in Ireland imitated their useful plan? Each of these convents or friaries derive their support chiefly from the interest of money given to them at different periods by our pious ancestors, also by the daily masses, and chaplaincies to wealthy families; and is it not a little re remarkable, that several Protestant gentlemen keep them as chaplains for the benefit of their servants, who are mostly Catholics. They also, agreeably to their vows of poverty, go questing or begging every year through the country, for money, sheep, grain, hay, potatoes, &c. &c. They also, in the fishing season, obtain herrings and other fish from the fishermen of the bay of Galway, who cheerfully share with them a part of their best fish, being firmly persuaded they shall have a blessing on their fishery that season. I am informed the Dominicans obtain more in that way than the other two orders. They also obtain some little addition to their scanty pittance by high masses chanted for the dead, voluntary offerings, mortuary money, remembrance masses, chapel rent collected annually, candle money twice a year, with some other little casualties, by which they contrive to live decently in community, and when at home dine in refectory.

The three orders may amount to thirteen or fourteen. Twenty years ago they were much more numerous. Each of these convents had formerly large estates attached to them, which were all swept away at the Reformation. The Dominicans and Augustinians are governed by priors, the Franciscans by a guardian, all annually chosen by their respective orders. The nuns of the four nunneries are also decently and comfortably lodged, and supported from the funds of their houses.

The mode of admission, time immemorial, or at least since they were deprived of their estates at the Reformation, is, on the admission of a novice, she or her friends hand over to the community her fortune of three or four hundred pounds at least, which is immediately added to the stock purse of the house, and put out at interest in safe hands for the support of the community at large. They are generally obliged to dine in refectory except they dine out or are sick. The mother abbess, who is chosen every third year, has the chief care of the house, and provides a well supplied but plain table. Each nun also will require to have a yearly pension paid by their friends for breakfast, clothing, &c. generally from twenty to sixty pounds a year, which enables many to support and educate a poor relation about them. They also have some little addition to their support from dieters and lodgers, females of known respectability.

Each Nunnery retains a chaplain. — On being deprived of their estates at the Reformation, and in Cromwell's usurpation, the Franciscans alone had the good fortune, about eighty years ago, to get back five or six acres of land, now called the Nuns' Island, opposite to where the town gaol stands; here they have a small house for valetudinarians, and a garden that produces plenty of vegetables for their use, besides pasture for a few milch cows to supply them with milk.

They petitioned George the Second's queen, by a deputation dressed in the costume of the order, stating their grievances and request, to which the queen acceded in the most gracious manner, and ordered a patent or grant to be immediately made out to them of these five or six acres, and which they still, and may they always, enjoy. — The Dominican nuns purchased the house they now reside in about the year 1806, for the sum of £800. forever: it is large and convenient, with good yard and offices in the rere (an accommodation by no means common in Galway), and, I am informed, would conveniently accommodate thirty nuns. The lower part is let for shops, which adds something to their comforts. It is a curious circumstance that the back house at the rere of their house, (usually called the slate nunnery) has been the estate of the nuns time immemorial, and the front house, which they purchased, was the estate of the late Robert Blake Forster. It seems the back house was formerly the properly of the Kirwans of Castle Hacket, to whom the nuns lent three hundred pounds, receiving the back house a security for the money. Mr. Kirwan never paid the money, and the nuns have retained quiet possession for upwards of 200 years.

The Protestant warden of Galway, who is appointed by the member for Galway, has eleven acres of glebe at Rosscom, (where the remains of an old abbey are still visible,) valued at three pounds an acre; seventeen acres of glebe at Royallen, between Galway and Oranmore, valued also at three pounds an acre; forty acres of glebe at Capanavagh, west of Galway, worth about £120. per annum; a glebe house called the warden's house, opposite the church of St. Nicholas, worth fifty pounds per annum, besides burial money in each of the church yards, and £10. for each corpse interred in the church, the amount not known. There has been an abatement lately of 10 percent. on the value of the tithes. Altogether his income, exclusive of

£150. to two vicars, is about £1000. per annum. Rahoon, or St, James' parish, and all the parishes in the wardenship, are exempt from the payment of vestry money except that of St. Nicholas, on paying an halfpenny an acre, a commutation long since established, and which they are very punctual in paying. — Note, a layman may hold the office of warden for the space of one year, by virtue of the original Bull appointing that office. — There are only two vicars under the charter; they rank as king's chaplains.

The vestry cess amounts to about £500. per ann. for the following purposes, and for the repairs of the church; it was formerly about £800. per. annum.

	£	s.	d.
Organist,	40	0	0
Keeper of the clock and chimes,	15	0	0
Clerk of the vestry,	11	7	6
Clerk of the church.	34	2	6
Sexton,	20	0	0
Henry Banks and choristers,	9	0	0
Door-keeper,	2	5	6
Sacramental bread and wine,	8	0	0
Candles,	9	0	0
Fuel,	8	0	0
Head nurse,	6	16	3
Support of foundlings,	113	15	0
Coffins for paupers,	36	16	3
Cleaning the branch	2	5	6
Flannel for foundlings,	10	0	0
Repairing crown post, glazing, &c.	30	0	0
Constables collecting the cess of the out parishes,	8	0	0

Of course the rates vary in some years.

The clergy of this county mostly reside; or procure curates who do. Some have glebes, as the united parishes of Killererun and Abbey have a handsome glebe house, and 40 acres of good land. Lickerrigh about 3½ acres, no house; Killconiran 2½ acres, no house. A parish church has been lately erected near Dunscandle. I am informed nothing can be more uncomfortable and damp: a handsome church, with a comfortable glebe house and 3 or 4 acres, has also lately been erected at Moylough. Another handsome church and glebe house near Ardrahan, with a good many acres of glebe. A very beautiful new church at Clifden in Connemara: another extremely handsome church at Gort: another at Ahascragh, very commodious. I trust before long, that under the auspices of the present archbishop of Tuam, there will not be a parish, or at least an union, without a church, a glebe, house and land, and an enforcement of residence by the incumbent.

There has been a great improvement in many of the Roman Catholic chapels; the generality of which, however, are disgraceful to the clergyman and his congregation:

though the parish priest may not be able to have his chapeline, he may have it clean and dry. I much fear it may be imputed to that indolence which prevents them from having any thing in their gardens but potatoes and cabbages, instead of setting an example to their flocks, like the priests on the continent, who generally have neat gardens, and every thing clean and comfortable about them. I cannot conceive why a priest may not say his prayers amidst good vegetables and sweet flowers, as well as amongst potatoes, cabbages, and all sorts of weeds. I presume to throw out a hint, that an arrangement in the College of Maynooth for giving the students a taste for, and knowledge of the cultivation of a garden, would be useful as well as healthful: probably an hour every day, would not interfere with their duties. There have been lately several handsome and comfortable chapels erected in this county; one at Galway; two at Loughrea; one at Oranmore; one at Laban near Ardrahan, towards the building of which Mr. Lambart of Creggclare gave £50. and the ground rent free; one at Mount Bellew, in a very superior style of finishing and arrangement.

Mr. Bellew gives to the Catholic incumbent 10 acres of land rent free. The old churches, and many of the new, though the elevation may be beautiful, are most uncomfortable in winter, both from want of studding the walls, without which no building of limestone can be dry, and from want of fires, and not frequently opening the windows on every fine day; instead of this they are usually shut up until a short time before service, and though some have fire places, the clergyman and church wardens seem to forget for what purpose they were erected. I really think that country churches are in general places of penance, especially in winter.

I can see no reason why a church, and a chapel too, should not be as comfortable as any room in a private house: a few hundred weight of Kilkenny coal would obviate every cause of complaint, and it would not in some measure countenance the hurried and incoherent manner of performing the service, in which some young gentlemen, and old ones too, indulge. I can not resist the temptation, whilst on this subject, to give the following excellent advice to parents and guardians from the Rev. Mr. John's introduction to bishop Massillon's address to his clergy.

> "What possible advantage can a congregation derive from having a young man, who is entirely unacquainted with the art of public speaking, read for fifteen or twenty minutes an elegant essay, or an ingenious disquisition equally adapted, with a few verbal alterations, to an assembly of Catholics, Jews, or Mahometans, ashamed all the time of looking them in the face? Such a one might have been active as a shopkeeper, skilful as a farmer, diligent as a tradesman, and may perhaps be distinguished as a philosopher; but it is with difficulty we can bring ourselves to believe that he was moved by the Holy Ghost to preach the gospel"

I shall only add, that the irritability of the congregation would be much increased in some of our country churches with wet walls and broken windows.

SECTION XXVI

WHETHER THE COUNTY HAS BEEN ACTUALLY SURVEYED

In addition to the Surveys of Dr. Beaufort and Major Taylor, made many years since, there has been an actual Survey of the county of Galway made by the late Mr. Larkin, under the auspices of the grand jury of the county. It supplies many omissions and errors of Dr. Beaufort's map, to which, as being chiefly an ecclesiastical one, it is probably liable, in the lines of roads, &c. and the multitude of alterations and additions made since the publication of the other, which is principally a map of roads, makes that of little use at present, especially on so small a scale. The map by Mr. Larkin will be sufficiently large, not only to supply the omissions of the former maps, but considerably to facilitate any change in the lines of roads and the adoption of new ones. As I have not seen the map, which is now engraving in London, I can only write from report.[1] It is intended by the grand jury to have maps of each barony, which will be highly useful in assisting in the detection of jobbing, if any such thing exists in this county. If the different changes in the mineral regions of the county, especially those of Connemara, as delineated by the very scientific Mr. Nimmo, in his luminous report to the commissioners for improving the bogs of Ireland, were distinguished by colouring, it would be highly useful. Several maps of the town have at different periods been published; I have a very small one of ancient Galway, very curious. There is also a very large and extremely interesting map of the town of Galway in the reign of Charles II. in the possession of colonel Browne of Castle Mountgarret; it would be highly desirous to have it copied, as it had a narrow escape from the flames when the house was consumed in 1812. I understand there are but two copies in existence, this, and another in a convent on the continent.[2] There is a remarkable map in the possession of Major Prendergast of the Tipperary militia, of the soundings and anchoring places on the coast of Ireland, taken from the French at Ballynamuck, on the 8th of September 1798.

The place where they landed at Killalla is thus marked, ‖ — A Frenchman, Monsieur De Latocnaye, published his travels through Ireland, and was in this county; he says Loughrea is superior to Galway: he mentions also near Ardrahan, a round fort, called the palace of Dunderlass, where tradition says Goora, king of Connaught, resided, and it was near the celebrated city of Ardrahan. Also a Cromlech, near the road of the plates, or *Boher lac dana mias*, of which he published

---

[1] This map has been finished, but, I regret to state, that there are so many errors, that it is in contemplation to have another and more correct one made. It will require great circumspection in the appointment, and particular care taken that the executive part of the Survey may not be made by young lads, to whom, if I am not misinformed, the Survey was mostly entrusted by the late Mr. Larkin, whose professional avocations probably presented a more constant personal superintendence than it received, [Original footnote].

[2] Mr. Hardiman discovered another copy in the College library in Dublin, of which he has given a facsimile, on a reduced scale, in his history of the town of Galway, highly interesting. If the scale had been the same as the modern map of Galway it would have been very desirable, [Original footnote].

a ridiculous legend not worth repeating. In another place, "On digging the ground of a little eminence, the only one in this stony place, a hideous statue, supposed to be that of Baal, has been found." He says that he met more barbarians in Paris, London, and Dublin than in Connemara. As a match for this marvellous account, I was favoured by a friend with the following from the manuscript of a natural history of the county of Galway intended to have been published.

"The islands in the lakes in Connemara are wooded with the *largest timber trees,*" again, "amongst which may be ranked the twelve pins in *the barony of Connemara*: they form what may be popularly called an Irish stone henge, much more stupendous than the English; *they stand at no great distance from each other*, and are disposed in an irregular line; they are not strictly pyramidal, not being acute at the top, but ending in rather an abrupt manner; they have an appearance of so many *steeples* when seen at a distance they are of so rude *workmanship*, that it is truly unaccountable, even miraculous, how such *structures, monstrous as an Egyptian obelisk, or Roman column*, each composed of a *single stone*, could be elevated by 94 such ignorant artificers, and fixed so accurately on" their centres of gravity, &c." What a public loss that those enlightened and accurate travels were not published! Baron Munchausen[1] might have turned them to some account; he might have tied his horse to one of those steeples. Those who have never seen those stupendous mountains called Binabola, or the twelve pins, must be informed, that one of those structures, monstrous as an Egyptian obelisk or Roman column, is a mountain upwards of 2400 feet high, and the twelve pins altogether occupy seven or eight miles square.

SECTION XXVII

WEIGHTS AND MEASURES, LIQUID OR DRY — IN WHAT INSTANCES ARE WEIGHTS ASSIGNED FOR MEASURES, OR VICE VERSA

The weights of this county are of the same standard as those used all over Ireland, but much use is made of stone weights, nominally of equal weight with those of metal; but although a stone may be throwing about the ground, and even pavement, and of course must be lessened by every collision, yet after suffering this for a year or more, it is still used under the original denomination. Weights are assigned for measure in potatoes, as in some places the barrel is forty-two stones weight, in others sixty-four stones, and sixteen pound to the stone. At Bunown forty stones of potatoes to the bushel. The pottle of milk in Ballinasloe is three quarts; in Eyrecourt four quarts; in Gort three quarts; in Loughrea six quarts: how ridiculous this is! how much better if the prices, as in the assize of bread, and not the measure changed. In some places five quarts of ashes (at 6½d.) to the pottle; eight quarts of oatmeal to the

---

[1] A fictitious character renown as a teller of exaggerated stories, based on a real traveller and storyteller, Hieronymus Carl Friedrich von Münchhausen, [Clachan ed.].

pottle in Loughrea; five in Eyrecourt; seven in Woodfort, &c. &c.: butter also is eighteen, twenty, and twenty-four ounces to the pound. Hay and straw is usually sold by the hundred weight, though sometimes straw is sold by the bundle. — Note, a cubic yard of hay sometime in the rick generally weighs about 1 cwt. 1 qr. 21 lb. Turf kishes, and baskets for horse loads, are of any size the owner chooses; but the statute turf kish, I understand, should be four feet six inches long, two feet and ten inches deep, and two feet and four inches broad.[1]

Salt is the only thing, I believe, in which measure is assigned for weight; it is usually sold by the quart. The barrel of wheat is twenty stones; of oats, fourteen stones; of barley, sixteen stones; of rape, sixteen stones; but in general every thing is sold by the stone, for as very few have scales, they put in any quantity the sack or bag will hold: two of our barrels of wheat weigh five hundred and sixty pounds, and the English quarter five hundred and sixteen pounds; I mention this because many imagine the English quarter is equal to two of our barrels. There are great frauds practised in the measurement of lime; every person should get a box made for this purpose. It would be highly desirable that Edward the Third's statute was renewed; he enacted that one weight, one measure, and one yard should be used all through the British dominions. Richard I. (1199) established one weight and measure throughout his dominions; but this was dispensed with by the profligate King John, for money.

The following table may be useful to those agriculturists who keep accounts, which I fear is not a general practice; I therefore publish it.

Relative weight of produce per Acre, English, Scottish and Irish from one ounce per square yard to one Pound calculated in stones. Pounds and ounces: and from one pound to one stone calculated in tons, cwt, stones and pounds — the former answering for wheat, barley, oats; the latter for cabbage, Turnips, potatoes, &c. &c.,

---

[1] The ancient way of measuring was by the Cronnoge, which was a basket lined with a skin, supposed to hold the produce of seventeen sheaves of corn, and equal to a Bristol barrel. The ancient *Suntmagiium*, Sagmegium, or Sauma, seems to have been a car or cart load, and is contradistinguished from *Onus* which was a horse load, called in this county an upload, [original footnote].

Per Sq. Yd.	English Acre. 4840 Sq. Yards.			Scotch Acre. 6150.			Irish Acre. 7840.	Per Sq. Yd.	English Acre. 4840.				Scotch Acre. 6150.				Irish Acre. 7840.	
Oz.	Stones.	lbs.	oz.	Stones.	lbs.	oz.	Stones.	lbs.	Tons.	Cwt.	St.	lbs.	Tons.	Cwt.	St.	lbs.	Tons.	Cwt.
1	21	8	8	27	6	6	35	1	2	5	1	10	2	14	7	4	3	10
2	43	3	0	54	12	12	70	2	4	6	3	6	5	9	6	2	7	0
3	64	11	8	82	5	2	105	3	6	9	5	2	8	4	5	12	10	10
4	86	6	0	109	11	8	140	4	8	12	6	12	10	19	5	2	14	0
5	108	0	8	137	5	14	175	5	10	16	0	8	13	14	4	6	17	10
6	129	9	0	164	10	4	210	6	12	19	2	4	16	9	3	10	21	0
7	151	3	8	192	2	10	245	7	15	2	4	0	19	4	3	0	24	10
8	172	12	0	219	9	0	280	8	17	5	5	10	21	19	2	4	28	0
9	194	6	8	247	1	6	315	9	19	8	7	6	24	14	1	8	31	10
10	216	1	0	274	7	12	350	10	21	12	1	2	27	9	0	12	35	0
11	237	8	8	302	0	2	385	11	23	15	2	12	30	4	0	2	38	10
12	259	4	0	329	6	8	420	12	25	18	4	8	32	18	7	6	42	0
13	280	12	8	356	12	14	455	13	28	1	6	4	35	13	6	10	45	10
14	302	7	0	384	5	4	490	14	30	5	0	0	38	8	6	0	49	0
15	324	1	8	411	11	10	525											
16	345	10	0	439	4	0	560											

RELATIVE VALUE IN ENGLAND, SCOTLAND AND IRELAND

If the Value of 10 Square Yards be	The English Acre, of 4840 Yards, will amount to			The Scotch Acre, of 6150 Yards, will amount to			The Irish Acre, of 7840 Yards, will amount to			The Irish Acre, in Irish Money, will amount to		
d.	£.	s.	d.	£.	s.	d.	£.	s.	d.	£.	s.	d.
0¼	0	10	1	0	12	9	0	16	3	0	17	7¼
0½	1	0	2	1	5	6	1	12	6	1	15	2½
0¾	1	10	3	1	18	3	2	8	9	2	12	9¾
1	2	0	4	2	11	0	3	5	0	3	10	5
1¼	2	10	5	3	3	9	4	1	3	4	8	0¼
1½	3	0	6	3	16	6	4	17	6	5	5	7½
1¾	3	10	7	4	9	3	5	13	9	6	3	2¾
2	4	0	8	5	2	0	6	10	0	7	0	10

This table may also be used for ascertaining the relative expense of labour per acre in the three countries.

SECTION XXVIII

MORALS, MANNERS, AND CUSTOMS OF THE PEOPLE

The morals of the people of this extensive county are at least on a par with the best of any other part of Ireland. That they are not better must be imputed to the deplorable ignorance in which they are permitted to live; they are merely the children of habit, for they owe little or nothing to instruction, and it is very remarkable that the inhabitants of every rank scarcely ever correct their children. They are very frequently admonished from the altar by their pastors[1], but any advice they may receive that is at variance with their very irritable feelings, dwells but a short time on their minds; they usually act from the impulse of the moment, and from a people so shamefully neglected by the landed proprietors, we ought to be astonished it has not led to more crime than can be attached to the character of the lower order of the people of this county; and those who exclaim that they are too much under the control of the catholic clergy, generally saying they are priest ridden, &c. expose their ignorance of the subject; the fact is the reverse; the younger part, especially, pay very little attention to their admonitions; if they did, we should hear little of ribbon men or any other disturbers of the public peace. There is, however, a most material change for the better since lord Chesterfield's administration, who says in one of his letters, "Let them make Connaught and Kerry know that there is a God, a King, and a Government, three things to which they seem to be at present utter strangers." It speaks highly in their favor that in the year 1798, and in the late ribbon business, they were the last in Ireland that permitted themselves to be influenced by demagogues and pedagogues, (a most dangerous class of people,) and had not leaders from adjoining counties corrupted them, they had remained peaceably occupied with their domestic labours. The general mass of the people were averse from any disturbance, but they were obliged, at the muzzle of the blunderbuss, to join all meetings, and were urged forward by a few desperate characters for their own emolument, and many of whom have justly paid the forfeit of their lives. Particular attention should be paid to the prohibition of strangers on every estate, and it would be a very useful duty of every clergyman to assist in their discovery and dismissal. A very lax observance of the Sabbath is amongst the vices of this county, and in many instances some holy days are observed more strictly, as far as an abstinence from work, which I much fear is the only duty thought necessary, except going to mass, where I also apprehend they go more from habit than from a feeling of what they owe to their Creator.

---

[1] Some years since on my way to Connemara I stopped at the inn at Oughterard, at the time that mass was performing in the parlour; some article of dress had been stolen from a female; a discourse was delivered from the altar by the parish priest, Rev. Mr. Martin, better calculated to produce a repentant restitution than any I ever remember to have heard. It spoke not only to the heart, but to the comprehension of the audience, [original footnote].

MANNERS.

In the manners of the people there is nothing more conspicuous than that universal wish to oblige; this is not confined to their intercourse with each other, but must be seen, and probably felt by every traveller; and in many instances this is so perfectly disinterested that, except amongst the very wretched, any attempt at remuneration for any trifling service would be considered as a lessening. Their good humour also is very remarkable; Mr. Young says, "they have none of that in civility of sullen silence in which so many Englishmen seem to wrap themselves up, as if retiring within their own importance." Any thing bad in Paddy's mind will out, and probably end in a broken head, and there is an end of it. In nothing is their gay humour more remarkable than whilst they are at work; in so much, that though their stories may be very pleasant and beguiling to themselves, they are a great obstacle to the quick performance of anything they may be doing: if you ask one of them a question, he never answers without looking you in the face, and stopping from his labour, which, though the very pink of politeness, delays the work greatly. It must be understood I confine those remarks to the country people; in towns they possess all the vices incident to such situations; and when any of the first class take an improper bias, it can be generally traced to a frequent intercourse with the latter. The general but indolent practice of letting land in villages, though latterly in most cases ruinous to the tenants of this county, yet it tends to encourage such strong attachments, generally strengthened by intermarriages, that though they may have some bickerings with each other, they will, right or wrongs keep their companions; this is frequently the source of much disturbance at fairs or any other public meeting. If Paddy gets a dose of the native whiskey, it sharpens his recollection of any former real or imaginary injury. This unhappy disposition, incidental to warm feelings in untutored minds, has led to the abolition of hurling matches (the Irish crickets), at which some years since it was the custom of ladies and gentlemen of the first rank to attend, to view feats of activity that would astonish those who think *potatoes and milk are only fit for swine*, but they have been obliged to give them up, and they are now seldom permitted to meet. The women of the county are remarkable for their conjugal fidelity and a strong and active attachment to their domestic concerns, and frequently they take a very severe part in the labours of the field. The unmarried women are also remarkably virtuous, especially if we consider the total neglect of their education; for although the boys are frequently sent to school, the girls, except in towns, very rarely receive any education. Even if they do, it is continued only until they are old enough to soften the labours of their mothers, and is generally forgotten in a short period. Where a female may have erred it usually terminates in matrimony, and it very seldom occurs that any impropriety can be attached to their character after their *amende honorable*. It must be confessed that an adherence to truth is not amongst their virtues, and from not considering it any crime, they are little concerned when detected. I regret to have to state that, in some instances, the example of breach of promise may be traced to those of a much higher rank; *slippery lads, that nothing will bind*, unless every agreement is in black and white; a meanness, not to say worse, that no person, especially one wishing to be considered a gentleman, should be guilty of. I am happy to say, this is by no means a general character; for in no part of Ireland can you meet more honorable men; to make use of a common expression, "men with whom you might deal in the dark." Pilfering is another vice, I must needs say, very frequently practised, but it is confined chiefly to articles of timber, or some kinds of vegetables, especially onions and turnips; but as to robbing on the high road, or in houses, it is never thought of by the country people, and if they were the only part of the population to apprehend, you might sleep safely with open doors, which many really do, but not so in or near town. A highwayman is unknown in the county, and indeed a footpad, except near large towns. The inhabitants of this county, of every rank, possess almost a veneration for those of what they call *old families*, insomuch that though the lower ranks must be sensible that they suffer every kind of injustice from many of them in all their dealings, and the higher ranks acknowledge that many are a disgrace to society, from a swindling non-observance of promises and other vices, yet if any person, not of the county, observes on them, they generally answer, "Why, I acknowledge that is but too true; Oh, but he's an old gentleman of the county". The very recollection of this should influence him to feel that a liar, though he may be a man of large fortune, even £10,000 a year, and trace back his pedigree as one of the tribes of Galway to 1280, cannot be a gentleman. I have been informed of a remarkable instance of presence of mind in a poor woman. The cook was preparing to heat the oven at the house of a man of large fortune, and had, for this purpose, placed some burning turf in the centre to kindle the remainder; this poor woman knew that her master had placed, unknown to the cook, a large quantity of gun-powder in a flower-pot in the oven to keep it dry, instantly perceiving that the property of her master and the lives of the family were at stake, nobly devoted herself, and with the assistance of some instrument she gradually stole the flower-pot round the edge of the oven, and wrapping it in her apron ran out of the house, threw it on the dunghill, and what had happened was only known when she recovered from a fainting fit. Her first exclamation was "Oh, thank God, I have saved my master." She had immediately a comfortable cottage built for her, and a few acres of land and a cow, with an annuity given to her, you will naturally say: no such thing; she was lately a poor, feeble, rheumatic old woman, living in a damp low hovel, superintendent of the fowl, amongst whose filth she might offer up her prayers for her kind master and mistress. If this should meet his eye, I trust he may have the grace to blush.

The disgraceful custom of loud crying at funerals, though practised in every part of Ireland, and that it may be traced as far back as holy writ, and to the days of Homer, yet calls loudly in those days of refinement for suppression. Another custom calls also equally loud for suppression; the attendance on those meetings where a corpse is laid out previous to interment, generally called *wakes*, and sometimes *corp house*; they are places where the young of both sexes meet, and the night is generally consumed in drinking whiskey, smoking tobacco, and playing different games of romps, &c. &c. and not infrequently some of the young couples contrive that the place of the deceased shall be supplied in a few months by a young substitute Those meetings are sometimes called *Hono's*, from the words *Ogh, hone*, oh, so frequently used at funerals.¹

In the island of Omey the men and women have separate burial places; probably originating when there were several religious residing in the island, many of whom would not permit a woman to come into their presence. In the parish of Moycullen there is, or was in 1818, great emulation amongst the parishioners who shall give most to their priest at a funeral or wedding; they often say, that at such and such people's funeral or wedding, so much was given; zounds, why should not we give more? surely we can afford it better: by this emulation the parish priest realised a good sum of money, which he lent out interest free to his parishioners in distress, but they were obliged to be punctual in the repayment at the stipulated period, or they received no future assistance; this was so well known, and so strictly observed, that they made every exertion to be punctual. Those who attend funerals in Galway wear crape in their hats for several days; if the deceased died unmarried, the crape is edged with white. Several villages pay the pound-keeper by the year, and the fences are so bad in general they are constant customers; sometimes they pay in money, but more frequently in grazing, or some other produce of the land.

Village tenants do not like tradesmen amongst them, as they do not assist in the labours of the field. Tombstones are frequently called *slates*. Women almost always ride to Galway market from the west, but the men seldom do. The general improvidence of Roman Catholics on fast days is very remarkable, even in the houses of those of large fortune it is nothing uncommon, if the fishman has disappointed them, that their dinner consists of dry ling, potatoes and butter, eggs, or buttered greens. A little forethought would never leave them without:

Potted lobster from 10d to 1s. each	Red herrings,
Pickled oysters.	Collard eel.
—— scollops.	Slauke
—— salmon.	Oyster soup and pye.
Cream cheese.	Pancakes.
Rice padding.	Apple fritters.
Plum pudding without suet, excellent	Jelly and blancmonge.
Apple pye and dumplings.	Spanish flummery
Cods sounds — to be had in casks	Muscle soup, as made in Galway, a

And many other things to be found in every cookery book. I cannot conceive why the table of a man of large fortune should ever be without some or most of those

---

¹ In the time of the Anglo Saxons this custom became too disgraceful to Christians, that Bishop Ælfric in his charge to his clergy says, "ye shall not make merry over the dead, nor resort to a corpse unless invited. Then shall ye forbid the heathenish songs of the laymen, and their loud shouts; and neither eat nor drink where the body lies, lest you partake in the superstitions which are practised on such occasions." Also in 1625, there was a fine of five shillings levied in Galway on any person using those hideous dry-eyed yells, [original footnote].

things on fast days; they are to be had easily in Dublin. As to cream cheese it is a rare thing except on gala days. It seems your very clever house keepers say it cuts too deep in the butter crock. Most Catholics either have, or work themselves up to have, an aversion to fish. They will, I hope, pardon me when I say that much of this proceeds from the expressions of disgust with which they always speak of fish before their children and servants. I have more than once or twice heard children not above six years old say, "oh mama that nasty fish." — There is also a deplorable want of winter fruit at the tables of most wealthy families; nuts and unripe apples generally constitute the desert. I am at a loss to conceive why every day in winter and spring, until the first fruit comes in, their tables should be without figs, raisins, almonds, chestnuts, wallnuts, oranges, French plums, &c. &c. which are easily got in Dublin, and would contribute materially to their health; they should consider them articles so necessary for their table as not to be introduced merely for parade. To Catholics on fast days they would be particularly grateful and wholesome, and might be well exchanged for the unwholesome second course, that grand source of bilious complaints. As for those delicious fruits, winter pears, I have scarcely ever seen them at any table in this county. Indeed, for some years past, they have been much neglected all through Ireland. Until within a few years the gardeners of this county were generally of that rank that totally prevented any knowledge of their proper management; — *they were too fond of the knife.*

A few years ago I was walking in a garden with the owner in the month of September. He went to several fine winter pears, Beaure, Chaumentelle, Crasare, Bergamotte, Colmar, &c. which had been brought into Ireland from France; after biting one of each, and of course finding them hard and ill tasted, like all unripe pears, he called to his gardener, equally ignorant as himself, and desired him instantly to throw all them damned pears out of the garden; and if I had not been there to explain the matter, several very find trees, just coming into bearing, would have been consigned to the faggot yard. If gardeners could be prevailed on to plant winter pears grafted on quince stocks, as those from France generally are, they would have them in bearing immediately, and they would ripen much better in wet cold seasons than those on free stocks, which, though they furnish the wall much sooner, yet they are frequently many years before they bear, and run so much to wood that none but the most intelligent gardener can manage them. I am aware that it will be said that the fruit of pears grafted on quince stocks are apt to be gritly. In some cases this may occur, but it is better to have plenty of ripe gritly pears than none, or a few badly ripened from those on free stocks. The quince stock throws out roots near the surface; the free stock is generally badly furnished with long forky roots running down perpendicularly like an oak, and soon reach the clay.

SECTION XXIX

CONCLUDING OBSERVATIONS

I cannot conclude my survey without bringing to the reader's knowledge, that almost perfect freedom from religious animosity that has disgraced some other parts of Ireland. That there are some sour bigots to be occasionally met with cannot be denied, but I regret to say, they are not confined to Roman Catholics; but a rapid and happy change for the better is taking place every day. Although we may have heard that some of this baneful ingredient was mixed up in the late ribbon business, and in some instances it was the case, yet from every thing I could learn it was by no means a general feeling, for no sort of distinction was made between Protestant and Catholic in the nocturnal depredations of this banditti; and I am well assured by Catholic gentlemen that the exhortations of the Catholic clergy were unceasing, but the irresistible torrent of turbulence carried those along that would otherwise have remained quietly at home. In the intermarriages of the better ranks, there is seldom any religious distinction made, and they unite as love or interest dictate. There is no difference made in the hiring of servants, for I have frequently seen Protestant servants in Catholic houses, and vice versa. As to the majority of the servants being Catholics, this must be the case in a county where the lower ranks are so decidedly of that persuasion. In the houses of Protestant clergymen the servants are mostly Catholics.

I have been well informed that on a Christmas day, the Protestant rector of a parish, on asking where the clerk was, was informed that he had not come from the chapel yet. The hospitality for which this county has long been celebrated, still maintains its place; but that mistaken idea of constraining a person to act against the dictates of reason or his health, has been abandoned in most houses of any respectability; at the same time the bottle is pushed about as fast, indeed faster than ever, as long sitting has been most happily changed for an early visit to the drawing room; and in most genteel houses music or dancing fill up the space between tea and the hour of repose, for suppers have been very generally abandoned, and scarce any house is without a piano forte and a good performer: our Irish ladies are all musical. The music of the lower ranks (the national music) is particularly sweet, but very plaintive. I have frequently listened for an hour with a delight mixed with subdued feelings to a young countryman whistling a plaintive Irish air, whilst leading a horse and car, that taught me to comprehend the feelings of the Swiss at hearing one of their national aire played in another country— the Kureiholan, or Ranz des Vaches. It also taught me to appreciate what Mr. Walker says of our national music.

"The Irish music is in some degree distinguished from the music of every other nation, by an insinuating sweetness, which forces its way irresistibly to the heart, and there diffuses an ecstatic delight that thrills through every fibre of the frame, awakens sensibility, and agitates or tranquillizes the soul. Whatever passion it may be intended to excite, it never fails to effect its purpose; it is the voice of nature, and will be heard. Mr. O'Connor says the Irish harp was introduced hither by the Celto-Phoenician colony of Milesius, which arrived before the Christian ara".

I need not bring to the recollection of an Irishman the effect of our sprightly airs; what youthful foot, or even old one, remains quiet when *"Patrick's day"* is lilted up by the bagpipes? Our women are all self-taught dancers; and it is remarkable that an instance can scarcely ever be perceived of the feet, even of the youngest, not keeping time to the music. I have often tried this, by frequently changing the time, but the motion of the feet uniformly changed with me. Probably I cannot conclude better than by an extract from my favourite author, Arthur Young's Irish Tour, to which, on a former occasion, I had to acknowledge my obligations. "That portion of national wealth which is employed in the improvement of the land of a state are the best employed for the general welfare of a country; whilst trade and manufactures, national funds, banking, &c. swallow up prodigious sums in England, but yield a profit of not above 5 to 10 percent: the lands of Ireland are unimproved, upon which money would pay 15 or 20 per cent, exclusive of a variety of advantages which must strike the most superficial reader. Hence the vast importance to England of the improvement of her Irish territory.

"It is an old observation that the wealth of Ireland will always centre in England; and the fact is true, though not in the way commonly asserted: no employment of an hundred millions, not upon the actual soil of Britain, can ever pay her a tenth of the advantages which would result from Ireland being in the above respects upon that par, which I have described, with England. The more attentively this matter is considered, I am apt to think the more clearly this will appear, and that when old illiberal jealousies are worn out, which, thanks to the good sense of the age, are daily disappearing[1], we shall be fully convinced that the benefit of Ireland is so intimately connected with the good of England, that we shall be as forward to give to that hitherto unhappy country as she can be to receive, from the firm conviction that whatever we there sow will yield to us a most abundant harvest."

---

[1] One would be apt to imagine this idea it not so well founded as the author seems to hope; for the celebrated Mr. Malthus permits himself to be so far influenced by those illiberal prejudices, as to call Ireland "a remote and inconsiderable country." But I leave him to Mr. Say. [original footnote].

APPENDIX

TRIBES AND NON-TRIBES

THE following papers have been put into my hands for publication. I merely state both sides of the question, leaving this weighty matter to the decision of those more immediately concerned. I did not intend to have published these documents, for I considered the affair of about as much consequence to the public as the fate of the battle between Homer's frogs and mice, but I was given to understand that it was expected I should publish the state of the case as follows: — "The Galway" tribes allege that they purchased their Bull for the sum-of fifteen hundred pounds (an enormous sum in those days) from Donates the then Archbishop of Tuam; for which sum he was induced to solicit the Court of Rome for the said Bull; and as the said Donates is said to have purchased a large tract of country for said money, which at this day comprises the best revenue of the See of Tuam, as an equivalent for the loss of Galway; by which act he conceived himself, absolved or saved from his oath on his induction into the See, which was to support and uphold, &c. and not to dispose or alienate any of the temporalities of his See; consequently the Roman Catholic tribes conceive that they alone have the exclusive right of voting in and electing their warden and vicars." — N. B. It must be understood that the Protestant warden and vicars have nothing to do with this affair. The following is the answer to the above: —

OBSERVATIONS on the disputes existing between the tribes and the non-tribes of Galway relative to the right of presenting a warden and vicars for the collegiate church of St Nicholas in Galway, submitted to the consideration of the public by

 A NON-TRIBE.
 Galway, July 1792.

As the first of August is rapidly advancing, and will probably be a day on which the election of a warden will again bring to light, and to the people's recollection, the disputes which have arisen on the death of the late Rev. Augustin Kirwan, deceased, relative to the right of election of a warden and vicars for the collegiate church of St Nicholas and town of Galway, and as that right or privilege has been exercised for some time past by a certain description of people, generally denominated the thirteen tribes of Galway, to the utter exclusion of their fellow citizens or townsmen, who are of different names or families, I think it incumbent on every person that wishes well to civil society; on every person divested of narrow prejudices and bigotry; on every person of a tolerant and enlightened mind; for the public good; for the benefit and advantage of himself, his contemporaries, the rising generation, and their posterity to the end of time, living in the town of Galway, to step forward and give whatever information and assistance in his power for the elucidation of an affair that has been buried in obscurity for so many years, and by which, without the smallest shadow of reason, justice, or equity, the larger part of the inhabitants of the town and parishioners of the said church of St Nicholas are excluded from a participation of the before mentioned privilege, which they undoubtedly have and ought to exercise for the presentation of a warden and vicars for the government of the said church.

Upon that presumption I have committed the following thoughts to paper, without the smallest intention of giving offence, for there are many individuals amongst the tribes for whom I have the greatest respect, and whose minds I am convinced are not narrowed by idle and vulgar prejudices, but enlarged by the tolerant and enlightened ideas of the age we live in. As some of the other inhabitants of Galway only behold the hardships and other oppressive circumstances of their situations, without making any particular enquiries into the merits of the case, some little explanation may be necessary to show them where the grievance lies, and if possible to do away a distinction so odious and disagreeable in itself, the bane of all society and connation amongst the inhabitants of the same place, and to bring them upon that equality with each other, which was the original institution of Pope Innocent VIII. when he constituted Galway with a wardenship; but we must first recur to whatever knowledge may exist relative and prior to that institution. Galway was built about the year 1300, by a colony of Englishmen, whose descendants at this day go by the name of the thirteen tribes of Galway, to distinguish them from the posterity of the other inhabitants of this county, but we have no account of its being erected into a wardenship until the year 1484; before that time (as is manifest by a Bull granted in the said year by the abovementioned Pope Innocent) it was commonly governed by vicars, but how they were elected or constituted does not appear, nor is it necessary for the present; however it is evident that a petition in behalf of that part of the parishioners living within the walk of the town was transmitted to the Pope, in which the petitioners took every care to represent themselves as modest and moral people, and to paint the inhabitants of the country near the town in the most dreadful and barbarous colours, as "A parcel of savages, brought up in woods and mountains, unpolished and illiterate; that they were disturbed in exercising the divine duties of their religion, according to the English decency, right, and, custom by those barbarians; that they were often robbed and murdered by them; that their lives were always in danger, and that they were likely to suffer many other losses and inconveniences for the future if not speedily succoured by the Court of Rome. That they had made an application to the Archbishop of Tuam, who commiserating their deplorable condition, had by his own proper authority erected the said church of St. Nicholas into a Collegiate, to be governed by a warden and vicars, who must be all learned, pious, and well bred men, and should be presented for institution to each other by the corporation of the town, or mayor, bailiff, and their equals, &c. The prayer of their petition was that his holiness would graciously confirm the said constitution of the Archbishop with his apostolic power, and protect them from the dangers those savages above mentioned threatened them with, in respect to the privilege of electing the said warden and vicars."

In consequence of a petition so speciously and pathetically put together, Pope Innocent VIII was pleased to grant a Bull, dated the sixth of the ides of February, in the year 1484, in which he confirms the continuation of the said Church of St. Nicholas into a collegiate church, to be governed by a warden and eight vicars, who must be moral, well bred, and virtuous men; and to follow the English decency rite and customs in celebrating the divine mysteries of their religion. He confirms the right of presentation to the corporation of Galway, or to the mayor, bailiffs, or sheriffs, and their equals, for ever, or in the words of the Bull, "Superiori proposito, sive majori, ballivis, et paribus dictae villae." The petitioners are styled in it, "Dilectorum filiorum universorum parochianorum parochialis ecclesiae St Nicolai villae Galviae," or "Our beloved children, all the parishioners of the parish Church of St Nicholas, of the village of Galway." And the people who by it are deprived of the right of franchise, are called in one part of the Bull" Montani et Sylvestres homines," men who live in woods and mountains, and in another place "indocti illiterate." Only for the democratical word "universorum," the thirteen tribes might boast that they were the only favourites of the Pope, and we might now find a curious aristocracy in the town, embodied and enabled by a patent granted 300 years ago in Rome; but unfortunately the word is of such a comprehensive signification as to prove that the Bull was granted at the request of the whole, and not of a part of the parishioners of St Nicholas, without any distinction or compliment being paid to any particular names, tribes, or families. It appears that the right of presentation was settled with the mayor, sheriffs, and their equals, who I conceive to be the common councilmen of the town; and the corporation of the town, consisting of the said mayor, sheriffs, bailiffs, &c. I consider to be the bulwarks by which the inhabitants were to be protected from encroachments of their troublesome neighhours; the people proscribed by the Boll are a parcel of savages without learning or education, who were brought up like wild beasts in the woods and mountains, supporting themselves by rapine, plunder and robbery, living on the prey they forcibly carried away from the people of Galway. In short they are represented in a greater state of barbarity than the Indians of North America, only they had not refined in cruelty so much as to scalp their unfortunate victims, and finish by devouring them like cannibals. However, certain it is that the Bull, in no particular part, makes the smallest mention of granting the privilege of presenting a warden or vicar to any particular name, tribe, or family, or any particular description of men whatsoever (the mayor, bailiffs, and their equals excepted). It does not even mention them at all except by the word "Pares," which in my opinion signifies equals. — The Pope meant the thirteen tribes of Galway, as I have heard very humoursly remarked.

But those advocates of the dignity of the thirteen tribes contend that their ancestors have been the original inhabitants of Galway, and that by right of inheritance they and no other are entitled to derive a privilege from any grant made in favor of their predecessors. Allowing them to be the Aborigines of the town, does it follow that those other names or families who since settled in Galway are entitled to no other privilege but that of occasional visitors? It cannot. They settled in it with their families and fortunes, they made it their place of residence and abode, and though they may not boast of the same antiquity in the town, its being a place of residence for themselves and successors for many generations, gives them a claim to the rights of naturalization. Will those advocates far the thirteen tribes candidly declare, if on their first arrival in Ireland they were prevented from settling in it? If they were prevented from sharing the liberties, privileges, and immunities of Irishmen, what would the consequence be, what would they do? Resort to other countries, perhaps to different parts of the world, according to their different inclinations, and as the custom is with all adventurers, ramble from country to country, from clime to clime, until they discover a place that would answer their wants and conveniences.

But the Irish, noted all over the old world for past ages, for their hospitality, generosity, and goodness to strangers, opened an asylum to them in the bosom of their country, and granted them a place of settlement and rest. The return they made them since their settlement in Galway is a trait in their characters that cannot bear the test of scrutiny or inquiry. By a sort of *Pacta conventa* they have, for 800 years and upwards, deprived them of a participation of those privileges which they arrogate entirely to themselves without justice or equity, and settled so long in Ireland they must enjoy the rights of Irishmen, and still consider themselves as an English colony, endowed with privileges peculiar to themselves, and as a right inherent in their families. A person might reasonably imagine that their remaining so long as five or six centuries in a country, would make them the natural born children of that country; but though they have been born in it for generations innumerable, they still must have the title of an English colony, with the annexed privileges of the Pope. Had the descendants of the first colonists of North America still assumed the names of the countries they went from, we should find in the new world a regeneration of all the nations of Europe, France, Spain, Germany, Holland, Sweden, England, Ireland, Scotland, &c. &c. Like the Phoenix from her ashes would each rise in America, and the Americans, instead of being a united independent people a people who have enlightened the eyes of all Europe, would be different distinct nations following different customs, bound by different laws, similar to the usage of their mother countries, and subject to all the divisions and distractions of an unconnected people. All those people that ever left one country and settled in another have become subjects to the country they settled in, and their posterity considered themselves as natural born subjects to it. Can the thirteen tribes show any exclusive right to the privilege of electing the clergy of the collegiate church of St. Nicholas? None, but a right of usurpation; they affirm it has remained in possession of their families time immemorial, that there has been an uninterrupted succession of clergy presented by their ancestors, and handed down inviolable to them; that their title before the present time has never been disputed, nor can the prejudiced part of them hear with any degree of patience any attempt made at what they term encroachment or innovation. "A long habit of not thinking a thing wrong gives it a superficial appearance of being right, and raises at first a formidable outcry in defence of custom; but the tumult soon subsides; time makes more converts than reason." —

Introduction to a pamphlet called *Common Sense*, published in Philadelphia in the year 1776.

The tribes are for many years in the above habit of thinking; it is the cause of their outcry against breaking through a privilege they imagine sanctioned by time and possession. Allowing them that possession since Galway was constituted into a wardenship, can that justify their exclusive title? In law I grant it may; limitation would then be in their favour, but in justice or equity it cannot; for I say that no limitation or presumption can justify what is wrong. They will appeal to the people in general whether the clergy they have at all times heretofore presented were not proper persons to fulfill the duties of their station; but that has nothing to do with the question; it is only declaration or affirmation on their side that they are more enlightened, and endued with a more particular share of grace, and know the pastors competent to preside over the church, direct their consciences, and take care of the people's souls better than the people do themselves. It is saying we are a body in ourselves, we are as one family, though of thirteen different names; we will make a monopoly of the church livings to ourselves, and when there is a child belonging to any of us, or of any of the name all over the world in orders, we are determined, be their qualifications what they may, they must be vicars of St Nicholas, to the total exclusion of any other names or families, whom we consider as so many strangers crept in among us, and as the descendants of those dangerous people who put our ancestors to so much trouble. Do the tribes of the present day consider the other inhabitants of the town to be such barbarians as their ancestors represented the former inhabitants of those parts to be to Innocent VIII? Do they imagine that they are mountaineers, wood rangers, or illiterate savages? They cannot. They know them to be a civilized people, as well acquainted with literature, as they are themselves. They know them to be a moral, industrious, and commercial people, rising into consequence before their eyes, and enriching the town with the rewards and blessings of industry and commerce. Some of the tribes behold it with eyes askew, and view their increasing prosperity with pain, malevolence and envy. But the day is nearly arrived that will do away every distinction. Tribes, tribunes, grumblers, and the discontented party of every description, will rank under the common title of fellow citizens. Distinctions so trifling, and all narrow and vulgar prejudices, shall sink into oblivion, to rise no more. We shall not behold the children of the brother and sister lose the ties of blood, kindred, and relationship, on account of such distinctions, and be as aliens or strangers to each other: Nature has made them cousins, but by a strange perversion of the intentions of God, Nature and the Church, the only cousins allowed a claim to relationship in Galway are the descendants of the thirteen families called tribes, — no matter if the degrees of kindred be as distant as the Poles; if the blood of their families has not been mixed or connected since the commencement of the Christian era, the name gives them a sufficient title, let them be born where they may, they are kindred souls to their Galway name sakes. Male and female are the distinctions of Nature; good and bad the distinctions of Heaven: but how a race of men, neither extraordinary in their size, endowed with no particular marks to distinguish them from their fellow creatures, should be so exalted above their contemporaries, is a matter that cannot be properly explained, and is well worthy of inquiry. There have been twelve tribes in Israel, who are scattered as children of wrath all over the world; after their dispersion, thirteen must be found in Galway, but how formed or embodied, is a question beyond my comprehension. I cannot think that the thirteen originals of those names were the children of one father, and that the thirteen names or tribes, are the descendants of those thirteen children. However, if not ashamed of humanity, they must positively be the descendants of Adam, and as such cannot pretend to be of a superior race of beings, endowed with any superior faculties; in fine, cannot have more sensibility, feelings, or rational qualifications than their fellow creatures.

Inthe beginning of the present controversy I heard some of the people, who now raise a great outcry against innovation, declare that their pretensions to those privileges were as strong and as well founded as a man's title to his family estate; that those privileges were purchased from his Holiness the Pope at a very great price, with the money of their ancestors, and that those people who require participation of those privileges with them, may put in as just and legal a claim to their properties. It is a charge on the Holy See that I shall not take upon me to justify; it is something akin to simony: it is besides selling the rights and privileges of unborn generations, and though not equally profitable with the sale of indulgencies, the trade is equally bad. It is an acknowledgment on our side of our being popish property, and when we consent that the Pope shall sell our liberties or privileges, the next thing he may attempt is to sell our persons and properties; the sale of one is as justifiable as a sale of the other; it is like what politicians in this kingdom call a sale of peerages; it is forming an hierarchy or church aristocracy in Galway; it is an encouragement to disputes, controversies, and civil distinctions; it is an encouragement to the spirit of contradiction, malevolence, and ill will; it is forming parties more detestable to each other than the Whigs and Tories of England, the Guelphs or Gibellines of Florence, or caps and hats of Sweden. But if those prejudiced people of the thirteen tribes who reproach the other inhabitants of the town with the vices, improprieties, or irregularities of the ancient possessors of the neighbourhood, consider but for a moment on the impropriety of such conduct, I am convinced they will for the future drop it. The crimes of former ages are not to reflect dishonour on the people of the present day. The customs or manners of ancient Britons may appear detest able now, and I believe that the thirteen tribes of Galway would not be at all pleased if they were to be censured for those customs I mention of the Britons, be cause they were the predecessors of the English colony that settled in this country. Julius Caesar in his commentaries gives the following description of the inhabitants of ancient Britain: — at the time of his invasion the interior parts of Britain were inhabited by people born in the country; the sea coast is inhabited by those who past over there from Belgium, with the intention of waging war and plundering the inhabitants, and they were generally called by the names of those states in which they lived, before they passed over into Britain, and when they had finished the war they remained in and began to cultivate that part of the country which they had conquered; and describing the inhabitants of the inland country, he says, most of the inland inhabitants sow no corn, but live on milk and flesh, and are clad with the skins of wild beasts; but all the Britons stain their skins with wood, which gives them a bluish colour, and makes them look more horrible in war; they all have long hair, and shave every part of their body but the head and upper lip; ten or twelve of them have their wives in common, but more particularly the brothers and fathers and sons; the offspring of such connections were considered to be the children of those who, first deprived the females of their Virginity. — I am convinced that the thirteen tribes of Galway are descended from them, for the custom of shaving the upper lip was introduced by them into this country, and was preserved in Galway for many years after the building of the town. Let those people who consider the present inhabitants of the town (lately dignified with the titles of Tribunes or Grumblers) to be the posterity of the mountaineers, plunderers, and murderers mentioned in the Bull of Pope Innocent VIII, but reflect for a moment on the above passage in Caesar, and I am sure they cannot object the crime of the ancient in habitants of this neighbourhood to the people of the present day. The characters of the ancients, in general, seem barbarous to those of the present age, and man kind more enlightened behold with hatred and detestation their barbarity, at the same time that they feel for, compassionate, and pity their savage customs, ferociousness, and ignorance; an ignorance the more deplorable, as it made them guilty of crimes which the custom of the times and the laws of the country they lived in sanctioned, privileged, and made habitual and honorable to them, instead of branding them with any degree of obloquy, detestation, or dishonour. My intention for mentioning the passage from Caesar, descriptive of the customs of the Britons, is by no means to offend any person who boasts of being descended from the English colony who settled in Galway with the barbarity, or with the horrid and incestuous customs of the ancient inhabitants of Britain; my reason for it was to rescue the memories of the ancient Irish from an imputation of being more wild, immoral, nd uncivilised than their neighbours Of the sister kingdom.

Upbraiding people with the crimes or misfortunes of their ancestors is unmanly, ungenerous, uncharitable, and scandalous retaliations are generally the offsprings of poor, vulgar, and narrow minds.

But to return to the dispute in question. Allowing that the thirteen tribes were the only inhabitants of Galway in the year 1484, and that it was at their request the Pope granted the present disputed privilege to the corporation of Galway, and that forever, does it follow that if they were scattered all over the world as the children of Israel, that they are the still existing corporation of Galway? The people unfortunately could not see so far into futurity as to consider them to be the only parishioners of St. Nicholas, nor keep them within the walls of the town shut up like a sorcerer in a magic circle; or does it follow that if any other persons of different names or families should at any time afterwards take up their residence in Galway, that they are not allowed to share in the privilege annexed to the inhabitants of the town. The laws of proscription or possession may determine that case in favor of the possessors, but the laws of God are most forcible against them. Considering all the other inhabitants in the light of neighbours, do not the commandments of Christ order us to love our neighbour as ourselves? — St. Mark, chap. xii. ver. 31. And the second is like, namely this, "Thou shalt love thy neighbour as thy self." In chap. xvi. ver. 3I, of St Paul to the Romans, we are desired to receive one another as Christ also received us to the glory of God; and considering them in the light of strangers, does not the Almighty, in the laws laid down for the instruction of the Israelites, speak most emphatically in favour of strangers? I shall mention some passages in holy writ to prove the validity of my assertion. Exodus, chap. xxii. ver. 21," Thou shalt neither vex a stranger nor oppress him, for ye were strangers in the land of Egypt" Also, "Thou shalt not oppress a stranger, for ye know the heart of a stranger, seeing ye were stranger in the land of Egypt" Exodus, chap, xxiii. ver. 9," And if a stranger sojourn with thee in your land, ye shall not vex him; but the stranger that dwelleth with you shall be unto you as one born amongst you, and thou shalt love him as thy self, for ye were strangers in the land of Egypt: I am the Lord your God." Leviticus, chap. xix. verses 33 and 34. "And if a stranger sojourn with you, or whosoever be among you in your generations, and will offer offering made by fire of a sweet savour unto the Lord, as ye do so he shall do." Numbers, chap. xiii. ver. 14. "One ordinance shall be both for you of the congregation, and also for the stranger that sojourneth with you, an ordnance for ever in your generations, as ye are, so shall the stranger be before the Lord. Numbers, chap. xiii. ver. 15. "One law and one manner shall be for you and the stranger that sojourneth with you." Numbers, chap. xiii. ver. 16. "And it shall be forgiven all the congregation of the children of Israel, and the stranger that sojourneth among them, seeing all the people were in ignorance." "You shall have one law for him that sinneth through ignorance, both for him that is born among the children of Israel and for the stranger that sojourneth among them." "But the soul that doeth aught presumptuously, (whether he be born in the land or a stranger,) the same reproacheth the lord, and that soul shall be cut off from among his people." Numbers, chap. xv. verses 26, 29, and 30. "Thou shalt not oppress an hired servant that is poof and needy, whether they be of thy brethren or of thy stranger that are in thy land within thy gates." "Thou shalt not pervert the judgment of the stranger nor of the fatherless, nor take a widow's raiment in pledge." Deuteronomy, chap. xxiv. verses 14 & 17. "Cursed be he that perverteth the judgment of the stranger, fatherless, and widow, and all the people shall say Amen," chap, xxvii. ver. 19." Gather the people together, men and women and children, and the stranger that is within thy gates, that they may learn and fear the Lord your God, and observe to do all the words of this law:" chap. xxxi. ver.12.

Had the Bull of 1484 been in favor of the thirteen tribes of Galway, had their names and families been particularly mentioned in it, the above passages taken from the Old Testament would be an evident contradiction to the authority of his holiness the Pope, or in other words, the Pope would act in direct opposition to the law of God.

Some learned caviller may say that these laws were made for the instruction of the Israelites, but not at all intended as a line of conduct for the observation of the thirteen tribes of Galway; but it is as easy and as just to say that the ten commandments given on Mount Sinai to Moses were not intended for them, and that is equally a matter of choice with them to observe or reject them in toto. I am sure the Pope was too well read in the sacred writings to form such an opinion himself, nor would he wish it should be the opinion of those he flattered with the title of "dearly beloved children". Any person who wishes to know how the warden and vicars had been elected for upwards of two hundred years after the Bull of 1484, by referring to the corporation books of the town shall find that the privilege of presenting them for institution was exercised by the corporation. They will not find them presented by the tribes as a right inherent in their families, but by the mayor, sheriffs, and freemen, or burgesses of the town, as a privilege annexed to their corporate body. While the tribes declare that the offices abovementioned were all centered in their families, but by the said corporation books it appears that there have been other names in the years prior to, at, and subsequent to the revolution of the corporation of Galway, that persons of other names and families exercised the privilege of presenting the clergy of the collegiate church of St. Nicholas; while it also is apparent that people of the thirteen names were not free of the town, for their petitions to the corporation of the town, praying for their freedom, are to be seen in the books above mentioned. Will any man assert that the tribes are the corporation of the town at this time? I know it would show such an absurdity that (though they may consider themselves the hereditary corporation) they will not venture to make the assertion. If they are not, on what principle do they assume a privilege annexed to it? Some of them say that the corporation, by renouncing the errors of the catholic church, have abdicated all pretensions to the privilege in dispute. I cannot imagine that by changing their religious opinions they resign any civil rights, and whilst they exercised the right in question without detriment to the catholic church, how ought they to be deprived of it? They must be deprived of it at any rate, and another set of people must become a body corporate for no other reason but to usurp a privilege to which they had no exclusive title, to the detriment of their fellow townsmen. What difference would it make to the people whether the tribes or protestant corporation elected the warden and vicars above mentioned? — The greatest. For whilst the corporation elected them, and let proper persons to preside over the church, they only exercised a right annexed or granted to them by the Pope, at the same time as a body corporate their actions are the less disgusting; but the exercise of it by the tribes is making a discrimination, and insultive to their under standings. If the corporation of Galway at present be composed of the established religion of the country, and that the Pope considered them as having no title to the privilege in question, was it not easy for him to issue another Bull, by which he could deprive diem of it, and settle it in any other body or description of men he pleased? But that has not been ever done, and the right, of consequence, has remained in the corporation, till they lately surrendered it up in as foil and ample a manner as they possibly could to the other inhabitants of the town, who claimed it from them, and began to look for that privilege to which they had as good a right and title as the thirteen tribes. In the year 1735, there was a second Bull issued at Rome by Urban VIII. then Pope, in consequence of a dispute about a privilege which the Archbishop of Tuam claimed in the wardenship. The parties were the Archbishop on the one part, and the clergy and people of Galway on the other. It is beyond a doubt, that in the year 1733, there were a great number of names and families living in the town besides the tribes, and if the people wished to consider the tribes as the people of the town, was it not as easy for him to mention the word *tribes*, or thirteen names of Galway, as the word *people*, which comprehends all names and families. If he did it would prevent a dispute between them who the people intended were; instead of that we find by the second Bull, that the first was pretended to be obtained at the request and for the benefit of the thirteen tribes, who might be the first inhabitants of the town; yet it is in the second Bull declared by the Archbishop then existing, that the first Bull never existed, and that if it did, it was surreptitiously obtained; there was no proof produced to support its authenticity, therefore I think that the word *people*, mentioned in the second Bull, destroys all the pretentions of the tribes. In the year 1733, it appears that a Rev. Mr. Bermingham was warden of Galway, but it is very surprising how he arrived at that dignity, as he could not be considered as one of the Galway families. Prior to that year Mr. Bermingham was parish priest of Bohermore, a parish belonging to the wardenship or collegiate church of St Nicholas, although he never was elected vicar of the town. But the above-mentioned dispute between the Archbishop of Tuam and the clergy and people of Galway, happening to arise at that time, at the same time that the other families of the town began to discover the impropriety of the tribes electing or presenting a warden and vicars to preside over them, the tribes in the first place, to stop the clamours of the people, gratified them by electing one who was considered to be of their party. In the second place they did it through a political motive, for Mr. Bermingham had a property which he mortgaged to defend the clergy and the town's people's privileges against what was considered the encroachments of the Archbishop. It was on that account, and not to please Mr. Bermingham, he was elected warden. I cannot say that there is another instance of a name different from the thirteen being warden of Galway. There are many instances of clergymen being deprived of the wardenship and vicarship, because they had the misfortune of being of other names. There is at present a clergyman in existence, and for upwards of twenty years in the service of the collegiate church of Galway, who was once proposed at an election for a vicar to fill a vacancy that happened at the time. The gentleman who proposed him, and the other who seconded his motion, declared that they had no intention in proposing him but the good of the church and the honor of their religion. But alas! he was rejected, not through any canonical faults, reasons or impediments, not in a blunt opposition to the proposers, but because his name was different from the thirteen tribes, and that they did not wish the name of a stranger should appear on the face of their books — to continue the blood of the Mirabels! Peace be to the shades of the honest men that proposed him, whose motives were so pious and religious, who preferred what was honourable to the service of the Almighty parent to all the selfish and paltry considerations of prejudice, intolerance, and family party. But that God, who was capable of seeing into their benevolent motives, is now rewarding them for their good intentions.

Another curious affair appears on all the elections of the clergy by the tribes. Any one of their name, be he from what part of the kingdom, nay, from what part of the world he may, if he appears in Galway at the time of election he has a right of franchise in consequence of his name; there is no other qualification necessary, neither property, rank, or fortune, his name alone is a sufficient title, and by this means are wardens and vicars elected in Galway. The greater part of the inhabitants of the town, let their respectability or consequence be ever so great, must patiently become spectators of an election in which people from different parts of the country, tribes by name, who have no interest in the conduct or behaviour of the clergy of the town — who never contribute to support or maintain them, who never contribute to keep our places of divine worship in repair, make their entry into the town with all the strut and parade of superior beings, and appoint clergy to preside over the people, who pocket the insult with the greatest humility, patience, and Christian resignation.

It is a most ridiculous absurdity to see a fellow well dressed, and his chin new reaped, a fellow who perhaps has seldom worn a tolerable coat in the country, but bedizened out for the occasion, come to town with his vote, whilst the man of property, wealth, or consequence in town, because he has not the honor to be of the thirteen names, is debarred a right to franchise, although be lives in the town, and gives his aid and assistance to support the warden and vicars of the tribes's appointment. What can be a greater inconsistency than for a people, a state, an empire, or government to raise supplies and send these supplies to the enemy that have declared open war against them, and are even in the very act of invasion. People may say that such inconsistency never existed, but I say it exists in the present instance, whilst those people who are looked upon as aliens or strangers, who are used worse than the most inveterate enemies of religion, are aiding, assisting, or contributing to the support of clergy appointed by persons the most of whom are in fact nothing but strangers. It is not many years ago since a perambulating country tailor, at an election in Galway, a creature that would remain in any country cabin whilst he could be employed, for few chose to trust their clothes out of their houses with him, passed his vote as one of the Galway names, whilst a very respectable merchant of the town's vote was rejected, because he wanted that title. On the late election we have seen the parish chapel crowded with strangers, appointing clergy for us; a few days after the doors have been contemptuously shut against us. It was the act of the vicars themselves at the request of the tribes, and whilst ever they consider themselves under obligations to them for the places they hold, their conduct will be much the same, it will be always influenced by them. And when the people unanimously and spiritedly keep up to the resolutions they formerly made, they may think proper to alter their conduct. It is in the people's power to make their own terms, as the defenders of a besieged fortress are often starved into a capitulation it could be so done with them; withhold the supplies, as had been before determined, and the clergy may become neuter, at least they will not take the active, open, and decided part they do at present. They would not acknowledge those of the tribes who do not contribute to support them as their parishioners; but at present they seem to be the active interested party themselves, and though the dispute originated between the tribes and the people, the present contesting party are the clergy of Galway on the one part, and the people on the other. I address myself to the tribes with the following: — If at the time the Catholic Committee and other Catholic bodies in the kingdom petitioned Parliament for a repeal of the penal laws, or a relaxation of some part of them in their favor, they had been the legislative body of the nation, in what manner they would behave? They may say that they would act upon the most tolerant principles; any other answer from them would be inconsistent, for they have been petitioners themselves.

But their narrow, confined, and limited ideas relative to the question at present in debate about privileges, argues the contrary. People that refuse a participation of the elective franchise for a warden and vicars for the government of the church of Galway would most undoubtedly refuse a right of franchises to their fellow subjects for returning members to serve in the grand inquest of the nation. If they could have the government of the kingdom in general in their possession, it would be no easy matter to wrest any privilege from them when they make such a difficulty of surrendering to their fellow townsmen a privilege trifling in itself, only for the curious distinctions it makes between them. But the people have the means of redress in their own power, and if they do not redress themselves, every future election for a warden or vicars will bring to their recollection their own littleness and insignificance.

They have discovered where the grievance lies, they have found out the seat of the distemper, and may with the more safety apply the remedy. There is no use in protraction, whatever is to be done let it be speedily determined on; the controverted affair must be settled one time or other, and the sooner the better. If it is properly determined now it will be serving posterity, it %ill be only recovering for them a right neglected by oar forefathers. They were, through necessity, obliged tamely to suffer it to be exercised by a few of the tribes in the late persecuting and intolerant times, who privately withdraw into holes and corners to elect their clergy, whilst they, not wishing to arrest the notice of persecutors or fanaticism, bore it in silence. Those days are now, thank God and a mild legislature, passed away, and at the same time that we behave like peaceable and thankful subjects for the favors we have received from government, let us not passively submit to have a civil right usurped from us by the few of our fellow citizens who are called tribes. *Rari apparent nantes in gurgite vasto*.— Virgil.[1] If ye neglect it now ye leave the work to be done by posterity, (for one time or other the distinction must be done away,) and they will blame their predecessors who neglected to complete a business they have began with such good auspices, and for handing down to them the trouble of rescuing themselves from the scandal and disgrace caused by such idle, vulgar, and insignificant distinctions.

Any person that can give a greater elucidation to this subject, owes it to whatever party he is attached, if there be such a person, (and I am confident there is, and many of them on both sides,) he ought to publish his opinions either for or against the right of patronage inhabitants in general, without respect to persons' names or families, have to the presentation of their clergy; for I am sure that if any of the right is exclusively in them, according to the bulls and charters of the town, it would be a great means of reconciling differences, though it could never satisfy the non-tribes that they ought to be excluded from an equal participation of rights and privileges in the town wherein they appear to be suffering or aggrieved, as if in *limbo partum*[2], rather than enjoying the equal liberties of their fellow subjects *interna partum*. There is a list of voters names for a warden annexed to the above, by which it appears that there were one hundred and twenty-nine for the Rev. John Joyce, and forty-four for the Reverend Patrick Kirwan; it consists mostly of those gentlemen living several miles from Galway, some in Loughrea, Castlebar, and other parts of Mayo, &c. &c.

---

[1] "they appear thinly scattered and swimming in the vast deep" (i.e., brilliant thoughts are sometimes lost in an ocean of words), [Clachan ed.].
[2] *in limbo*, meaning *on the border*, as Limbo was imagined to form the borderland of Hell, [Clachan ed.].

POPE'S BULL

Innocent, Bishop

Servant of the Servants of God, &c.

We exercising the office of a watchful sentinel, as it is granted to us from above, over the Lord's flock, committed by the Divine Power to our vigilance, do willingly mind those things by which Divine Worship is augmented, and the salvation of souls is hoped to proceed from, and we cheerfully add the strength of our power to such measures as we have found out these providentially to have sprung from, to the end that they may last the firmer uncorrupted, by being the more strengthened, and for as much as a petition hath been lately preferred unto us on behalf of our beloved children, all the Parishioners of the Parish church of St Nicholas of the town of Galway and the diocese of Annadown, setting forth, that our venerable Brother Donatius, Archbishop of Tuam, who is known to be Prelate of the See of Annadown, perpetually united to the See of Tuam, has seriously considered some time ago, that the parishioners of the said church of St Nicholas were modest and civil people, and that they lived in the said town surrounded with walls, not following the custom of the mountainous and wild people of those parts; and that by reason of the impetration or provisions of the afore said mountainous and wild people to the vicarage of the said church of St Nicholas, commonly governed before by vicars, they were so much disturbed, that they could not assist at divine service, nor receive the holy sacrament, according to the English decency, rite, or custom, which the afore-said inhabitants and their ancestors always used, they being much disquieted therein, and sometimes robbed of their goods, and killed by those unlearned men, and likely to sustain many other damages and inconveniences, both in person and substance from them, and fearing to suffer more for the future if not speedily succoured. This matter being providentially considered, the said Donatius, at the humble request of the aforesaid parishioners, has constituted and created, by his proper authority, the aforesaid church of St. Nicholas into a collegiate, and therein a college of one warden and eight vicars, and for their support he hath applied the fruits, rents, and incomes of the said vicarage, and the half quarter which the incumbents of the said church of St Nicholas had been for a long time accustomed to have from our beloved children the abbot and convent of Knockmoy, of the Cistercian order, and diocese of Tuam, he has also appropriated to the capitular table of the said church of St. Nicholas, other good lands, rights, tithes, and services there expressed, which have been bestowed and offered to himself. And having providentially considered that the said premises were scarcely sufficient to support decently four of the said priests, it is his will that whatever any of the said parishioners might chance to bestow for the future, should belong in full right to the said church of St Nicholas; and he has likewise so united, annexed, and incorporated forever to the said church of St. Nicholas, the vicarage of the parish church of Ballinclare, (Clare-Galway,) of the said diocese of Annadown, by consent of his vicar thereof, for the sustenance of the warden and eight priests aforesaid, in the said church of St Nicholas. And by the same proper authority, the archbishop (as it is said to be more amply contained in certain authentic letters under his own seal) has ordered that the said church of St Nicholas, erected into a collegiate aforesaid, should be governed and ruled for the future, not by one vicar, but by the said eight priests or vicars, who ought to be virtuous, learned, and well bred men, and by one warden or custos, who all must rightly observe the English rite and custom in divine service; and he has likewise ordered that the said priest should be presented by the chief magistrate or mayor, bailiffs, and burgesses, or equals, of the common council of the aforesaid town to the aforesaid warden or custos, who is removeable every year at the presentation of the aforesaid superiors, or of the mayor and burgesses, and should be instituted by the said vicars. And the said warden being thus instituted, is to have power over all the said vicars and parishioners, and exercise the care of souls, wherefore there has been an humble address made unto us, on behalf of the aforesaid parishioners, that we might be pleased by our apostolical favor to add the authority of our confirmation, will, and ordination, to the end, therefore, they may exist more firmly, and that we might be further pleased to provide what may seem fit in relation to the premises. We, therefore, who love the advancement of the divine worship, and have been always willing that whoever would have ecclesiastical benefices united to others, should, among other things, tell the clear yearly value of the fruits, rents, and incomes of the benefices, for which no union should be made other wise, and that always in case of unions, matters should be made known to the parties concerned, as is observed in the confirmations of unions already made. We having an account of the true yearly value, of the fruits, rents, and incomes of the said vicarage of the said church of St. Nicholas and college thereof, and of the other donations and oblations, and of the manner of the last vacation of the said vicarages of the churches of St Nicholas and St James, and having before us expressly the tenor of the letters of the aforesaid erection, donation, application, appropriation, union, connection, and incorporation, ordination and will, and in regard to the aforesaid petition, We by our apostolical authority in virtue of these presents, do confirm and approve, and by force of this writing do strengthen the aforesaid creation, donation, application, appropriation, union, connection, incorporation, will, and ordination, and all and every thing contained in said letters; and we supply all and every defect, as well of law as of fact, and even of any other solemnity whatsoever omitted; and if any has happened therein, and for further security of the premise, we, by the aforesaid apostolical authority, do erect it *de novo* without prejudice to any other, the said church of St Nicholas into a Collegiate, and therein do appoint one wardenship, for one warden or custos, and eight perpetual vicarages for so many priests, who as head and members of the said Collegiate, do make a chapter, having privilege of a common seal, a chest or burse, a table and other Collegiate ornaments. We also forever unite, annex, and incorporate anew, the aforesaid vicarage of St. James, with all its rights and appurtenances, and all other fruits, rents, and incomes thereof, not exceeding the value of six marks sterling, according to the common estimation as the aforesaid parishioners allege, to the said church of St Nicholas, to whom the care of souls appertains; and though the vicarage of St. James should be vacant for so long a time, as that the collation thereof should lawfully devolve to the Apostolical See, according to the statutes of the Lateran council, it is especially reserved to the afore said church, and by the same authority. We appoint and order that the aforesaid church of St Nicholas, so erected into a Collegiate, according to the aforesaid ordination of the said Archbishop, be for the time to come, perpetually ruled and governed by eight priests, who must be learned, virtuous and well-bred men, and accustomed to the English rite and manner of divine service; and that the aforesaid priests be presented by the chief magistrate, or mayor, bailiffs and burgesses of the said town, to the aforesaid warden or custos for the time being, and that on the same presentation they may be instituted by the said warden, perpetual priests or vicars in the said college. But the aforesaid warden or custos, who is every year removeable, ought to be presented to the aforesaid priests or vicars by the said superior or mayor, and burgesses, and at the said presentation to be by the said priests or vicars instituted warden for that year in the said college; and the said warden, after having obtained his institution, should have during the year for which he is elected or instituted, power over all the said priests or vicars of the said church of St Nicholas, and over all the parishioners, and exercise the cure of souls of both the said priests and parishioners, without prejudice to the right of any other parishioner, or any other. We by the aforesaid authority, do grant forever, to the aforesaid chief magistrate or mayor, bailiffs and equals, of the said town, a right of patronage, and presenting the aforesaid priests to the warden, to be instituted vicars by him, and of presenting the warden to the priests or vicars to be instituted by them. And if any attempt happens to be made contrary to those, knowingly or ignorantly by any person of what authority soever. We from this time forth decree the same to be void and of no force, notwithstanding any other former will, or any other apostolical constitutions or ordinations to the contrary; and if any person that was to be provided for, has obtained special or general letters of the said See, or its legates, to this or the other annexed ecclesiastical benefices, and by the said letters proceeded to an inhibition, reservation, and decree, or otherwise, it is our will that the said letters, and the prosecutions made by them, be not from henceforth extended to the aforesaid united vicarages. But by this we would have no prejudice done to them, as to their obtaining other benefices, privileges, indulgencies, or any other apostolical letters, special or general, of whatsoever tenor they be, or that their effect may be any ways hindered, or deferred in relation to any other matter but what is expressed, or totally inserted in those presents, of which, and their tenor, a special recital may be found in our letters, provided by this union the church of St. James be not deprived of the due service, and the cure of souls be by no means neglected, but the accustomed charges thereof be graciously supported.

Let it not be lawful for any persons whatsoever, to break or by a rash boldness, oppose these letters of our confirmation, approbation, communication, application, union and connection, incorporation, institution, ordination, confession, decree and will; and if any one will presume to attempt it, let him know that he incurs the indignation of Almighty God, and of his blessed Apostles Peter and Paul.

Dated at Rome, at St Peter's, in the year of our Lord's incarnation 1484, the 6th of the ides of Fe bruary, and the first year of our popedom.

L. GRIFUS.

CHARTER GRANTED BY QUEEN ELIZABETH TO THE TOWN OF GALWAY.

ELIZABETH, by the grace of God, of England, France and Ireland Queen, defender of the faith, and so forth, to all unto whom these present letters shall come, greeting. We have inspected letters patent of our most dear brother, our Lord Edward VI. late king of England, to the mayor, bailiffs, burgesses, and commonalty of the town of Galway, in our kingdom of Ireland, the tenor whereof follows in these words:

EDWARD VI. by the grace of God, of England, France and Ireland King, defender of the faith, and of the Church of England supreme head on earth, to all unto whom these present letters shall come greeting. We have inspected into the letters patent of our Lord Henry the Eighth late King of England, our dearest father made in these words: Henry by the grace of God of England, France and Ireland King, Defender of the Faith, and of the Church of England and Ireland supreme head on earth, to all onto whom these present letters shall come greeting; Know ye, that whereas Lord Richard, late King of England, the second after the conquest, having taken it into consideration the town of Galway in Connaught, which is the key of those parts of his lands of Ireland (in which town all his faithful and loyal people, as well foreigners as others coming into the said parts, were received, saved, comforted and relieved) lay exposed as well to Irish enemies as English rebels on all sides, and the burgesses of said town and others dwelling therein, and coming thereunto, dare not without great conduct come to the said town either by land or by water, nor go out of the same to exercise merchandizing or other necessary affairs, and that the said burgesses, for the safe custody of the said town, have against the malice of the said enemies and rebels continually, by day and night, maintained and supported men for defence in the said town at their own proper cost, to the manifest impoverishment of their state, hath towards the assistance, relief, and comfort of the said town, that merchants and others may be the more encouraged and comforted to dwell and inhabit in the said town, for the better resistance of the malice of the said enemies and rebels; by his letters patent, dated at Dublin the 26th day of January in the 19th year of his reign, of his special grace granted and given license for him and his heirs, as much as in him lay, to the portrieve and common burgesses of the said town of Galway, that they and their heirs and successors, common burgesses therein, may from thenceforward, perpetually every year, from year to year, by their common consent among themselves, be able to choose one chief or sovereign, of the said town, and that the said chief or sovereign when he should by them be so chosen, viz. after the first election of chief before the said provost of the said town, should from thenceforward every year take his corporal oath before the chief or sovereign of said town, for the year last past, to rule and govern well and faithfully the said town, and to maintain the laws of the said late King and the good and usual and approved customs of the said town, and all other things whatsoever concerning the office of such chief or sovereign rightly, for the good government and profit of the said town; and he hath further granted for him, and his heirs to the said co-burgesses, their heirs and successors burgesses therein, that no merchant or other person whatsoever, whether foreign or native, of what state or condition so ever he should be, who continually residing in the said town, and as co-burgess of the said town should not be sworn to support and sustain from time to time all burthens in the said town, as the burgesses themselves would or should do within the liberty of the said town, by land or by water; buy nor sell any merchandize or victuals for retail after any manner whatsoever, except only in gross; and likewise that they, their heirs and successors fellow burgesses of the said town, from henceforth for ever freely have, enjoy, and use in the said town, and whosesoever the government, power, and dominion of the said late King should reach, all and singular such liberties, franchises, and jurisdictions, privileges, cognizances, pleas, customs, and free customs, as freely and quietly as the burgesses of his town of Drogheda, on both sides of the water, have hitherto enjoyed and used, and by their ancestors charters of confirmation, had or of right were accustomed to have so freely and quietly, and after the same manner as the said burgesses or town of Drogheda have used and enjoyed them, saving unto the lord of the town of Galway aforesaid, and unto his heirs, his and their rents, services, fine, amercements, issues, and other profits to him and them the lords of the said town, out of the said town and the commons thereof appertaining and belonging, and after such manner as they and their ancestors, lords of the said town, have more freely and quietly had, or of right were accustomed, ought and were wont to receive and enjoy them; and he hath like wise granted for him and his heirs to the said burgesses of the town of Galway, that also if they or their heirs or successors, burgesses of the said town, should upon any emergency whatsoever, from thenceforward, have abused or not used the liberties, franchises, jurisdictions, privileges, cognizances, customs, and free customs of the said town or any of them, that they may from thenceforth freely use and enjoy the liberties, franchises, jurisdictions, privileges, cognizances, customs, free customs aforesaid, without the impeachment or hindrance of him, his heirs, or ministers whatsoever, as in said letters is more fully contained. And whereas our said Lord, Richard II. late King of England, hath on the 18th day of November in the 19th year of his reign, (1396,) by other his letters patents to help the said town of Galway, which trade among divers enemies and rebels, both English and Irish, and being exposed to their daily assaults was reduced to great poverty, to be for the safety of his faithful people of the said town enclosed with a stone wall, and to help the paving of the said town granted to his beloved the portrieve, the bailiffs, sheriffs, communities, and corporation of the town of Galway, and to their successors, that they may by themselves, or by those who shall be by them thereto deputed, take for goods to be sold coming to the, or going from the said town by land or water, the customs or tolls under written, via,

for every pound of ginger to be sold, 1d.,
for every pound of saffron to be sold, 2d.;
for every pound of pepper to be sold, ¼d;

for every pound of galengale[1] to be sold, 1d;
for every pound of cloves to be sold, 1d.;
for every pound of grains of paradise to be sold, 1d.;
for all other sorts of spices of the value of twelve pence to be sold, ¼d.;
for one hundred pounds of wax to be sold, 6d.;
for one hundred pounds of allum to be sold, 3d.;
for every hyde tanned, fresh, green, or salted, and put or to be put into juice in the said town, or without as far as the island which is called Inniskeragh, ½d.;
for every pound of silk to be sold, 3d.;
for every piece of English cloth to be sold, 3d.; for every piece of Irish linen containing twelve yards, ½d.;
for every hundred of iron to be sold, 2d.;
for every bend of pieces of iron to be sold, 1d.; for every hundred sable skins to be sold, 1d.;
for one hundred stones of Spanish iron to be sold, 4d;
for every fuder of lead to be sold, 2d.; for one hundred pounds of ceruse[2], 1d.;
for a thousand nails spikeings to be sold, 1d.;
for every fayel or battery to be sold, 8d.;
for every great cauldron or grann to be sold, 4d.;
for every hundred of barley to be sold, 4d.;
for every tun of wine to be sold, 6d;
for every pipe of wine to be sold, 3d.;
for every short small curnock, four bushels, of malt to be sold, 1d;
for every capital large curnock of malt to be sold, 2d.;
for every ditto of wheat to be sold, 2d.;
for every sumage[3] horseload of blade, any sort of corn that grows in blade to be sold, ½d.;
for sumage of batery[4], 1d.;
for every lest or load of butter to be sold, 1d.;
for every stone of tallow to be sold, ½d.;
for every mease (500) of herrings to be sold, ½d.;
for every curnock of salt to be told, 1d.;
for every curnock of barley, bere, beens, and peas to be sold, 1d.;
for every curnock of oats and other corn to be sold, 1d.;
for every stone of wool to be sold, 1d.;
for every sack of wool to be sold, 4d.;
for every hyde tanned fresh or sallied to be sold, ½d.;
for all sorts of hydes of the value of twelve pence, and of other skins of shorlings to be sold, 1d.;
for one hundred wooled duns to be sold, 1d.;
for one hundred lamb skins to be sold, 2d.;
for the value of twelve pence of other skins, ¼d.;
for every horse worth forty shillings and upwards to be sold, 6d.;
for every plough horse or plough bullock, ox and cow to be sold, 1d. ,

---

[1] A root similar to ginger and used for the same purposes, [Clachan ed.].
[2] White lead used as pigment, [Clachan ed.].
[3] Toll for carriage on horseback, [Clachan ed.].
[4] Perhaps artillery and military equipment, [Clachan ed.].

for every calf to be sold, ¼d.;
for every large hog, 1d.;
for every sheep or goat to be sold, ½d.;
for every small hog or pig to be sold, ½d.;
for every hundred of rabbit skins, 2d.;
for one hundred skins of woolfells[1] to be told, 3d.;
for every horse load of fish to be sold, ½d.;
for one hundred dry fishes to be sold, 2d.;
for every salmon to be sold, ¼d.;
for every thousand eels and merlings to be sold, 1d.;
for every sort of timber, and also carts, chairs, and tables of the value of four shillings, 1d.;
for every falcon or hawk to be sold, 1d.;
for every tercil[2] or tercillet to be sold, ½d.;
for every mill quern[3], 1d.;
for two hand querns, ¼d.;
for twelve curnochs of coals to be sold, 1d.;
for every stone of butter* tallow* and cheese to be sold, ½d.;
for every tun of honey to be sold, 3d.;
for every pipe of salmon to be sold, 1s. 6d.;
for every hundred of glass to be sold, 1d.;
for every hundred of scollops, or other fish, salted dry, or hard, to be sold, 1d.;
for two thousand onions to be sold, 1d.;
for 8lb. hemp and flax to be sold, 1d.;
for every new chest or ark, and every 1000 dishes and platters of wood, ¼d.;
for 100 pounds of pitch or resell to be sold, one halfpenny!
for 100 gads of boards or planks to be told, one halfpenny;
of all torts of wares of the value of 12s. of which there is no mention made above one farthing;
for all wares of the value of 6s. 8d. to be sold, not expressed above, one half penny;
for all wares of the value of 13s. 4d. to be sold, likewise not mentioned before, 1d.

And therefore, the said portrieve shall command the bailiffs and corporation of the said town of Galway to cause and order the said customs and tolls, and every of them, to be from day to day levied, collected, received, and had in the said town in manner aforesaid; *provided always, that the money pence arising from thence be faith fully laid out towards the walling and paving the said town, and not otherwise,* as in the same letters is more fully contained, both which letters patent, and all grants in them contained, our Lord Henry, late King of England, our predecessor, hath by his letters patent, dated at Westminster the 12th day of March, in the third year of his reign, accepted, approved, and ratified, and hath granted and confirmed unto the aforesaid portrieve, bailiffs, sheriffs, burgesses, and corporation of the said town, as the said letters shall reasonably testify, and as the said portrieve, bailiffs, sheriffs,

---

[1] Skin of a sheep or similar animal with the fleece still attached, [Clachan ed.].
[2] tercil - a type peregrine falcon, [Clachan ed.].
[3] quern – stone for grinding corn etc. , [Clachan ed.].

burgesses, and corporation have always reasonably used and enjoyed, the liberties, franchises, jurisdictions, privileges, cognizances, custom and free customs aforesaid, as in the said letters of confirmation is likewise more fully contained; And whereas afterwards our Lord Edward the Fourth, our grandfather, late King of England, hath by his letters patent, dated at Woodstock the 28th day of August, in the fourth year of his reign, accepted, approved, ratified and granted, and confirmed unto the said chief magistrate, bailiffs, burgesses, and corporation of the said town of Galway, and their successors, all and singular the letters patent aforesaid, and all and singular in them contained and hath also pardoned, remitted, and released unto them all, and all manner of actions and demands which appertain or may appertain unto him, our said grandfather, against the said then chief magistrate, bailiffs and corporation, or their successors, upon account of the premises, or any of them; and he hath further, for the greater security of them the then chief magistrate, bailiffs, burgesses, and corporation of the said town of Galway, and their successors aforesaid, of his more bountiful grace granted unto them, that they and their successors may have all and singular the said customs and tolls in said letters patent, dated the 18th day of Nov. aforesaid, specified to the said chief magistrate, bailiffs, and corporation, granted as is aforesaid, concerning goods to be sold coming into or passing from said town of Galway by land or by water, by themselves or their servants, for that purpose to be deputed herein, from time to time, to take, receive, levy, have, and raise freely, quietly, well and peaceably for ever, without the impeachment, impediment, contradiction of his heirs or other his officers or ministers whatsoever; *provided always, that the money pence from thence arising be lend out in the walling and paving of the said town,* and not elsewhere, as is afore said; and further, for the greater security and safeguard of our said town, our said Lord Edward, our grand father, hath willed and ordained that no power of what state, degree, or condition soever, his lieutenant and chancellor of our said land only excepted, should after any manner whatsoever enter into our said town but by the licenses and consent of said chief magistrate, bailiffs, and corporation of said town, as in said letters of confirmation of our grandfather is likewise more fully contained. And whereas afterwards Richard the Third, late King of England, by his letters patent, dated at Westminster, the 15 th day of December, in the second year of his reign, having previous confederation, and that the said town of Galway might the better resist the enemies and rebels aforesaid, of his special grace ratifying and agreeing to all and singular the letters patent above mentioned, and all and singular in them contained, hath for him and his heirs, as much as in him lay, accepted, approved, and ratified, and hath to the then chief magistrate, bailiffs, and burgesses, and corporation of the said town, confined all and manner of actions and demands, and hath pardoned, remitted, and released unto them all that which doth or may appertain unto him the said King Richard against the said chief magistrate, bailiffs, burgesses, corporation, and their successors, upon account of the premises, or any of them; and he hath further, for the greater security of the then chief magistrates, bailiffs of said town, and their successors aforesaid, of his greater grace granted that they and their successors may have all and singular the said customs and tolls in said letters patent of the 18th day of Nov. aforesaid to the chief magistrate, bailiffs, burgesses, and corporation granted and aforesaid specified, concerning goods to be coming into or passing from said town of Galway by land or by water, by themselves or by their servants for that purpose, to be deputed herein, from time to time, to take, receive, levy, have and raise, freely, quietly, well and peaceably for ever, without the impeachment or contradiction of him the King, his heirs or ministers whatever; provided always, the pence money from thence arising be laid out on the murage and paveage of said town, and not elsewhere, as aforesaid; and further, for the greater security and safeguard of the town of Galway aforesaid, the late King hath willed and ordained, and by his said letters patent given and granted licence unto the chief magistrate, sovereign, portrieve, bailiffs, and corporation of said town of Galway, that they may yearly for ever, by their common consent, choose one mayor and two bailiffs, sheriffs, within the said town of Galway, as is accustomed to be done in the town of Bristol, for to rule and govern well and laudably the said town of Galway, and the laws and good customs therein, anciently used and approved, to maintain and administer in all things as becometh; and also for the greater security and safeguard of the said town of Galway, he hath willed and ordained that no one of what state, degree, or condition soever he should be, for the future, in any manner whatsoever, enter the said town of Galway except by the license and consent of said mayor, sheriffs and corporation of said town: besides of greater grace, and for the greater security and safeguard of said town of Galway, he hath willed and ordained, and hath for him and his heirs as much as in him lay granted, that from thenceforth that neither lord M'William of Clanricard, nor his heirs, should have any government or power within the said town of Galway to act, perceive, exact, ordain or dispose of any thing therein, by land or by water, in asmuch as he, the said lord and his predecessors were anciently accustomed to receive and exact, without the special license, and by the consent and survizal [sic?] of the mayor, sheriffs, and corporation of said town of Galway, unto whom he hath given, granted, and attributed plenary power and authority to rule and govern said town well and laudably in all things as becometh, as in his said letters patent is more fully contained: and we likewise considering the premises as for the assistance and relief of our town of Galway aforesaid, that merchants and others may be the more encouraged to inhabit and dwell in said town, and be he better enabled to resist the malice of all enemies and rebels whatsoever, and especially of other ports, of our special grace, ratifying and approving of all and singular the letters patent above recited, and all and singular in them contained, do for us, our heirs and successors, as much as in us lyeth, accept, approve, and ratify them, and now do, by the tenor of these presents give, grant, and confirm unto the mayor, sheriffs, burgesses and corporation of said town of Galway, their heirs and successors, and have pardoned, remitted and released, and by these presents do pardon, remit and release unto them and every of them all and all manner of actions and demands, and all and every thing which did or may appertain to us against the said mayor, sheriffs, burgesses and corporation, or any of them, their or any of their heirs or successors, by reason or upon account of the premises, or any of them; and further, for the greater security of said mayors sheriffs, burgesses and corporation of our town of Galway aforesaid, their said heirs and successors, we do of our further grace, certain knowledge, and mere motion, give and grant unto the said mayors, sheriffs, burgesses and corporation, their heirs and successors, all and singular the liberties, franchises, customs, advantages, profits, things tollable, and all other things whatsoever, or any of them notwithstanding; we have likewise granted, and do by these presents give and grant unto the said mayor, sheriffs, burgesses and corporation, our port of Galway aforesaid, and the bay or arm of the sea which enters between the islands of Arran, and from thence runs or flows into our town of Galway aforesaid; and that all ships and boats which enter the port, bay, or arm aforesaid, whether loading or unloading at our town of Galway aforesaid, and no where else within the port, bay, or arm aforesaid, in any land adjacent, or being nigh the bay or arm, or any water or rivulet running into, or from said bay or arm; and that the said burgesses and corporation, and their heirs and successors for ever, to be eased of the toll, lastage[1], passage, portage, murage, pavage, poundage, and all other customs throughout all our kingdoms and powers; and that every mayor of said town to be elected for the future, shall effectually take and perform the oath accustomed to be taken in that office before that person who hath been next before him in the office of mayor of the said town, or before two others who have before bore that office of the said town; and that no person or persons who shall for the future import wines in any ship or boat to the quay or port of Galway aforesaid, and there unload the said wines, shall not pay prizage for said wines, because prizage hath not hitherto been accustomed to be paid there; and that no merchant or merchants, foreign or native, who shall import into, or unload, or export from, or load at the said town, or the port or quay of the said town, any merchandizes or wares, shall pay any custom, poundage or tonnage, nor any other thing for the said wares or merchandizes, except such customs, poundage or tonnage, as were mentioned to be paid there in times past for such merchandizes or wares; and that the said mayor, sheriffs, burgesses, and corporation of said town, their heirs and successors, and every of them, shall and may load and transport whithersoever they shall please, all and all manner of merchandizes and wares, as well staple as otherwise, (woollen and linen only excepted), any statute, act or ordinance to the contrary hereof made notwithstanding: we have moreover granted, and do by these presents give and grant to the said mayor, sheriffs, burgesses and corporation of our town of Galway aforesaid, to their heirs and successors, and every of them, all and singular such liberties, uses, jurisdictions, privileges, customs, cognizances and pleas, as the mayor, sheriffs burgesses and corporation of ear town of Drogheda, on both sides of the water in our kingdom of Ireland aforesaid, have or have had, or reasonably used and enjoyed, as freely and quietly, and after the same manner as the said mayor, sheriffs, burgesses

---

[1] A duty exacted, in fairs or markets, for the right to carry things where one will, [Clachan ed.].

and corporation of our said town of Drogheda have used and enjoyed them, without the impeachment, occasion, disturbance, molestation, hindrance or grievance of us, our heirs or successors, or of the lieutenant or deputies of our kingdom of Ireland aforesaid, of our justices, sheriffs, executors, coroners, seneschals[1], bailiffs, or other ministers or officers of us, our heirs or successors whatsoever, or any other whatsoever, saving to us and our heirs the rents, fees, farms, services, amercements, issues and other profits to us and our ancestors lords of the town, oat of the said town and county thereof issuing, belonging, or appertaining, as we and our ancestors lords of said town have freely and quietly, or of right ought and were accustomed to have claimed them; saving likewise to us, our heirs and successors, the custom of every castage of cockets[2] in the port of said town, which is called the cocket, which we have, or of right ought to have received the same; saving likewise to the portriere or burgesses of the town of Athenry, and their successors in our said town of Galway and port thereof, and all and singular such liberties, franchises, and privileges as the said portrieve and burgesses of Athenry aforesaid, or any one or more of them were accustomed or were used to have in times past in oar said town of Galway, or in the port thereof, these our letters patent, nor any thing in them contained, specified in any wise notwithstand, and that express mention of the true yearly value, or any other value, or of the certainty of the premises or any of them, or of other gifts or grants made by us or by any of our progenitors or predecessors to said mayor, sheriffs, burgesses, and corporation of Galway aforesaid, or to any of them before these times, is not made in or by these presents, or any statute, act or ordinance, provision or restriction to the contrary made, published, ordained, or provided, or any other thing, cause, or matter whatsoever in any wise notwithstanding. In witness whereof we have caused these our letters patent to be passed, witness myself at Westminster, the third day of July, the 36th of year of our reign; and we ratifying and approving the said letters, and all and singular in them contained, do for us and our heirs, as much as in us lieth, accept and approve them, and they are by the tenor of these presents ratified and confirmed unto our beloved the present mayor, sheriffs, burgesses, and corporation of Galway aforesaid, and their successors of the said town, as the said letters do reasonably testify.

In witness whereof we have caused these our letters patent to be passed for us and our heirs, witness myself at Westminster, the 18th day of November, in the third year of our reign. Know ye that we, of our special grace, certain knowledge, and mere motion, have given, granted, confirmed, ratified, and approved, and as by these present letters patent for us, our heirs and successors, as much as in us lyeth, give, grant, confirm, ratify, and approve unto Peter Lynch, now mayor of our said town of Galway in our said kingdom of Ireland, to John Blake and Francis Martin, now

---

[1] An officer in the houses of important nobles in charge of domestic arrangements and the administration of servants, [Clachan ed.],
[2] A customhouse seal; a certified document given to a shipper as a warrant that his goods have been duly entered and have paid duty, [Clachan ed.],

sheriffs of our said town of Galway, to the burgesses and corporation of said town and their successors for ever, by what name or names soever of corporation or corporations, or other name, they or any of them is, are, or shall ever, or at any other time, be incorporated, named, or called in any letters patent of any of our progenitors or predecessors, or in or after any other manner, all and singular the privileges, franchises, liberties, advantages, jurisdictions, customs, emoluments, forfeitures, prescriptions, uses, customs, cognizances, pleas, honors, dignities, elections of dignities, denominations, grants, annihilations, fines, redemptions, amercements, issues, and all other profits and hereditaments whatsoever in said letters patent, and in all and singular the other letters patent, in the same inspected and recited, contained, granted, specified, and expressed in such ample manner and form, and so freely, fully, and entirely as the said letters patent do testify, and also in so ample manner and form as they or their predecessors have or ought to have at any time had, held, occupied, used, or enjoyed by reason of any prescription, use or custom, or by reason or pretext of any other thing, cause, or matter whatsoever, though they or their predecessors, or any one or more of them have or hath ill-used or abused the premises, or any of them. And further of our greater special grace, of our certain knowledge and mere motion, we have given and granted, and by these our letters patent do for our heirs and successors, as much as in us lyeth, give and grant unto the said mayor, sheriffs, burgesses, and corporation, and their successors for ever, full power and authority to choose, make, constitute, and create yearly on the Monday next after the feast of St Michael the archangel, in the court hall or tholsel of the said town, a recorder, coroner, escheator, customer, comptroller of customs, gauger, and all other officers and ministers whatsoever, necessary and convenient in said town, and the franchises and liberties thereof; and that the said recorder, coroner, exacter of custom, comptroller and searcher of customs, gauge, and all other officers and ministers whatsoever, so by said mayor, sheriffs, burgesses, corporation, and their successors from time to time, chosen, made, constituted, and created, and every of them, have full power and authority to do and exercise all and singular the things which may or ought to appertain or belong to said office and officer, and every of them, and to receive, have, and levy for their proper use, all and singular fees, records, advantages, and profit whatsoever, appertaining and belonging to said office and officer, and every of them, as fully, freely, and entirely, and in as ample a manner and form as any other recorder, coroner, exacted of customs, comptroller, searcher of customs, gauger, or any other such officers or ministers, or any of them, can or may make, exercise, have or receive, levy and enjoy in any town, city, or other place within our said kingdom of Ireland; and that no other recorder, coroner, exacted of customs, comptroller, and searcher of customs, gauger, or any other such officers or ministers of us, our heirs or successors, enter or in any wise intrude themselves to exercise, or have said offices within said town, the franchises or liberties thereof.

And moreover of our greater grace, certain knowledge, and meer motion, we have given and granted, and by these our present letters patent, we do for us, our heirs and successors, as much as in us lyeth, give and grant to said mayor, sheriffs, burgesses, and corporation, and their successors for ever, full power and authority to give and grant, with the license of our deputy or governor of our kingdom of Ireland, from time to time, in writing first obtained, as well in time of war as in time of peace, to all and singular foreign merchants coming from time to time, willing to come to said town, for the sake of merchandizing, or with merchandize, a safe and secure conduct and protection to come into and go back from said town safely and securely with their ships, boats, goods, and merchandise, as freely and quietly without the hindrance, impeachment, calumny, molestation, and grievance of us, our heirs or successors, or of any lieutenants, deputies, justices, or other officers or ministers of ours, our heirs or successors whatsoever. And further of our greater grace and certain knowledge and meer motion, we have given, granted, and by these our present letters patent we for us, our heirs and successors, as much as in us lyeth, give and grant to the aforesaid mayor, sheriffs, burgesses, and corporation of our said town, and their successors for ever, that the said mayor of our said town, whosoever he be, during the time he shall be mayor of said town, be our Admiral for us, our heirs and successors within said town, and the liberties and franchises thereof, and within and enter the islands of Arran, and from the said islands to Galway aforesaid, on both sides of the water, there as well by sea and as by land, and fresh waters, and that all and singular the other mayors of our said town, who for the time being, as long as they shall be mayor of said town, be our Admirals, their heirs and successors, and every of them, who shall be for the time being mayor of said town, be our Admiral, and that of our heirs and successors, within the port, bay, town, liberties, franchises, and suburbs of Galway aforesaid, and within and over the islands of Arran, and from the said islands to Galway aforesaid, on both sides of the water there, both by sea and land, and fresh water, and that the said mayor who is now, and every other mayor, who for the time being shall be in said town, have full power, authority, and jurisdiction from time to time to enquire, hear, determine, exercise, execute, all and every thing appertaining and belonging to the office and jurisdiction of Admiral within the port, bay, town, liberties, franchises, suburbs, islands, and places aforesaid, both by sea and by land, and fresh water aforesaid, in as ample manner and form, and as fully, freely, and entirely as our admiral of our heirs and successors for the time being in any place within our kingdom of England, or within our kingdom of Ire land, can or may enquire, hear, determine, do, exercise or execute; and that no admiral of ours, our heirs or successors, have or exercise any power, authority, or jurisdiction within the port, bay, liberties, suburbs, islands, and places aforesaid, by sea or land, or fresh waters, nor intrude nor concern himself, nor can or may intrude or concern himself, in any manner whatsoever, in or concerning any thing which appertained or belonging to the office of Admiral within the port, bay, liberties, franchises, suburbs, islands, and places aforesaid; and that the said mayor, sheriffs, burgesses, and corporation, and their successors for ever, have, enjoy, receive, and levy, for the common use of said town, all and singular, the wrecks of the sea, forfeitures, fines, amercements redemptions, issues, commodities, advantages, emoluments and prescriptions whatsoever within the port, bay, and town, liberties, franchises, suburbs, islands, and places aforesaid, both by sea and by land, and fresh waters, forfeited, accruing, or arising, or to be for the future forfeited, accruing, or arising to him, by reason of his admiralty or jurisdiction of admiral; and that the said mayor, sheriffs, burgesses, and corporation and their successors for ever, can and may from time to time, put themselves in full possession and seisin[1] of, and in all and singular the said wrecks of the sea, forfeitures, fines, amercements, redemptions, issues, advantages, emoluments and profits whatsoever, and the same to raise, receive, take, collect, and have by themselves, or to employ some officer tor that purpose, without account or other thing to us, our heirs and successors, or to any admiral of ours, our heirs or successors, to be rendered paid off or made. And further, of our greater special grace and certain knowledge and meer motion, we do for us, our heirs and successors, give and grant unto said mayor, sheriffs, burgesses, and corporation, and their successors for ever, that no burgesses, inhabitants, dwellers, or residents within the town, franchises and liberties of Galway aforesaid, nor any of them, be at any time to come, drawn or compelled to come with out the town, franchises, and liberties of Galway afore said, nor any of them be at any time to come, drawn, or compelled to come without the town, franchises, and liberties of Galway aforesaid, before any justices, barons, commissioners, and other our officers whatsoever, to any assizes, sessions, enquiries, juries in the city of Dublin, or in the county of Dublin, or else where within our kingdom of Ireland, to be held concerning any thing or things, cause or causes, matter or matters, risen, done or committed to arise to be done or committed within our said town, the franchises or liberties thereof; nor shall the said burgesses, inhabitants, dwellers or residents, nor any of them within the said town, the franchises and liberties thereof, be put, impannelled, returned or sworn without the town of Galway aforesaid for any thing or things, forfeit or forfeitures, cause or causes, matter or matters, arisen, done, happening or accruing to arise to be done, committed, happen, or accrue within said town of Galway, the franchises and liberties thereof, before any justices, barons, commissioners, or other our officers whatsoever, in any assizes, juries, attaints, recognizances, or other enquiries whatsoever, to be taken, arraigned, or returned in said city or county of Dublin, or elsewhere within our said kingdom of Ireland aforesaid, though they should touch or concerns us, our heirs and successors, or any others whatsoever, but only within our town of Galway aforesaid, the franchises and liberties thereof, before our justices, barons, commissioners, or other officers whatsoever, when we our heirs and successors shall from time to time see expedient Further, of our special grace and certain knowledge and meer motion, we have given, granted, and by these present letters patent do for us, our heirs and successors, as much as in us, our heirs and successors lyeth, give and grant unto our said mayor, sheriffs, burgesses, and corporation, and their successors for ever, that no merchant

---

[1] A feudal term for having both possession and title of real property, [Clachan ed.].

or merchants, foreign or native, who shall import or unload, transport or load any merchandizes, goods to be sold, or wares whatsoever, into or from said town, or port or bay of the said town, by land or by water, shall pay, give, or be compelled to pay or give custom, poundage, tonnage, or other burthens, things, or duties whatsoever to us, our heirs and successors, or to any other person or persons for said merchandises, goods to be sold, or wares, or for any part thereof except only the customs and burthens following, viz. —

for every pound of ginger to be sold, 1d.;
for every pound of saffron to be sold, 2d.;
for every pound of cloves to be sold, 1d.;
for every pound of grains of paradise to be sold, 1d.;
for all other kinds of spices of the value of 12d. to be sold, one farthing;
for an hundred pounds of wax to be sold, 6d.;
for an hundred pounds of allum to be sold, 3d.;
for every hide tanned, fresh or salted, put or to be put in ouze or juice in said town, within or without, as far as the is land called Inniskeragh, one halfpenny;
for every pound of silk to be sold, 3d;
for every piece of Irish linen containing twelve yards, one halfpenny;
for every hundred of iron to be sold, 2d.;
for every bend of pieces of iron to be sold, 1d.;
for every hundred of sable skins to be sold, 1d.;
for every hundred stones of Spanish iron to be sold, 4d.;
for every fodder of lead to be sold, one halfpenny;
for an hundred pound of ceruss, 1d.;
for all sorts of anodynes of the value of 12d. to be sold, one farthing;
for an hundred nails of spikings, one penny;
for every trayl of barley to be sold, 8d.;
for every large cauldron and pan to be sold, 4d.;
for every hundred battery to be sold, 4d.;
for every tun of wine to be sold, 6d.;
for every pipe of wine to be sold, 3d.;
for every small curnock of malt to be sold, 1d.;
for every large curnock of malt to be sold, 2d.;
for every curnock of wheat to be sold, 2d.;
for every summage (horse load) of corn to be sold, one halfpenny;
for every summage of butter to be sold, one penny;
for every last of butter[1] to be sold, 1d.;
for every stone of tallow to be sold, one halfpenny;
for every mease[2] of herrings to be sold, one halfpenny;
for every curnock of salt to be sold, 1d.;
for every stone of wool, 1d.;
for every sack of wool, 4d.;

---

[1] According to the "Report on the manuscripts of the Marquess of Downshire, vol. 3", (Internet Archinve), there are eight hogsheads in a 'last' of butter, [Clachan ed.].
[2] a 'mease' of herrings measures five hundred, [Clachan ed.].

for every hide tanned fresh or salt to be sold, one halfpenny;
for all hides whatsoever of the value of 12d. or other skins of shorlings to be sold,- 1d;
for an hundred wooled skins to be sold, \d.;
for an hundred lamb skins to be sold, 2d.;
for the value of 12d. of other skins to be sold, one farthing;
for every horse of the value of 40s. sterling, and upwards to be sold, 6d.
for every plough horse or plough beast, bull or ox or cow to be sold, 1d.;
for every calf to be sold, one farthing;
for every large hog to be sold, 1d.;
for every sheep and goat to be sold, one halfpenny;
for every small hog to be sold, one halfpenny;
for an hundred rabbit skins, 2d.;
for an hundred skins of woolfell 3d;
for every sum mage of fishes to be sold, one half penny;
for an hundred of dry fishes to be sold, 2d.;
for every salmon to be sold, one farthing;
for a thousand eels and merlins to be sold, 1d.;
for all sorts of draughts, cars, &c. of the value of 4s., 1d.;
for every falcon and hawk to be sold, 1d.;
for every tercel or tercillet to be sold, one halfpenny;
for every mill quern, 1d.;
for two hand querns, one farthing;
for twelve curnocks of coals to be sold, 1d.;
for every stone of butter, tallow, and cheese to be sold, one halfpenny;
for every tun of honey to be sold, 3d.;
for every pipe of salmon to be sold, 18d.;
for every hundred of glass to be sold, 1d.;
for every hundred of scollops or other fish, salt, dry, or hard, to be sold, 1d.;
for two thousand onions to be sold, one farthing;
for eight pounds of flax or hemp to be sold, 1d.;
for eight bands of garlick to be sold, one farthing;
for every new chest and ark, and every thousand of dishes and platters of wood to be sold, one farthing;
for an hundred pound of pitch and rosin to be sold, one half penny;
for a thousand of gads of boards to be sold, one halfpenny;
for all wares of the value of twelve pence, of which mention is not above made, one farthing;
for all wares of the value of six shillings and eight pence to be sold, not expressed above, one half penny;
for all wares of the value of thirteen shillings and four pence to be sold, likewise not contained above, one penny:

all and singular which custom, burdens and uses aforesaid, we do of our special grace, and of our certain knowledge and meer motion, give and grant for us, our heirs and successors, to said mayor, sheriffs, burgesses and corporation, and their successors that they shall cause and order the usance, burthens and customs aforesaid, and every of them, to be from day to day raised, collected, received and had in said town, in manner and form aforesaid; *provided always, that the pence money, from thence arising, be faithfully expended on the murage and parage of said town, and not elsewhere nor otherwise;* moreover, we have of our special grace and certain knowledge, and our meer motion, given and granted, and by these our present letters patent for us, our heirs and successors, as much as in us lyeth, give and grant unto the aforesaid mayor, sheriffs, burgesses and corporation, and their successors for ever, that they the now mayor, sheriffs, burgesses and corporation of the aforesaid town, and their successors, and every of them, may and be able, from time to time, to assemble, prepare, and gather themselves and every of them; and all and singular the other inhabitants of said town, together with all and singular their friends, servants, tenants and adherents, and every of them, at their and every of their wills and pleasures, with defensive arms, or otherwise, as to them or any one or more of them shall seem most expedient, within the said town, the liberties and suburbs thereof, or without in any other place whatsoever, as well by sea as by land, and fresh waters, to assist, repel, recover and vindicate all and singular the robberies, spoils, depredations and other injuries, losses, damages and crimes whatsoever made, perpetrated, offered or committed, or for the time to come to be made, perpetrated, offered and committed against them, or any one or more of them, by any Irish neighbours, or by any rebels, malefactors and disturbers of our peace, or of that of our successors; and all and singular the other inhabitants of said town, and every of them, together with their friends, servants, tenants and adherents, from time to time for ever, to pass, ride, sail, and go beyond the seas, either with aims, ammunition, with double flags in hostile manner or otherwise, as they and every of them shall please, to any country, island, arm of the sea, or any other place whatsoever, to prosecute, take, recover, vindicate and claim all robberies, felonies, spoils, depredations, injuries and crimes whatsoever made, offered or committed against them or any of them; and to have, recover, distrain, make and receive recompense, distresses, restitution, evictions for said robberies, felonies, spoils, depredations, injuries and crimes aforesaid, against the said rebels, robberies, depredations and malefactors, and every of them, lawfully and unpunished, without the impeachment, calumny, molestation, grievance, disturbance or vexation, disquieting or hindrance of us, our heirs or successors, lieutenants, deputies, justices, sheriffs, or other our officers or ministers, or those of our heirs or successors whatsoever, any statute, act, ordinance, restrictions, law, proscription, proclamation or other thing, cause or matter whatsoever in anywise notwithstanding. — Further, we have of our great grace and certain knowledge and meer motion, given and granted, and do by these our present letters patent for us, our heirs and successors, as much as in us lyeth, give and grant unto said mayor, sheriffs, burgesses and corporation, and their successors for ever, that every mayor, and every recorder of said town for the time being, during the time which they severally and every or any of them, or their successors, shall be mayor and recorder of said town, or they or any of them shall bear and exercise the office of mayor or recorder of said town, they and every of them shall be, and are keepers and justices of our peace, and of our heirs and successors, and justices for our gaol and gaol delivery, of our heirs and successors, from time to time for ever within said town, the franchises, liberties and suburb thereof, as well by sea as by land and fresh waters, for felonies and other misdeeds committed within said town, the franchises, liberties, and suburbs thereof.

And we do for us, our heirs and successors, as much as in us lyeth, give, make, constitute, create, and ordain all and every mayor and mayors, recorder and recorders of the said town for the time being, and every of them, for ever, keepers and justices of our heirs and successors gaol delivery from time to time within said town, the franchises, liberties, and suburbs thereof, as well by sea as by land and fresh waters for the felonies and misdeeds aforesaid; and that all and singular the mayors and recorders of said town for the time being, and every of them for ever have, and shall have full power and authority and jurisdiction to enquire and examine by oath of good and lawful men of said town, the liberties, franchises, and suburbs thereof, concerning all and singular and every felonies, murders, rebellions, transgressions, riots, routs, conventicles, ambuscades, conspiracies, outcries, misprisions, and other crimes, offences, and misdeeds whatsoever made, committed, or perpetrated, or for the future to be made, committed or perpetrated within the said town, the franchises, liberties, and suburbs thereof, as well by sea as by land and fresh waters, and concerning all and singular entries to any lands and tenements by strong hand, and also concerning entries into such lands or tenements peaceably, and afterwards held or to be held by force, power, or strong hand made or to be made within said town, the franchises, liberties or suburbs thereof, concerning all singular articles, statutes, deliberation of clothiers and inn-keepers, and concerning labourers, servants, vagabonds, carpenters, artisans, weights, measures, victuals, tanners, carriers, slaters, ostlers[1], huxters and concerning all and singular the articles and privileges contained in any statutes whatsoever already set forth, and also concerning all and singular articles and things whatsoever, concerning which any justices or keepers of our peace, or any justices of the gaol delivery in any other place within our kingdom of England, or within our kingdom of Ireland, can enquire or examine, and to do, exercise, and execute the premises, and all and singular other matters within said town, the franchises, liberties, and suburbs thereof, as well by sea as by land and fresh waters, which appertained or belongeth to the office of a keeper or justice of the peace, or justice of the gaol delivery, or to any of them, and to hear, determine, and adjudge them all according to the law and custom of our kingdom of Ireland, and that no keeper or justice, keepers or justices of our heirs or successors' peace, or our heirs and successors' justice or justices for our heirs or successors' gaol delivery, assigned or to be assigned in any county or any other place within our kingdom of Ireland aforesaid, shall enter, nor in any wise intrude or concern himself to enquire or examine concerning the premises or any of the premises, or to hear, determine, or adjudge them or any of them, or to do, exercise, or execute any other thing which appertained or belongeth to the office of a keeper or justices of the peace, or to the

---

[1] A stableman, esp. one at an inn, [Clachan ed.].

office of a justice of gaol delivery within the said town, franchises, liberties, and suburbs thereof, by sea, land, or fresh waters; and that if any enquiry, or any indictment to be presented, or any other thing whatsoever within the said town, the franchises, liberties, or suburbs thereof, before any other keepers or justices of our heirs or successors' peace, or before our heirs or successors, justices of our heirs or successors' gaol delivery, or before any of them, assigned or to be assigned in any other county or place, such enquiry, indictment, and other thing whatsoever, it shall be made, determined, or adjudged within said town, the franchises, liberties, and suburbs thereof, before the said other keepers or justices of our heirs or successors' peace, or before our heirs or successors, justices for our heirs and successors' gaol delivery, shall be, and are void and of no virtue or force, and to be accounted for void and null, and every of them shall be and are void, and of no virtue or force, and to be accounted as void and null. And moreover we have of our special grace, certain knowledge and mere motion given and granted, and do by these our present letters patent, for us, our heirs and successors, as much as in us lyeth, give and grant unto said mayor, sheriffs, burgesses, and corporation, and their successors for ever, that no sheriff executor, or other our officer or minister, or our heirs, or successors, nor any of them, except the bailiff or sheriffs, or other officers of said town shall enter in any manner whatsoever within the said town, the franchises, liberties, and suburbs thereof, in any manner whatsoever, nor shall they or any of them intermeddle, or they or any of them in any thing or manner whatsoever within the said town, the franchises, liberties, and suburbs thereof. And that the mayor, sheriffs, burgesses, and corporation, and their successors for ever, have and hold a gaol or prison within the said town, the franchises, liberties, and suburbs thereof, where they shall think expedient, and that they have and hold for them and successors for ever, a keeper of the gaol and prison aforesaid, to commit to gaol, and imprison in said gaol or prison, from time to time, prisoners for what cause or crime soever they or any of them shall be taken, attached, or arrested within the said town, the franchises, liberties, and suburbs thereof, and likewise to secure, detain, and keep them, and every of them by themselves, or by their ministers thereto deputed, and also to give up and deliver or enlarge them so committed to gaol, and imprisoned according to due form of law in bail, or otherwise, according to their direction. And further, of our greater grace, certain knowledge and meer motion, we have given and granted, and as by these our present letters patent, for us, our heirs and successors, as much as in us lyeth, give and grant unto the said mayor or sheriffs, burgesses and corporation of our said town of Galway, and their successors for ever, all and singular such and such like other liberties, franchises, and privileges, preeminences, jurisdictions, authorities, easements, immunities, profits, commodities, advantages, customs and usances, forfeits and forfeitures, fines, redemptions and other hereditaments and things which the mayor, sheriffs, and citizens of our city of Waterford in our kingdom of Ireland afore said, or the mayor, sheriffs and corporation of our town of Drogheda in our kingdom of Ireland aforesaid, and every of them have, hold, enjoy or use, or ought to have held, enjoyed or used, by reason, virtue or pretence of any grant or letters patent of ours, or any of our progenitors or predecessors whatsoever, or by reason, virtue or pretence of any use, custom, statute, or any other thing, cause or matter whatsoever, within our said city of Waterford, the franchises, liberties and suburbs thereof, and within our said town of Drogheda, the franchises, liberties and suburbs thereof. And that the said mayor, sheriffs, burgesses and corporation of our said town of Galway, and their successors for ever have full power and authority to do, receive, deliver, administer, exercise and execute all and singular and every thing which appertained and belonged] to the said liberties franchises, privilege, preeminences, jurisdictions, authorities, easements, immunities, profits, commodities, advantges, customs, usages, forfeitures, fines, issues, redemptions, and other hereditaments and things what soever within our town of Galway aforesaid, the franchises, liberties, and suburbs thereof, as well by sea as by land and by fresh waters, in as ample manner and form, and as fully, freely, and entirely and un punished as the said mayor, sheriffs and citizens of our said city of Waterford, within the said city of Waterford, the franchises, liberties and suburbs thereof, or the said mayor, sheriffs and corporation of our said town of Drogheda, within said town, the franchises, liberties and suburbs thereof, can or ought, or any of them can or ought in any manner to do, receive, deliver, administer, exercise, and execute. And further, of our special grace and certain knowledge and mere motion, we have given, granted, and do by these our present letters patent for us, our heirs and successors, for ever, as much as in us lyeth, give and grant to the said mayor, sheriffs, burgesses, and corporation of our town of Galway aforesaid, and their successors for ever, that all and singular the articles, clauses, sentences and grants in these letters patent, and in all and singular the other letters patent by us, or by any of our progenitors or predecessors, to said mayor, sheriffs, burgesses and corporation of our town of Galway aforesaid, or to their or any of their predecessors granted, be excepted, judged, understood, interpreted and construed in as bountiful and favourable a manner as may be, and not otherwise, nor in any other manner, to the advantage and profit of the said mayor, bailiffs, burgesses and corporation of our said town of Galway, against us, our heirs and successors in all our heirs and successors' courts whatsoever, and before all our heirs and successors, judges, justices, barons of the Exchequer, and others our heirs and successors ministers whatsoever; and that express mention of the true yearly value, or of the certainty of the premises of any of them of the other gifts or grants by us or by any of our ancestors aforesaid, made to said mayor, sheriffs, burgesses and corporation of our town of Galway afore said, or to any of them from time to time, is not made in these presents, or any statute, act, ordinance, provision, proclamation or restriction to the contrary made, published, set forth, ordained or provided, or any thing, cause or matter whatsoever, in any wise notwithstanding. In witness whereof we have caused these our letters patent to be passed. Witness myself at Grainbury the fourteenth day of July, in the twentieth year of our reign.

Copy of Mr. Cole's certificate of the translation.

I do hereby certify that I have carefully translated the above charter from the original, with due circumspection, correction, and to the best of my skill and knowledge in the Latin tongue. Witness my hand, this 27th day of June, in the year of our Lord God, 1693.

ELISHA COLE.

(CopiaVera.)

CHARTER GRANTED BY CHARLES THE SECOND TO THE TOWN OF GALWAY

Charles the Second, by the grace of God of England, Scotland, France, and Ireland King, Defender of the Faith, &c. to all whom these presents shall come greeting. Whereas by letters patent under our royal signet and sign manual, bearing date at our court at Whitehall the 16th day of August, in the three and twentieth year of our reign, directed to our right trusty and well beloved councellor John Lord Berkelly, our lieutenant general and general governor of our said kingdom of Ireland, and to the chief governor or governors there for the time being, we did signify our royal will and pleasure therein, that whereas many of the charters of the several cities and towns formerly corporate in our said kingdom of Ireland have been by reason of the several misconducts and misdemeanors of the said cities and towns during the time of the late horrid rebellion in that our kingdom forfeited unto us, and other of the said corporations are dissolved or otherwise determined, so that we may justly seize all the said liberties and franchises that have been by any of our royal ancestors granted to the said corporations if we would take the full and utmost advantage that we legally may against them. And that whereas we were graciously pleased, for the encouragement of trade in our said kingdom of Ireland, to extend our favour to such of the said corporations as our said lieutenant general and general governor of our said kingdom of Ireland shall judge best meriting the same, &c. to grant unto them new charters, with such lands and other privileges, liberties, and advantages formerly belonging unto them, as should appear unto our said lieutenant general and general governor of Ireland to be fit and reasonable to be granted unto them, we did therefore, by our said letters, declare our royal will and pleasure, and did thereby give unto our said lieutenant general and general governor of our said kingdom of Ireland full power and authority to make due inspection unto the several charters formerly granted by any of our royal ancestors to the several cities and towns corporate in our said kingdom of Ireland and upon humble suit made unto our said lieutenant general and general governor of our said kingdom of Ireland, by the members of the said cities and towns, to cause new charters, by the advice of our learned council in that our kingdom, or some of them, to be passed unto the said cities and towns formerly corporate, respectively, and the great seal of our said kingdom of Ireland, in such manner as our said lieutenant general and general governor of our said kingdom of Ireland should think fit, and thereby to grant unto the said cities and towns formerly corporate, respectively, such of the lands, tenements, and hereditaments formerly belonging unto them, and also such liberties, franchises, privileges, and advantages formerly granted unto or conveyed by them, and also such restrictions, limitations, and exceptions as our said lieutenant general and general governor of our said kingdom of Ireland should think fit and most conducing to our service and the better support of the corporation.

And whereas the mayor, sheriffs, burgesses, and commonality of our said town and county of our town of Galway, taking notice of our princely grace and favour intended to our cities and towns corporate in our realm of Ireland, by our said letters of the 16th day of August in the twenty-third year of our reign, have humbly petitioned our right trusty and right well beloved cousin and counsellor Arthur Earl of Essex, our lieutenant general and general governor of our said kingdom of Ireland, that we would be graciously pleased to grant unto them a new charter, and thereby incorporate them and their successors to be one body corporate and politic within our said town and county of our said town of Galway, in succession for ever, and to have and enjoy such lands, tenements, and hereditaments, royalties, franchises, liberties, and privileges as our said lieutenant general and general governor of our said kingdom of Ireland should think fit for the encouragement of trade and the advantage of our service there; and have also since made it their humble and express desire that we should be graciously pleased to make some provision in our said new charter for securing the disbursements and charges which Theodorus Russell, esq. their present mayor, hath been at in laying out serviceable great sums of money to redeem them from their lost condition, by purchasing it from Elizabeth Hamilton, the widow and relict of James Hamilton, esq. lately deceased, the estate, right, title, and interest in and onto such charter, market, and petty duties formerly belonging unto the said corporation, which were forfeited unto and granted by us unto the said Elizabeth, by letters patents and our great seal of Ireland, bearing date the 5th of December in the twenty-fifth year of our reign, and for a further compensation of his great pains and favour therein showed unto them. And whereas we have graciously pleased, for the better improving the said town and settling of trade and manufactures therein, to condescend to the humble desires of the said petitioners. Now know ye that we, of our special grace, certain knowledge, and mere motion, by and with the advice and consent of our right trusty and well beloved cousin and counsellor Arthur Earl of Essex, our lieutenant general and general governor of our said kingdom of Ireland and according to the tenor of our said letters and our royal signet and sign manual, bearing date at our court at Whitehall the 16th day of August in the 23rd year of our reign, and enrolled in rolls of our high court of Chancery in our said kingdom of Ireland, have willed, declared, and constituted and granted, and by these presents do will, declare, ordain, constitute, and grant that our said town of Galway, and all and singular castles, houses, messuages, tufts, mills, edifices, structures, curtilleges[1], gardens, waste grounds, lands, tenements, and hereditaments situated, lying and being within the town of Galway, shall be at all times hereafter one entire and free borough of itself, by the name of the town and borough of Galway, and shall from thence be called and known by the name of the town and borough of Galway, and all and singular the premises, into one entire borough of itself, by the name of the town and borough of Galway, we do erect, constitute, make, and ordain by these presents and of our special grace, certain knowledge and meer motion, by and with the advice and consent aforesaid, we have willed ordained and constituted, and by these presents for us, our heirs and successors, we do will ordain and constitute, that the said town of Galway, and all castles, messuages, waters, rivers, lands, tenements and other hereditaments whatsoever, lying and being within the space of two miles from every part of the town of Galway, in a direct line from henceforth, to be one entire county of itself corporate in deed and in name, and shall be for ever distinct and altogether separate from the county of Galway, and that the said county of the town so corporate, distinct and separate from the said county of Galway, shall for ever hereafter be called, , taken, and known to be the county of the town of Galway; provided always nevertheless, our will and pleasure is, and we do hereby declare, institute and appoint, that our justices of assize and goal delivery, and our justices of the peace in the sessions for business touching the county of Galway at large, and also the sheriffs of the said county at large, for the time being, in holding his terms or other his courts, and also their commissioners, enquiries, and other offices of us our heirs and successors, and every of them, who have heretofore held their courts within the county of Galway at large, and shall and may have free ingress and regress into the town of Galway, and there hold their sessions of all matters or things whatsoever, which shall or may happen to be done or arise without the said county of the town of Galway, and within the county of Galway at large, in such place as they shall think fit, and in as ample manner, to all intents and purposes, as they did heretofore hold the same in Su Francis Abbey, or any part of the county of Galway at large, or as they might have held the same in case the said town and precincts of the same were not hereby made an entire county of itself but remained part of the said county of Galway at large, any thing in our letters patents contained to the contrary thereof in any wise notwithstanding. And further of our special grace, certain knowledge and meer motion, by and with the advice and consent aforesaid, we have given and granted, and by these presents for us, our heirs and successors do give and grant, that in our said town and county of our said town of Galway, there shall be for ever after one new body corporate and politique in deed and name, consisting of one mayor, two sheriffs, three burgesses and commonality of the said town and county of said town of Galway, and that the said mayor, sheriffs, free burgesses and commonality of the said town and county of our said town of Galway, and their successors, be one

---

[1] The area of land occupied by a dwelling and its yard and outbuildings, actually enclosed or considered as enclosed, [Clachan ed.].

body corporate fend politique for ever to endure, we do by these presents folly make, create and establish, that the same body corporate shall for ever be called and known by the name of the mayor, sheriffs free burgesses and commonality of the said town and county of the said town of Galway, and that by the same name they and their successors shall have perpetual succession, and shall have, and shall be able and capable in law to have, purchase, receive and possess lands, tenements, liberties, privileges, jurisdictions, franchises, and hereditaments whatsoever, of what kind or nature soever, unto them and their successors in fee or perpetuity, and also goods and chatties and all other things whatsoever, of what nature or kind soever, and also to give, grant, demise and assign lands, tenements, and hereditaments, goods and chattels, and do and execute all other matters and things by the name aforesaid, as any other person or natural body politique lawfully could or might do in anywise; and likewise that they and their successors, by the name of the mayor, sheriffs, free burgesses, and commonality of said town and county of the said town of Galway, may plead and be impleaded, answer and be answered before us, our heirs and successors, and before any of the justices, coroners, and judges, as well ecclesiastical as secular of us, our heirs and successors, or else wheresoever, of and in all manner of accounts, real, personal, or mixt suits, quarrels, and demands whatsoever against them or by them to be prosecuted; and further, of our like especial grace, certain knowledge, and meer motion, by and with the advice and consent aforesaid, we have given and granted, and by these presents, for us our heirs and successors, we do give and grant unto the said mayor, sheriffs, free burgesses and commonalty of the said town and county of our said town of Galway, and their successors for ever, shall and may have full power and authority to choose, send and return in full and effectual manner, to all intents and purposes, as formerly they did, or at any time heretofore have done, two discreet fit persons to serve and attend in every parliament hereafter to be held in our said kingdom of Ireland; and that the said persons so elected, sent and returned, shall have full power and authority to treat and consent upon such things and matters as shall be to them there proposed, or declared, and thereupon freely give their votes and suffrages, and to do and execute all other things whatsoever, as fully and freely as any other burgess of any ancient borough in the said realm of Ireland, or in our said realm of England, in the parliament there are wont to do and execute; and to the intent that in time to come it may appear that the said new charter was granted unto honest discreet men, we do by these presents make, nominate and constitute Theodore Russell, Esq. to be the first and modern mayor of said town and county of said town of Galway, to continue in the said office until the feast of Saint Michael the Archangel, which shall be in the year of our Lord God 1678; and we do likewise by these presents make, nominate and constitute and appoint John Clarke and Richard Browne to be first and modern sheriffs of the town and county of the said town of Galway, to continue in the said office until the feast of Saint Michael the Archangel which shall be in the year of our Lord God 1678; and likewise we do by these presents make, nominate and constitute Sir Oliver St George, Bart. Sir James Cuff and Sir Thomas Newcom, knights, Vere Essex

Cromwell, Esq. Richfird Coote, Esq. Sir Henry Waddington, Sir Charles Holecraft, John Eyre, Edward Eyre, John Mayort and William Hamilton, Esqrs. George Hull, gentleman, and George Lesson, Esq. and such other as the mayor and sheriffs, and the major part of the free burgesses for the time being shall choose to be the first and modern free burgesses of the said town and county of the said town of Galway, to continue in the said offices of free burgesses, during their respective lives, until they shall, in the mean time, for their misbehaviour, or any other reasonable cause, be removed from the said office or offices, and also all such inhabitants of the said town, and so many others as the said mayor, sheriffs and free burgesses of the said town and county of the said town of Galway for the time being shall admit into the freedom of the said town and we do by these presents make and ordain to be of the commonality of the said town of Galway. And further, we do by these presents make, nominate and constitute William Sprigg, Esq. to be recorder of the said town of Galway, and to continue the said office until the feast of Saint Michael the Archangel which shall be in the year 1678; and Jerom Russell, Gentleman to be sworn clerk of our said town of Galway, and to continue in the said office until the feast of Saint Michael the Archangel which shall be in the year 1678; and further, we will that the said Theodore Russell, whom we have by these presents constituted mayor of the said town of Galway, and the said William Sprigg, whom we have constituted recorder of the said town, shall, within one month after the date of these our letters patent, come before Sir Henry Waddington, knight, Charles Holecraft, Esq. now high sheriff of the said county of Galway, and John Eyre. Esq. or any two of them, and in due manner take the oath of supremacy established by act of parliament second Elizabeth, in our said kingdom of Ireland, and the oath of allegiance, and also this ensuing oath (viz.) "I, A.B. do declare and believe that it is not lawful, upon any pretence whatsoever to take up arms against the king, and that I do abhor that traitorous position of taking arms by his authority against his person, or against those that are commissioned by him, so help me God," — shall likewise respectively take the several oaths heretofore usually taken for the due execution of the several offices of the mayor and recorder of the said town and county of the said town of Galway, and that the said John Clarke and Richard Browne, whom we have by these presents constituted sheriffs of the said town and county of the said town of Galway and their successors; and the said Jerom Russell, whom we have constituted town clerk of our said town of Galway, and his successors, and the said Sir Oliver St. George, Sir James Cuff, Sir Thomas Newcom, Vere Essex Cromuck, Richard Coote, Sir Henry Waddington, Charles Holecroft, John Eyre, Edward Eyre, John Mayort, William Hamilton, George Hall, and George Lesson, whom we have made present free burgesses of the said town, as also their successors, in the place and places of free burgesses at all times, to come before they be admitted to execute their respective offices, places and employments; and likewise all and every such person and persons as shall be of the said common council of the said town and borough, as also their successors in the place of common councilmen, at all times to come before they be admitted into their respective offices, places and employments, shall severally and respectively take as well the several oaths particularly mentioned, as also the other heretofore usually taken for the due execution of their several offices, places or employments; the said to be administered by the mayor and recorder, or by the mayor and two of the burgesses of the said town and county of the town of Galway for the time being, whom we do by these presents authorise and require to administer the same in the tholsel, or in any other convenient place within the said town: and it is our further will and pleasure that said office and offices of mayor, recorder, sheriffs and town clerk of the said town and county of the said town of Galway, be for ever hereafter elective. And we do by these presents for us, our heirs and successors, give and grant unto the said mayor, sheriffs, and free burgesses and commonality counsel of the said town of Galway, and their successors, that the said mayor, sheriff, free burgesses and commonality, counsel for the time being, yearly, for ever, at the feast of St Peter *ad vincula*, commonly called Lamass day, from and after the five and twentieth day of March next ensuing the date hereof, shall and may assemble themselves in the tholsel of the said town, or any other convenient place within the said town of Galway, and being so assembled may, or the greater part of them, before they depart thence, choose one of the discreet free burgesses of the said town to the office of mayor of the said town, who being presented, approved and sworn in manner as hereafter is expressed, may hold, exercise, and enjoy the same for one whole year, from the feast of St Michael the Archangel then next following, and until another of said burgesses shall be duly elected, presented, approved, sworn in the said office in manner and form as hereafter is set forth, and may also then and there elect some discreet person learned in the laws to be recorder of the said town, as also some discreet person to be town clerk of the said town, who being respectively presented, approved and sworn in manner and form as hereafter is expressed, may hold, exercise and enjoy the same for one whole year from the feast of St Michael the Archangel then next following, and until two others shall be duly elected, presented, approved, and sworn into the said offices respectively, in manner as hereafter is set forth and appointed; that it shall and may be lawful for the mayor and recorder of the said town for the time being respectively, in case of sickness or any urgent and important occasion of their own to be absent from the said town, to appoint their respective deputies during the time of his or their sickness or absence from the said town, who taking the several oaths herein formerly appointed to be taken by the mayor and recorder of the said corporation respectively, shall and may execute the place and office of deputy mayor and deputy recorder of the said corporation in all things during the time of such mayor's and recorder's sickness or absence respectively, as fully and amply to all intents and purposes as such sick or absent mayor or recorder might have done if he or they were well and personally present; such deputy mayor and deputy recorder respectively, first taking all the several oaths formerly mentioned to be taken by the mayor and recorder of the said town before the sheriffs of the said town for the time being, and any three or more of the free burgesses of the said town, whom we do hereby fully authorize and require to administer the same unto them respectively, on the Holy Evangelists; and our will and pleasure is, that the mayor and recorder of our said town of Galway, and their deputies for the time being respectively, shall be justices of the peace of said county of Galway at large, during their continuance in their respective offices: and further, of our abundant grace, certain knowledge, and mere motion, by and with the advice and consent aforesaid, we will, and by these presents for us our heirs and successors, do give and grant unto the said mayor, sheriffs, free burgesses, and commonality of the said town and county of the said town of Galway and their successors, that when and so often as it shall happen that the mayor of the said town of Galway, for the time being, shall die, or the said office become void within the compass of the same year after he shall be elected, presented, approved, and sworn as aforesaid, that then in such case it shall and may be lawful to and for the sheriffs, free burgesses, and common council of the said town and their successors, within fifteen days after such death or vacancy, to choose some other fit person out of the number of free burgesses to the office of mayor of the town, and that such person being so elected and chosen, and taking the several oaths before mentioned before the sheriffs, and any seven or more of them, free burgesses of the said town for the time being, whom we do hereby authorize and require to administer the same on the Holy Evangelists, shall and may execute the said office of mayor of the said town and county of the said town of Galway until the feast of St. Michael archangel next following, until new election business. And further of our abundant grace, certain knowledge, and mere motion, by and with the advice and consent aforesaid, we have granted, and by these presents for us, our heirs, and successors, do give and grant unto the mayors, sheriffs, free burgesses, and commonality of the said town of Galway and their successors for ever, that the said mayors, sheriffs, and common council, and their successors for ever, shall have full power and authority from time to time every year at the feast of Lamass, to choose and nominate two honest discreet free burgesses of the said town to be sheriffs of the said county of the said town of Galway aforesaid, to continue for one whole year from the feast of St Michael the archangel then next following inch election inclusive; and that such persons so elected, presented, approved, and sworn in manner as hereafter is set forth, may take upon them the execution of the said office of sheriff, and may hold, execute, and enjoy the said office of sheriff of the county of the town of Galway for one whole year, from the feast of Saint Michael the archangel, then next following, until others be elected, presented approved, and sworn in the said office in manner as hereafter is expressed, and that such sheriffs of the county of said town of Galway shall and may have and exercise all manner of instructions, powers, authorities, liberties, and other things whatsoever to the said office of sheriff belonging or appertaining within the said town and county of the town of Galway, and the limits, means, and bounds of the same, as other sheriffs of us, our heirs and successors within our said kingdom of Ireland have, or ought to have within their bailiwick; and that our heirs and successors from time to time, *for ever hereafter,* shall and will direct and cause to be made to the sheriffs of the said county of the said town of Galway for the time being, all and singular writs, bills and precepts, warrants, summons, attachments, distresses, estreats and mandates of us, our heirs and successors; and the summons, attachments and distresses of the exchequer of us, our heirs and successors, and other the courts of us, our heirs and successors, arising from any matters and things within the said town and company of the said town of Galway, or within the precincts or limits of the same for the future, which ought to be directed to and executed by the sheriffs of the county of Galway if the town of Galway and precincts of the same were not made in an entire county of itself to that no other sheriffs in our said realm of Ireland, or bailiff or sergeant of any sheriff in said realm of Ireland, except the sheriffs of us, our heirs and successors of the said county of the town of Galway, and their bailiffs, ministers, or sergeants, shall for the future enter into the said town or precincts of the same (except as before is excepted) to exercise or execute any thing that belongs to the office of the said sheriff, nor shall any way enter or meddle therein. And we do further will, institute and ordain, and our royal will and pleasure is, that upon all elections to be hereafter made after the 25th day of March next of any person or persons to serve in any of the offices of mayor, sheriffs, recorder, or town clerk of the said corporation, the names of the persons so elected to serve in the said several offices of mayor, sheriff or recorder, shall be by said corporation forthwith presented to our lieutenant or the chief governor or governors of the said privy council of our said kingdom of Ireland, to be approved of by them; and that the said persons so elected for any of the said offices shall be for ever hereafter incapable of serving in the said several offices, or any of them, until they shall be respectively approved of by the said lord lieutenant or chief governor or governors of the privy council of our said kingdom of Ireland, by order, or under their hands; and in case the persons, or any of them whose names shall be presented to our lieutenant or other chief governor or governors and council of our said kingdom of Ireland shall not be so approved of within ten days after their names shall be so presented, then in such case the said corporation shall, from time to time, proceed to a new election of fit persons for the said respective offices for which the said persons, so presented shall not be approved of and shall in like manner present their names to the said lieutenant or other chief governor or governors and council of our said kingdom of Ireland until they shall have chosen such persons for the said respective offices as shall be approved of as aforesaid; provided always, that this shall not extend to the elections of any persons that shall be elected in the place of any the said officers annually chosen who shall die within the year of their election of the said respective offices, or within one month before they are to enter upon the execution thereof; and our further will and pleasure is, that no person shall be hereafter chosen warden of the said town of Galway but such person as shall be nominated to the said office by our lieutenant or other chief governor or governors of our said kingdom of Ireland for the time being. And our further will and pleasure is, and we do hereby declare and ordain that no person or persons that shall be hereafter elected either mayor, recorder, sheriffs, aldermen, town clerk, free burgesses, or one of the common council within the said town or corporation, or master or wardens of any corporation, guild, or fraternity within the said town and corporation, shall be capable of holding, enjoying, or executing any of the said offices, places or employments, until he or they shall take the oath of supremacy established by Act of Parliament second Elizabeth in this kingdom, and the oaths of allegiance, besides the oaths usually taken upon the admission of any person unto the said respective offices, places, or employments, and also the ensuing oath, viz. "I, A.B. do declare and believe, that it is not lawful upon any pretence whatsoever to take up arms against the King, and that I. do abhor that traitorous position of taking arms by his authority, against his person, or against those that are commissioned by him, so help me God:" the said oaths to be taken before such person or persons as shall admit them to their several offices and employments, who are hereby empowered, authorised, and required to administer to them the said oaths; and upon any such person or persons refusal to take the said oaths, the election of said such person or persons unto any of the said offices, places, and employments, is hereby declared to be absolutely null and void, such persons only excepted, with whose taking the said oath of supremacy, our lieutenant or other chief governor or governors of our said kingdom, for the time being, for some particulars shall think fit, by writing under his or their hands by name to dispense; and for the avoiding of such tumults and discords, wherewith popular election of magistrates and other officers are often attended, we do hereby further order and direct, for ever hereafter, the mayor, sheriffs, recorder, and town clerk, shall be elected and chosen by the mayor, sheriffs, and common council of the said town, or the greater number of the votes of such of the common council of the said town that shall be present at the days whereon such election are and ought usually to be made; and that no freeman of the said town, or other person who shall not be of the common council of the said town, shall at any time hereafter have any vote in the election of any mayor or sheriffs, recorder or town clerk, or other officers in the said town of Galway; and that no matter or thing relating in any wise, to affairs of said town shall be hereafter pro pounded or abated in the tholsel or general assembly of the said town until the same shall have first passed the common council of the said town, and the persons offending against the rule to be enfranchised by the mayor and common council of the said town, any law usage or custom of the said town to the contrary not withstanding. And further, we will and ordain that the said mayor, sheriff, free burgesses, and commonality, for them and their successors, do accordingly covenant and agree to and with us, our heir and successors, that:

"all foreigners, strangers, aliens, as well others as protestants, who are or shall be merchant, factor, artifice, artificers, seamen or otherwise skilled or exercised in any mysteries, craft or trade, in working or making any manufactory, or the art of navigation, who are at present residing and inhabiting within the said town of Galway, or who shall at any time after come unto the said town of Galway, with intent and resolution there to inhabit, reside or dwell, shall upon his or their reasonable suit or re quest made, and upon payment due or tendered of 20s. sterling, by way of a fine unto the chief magistrate or magistrates, common council or persons authorised to admit and make freemen of the said town of Galway, be admitted a freeman of our said town of Galway and if he or they shall desire it of all or any guild, brotherhood, society, or fellowship of any trade, craft, or other mystery within the same *during his or their residence for the most part, and his and their families constant inhabiting within the said town of Galway , and no longer, and shall have* exercise and enjoy all privileges and immunities of trading, working, buying and selling in as large and ample manner as any freeman of said town of Galway might have, exercise and enjoy, by virtue of his or their freedom; and that every such person or persons who shall be admitted to be free as aforesaid, shall henceforth be deemed, esteemed, and taken to be denisen and denisens within this kingdom, any law statute, charter, usage, or custom of this kingdom, or of any city, walled town or corporation of the same, to the contrary in any wise notwithstanding; provided always, that all such strangers, artificers, and others to be admitted freemen as aforesaid, shall take the oath of allegiance, and also all such oaths as are accustomably taken by all or any freeman or members of the said town of Galway, or by all or any such guild or brotherhood, society or fellowship of the traders crafts or other mysteries which he or they shall occupy or exercise, in case he or they shall desire to be incorporated into any such guild, brotherhood, society or fellowship aforesaid, and shall pay all such and like charges as all freemen or subjects of the like trade, craft, or any mystery shall do use to pay, and no other nor no more; and that if the chief magistrate or magistrates, or any person authorised as aforesaid of the said town of Galway, or any master, warden, or other governor of any brotherhood, society or fellowship, or any trade, craft, or mystery within the said town of Galway, shall refuse to admit any such stranger, being a merchant, trader, artificer, workman or seaman, residing or coming into our said kingdom of Ireland with intent as aforesaid to be a freeman of our said town of Galway, or to be a brother or member of any brotherhood, society, or fellowship within the same, every such chief magistrate or magistrates, masters, wardens, or other governors respectively, shall upon complaint and due proof made of such refusal before our lieutenant or chief governor or governors and council of our said kingdom of Ireland, be by their order disfranchised, and from thenceforth, incapable, without their licence, of being a freeman or member of the said town; and every such stranger being a merchant, trader, artificer, workman or seaman, upon tender made by him of twenty shillings by way of fine as aforesaid, and taking the oath of allegiance before any justice of the peace of the county of Galway, who is hereby authorised and appointed to administer the said oath, shall thereupon by virtue hereof, be deemed, reputed, and taken to all intents and purposes to be a freeman or member of our said town of Galway, and of the brotherhood, society, and fellowship of any trade, craft or mystery where he or others shall be denied admission as aforesaid, and from henceforth have, exercise, and enjoy the liberty and privilege of trading, working, buying and selling of any commodities whatsoever in as large and ample manner as if he had been admitted a freeman of the said town of Galway, a brother or member of such brotherhood, society, or fellowship, or trade or craft, or mystery within the same, taking the usual oaths of such free brothers or members, which oath any one justice of peace of our said county of Galway is by these presents empowered to administer, and paying all such charges as aforesaid, any law, custom or usage to the contrary in anywise notwithstanding; and in case any person or persons shall give any disturbance or interruption to any such stranger, being a merchant, trader, artificer, artisan, workman or seaman as aforesaid, to the hindering of him in his trading, working, buying or selling as aforesaid, contrary to the intent and meaning of these presents, all and every such person or persons so offending shall, upon the complaint and proof made of his or their offence therein before our lieutenant or other chief governor or governors and council of our said kingdom of Ireland, for the time being, by their order be disfranchised, and from thenceforth incapable without their licence of being made a freeman or member of our said town of Galway."

And further, of our abundant grace, certain knowledge, and meer motion, by and with the consent aforesaid, we have given, granted, and by these presents for us, our heirs and successors, we do give and grant unto the said mayor, sheriffs, free burgesses and commonality of the said town and county of the said town of Galway, and their successors for ever, that there be within the said town and county of the said town of Galway, and the franchises of the same, one guild of merchants of the staple consisting of one mayor, two constables, and of such number of merchants of the said town as the said mayor and constables of the said guild of merchants of the staple for the time being shall think fit; and therefore we will, and by this our charter we do for us, our heirs and successors, make, constitute and ordain Charles Holecroft, esq. mayor of the said guild of merchants of the staple of the said town of Galway, to continue from the date of these our letters patents to the feast of Saint Michael the Archangel which shall be in the year of our Lord 1678; and also we do by these presents make, constitute and ordain John Flower and Thomas Poole constables of the said guild of merchants of the staple of the said town of Galway, to continue until the feast of Saint Michael the Archangel which shall be in the year of our Lord 1678; and that after the feast of Saint Michael the Archangel in the year 1678, the mayor and constables of the said guild of merchants of staple to be yearly ordained in manner following; that is to say, the mayor of said town of Galway for the proceeding year shall be, and is hereby appointed to be mayor of the said guild of merchants of the staple for one year then next following; and the sheriffs of the said town for the proceeding year shall be, and are hereby appointed to be constables of the said guild of merchants for one year then next following, and no longer; and that the mayor and constables, and mayor and one constable of the said guild of merchants of the staple of the said town for the time being, for ever, shall have foil and absolute power and authority, from time to time, to take and receive all and singular statutes, recognizances of the staple taken, or to be taken within the said town and borough, and thereupon to certify the same into the high court of chancery in our said realm of Ireland, and further to do and execute all and singular other matters and things which do any wise belong or appertain to the office of mayor and constables of the guild of merchants of the staple, according to the form of the statute in that case made and provided, in as ample manner and form as the mayor and constables of the staple in our city of Waterford, or any other town or city within our said realm of Ireland do use or execute, or heretofore might or could do or execute in any wise. And further, of our more ample grace, certain knowledge, and mere motion, by and with the advice and consent aforesaid, we will, and by these presents for us, our heire and successors, do grant unto the said mayor, sheriffs, free burgesses and commonality of the said town and county of the said town of Galway, and their successors, that they and their successors for ever shall and any have and use such several vestments, ensigns and ornaments within the said town and county of the town of Galway, and the franchises of the same, for honour and dignity of the said town and county of the said town of Galway, and the mayor and sheriffs, free burgesses, and commonality of the said town, as the mayor, sheriffs, burgesses and commonality had used, or might or could have had or used within the said town of Galway at any time before the said 23rd of October which was the year 1641. That the said mayor of the paid town of Galway may have a sword-bearer before him at all places within the said town of Galway and county of the said town of Galway, and all the franchises thereof, for the greater eminence of the mayoralty or office of mayor of the said town, and authority thereunto belonging: and to this end we will, and by these presents do grant that the mayors, sheriff, free burgesses and commonality of the said town, and their successors from time to time for ever, may constitute and have one officer or sword-bearer to carry the sword before the mayor of of the said town for the time being in manner and form aforesaid: and further we will, and by these present for us, our heirs and successors, do grant unto the said mayor, sheriffs, free burgesses and commonality of the said town and county of the said town of Galway, and their successors, that they and their successors shall and may have, for ever hereafter, within the said town of Galway, or the liberties and precincts thereof, one house of common meeting or convocation, which shall be called the Tholsel of said town of Galway: and that it shall and nay be lawful to and for the said mayor, sheriffs, free burgesses and commonality, and their successors, and to and for the recorder of the said town for the time being, or the major part of them, as often as to them or the major part of them shall seem meet or requisite, to meet and assemble themselves in the aforesaid house called the Tholsel, or in any other convenient place within the said town, the liberties and precincts thereof; and that the said mayor, sheriffs, free burgesses and commonality of the said town, or thee major part of diem so assembled, whereof the said mayor and recorder of the said town of Galway for the time being to be two, may and shall have full power and authority from time to time, then and there to ordain, make, constitute and establish such reasonable laws, statutes, constitutions, decrees and ordinances whatsoever, as they or the major part of them shall, in their discretions, see good, wholesome, profitable, honest and necessary as well for the good rule and government of our said town and county of Galway, and the liberties and precincts thereof, and of all and singular the officers, members and ministers of the said town and liberties and precincts thereof, as also for the declaring, setting down, and appointing in what order, manner and form the said mayor, sheriffs and free burgesses and commonalty, and other officers and ministers of our said town and county of our said town of

Galway, the liberties and precincts thereof, shall and may from time to time demean and behave themselves in their several and respective employments, and also for the common profit, advantage and good government of the said town and liberties and precincts thereof as also for the better preserving, governing and disposing and placing, selling, or letting of all or any lands, tenements and hereditaments within, and by these presents or otherwise are and have been granted, assigned, or confirmed, or which at any time hereafter shall be given, granted, assigned or confirmed to the said mayor, sheriff, free burgesses and commonality of our said town and county of our said town of Galway, as also for the better governing, ordering and disposing of all and singular other matters, causes and things whatsoever touching or concerning the estate, right or interest of said town of Galway. And that it shall and may be lawful to and for the said mayor, sheriffs, free burgesses, recorder and commonality of our said town and county of our said town of Galway for the time being, or the major part of them, whereof the mayor and the recorder of said town for the time being to be two, at such time and times and places as they, or the major part of them shall think fit, to make, ordain, and establish such laws, statutes, and ordinances, as aforesaid, and to impose and cesss [sic] upon all and every person and persons that shall offend against the said laws, statutes, ordinances, or any of them, such reasonable payments penalties and punishments as to the mayor, sheriffs, free burgesses, recorder and commonality for the time being, or the major part of them as aforesaid, shall seem requisite and expedient in that behalf; all and singular which said laws, statutes, and ordinances for to be made, constituted and ordained as aforesaid, we will and command to be observed, obeyed and performed under the payments, penalties and punishments therein to be contained as aforesaid; provided that the said laws, statutes, ordinances, payments, penalties and punishments be reasonable, and not repugnant nor contrary, but agreeable to the laws, statutes, customs, rights and usages of our said kingdom of Ireland, and unto the rules, ordinances and directions made and established by our lieutenant and council of our said kingdom of Ireland, bearing date the 29th day of September in the year 1662, for the better regulation of the said corporation of our said town of Galway, and the electing of magistrates and officers there. And we further will, and by these presents for us, our heirs and successors, do grant unto the said mayors, sheriffs, free burgesses and commonality of our said town and county of our said town of Galway, and their successors, that they and their successors shall and may for ever hereafter have, hold, and keep in the tholsel of our said town of Galway, or any other convenient place within the said town, the liberties and precincts thereof, a weekly court of record on every Tuesday and Friday in the week before the mayor or his deputy and the recorder of the said town for the time being, or his deputy; and that in the same court they may hold and may have cognizance of all and all manner of pleas and actions upon the case, deceipt, debts, accounts, detinues[1] and trespasses, taking and detaining of goods and chattels and other contracts whatsoever, for any causes, matters or things arising, happening, or growing within our said town and county of our said town of Galway, the liberties and precincts thereof; and that in the said court the said mayor and recorder of the said town for the time being, and their respective deputies as aforesaid, and may cause all and every person and persons against whom such suits, plaints, actions and demands as aforesaid shall be brought, sued or demanded to be attached according to the due course and process of law, by their goods and chattels within the said town and county of the said town of Galway, the liberties and precincts thereof, or shall and may cause the bodies of such persons to be arrested, and the bodies of such persons so arrested, to be committed and sent to prison, and by and according to the like due course of law shall and may have and determine all and singular such pleas, actions, plaints, suits and demands, and cause execution to be thereof made in as ample manner and form as hath been done, used, and accustomed in any court of record now, or at time heretofore held or kept within our said town and county of our said town of Galway, or any court of record now, or at any time heretofore holden or kept in any other city or borough or town corporate within our said kingdom of Ireland; and our further will and pleasure is, and we do by these presents for us, our heirs and successors, grant, restore, ratify, and confirm to the aforesaid mayor, sheriffs, free burgesses, and commonality of our said town and county of our said town of Galway, and their successors for ever, all the manors, messuages, houses, chantries, lands, tenements, wastes, waste grounds, common pastures, purprestures[2], reversions, rents, services and hereditaments whatsoever, which in and upon the 22nd of October 1641 were lawfully held and possessed or enjoyed by the mayor, sheriffs, free burgesses and commonality of the said town and county of the said town, in their politique capacity; and also all and all manner of such and the same liberties, franchises, free customs, immunities, usages, exemptions, easements, jurisdictions, fairs, markets, courts of pypowder[3], weyers, fishings, waters, wharfs, keys, customs, tolls, pickage[4], stallage[5], passage, pontage[6], paveage[7], goods and chattels wayved, strayes, treasuretrove, profits, commodities, advantages, benefits, emoluments, liberties, powers, authorities, privileges, duties, rights and hereditaments, lawfully had, held, used, received, possessed or enjoyed by the mayor, sheriffs, free burgesses, and commonality of the said town and county of the said town of Galway, in or upon the said two and twentieth day of October 1641, by

---

[1] Action to regain personal property, [Clachan ed.].
[2] The wrongful enclosure of or intrusion upon lands, waters, or other property rightfully belonging to the public at large, [Clachan ed.].
[3] The Pypowder Court's function was to deal with disputes with itinerant pedlars and it could impose fines, [Clachan ed.].
[4] A toll paid at fairs for leave to break ground for booths, [Clachan ed.].
[5] The right of erecting a stall or stalls in fairs; rent paid for a stall, [Clachan ed.].
[6] A toll levied for the building or repair of bridges, [Clachan ed.].
[7] A toll for the maintenance or improvement of a road or street, [Clachan ed.].

force and virtue of any charters or letters patents heretofore made or granted, or confirmed by any of our royal predecessors, late Kings and Queens of England, by whatsoever name or names, or by whatsoever incorporation they have been incorporated or known, or by force of or virtue of any lawful right, title or acquisition, purchase, usage, custom, prescription, or other lawful means whatsoever, although they or any of them have been abused, disused and discontinued: Wherefore we do will, and by these presents for us, our heirs and successors, do strictly enjoin and command that the mayor, sheriffs, free burgesses, and commonality of the said town and county of the said town of Galway, and their successors for ever, shall and may freely and entirely have, hold, use and enjoy all the liberties and free contents, privileges, authorities, jurisdictions, freedoms, manors, messuages, chantries, lands, tenements, and common pasture, fishings, wiers and hereditaments aforesaid, according to the tenor, effect, true intent and meaning of these our letters patents, without the least impeachment or hindrance of us, our heirs and successors, or any of the officers or ministers of us, our heirs and successors whatsoever, willing that the said mayor, sheriffs, free burgessers, and commonality of our said town and county of our said town of Galway or their successors, or any of them, be not at any time hereafter impleaded, molested, vexed, aggrieved, or in any ways troubled for or by reason of the premises, or any of them, by us, our heirs, and successors, or the sheriffs, escheaters[1], bailiffs, coroners or other officers or ministers whatsoever for us, our heirs and successors; saving nevertheless to every person or persons, their heirs and assigns, who have or claim any lands, tenements, or hereditaments formerly belonging to the said corporation of Galway in their politique capacity, by force and virtue of any letters patents under our great seal of Ireland, grounded on any certificate past by our late commissioners of our court of claim sitting at Dublin, all such estate, right, title, and interest as they and their heirs and assigns have or ought to have in law or equity, of, in, and unto such lands, tenements, or hereditaments, by force and virtue of any such certificates, and letters patents made unto them in manner as aforesaid; saving also unto Mrs. Elizabeth Hamilton, the widow and relict of James Hamilton, one of the grooms of our bed chamber, lately deceased, her heirs and assigns, all and such estate, right, title, and interest as she and they have in and unto any the lands, tenements, and hereditaments formerly belonging unto the said corporation of Galway, and which were lately given by us unto the said Elizabeth Hamilton, her heirs and assigns, by certain letters patents under our great seal of Ireland, bearing date the 5th day of September which was in the 25th year of our reign; saving also unto Colonel Theodore Russell, his heirs and assigns, all such estate, right, title, and interest as the said Theodore Russell, or the assigns of the said Elizabeth Hamilton hath, or ought to have in law or equity in and unto the duties, fees, and perquisites of the market of Galway, together with the market-house lately mortgaged by the corporation of

---

[1] Officers who had the duty of looking after the Kings escheats. Their abuses for personal gain led to the coining of the word 'cheater',

Galway to John Blake, esq. late recorder of Galway, for the sum of £400. sterling, and in and unto the charter and petty customs of Galway lately mortgaged by the said corporation unto Nicholas Blake and Gregory Lynch, and others, for the sum of £2000. sterling, all which said charter, market and petty duties and customs, were to be amongst other things granted by us to the late Elizabeth Hamilton, her heirs and assigns as aforesaid, and by her assigned or articled, and agreed to be assigned unto the said Theodore Russell, his heirs and assigns, for a great and valuable consideration laid out and paid by him for the same at the instance and desire of the said corporation; and therefore we do hereby ordain and appoint the said mayor, sheriffs, free burgesses and commonality of our said town and county of our said town of Galway, do accordingly for them and their successors covenant, promise, grant and agree to and with us, our heirs, and successors, that neither they the said mayor, free burgesses and commonality, nor their successors or any of them, nor any person or persons whatsoever claiming the premises, or any part thereof by freedom from them or any of them, or by or with their privity[1] or procurement, shall or will by virtue of these presents or otherwise, demand, levy, collect, or recover the charter, market and petty duties or customs aforesaid, or any of them, or wittingly or willingly interrupt, molest, or disturb, or give any interruption or disturbance at any time unto the said Theodore Russell, his heirs and assigns, or his or their agents and receivers in having, collecting, and receiving the aforesaid charter, market, and petty duties and customs, and every of them, until he and they have first levied, collected, and received out of all and singular the issues, perquisites, and profits that shall arise out of the said charter, market, and petty duties and custom of the said town of Galway to his or their own use, the full and entire sum of £2500. sterling, which hath been expended by him by purchasing the said charter, market, and petty duties from the said Mrs. Elisabeth Hamilton in manner as aforesaid; and also all such other sum or sums of money as he the said Theodore Russell shall upon oath account to have pended and laid out in and concerning the same, and until the said mayor, sheriff, free burgesses and commonality of the said town and county of the said town of Galway shall likewise have satisfied and paid to the said Theodore Russell, either out of the issues and profits of the said charter, market, and petty duties and customs aforesaid, or otherwise the full stun of £300. sterling over and above his disbursements, as a reasonable composition for his great pains and trouble undergone on the behalf of and for the good of that corporation; *and from and after such satisfaction of the same aforesaid, to the said Theodore Russell, his heirs and assigns, the said charter, market, and petty duties and customs of the town, to remain to the mayor, sheriffs, free burgesses and commonality of the said town, and their successors, to such uses whereunto the same were by any former charter of the said town granted or designed.* And our farther will and pleasure is, and we do hereby will and require our lieutenant general, or any other thief governor or

---

[1] A close, direct, or successive relationship; having a mutual interest or right, a connection or bond between parties to a particular property, [Clachan ed.].

governors of our said kingdom of Ireland, and our privy council there for the time being, that they and every of them do take care that the said mayor, sheriffs, free burgesses and commonality of our said town of Galway, and their successors, do hereby and truly observe, fulfill and perform and keep the several articles and Agreements by them made with us for satisfying the said Theodore Russell in manner as aforesaid; and that they pursue all fitting means for his security, and keep him in the quiet and full possession of the said duties and customs, either by an annual electing him unto the office or place of mayor of the said corporation in succession, until he is satisfied in all and singular the aforesaid sums and engagements or otherwise by such other reasonable and fitting ways and means as they shall judge to be most expedient and conducing to the ends and purposes aforesaid. And further, of our more ample grace, certain knowledge, and meer motion, by and with the advice and consent aforesaid, we do by these presents for us, our heirs and successors, grant unto the mayor, sheriff, free burgesses, and commonality of the; said town and county of the said town of Galway, and their successors for ever, that these our letters patents, or the emoluments thereof and every clause and covenant therein contained, shall be construed, interpreted, and read to the greatest advantage, benefit and favour of the said mayor, sheriffs, free burgesses and commonality of the said town of Galway, and their successors, against us our heirs and successors, as well in all our courts in our said kingdom of Ireland, as elsewhere soever, without any other confirmation, licence or toleration hereafter to be procured or obtained, notwithstanding any defect or default whatsoever in these our letters patents, or any other clause, matter or thing whatsoever to the contrary whatsoever, although no express mention, &c. And we further will, &c. without fine in our hanaper[1], &c. Provided always, that these our letters patent be enrolled in the rolls of our high court of chancery in our said kingdom of the land, within the space of six months next ensuing the date of these presents; any statute, &c. In witness whereof we have caused our letters to be made patent unto our aforesaid lieutenant general and general governor of our said kingdom of Ireland, at Dublin, the 14th day of August, in the twenty-ninth year of our reign.

The words of the charter of Richard II. after enumerating the tolls and customs, are, "Provided always that the "money pence" arising from thence to be laid out towards the walling and paving of the said town, and not otherwise. Those tolls and customs were first granted by Richard the Second's charter, the 18th of November 1396; Henry the Sixth's charter, 12th of March 1425; Edward the Fourth's charter, granted 28th of August 1464; Richard the Third's charter, granted the 15th of December, 1484, confirmed and enlarged the former charter of Richard the Second. But Richard the Third's charter says, "Provided always, that the pence money from thence arising be laid out on the murage and pavage of the said town, and not elsewhere or otherwise." The last charter gave the title of Maya and Courts. The Lord Mac

---

[1] A small wicker case used as a repository for legal documents, [Clachan ed.].

William of Clanrickard is deprived of all authority in Galway, and first uses the words murage and pavage. Henry the Eighth's charter, granted the third of July in the 56th year of his reign, greatly enlarged the former charters, which he has all respectively confirmed.

Edward the Sixth did the same. Elizabeth's charter, granted the 14th of July and 20th of her reign, greatly enlarged the former charters, and as to the tolls and customs, expressly says, "Provided always, that the pence money from thence arising *be faithfully* expended on the murage and pavage of the said town of Galway, and not elsewhere or otherwise." I have been favoured with copies of many other charters; but as they have been all recited in the subsequent charters of Elizabeth and Charles the Second, they would be merely literary curiosities, for which I did not think myself warranted in laying my friends under contribution.

The following poems I give as a specimen of county of Galway poetry. I fear the talent has died with their author.

APPENDIX

THE BATTLE OF THE CHAUNTERS.

BY DR DOMINICK O'KELLY OF BALLYGLASS,

A CELEBRATED PHYSICIAN.

(Fought near Castle Blakeney, in the county of Galway, 27th July, 1767.)

Now shield with shield, with helmet helmet doted,
To armour armour, lance to lance opposed;
To Greece and Troy the field of war divide,
And foiling ranks are strewed on either aide
None stoops a thought to base inglorious flight.
But horse to horse and man to man they fight
Not rabid wolves more fierce contest their prey.
Each wounds, each bleeds, but none resign the day.
                                        POPE'S HOMER.

THE sun was set, the busy fair was o'er,
And hawkers strained their weary lungs no more.
With tents well stored each neighboring road was lin'd,
And ev'ry ale-wife was exceeding kind.
Of these, Black Moll the purest liquor sold;
Rich, ripe, and clear, although not five days old.
Her spacious tent had seats for soft repose,
And from her pots a grateful steam arose.
Before her door she sate, with gracious air,
To greet her friends returning from the fair.
Hard task! her tongue was not a moment mute,
For who could pass without a kind salute?
Scarce could the tent her crowding guests contain,
Scarce could her hands supply the cheerful train:
From friend to friend, while foaming cups went round,
In songs the music of the drones was drown'd.
Ah, how Tarn Tip taught ev'ry note to thrill,
While Munster Jack exerted all his skill!
Both pipers, both well known o'er all the land,
For cards and dice, low wit, and slight of hand.
Both drunkards, am'rous, vers'd in ev'ry art,
To drain a cask, or wound a female heart.
Tom's softer strains young simple maids allure,

And Munster Jack no rival can endure:
Hence discord and disdain. The greatest wits
Are oft tormented with these jealous fits.
What wonder, then, if Jack should swell with pride?
Hear how he spoke; and bow Tom Tip replied.

MUNSTER JACK.

On thee, Clonmell! sure ev'ry blessing falls,
And joy for ever dwells within thy walls;
Nor less delightful are thy neighb'ring bow'rs,
Where merry sportsmen pass their careless hours,
Where sprightly notes set youthful hearts on fire,
And ev'ry shepherd dances like a squire.
There, bred with gentle folks, I learn'd my trade;
Nor were my fingers hardened by the spade.
Yield now, ye bagpipes! to the noisy drum,
And let spring water be prefered to rum;
Let th' ace of hearts, the clubs' black knave defy,
Since poor Tom Tip with Munster Jack can vie.

TOM TIP

Thy praise, Loughbrea! let ev'ry stranger tell,
Whose maids in beauty as in wealth excel;
Whose air no clouds, nor morning fogs obscure,
Whose bread is wholesome, and whose drink is pure.
Within thy walls, to priest-catchers unknown,
All things are safe but M—d— n h—ds alone.
'Tis there my pipe for ranting bucks I sound;
How shillings jingle when the plate goes round.
Sure low mushrooms like mountain oaks may rise,
And Eyre from Daly snatch the Galway prize;
Yon moon so pale, may teach the sun to see,
Since Munster Jack pretends to cope with me.

MUNSTER JACK

An iv'ry flute, with silver tip'd I boast,
A fairy brought it from Arabian coast:
How straight and smooth! this, while my breath inspires,
Old wives grown youthful, feel their former fires.

TOM TIP

My drone, 'tis true, no silver rings embrace,
Nor is my chaunter of the fairy race;
Yet honest maids, whose hearts to truth incline,
Will swear no music is more sweet than mine. (Bravissimo)

MUNSTER JACK

To me young Ross a dainty nag bestow'd,
Fit for the plough, but fitter for the road.
French gives me wine, nor is the wine misplac'd,
The good old colonel is a man of taste.
While men like these my lofty notes admire,
Poor Tom sits tip'ling at an ale-house fire.

TOM TIP

On Lombards ground three pye-bald cows I feed,
And three young heifers of Nic Lynch's breed
Nor think my bags are dry for want of wine,
For know Tom Garret and young Persse are mine.
If with Black Moll I pass an idle day,
For Moll what piper could refuse to play?

MUNSTER JACK

Gods! how Pegg Walker fills my heart with glee,
So kind, so fond, and of her punch so free!
Yet more than Pegg her servant maid I prize,
For smooth as doe skin are her legs and thighs:
And sure no doe with greater speed can run,
A smock she ran for, and the smock she won.

TOM TIP

A butcher's niece was once my soul's delight,
But out of mind, soon follows out of sight.
To good Kate Kearney my respects I paid,
And now I love the miller's blooming maid,
Whose limbs in beauty with her face agree;
No Munster lass hath lighter heels than she.

MUNSTER JACK

I grant her heels were lighter than her head,

When Lambart found her with his groom in bed,
And when the cook Alas! no more he sung!
Against the floor his guiltless pipes were flung:
The chaunter perished with a mournful sound,
And half the reed was buried in the ground.
Ah whence this civil rage? Ah Tom forbear!
And let a knave, a brother knave revere.
Up rose Black Molly the rising fray to quell,
And as she rose, her pipe in splinters fell;
Tom's arm she seized, and while she held it fast,
An earthen jug the Munster piper cast,
But missed his aim; for rolling as it went,
On a poor cotter's cheek its force was spent:
Two pond'rous grinders from their seats it tore,
Ah! doomed to stretch a bullock's hide no more!
The crowd stood up, men, women, took th' alarm
All wedged together like a clust'ring swarm;
The graver sort restrain, reproach, advise,
And trembling maidens join their feeble cries.
When lo! the Cobler from his seat arose,
The blood yet gushing from his mouth and nose,
All pale with rage, he rushed upon the crew,
With head, hands, feet, and friends and foes o'er threw.
Then all alike with thirst of vengeance burn'd,
The seats were shattered, and the pots o'erturned;
With one loud crash, the bulging tent was broke,
Tho' formed of canvas, and strong ribs of oak.
Reeling and tumbling o'er each other's heads,
Wide o'er the green the mad battalion spreads:
So waters gather'd on a rising ground,
Rush through their dams, and float the vales around.
And now the Cobler lifts a pond'rous stone,
Which with full force at Munster Jack was thrown;
But while to earth the cautious piper bends,
The rough, round bullet on a cask descends;
The vessel bursted with a dreadful sound,
Like yawning ice when heedless boys are drown'd,
The beer, that pleasing cordial of the poor,
In frothy torrents pour'd along the floor.
Black Moll beheld, and felt more grief no doubt,

Than if her husband's brains were dash'd about.
As Indian dames, their sons, or brothers slain,
In frantic gestures to their gods complain,
So to the skies her plaintive paws she spread,
Her eyes with fury starting from her head;
Then seized a tankard, which by chance was full,
Resolved to crush the crazy cobler's skull,
The tankard flies, but erring as it goes,
Falls like a bomb, on George the taylor's nose.
Ill fated youth! the darling of the fair,
For snuff, white stockings, and well powder'd hair;
In vain alas! the useful art he found,
To pinch his hat, and circumcise it round:
In dust he lay, the fustian frock he wore
Was drench'd with beer, and stained with purple gore;
Now Munster Jack to his associates cries,
See where my drone, unhappy victim! lies.
So great a conquest shall a scoundrel boast?
And shall my chaunter unrevenged be lost?
As thick as watchmen to a rising flame,
His dear comrades (all dear to mischief) came:
At Tom they flew, (so dogs a bull surround)
On his broad back their rattling cudgels bound.
While Tom defenceless, for assistance calls,
Full on his arm a ponderous cleaver fells;
Down drops his chaunter, (once so soft and sweet)
And the bag squeaks beneath its master's feet.
'Twas then Kate Kearney felt the dreadful fray,
Where stretch'd at ease beside the road she lay,
Not spent with too much toil, but overcome,
By treach'rous Hermes, in the form of rum.
With hair disordered in a thrice she rose,
And saw Top Tip encompassed by his foes;
Tom once so dear! henceforth ye nymphs be brave!
And learn, like Kate, your lovers' lives to save.
With strength endued, tho' frail about her waist,
A beggar's crutch she snatched with furious haste,
Fierce as a bitch, whose whelps are stolen away,
The young virago mingled in the fray:
Her stiff strong arms the jostling crowd divide,

And strokes on strokes she deals on ev'ry side.
First Nic the barber felt her vengeful ire,
Nic the gay cricket of each neighbour's fire;
Whose merry tales make mournful faces bright,
The miller's solace, and the smith's delight.
Next on a pedagogue her fury fell,
Who thought Alecto was let loose from hell.
No trope nor figure could her rage withstand,
And sure each neighbour schoolboy blest her hand.
As Dick the dancer rolled his watchful eye,
Trembling with fear, and yet ashamed to fly,
Prostrate he sunk beneath a thund'ring stroke,
His arm was batter'd, and his strings were broke.
Who now alas! shall charm the vulgar crew,
With strains which Handel or Duburgh ne'er knew;
Ah can his labours be so soon forgot?
Spare him O Kate who taught thee first to trot.
Nor could Black Tim, without a wound escape,
A fresh young shepherd of a comely shape,
Whose lungs are strong, although his arms be weak,
And on his lips the Jew harp seems to speak.
What grief, Black Moll I thy tender bosom tore
To see thy brother welt'ring in his gore?
Yet not in fruitless tears that grief was spent,
To sweet revenge her rising wrath she bent.
With all her might she struck the unguarded foe,
The cudgel cracked, Kate reel'd beneath the blow,
'Till, like a tree that struggles with the blast,
And falls uprooted by the storm at last,
Headlong she fell before the gazing crowd,
O! had the moon been hid behind a cloud.
Now Moll exalting urged her friend to rise,
And chear'd the rest with animating cries.
Not sturdy Sancho in a blanket tost,
Nor e'en Don Quixote when his teeth he lost,
Felt such resentment as this warlike band,
All sorely wounded by a female hand.
At helpless Kate a shower of dirt was thrown,
And all their rage was aim'd at her alone.
Straight th' adverse party to her rescue flew,

The tumult spread, the battle blazed anew,
Shouts followed shouts, taught ev'ry throat to roar,
And those engaged, that shun'd the fray before.
Thicker than fops that for precedence strive,
Thicker than bees, when crowding to their hive,
They mix'd in fight, a wild tempestuous throng,
Stick clash'd with stick, and clown drove clown along.
Kate roared for help; (not sailors half so loud,
When the red lightnings flash from shroud to shroud,)
Nor cries nor tears her brutal foes could charm,
One seiz'd her leg, one fastened on her arm.
To Heaven at length, with upward eyes she pray'd,
And Heaven sure loves a charitable maid:
For lo! descending from his steed appeared
The rough good priest, whom all his people fear'd.
His lash he whired amidst the warring crew,
The clamour ceas'd, the combatants withdrew.
With wrathful eyes he view'd the dismal scene,
Hats, hoods, cloaks, cravats, scattered o'er the green!
Then fir'd with zeal, the list'ning crowd he charged,
And chose a text, and on that text enlarged:
"Beer makes young men the foulest crimes commit;"
Ah! think what Lot did in a drunken fit!".
Moll broached a cask. — The man of God drew nigh,
For after preaching ev'ry pipe is dry.
Around their guardian flock'd the wounded swains.
And beer and music banish'd all their pains.
The social pipe diffus'd a grateful smoak,
The milk-maid laugh'd, the 'ploughman crack'd his joke.
Tom Tip and Jack, eternal friendship swore,
And Moll embrac'd her gossips o'er and o'er.
The skilful Dick, once more his art displayed,
While Tom with Kate a tuneful concert made.
Each am'rous heart was tickl'd with the sound,
And kisses strait, instead of kicks, went round.
At length the cask was drain'd of all its store,
(How Moll was curs'd, when she could give no more)
Each guest departed with an aching head,
And rising Phoebus lighted all to bed.

>   ——— Quis talia fando
>   Temperet a lacrymis?[1]
> *The humble petition of Cornelius O'Clummughan,[2] the famous poor scholar, to the priest of the parish.*

Humbly sheweth,

That I went to Ballynahan th'other day ('twas Sunday morning I remember,
For I was not there you must know, before, since the latter end of September,)
There was a desperate fire in the kitchen; so myself sat down very snug,
'Till Miss Peggy (God bless her) came down, and brought me the bracket jug.
"Is that Cornelius," says she, "'tis good for sore eyes to see the stranger."
'Twas the want of health, madam," says myself, "that made me become a stranger,
I travell'd many a weary step between Caltragh and Kinclare,
And went to Ballinlass itself, but Doctor Dillon was not there.
"He's here in the house," says she, "as good a man as ever trod in leather,
For he cures all the common people without asking a feather."
"Common people!" says myself, "I know what that expression means:"
"Pardon me, Cornelius," says she, "to be sure there is good blood in your veins:"
"The O'Clummoghans, madam," says myself, "are the most populous people in the land;"
"Indeed I meant no harm," says Miss Peggy, so with that she shook my hand.
Then I went up to the parlour; and to be sure they were all very glad,
"Your welcome," says Master Lacky, (indeed a very courteous lad.)
Then the doctor looked at myself, as who should say, "what brought you here?"
"Most noble sir!" says myself, "I'm sick these three quarters of a year:
My father wore cloth of gold, although myself be clad in a homely frize,"
"That's not the thing," says the doctor, "but tell me where your disorder lies."
"Why, sir? you must know," says I, "that I was three years and a half with Mr. Dunn;
As stout a scholar, by St. Bridget, as ever saw the noon day sun;
But now the small of my back is weaker than an osier twig,
And I cannot go to school, nor read, nor write, nor dig."
So the doctor looked at Mr. Fallon, and began to smile and wink;
"Ah! gentlemen,!" says myself, "I'm not such a man as you think,
It was reading Horace very fast, and lying often on the ground,

---

[1] "Who, in speaking such things, can abstain from tears?" (Virgil), [Clachan ed.].
[2] O'Clummugban is a rough, ugly, fellow, [original footnote].

That gave my constitution, at last, a mortiferous wound."
"Well," says the doctor, "bathe in cold water, 'tis the best thing you can do;
And I'll engage your back will be strong enough in a month or two."
"Celeberrime vir!" says myself "is it safe to dip in the frigid wave?"
"Yes, yes," says he, "my good lad," so with that myself took leave.
'Twas then at Clunagh house I saw the chimnies greatly smoking:
"Well, well," says I to myself, "that I'll dine there is past all joking."
So I went in at the kitchen door, and being a lad of an excellent shape,
I bowed down my head, as you understand, and made a very courteous scrape.
Then I took out my book of knowledge, and fell a reading very loud,
'Till all the servants gathering round me, look'd like a fair day crowd.
 "O Gemni!" cried the cook maid, "I'd give my green gown to read so gay;"
"Pugh!" says the tea boy, "that lad would speak Latin 'with a face of clay'?
"Pray, sir," says Molly Walsh, "what's it you read in Arristottle?"
"That you'll be married to a taylor," says myself, "without cow, sheep, or cattle."
"To a taylor?" says the tea boy, "pray, friend! what trade do you follow?"
"I'm no mechanic," says myself, "but a true son of Apollo."
"What Pollo?" says he very fiercely, "damn me, you look like a goose"—
"Harkee, sirrah," says myself, "do you know to whom you give that abuse?
I'm none of your greasy grooms, nor your lick plate liv'ry fops"—
So I up's with my fist, and gives him a lick across the chops.
"Murther!" says he, "murther! "says myself; so to it we fell clutter, clatter,
'Till Mrs. Fallon herself run down, and asked what was the matter?
But when she saw myself over head and ears in a pot of broth.
"O God!" says she, "the scholar's drown'd, 'tis a pity, faith and troth."
"Faith, madam," says Molly Walsh, "twas himself struck Jack across the pate"—
"Jack is a rogue," says she, "by the same token he ne'er shall taste my meat."
So getting a short discharge (now this is truth as I'm a sinner)
He went off with a flea in his ear, and, as the saying is, without his dinner.
At length Miss Betty came down (to be sure I never saw her such)
"O Lord!" says she "Mr. Scholar! I admire your courage very much."
"Fie, Molly do not weep; fare you can take himself for a spark;
"Ton my honor he'll write a ballad with any man from this to Cork."
"Bright goddess!" says myself, "who art much fairer than Britomartis
 "I adore thy worshipful face, opus naturae non artis?
When Mrs. Fallon heard the Latin, as she's always very discerning,
And extremely civil to lads (such as myself) of polite learning;
"Come, Tom," says she, "lay the cloth: may the weavers steal my yarn,
"If I don't respect him more than one with gold lace, hounds, and horn."
So when myself had done my best, and found that I could do no more,

I put my leavings in my satchel, as I often did before.
Then I went to the river's side; the Suck was full up to the brim,
I strip'd off what clothes I had, and so I began to swim.
But little did I dream that all my substance could be taken,
When I saw the great house dog running off with my books and my bacon.
"O Hector!" says I, "O murther!" says I, "what's this your going to do?'
So he turned about his angry nose, as who should say,
"what's that to you?"
Myself was in such a fright, I did not know where to sit or stand,
So at length I met John the clerk, with a pole in his hand.
"Well John," says I, "it can't be help'd, to be snre 'tis a desperate case,"
Do you know that Hector took my satchel, and eat it up before my face?"
"I knew that rogue" said John, "since first he wore a leathern collar,
And I'll take my Bible book, he plundered many a ragged scholar."
"A ragged scholar!" says myself, "pon my soul John I never liked your prate,"—
So then I went to a shepherd's house, for you must know 'twas very late;
The woman prepared a supper that was fit for the lord of the manor;
"Mr. O'Clummughan," says she, "your learning deserves a greater honor,"
But what you'll do for a bed, is a thing myself does not know;
For the cows eat all our straw last week, in the time of the snow.
But sure you can lye with ourselves, as Tom won't come to night from the mill,"
"Quid tibi vis mulier?"[1] says myself, "have you a mind to try my skill?"
"Odi profanum vulgus — don't you know that I'm a man of letters?
And therefore, good woman," says I, "you should never think of your betters."
Then I stretched my weary limbs by the fire side, and fell asleep in a thrice,
For my satchel, as you know, being lost, I was not afraid of the mice.
So I dream'd the house of Clunagh was full of ladies and people,
And that every candle in the parlour was higher than any steeple.
Myself stood gaping at the door, when Mrs. Fallon bounced up from the table,
"Gentlemen and ladies," says she "upon my honor I'll tell you no fable.
Behold that worthy youth; although he cannot dance or caper,
He'll write a verse with any man that ever set pen to paper.
But Hector eat his satchel, (for which I'll hang the nasty thief,)
And four or five shillings from you would be a very great relief."
So when the ladies felt their pockets, and each brought out a goodly piece,
Myself was as proud as if I got Jason's golden fleece.
And now if you would speak to Mrs. Fallon to make this my vision true,
Poor Cornelius, as in duty bound, would ever pray for her and you.

---

[1] "What do you want, woman?", Latin, Horace, [Clachan ed.].

The author of the two foregoing poems was in his early days a physician of the county of Galway, well remembered for his satirical wit, eccentricities and misfortunes. No man who has a strong feeling of the vices or follies of the inhabitants of a country, and is also weak enough to publish them, can expect to be a favorite. This operated against poor Dr. O'Kelly, and he lived long enough to feel the effects of it. Many anecdotes of him are still remembered. He called at a house near Caltra, the lady of which was not as liberal of her strong beer (of which the Doctor was very fond,) as he wished: after being regaled with some eatables and very weak small beer, he left behind on the table at his departure, a slip of paper, with

> *Your ale to make small beer next akin,*
> *Is like yourself, sour, spiritless and thin.*

The apprehension of his satirical pen was so great, that tradition says a propitiatory fat sheep was sent to him the following day. The Battle of Chaunters loses something of its point at this distance of time, from the characters being almost unknown to the present generation; but sufficient I imagine remains to place his talent for genuine humour on such high ground, as none since his day could reach. The petition of Cornelius O'Clammughan is founded on a humorous fact of the day, and also loses something by time; but enough remains to show the rich mine from which it was attracted. There are many other things of the same author floating about the country, that escaped my research, particularly another battle of the chaunters between two other pipers at a much later period, of which I have not been able to procure a copy.

It would be unpardonable to omit mentioning Cormac Common, celebrated by the elegant pen of Mr. Walker in his Irish Bards, as probably the last of the order of minstrels called *Tale-tellers*.

He died at Sorreltown near Dunmore, in the county of Galway, where he lived with one of his daughters. "It was in singing some of our native airs that he displayed the powers of his voice; on these occasions his auditors were always enraptured. I have been assured that no singer ever did Carolan's airs or Ossian's celebrated hunting song more justice than Cormac. His musical powers were not confined to his voice; he composed a few airs, one of which Mr. Ousley thinks extremely sweet. It is to be feared those musical effusions will die with their author." "But it was in poetry that Cormac delighted to exercise his genius. He has composed several songs and elegies, which have met with applause. As his muse was generally awakened by the call of gratitude, his poetical productions are mostly panegyrical or elegiac; they extol the living or lament the dead. Sometime he indulged in satire, but not often, though indued with a rich vein of that dangerous gift." His moral character was unstained; his person was large and muscular.

MR. KNIGHT'S DIRECTIONS FOR MAKING CIDER

"The merit of cider will always depend on the proper separation of the fruits: those only whose fruit is yellow or yellow mixed with red, are proper to make the fine cider; those whose flesh and rind are green are very inferior. The fruit should remain on the tree until a slight shake will disengage them from the tree.

Each kind should be kept separate in layers eight or ten inches thick, exposed to the sun and air, and not pressed until they are perfectly mellow without being decayed. Except the fruit can be exposed to a free current of air, they had better not be put under cover; but where this can be effected it is an improvement. Fruit improves as long as it continues to increase in colour without decaying, and before grinding they should be carefully examined, and any green or decayed fruit carefully separated from them; this will not only greatly improve the flavour of the cider, but prevent too great a degree of fermentation. Each kind of fruit should be ground separately, or mixed only with such as become ripe at the same time. By a judicious mixture of fruits, the requisite qualities of richness, astringency, and flavour are obtained; which seldom can be had from one kind. In grinding, the fruit should be so reduced that the rind and kernels should be scarcely discernable. In such a complete mixture, it seems probable that new elective attractions will be exerted, and compounds formed, which did not exist previously to the fruit being placed under the roller. The process of slow grinding, with free access of air, giving the cider good qualities it did not possess before, probably by the absorption of oxygen. To procure very fine cider, the fruit should be ground and pressed imperfectly, and the pulp spread as thin as possible, exposed to the air, and frequently turned during twenty-four hours, to obtain as large an absorption of air as possible. The pulp should be ground again, and the liquor formerly expressed added to it, by which the liquor will require an increase of strength and richness. Whilst fermentation is proceeding the casks should be kept in the open air, or in airy sheds, and racked when it becomes clear; before this it is useless to rack, as the fermentation begins again. The instant fermentation stops, which may be known by the clearness of the liquor, it should be drawn off into a clear cask, and the lees put into flannel bags, the clear liquor from those should be returned to the cask; but it must have great attention paid to it that it has not the least tendency to become acetous, which it will frequently do in forty-eight hours; if so it must on no account be added to the cider in the cask. If the cider after being racked remains bright and quiet, nothing more is to be done until spring; but if a scum collects on the surface, it must immediately be racked off into another cask; as this would produce bad effects if suffered to sink. If a disposition to ferment with violence again appears, it will be necessary to rack off from one cask to another as often as a hissing noise is heard. When cider is not disposed to ferment, it is probable that a small quantity of yeast or the lees of good cider will produce that effect, which is desireable before the commencement of cold weather. In April the cider should be racked into the casks in which it is to remain. They should be previously well scalded and dried, and filled nearly to the bung, and stopped closely if all danger of fermentation is over, but not so tightly as to endanger the casks in case of a renewed fermentation. Cider, which has been made from good fruits and properly manufactured, will retain a considerable portion of sweetness in the cask for three or four years. It is usually in the best state to be bottled at two years old, when it will become brisk and sparkling, and if it possesses much richness will remain with scarcely any change for twenty or thirty years if well corked. The specific gravity of the juice of any apple recently expressed, indicates with very considerable accuracy the strength of the future cider."

Every person knows that few if any of those directions are observed in the county of Galway, therefore the cider is very inferior.

FINIS

Index

Absenteeism, 229
Agents, 37, 45, 59, 65, 84, 86, 87, 97, 104
Aghrim, 10, 67, 209, 248, 266
Aghrim, battle of, 165, 166
Ahaseragh, 19, 97
Amicable Society, the, 115
Anderson of Fermoy, 188
Annals of Ulster, 271
Appleyard, Mr. Thomas, 53
Archbishops of Tuam, 136, 146, 153, 154, 160, 187
Ardagh, 269, 270
Ardbear, 15, 21, 25, 217, 257
Arderrow, 25
Ardfroy, 20
Ardfry, 123
Ardrahan, 40, 58, 67
Arran islands, 1, 2, 15, 62, 90, 108, 135, 139, 156, 158, 161, 175, 194, 221, 226, 233, 254, 263, 269, 276, 279, 320, 323
Ashtown, Lord, 10, 46, 54, 56
Athenry, 3, 5, 18, 32, 40, 58, 67
Athenry, Baron of, 121
Athlone, 10, 28, 81, 134, 138, 139, 155, 160
Athy, 84, 119, 120, 126, 127, 128, 139, 151
Augustinians, 126

Ballinaboy, 25
Ballinakill, 21
Ballinasloe, 7, 10, 51, 52, 61, 64, 66, 67, 69, 70, 81, 88, 89, 109, 137, 184, 189, 209, 211, 212, 234, 235, 251
Ballinasloe fair, 10, 61, 81, 88, 235
Ballybanemore, 227
Ballyclare, 132, 137
Ballydonndan, 10
Ballydonnelan, 58
Ballyfenton, 138
Ballymackward, 19
Ballymanagh Fort, 148
Ballynahinch, 1, 3, 4, 9, 13, 18, 21, 22, 25, 27, 46, 58, 61, 90, 101, 232, 254
Ballynakill, 15, 22, 100
Banagher, 41
Bank of Ireland, 233, 234
Bank of Tuam, 234
Banking, 233
Bannagher, 7

Barrett family, 162, 168, 172
Battle of Chaunters, 359
Beggars, 118, 149, 196
Begge, 125
Bellew, Mr., x, 11, 46, 95, 285
Bencoona, 22
Bengower, 22
Bermingham, 119, 151, 154, 187, 188. See also *de Bermingham.*
Bird family, 162, 169, 172
Bishops of Clonfert, 56, 72, 136, 187
Bishops of Killaloe, 157
Bishopric of Mayo, 269
Bishops of Meath, 138
black mud / *mooreen*, 43, 96, 97
Blakes, the, , 20, 64, 119, 120, 122, 123, 124, 126, 129, 130, 131, 135, 136, 138, 143, 144, 145, 146, 147, 148, 149, 151, 153, 154, 165, 171, 172, 174, 175, 176, 179, 180, 181
Blake of Furbough, 227
Blake of Merlin Park, x, xiv, 227
Blake, Mr. Francis, 112
Blake, Sir Richard, 148, 150
Blake-Fitz-Andrew, 150, 154
Blake-Fitz-Christopher, 148
Blake-Fitz-Nicholas, 153, 154
Blake-Fitz-Robert, 153
Blake-Fitz-Robert-Fitz-Walter-Fitz Andrew, 148
Blake-Fitz-Walter-Fitz-Thomas, 149
Blakes, 119, 123, 132
Bodkin-Fitz-David, 153
Bodkin-Fitz-Domnick, 151
Bodkin-Fitz-Thomas, 150
Bodkins, 119
Bog timber, 253
Bogland, xi, 3, 5, 8, 9, 10, 11, 12, 13, 15, 30, 36, 45, 57, 86, 91, 94, 96, 97, 101, 102, 239, 244, 247, 253, 254, 255, 256, 257, 258
Boheshul, 25
Boyce family, 159
Brabazon, Mr, 226
Brandy, 109, 196
Brehon laws, 128
Briarfield, 211
Bricknells, 178, 179
Brock family, 162
Brown Fitz-Oliver, 149

Browne, Mr., of Moyne, 46, 62
Browne, Sir Domnick, 150
Browne-Fitz-James, 154
Browne-Fitz-Nicholas, 153
Browne-Fitz-Thomas, 148
Buachaly, 28
Bulteel, Mr., 5
Burkes, 121, 126, 128,132, 133, 135, 138, 139, 148, 152, 154, 158, 161, 172, 175, 177, 179, 181, 184, 277, 278, 279
Burke of Murrough, 227
Burke, Rev. Bartholomew, 228
Burke, Rickard, 242
Burke, Sir John, 10, 18, 46, 147, 232, 246, 247
Burke, Sir Thomas, 18, 19
Burke, Ulick, 132, 139, 161
Burkes of St. Clerans, 10
Burrin, 2, 8, 161, 263
Bushell familt, 162
Butler, 2, 119, 125, 138, 232, 277, 278
Butler, Dr. Ledwich, xiii

Caddells, (Blakes), 119
Caeggclare, 40
Cahir, 58
Canmore, 121
Cappahoosh, 25
Cappard, 186
Carew, Sir George, 136
Carlow, 78, 79
Carts, 51
Castle Hacket, 9, 31
Castle Taylor, 8
Castlebar, 23, 58
Castleboy, 186
Castlecoote, 153
Castlekirk, 27
Castles, 260, 261
Cattle, xii, 2, 8, 10, 11, 14, 27, 42, 43, 46, 47, 48, 50, 57, 59, 60, 61, 62, 63, 65, 66, 69, 70, 71, 72, 73, 74, 75, 76, 82, 88, 90, 92, 93, 94, 95, 100
Chalybeate wells, 31
Charter schools, 228
Chisterman, Mr, 101
Cicero, 229
Claddagh, 109, 110
Clancarty, Earl, 7, 10
Clancarty, Lord, 184, 185, 188
Clandonnels, 137
Clane, 7

Clanmacnois, 136
Clanmorris, Lord, 123, 152
Clanrickard, 3, 4, 18, 32, 126, 133, 137, 138, 139, 150, 152, 153, 156, 159, 161, 162, 163, 165, 182, 230, 249, 260, 278, 280, 348
Clanrickard, Countess of, 183
Clare County, x, xii, 1, 2, 3, 5, 8, 9, 10, 15, 16, 20, 24, 42, 49, 58, 60, 86, 97, 123, 129, 144, 145, 160, 186, 198, 204, 208, 216, 220, 233, 254, 255, 263, 266, 310
Clare-Galway, 27, 58, 278
Clarke, Messrs., of Galway, 183
Cleggan, 21
Cleggan Head, 21
Clifden, x, 7, 25, 61, 188, 208, 230
Clifton [?], 21, 100
Climate, 5, 6, 14
Clonbrock, Lord, 10, 56, 230
Coke, Mr, of Holkham, 82
Conbrock, Lord, 101
Cong, 15, 18, 23, 27
Conmacne-Ira, 4
Conmacnemara, 4
Connemara, xi, 2, 4, 6, 7, 8, 12, 13, 14, 17, 18, 20, 21, 25, 32, 37, 51, 58, 62, 63, 64, 65, 68, 81, 82, 100, 101, 102, 103, 104, 3, 42, 78, 82, 87, 88, 90, 92, 98, 102, 103, 108, 109, 110, 111, 115, 118, 122, 131, 132, 134, 152, 153, 154, 157, 158, 178, 180, 181, 184
Connor-mac-a-Righ, 139
Cork, 66, 78, 84, 221, 239
Cormac Common, 359
Corn, 7, 8, 9, 12, 33, 38, 40, 42, 43, 48, 50, 52, 53, 66, 75, 86, 87, 91, 97, 102, 105
corn acres (conacre), 88
Costellos, 119
Council of Cashel, 229
Court houses, 114, 117
Cower, 22
Creggan, 160
Creran, 92
Croagh Patrick, 21
Croghwell, 58
Cromlechs, 263
Cromwell, Oliver, 111, 118, 119, 158, 159, 161, 224, 247, 253, 260, 261
Culliagh, 209
Cunnine, Manus, 147
Curry's Review, 203
Curwen, Mr., of Workington, 57

D'Arcey, 138, 144, 153, 154, 188
D'Arcey Fitz-Nicholas, 153
D'Arcy, Mr. of Clifden Castle, x
D'Arcy, Mr., of Galway, x
D'Arcys, x, 12, 20, 32, 65, 120, 126, 144, 230
D'Ussona, a French, 165
D'Arcey, 145, 147
D'Arcy, of Clifden, 63
Dairies, 78
Daly of Dunsandle, 34
Daly of Mount Shannon, 238
Daly, Right Hon. D. B., 10
Dalyston, 7, 10, 29, 250, 263
Davis of Hampstead, 1
de Bermingham, 121, 278
De Bry's *Collection of Voyages*, Vol. 1, 35
De Mareschall, 121
Deane family, 120, 125, 126, 128, 159
Deer, 64, 65
Derryclare, 21
Derryvreeda, 22
Digby, 1, 233
Diocesan schools, 228
Dominicans, 177, 187, 188
Drill machines, 50
Dublin, i, ii, viii, xi, 16, 17, 18, 45, 47, 53, 59, 64, 65, 71, 72, 79, 81, 84
Dublin Society, the, 12, 16, 210
Ducket, Mr, of Esher, 90
Duff, 135
Dunboyne, Lord, 122
Dunbrody Abbey, 265
Dundonald, Lord, 97
Dunlo, 66, 67
Dunmore, 7, 10, 18, 242, 266
Dunsandle, 32, 102
Dysart, 120

Eagers, 178, 179
Earl of Essex, 135
Earl of Thomond, 139, 146
Earls of Desmond, 279
Earls of Kildare, 279
Eastwell, 10, 230
Edmund, Mr. Costello of Galway, x
Education, 222, 226, 227, 228
Edward IV, 119, 122
Elkington, Mr., 11, 56, 94, 95
Ely, Viscount, 151
Emmet, Mr., 202
Emuin a Thuane, 121

Enachdoen, 269
Endeus, 2, 276
Exports, 201, 235, 241
Eyre family, 159, 162, 168, 169, 173, 174, 178, 179, 180, 181
Eyrecourt, 10, 19, 52, 63, 67, 180, 224, 231

Fairs, 6, 10, 47, 56, 61, 66, 70, 75, 81, 86, 88, 105, 222, 233, 235, 236, 238
Farm houses, 83
Farmer's Kalendar, 75, 106
Farmers Journal, 39
Farming Societies, ix, 38, 39, 46, 47, 49, 51, 64, 95, 100, 101, 229, 234
Farming Society of Ireland, ix, 39, 46, 47, 49, 51, 64, 73, 95, 234, 235, 236, 257
Faunt, 119, 126, 128, 129, 133, 134, 136, 146, 151
Fermnamore, 24
Fingal, 41, 49, 93
Finniesglen, 22
Fiorin grass, 12, 36, 45, 54, 55, 57, 60, 73, 74, 89, 96, 100
Fish markets, 6, 113, 114, 242
Fisheries/Fishing, 12, 103, 213, 214, 223, 224, 225

Fitzgerald, Mr., 114
Flax, 46, 51
Fleming, 162
Flour mills, 30
Font, 119, 145
Forbes, Lord, 153, 261
Franciscan Abbey, 110, 178
Franciscans, 224
French, 120, 125, 126, 127, 129, 131, 132, 133, 134, 135, 136, 137, 138, 139, 143, 144, 145, 146, 147, 148, 149, 151, 153, 154, 155, 158, 159, 165, 170, 174, 175, 176, 179, 180, 181, 182
French, of French Park, 63
French, of Monivae, 101
French, Sir Oliver, 155
Frenches of Monivae, 10, 209
French-Fitz-Edmond, 155
French-Fitz-George, 150
French-fitz-Marcus, 147, 148
French-Fitz-Patrick, 149, 150
French-Fitz-Peter, 158
French-Fitz-Stephen, 149
Fuller, Mr., M.P., 229

Galtrim, 121
Galway Bay, 1, 2, 130, 143, 153, 177, 193, 222, 225, 226, 247, 264, 279, 282
Galway fish market, 112
Galway Hospital rules, 116
Galway meat market, 112
Galway merchants, 201
Galway names - pre 'the tribes', 119
Galway. meaning of, 4
Gaols, 113, 114, 117, 118, 165, 178
Garomin, 25
Ginkle, General, 165
Glan, 15, 21, 23, 24
Glan Ina, 21
Glen Hoghan, 21
Glentrasna, 26
Gort, 3, 7, 8, 10, 16, 17, 18, 52, 56, 64, 67, 154, 155, 186, 230, 261, 284
Gort, Lord, 16, 17, 20, 30
Governors of Connaught, 138
Grand Jurors, xi
Grasses, 72
Graziers, 1, 10, 48, 59, 60, 61, 62, 66, 69, 70, 81, 86, 90
Greenway family, 162
Grouse Lodge, 29

Hampstead, 19, 32
Hanging gales, 87
Hardiman, James, xiii, xiv, 4, 6, 108, 120, 122, 124, 179, 232, 261, 270, 286
Harriott, Thomas, 35
Harrows, 50, 52, 89
Hayes of Avondale, 245
Headford, 123, 160, 165, 184, 189
Holkham Cattle Show, 62
Holy days, 258
Horse-leap, 208, 211, 212
Houses of Galway, 114
Hurd, Humphry, 160
Hy-Fiacria Aidne, 4
Hy-Tartagh, 4

Iar-Connaught, 4, 109, 133, 134, 277, 278
Imlagh, 25
Infirmaries, 110, 116, 174
Ingoldsby, Colonel Henry, 158
Inishgan, 28
Inishgile, 28
Innis Leer, 1
Innishgoile, 264
Innismore, 1

Iron ore, 18

Jobbing, xi, 207, 209, 286
Joyce and Co., 233
Joyce, Messrs, 114
Joyce's country, 13, 14, 22, 24, 27
Jurors, 207, 229

Kaims, Lord, 229, 255
Keatinge, Dr., 152
Kelp, 14, 102, 103, 104
Kilcolgan/Kilcogan, 30, 38
Killery, 21
Killery Bay, 21, 24
Killimor, 32
Killrinckle, 10
Kilmacduagh, 186

Kiltulla/Kiltolla, 32, 65
King John, 119, 187
King of Denmark, 136
Kings of Connaught, 121, 134, 188, 274, 275, 277, 286
Kings of Immany, 278
Kings of Ireland, 269, 273, 276, 279, 280
Kings of Leinster, 273
Kings of Ulster, 273
Kinvara, 58
Kinvara castle, 261
Kirvara, 40
Kirwan, Mr. , of Dalgin, 10
Kirwan, Mr. Joseph, 99
Kirwan, Richard, 2, 130, 134, 149, 155, 261
Kirwan-Fitz-Andrew, 153
Kirwans, 130
Knock-Lynch, 152
Knockmoy, 20
Knocknay, 31
Knocktopher, 24
Kylemore, 21

Lack liagh, 97
Laganians, 273
Lake Ina, 21
Lake, General, 177
Lambart, of Creggclare, 50
Larkin, Mr., 1, 26, 286
Lawrence at Lawrencetown, 238
Le Petit, William, 120
Le Poer Trench, 212, 221
Le Power Trench, Rev. Charles, 184
Leam, 26

Leggett, Thomas, 178
Leinster cars, 51
Letterbrickaun, 22
Letterfore, 26
Letterfragh, 22
Lettery, 21
Limerick, 66, 78, 221, 239
Limerick County, 10, 75
Linchee, 121, 135
Linen, 236, 238, 239
Liscopel, 209
Littery, 22
Lord Galway, 166
Lord Mayo, 157
Lough Contra, 186
Lough Corrib, 7, 9, 13, 14, 15, 17, 21-27, 143, 182, 184, 212, 225, 260, 264
Lough Coutra, 30
Lough Elan, 25
Lough Mask, 14, 15, 21, 23, 24, 27
Lough Oured, 25
Loughcoutra, 3, 20, 56
Loughrea, 3, 10, 19, 29, 30, 52, 66, 68, 102
Lowville, 19
Lynch-Fitz-James, 151
Lynch Dubh, William, 122
Lynch Fitz Thomas, Edmond, 121
Lynch Fitz-Marcus-Fitz-Martin, 155
Lynch, Gorman, 122
Lynch, Gormyn, 119
Lynch, Nicholas More, 115
Lynch, Pierce, 122, 123, 135, 137, 138, 143, 145, 147
Lynch, Sir Robert, 156
Lynch's castle, 261
Lynch-Fitz-Ambrose, 151, 158
Lynch-Fitz-Andrew, 150, 157
Lynch-Fitz-Anthony, 155
Lynch-Fitz-Arthur, 130, 148
Lynch-Fitz-James-Fitz-Ambrose, 151
Lynch-Fitz-John, 147, 149, 150, 155
Lynch-Fitz-Jonakine, 149
Lynch-Fitz-Nicholas, 148, 151, 155
Lynch-Fitz-Nicholas-Fitz-Stephen-Fitz Arthur, mayor, 148
Lynch-Fitz-Patrick, 135, 155
Lynch-Fitz-Peter, 151
Lynch-Fitz-Pierce, 150
Lynch-Fitz-Richard, 148
Lynch-Fitz-Stephen, 130, 150, 151, 155
Lynch-Fitz-Stephen -Fitz-Nicholas, 157
Lynch-Fitz-Thomas, 158

Lynch-Fitz-William, 151
Lynsky, 121

Maam, 21
Maam Ina, 21
Maamgawney, 22
Mac Dermotts, 144
Mac William Eighter, 121, 135, 137
Mac William Oughter, 121, 138
Macan Earlas, 137, 138
Macherithimar, 120
Maclachlan, Mr., xii
Magheridernan, 120
Mahon, Rev. Dean, 11, 231
Mahons of Castlegar, 11
Malthus, 10, 99
Mamturk, 13, 22
Mananan Mac Lir, 28
Mangel worzel, 43, 89
Mannin Bay, 21
Manuscripts, 136
Maps of Galway, 286
Marble, 18
Marblehill, 10, 19, 46
Marl, 19
Martin-Fitz Jasper, 153
Martin-Fitz-Geoffry, 151
Martin-Fitz-Nicholas, 151
Martin-Fitz-Stephen, 151, 157
Martin-Fitz-Thomas, 154
Martin-Fitz-Walter, 147, 150
Martins, 7, 9, 17, 18, 20, 46, 63, 101, 120, 125-131, 134-139, 142-151, 154, 165, 174-176, 179, 180, 189
Mausergh St George, 184
May family, 110, 147, 149, 155, 157, 161, 162
Mayo County, 1, 4, 7, 9, 21, 24, 27, 29, 31, 56, 95, 109, 129, 135, 137, 140, 148, 152, 157, 165, 176, 182, 184, 255, 263, 277, 309
McEvoy, *Survey of the County of Tyrone*, 45
McRoebuck Bermingham, Donell, 148
Meath, 11, 41, 66, 92, 93
Merlin Park, 18
Milk, 21, 36, 62, 79, 80, 83
Mill, bleach, 241
Millers, 201, 224, 241
Mills, flour, 241, 242
Mills, malt, 241
Mills, oat, 241
Mills, paper, 241

Mills, tuck, 241
Minterowen, 24
Miveel, 22
Monasteries, 116, 145, 164
Moncktons, the, 117
Monivue, 8
Moore, Charles, 166
Moore, Mr., 114
More-Lynch-Fitz-Marcus, 150
Morgan family, 114, 162, 169, 171, 172, 173, 175, 176, 177, 179
Morgan, Mr., of Monksfield, 114
Morris, 58, 119, 120, 123, 125, 126, 128, 129, 130, 136, 143, 144
Mount Bellew, 11, 19, 46, 52, 54, 57, 72, 95, 184, 188, 189
Mountshannon, 7, 18, 19, 31
Moycastle, 31
Moycullen, 1, 3, 4, 7, 13, 58, 61, 90, 231, 293
Mulloy, Sir Nicholas, 138
Munga, 25
Murry family, 162
Mutton Island, 168, 178
Mylough, 19

Netterville estate, 200
Netterville, Misses, 18
Newcastle, 7, 28
Newcastle brewery, 38
Nimmo, Mr., xi, 1, 4, 13, 20, 29, 102
Nuad, 28
Nunneries, 116
Nuns, 221, 224, 228
Nuns' Island, 178
Nurseries, 248, 249, 251, 252

O'Briens, 135
O'Connor, Phelimy, 121
O'Connor-roe, 144
O'Dalys, 3
O'Donnel, Balderoy, 165
O'Flaherty, 126
O'Flaherty, Murrough, 260
O'Flahertys, 4, 135, 144, 260, 264, 278, 279, 281
O'Hallorans, 3, 119, 278
O'Kellys, 278
O'Layns, 3
O'Maddens, 4, 135
O'Shaughnessy, Roger, 146, 152
O'Vologhan (O'Nolan), 125
O'Flahertys, 2, 4, 118, 277

O'Kellys, 3
O'Maddens, 118, 135, 278
O'Neill, Mr. Geoghegan, 256
O'Shaughnessy, 126
Oatfield, 10
Oath of supremacy, 146, 147, 149
Oats, 33, 40, 41
Oliver St John, Sir, 146
Omey Island, 22
Ormsby family, 161, 162, 179, 180
Oughterard, 7, 15, 17, 18, 20, 23, 25, 27, 32, 46, 63, 100, 101, 208, 225, 254, 260

Pallas, 10
Papal Nuncio, 153, 154
Patten of Wesport, 188
Patterson of Kilrosh, 188
Persse, Robert, 16, 230
Petersburgh, 23
Pigs, 65, 69, 75, 83
Pimento, 205
Pitchforks, 52
Ploughing matches, 49
Ploughs, 33, 34, 37, 38, 44, 46, 47, 48, 49, 50, 52, 61, 82, 87, 89, 90, 95, 97
Pope family, 121, 153, 162
Pope Gregory I, 228
Portumna/Potumna, 10, 19, 31, 67
Potatoes, 8, 12, 33, 34, 35, 36, 37, 40, 41, 42, 43, 44, 45, 48, 49, 51, 54, 58, 62, 71, 75, 80, 83, 88, 89, 90, 97, 99, 100, 102, 103
Poteen, 204

Poulacopple, 22
Presbyterian, 159
Presentation convent, 177
Presentation order, 228
Protestant clergy, xi, 107
Protestants, 115, 148, 152, 158, 162, 163, 166, 169, 172, 226, 261

Rahasane, 8, 9, 27, 231
Rape (crop), 11, 43, 45, 47, 54, 57, 70
Raths, 262
Reddington, Mr. of Ryehill, x
Rents, 1, 10, 14, 34, 37, 39, 40, 44, 59, 64, 85, 86, 87, 97, 105
Renville, 22
Resident Proprietors, list of, 230
Ribbonmen, 185
Richardson, Dr., 12, 55, 73, 74
Riverston, Lord, 12, 19, 46, 230, 249

Roman Catholic clergyman, 6
Roman Catholics, xi, 115, 145, 153, 154, 156, 165, 223, 227, 228, 258
Roman Catholics as "Papists", 115
Roscommon County, 1, 30, 132, 137, 140
Ross, 1, 3, 7, 22, 56, 58, 61, 90, 122, 231, 232, 239, 254, 351
Ross Lake, 23
Ross Mahon, 11, 19
Ross, Abbey of, 184
Rotheram, 149
Rotheram, Sir Thomas, 146, 149
Round towers, 261
Roxborough, 7, 10, 18, 101, 183, 230, 250
Royal Dublin Society, i, ii, viii, xi, 119, 248
Running-out system, 12, 58
Russell, Colonel, 163
Russell, Rev., Mr., x, , 202, 221
Ryndifin, 186

Saunder's Grove, 74
Saunders, Mr. Morley, 74
Schools, 226, 227, 228, 248
Scotch ploughs, 41, 49
Scourging system, 10, 12, 36, 39
Scutching, 52
Semper, 147, 162, 187
Shanley and Leggett, 243
Shannon, the, 18, 19, 28, 30, 31
Shanonafola, 13, 22
Sheep, 8, 9, 10, 12, 27, 55, 58, 59, 61, 63, 64, 65, 66, 69, 70, 71, 74, 75, 88, 90, 92, 93, 94
Sheep, Merino, 237
Shindela, 25
Shovels, 52
Shruel, 9, 10, 31, 58, 135, 157, 207
Shruel, massacre at, 152
Silanchia, 135
Skerrett-Fitz-Edmond, 151
Sliebhbaughta, 7
Sliebh-Baughta mountains, 7, 29
Slieve Meesh, 24
Sline Head, 21, 220
Smyth/Smith, Erasmus
Society of Friends, 120
spalpeens, 199
Spas, 17, 32
Speed family, 162
Spencer, 162
St Francis Abbey, 146
St George Daly, 176, 177, 181

St Iarloth/Jarlath College, 182, 228
St Kieran, 2
St. Clerans, 30
St. Colman, 274
St. Francis' Abbey, 148
St. Nicholas Church, 115, 123, 127, 132, 133, 138, 167, 170, 179
Strawlodge, 28
Strogen, John, 177, 178
Strongbow, 124, 126, 129, 132, 137
Stubbers, 156, 158
Survey of the County of Clare, 245
Surveyors of Roads, 210

Tale-tellers, 359
Tartarian oats, 38
Taverns, 114, 132
Terrylan, 29
Thirteen tribes, the, 119
Thomastown, 31
Tintrim, 32
Tipperary, 1, 263, 265, 286
Tithes, 201, 202, 203, 214
Topiary, 243
Tour in Ireland, 10
Townlands, 90
Trench, Esq., Richard, 66
Trench, William Le Poer, 113
Tribune Society, the, 115
Tuam, 7, 9, 10, 27, 31, 52, 56, 58, 67, 99, 133, 167, 172, 182, 188, 204, 207, 208, 209, 211, 228, 229, 230, 234, 236, 239, 260, 268
Tuam Cathedral, 265
Turf, 3, 13, 15, 49, 73, 86, 96, 98, 100, 103, 105
Turloghmore, 27
Turloghs, 27
Turloughmore, 58
Turnips, 43, 48, 54, 57, 70, 79, 89, 98
Twelve Pins, the, 9, 21, 22

Ulinn, 28

Veil family, 162
Veitch, Dr., 116
visiting roads, xii

Waddlesworth, Mr., 242
Walcott family, 162
Wandesford, Sir Christopher, 151
Ward, Patrick, 242

Waterford, 238, 239
Weights and Measures, 237
Wellpark, 28
Wentworth, Thomas, 150
West Meath, 1
Westport, 23, 214, 216, 217, 221
Wexford, 19
Whaley family, 159
Whaley, Mr., of Claddagh, 111

Wheat, 33, 41
Whiskey, 204, 205
Wine, 109, 131, 140, 142, 147
Woodbrook, 18, 32
Woodford, 18, 31, 67
Woodlawn, 10, 54, 101, 183, 189, 233, 247
Woollen manufacture, 237

Younghusband, 162

Books in the Clachan 'Historic Irish Journeys' series

Travels In Ireland - J.G. Kohl
A very readable account by a German visitor of his tour around Ireland immediately before the Great Famine.

Disturbed Ireland – 1881 - Bernard Becker
Letters written on a tour of the West of Ireland, visiting key places in the 'Land War'. We meet Captain Boycott and other members of the gentry, as well as a range of small farmers and peasants.

A Journey throughout Ireland, During the Spring, Summer and Autumn of 1834, - Henry D. Inglis
Inglis travels Ireland attempting to answer the question, 'is Ireland and improving country?' using discussion with landlords, manufacturers and tenants plus his own insightful observations.

The West Of Ireland: Its Existing Condition and Prospects - Henry Coulter
This is a collection of letters from *Saunders's News-Letter* relating to the condition and prospects of the people of the West of Ireland after the partial failure of the harvests of the early 1860s.

* * * * *

Also in the 'Local History' Series

Henry Coulter's account has been sub-divided for the convenience of local and family historians.

The West of Ireland: Its Existing Condition and Prospects, Part 1, by Henry Coulter
This is an extract from the complete edition dealing with Athlone, Co. Clare and Co. Galway.

The West of Ireland: Its Existing Condition and Prospects, Part 2, by Henry Coulter
This is an extract from the complete edition dealing with Co. Mayo.

The West of Ireland: Its Existing Condition and Prospects, Part 3, by Henry Coulter
The final extract from the complete edition dealing with Counties Co Sligo, Donegal, Leitrim and Roscommon.

* * * * *

J.G.Kohl's account has been sub-divided for the convenience of local and family historians.

Travels in Ireland – Part 1, takes us through Edgeworthtown, The Shannon, Limerick, Edenvale, Kilrush and Father Mathew.

Travels in Ireland – Part 2, his journey continues through Tarbet, Tralee, Killarney, Bantry, Cork, Kilkenny and Waterford.

Travels in Ireland – Part 3, this section deals with Wexford, Enniscorthy, Avoca, Glendalough and Dublin.

Travels In Ireland - Part 4 – he goes north for the last part of his journey through Dundalk, Newry, Belfast, The Antrim Coast, Rathlin, The Giant's Causeway.

* * * * *

Henry D. Inglis' account has also been sub-divided for the convenience of local and family historians.

A Journey throughout Ireland, During the Spring, Summer and Autumn of 1834, Part 1 takes us from Dublin. Through Wexford, Waterford and Cork.

A Journey throughout Ireland, During the Spring, Summer and Autumn of 1834, Part 2 is an account of Kerry, Clare, Limerick and the Shannon and concludes in Athlone.

* * * * *

Aghaidh Achadh Mór, The Face of Aghamore – edited by Joe Byrne. This is a reproduction of a title originally published in 1991 and is of enduring interest to local historians and to those with ancestral roots in East Mayo. It covers such topics as Stone Age archaeology, family history, local hedge schools, O'Carolan's connection with the parish, the Civil War and townland surveys.

Inishowen, Its History, Traditions and Antiquities, by 'Maghtochair'. A record of the history of Inishowen, its typography and archeology as well as its peoples and traditions.

Lough Corrib, Its Shores and Islands: with Notices of Lough Mask - by William R. Wilde, first published in 1867. In the words of the author: 'A work intended to … rescue from oblivion, or preserve from desecration, some of the historic monuments of the country'.

* * * * *

Ballads and Songs

Songs of the Glens of Antrim, Moiré O'Neill

These Songs of the Glens of Antrim were written by a Glenswoman in the dialect of the Glens, and chiefly for the pleasure of other Glens-people.

Clachan Publishing, Ballycastle, Glens of Antrim.

www.ingramcontent.com/pod-product-compliance
Lightning Source LLC
Chambersburg PA
CBHW081838230426
43669CB00018B/2743